MASTER THE SAT

2005

MASTER THE SAT

2005

Phil Pine

THOMSON ™

PETERSON'S

Australia • Canada • Mexico • Singapore • Spain • United Kingdom • United States

An ARCO Book

ARCO is a registered trademark of Thomson Learning, Inc., and is used herein under license by Peterson's.

About The Thomson Corporation and Peterson's

With revenues of US$7.8 billion, The Thomson Corporation (www.thomson.com) is a leading global provider of integrated information solutions for business, education, and professional customers. Its Learning businesses and brands (www.thomsonlearning.com) serve the needs of individuals, learning institutions, and corporations with products and services for both traditional and distributed learning.

Peterson's, part of The Thomson Corporation, is one of the nation's most respected providers of lifelong learning online resources, software, reference guides, and books. The Education Supersite[SM] at www.petersons.com—the Internet's most heavily traveled education resource—has searchable databases and interactive tools for contacting U.S.-accredited institutions and programs. In addition, Peterson's serves more than 105 million education consumers annually.

For more information, contact Peterson's, 2000 Lenox Drive, Lawrenceville, NJ 08648; 800-338-3282; or find us on the World Wide Web at: www.petersons.com/about.

Petersons.com/publishing

Check out our Web site at www.petersons.com/publishing to see if there is any new information regarding the test and any revisions or corrections to the content of this book. We've made sure the information in this book is accurate and up-to-date; however, the test format or content may have changed since the time of publication.

Acknowledgments

We would like to thank Judith Berg, Charlotte Klaar, and Andrew Bryan for their invaluable help, insight, and advice in creating this book. Their knowledge and experience provided us with critical feedback during all stages of this book's production and ultimately helped us create a comprehensive yet concise test-prep resource.

ISSN: International Standard Serial Number information available upon request.

ISBN (book only): 0-7689-1712-3

ISBN (book with CD-ROM): 0-7689-1711-5

Printed in the United States of America

10 9 8 7 6 5 4 3 2   06 05 04

Contents

Contents

PART II DIAGNOSING STRENGTHS AND WEAKNESSES

PART III SAT VERBAL STRATEGIES

PART VII PRACTICE TESTS

Contents

COLLEGE ADMISSIONS/FINANCIAL AID COUNTDOWN SENIOR YEAR

SEPTEMBER

☐ Continue honing list of target schools, on-campus interviews, and alumni interviews.

☐ Get financial aid information from guidance counselors and give teacher recommendations to appropriate teachers.

☐ Register for October ACT Assessment, October SAT I, or November SAT I.

☐ Begin Early Action/Early Decision steps now. Check deadlines with appropriate schools.

OCTOBER

☐ Register for December ACT Assessment, December SAT I, or November SAT II.

☐ Take October ACT Assessment, October SAT I exam.

☐ Draw up a master schedule of application and financial aid due dates and mark them on your calendar.

☐ Continue working on college essays and personal statements. Follow up on teacher recommendations.

☐ Submit Early Decision (ED) and Early Action (EA) applications.

NOVEMBER

☐ Reduce college "long list" to "short list" where applications will be sent.

☐ Plan Thanksgiving-break visit to college campuses.

☐ Get someone to proofread your applications and essays.

☐ Take the November SAT I or SAT II; prepare for December ACT Assessment.

☐ Send first-quarter grades to colleges; send test scores (include ETS numbers) for ED/EA applications and regular admissions.

DECEMBER

☐ Pick up any additional financial aid forms you need and attend financial aid workshops, if possible. Follow up with guidance counselors and teachers on references letters and transcripts.

☐ Take ACT Assessment, SAT II subject tests this month.

☐ Submit all regular applications.

☐ If accepted on Early Decision, withdraw remaining applications. If deferred on Early Decision, send follow-up letter to college.

JANUARY

☐ Fill out financial aid forms. Finish and mail as soon as possible. Never be late with these.

☐ Complete all applications regardless of later deadlines. Photocopy everything. If taking SAT this month, are RUSH scores required? Ask target colleges if you're not sure. Register for February ACT Assessment now.

FEBRUARY

☐ ACT Assessment administered this month.

☐ Call those colleges that didn't confirm receipt of completed applications.

MARCH

☐ It's not too late to apply to more schools—get any remaining applications out this month.

☐ Actively seek and pursue scholarship opportunities and draw up your financial aid plan to pay for next year's expenses.

APRIL

☐ Prepare for May AP exams.

☐ Plan "crunch time" visits to campuses and compare financial aid decisions.

☐ Return "wait list" cards as needed. Check admissions offices for wait-list status.

☐ *Make your decision!* Send the deposit or your place won't be held; for most schools *May 1st* is the deadline, so do it now.

☐ Notify those schools you won't be attending.

MAY

☐ Take AP exams where appropriate.

☐ Check housing options: When will forms be mailed? Should you check alternative arrangements?

☐ Start thinking about summer employment—last chance to build up a "nest egg" for freshman year!

JUNE

☐ Write thank-you notes to anyone who helped you: guidance counselors, teachers, admissions counselors, etc.

☐ Make sure final high school transcripts are sent to the college you'll attend.

Introduction

ARCO's *Master the SAT* was prepared by SAT experts who have spent thousands of hours researching the SAT and studying its patterns—and teaching people just like you to get the highest scores on the exam. In this book, they share the *most innovative test-taking techniques* available and give you an opportunity to apply them. The book also includes a review of all of the mathematical concepts ever tested on the SAT as well as a list of the 500 *most popular SAT vocabulary words*. And this book won't just boost your test scores—it also offers you valuable information and advice for life "after the SAT." You get real information on the college application process, and how to search for and secure financial aid. And if you're getting an early start on preparing for the exam, there's even a chapter at the end of the book about the changes that will go into effect with the 2005 SAT.

Master the SAT does not offer an "easy way" to improve your SAT scores. That's because there really is no "easy way out" when it comes to SAT preparation. But for students who take their preparation seriously, *Master the SAT* can help dramatically improve their scores.

HOW THIS BOOK HELPS YOU SUCCEED ON THE EXAM

Whether you have three months or four weeks to prepare for the exam, *Master the SAT* helps *develop a study plan* that caters to your individual needs and time table. These step-by-step plans are easy to follow and remarkably effective. No matter which plan you select, you begin the ARCO program by taking a diagnostic exam. The diagnostic does more than give you testing experience. Easy-to-use *diagnostic tables* help you track your performance, convert your scores, identify your strengths, and pinpoint your weaknesses. At the end of the diagnostic test, you will know whether you are weak in verbal topics such as analogies, sentence completions, or critical reading. And you will know whether multiple-choice math, quantitative comparisons, or grid-ins are giving you the most trouble. Moreover, you will receive deeper insight into your vocabulary, arithmetic, geometry, and algebra needs. No other book helps you identify your weaknesses as painlessly and completely. By understanding your testing profile, you can immediately address your weak areas by reading the relevant chapters, learning the relevant techniques, and doing additional *practice exercises*.

When you have completed your formal review, it's time to use the book's *practice tests* to sharpen your skills. Because even if you understand the SAT, you need to practice applying the methods you have learned. *Master the SAT* teaches you how to take these exams under simulated test conditions. And because we made sure that our practice tests perfectly mirror the content and format of the SAT, there will be no surprises for you on test day. At the end of each practice test, you not only have access to the correct answers, but also to *comprehensive explanations* of every one of the book's 1,000+ test questions! This way, you can really learn from your mistakes. If you don't have the time to take full-length practice tests, *Master the SAT* explains how to use *timing drills* to take shorter sections of exams to combat your weaknesses, work on your pacing, and increase your level of confidence.

You'll also find that *Master the SAT* discusses all of the "big picture issues" other books ignore. For example, it addresses questions such as:

- How is the SAT really used for college admission?
- When should you take the test?
- How many times should you plan to take the SAT?
- How do the PSAT and SAT differ from each other?
- Do all PSAT, SAT, and SAT II scores "count" in the college admissions game?

By addressing these questions, *Master the SAT* debunks prevailing myths and helps you put the SAT into its proper perspective. It also serves as your "college guidance counselor," giving you the expert advice you need to apply to college. And when you think about it, that's our number-one goal here. Our objective is to help you dramatically raise your scores so that you can maximize the likelihood of getting into the college of your choice. And if you use this book properly, we can help you reach that goal.

HOW TO USE THIS BOOK

Master the SAT was designed to be as user friendly as it is complete. Its design is contemporary and its voice is approachable. Each chapter begins with a *bulleted overview* that highlights what will be covered; and each chapter ends with a point-by-point summary that captures the essence of what was discussed. These *chapter summaries* reflect ARCO's belief in the value of repetition and reinforcement. You can use these summaries to supplement your understanding of a chapter, and you can revisit them as an effective means of review.

Master the SAT includes several different features to make your preparation easier. *Practice questions* give you instant insight into the SAT question types, and our walk-through answer explanations let you know exactly how you can arrive at the right answers on test day. In addition, look to the margins for these special test-prep tools.

Note

Notes highlight critical information about the SAT format—things you need to know that may be overlooked in other test-prep books and programs.

Tip

Tips draw your attention to valuable concepts, advice, and shortcuts for tackling the SAT and PSAT. By following the tips, you will learn how to approach different question types, use process-of-elimination techniques, pace yourself, and guess most effectively.

Alert!

Wherever you need to be wary of a common pitfall or test-taker trap, you'll find an *Alert!*. This information reveals and eliminates the misperceptions and wrong turns so many people take on the exam. By taking full advantage of all of the book's features, you will become much more comfortable with the SAT and considerably more confident about your ability to defeat it.

YOU'RE ON YOUR WAY TO SUCCESS

By providing you with the most comprehensive and usable SAT preparation guide, we hope that you can actually learn to enjoy the SAT process. After all, knowledge is power. And by reading this book, you will become extremely knowledgeable about the SAT. We look forward to helping you raise your SAT scores and improve your college prospects. Good luck!

ABOUT THE CD

If you have the CD edition of this book, you have purchased additional SAT test preparation. On this CD you will find practice tests, tutorials, and exercises to help you study for the SAT I examination.

We suggest that you begin by taking the diagnostic test at the beginning of the book. Once you have an idea of how you did and where to focus your studying, review the material in the book, and then supplement your studies with the CD lessons. Then take the other tests in the book and on the CD. Very little has been left to chance here, and you have been given a wide range of preparatory materials, both on the CD and in this book. Try to review as much as possible.

PART I
SAT BASICS

Getting Started

OVERVIEW

- Learn how the SAT is used for college admission
- Decide when you should take the SAT (and SAT II)
- Understand how many times you should take the SAT
- Learn how to register for the SAT
- Make an SAT study plan
- Measure your progress

HOW THE SAT IS USED FOR COLLEGE ADMISSION

One explicitly stated purpose of the SAT is to predict how students will perform academically as college freshmen. But the more practical purpose of the SAT is to help college admissions officers make acceptance decisions. When you think about it, admissions officers have a difficult job, particularly when they are asked to compare the academic records of students from different high schools in different parts of the country taking different classes. It's not easy to figure out how one student's grade point average (GPA) in New Mexico correlates with that of another student in Florida. Even though admissions officers can do a good deal of detective work to fairly evaluate candidates, they benefit a great deal from the SAT. The SAT provides a single, standardized means of comparison. After all, virtually every student takes the SAT, and the SAT is the same for everyone. It doesn't matter whether you hail from Maine, Maryland, or Montana.

So the SAT is an important test. But it is not the be-all, end-all. Keep it in perspective! It is only one of several important pieces of the college admissions puzzle. Other factors that weigh heavily into the admission process include GPA, difficulty of course load, level of extracurricular involvement, and the strength of the college application itself.

WHEN YOU SHOULD TAKE THE SAT (AND SAT II)

When you decide which schools you're going to apply to, find out if they require the SAT. Most do! Your next step is to determine when they need your SAT scores. Write that date down. That's the one you *really* don't want to miss.

You do have some leeway in choosing your test date. The SAT I (that's the basic test this book addresses) is offered on one Saturday morning in October, November, December, January, March, May, and June. Check the exact dates to see which ones meet your deadlines. To do this, count back six weeks from each deadline, because that's how long it takes ETS to score your test and send out the results.

What if you don't know which schools you want to apply to? Don't panic! Even if you take the exam in December or January of your senior year, you'll probably have plenty of time to send your scores to most schools.

When you plan to take the SAT, there is something even more important than the application deadlines of particular schools. You need to select a test date that works best with your schedule. Ideally, you should allow yourself at least two to three months to use this book to prepare. Many students like to take the test in March of their junior year. That way, they take the SAT several months before final exams, proms, and end-of-the-year distractions. Taking the test in March also gives students early feedback as to how they are scoring. If they are dissatisfied with their scores, there is ample opportunity to take the test again in the spring or following fall. But your schedule might not easily accommodate a March testing. Maybe you're involved in a winter sport or school play that will take too much time away from SAT studying. Maybe you have a family reunion planned over spring break in March. Or maybe you simply prefer to prepare during a different time of year. If that's the case, just pick another date.

If the schools you've decided on also require SAT II (subject tests), here's one good piece of advice: try to take SAT II tests immediately after you finish the subject(s) in school. For most of you, this means taking the SAT II exams in June. By taking the exam then, you'll save an awful lot of review work. Remember this, too: you have to register for the SAT II tests separately, and you can't take the subject tests on the same day as the SAT. So check the dates, think ahead, and plan it out. It's worth it in the end.

HOW MANY TIMES YOU SHOULD TAKE THE SAT

Different colleges evaluate the SAT I in different ways. Some will take your highest math and verbal scores, even if they were earned on different test days. So if you nailed the math portion in March and the verbal portion in October, they will combine those two numbers to maximize your overall score. Not bad, huh? But many other schools don't do that. Some pay most attention to your highest combined score on a particular day. Many others will average all of your scores or lend equal weight to all of them.

So what does this mean? It means that you should only take the SAT I when you are truly prepared. Because no matter what each school's individual policy tends to be, every single SAT I score you earn is part of your permanent transcript, so colleges see them all. Ideally, you should try to earn your "goal score" sooner rather than later. For example, a student who hits his objective of 1100 in one sitting certainly has an advantage over a student who needed five tries to squeeze out 1100.

There is nothing wrong with taking the SAT two or three times, so long as you are confident that your scores will improve substantially each time. Let's say that you scored a 1080 on your first SAT. If you would have been thrilled to have hit 1100, it's probably not worth taking again. Most colleges look at SAT scores in ranges and will not hold 20 points against you. They understand that scoring 1080 means that you were only one or two questions away from 1100; and no sane admissions officer would deny you admission based on one or two questions! But if you scored 1080 and expected to score closer to 1150 or 1200 based on practice testing, then you should probably retake the exam. In other words, it is of little value to take the SAT multiple times if you expect to earn roughly the same score. But it is worthwhile if you expect to score significantly higher on a second or third try. For more advice about this, see your high school guidance counselor.

HOW TO REGISTER FOR THE SAT

You should register for the SAT at least six weeks before your testing date. That way you will avoid late registration fees and increase your chances of taking the exam at your first-choice testing center. You can register through the mail by completing the SAT registration form found inside the annual SAT bulletin. Your high school guidance office should have plenty of extra copies of the SAT bulletin. If you'd like, you can also painlessly register online or by telephone. Please note, however, that you cannot register for the SAT by phone the first time you register—you can only re-register. The mailing address, phone numbers, and Web address for the SAT registration center is shown in the following table.

College Board SAT Program Addresses

P.O. Box 6200
Princeton, NJ 08541-6200
(800) 728-7267 (re-register only)
(609) 771-7600 (re-register only)
(7:00 a.m. to midnight Eastern Time)
www.collegeboard.com

MAKE AN SAT STUDY PLAN

As with almost any form of learning, preparing for the SAT is an investment of time. The more you have, the better your chances of boosting your score significantly. Next, we'll walk you through two different study plans, each tailored to a specific amount of preparation time. Find the plan that fits your circumstances and adapt it to your needs.

Regardless of how much time you have before the actual exam, your first step should be to take the *Diagnostic Test* in Part II of this book. After you score it, compute your category percentages to assess your relative strengths and weaknesses. Hang on to the scoring sheet so you know where to get started.

If you are using this book to get early preparation for the PSAT, you should take the *PSAT Diagnostic Test* in Part VIII. After you score it, compute your PSAT category percentages to assess your relative strengths and weaknesses.

The Complete Course

If you have three or more months to prepare, you should congratulate yourself! This will give you sufficient time to familiarize yourself with the test, learn critical strategies, review vocabulary and mathematical fundamentals, and take full-length practice tests.

You'll get the most out of your SAT preparation if you read this whole book from cover to cover. No, you can't do that in a weekend! But if you have two or three months, you'll have enough time to read and reread at your own pace and work through all of the examples, exercises, and practice exams without breaking a sweat.

The Accelerated Course

If you have one month or less to prepare for the SAT, you shouldn't even attempt to read this book from cover to cover. Or if you have several months, but can't devote too much time to SAT study, you should opt for the accelerated course. Take the diagnostic exam. Read Chapter 2 to ensure that you understand the format, structure, and scoring of the SAT. Then visit the chapters that cover material that is most problematic for you.

WORKING THROUGH YOUR STUDY PLAN

It does seem like you're on a treadmill sometimes, doesn't it? Question after question after question—are you really getting anywhere? Is all of this studying really working?

The way to find out is to monitor your progress throughout the preparation period, whether it's three months or four weeks. By taking a diagnostic examination at the beginning, you'll establish your "home base" of skills, and you'll be able to craft the study plan that's right for you. Then, you can either start to read the entire book (if you are taking the complete course) or go directly to the chapters that address your weaknesses (if you are taking the accelerated course). At the end of each chapter, complete the exercises and compare your percentages to your original diagnostic percentages. How have you improved? Where do you still need work? Even if you haven't reached your ultimate performance goal, are you at least applying new test-taking methods?

When you are approximately one third of the way through your course of study—this can be after ten days or a month—it's time to take one of the practice examinations in Part VII. Compare your overall scores with your original diagnostic scores. Then compare subcategories. Hopefully you're doing better. But if you're not, don't panic. At this stage in the game, it's not unusual to score roughly the same as you did at the beginning. What's more important than *what* you score is *how* you take the test. Are you really using the test-taking strategies to which you've been introduced? If you aren't, it's time to go back and either reread chapters or their summaries. Then continue your review. Read more chapters, do exercises, and compare your percentages with your diagnostic percentages.

After you have reviewed the vast majority of the chapters (under the complete course) or all of your weaknesses (under the accelerated course), it's time to take another practice examination. By now you should be seeing some real score improvement. If your weaknesses continue to plague you, revisit problematic material. But for the most part, this last phase of study should involve *less learning* and *more practice*. Take more practice examinations! By now, you probably understand how to take the SAT. What you need is more practice actually taking the test under simulated test-day conditions.

When you take additional practice exams, be sure you do so in a near-test environment (see the beginning of Part VII for ways to do this). Keep analyzing your scores to ensure that all of this practice is working. Determine which areas need additional work. Now is probably the perfect time to take timing drills. (For more information about timing drills, see the beginning of Part VII.) Because you have already reviewed the chapters, work on your weaknesses by doing timing drills.

One last word of advice: no matter what study plan you select, you should probably take one full-timed SAT the week before the SAT. This will get you ready for the big day. But don't take that test the day before the SAT. That's a time when you should be relaxing, not cramming.

For more information about what to do the day before the SAT, see "Some Test-Wise Strategies for SAT Success" on page 15.

Here's a list that highlights your goals for forming and following an SAT study plan:

WORKING THROUGH YOUR STUDY PLAN: THE KEY POINTS
- Get started by taking the diagnostic examination in Part II (or PSAT test in Part VIII).
- Compute your category percentages to assess your relative strengths and weaknesses.
- If you have sufficient time and initiative, take the complete course. Do the book from cover to cover. You can read the book in order, or you can start with the kind of question you find most difficult. At the end of each chapter, do exercises and assess your performance.
- If you have one month or less, follow the accelerated course. Read Chapter 2 to familiarize yourself with the SAT. Then visit the chapters that cover material that is most problematic for you. At the end of each chapter, do exercises and assess your performance.
- When you are one third of the way through your preparation, take a practice test. Compare your scores with your original results. Make sure you are applying new test-taking strategies.
- Revisit problematic chapters and chapter summaries. Then read additional chapters, do exercises, and compare your percentages with your original category percentages.

TIP

Here's an important point: you don't have to go through the parts in order. You might want to start with the kind of question you find most difficult, such as critical reading or quantitative comparisons. Then you can move to the next most difficult and so on down the line, saving your best stuff for last. If you take the accelerated course, you should definitely take this approach.

TIP

Based on the results of your SAT diagnostic test, rank the six question types in order of priority, from the one on which you need the greatest improvement to the one on which you currently perform the best.

TIP

Don't forget that the anxiety you feel is completely natural! If you are well prepared for the test, anxiety can be a great aid to you on test day! But too much anxiety can really hurt your performance. That's why you're smart to be using this book; the strategies you'll learn and the practice and in-depth reviews you'll work through will boost your confidence on test day. When you're prepared for the test, you have much less to feel anxious about.

- After you have reviewed all of the chapters (the complete course) or all of your weaknesses (the accelerated course), take another practice examination.

- During the last phase of your review, take as many complete practice tests as possible under simulated test conditions. For more information about simulating test conditions, see Part VII.

- If you continue to have weak areas, take timing drills to pinpoint your study. For more information about timing drills, see Part VII.

- The week before the SAT: take a full exam to make sure you're ready. Don't take this exam the night before when you should be relaxing!

What You Need to Know about SAT Preparation

- Don't be intimidated! The SAT is a coachable test that you can prepare for!

- Although the SAT is the most important test you'll take in high school, it is not the most important factor in getting into college. So study seriously, but keep it in perspective.

- You should only take the SAT when you are adequately prepared because every score you earn is part of your transcript.

- Most people take the SAT more than once. There is nothing wrong with taking the exam a couple of times, as long as you are confident that your scores will improve. To take the test multiple times and earn roughly the same score is a waste of time, money, and energy.

- Register for the SAT at least six weeks before the test date to ensure that you can take the test at a familiar test center.

- Make certain that you take the SAT early enough to fulfill the application requirements of the colleges you're interested in.

- Make an SAT study plan! Depending upon your time and initiative, select either the complete course or the accelerated course. For more information about these study plans, revisit the last section of this chapter.

Inside the SAT

OVERVIEW

- **Learn about the SAT format**
- **Learn about the SAT question types**
- **Take a look at the SAT answer sheet**
- **Understand how the SAT is scored**
- **Some test-wise strategies for SAT success**
- **Educated guessing will boost your score!**
- **Get ready for test day**

GET TO KNOW THE SAT FORMAT

The SAT has seven sections. This seems like a lot, but there are really just three math sections and three verbal sections, plus a "wild card" section. The wild card can be another math section or another verbal section. This is where ETS—the company that writes the SAT—tries out questions that might be used on future tests. Even though the wild card section doesn't count toward your score, you won't know which section it is. ETS does this on purpose. It knows that if you knew which section did not count, you probably wouldn't try your hardest on it! So you'll have to do your best on all seven SAT sections.

Each section is timed to take either 15 or 30 minutes. The whole test will take you three hours to complete. This chart will give you a good idea of what to expect. Note, though, that the order of the sections can vary. In other words, don't memorize the chart, just use it as a guide.

FORMAT OF A TYPICAL SAT I

Section #/Content	# of Questions	Time
(1) Verbal Reasoning	30 or 31	30 min.
Sentence Completions	9	
Analogies	6	
Critical Reading	15	
(2) Mathematical Reasoning	25	30 min.
Standard Multiple-Choice		
Mathematics		

FORMAT OF A TYPICAL SAT I (continued)

Section #/Content	# of Questions	Time
(3) Verbal Reasoning	35 or 36	30 min.
Sentence Completions	10	
Analogies	13	
Critical Reading	12	
(4) Mathematical Reasoning	25	30 min.
Quantitative Comparisons	15	
Grid-Ins	10	
(5) "Wild Card" Section	varies	30 min.
(6) Verbal Reasoning	12 or 13	15 min.
Critical Reading		
(7) Mathematical Reasoning	10	15 min.
Standard Multiple-Choice		
Mathematics		

GET TO KNOW THE SAT QUESTION TYPES

The question types in the SAT don't cover a wide variety of topics. Actually, the field is pretty limited—no science, no foreign languages, no social studies. You'll just find questions testing verbal and math skills—skills you've been working on since you were 6 years old.

Most of the questions are multiple choice. That's good; it means that you have four or five answers to choose from—and the right answer is always given to you! Only 10 questions in one of the math sections ask for "student-produced" answers. This means you need to do the calculations and then fill in bubbles to show your answers. (More about the bubbles later!) In this section of the chapter, we take a closer look at the individual question types you'll encounter in each of these two SAT subject areas.

The information in this chapter is just an overview of the SAT and its contents. In Chapter 3, "SAT Questions: A First Look," you'll see examples of the SAT question types and learn how to tackle them.

The SAT Verbal Reasoning Question Types

All right, so what exactly will you find in a "verbal reasoning" section? Well, this section has questions that test reasoning, vocabulary, and reading comprehension. The three types of questions are analogies, sentence completions, and critical reading. Briefly, here's what these question types involve:

- **Analogies** present a pair of words that have some logical relationship. Then the choices present other pairs of words. You have to choose the pair that has the same kind of relationship as the first pair.

- **Sentence completion** questions ask you to choose a word or words that fill in the blanks in a given sentence. They test how well you can use context clues and word meanings to complete a sentence.

- **Critical reading** questions relate to a passage that is provided for you to read. The passage can be about almost anything, and the questions after it test how well you understood the passage and the information in it.

NOTE

In 2005, the College Board will be revising the SAT. See Appendix A, *The New SAT and PSAT,* for more information.

The SAT Math Questions

Now, let's talk a minute about the math questions. The questions in this section are about problem solving in arithmetic, elementary algebra, and geometry. Here are some details about the three kinds of questions you'll find—standard multiple-choice, quantitative comparison, and grid-ins:

- **Standard multiple-choice questions** give you a problem in arithmetic, algebra, or geometry. Then you choose the correct answer from the five choices.

- **Quantitative comparison questions** test your skills in comparing information and in estimating. You'll see two quantities, one in Column A and one in Column B. Your job is to compare the two quantities and decide if one is greater than the other, if they are equal, or if no comparison is possible.

- **Grid-Ins** do not give you answer choices. You have to compute the answer and then use the bubbles on the answer sheet to fill in your solution.

THE SAT ANSWER SHEET

This is where we get to the bubbles. When you get the test booklet, you'll also get a separate sheet on which you'll mark your answers.

For each multiple-choice question, you'll see a corresponding set of answer ovals. (These are the bubbles!) The ovals are labeled from A to D or E, depending on the number of answer choices given for the question. Here's the main point to remember: answer sheets are read by machines—and machines can't think. That means it's up to you to make sure you're in the right place on the answer sheet every time you record an answer. The machine won't know if you really meant Question 25 when you marked the space for Question 26. Another thing to remember: don't be a wimp with that pencil. Fill in your chosen answer ovals completely and boldly so there can be no mistake about which one you chose.

TIP

Make sure you're in the right place! Always check to see that the answer space you fill in corresponds to the question you are answering.

Take a look at this sample answer sheet. You can just imagine what the machine will do with it.

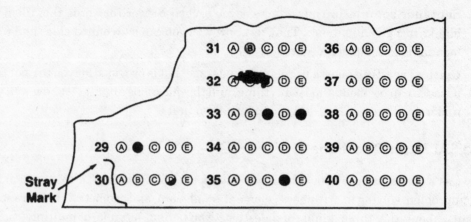

In the answer-sheet example we show you here, the only answers that will be registered correctly are 29 and 35. Question 30 isn't filled in completely, and Question 31 isn't dark enough, so the machine might miss it. Question 32 is a total mess—will the machine choose A, B, or C?

Since Question 33 has two ovals filled in, they cancel each other out and this is registered as an omitted question. There's no penalty, but there's no credit either. The same will happen with Question 34; no answer, no credit.

Let's move on to the student-produced responses. You'll still be filling in ovals, but they will look a little different from the multiple-choice ovals. Here's a sample of the special grid you will use.

TIP

You are allowed to use a four-function, battery-powered, scientific or graphing calculator for the math sections of the SAT. You may *not* use the following: hand-held mini-computers, laptop computers, pocket organizers, calculators that print or "talk," or calculators with letters on the keyboard.

← boxes to write your numerical answer
← fraction lines—use at most one per answer
← decimal points—use at most one per answer

At the top of the grid, you'll write in the actual numerical answer. The slashes are used for answers with fractions. If you need one of these fraction lines in your answer, darken one of the ovals. The ovals with the dots are for answers with decimal points—use these ovals just as you do the fraction line ovals. Then you use the number ovals to represent the actual numbers in your answer. Chapter 10 has more details about these special grids, and you'll be able to see some samples, too.

HOW THE SAT IS SCORED

OK, you've filled in all your ovals, the three hours are up (and not a moment too soon), and you turn in your answer sheet. What next? Off it goes to the machines at ETS. The machines scan the sheets in seconds (aren't you glad you were careful with those ovals?) and calculate a score. In this calculation, you get one point for each correct answer, and you lose one quarter of a point for each incorrect answer to a standard five-choice question. (For incorrect answers to four-choice quantitative comparison questions, you lose one third of a point; incorrect answers to grid-in questions have no effect on your score.) The result of these calculations is your raw score, which is then converted to a scaled score between 200 and 800. This is the score that is reported to you and to the schools you have designated.

SOME TEST-WISE STRATEGIES FOR SAT SUCCESS

What makes some people better test-takers than others? The secret isn't just knowing the subject; it's knowing specific test-taking strategies that can add up to extra points. This means psyching out the test, knowing how the test-makers think and what they're looking for, and using this knowledge to your advantage. Smart test-takers know how to use pacing and guessing to add points to their score.

Pace Yourself

As any comedian will tell you, it's all in the timing. For example, the scored sections of the SAT contain 78 verbal questions to be answered in 75 minutes. That means that you have nearly a minute to answer each question. But smart test-takers know that that's not the best way to use their time. If you use less than a minute to answer the easier questions, you'll have extra time to help you answer the more difficult ones. That's why learning to pace yourself is so important. Here are some pacing guidelines you need to remember.

Question Sets Usually Go from Easiest to Most Difficult— You Should, Too

Except for the critical reading questions, SAT questions follow this pattern. So work your way through the earlier, easier questions as quickly as you can. That way you'll have more time for the later, more difficult ones.

NOTE

Because the SAT can vary in format, scaled scores allow the test-maker to account for differences from one version of the SAT to another. Using scaled scores ensures that a score of 500 on one SAT is equivalent to 500 on another.

You Can Set Your Own Speed Limit

All right, how will you know what your speed limit is? Use the practice tests to check your timing and see how it affects your answers. If you've answered most of the questions in the time limit, but also have a lot of incorrect answers, better slow down. On the other hand, if you are very accurate in your answers but aren't answering every question in a section, you can probably pick up the pace a bit.

It's Smart to Keep Moving

It's hard to let go, but sometimes you have to. Don't spend too much time on any one question before you've tried all the questions in a section. There may be questions later on in the test that you can answer easily, and you don't want to lose points just because you didn't get to them.

The Easy Answer Isn't Always Best

Are you at the end of a section? Remember, that's where you'll find the hardest questions, which means that the answers are more complex. Look carefully at the choices and really think about what the question is asking.

You Don't Have to Read the Directions

What? Yes, you read it correctly the first time—you don't have to read the directions. Look, by the time you actually sit down to take the SAT, you've read this book, you've taken all the practice tests you could find, and you've read enough SAT directions to fill a library. So when the exam clock starts ticking, don't waste time rereading directions you already know. Instead, go directly to Question 1.

You're Going to Need a Watch

If you're going to pace yourself, you need to keep track of the time—and what if there is no clock in your room or if the only clock is out of your line of vision? That's why it's a good idea to bring a watch to the test. A word of warning: don't use a watch alarm or your watch will end up on the proctor's desk.

EDUCATED GUESSING WILL BOOST YOUR SCORE!

The fractional deduction for wrong answers makes random guessing a wash—statistically speaking, you're unlikely to change your score. This means that if you come to a question that you have absolutely no idea how to answer, you're probably better off skipping it and moving on, rather than just choosing an answer at random.

Although random guessing won't help you, anything better than random guessing will. On most questions, you should be able to guess better than randomly by using common sense and the process-of-elimination techniques that are developed throughout this book. Even if you aren't certain which answer is correct, you might be certain that one or more of the answer choices is definitely *wrong*. If you can knock out one choice out of five, you have a 25-percent chance of guessing correctly. If you can knock out two choices, the odds go up to $33\frac{1}{3}$ percent. If you can knock out three, you have a 50/50 chance of guessing the right answer. With odds like this, it makes sense to guess, especially when you realize that a single correct guess can raise your scaled scored as much as 10 points.

How Educated Guessing Can Help

Let's take a sample situation to demonstrate the effectiveness of educated guessing. Let's say that on the entire SAT there were forty questions you were unsure of. Now we know what you're thinking. Forty questions seem like an awful lot of questions with which to have difficulty. But think about it: if you answered every other one of the SAT's 138 questions correctly, you'd already be scoring over 1200! So to have trouble with forty questions is not only possible, it's likely.

Now remember how the SAT is scored. Every question you answer correctly is worth one raw score point, which corresponds to roughly 10 scaled score points. For every question you leave blank, you gain nothing and lose nothing. And for every incorrect answer you mark down, you lose $\frac{1}{4}$ of a raw score point, which corresponds to approximately 2.5 scaled score points. When students first learn this, they usually get nervous about guessing. After all, who wants to lose points on questions you're unsure of? However, a more careful look demonstrates the exact opposite: educated guessing can dramatically improve your score even if you make many incorrect guesses along the way.

Let's get back to those forty difficult questions. You basically have three choices: you can leave them all blank in fear of losing points; you can guess randomly; or you can use process-of-elimination techniques to make educated guesses. Let's examine the outcome of each approach:

The *fearful student* takes the first approach and leaves all forty questions blank. For his effort, he receives no points and loses no points. So he breaks even.

The *random guesser* picks the answers for random reasons. Maybe he picks choice (C) for every one. Or maybe he fills his answer sheet in such a way as to make a visually appealing pattern. What will happen to the random guesser? Well, statistically speaking, he will answer one out of every five questions correctly, since most questions have five answer choices. That means he will answer 8 questions correctly out of 40 ($\frac{1}{5}$ out of 40). For his effort, the random guesser will pick up 80 points for the questions he got right (8×10 points) and lose 80 points for the 32 questions he got wrong (32×2.5 pts). So the random guesser ends up in the exact same position as the fearful student.

The *smart test-taker* will take advantage of what he *does* know to make educated guesses. You will become the smart test-taker! You will use the process-of-elimination techniques that we develop in this book. On virtually every question, you will eliminate one, two, or three poor choices. Let's say that you answer 16 questions correctly out of the 40 you're unsure of. Even though that's a pretty low percentage, you will do considerably better than the fearful student or the random guesser. For the 16 questions you answer correctly, you will receive 160 points (16 × 10 pts), and for the 24 questions you answer incorrectly, you will lose 60 points (24 × 2.5 pts). So by doing nothing more than answering questions you've already thought about, you pick up 100 scaled score points. Here's a table that might make more sense of these numbers:

Guessing on 40 Difficult Questions

	#Right	#Wrong	#Blank	Total Pts.
The Fearful Student	0	0	40	0 pts
The Random Guesser	8 (+80)	32 (−80)	0	0 pts
The Smart Test-Taker	16 (+160)	24 (−60)	0	100 pts

Obviously, the better you get at eliminating implausible choices, the more points you will pick up from educated guessing. But no matter what, if you have time to read through a question and eliminate at least one choice, it is always to your benefit to guess. Don't worry about the fact that you will probably get the question wrong, because you don't need to guess correctly on too many questions to gain points. As long as you are guessing better than randomly, you will do considerably better.

GETTING READY: THE NIGHT BEFORE AND THE DAY OF THE TEST

If you follow the guidelines in this book, you will be extremely well prepared for the SAT. You will know the format inside and out; you will know how to approach every type of question; you will have worked hard to strengthen your weak areas; and you will have taken multiple practice tests under simulated testing conditions. The last 24 hours before the SAT is not the time to cram—it's actually the time to relax. Remember that the SAT is primarily a test of how you think, not what you know. So last-minute cramming can be more confusing than illuminating.

That said, there are plenty of steps you can take over the final 24 hours to get ready. For one thing, don't do anything too stressful. On the night before the big day, find a diversion to keep yourself from obsessing about the SAT. Maybe stay home and watch some of your favorite television shows. Or go out to an early movie. Or talk for hours and hours on the phone about a subject other than the SAT. Do whatever is best for you. Just make sure you get plenty of sleep.

You should also lay out the following items before you go to bed:

- **Registration ticket:** Unless you are taking the test as a "standby" tester, you should have received one of these in the mail.

- **Identification:** A driver's license is preferable, but anything with a picture will do.

- **Pencils:** Make sure you bring at least three number-2 pencils; those are the only pencils that the machines can read.

- **Calculator:** Bring the calculator that you're most comfortable with. Don't pack a scientific or graphing calculator if you're unfamiliar with how it works. And don't take any calculator that beeps, produces a paper tape, makes any noise at all, or that is a part of a computer or other device. You won't be allowed to use such a calculator on the SAT.

- **Layered clothing:** You never know what the test-taking temperature will be. By dressing in layers, you can adapt to extreme heat or cold.

- **Wristwatch:** Your classroom should have an operational clock, but if it doesn't, you want to come prepared. Again, don't wear a watch that beeps, unless you can turn off the alarm function. You won't be allowed to wear a noise-making watch during the exam.

- **Snack:** You're not allowed to eat during the test administration in your test room, but you are given a 5- to 10-minute break after Section 2. So be armed with a fortifying snack that you can eat quickly in the hallway.

When you awake on test day, make sure you allow enough time to comfortably arrive at the test site by 8:00 a.m. (If you're uncertain how long the trip from your home to the site will take, practice the drive ahead of time.) Take a shower to wake up and then eat a sensible breakfast. If you are a person who usually eats breakfast, you should probably eat your customary meal. If you don't usually eat breakfast, don't gorge yourself on test day, because it will be a shock to your system. Eat something light (like a granola bar and a piece of fruit) and pack that snack.

SUMMARY

Understand the SAT and Conquer Test Anxiety

- Familiarize yourself with the SAT's seven sections. Knowing the test format will relieve test anxiety because you will know exactly what to expect on test day.

- Within each question set (except critical reading), questions are arranged from easiest to most difficult. So where a question is placed provides an instant indication of how difficult it is.

- Remember that all SAT questions count the same, so you receive the same number of points for an easy question as for a more difficult one. So nail the easier questions—they're a good source of points!

- Make sure that you fill in the answer bubbles cleanly and completely. Otherwise, the machine won't give you credit for your answers.

- Remember that random guessing will have no effect on your score, but educated guessing will boost your score. So if you've had time to read through a question and eliminate at least one choice, guess!

- It pays to pace yourself and move through the test relatively quickly. But you can get a very good score even if you don't answer every question. As a matter of fact, a raw score of 36 out of 78 on verbal—or 27 out of 60 on math—is equivalent to a 500!

- Relax the day before the SAT. Before you go to bed the night before the exam, however, check through the list of things you need to take with you to the test site. Make sure your calculator has fresh batteries, eat breakfast, and head for the site.

- Remember—if you're working through this book, you're giving yourself the best preparation available for succeeding on the SAT. Let your preparation give you the confidence you need to be calm and focused during the exam.

SAT Questions:
A First Look

OVERVIEW

- Learn how the SAT tests verbal reasoning
- Understand analogies
- Understand sentence completions
- Understand critical reasoning
- Learn how the SAT tests mathematical reasoning
- Understand multiple-choice math
- Understand quantitative comparisons
- Understand grid-ins

HOW THE SAT TESTS VERBAL REASONING

The SAT exam determines your verbal reasoning skills in three ways. You will
be tested using the following types of questions:

1. Analogies
2. Sentence completions
3. Critical reading

The scored sections of the test will contain a total of 19 analogies, 19 sentence
completions, and 40 critical reading questions. Even if you're not a math whiz,
you can see that critical reading accounts for more than half of your total verbal
score. The following sections discuss each of the verbal reasoning question types,
to give you a clear idea of what you can expect on the verbal sections of the SAT.

UNDERSTANDING ANALOGIES

SAT analogy questions ask you to match up pairs of words that are related in the
same way. Each question starts with a word pair. You have to pick the pair of words
from five answer choices that has the same logical relationship.

The directions for SAT analogy questions look like this:

Directions: Each question below consists of a related pair of words
or phrases, followed by five pairs of words or phrases labeled (A)
through (E). Select the pair that best expresses a relationship similar
to that expressed in the original pair.

chapter 3

NOTE

When you've finished this chapter, you can rest assured that you have learned about every type of SAT question. No need to worry what the test will "really" be like— this book will present everything as it appears on the test!

Here are three sample SAT analogy questions. Try each one on your own, then read the explanation that accompanies it.

1. HORSE : UNICORN ::
    (A) lizard : dragon
    (B) ram : stallion
    (C) sheep : lamb
    (D) reptile : scale
    (E) mare : mermaid

The correct answer is (A). A horse is a real animal and a unicorn is an imaginary horselike animal, just as a lizard is a real animal and a dragon is an imaginary lizardlike animal. Let's look at the other answer choices to see why they are wrong. Choice (B) is wrong because the only relationship between ram and stallion is that they are both male animals. In choice (C), the relationship is that a sheep is an adult lamb. In answer (D), the relationship is that a reptile is covered with scales. Choice (E) is close. A mare is real and a mermaid is imaginary, but a mermaid bears no resemblance to a female horse. So, choice (E) is not the best answer.

2. SPOOL : THREAD ::
    (A) bale : hay
    (B) sack : potatoes
    (C) verse : song
    (D) coil : rope
    (E) reel : line

The correct answer is (E). Thread is wrapped around a spool, just as a fishing line is wrapped around a reel. Choice (A) is wrong because hay is bundled, not wrapped, in a bale. Choice (B) is wrong because potatoes are stored in, not wrapped around, a sack. In choice (C), the only relationship is that a verse is part of a song. And choice (D) is wrong because the relationship is only that rope can be shaped into a coil.

3. RICE : WEDDING ::
    (A) food : groom
    (B) celebration : ceremony
    (C) wheat : meal
    (D) bran : cereal
    (E) confetti : parade

The correct answer is (E). Rice is often thrown at a wedding, just as confetti is often thrown at a parade. Just try this sentence with the other choices and you'll see that none of them even comes close to working.

UNDERSTANDING SENTENCE COMPLETIONS

Just as the name implies, sentence completions are "fill-in-the-blank" questions. SAT sentence completion questions may have one or two blanks. Your job is to choose from among the answer choices the word or words that best fit each blank.

The directions for SAT sentence completion questions look like this:

> **Directions:** Each of the following sentences contains one or two blank spaces to be filled in by one of the five choices listed below each sentence. Select the word or words that best complete the meaning of the sentence.

Here are three sample SAT sentence completion questions. Try each one on your own, before you read the explanation that accompanies it.

1. Many hours of practice are required of a successful musician, so it is often not so much _____ as _____ that distinguishes the professional from the amateur.

    (A) genius..understanding

    (B) money..education

    (C) talent..discipline

    (D) fortitude..mediocrity

    (E) technique..pomposity

The correct answer is (C). How do you know this? The sentence gives you a clue. The "not so much . . . as . . ." lets you know that there is some kind of contrast here. Choices (B) and (C) both show a contrast, but choice (C) is the only one that makes sense in the sentence.

2. The sudden death of the world-renowned leader _____ his followers, but it _____ his former opponents.

    (A) saddened..devastated

    (B) shocked..encouraged

    (C) depressed..tempered

    (D) satisfied..aided

    (E) prostrated..depressed

The correct answer is (B). The word *but* is your clue that the word in the second blank will contrast with the word in the first blank. Only the words *shocked* and *encouraged* offer the logical contrast that is expected between the feelings of followers and opponents on the death of a leader.

NOTE

These directions ask you to choose the best answer. That's why you should always read all the answer choices before you make your final selection.

NOTE

It's an open-book test. In SAT critical reading questions, the answers will always be directly stated or implied in the passage.

3. Despite his valor on the football field, the star athlete _____ when forced to take a flu shot.

    (A) relaxed

    (B) trembled

    (C) hustled

    (D) sidled

    (E) embellished

The correct answer is (B). The word *despite* is your clue that the athlete will do something less than heroic when confronted with the flu shot. *Trembled* completes the sentence and continues the strong tone of irony.

UNDERSTANDING CRITICAL READING

SAT critical reading questions present a passage that you are to read and answer questions about. The questions follow the order in which information appears in the passage. The directions for critical reading questions look like this:

> **Directions:** The passage below is followed by a set of questions. Read the passage and answer the accompanying questions, basing your answers on what is stated or implied in the passage.

Here is a sample of what to expect. (Note that this passage is much shorter than a standard SAT passage.)

The following passage discusses the mythical island of Atlantis.

A legendary island in the Atlantic Ocean beyond the Pillars of Hercules was first mentioned by Plato in the Timaeus. Atlantis was a fabulously beautiful and prosperous land, the seat of an empire nine thousand years before Solon. Its
(5) inhabitants overran part of Europe and Africa, Athens alone being able to defy them. Because of the impiety of its people, the island was destroyed by an earthquake and inundation. The legend may have existed before Plato and may have sprung from the concept of Homer's Elysium. The possibility that such an island once existed has caused much speculation, resulting in a theory that pre-
(10) Columbian civilizations in America were established by colonists from the lost island.

1. The main purpose of the passage is to discuss

    (A) the legend of Atlantis.

    (B) Plato's description of Atlantis in the Timaeus.

    (C) the conquests made by citizens of Atlantis.

    (D) the possibility that the Americas were settled by colonists from Atlantis.

    (E) the destruction of Atlantis.

The correct answer is (A). The main purpose should be represented by an overall statement. While the details in choices (B), (C), (D), and (E) are all mentioned in the text, choice (A) is the only overall statement.

2. According to the passage, we may safely conclude that the inhabitants of Atlantis

    (A) were known personally to Homer.

    (B) were a peace-loving people who stayed close to home.

    (C) were a religious and superstitious people.

    (D) used the name Columbus for America.

    (E) were never visited by Plato.

The correct answer is (E). At the time Plato mentioned Atlantis, it was already legendary. Therefore, Plato could not have visited the island.

3. According to the legend, Atlantis was destroyed because the inhabitants

    (A) failed to obtain an adequate food supply.

    (B) failed to conquer Greece.

    (C) failed to respect their gods.

    (D) believed in Homer's Elysium.

    (E) had become too prosperous.

The correct answer is (C). The only cause that's mentioned in the passage is the "impiety" of the people of Atlantis.

HOW THE SAT TESTS MATHEMATICAL REASONING

The SAT tests your mathematical reasoning ability with these three question types:

*   Standard multiple-choice
*   Quantitative comparisons
*   Student-produced response

The scored sections of the test will contain a total of 35 standard multiple-choice questions, 15 quantitative comparisons, and 10 student-produced response questions.

UNDERSTANDING MULTIPLE-CHOICE MATH

SAT standard multiple-choice math questions look like all the other multiple-choice math questions you've ever faced, but they usually require some logical thinking to solve them. The directions for SAT math questions include many of the concepts you need to know. Here's what they look like:

Directions: Solve the following problems using any available space on the page for scratchwork. On your answer sheet, fill in the choice that best corresponds to the correct answer.

Notes: The figures accompanying the problems are drawn as accurately as possible unless otherwise stated in specific problems. Again, unless otherwise stated, all figures lie in the same plane. All numbers used in these problems are real numbers. Calculators are permitted for this test.

Circle: $C = 2\pi r$ $A = \pi r^2$

Rectangle: $A = lw$

Rectangular Solid: $V = lwh$

Cylinder: $V = \pi r^2 h$

Triangle: $A = \frac{1}{2}bh$

$a^2 + b^2 = c^2$

The number of degrees of arc in a circle is 360.
The measure in degrees of a straight angle is 180.
The sum of the measures in degrees of the angles of a triangle is 180.

Here are some sample multiple-choice math questions. Try them yourself before looking at the solutions that are given.

1. A certain triangle has sides that are, respectively, 6 inches, 8 inches, and 10 inches long. A rectangle with an area equal to that of the triangle has a width of 3 inches. What is the perimeter of the rectangle, in inches?

   (A) 11
   (B) 16
   (C) 22
   (D) 24
   (E) 30

Note: A [calculator] following a math answer explanation indicates that a calculator could be helpful in solving that particular problem.

The correct answer is (C). The area of the triangle is $\frac{1}{2}bh$, which in this case is $\frac{1}{2} \times 6 \times 8 = 24$. The area of a rectangle is $A = l \times w$. Since we know the width and area, $24 = l \times 3$; therefore, $l = 8$. The perimeter of the rectangle is $P = 2l + 2w$, which we find to be $(2 \times 8) + (2 \times 3) = 16 + 6 = 22$. [calculator]

2. A room 27 feet by 32 feet is to be carpeted. The width of the carpet is 27 inches. What is the length, in yards, of the carpet needed for this floor? (1 yard = 3 feet = 36 inches)

   (A) 1,188
   (B) 648
   (C) 384
   (D) 128
   (E) 96

The correct answer is (D). The length of one side of the room in inches is 27 ft. × 12 in. = 324 in. The width of the carpet is 27 in.; therefore, it takes 324 ÷ 27 = 12 lengths of carpet at 32 ft. per length, or 12 × 32 = 384 ft. The length needed in yards is 384 ft. ÷ 3 ft./yd. = 128 yards.

3. Given: Right $\triangle ABC$ with $AB = 6$ and $AC = 7$. What does BC equal?

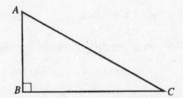

   (A) 1
   (B) $\sqrt{13}$
   (C) 6
   (D) $\sqrt{29}$
   (E) $\sqrt{98}$

The correct answer is (B). By the Pythagorean theorem, $(AB)^2 + (BC)^2 = (AC)^2$, or $(BC)^2 = (AC)^2 - (AB)^2$. Substituting the values in this equation yields $(BC)^2 = (7)^2 - (6)^2 = 49 - 36 = 13$, and $BC = \sqrt{13}$.

4. The closest approximation to the correct answer for $5 - \sqrt{32.076} + 1.00017^3$ is

   (A) 9
   (B) 7
   (C) 5
   (D) 3
   (E) 0

The correct answer is (E). $\sqrt{32.076}$ is slightly more than halfway between 5 and 6, say 5.6. Also, 1.00017^3 is very slightly over $1^3 = 1$. Therefore, $5 - 5.6 + 1 = 0.04$. The closest answer given is 0.

5. If the numerator and denominator of a proper fraction are increased by the same quantity, the resulting fraction is
    (A) always greater than the original fraction.
    (B) always less than the original fraction.
    (C) always equal to the original fraction.
    (D) one half the original fraction.
    (E) not determinable.

The correct answer is (A). If the numerator and denominator of the fraction $\frac{n}{d}$ are increased by a quantity q, the new fraction is $\frac{(n+q)}{(d+q)}$. Compare this to the old fraction by finding a common denominator $d(d+q)$. The old fraction is $\frac{n(d+q)}{d(d+q)} = \frac{(nd+nq)}{d(d+q)}$; the new fraction is $\frac{d(n+q)}{d(d+q)} = \frac{(nd+dq)}{d(d+q)}$. Comparing the old numerator $(nd+nq)$ with the new, the new fraction is larger, since $d > n$. The fraction in this example must be a proper fraction.

6. The total number of feet in x yards, y feet, and z inches is (1 yard = 3 feet = 36 inches)
    (A) $3x + y + \frac{z}{12}$
    (B) $12(x + y + z)$
    (C) $x + y + z$
    (D) $\frac{x}{36} + \frac{y}{12} + z$
    (E) $x + 3y + 36z$

The correct answer is (A). x yards = $3x$ feet; z inches = $\frac{z}{12}$ feet. Therefore, x yards + y feet + z inches = $3x$ feet + y feet + $\frac{z}{12}$ feet, or $3x + y + \frac{z}{12}$ feet.

UNDERSTANDING QUANTITATIVE COMPARISONS

SAT quantitative comparisons are probably not like any other math question you've ever seen. These questions present you with two quantities, one quantity is presented in Column A, and the other in Column B. Your job is to decide which quantity is greater, whether the two quantities are equal, or whether no comparison is possible. There are only four answer choices for this question type, and they are always the same. Here is what the directions look like:

> **Directions:** For each of the following items, compare the quantity in Column A with the one in Column B and determine whether:
>
> **(A)** the quantity in Column A is greater
>
> **(B)** the quantity in Column B is greater
>
> **(C)** if the two quantities are equal
>
> **(D)** if the relationship cannot be determined from the information given
>
> **Notes:**
>
> **(1)** Information concerning one or both of the compared quantities will be centered between the two columns for some of the items.
>
> **(2)** Symbols that appear in both columns represent the same thing in Column A as in Column B.
>
> **(3)** Letters such as x, n, and k are symbols for real numbers.

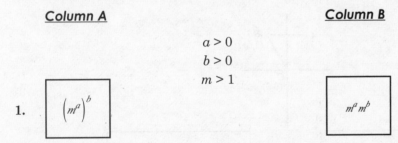

Column A

$$a > 0$$
$$b > 0$$
$$m > 1$$

1. $\left(m^a\right)^b$ | $m^a m^b$

The correct answer is (D). In Column A, $\left(m^a\right)^b = m^{ab}$, with $ab > 0$, since $a, b > 0$. In Column B, $m^a m^b = m^{a+b}$, with $a + b > 0$ since $a, b > 0$. Since we know nothing else about a and b, we cannot tell if $ab > a + b$ or vice versa.

<u>Column A</u>   <u>Column B</u>

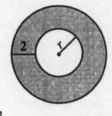

2. | Area of | | Area of |
      | smaller circle | | shaded portion |

The correct answer is (D). The area of the larger circle is $\pi(r+2)^2$. The area of the smaller circle is πr^2. The area of the shaded region is:

$$\pi(r+2)^2 - \pi r^2$$
$$= \pi(r^2 + 4r + 4) - \pi r^2$$
$$= \pi r^2 + 4\pi r + 4\pi + \pi r^2$$
$$= 4\pi r^2 + 4\pi = 4\pi(r+1)$$

Since we know nothing about the radius r, we cannot tell which area is larger.

3. | 39% of 87 | | 87% of 39 |

The correct answer is (C). The trick to the problem is realizing that in both columns you will multiply 39×87 and move the decimal point two places to the left.

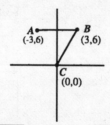

4. | Distance from A to B | | Distance from B to C |

The correct answer is (B). The distance from A to B is

$$\sqrt{(3+3)^2 + (6-6)^2} = \sqrt{36} = 6.$$

The distance from B to C is

$$\sqrt{(0-3)^2 + (0-6)^2} = \sqrt{9+36} = \sqrt{45}.$$

The square root of 45 is greater than 6. Therefore, the distance from B to C is greater than the distance from A to B.

UNDERSTANDING GRID-INS

SAT grid-in questions are the only SAT questions that don't give you the answers. That is your job. You do the calculations, you find the answer, and you write the information on a special part of the answer sheet. You do this by filling in ovals that correspond to your answer. These examples and explanations will help prepare you for the questions to come.

> **Directions:** Solve each of the following problems and write the arithmetic value of your answer in the open spaces at the top of the correspondingly numbered grid on your answer sheet. Then grid your answer by blackening the ovals that correspond to the decimal point, fraction line, and numbers in your answer.
>
> **Notes:** If a question has more than one correct answer, grid only one of them.
> To grid $4\frac{1}{4}$ use 4.25 or $\frac{17}{4}$. Do not use $4\frac{1}{4}$ as it will be read as $\frac{41}{4}$.
> None of these answers requires a minus sign.
> Answers may begin in any grid column.
> Decimal answers should be entered with the greatest accuracy allowed by the grid.

1. The circumference of a circle is 20π. If the area of the circle is $a\pi$, what is the value of a?

   $C = 2\pi r = 20\pi$
   $r = 10$
   $A = \pi r^2 = \pi(10)^2 = 100\pi = a\pi$

   $\therefore a = 100$

2. If 35% of a number is 70, what is the number?

   $\frac{35}{100} \bullet x = 70$
   $\frac{35x}{100} = 70$
   $x = 200$

3. Find the mode of the following group of numbers: 8, 8, 9, 10, 11

The mode is the number that occurs the most frequently. The mode = 8.

SUMMARY

What You Need to Know about the SAT Question Types

This information is the foundation that you're going to build on as you prepare for the SAT.

- Learning the SAT question types is the best way to prepare for the SAT. Since the question types never change, you'll know exactly what to expect on test day.

- There are 19 analogies on the SAT. Each question asks you to find the answer choice that best expresses a relationship similar to the one expressed by the capitalized pair.

- There are 19 sentence completions on the SAT. Each question asks you to find the answer choice with the word or words that best fit into each blank.

- There are 40 critical reading questions on the SAT. Remember that the answers to every question will always be directly stated or implied in the passage. So find them.

- There are 35 multiple-choice math questions on the SAT. Remember to use the reference formulas at the beginning of each math section to help you with these questions.

- There are 15 quantitative comparison questions on the SAT. Each one asks you to compare two quantities and decide which is greater. Remember that there are only four answer choices for this question type!

- There are 10 grid-in questions on the SAT. Unlike other math questions, grid-ins require that you provide your own answer by filling in the ovals of a special grid. Remember that only the ovals count, so make sure you fill them in correctly.

- You can use a calculator to tackle SAT math questions. While a calculator may be helpful on some problems, it isn't *absolutely necessary* for any of them. So use your calculator, but don't rely on it too much.

PART II

DIAGNOSING STRENGTHS
AND WEAKNESSES

CHAPTER 4   Diagnostic Test

Diagnostic Test

SECTION 1

31 Questions • Time—30 Minutes

Directions: Each of the following questions consists of an incomplete sentence followed by five words or pairs of words. Choose that word or pair of words that, when substituted for the blank space or spaces, best completes the meaning of the sentence and mark the letter of your choice on your answer sheet.

Example

Q In view of the extenuating circumstances and the defendant's youth, the judge recommended ____.

(A) conviction

(B) a defense

(C) a mistrial

(D) leniency

(E) life imprisonment

A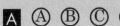

1. Her position in the agency authorized her to award contracts and to ____ obligations for payment of expenses.

(A) rescind

(B) incur

(C) procure

(D) recur

(E) resume

2. Despite all his courtroom experience, the attorney was able to pry very little information out of the ____ witness.

(A) cooperative

(B) recalcitrant

(C) reactionary

(D) presumptive

(E) credulous

3. Although over the years ____ resources had been devoted to alleviating the problem, a satisfactory solution remained ____.

   (A) natural..costly
   (B) adequate..probable
   (C) substantial..elusive
   (D) capital..decisive
   (E) conventional..abstract

4. The team attributes its ____ season to a number of ____ factors.

   (A) losing..propitious
   (B) long..irrelevant
   (C) remarkable..derogatory
   (D) embarrassing..optimistic
   (E) winning..favorable

5. While fewer documents are being kept, the usefulness of those ____ is now ____ by an improved cataloging system.

   (A) printed..documented
   (B) discarded..concurred
   (C) read..emblazoned
   (D) retained..insured
   (E) received..negated

6. The ____ with which the agent calmed the anxieties and soothed the tempers of the travelers ____ by the delay was a mark of frequent experience with similar crises.

   (A) evasiveness..angered
   (B) reverence..pleased
   (C) facility..inconvenienced
   (D) mannerism..destroyed
   (E) acuity..accommodated

7. The lover of democracy has an ____ toward totalitarianism.

   (A) antipathy
   (B) empathy
   (C) equanimity
   (D) idolatry
   (E) obstinacy

8. A ____ of employment opportunities ____ prospective employees entering the job market.

   (A) surfeit..impedes
   (B) paucity..discourages
   (C) plethora..deters
   (D) dearth..inspires
   (E) deluge..enervates

9. In truth, ____ has a cost; for every free person we pay with the ____ of fifty others.

   (A) liberty..subjection
   (B) liberalism..environmentalism
   (C) capitalism..punishment
   (D) independence..individualism
   (E) authority..autonomy

Directions: Each of the following questions consists of a capitalized pair of words followed by five pairs of words lettered (A) to (E). The capitalized words bear some meaningful relationship to each other. Choose the lettered pair of words whose relationship is most similar to that expressed by the capitalized pair and mark its letter on your answer sheet.

Example

Q DAY : SUN ::

(A) sunlight : daylight

(B) ray : sun

(C) night : moon

(D) heat : cold

(E) moon : star

A   ● (D) (E)

10. POWERFUL : MIGHTY ::

(A) muscular : alert

(B) mediocre : ordinary

(C) tense : springy

(D) weak : small

(E) deep : murky

11. HAIR : HORSE ::

(A) feather : bird

(B) wool : sheep

(C) down : pillow

(D) fuzz : peach

(E) fur : animal

12. GOBBLE : TURKEY ::

(A) shed : cobra

(B) chop : tree

(C) graze : elephant

(D) twitter : bird

(E) sleep : lion

13. SELL : PURCHASE ::

(A) pay : charge

(B) offer : bid

(C) buy : earn

(D) donate : demand

(E) give : receive

14. NOVEL : BOOK ::

(A) act : play

(B) article : magazine

(C) mitten : hand

(D) sock : foot

(E) loafer : shoe

15. TEMERITY : CAUTION ::

(A) trepidation : fear

(B) effrontery : shame

(C) cacophony : dissonance

(D) capriciousness : whimsy

(E) adulation : praise

> **Directions:** Each passage below is followed by a set of questions. Read each passage; then answer the accompanying questions, basing your answers on what is stated or implied in the passage and in any introductory material provided. Mark the letter of your choice on your answer sheet.

Questions 16–22 are based on the following passage.

The principles of classical architecture have endured over time. Modern buildings built in the classical style still adhere to architectural principles established during the times of the ancient Romans. The following passage considers some of those principles.

Classical architecture, the origins of which can be traced to ancient Rome, was the type of architecture embraced by the very highest social levels of that
(5) ancient civilization. As such, classical architecture was characterized by a rigorous adherence to the principles of coherence, exactness, and detail.

The basis of the classical style was
(10) the manner in which a building's space was divided so as to create a coherent whole. An example of a plan for the division of a building's space was the *tripartite* plan, which would divide the space in
(15) a particular building into three equal parts. Such a plan would be followed no matter what the purpose of the building—churches, homes, or public government buildings could all be designed with
(20) such a plan. Even gardens, designed in the classical style, might have a three-part plan. It is interesting, too, that the classical *tripartite* plan spilled over from architecture to other arts—music, poetry,
(25) and dance—so that it is not uncommon to have a three-part hierarchy within those artistic areas as well.

Once the framework of a building designed in the classical style was estab-
(30) lished, architectural elements were added. Columns are fairly typical architectural elements, with the five most common column types being the *Doric,*

Ionic, Corinthian, Tuscan, and *Compos-*
(35) *ite.* Each column was distinctive and of a certain specified proportion, base to top. Just as the building itself might embody a tripartite plan, so did the columns themselves have a three-part
(40) organization. Above the column is a horizontal piece, called the *entablature,* then comes the column itself, which is tall and cylindrical, and finally comes the three-step platform upon which the col-
(45) umn rests, called the *crepidoma.* The top piece is further divided into three parts—the cornice, the frieze, and the architrave. The column breaks down into three parts—the capital, the shaft, and the base.
(50) The crepidoma maintains the three-part division with its three steps.

Symmetry was also an important element in classical architecture. The relationship between architectural ele-
(55) ments and the whole edifice was conceived, studied, and implemented with a great deal of attention paid at each stage of the plan to assuring that balance was achieved. Proportion and parallelism
(60) were critical in the achievement of the plan's coherence as well.

Classical architecture was filled with conventions, scrupulously adhered to, which although perhaps not obvious
(65) to the viewer become apparent upon closer analysis. For example, classical buildings must stand free; they cannot touch the sides of other buildings. This is so because in the view of the classicist, the
(70) building was a world within a world of its own. Thus, the building had to stand alone, an example of its singular world. Consequently, groups of classical buildings became problematic because of per-
(75) ceived violations of spatial conventions that troubled rule-based classical architects. The classical mode required an adherence to formal patterns and sym-

metry sometimes not possible to impose
(80) on groups of buildings.

Classical architects longed to bring
order to the world through designs that
struggled for consistency and complete-
ness. The classical plan was a disci-
(85) plined plan requiring the ability to divide,
relate, and align elements. The resulting building was thus created in a way
pleasing to the eye and appropriate to
the time and place in which it was placed.

16. The origins of classical architecture date
back to the time of ancient

    (A) Egypt.
    (B) Greece.
    (C) Sumeria.
    (D) Rome.
    (E) Mesopotamia.

17. Classical architecture is characterized by
all of the following EXCEPT

    (A) attention to detail.
    (B) rigorous exactness.
    (C) different spatial divisions for differ-
    ent types of buildings.
    (D) attention to a coherent whole.
    (E) use of a *tripartite* division of spaces.

18. The word *tripartite* in lines 13 and 14
most nearly means

    (A) geometric.
    (B) three-part.
    (C) political.
    (D) spatial.
    (E) mathematical.

19. All of the following are column types
EXCEPT

    (A) Egyptian.
    (B) Doric.
    (C) Ionic.
    (D) Tuscan.
    (E) Corinthian.

20. Which of the following is one of the three
parts of the column proper?

    (A) The cornice
    (B) The capital
    (C) The frieze
    (D) The architave
    (E) The detail

21. The word *symmetry* in line 52 most nearly
means

    (A) absence of proportion.
    (B) lack of parallelism.
    (C) spatial qualities.
    (D) architectural element.
    (E) balance.

22. The main idea of this passage is that

    (A) classical architecture is out of fashion.
    (B) the classical approach to architecture
    allows for much freedom of expression.
    (C) there is no place for architectural
    elements in the classical scheme.
    (D) the Ionic column is the most perfect
    example of a classical element.
    (E) the conventions of classical architec-
    ture are scrupulously followed.

Questions 23–31 are based on the following passage.

Angel Decora was born Hinookmahiwikilinaka on the Winnebago Reservation in Nebraska in 1871. She worked as a book illustrator, particularly on books by and about Native Americans, and lectured and wrote about Indian art. The story from which this excerpt is taken, "The Sick Child," may be autobiographical.

It was about sunset when I, a little
child, was sent with a handful of pow-
dered tobacco leaves and red feathers to
make an offering to the spirit who had
(5) caused the sickness of my little sister. It
had been a long, hard winter, and the

snow lay deep on the prairie as far as the eye could reach. The medicine-woman's directions had been that the offering
(10) must be laid upon the naked earth, and that to find it I must face toward the setting sun.

I was taught the prayer: "Spirit grandfather, I offer this to thee. I pray
(15) thee restore my little sister to health." Full of reverence and a strong faith that I could appease the anger of the spirit, I started out to plead for the life of our little one.
(20) But now where was a spot of earth to be found in all that white monotony? They had talked of death at the house. I hoped that my little sister would live, but I was afraid of nature.
(25) I reached a little spring. I looked down to its pebbly bottom, wondering whether I should leave my offering there, or keep on in search of a spot of earth. If I put my offering in the water, would it
(30) reach the bottom and touch the earth, or would it float away, as it had always done when I made my offering to the water spirit?

Once more I started on in my search
(35) of the bare ground.

The surface was crusted in some places, and walking was easy; in other places I would wade through a foot or more of snow. Often I paused, thinking
(40) to clear the snow away in some place and there lay my offering. But no, my faith must be in nature, and I must trust to it to lay bare the earth. It was a hard struggle for so small a child.
(45) I went on and on; the reeds were waving their tasselled ends in the wind. I stopped and looked at them. A reed, whirling in the wind, had formed a space round its stem, making a loose socket. I
(50) stood looking into the opening. The reed must be rooted in the ground, and the hole must follow the stem to the earth. If I poured my offerings into the hole, surely they must reach the ground; so I said the
(55) prayer that I had been taught, and dropped my tobacco and red feathers into the opening that nature itself had created.

No sooner was the sacrifice accom-
(60) plished than a feeling of doubt and fear thrilled me. What if my offering should never reach the earth? Would my little sister die?

Not till I turned homeward did I
(65) realize how cold I was. When at last I reached the house they took me in and warmed me, but did not question me, and I said nothing. Everyone was sad, for the little one had grown worse.
(70) The next day the medicine-woman said my little sister was beyond hope; she could not live. Then bitter remorse was mine, for I thought I had been un-faithful, and therefore my little sister
(75) was to be called to the spirit land. I was a silent child, and did not utter my feelings; my remorse was intense. . . .

23. The word *offering* (line 4) means

   (A) proposal.

   (B) bid.

   (C) advance.

   (D) tribute.

   (E) suggestion.

24. By "naked earth" (line 10), the medicine-woman meant

   (A) the bare ground.

   (B) an eroded streambed.

   (C) a treeless plain.

   (D) the dirt floor of the house.

   (E) a patch of snow.

25. The narrator's journey could be called a

   (A) reverie.

   (B) retreat.

   (C) junket.

   (D) quest.

   (E) jaunt.

26. "White monotony" (line 21) refers to the fact that

(A) the family lives on a reservation.

(B) white people find Nebraska dull.

(C) snow covers the landscape.

(D) the narrator is blind.

(E) nothing happens in the story.

27. Lines 43–44 ("It was a hard struggle for so small a child") are

(A) an aside by an omniscient narrator.

(B) the adult narrator's realization that saving her sick sister was too big a task for the child.

(C) an ironic statement by an outside observer.

(D) the adult narrator's excuse for placing the feathers and tobacco in a poor spot.

(E) the adult narrator's explanation for the young girl's silent remorse.

28. The word *thrilled* (line 61) is used to mean

(A) delighted.

(B) exhilarated.

(C) inflamed.

(D) enraptured.

(E) inspired.

29. The narrator's remorse is due to her

(A) uncaring attitude toward her sister.

(B) mixed feelings toward her own religion.

(C) secret longing for attention.

(D) perceived failure at following instructions.

(E) mistrust of the medicine-woman.

30. If her sister died, you would expect the narrator to feel

(A) relieved.

(B) elated.

(C) surprised.

(D) confused.

(E) guilty.

31. What feeling does the narrator have toward the child?

(A) shame

(B) bewilderment

(C) forgiveness

(D) irritation

(E) anxiety

STOP

END OF SECTION 1. IF YOU HAVE ANY TIME LEFT, GO
OVER YOUR WORK IN THIS SECTION ONLY. DO NOT
WORK IN ANY OTHER SECTION OF THE TEST.

SECTION 2

25 Questions • Time—30 Minutes

Directions: Solve the following problems using any available space on the page for scratchwork. On your answer sheet fill in the choice that best corresponds to the correct answer.

Notes: The figures accompanying the problems are drawn as accurately as possible unless otherwise stated in specific problems. Again, unless otherwise stated, all figures lie in the same plane. All numbers used in these problems are real numbers. Calculators are permitted for this test.

Reference Information

Circle: Rectangle: Rectangular Solid: Cylinder: Triangle:

$C = 2\pi r$ $A = lw$ $V = lwh$ $V = \pi r^2 h$ $A = \frac{1}{2}bh$ $a^2 + b^2 = c^2$
$A = \pi r^2$

The number of degrees of arc in a circle is 360.
The measure in degrees of a straight angle is 180.
The sum of the measures in degrees of the angles of a triangle is 180.

1. Which of the following fractions is more than $\frac{3}{4}$?

   (A) $\frac{35}{71}$

   (B) $\frac{13}{20}$

   (C) $\frac{71}{101}$

   (D) $\frac{19}{24}$

   (E) $\frac{15}{20}$

2. If $820 + R + S - 610 = 342$, and if $R = 2S$, then $S =$

   (A) 44

   (B) 48

   (C) 132

   (D) 184

   (E) 192

3. What is the cost, in dollars, to carpet a room x yards long and y yards wide, if the carpet costs five dollars per square foot?

   (A) xy

   (B) $5xy$

   (C) $25xy$

   (D) $30xy$

   (E) $45xy$

4. If $7M = 3M - 20$, then $M + 7 =$

   (A) 0

   (B) 2

   (C) 5

   (D) 12

   (E) 17

5. In circle *O* below, *AB* is the diameter, angle *BOD* contains 15°, and angle *EOA* contains 85°. Find the number of degrees in angle *ECA*.

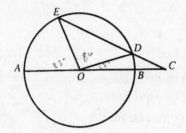

   (A) 15
   (B) 35
   (C) 50
   (D) 70
   (E) 85

6. What is the smallest positive number, other than 2, which, when it is divided by 3, 4, or 5, will leave a remainder of 2?

   (A) 22
   (B) 42
   (C) 62
   (D) 122
   (E) 182

7. A taxi charges 75 cents for the first quarter of a mile and 15 cents for each additional quarter of a mile. The charge, in cents, for a trip of *d* miles is

   (A) $75 + 15d$
   (B) $75 + 15(4d - 1)$
   (C) $75 + 75d$
   (D) $75 + 4(d - 1)$
   (E) $75 + 75(d - 1)$

8. In a certain army post, 30% of the enlistees are from New York State, and 10% of these are from New York City. What percentage of the enlistees in the post are from New York City?

   (A) .03
   (B) .3
   (C) 3
   (D) 13
   (E) 20

9. The diagonal of a rectangle is 10. What is the area of the rectangle?

   (A) 24
   (B) 48
   (C) 50
   (D) 100
   (E) It cannot be determined from the information given.

10. In triangle *PQR* below, angle *RPQ* is greater than angle *RQP*, and the bisectors of angle *P* and angle *Q* meet in *S*. Therefore,

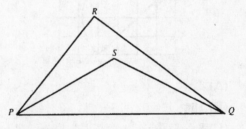

   Note: Figure not drawn to scale.
   (A) $SQ > SP$
   (B) $SQ = SP$
   (C) $SQ < SP$
   (D) $SQ \geq SP$
   (E) No conclusion concerning the relative lengths of *SQ* and *SP* can be determined from the information given.

11. Which of the following is equal to 3.14×10^6?

(A) 314

(B) 3,140

(C) 31,400

(D) 314,000

(E) 3,140,000

12. $\dfrac{36}{29 - \frac{4}{0.2}} =$

(A) $\dfrac{3}{4}$

(B) $\dfrac{4}{3}$

(C) 2

(D) 4

(E) 18

13. In terms of the square units in the figure below, what is the area of the semicircle?

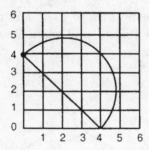

(A) 32π

(B) 16π

(C) 8π

(D) 4π

(E) 2π

14. The sum of three consecutive odd numbers is always divisible by

I. 2

II. 3

III. 5

IV. 6

(A) I only

(B) II only

(C) I and II only

(D) I and III only

(E) II and IV only

15. In the diagram, triangle ABC is inscribed in a circle and CD is tangent to the circle. If angle BCD is 40°, how many degrees are there in angle A?

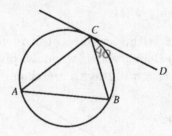

(A) 20

(B) 30

(C) 40

(D) 50

(E) 60

16. If a discount of 20% off the marked price of a jacket results in a savings of $15, what is the discounted price of the jacket?

(A) $35

(B) $60

(C) $75

(D) $150

(E) $300

17. While researching a term paper, a student read pages 7 through 49 and pages 101 through 157 of a particular source book. Altogether, how many pages from this book did this student read?

(A) 98

(B) 99

(C) 100

(D) 101

(E) 102

18. If $\dfrac{P}{Q} = \dfrac{4}{5}$, what is the value of $2P + Q$?

(A) 14

(B) 13

(C) 3

(D) –1

(E) It cannot be determined from the information given.

19. A 15-gallon mixture of 20% alcohol has 5 gallons of water added to it. The strength of the mixture, as a percent, is approximately

(A) $12\dfrac{1}{2}$

(B) $13\dfrac{1}{3}$

(C) 15

(D) $16\dfrac{2}{3}$

(E) 20

20. In the figure below, $QXRS$ is a parallelogram and P is any point on side QS. What is the ratio of the area of triangle PXR to the area of $QXRS$?

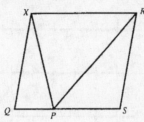

(A) 1:4

(B) 1:3

(C) 1:2

(D) 2:3

(E) 3:4

21. If $x(p + 1) = M$, then $p =$

(A) $M - 1$

(B) M

(C) $\dfrac{M-1}{x}$

(D) $M - x - 1$

(E) $\dfrac{M}{x} - 1$

22. If T tons of snow fall in 1 second, how many tons fall in M minutes?

(A) $60MT$

(B) $MT + 60$

(C) MT

(D) $\dfrac{60M}{T}$

(E) $\dfrac{MT}{60}$

23. Which of the following is the graph of $x \geq -2$ and $x \leq 3$?

(A)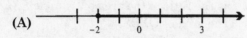

(B)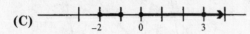

(C)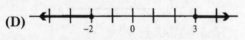

(D)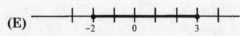

(E)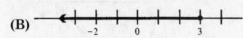

24. From 9 a.m. to 2 p.m., the temperature rose at a constant rate from $-14°F$ to $+36°F$. What was the temperature at noon?

(A) $-4°$

(B) $+6°$

(C) $+16°$

(D) $+26°$

(E) $+31°$

25. What is the sum of $\angle EBA + \angle DCF$?

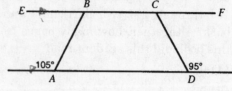

(A) $160°$

(B) $180°$

(C) $195°$

(D) $200°$

(E) It cannot be determined from the information given.

STOP

END OF SECTION 2. IF YOU HAVE ANY TIME LEFT, GO OVER YOUR WORK IN THIS SECTION ONLY. DO NOT WORK IN ANY OTHER SECTION OF THE TEST.

SECTION 3

35 Questions • Time—30 Minutes

Directions: Each of the following questions consists of an incomplete sentence followed by five words or pairs of words. Choose that word or pair of words that, when substituted for the blank space or spaces, best completes the meaning of the sentence and mark the letter of your choice on your answer sheet.

Example

Q In view of the extenuating circumstances and the defendant's youth, the judge recommended ____.

(A) conviction

(B) a defense

(C) a mistrial

(D) leniency

(E) life imprisonment

A Ⓐ Ⓑ Ⓒ ● Ⓔ

1. Human survival is a result of mutual assistance, since people are essentially ____ rather than ____.

    (A) superior..inferior

    (B) cooperative..competitive

    (C) individualistic..gregarious

    (D) physical..mental

    (E) dependent..insensate

2. For centuries, malnutrition has been ____ in the drought-stricken areas of Africa.

    (A) impalpable

    (B) evasive

    (C) endemic

    (D) divisive

    (E) redundant

3. Even as they ____ their pledges of support, they secretly planned a betrayal; their actions ____ their words.

    (A) demonstrated..echoed

    (B) confirmed..reinforced

    (C) compromised..precluded

    (D) reiterated..belied

    (E) submitted..emphasized

4. The day will come when our ____ will look back upon us and our time with a sense of superiority.

    (A) antecedents

    (B) descendants

    (C) predecessors

    (D) ancestors

    (E) contemporaries

5. Their ____ debate, billed as a(n) ____ of their opinions, was only needless repetition.

   (A) senseless..exoneration

   (B) national..travesty

   (C) incessant..distillation

   (D) primary..renunciation

   (E) final..clarification

6. With the ____ of winter storms, all drivers should take extra ____ while on the road.

   (A) demise..caution

   (B) approach..precautions

   (C) waning..care

   (D) proximity..leisure

   (E) duration..heed

7. Despite our ____, Eva ____ the stranger for directions.

   (A) compliance..harrassed

   (B) encouragement..questioned

   (C) entreaties..pinioned

   (D) intentions..assailed

   (E) warnings..approached

8. The young man was very unlikely to be hired; his appearance was disheveled, slovenly, and ____.

   (A) tousled

   (B) harried

   (C) beleaguered

   (D) mortified

   (E) despondent

9. The use of trained bears in circuses was once a ____ but has now almost ____.

   (A) menace..diminished

   (B) precedent..extinguished

   (C) sinecure..vanquished

   (D) commonplace..ceased

   (E) legacy..vanished

10. Although he has a reputation for aloofness, his manner on that occasion was so ____ that everyone felt perfectly at ease.

   (A) reluctant

   (B) gracious

   (C) malign

   (D) plausible

   (E) spurious

Directions: Each of the following questions consists of a capitalized pair of words followed by five pairs of words lettered (A) to (E). The capitalized words bear some meaningful relationship to each other. Choose the lettered pair of words whose relationship is most similar to that expressed by the capitalized pair and mark its letter on your answer sheet.

Example

Q DAY : SUN ::

   (A)   sunlight : daylight

   (B)   ray : sun

   (C)   night : moon

   (D)   heat : cold

   (E)   moon : star

A

11. NEST : BIRD ::

   (A) lair : lion

   (B) kennel : dog

   (C) ring : elephant

   (D) corral : horse

   (E) coop : chicken

12. HAMMER : HIT ::
    (A) screw : replace
    (B) wrench : leak
    (C) glue : paste
    (D) saw : cut
    (E) heat : melt

13. ANGER : DISPLEASURE ::
    (A) ignorance : knowledge
    (B) hatred : understanding
    (C) ecstasy : happiness
    (D) patience : fury
    (E) indicate : triumph

14. TRICKLE : GUSH ::
    (A) flow : stream
    (B) listen : hear
    (C) soar : dive
    (D) touch : collide
    (E) drive : ride

15. WINK : EYE ::
    (A) swallow : food
    (B) tap : toe
    (C) flirt : hand
    (D) hit : nail
    (E) smell : nose

16. BOWLING : PIN ::
    (A) basketball : center
    (B) tennis : racket
    (C) baseball : glove
    (D) archery : arrow
    (E) golf : hole

17. LAKE : WET ::
    (A) electricity : nuclear
    (B) ice : cold
    (C) fog : unavoidable
    (D) sand : dry
    (E) jewel : expensive

18. TOOTH : COMB ::
    (A) book : store
    (B) horse : race
    (C) cog : gear
    (D) hair : brush
    (E) dog : hound

19. MISER : STINGINESS ::
    (A) dilettante : skill
    (B) demagogue : passivity
    (C) tyrant : dignity
    (D) altruist : selflessness
    (E) miscreant : honesty

20. CHIVALROUS : GALLANT ::
    (A) sanguine : cheerful
    (B) doleful : happy
    (C) tardy : early
    (D) mercurial : slow
    (E) rich : degenerate

21. LAVA : VOLCANO ::
    (A) snow : mountain
    (B) water : spring
    (C) balloon : air
    (D) eyes : makeup
    (E) chimney : smoke

22. DIFFIDENT : CONFIDENCE ::
    (A) magnificent : beauty
    (B) voluminous : size
    (C) gloomy : cheer
    (D) meticulous : care
    (E) athletic : strength

23. CONDUCTOR : ORCHESTRA ::
    (A) violinist : bow
    (B) pianist : hands
    (C) author : books
    (D) president : country
    (E) school : principal

Questions 24–35 are based on the following passage.

Stephen Crane (1871–1900) wrote a number of novels, short stories, and poems in his short life, as well as working as a war correspondent overseas. "The Bride Comes to Yellow Sky" (1898) is the story of a small-town sheriff who brings home a bride, changing his frontier home forever. It opens with this scene.

The great Pullman was whirling onward with such dignity of motion that a glance from the window seemed simply to prove that the plains of Texas were
(5) pouring eastward. Vast flats of green grass, dull-hued spaces of mesquite and cactus, little groups of frame houses, woods of light and tender trees, all were sweeping into the east, sweeping over
(10) the horizon, a precipice.

A newly married pair had boarded this coach at San Antonio. The man's face was reddened from many days in the wind and sun, and a direct result of his
(15) new black clothes was that his brick-colored hands were constantly performing in a most conscious fashion. From time to time he looked down respectfully at his attire. He sat with a hand on each
(20) knee, like a man waiting in a barber's shop. The glances he devoted to other passengers were furtive and shy.

The bride was not pretty, nor was she very young. She wore a dress of blue
(25) cashmere, with small reservations of velvet here and there, and with steel buttons abounding. She continually twisted her head to regard her puff sleeves, very stiff, straight, and high.
(30) They embarrassed her. It was quite apparent that she had cooked, and that she expected to cook, dutifully. The blushes caused by the careless scrutiny of some passengers as she had entered the car
(35) were strange to see upon this plain, under-class countenance, which was drawn in placid, almost emotionless lines.

They were evidently very happy.
(40) "Ever been in a parlor-car before?" he asked, smiling with delight.

"No," she answered; "I never was. It's fine, ain't it?"

"Great! And then after a while we'll
(45) go forward to the diner, and get a big lay-out. Finest meal in the world. Charge a dollar."

"Oh, do they?" cried the bride. "Charge a dollar? Why, that's too much—
(50) for us—ain't it Jack?"

"Not this trip, anyhow," he answered bravely. "We're going to go the whole thing."

Later he explained to her about the
(55) trains. "You see, it's a thousand miles from one end of Texas to the other; and this train runs right across it, and never stops but for four times." He had the pride of an owner. He pointed out to her
(60) the dazzling fittings of the coach; and in truth her eyes opened wider as she contemplated the sea-green figured velvet, the shining brass, silver, and glass, the wood that gleamed as darkly brilliant as
(65) the surface of a pool of oil. At one end a bronze figure sturdily held a support for a separated chamber, and at convenient places on the ceiling were frescoes in olive and silver.

(70) To the minds of the pair, their surroundings reflected the glory of their marriage that morning in San Antonio; this was the environment of their new estate; and the man's face in particular
(75) beamed with an elation that made him appear ridiculous to the negro porter.

This individual at times surveyed them from afar with an amused and superior grin. On other occasions he bullied them *(80)* with skill in ways that did not make it exactly plain to them that they were being bullied. He subtly used all the manners of the most unconquerable kind of snobbery. He oppressed them; but of *(85)* this oppression they had small knowledge, and they speedily forgot that infrequently a number of travelers covered them with stares of derisive enjoyment. Historically there was supposed to be *(90)* something infinitely humorous in their situation.

24. Crane highlights the newlyweds'

(A) tactlessness.

(B) unsophistication.

(C) wealth.

(D) merriment.

(E) fear.

25. The bride's dress is clearly

(A) beautiful.

(B) torn.

(C) red.

(D) comfortable.

(E) unfamiliar.

26. The line "It was quite apparent that she had cooked, and that she expected to cook, dutifully" (lines 30–32) shows the bride's

(A) natural talent.

(B) submissiveness.

(C) commonness.

(D) Both A and B

(E) Both B and C

27. When the bridegroom answers his bride "bravely" (line 52), the implication is that

(A) he has overcome his fear of her.

(B) his usual posture is weak and sniveling.

(C) gallantry is his natural mode.

(D) he will conquer his anxiety about money for her sake.

(E) it takes courage to speak forthrightly.

28. The line "He had the pride of an owner" (lines 58–59) is ironic because

(A) the bride has no sense of style.

(B) the bridegroom could never own anything so fine.

(C) Crane prefers workers to owners.

(D) the owners of the train take no pride in it.

(E) the bridegroom is not proud of his own belongings.

29. The word *estate* (line 74) is used to mean

(A) property.

(B) inheritance.

(C) status.

(D) statement.

(E) manor.

30. The figure of the porter is used to indicate

(A) a parallel between slavery and marriage.

(B) where the line between worker and owner is drawn.

(C) the absurdity of young love.

(D) that the newlyweds are not alone in the world.

(E) just how unworldly and lower class the newlyweds are.

31. The last sentence of the passage refers to

    (A) the fact that newlyweds are figures of fun.

    (B) Crane's amusement at the behavior of the travelers.

    (C) people's delight at others' misfortunes.

    (D) the joy of the newlyweds despite their surroundings.

    (E) readers' sympathy with the characters.

32. Crane uses the word *historically* (line 89) to mean

    (A) importantly.

    (B) famously.

    (C) customarily.

    (D) prominently.

    (E) ritually.

33. Crane's feeling toward the newlyweds is one of

    (A) amused sympathy.

    (B) disgusted revulsion.

    (C) weary resignation.

    (D) scornful derision.

    (E) honest hatred.

34. Crane probably does not name the newlyweds in this part of the story

    (A) because he does not know who they are.

    (B) to make them seem ordinary and universal.

    (C) because he wants to surprise the reader.

    (D) to prove that they are worthless in his eyes.

    (E) to focus attention on the peripheral characters.

35. The main goal of this passage is to

    (A) introduce characters and setting.

    (B) illustrate a conflict between two characters.

    (C) resolve a crisis.

    (D) express an opinion.

    (E) instruct the reader.

STOP

END OF SECTION 3. IF YOU HAVE ANY TIME LEFT, GO OVER YOUR WORK IN THIS SECTION ONLY. DO NOT WORK IN ANY OTHER SECTION OF THE TEST.

SECTION 4

25 Questions • Time—30 Minutes

Directions: Solve the following problems using any available space on the page for scratchwork. On your answer sheet fill in the choice that best corresponds to the correct answer.

Notes: The figures accompanying the problems are drawn as accurately as possible unless otherwise stated in specific problems. Again, unless otherwise stated, all figures lie in the same plane. All numbers used in these problems are real numbers. Calculators are permitted for this test.

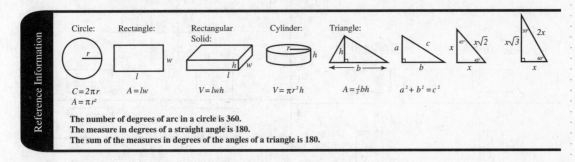

Reference Information

Circle: $C = 2\pi r$ $A = \pi r^2$

Rectangle: $A = lw$

Rectangular Solid: $V = lwh$

Cylinder: $V = \pi r^2 h$

Triangle: $A = \frac{1}{2}bh$ $a^2 + b^2 = c^2$

The number of degrees of arc in a circle is 360.
The measure in degrees of a straight angle is 180.
The sum of the measures in degrees of the angles of a triangle is 180.

Part 1: Quantitative Comparison Questions

Directions: Questions 1–15 each consist of two quantities—one in Column A, the other in Column B. Compare the two quantities and mark your answer sheet as follows:

(A) if the quantity in Column A is greater

(B) if the quantity in Column B is greater

(C) if the two quantities are equal

(D) if the relationship cannot be determined from the information given

Notes:

(1) Information concerning one or both of the compared quantities will be centered above the two columns for some items.

(2) Symbols that appear in both columns represent the same thing in Column A as in Column B.

(3) Letters such as x, n, and k are symbols for real numbers.

Examples

Column A	Column B	Answers
	$a > 0$	
	$x > 0$	
E1. $\boxed{a - x}$	$\boxed{a + x}$	(A) (B) (C) (D)
E2. $\boxed{\text{The average of } 17, 19, 21, 23}$	$\boxed{\text{The average of } 6, 18, 20, 22}$	(A) (B) (C) (D)

Do not mark choice (E) for these questions. There are only four answer choices.

Column A   **Column B**

1. $\boxed{2x - 1}$ $\boxed{2x + 1}$

$x < -1$

2. $\boxed{\dfrac{1}{x^2}}$ $\boxed{x}$

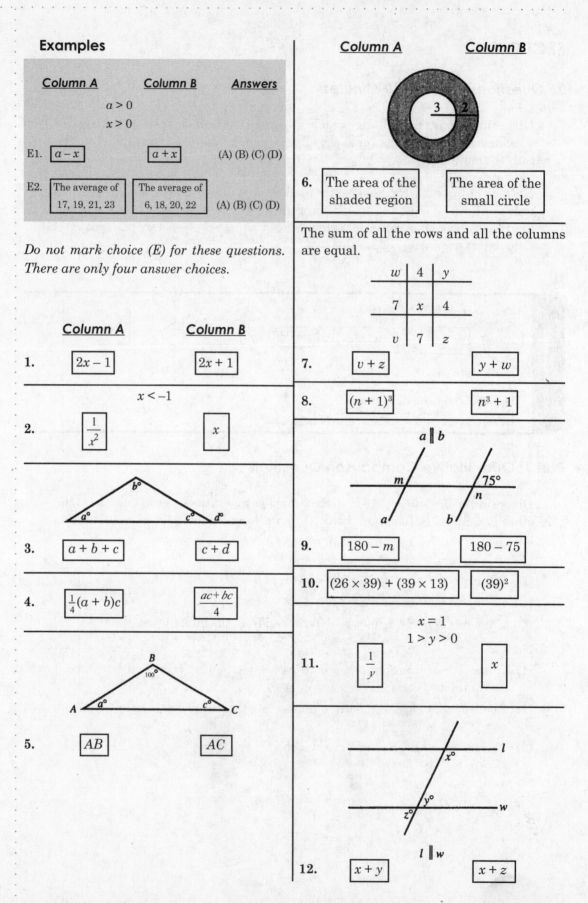

3. $\boxed{a + b + c}$ $\boxed{c + d}$

4. $\boxed{\frac{1}{4}(a + b)c}$ $\boxed{\dfrac{ac + bc}{4}}$

5. $\boxed{AB}$ $\boxed{AC}$

Column A   **Column B**

6. $\boxed{\text{The area of the shaded region}}$ $\boxed{\text{The area of the small circle}}$

The sum of all the rows and all the columns are equal.

w	4	y
7	x	4
v	7	z

7. $\boxed{v + z}$ $\boxed{y + w}$

8. $\boxed{(n + 1)^3}$ $\boxed{n^3 + 1}$

9. $\boxed{180 - m}$ $\boxed{180 - 75}$

10. $\boxed{(26 \times 39) + (39 \times 13)}$ $\boxed{(39)^2}$

$x = 1$
$1 > y > 0$

11. $\boxed{\dfrac{1}{y}}$ $\boxed{x}$

$l \parallel w$

12. $\boxed{x + y}$ $\boxed{x + z}$

	Column A	Column B
13.	$(m^2 - 1)(2m + 2)$	$(m + 1)^2(2m - 2)$
14.	0.7% of 62	70% of 6,200
15.	The area of a square with side s	The area of an equilateral triangle with side $2s$

Part 2: Student-Produced Response Questions

Directions: Solve each of these problems. Write the answer in the corresponding grid on the answer sheet and fill in the ovals beneath each answer you write. Here are some examples.

Answer: $\frac{3}{4}$ (= .75; show answer either way)   Answer: 325

Note: A mixed number such as $3\frac{1}{2}$ must be gridded as 7/2 or as 3.5. If gridded as "3 1/2," it will be read as "thirty-one halves."

Note: Either position is correct.

16. In the figure below, $l_1 \parallel l_2$. If the measure of $\angle x = 70°$ and the measure of $\angle y = 105°$, what is the measure of $\angle r$? (Disregard the degree symbol when you grid your answer.)

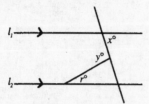

17. What is the value of $-x^2 - 2x^3$ when $x = -1$?

18. Jessica received marks of 87, 93, and 86 on three successive tests. What grade must she receive on a fourth test in order to have an average of 90?

19. In a circle with radius 6, what is the measure (in degrees) of an arc whose length is 2π? (Disregard the degree symbol when you grid your answer.)

20. If $\dfrac{2x}{3\sqrt{2}} = \dfrac{3\sqrt{2}}{x}$, what is the positive value of x?

21. Using the table below, what is the median of the following data?

Score	Frequency
20	4
30	4
50	7

22. If A * B is defined as $\dfrac{AB - B}{-B}$, what is the value of $-2 * 2$?

23. A man travels 320 miles in 8 hours. If he continues at the same rate, how many miles will he travel in the next 2 hours?

24. A booklet contains 30 pages. If 9 pages in the booklet have drawings, what percent of the pages in the booklet have drawings? (Disregard the percent symbol when you grid your answer.)

25. If 3 copier machines can copy 300 sheets in 3 hours, assuming the same rate, how long (in hours) will it take 6 such copiers to copy 600 sheets?

STOP

END OF SECTION 4. IF YOU HAVE ANY TIME LEFT, GO OVER YOUR WORK IN THIS SECTION ONLY. DO NOT WORK IN ANY OTHER SECTION OF THE TEST.

SECTION 5

12 Questions • Time—15 Minutes

Directions: The two passages given below deal with a related topic. Following the passages are questions about the content of each passage or about the relationship between the two passages. Answer the questions based upon what is stated or implied in the passages and in any introductory material provided. Mark the letter of your choice on your answer sheet.

Questions 1–12 are based on the following passages.

Matthew Henson was born in 1866 of free black parents in Maryland. He met Commander Robert Peary in 1888 and became first his servant, and then his assistant, on Peary's major expeditions to the Arctic. In these two passages, Henson and Peary describe the same area in Greenland, a place known as Karnah.

Passage 1—from Henson's Account of the 1908 Expedition

We stopped at Kookan, the most prosperous of the Esquimo settlements, a village of five tupiks (skin tents), housing twenty-four people, and from there
(5) we sailed to the ideal community of Karnah.

Karnah is the most delightful spot on the Greenland coast. Situated on a gently southward sloping knoll are the
(10) igloos and tupiks, where I have spent many pleasant days with my Esquimo friends and learned much of the folklore and history. Lofty mountains, sublime in their grandeur, overtower and sur-
(15) round this place, and its only exposure is southward toward the sun. In winter its climate is not severe, as compared with other portions of this country, and in the perpetual daylight of summer, life here
(20) is ideal. Rivulets of clear, cold water, the beds of which are grass- and flower-covered, run down the sides of the mountain and, but for the lack of trees, the landscape is as delightful as anywhere
(25) on earth.

Passage 2—from Peary's Account of the 1891 Expedition

From the eastern point of Academy Bay the main shore of the gulf extends, due east, to the face of the great Heilprin Glacier, and then on beside the great ice-
(30) stream, until the crests of the cliffs disappear under the white shroud of the "Great Ice." From here on, the eastern and northern sides of the head of the gulf are an almost continuous glacier face, six great
(35) ice-streams, separated by as many precipitous nunataks, flowing down from the interior ice-cap to discharge an enormous fleet of bergs. As a result of this free discharge, the great white viscosity of the
(40) interior has settled down into a huge, and in clear weather easily discernible, semicircular basin, similar to those of Tossukatek, Great Kariak, and Jacobshavn. In this head of the gulf,
(45) situated some in the face of the glaciers, and others a short distance beyond them, are seven or eight islands, most of which bear proof of former glaciation. Along the north-western shore of the gulf, the ver-
(50) tical cliffs resume their sway, back of which rise the trio of striking peaks, Mounts Daly, Adams, and Putname. The cliffs continue westward for some little distance, then gradually merge into a
(55) gentle slope, which is in turn succeeded by the face of the Hubbard Glacier. West of the glacier, cliffs of a different character (red and grey sandstone) occur, and extend to the grand and picturesque red-

brown Castle Cliffs at the entrance to
(60) Bowdoin Bay. At these cliffs, the shore
takes an abrupt turn to the northward,
into the now familiar but previously unknown Bowdoin Bay, in which was
(65) located the headquarters of my last
Expedition.

This bay has an extreme length of
eleven miles, and an average width of
between three and four miles. What
(70) with its southern exposure, the protection from the wind afforded by the cliffs
and bluffs which enclose it, and the
warmth of colouring of its shores, it
presents one of the most desirable loca-
(75) tions for a house. The scenery is also
varied and attractive, offering to the eye
greater contrasts, with less change of
position, than any other locality occurring to me. Around the circuit of the bay
(80) are seven glaciers with exposures to all
points of the compass, and varying in
size from a few hundred feet to over two
miles in width.

The ice-cap itself is also in evi-
(85) dence here, its vertical face in one place
capping and forming a continuation of a
vertical cliff which rises direct from the
bay. From the western point of the bay,
a line of grey sandstone cliffs—the Sculp-
(90) tured Cliffs of Karnah—interrupted by
a single glacier in a distance of eight
miles, and carved by the restless arctic
elements into turrets, bastions, huge
amphitheatres, and colossal statues of
(95) men and animals, extends to Cape
Ackland, the Karnah of the natives. Here
the cliffs end abruptly, and the shore
trending north-westward to Cape Cleveland, eighteen miles distant, consists of
(100) an almost continuous succession of fan-
shaped, rocky deltas formed by glacier
streams. Back of the shoreline is a gradually sloping foreshore, rising to the foot
of an irregular series of hills, which rise
(105) more steeply to the ice-cap lying upon
their summits. In almost every depres-
sion between these hills, the face of a
glacier may be seen, and it is the streams
from these that have made the shore
(110) what it is, and formed the wide shoals off
it, on which every year a numerous fleet
of icebergs becomes stranded.

1. Henson uses the word *exposure* (line 15)
   to mean
   (A) denunciation.
   (B) unmasking.
   (C) emptiness.
   (D) danger.
   (E) openness.

2. Henson's main impression of Karnah is
   one of
   (A) apprehension.
   (B) dismay.
   (C) indifference.
   (D) pleasure.
   (E) tolerance.

3. Henson might prefer that Karnah
   (A) were not so far north.
   (B) were warmer.
   (C) were uninhabited.
   (D) lay further inland.
   (E) had more trees.

4. Peary admires Bowdoin Bay for its
   (A) diverse vistas.
   (B) incredible length.
   (C) calm waters.
   (D) impressive tides.
   (E) great ice-streams.

5. Peary compares the arctic elements to
   (A) avenging Furies.
   (B) athletic challenges.
   (C) stonecarvers.
   (D) wild horses.
   (E) ice palaces.

6. Future explorers might use Peary's description to
   (A) locate their ships in Karnah's harbor.
   (B) find their way around Greenland's shoreline.
   (C) decide the future of native settlements.
   (D) identify trees and vegetation on the island.
   (E) reenact Peary's discovery of the North Pole.

7. In general, Peary's description is in
   (A) chronological order, according to his various trips.
   (B) spatial order, proceeding along the coastline.
   (C) chronological order, moving from past to present.
   (D) spatial order, moving from west to east.
   (E) spatial order, moving in a circle around the ship.

8. The "lofty mountains" described by Henson (line 13) are probably Peary's
   (A) Sculptured Cliffs (lines 89–90).
   (B) Cape Cleveland (lines 98–99).
   (C) Heilprin Glacier (lines 28–29).
   (D) Mount Daly (line 52).
   (E) Great Kariak (line 43).

9. Unlike Henson, Peary seems intent on
   (A) snubbing the natives.
   (B) discussing flora and fauna.
   (C) focusing on geology.
   (D) raising political issues.
   (E) extolling the delights of Karnah.

10. Peary and Henson seem to agree on
    (A) the severity of Greenland's weather.
    (B) the area's attractiveness.
    (C) the need for future exploration.
    (D) both A and B.
    (E) both B and C.

11. Unlike Peary's account, Henson's tone is primarily
    (A) humorous.
    (B) objective.
    (C) scientific.
    (D) appreciative.
    (E) technical.

12. Unlike Henson's account of his 1908 expedition, Peary pays considerable attention to
    (A) Esquimo settlements.
    (B) Esquimo folklore.
    (C) Esquimo dietary restrictions.
    (D) glaciers and ice formations.
    (E) Karnah's overall physical characteristics.

STOP

END OF SECTION 5. IF YOU HAVE ANY TIME LEFT, GO OVER YOUR WORK IN THIS SECTION ONLY. DO NOT WORK IN ANY OTHER SECTION OF THE TEST.

SECTION 6

10 Questions • Time—15 Minutes

Directions: Solve the following problems using any available space on the page for scratchwork. On your answer sheet fill in the choice that best corresponds to the correct answer.

Notes: The figures accompanying the problems are drawn as accurately as possible unless otherwise stated in specific problems. Again, unless otherwise stated, all figures lie in the same plane. All numbers used in these problems are real numbers. Calculators are permitted for this test.

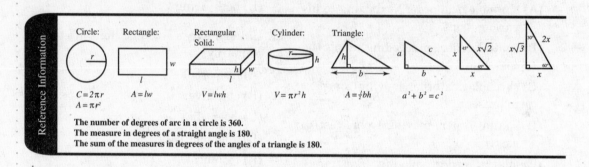

The number of degrees of arc in a circle is 360.
The measure in degrees of a straight angle is 180.
The sum of the measures in degrees of the angles of a triangle is 180.

1. The coordinates of vertices X and Y of an equilateral triangle XYZ are $(-4,0)$ and $(4,0)$, respectively. The coordinates of Z may be
   (A) $(0, 2\sqrt{3})$
   (B) $(0, 4\sqrt{3})$
   (C) $(4, 4\sqrt{3})$
   (D) $(0, 4)$
   (E) $(4\sqrt{3}, 0)$

2. There are just two ways in which 5 may be expressed as the sum of two different positive (nonzero) integers, namely, $5 = 4 + 1 = 3 + 2$. In how many ways may 9 be expressed as the sum of two different positive (nonzero) integers?
   (A) 3
   (B) 4
   (C) 5
   (D) 6
   (E) 7

3. A board 7 feet 9 inches long is divided into three equal parts. What is the length of each part?
   (A) 2 ft. $6\frac{1}{3}$ in.
   (B) 2 ft. 7 in.
   (C) 2 ft. 8 in.
   (D) 2 ft. $8\frac{1}{3}$ in.
   (E) 2 ft. 9 in.

4. What is the smallest possible integer $K > 1$ such that $R^2 = S^3 = K$, for some integers R and S?
   (A) 4
   (B) 8
   (C) 27
   (D) 64
   (E) 81

5. The number of square units in the area of triangle *RST* is

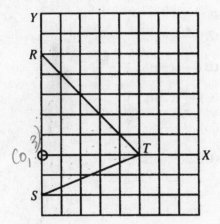

(A) 10

(B) 12.5

(C) 15.5

(D) 17.5

(E) 20

6. Which of the following has the same value as $\frac{P}{Q}$?

(A) $\frac{P-2}{Q-2}$

(B) $\frac{1+P}{1+Q}$

(C) $\frac{P^2}{Q^2}$

(D) $\frac{3P}{3Q}$

(E) $\frac{P+3}{Q+3}$

7. In the accompanying figure, $\angle ACB$ is a straight angle and $\overline{DC}$ is perpendicular to $\overline{CE}$. If the number of degrees in angle ACD is represented by x, the number of degrees in angle BCE is represented by

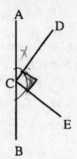

(A) $90 - x$

(B) $x - 90$

(C) $90 + x$

(D) $180 - x$

(E) $45 + x$

Questions 8 and 9 refer to the following drawing:

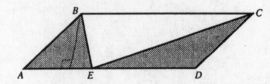

8. In parallelogram *ABCD*, what is the ratio of the shaded area to the unshaded area?

(A) 1:2

(B) 1:1

(C) 4:3

(D) 2:1

(E) It cannot be determined from the information given.

9. If the ratio of AB to BC is 4:9, what is the area of parallelogram $ABCD$?

   (A) 36

   (B) 26

   (C) 18

   (D) 13

   (E) It cannot be determined from the information given.

10. A store owner buys eggs for M cents per dozen and sells them for $\frac{M}{6}$ cents apiece. At this rate, what is the profit on a dozen eggs?

   (A) $\frac{M}{12}$ cents

   (B) $\frac{M}{6}$ cents

   (C) $\frac{M}{2}$ cents

   (D) M cents

   (E) $2M$ cents

STOP

END OF SECTION 6. IF YOU HAVE ANY TIME LEFT, GO OVER YOUR WORK IN THIS SECTION ONLY. DO NOT WORK IN ANY OTHER SECTION OF THE TEST.

ANSWER KEY

Section 1: VERBAL

1. B	8. B	15. B	22. E	29. D
2. B	9. A	16. D	23. D	30. E
3. C	10. B	17. C	24. A	31. C
4. E	11. B	18. B	25. D	
5. D	12. D	19. A	26. C	
6. C	13. E	20. B	27. B	
7. A	14. E	21. E	28. C	

Section 2: MATH
(Code: A = Arithmetic; AL = Algebra; G = Geometry; O = Other)

1. D (A)	6. C (O)	11. E (A)	16. B (A)	21. E (AL)
2. A (AL)	7. B (AL)	12. D (A)	17. C (O)	22. A (A)
3. E (G)	8. C (A)	13. D (G)	18. E (A)	23. E (O)
4. B (AL)	9. E (G)	14. B (O)	19. C (A)	24. C (A)
5. B (G)	10. A (G)	15. C (G)	20. C (G)	25. A (G)

Section 3: VERBAL

1. B	8. A	15. B	22. C	29. C
2. C	9. D	16. E	23. D	30. E
3. D	10. B	17. B	24. B	31. A
4. B	11. A	18. C	25. E	32. C
5. E	12. D	19. D	26. E	33. A
6. B	13. C	20. A	27. D	34. B
7. E	14. D	21. B	28. B	35. A

Section 4: MATH

Part 1

1. B	4. C	7. B	10. C	13. C
2. A	5. B	8. D	11. A	14. B
3. C	6. A	9. B	12. C	15. B

Part 2

16. 35	18. 94	20. 3	22. 3	24. 30
17. 1	19. 60	21. 30	23. 80	25. 3

Section 5: VERBAL

1.	E	4.	A	7.	B	9.	C	11.	D
2.	D	5.	C	8.	A	10.	D	12.	D
3.	E	6.	B						

Section 6: MATH
(Code: A = Arithmetic; AL = Algebra; G = Geometry; O = Other)

1.	B (G)	3.	B (G)	5.	D (G)	7.	A (G)	9.	E (G)
2.	B (O)	4.	D (A)	6.	D (AL)	8.	B (G)	10.	D (AL)

EXPLANATORY ANSWERS

Note: A ⊞ following a math answer explanation indicates that a calculator could be helpful in solving that particular problem.

Section 1: VERBAL

1. **The correct answer is (B).** A position that provides authority to award contracts is also likely to allow the holder to *incur* (take on) obligations to pay bills.

2. **The correct answer is (B).** A witness who reveals very little information, even when questioned by an experienced attorney, is *recalcitrant* (stubborn).

3. **The correct answer is (C).** The word *although* signifies a shift in meaning. Even though *substantial* (large) resources had been applied, the solution was still *elusive* (hard to determine).

4. **The correct answer is (E).** The only logical choice is the one in which both words have the same connotation; both must be either positive or negative. Only choice (E) satisfies this condition with two positive words.

5. **The correct answer is (D).** The word in the first blank must be a synonym for *kept. Retained* and *received* both might satisfy this condition, but only *insured* makes sense in the second blank.

6. **The correct answer is (C).** The first blank needs a positive word to describe the way the agent calmed the travelers; the second blank needs a negative word to describe the delayed travelers. Only choice (C) meets both conditions.

7. **The correct answer is (A).** The lover of democracy has an aversion or *antipathy* toward totalitarianism.

8. **The correct answer is (B).** This answer needs either two negative or two positive words. The other four choices have a combination of positive and negative words. Since choice (B) has two negative words describing the situation, it is the only correct response.

9. **The correct answer is (A).** The words need to be opposites. One word needs to be supportive of free individuals and the other needs to undermine it.

10. **The correct answer is (B).** Those who are *powerful* are also *mighty*. Those who are *mediocre* are also *ordinary*.

11. **The correct answer is (B).** A *horse* is a four-legged animal that is covered with an outer growth of *hair*. A *sheep* is a four-legged animal that is covered with an outer growth of *wool*.

12. **The correct answer is (D).** A *gobble* is a sound made by a particular kind of bird, a *turkey*. A *twitter* is a sound made by some *birds*.

13. **The correct answer is (E).** One *sells* something to someone else, who thereby *purchases* it. One *gives* something to someone else, who thereby *receives* it.

14. **The correct answer is (E).** A *novel* is a type of *book*, just as a *loafer* is a type of *shoe*.

15. **The correct answer is (B).** *Temerity* is a lack of *caution; effrontery* is a lack of *shame*.

16. **The correct answer is (D).** The roots of classical architecture date back to ancient Rome, when people of the highest social orders embraced its style.

17. **The correct answer is (C).** This answer is the exception because just the opposite is true—the same spatial divisions were applied no matter what the type of building.

18. **The correct answer is (B).** The context of the sentence indicates that *three-part* is the only possible answer.

19. **The correct answer is (A).** The passage mentions all of the columns by name with the exception of Egyptian. (See lines 33–35.)

20. **The correct answer is (B).** *Capital* is the answer. Line 49 defines the parts of the column as the capital, the shaft, and the base.

21. **The correct answer is (E).** The context of the sentence indicates that *balance* is the only possible answer.

22. **The correct answer is (E).** Throughout the passage the idea that classical architecture is filled with rules that must be followed is stressed.

23. **The correct answer is (D).** The word is used several times to refer to the feathers and leaves with which the narrator will appease the spirit. It is thus a *tribute* rather than any of the other synonyms.

24. **The correct answer is (A).** This interpretation question is quite literal. Go with your first answer on questions of this kind. The narrator's entire dilemma surrounds the difficulty of finding *bare ground* in a snowy landscape.

25. **The correct answer is (D).** It is a *quest*, because she is looking for a patch of bare ground where she can perform a religious rite.

26. **The correct answer is (C).** This is the essential problem of the story: How can bare ground be found in this snowy landscape?

27. **The correct answer is (B).** Looking back on the events, the adult narrator feels sorry for the small child she was. She now sees that the task was too great for someone so small—that a child could not hope or be expected to save her sister's life.

28. **The correct answer is (C).** Try the various synonyms in context, and you will see that only *inflamed* makes any sense.

29. **The correct answer is (D).** The child is afraid that the offering did not reach the ground, and therefore, her sister will not be saved. If it did not reach the ground, perhaps it is because she did not have faith in nature to show her a bare patch of ground and did not follow the medicine-woman's instructions.

30. **The correct answer is (E).** If you understand question 28, you probably answered this question correctly. The small child blames herself for her lack of faith, which she sees as causing her sister's turn for the worse.

31. **The correct answer is (C).** This evaluation question is a restatement of interpretation question 26. Throughout the passage, the reader is made aware of the child's struggle and her essential decency. The author wants us to like the child and forgive her as she herself has done.

Section 2: MATH

1. **The correct answer is (D).**

$$\frac{3}{4} = .75$$

$\frac{35}{71}$ is slightly less than $\frac{35}{70} = .5$

$\frac{13}{20} = \frac{13 \times 5}{20 \times 5} = \frac{65}{100} = .65$

$\frac{71}{101}$ is very close to $\frac{7}{10}$ or .7

$\frac{15}{20} = \frac{15 \times 5}{20 \times 5} = \frac{75}{100} = .75$

$\frac{19}{24} = 24\overline{)19.00}$ which is more than $\frac{3}{4}$

$$\begin{array}{r} .79 \\ 24\overline{)19.00} \\ \underline{168} \\ 220 \\ \underline{216} \end{array}$$

2. **The correct answer is (A).**

$$820 + R + S - 610 = 342$$
$$R + S + 210 = 342$$
$$R + S = 132$$
If $R = 2S$, then $2S + S = 132$
$$3S = 132$$
$$S = 44$$

3. **The correct answer is (E).**

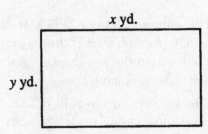

x yd.

y yd.

Area = xy sq. yd. = $9\,xy$ sq. ft.

$9\,xy \cdot 5 = 45\,xy$

4. **The correct answer is (B).**

$$7M = 3M - 20$$
$$4M = -20$$
$$M = -5$$
$$M + 7 = -5 + 7 = 2$$

5. **The correct answer is (B).** Arc $EA = 85°$ and arc $BD = 15°$. Since a central angle is measured by its arc, then

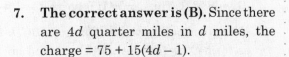

$$\text{angle } ECA = \tfrac{1}{2}\left(AE - BD\right)$$
$$= \tfrac{1}{2}\left(85 - 15\right)$$
$$= \tfrac{1}{2} \bullet 70$$
$$= 35°$$

6. **The correct answer is (C).** The smallest positive number divisible by 3, 4, or 5 is $3 \cdot 4 \cdot 5 = 60$. Hence, the desired number is $60 + 2 = 62$.

7. **The correct answer is (B).** Since there are $4d$ quarter miles in d miles, the charge $= 75 + 15(4d - 1)$.

8. **The correct answer is (C).** Assume that there are 100 enlistees on the post; then 30 are from New York State and $\frac{1}{10} \times 30$ are from New York City. $\frac{3}{100} = 3\%$.

9. **The correct answer is (E).** If you know only the hypotenuse of a right triangle, you cannot determine its legs. Hence, the area of the rectangle cannot be determined from the data given.

10. **The correct answer is (A).** If angle $RPQ >$ angle RQP, then $\frac{1}{2}$ angle $P > \frac{1}{2}$ angle Q; then angle $SPQ >$ angle SQP. Since the larger side lies opposite the larger angle, it follows that $SQ > SP$.

11. **The correct answer is (E).**

$$3.14 \times 10^6 = 3.14 \times 1,000,000$$
$$= 3,140,000$$

12. **The correct answer is (D).**

$$\frac{36}{29 - \frac{4}{0.2}} = \frac{36}{29 - 20} = \frac{36}{9} = 4$$

13. **The correct answer is (D).** Diameter = $4\sqrt{2}$, since it is the hypotenuse of a right isosceles triangle of leg 4. Then the radius = $2\sqrt{2}$.

$$\text{Area of semicircle} = \frac{1}{2} \times \pi \times \left(2\sqrt{2}\right)^2$$
$$= \frac{1}{2} \times \pi 8 = 4\pi$$

14. **The correct answer is (B).** Consecutive odd numbers may be represented as

$$2n+1$$
$$2n+3$$
$$\underline{2n+5}$$
$$\text{Sum} = 6n+9$$

Divide by 3. Thus, only II is correct.

15. **The correct answer is (C).** Angle BCD is formed by tangent and chord and is equal to one half of arc BC. Angle A is an inscribed angle and is also equal to one half of arc BC. Hence, angle A = angle $BCD = 40°$.

16. **The correct answer is (B).** Let x = amount of marked price. Then:

$$\frac{1}{5}x = 15$$
$$x = 75$$
$$75 - 15 = \$60$$

17. **The correct answer is (C).** This problem cannot be solved by simply doing subtraction. To give an example: if you read pages 1 and 2 of a book, how many pages have you read? The answer is obviously 2; we can conclude then that we do not obtain the answer by subtracting 1 from 2. Instead we subtract 1 from 2 and add 1.

$$49 - 7 + 1 \quad = \quad 43$$
$$157 - 101 + 1 = \quad 57$$
$$43 + 57 \quad\quad = \quad 100$$

18. **The correct answer is (E).** If $\frac{P}{Q} = \frac{4}{5}$, then $5P = 4Q$. However, there is no way of determining from this the value of $2P + Q$.

19. **The correct answer is (C).** The new solution is $\frac{3}{20}$ pure alcohol or 15%.

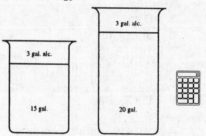

Starting Sol.   Resulting Sol.

20. **The correct answer is (C).** Area of $QXRS = XR \times$ altitude from P to XR. Area of $\triangle PXR = \frac{1}{2} XR \times$ altitude from P to XR. Hence, ratio of area of $\triangle$ to $QXRS = 1:2$.

21. **The correct answer is (E).** $x(p + 1) = M$ Divide both sides by x.

$$p + 1 = \frac{M}{x} \text{ or } p = \frac{M}{x} - 1$$

22. **The correct answer is (A).**

$$\frac{T}{1} = \frac{x}{60M}$$
$$x = 60MT$$

23. **The correct answer is (E).** It can be helpful to graph each of the inequalities and then put the two graphs together to find the overlapping area.

24. **The correct answer is (C).** Rise in temperature = $36 - (-14) = 36 + 14 = 50°$. $\frac{50}{5} = 10°$ (hourly rise) Hence, at noon, temperature = $-14 + 3(10) = -14 + 30 = +16°$.

25. **The correct answer is (A).** When we are asked for the sum of two items, we often *cannot* state the values of the individual items. This is the case in this problem. We can say $\angle BAD$ is 75° and $\angle CDA$ is 85°. We

also know that *ABCD* is a quadrilateral and must contain 360°. Therefore:

$\angle ABC + \angle BCD = 200°$

$\angle EBA + \angle ABC = 180°$

$\angle BCD + \angle DCF = 180°$

$\angle EBA + \angle ABC + \angle BCD + \angle DCF = 360°$

$\angle EBA + 200° + \angle DCF = 360°$

$\angle EBA + \angle DCF = 160°$

Section 3: VERBAL

1. **The correct answer is (B).** "Mutual assistance" implies that people are *cooperative*. Since "rather than" indicates a shift in meaning, the word in the second blank must have an opposing connotation; only *competitive* satisfies this condition.

2. **The correct answer is (C).** A condition that has existed for a long time in a particular place is said to be *endemic* to that location.

3. **The correct answer is (D).** The first blank could logically be filled by any of the choices. However, the secret betrayal implies that the actions *belied* (showed to be untrue) the words of the *reiterated* (repeated) pledges of support.

4. **The correct answer is (B).** Of the choices, the only one that could "look back upon us and our time" is our *descendants*.

5. **The correct answer is (E).** Choices (B), (D), and (E) are possibilities for the first blank. However, the second words in choices (B) and (D) make no logical sense. A *final* debate is likely to offer *clarification* of opinions.

6. **The correct answer is (B).** This is the only logical answer. "With the *duration*" is poor diction.

7. **The correct answer is (E).** The sentence establishes an opposition between "our" wishes and Eva's action. Only (E) satisfies this requirement.

8. **The correct answer is (A).** A key word in this sentence is *appearance*. The words following all tell how a person physically looks. Choices (B), (C), (D), and (E) describe feelings or behaviors. The only word describing physical appearance is *tousled* (A), which means "unkempt."

9. **The correct answer is (D).** The word *but* is your clue that the two words must have opposite connotations. The only choice that satisfies this condition is (D): the use of trained bears was once a *commonplace* (ordinary occurrence) but has now almost *ceased* (stopped).

10. **The correct answer is (B).** The word *although* signals that the second part of the sentence will describe the opposite of *aloofness* (coldness of manner). Therefore, the correct answer is *gracious* (courteous and kind).

11. **The correct answer is (A).** A *nest* is a structure built by a *bird* as a place to live and raise young. A *lair*, or *den*, is a place created by a *lion* for similar purpose. All the other choices include structures that are man-made.

12. **The correct answer is (D).** A *hammer* is used to *hit* an object. A *saw* is used to *cut* an object.

13. **The correct answer is (C).** The capitalized words are degrees of each other. *Ecstasy* is a stronger form of *happiness*.

14. **The correct answer is (D).** To *trickle* is to flow slowly; to *gush*, to flow profusely. Similarly, to *touch* is to come into gentle contact and to *collide* is to come into violent contact.

15. **The correct answer is (B).** We intentionally use the *eye* to *wink* and the *toe* to *tap* but we couldn't be said to intentionally use the *nose* to *smell*.

16. **The correct answer is (E).** In *bowling* you aim at the *pin* as in *golf* you aim at the *hole*.

17. **The correct answer is (B).** A *lake* will necessarily be experienced as *wet*, and *ice* necessarily as *cold*.

18. **The correct answer is (C).** A *tooth* is part of a *comb*; a *cog* is part of a *gear*.

19. **The correct answer is (D).** A *miser* is characterized by *stinginess*. An *altruist* (a person concerned with the welfare of others) is characterized by *selflessness*.

20. **The correct answer is (A).** One who is *chivalrous* is *gallant* and one who is *sanguine* is *cheerful*. Choices (B), (C), and (D) are antonyms.

21. **The correct answer is (B).** *Lava* flows out of a *volcano* and *water* flows out of a *spring*. Although answer choice (E) has some appeal, it reverses the order.

22. **The correct answer is (C).** To be *diffident* (timid) is to be lacking in *confidence*. Similarly, to be *gloomy* is to be lacking in *cheer*.

23. **The correct answer is (D).** A *conductor* leads an *orchestra* and a *president* leads a *country*.

24. **The correct answer is (B).** Their preoccupation with their stiff, new clothing, their awe at the train's typical conveniences, and their blushes at the glances of travelers—all of these combine to paint the picture of an innocent, unworldly pair.

25. **The correct answer is (E).** The bride constantly "twisted her head to regard her puff sleeves" (lines 28–29) and is embarrassed by them. Her dress is probably brand new, and she is certainly unused to such finery.

26. **The correct answer is (E).** With this single line, Crane paints a life of hard work and resignation.

27. **The correct answer is (D).** The bridegroom is putting on a brave face for the sake of his bride, who is even more unsophisticated than he.

28. **The correct answer is (B).** The bridegroom's pride is part of his delight in his "new estate" of marriage. He can show off for his bride, but there is no doubt that such elegance is rare for him.

29. **The correct answer is (C).** The charmingly decorated train is thought by the newlyweds to be indicative of their new status in life. Because they feel exalted by their new marriage, they imagine that they deserve such luxury.

30. **The correct answer is (E).** The porter is a lower-class working man, and is probably looked down upon by travelers, but he welcomes this opportunity to sneer at those lower on the ladder than himself.

31. **The correct answer is (A).** Travelers look at the newlyweds with "derisive enjoyment" (line 88). It is clear that they are just married, and there is something amusing about this.

32. **The correct answer is (C).** Customarily, people in the position of the newlyweds are amusing to others. None of the other synonyms makes sense in this context.

33. **The correct answer is (A).** Crane is not derisive (D); he leaves that to the other travelers and the porter. On the contrary, his attitude seems to be a slightly detached air of sympathy at the newlyweds' embarrassment and innocence.

34. **The correct answer is (B).** Their names are unimportant; what is vital is their provincialism and ordinariness. The reader can thus identify a type without feeling overly empathetic.

35. **The correct answer is (A).** This is, in fact, the beginning of the story, and, as with most short stories, its object is to introduce characters and setting. No opinion is expressed (D); the passage is simply descriptive.

Section 4: MATH

Part 1

1. **The correct answer is (B).** Since $2x$ is the same in both columns, adding 1 to $2x$ will surely be larger than subtracting 1 from it. The answer is (B).

2. **The correct answer is (A).** In Column A, x^2 will be a positive number, therefore $\frac{1}{x^2}$ will also be positive. In Column B, x will always be negative, so (A) is greater.

3. **The correct answer is (C).** $a + b + c$ is the sum of the angles of a triangle and therefore equals $180°$. $c + d$ is the sum of supplementary angles and, therefore, also equals $180°$.

4. **The correct answer is (C).** Using the distributive property in Column A, $(a + b) c = ac + bc$. Therefore $\frac{1}{4}(ac + bc) = \frac{ac+bc}{4}$. Column A and Column B are equal.

5. **The correct answer is (B).** Angle B is the largest in the triangle, so the side opposite B, side AC, is the largest side of the triangle. Therefore, AC is larger than AB.

6. **The correct answer is (A).** The area of the small circle is $\pi(3)^2 = 9\pi$. The area of the shaded region is the area of the large circle minus that of the small circle. The area of the large circle is $\pi(5)^2 = 25\pi$. The area of the shaded region is $25\pi - 9\pi = 16\pi$. The area of the shaded region is larger than that of the smaller circle.

7. **The correct answer is (B).** We are told that the sums of all the rows and columns are the same. We could set up an equation:

$$\frac{v+z+7}{-4} = \frac{w+y+4}{-4}$$
$$v+z+3 = w+y$$

Therefore, $w + y$ must be greater than $v + z$.

8. **The correct answer is (D).** It is impossible to determine which is larger. Taking two examples:

$$n = -\tfrac{1}{2}; (n+1)^3 = \left(\tfrac{1}{2}\right)^3 = \tfrac{1}{8}$$
and
$$n^3 + 1 = \left(-\tfrac{1}{2}\right)^3 + 1 = -\tfrac{1}{8} + 1 = \tfrac{7}{8}.$$

In this example, Column B is greater than Column A. However,

$$n = \tfrac{1}{2}, (n+1)^3 = \left(1\tfrac{1}{2}\right)^3 = 3\tfrac{3}{8} \text{ and}$$
$$n^3 + 1 = \left(\tfrac{1}{2}\right)^3 + 1 = 1\tfrac{1}{8}.$$

In this example, Column A is greater than Column B.

9. **The correct answer is (B).** m and n are alternate exterior angles, so $m = n$. n and $75°$ are supplementary angles, so $n = 180° - 75° = 105° = m$ and $180° - m = 75°$. Therefore, $180° - 75° > 180° - m$, and (B) is the correct choice.

10. The correct answer is (C). Using the distributive property, $(26 \times 39) + (39 \times 13)$ $= 39(26 + 13) = 39 \times 39 = (39)^2$. Therefore, Column A and Column B are equal.

11. The correct answer is (A). Since y is a positive fraction less than 1, $\frac{1}{y}$ is a positive fraction greater than 1. Therefore, $\frac{1}{y} > x$.

12. The correct answer is (C). y and z are vertical angles and therefore equal angles. Thus, $x + y$ and $x + z$ are equal sums.

13. The correct answer is (C). Factoring Column A $(m^2 - 1)(2m + 2) = (m - 1)(m + 1) \cdot 2(m + 1)$. Rearrange the factor so that $(m + 1)^2 \cdot 2(m - 1) = (m + 1)^2(2m - 2)$, which is equal to Column B.

14. The correct answer is (B). In Column A, 0.7% of 62 is $(0.007) \times (62) = 0.434$. In Column B, 70% of 6,200 is 4,340. Column B is larger.

15. The correct answer is (B). The area of a square with side s is s^2. The height of the triangle, using the Pythagorean theorem, is $\sqrt{(2s)^2 + s^2} = \sqrt{3s^2} = s\sqrt{3}$. The area of the triangle is $\frac{1}{2}(2s)(s\sqrt{3}) = s^2\sqrt{3}$. Thus, the area of the triangle (Column B) is larger.

Part 2

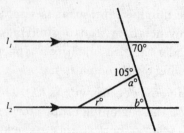

16. The measure of $\angle b = 70°$. It is an alternate interior angle with angle x.

The measure of $\angle a = 75°$. It is the supplement of angle y.

$\angle r + \angle a + \angle b = 180°$. They form a triangle.

$\angle r + 75° + 70° = 180°$

$\angle r = 35°$

17. $-x^2 - 2x^3$

Substitute the value -1 for x.

$-(-1)^2 - 2(-1)^3 =$

$-(-1) - 2(-1) =$

$-1 + 2 = 1$

18. $\text{Average} = \dfrac{\text{Sum of the test scores}}{\text{Quantity of tests}}$

$90 = \dfrac{87 + 93 + 86 + x}{4}$

By cross-multiplication:

$4(90) = 87 + 93 + 86 + x$

$360 = 266 + x$

$x = 94$

19. Circumference $= 2\pi r = 2\pi(6) = 12\pi$.

2π is $\dfrac{2\pi}{12\pi} = \dfrac{1}{6}$ of the circumference. In turn, the central angle is:

$\dfrac{1}{6}(360°) = 60°$, or $\dfrac{\text{arc length}}{\text{circumference}} = \dfrac{x°}{360°}$

$\dfrac{2\pi}{12\pi} = \dfrac{x}{360}$

$\dfrac{1}{6} = \dfrac{x}{360}$

$6x = 360$

$x = 60$

20. $\dfrac{2x}{3\sqrt{2}} = \dfrac{3\sqrt{2}}{x}$

By cross-multiplication:

$$2x(x) = \left(3\sqrt{2}\right)\left(3\sqrt{2}\right)$$

$$2x^2 = 9(2) = 18$$

$$x^2 = 9$$

$$x^2 = \pm 3$$

The positive value of x is 3.

21. The median is the "middle" data element when the data is arranged in numerical order.

$$20, 20, 20, 20, 30, 30, 30, 30, 50, 50, 50, 50, 50, 50, 50$$
$$\uparrow$$

The "middle" data element is 30.

22. $A * B = \dfrac{AB - B}{-B}$

$$-2 * 2 = \dfrac{(-2)(2) - 2}{-2} = \dfrac{-4 - 2}{-2} = \dfrac{-6}{-2} = 3$$

23. distance = rate × time → rate = $\dfrac{\text{distance}}{\text{time}}$

$$\dfrac{320 \text{ miles}}{8 \text{ hrs}} = 40 \text{ miles}$$

$$40 \text{ mph} \times 2 \text{ hrs} = 80 \text{ miles}$$

24. $\dfrac{\text{part}}{\text{whole}} \times 100 = \dfrac{9}{30} \times 100 = 30\%$

25. The number of sheets is directly proportional to the number of machines and also directly proportional to the amount of time. Mathematically this can be expressed as:

$$\dfrac{\text{sheets}}{(\text{number of machines})(\text{time})} = \dfrac{\text{sheets}}{(\text{number of machines})(\text{time})}$$

$$\dfrac{300}{3(3)} = \dfrac{600}{6(t)}$$

$$\dfrac{300}{9} = \dfrac{600}{6t}$$

Simplify the fractions and then cross-multiply:

$$\dfrac{100}{3} = \dfrac{100}{t}$$

$$100t = 300$$

$$t = 3$$

Section 5: VERBAL

1. **The correct answer is (E).** The town's only exposure is southward toward the sun; it is open only on the south side.

2. **The correct answer is (D).** Henson calls Karnah "pleasant," "delightful," even "ideal."

3. **The correct answer is (E).** The lack of trees (line 23) is the only thing that keeps Karnah from having a landscape "as delightful as anywhere on earth."

4. **The correct answer is (A).** "The scenery is also varied and attractive, offering to the eye greater contrasts. . . ." (lines 75–77), writes Peary. This diversity is one of the attractions of the bay.

5. **The correct answer is (C).** Lines 92–93 describe the "restless arctic elements" carving the cliffs into "turrets, bastions, huge amphitheatres, and colossal statues. . . ."

6. **The correct answer is (B).** Peary does not talk about vegetation (D), nor is this passage about the North Pole (E). The passage follows the coast of Greenland with enough specific detail that a reader could use it as a map.

7. **The correct answer is (B).** The description of the geology and scenery of Greenland seems to be from the vantage point of a ship traveling along the coastline. Everything that is mentioned is along the shore.

8. **The correct answer is (A).** Henson's "lofty mountains" surround Karnah; the only mention of landmarks around Karnah in Peary's description is to the "Sculptured Cliffs of Karnah."

9. **The correct answer is (C).** Peary's descriptions are much more technical than Henson's; his purpose is not to write a simple travelogue, but to detail an expedition for future explorers.

10. **The correct answer is (D).** Both writers mention the severity of most of the arctic, Henson in comparing it to Karnah's more moderate climate (lines 16–18), and Peary in his description of the restless arctic elements. Both, too, remark on the unusual attractiveness of Karnah and the bay.

11. **The correct answer is (D).** As was previously mentioned, Peary's descriptions are more objective and technical than those of Henson. Henson's sound more like the appreciative words of a casual traveler.

12. **The correct answer is (D).** Although Henson's account discusses the "rivulets of clear, cold water," he does not focus on the impact of glacial and iceberg activity, as does his counterpart.

Section 6: MATH

1. **The correct answer is (B).** Since Z is equidistant from X and Y, it must lie on the y-axis. Then $\triangle OZY$ is a $30° - 60° - 90°$ triangle with $YZ = 8$. Hence, $OZ = \frac{8}{2}\sqrt{3} = 4\sqrt{3}$.

Coordinates of Z are $(0, \ 4\sqrt{3})$.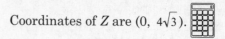

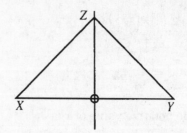

2. **The correct answer is (B).** $9 = 8 + 1 = 7 + 2 = 6 + 3 = 5 + 4$.

   Thus, 4 ways.

3. **The correct answer is (B).**

   $$\frac{7 \text{ ft. } 9 \text{ in.}}{3} = \frac{6 \text{ ft. } 21 \text{ in.}}{3} = 2 \text{ ft. } 7 \text{ in.}$$

4. **The correct answer is (D).** Since K is an integer and R and S are integers, K must be a perfect square and perfect cube. The smallest such number listed is $64 = 8^2 = 4^3$.

5. **The correct answer is (D).** The $\triangle RST$ has a base of 7 and an altitude of 5. Hence, the area $= \frac{1}{2} \bullet 7 \bullet 5 = 17\frac{1}{2}$.

6. **The correct answer is (D).** $\frac{3P}{3Q}$ is obviously reducible to $\frac{P}{Q}$. The others cannot be reduced.

7. **The correct answer is (A).** ACB is a straight angle and angle DCE is a right angle, then angle ACD and angle BCE are complementary. Hence, $BCE = 90 - x$.

8. **The correct answer is (B).** When a triangle is inscribed in a parallelogram or a rectangle, the area inside the inscribed triangle will always be the same

as the area outside the inscribed triangle. All three triangles have the same altitude. Since AE plus ED equals BC, the two shaded triangles combined have the same base as the unshaded triangle. If the base and the altitude are the same, then the area is the same.

9. **The correct answer is (E).** The most important point here is that we do not know the altitude of the parallelogram; the area of a parallelogram is altitude times base. A secondary point would be that we do not know the lengths of AB and BC; we only know the ratio of the two sides. The actual lengths of the sides could be, for example, 8 and 18.

10. **The correct answer is (D).** If a dozen eggs cost M cents, then 1 egg costs $\frac{M}{12}$ cents (there are 12 items in a dozen). The profit per egg would be Selling Price – Cost or $\frac{M}{6} - \frac{M}{12}$. Using a common denominator of 12, the profit per egg would be $\frac{M}{12}$ cents. Then the profit on a dozen eggs would be $\frac{M}{12} \times 12$, which is M cents.

COMPUTING YOUR SCORES

To get a sense of where you are scoring, you need to compute individual verbal and mathematical raw scores. Once you have computed these, refer to "Conversion Scales" to compute your SAT scaled scores (200–800). Keep in mind that these formulas have been simplified to give you a "quick and dirty" sense of where you are scoring, not a perfectly precise score.

Compute Your Raw Scores

Verbal Section	Total Number of Questions	Number of Questions Correct	Number of Questions Incorrect
1	31		
3	35		
5	12		
Totals	**78**	**Total Correct:**	**Total Incorrect:**

Verbal Raw Score = Total Correct – ($\frac{1}{4}$ × Total Incorrect) =

Math Section	Total Number of Questions	Number of Questions Correct	Number of Questions Incorrect
2	25		
4	25		
6	10		
Totals	**60**	**Total Correct:**	**Total Incorrect:**

Math Raw Score = Total Correct – ($\frac{1}{4}$ × Total Incorrect) =

CONVERSION SCALES

VERBAL REASONING

Raw Score	Scaled Score	Raw Score	Scaled Score
75	800	40	540
70	740	35	510
65	690	30	480
60	650	25	450
55	620	20	410
50	600	15	380
45	570	10	340
		5	290
		0	230

MATHEMATICAL REASONING

Raw Score	Scaled Score	Raw Score	Scaled Score
60	800	25	470
55	730	20	440
50	670	15	400
45	620	10	360
40	580	5	310
35	550	0	240
30	510		

Although you now have some idea of what your scores would look like had they been scaled according to unofficial ETS standards, you will probably want to know how to interpret your raw scores in more familiar terms. If so, use the following Self-Evaluation Charts to see what your raw scores actually mean.

SELF-EVALUATION CHARTS

VERBAL REASONING: Raw Score

Excellent	60–75
Good	50–59
Average	30–49
Fair	20–29
Poor	0–19

MATHEMATICAL REASONING: Raw Score

Excellent	50–60
Good	40–49
Average	20–39
Fair	10–19
Poor	0–9

PINPOINTING RELATIVE STRENGTHS AND WEAKNESSES

You can pinpoint how to focus your review time by calculating the percentage of each type of question you answered correctly. For each question type, divide the number of correct questions by the total number of questions.

Verbal Question Types

Type of Verbal Question	Number of Questions Correct	Total Number of Questions	Percent Correct (number correct ÷ total)
Sentence Completions		19	
Analogies		19	
Critical Reading		40	

Compare these three percentages to assess your relative strengths and weaknesses. If any individual percentage was considerably lower than others, you should concentrate your further study of SAT verbal topics in that area. You can do so by reading the appropriate strategy chapter in Part III and completing the exercises that accompany it.

If sentence completions and/or analogies gave you difficulty, you should work through Part 5 to bolster your vocabulary. Learning vocabulary words is a critical step to improving on these sections.

Math Question Types

Type of Math Question	Number of Questions Correct	Total Number of Questions	Percent Correct (number correct ÷ total)
Multiple Choice		35	
Quantitative Comparison		15	
Grid-In		10	

Compare these three percentages to assess your relative strengths and weaknesses. If any individual section produced a percentage that was considerably lower than others, that's a weakness you can—and should—eliminate. To improve your skills in any area of SAT math, read the appropriate strategy chapter in Part IV and do the exercises.

Math Subtopics

To get an even more in-depth look at your performance, look back at the answer key to the multiple-choice math questions (Sections 2 and 6) on page 65–66. You'll notice that each question has been subdivided into one of four categories—arithmetic, algebra, geometry, and other.

Type of Math Subtopic	Number of Questions Correct	Total Number of Questions	Percent Correct (number correct total)
Arithmetic (A)		10	
Algebra (AL)		6	
Geometry (G)		14	

Compare these three percentages to assess your relative strengths and weaknesses by mathematical subcategory. If an individual percentage is considerably lower than others, you've found an area for further study. Read the appropriate math chapter in Part VI and do the exercises.

MEASURING YOUR PROGRESS

As you visit chapters and do exercises, don't forget to compare your performance on those exercises with the verbal and mathematical percentages you calculated here. Down the road, you can also measure your progress very easily by comparing how you did on this test with how you do on other practice examinations.

Take note of whether you had difficulty finishing any particular part of the test. It might be that you are spending too long on certain questions and not allotting enough time for others. This should improve as you work through the strategy sections of this book and increase your familiarity with the test and question format. If you are worried about spending too long on particular question types, see Part VII for a discussion of timing drills.

PART III

SAT VERBAL STRATEGIES

SAT Analogy Strategies

OVERVIEW

- **Take a closer look**
- **Learn to solve analogies**
- **Solve analogies even when you don't know the capitalized words**
- **Review what you need to know about analogies**
- **Practice your skills on analogies exercises**

A CLOSER LOOK AT ANALOGIES

Analogies test your ability to recognize the relationships between pairs of words. You'll be given a pair of words in capital letters (the stem pair) that have a particular relationship to each other. You'll then be given five additional pairs of words, labeled (A), (B), (C), (D), and (E) (the answer choices). Your job is to select that answer choice with a pair of words whose relationship is similar to the relationship between the words in the stem pair.

SAT Analogy Questions

Your SAT examination will probably have a total of 19 analogy questions. In one verbal section, you can expect six analogies out of 30 total questions; in another verbal section, expect 13 analogies out of 35 total questions.

Question Format

A sample analogy question has been provided below to help you to familiarize yourself with the format.

> **Directions:** Each question below consists of a related pair of words or phrases, followed by five pairs of words or phrases labeled (A) through (E). Select the pair that best expresses a relationship similar to that expressed in the original pair.

chapter 5

NOTE

Analogies are 19 out
of 78 total verbal
questions. They count
as 24% of your overall
verbal score.

Example

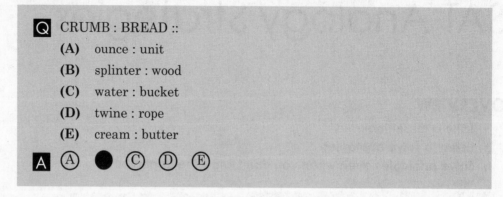

Q CRUMB : BREAD ::
(A) ounce : unit
(B) splinter : wood
(C) water : bucket
(D) twine : rope
(E) cream : butter

A Ⓐ ● Ⓒ Ⓓ Ⓔ

SOLVING ANALOGIES: STRATEGIES THAT REALLY WORK

Build a Bridge

A bridge is a short sentence that contains both words in the stem pair and shows how they are related. Let's call the two words in the stem pair "X" and "Y." A typical bridge would define X in terms of Y. So, for the sample question from the directions above, the bridge might say, "A CRUMB is a very small piece that falls off or breaks off a piece of BREAD." Notice how this sentence explains the relationship between the two words. It also defines CRUMB (tells what a crumb is) in terms of BREAD. A lovely bridge! (No wonder: It's the test-makers' own example.)

Here are a couple of other examples. Suppose the stem pair was "OPERA : MUSIC." (By the way, you would read this aloud, "opera is to music.") The bridge might say, "An OPERA is a long, elaborate, classical work of MUSIC." If the stem pair was "SURGEON : SCALPEL," the bridge might be, "A SURGEON is a professional who uses a SCALPEL." Get the idea?

Plug in the Answer Choices

After you've created a bridge, turn to the answer choices. One by one, try to plug in the words from the answer choices into the same sentence. If your bridge is a strong one, only one pair of words will make sense.

Try this with the five answer choices for the sample question above. Only the words in choice (B) fit comfortably into the bridge: "A SPLINTER is a very small piece that falls off or breaks off of a piece of WOOD." Think about the others. Is an OUNCE a very small piece of a UNIT (choice A)? No; an ounce is a kind of unit—a unit of weight. Is WATER a very small piece of a BUCKET (choice C)? No; water might be carried in a bucket. The same with the other answers. So choice (B) is correct. (By the way, you would read the stem pair and the correct answer this way: "CRUMB is to BREAD as SPLINTER is to WOOD.")

NOTE

A strong bridge
explicitly defines the
relationship between
the two words in the
stem pair. By building
a bridge, you force
yourself to explain (to
yourself) exactly how
the two words logi-
cally fit together—the
first step to solving any
analogy question.

What if our stem pair is OPERA : MUSIC?

Which of these five answer choices fits the same bridge?

(A) novel : artistry

(B) painting : landscape

(C) oboe : instrument

(D) epic : poetry

(E) microphone : recording

The correct answer is (D), because only that word pair fits into the same bridge: "An EPIC is a long, elaborate, classical work of POETRY."

Get Narrow as Needed

Sometimes the differences among the answer choices will be subtle—so subtle that the first bridge you've built won't eliminate the wrong answers. When that's the case, two or more answer choices may fit the bridge. Here's an example:

SURGEON : SCALPEL ::

(A) judge : gavel

(B) painter : canvas

(C) executive : computer

(D) farmer : fertilizer

(E) carpenter : saw

If you built the bridge "A SURGEON is a professional who uses a SCALPEL" and then tried plugging each of the answer pairs (A) through (E), you'd be dismayed to find that all five answer pairs could fit the bridge! A judge uses a gavel (it's the hammer a judge uses to pound on the bench); a painter (often) uses a canvas; an executive (often) uses a computer; a farmer uses fertilizer; and a carpenter uses a saw. Based on this bridge, all five answer choices could be considered correct! Now what?

Solution: narrow your bridge—that is, add details to the sentence to make it more specific. In this case, you might narrow the bridge in this way: "A SURGEON is a professional who uses a SCALPEL as a tool for cutting." Now plug in the answer choices. Only one fits the new, narrower bridge: choice (E). That's the correct answer.

Of course, picking the correct answer depends on your narrowing the bridge correctly. You could concoct, a misleading bridge that included details that pointed to a different answer. For example, you could say, "A SURGEON is a professional who wears a protective smock while using a SCALPEL." With that bridge, choice (B) is arguably correct, since artists, like surgeons, do often wear protective smocks. (The robe a judge wears isn't "protective," so choice (A) doesn't work. And the people in the other choices don't wear smocks at all.) Does this mean that choice (B) is just as good as choice (E)?

TIP

Think of analogies as resembling proportions in math. A proportion like $\frac{2}{3} = \frac{4}{6}$ also describes analogous logical relationships among things. Do you see the similarity?

TIP

If the correct answer for an analogy "jumps out at you" without the bridge-building step, great—go for it! But the more you practice bridge-building *before* the test, the faster your instincts will supply answers on SAT day.

No—in fact, if you think about it, you probably find answer (B), and the bridge we made up that points to it, a little silly. The smock that a surgeon (or an artist) wears isn't central to his or her work; and it certainly has little to do with the use of the scalpel. The first narrow bridge we created—the one that refers to the scalpel as a cutting tool—seems more sensible. It defines exactly what the scalpel does in the hands of the surgeon—which is similar to what the saw does in the hands of the carpenter.

The point is that it takes a bit of judgment to build the right bridge. You want to focus on the central, basic nature of the relationship between the two words—not on side issues that are irrelevant (like the surgeon's smock). It's a little subjective, yes. But nine times out of ten, devising the right bridge will strike you as a matter of "common sense."

In fact, in the example we've been looking at, you may have been able to "see" the similarity between SURGEON : SCALPEL and carpenter : saw even without consciously building the new, narrow bridge. That's fine. But as you prepare for the test, practice your bridge-building technique. It'll give you crucial help on the handful of really tough analogies your test will contain.

Look for the Test-Makers' Favorite Relationships

Pity the people at ETS. They write test questions by the hundred, week in and week out. Like anyone else, they eventually start to repeat themselves. (Ever notice how the third CD by your favorite pop group sounds a lot like their first and second CDs—only less interesting?) But this is a good thing for you, the test-taker. It means that analogies fall into repeated patterns that you can practice and learn. If you know and understand the test-makers' favorite analogy relationships, you'll quickly pounce on them if they pop up on your exam. And they will, they will!

Here are the top nine analogy relationships we've found on past and current SATs. (If any of the examples that follow contain words you're not sure about, you know what to do: grab your dictionary!)

Part : Whole

In this kind of analogy, one word names something that is part of what's named by the other word—usually a specific kind of part. Here are a couple of examples:

LID : POT :: roof : house
MOVEMENT : SYMPHONY :: scene : play

Opposites

Here, the two words in the pair are opposite or opposed in meaning. Examples:

NAIVE : SOPHISTICATED :: untutored : educated

WATER : DROUGHT :: food : famine

Actor : Action

This kind of analogy links a person or thing with what that person or thing commonly does. Examples:

COUNTERFEITER : FAKE :: blackmailer : extort

DETERGENT : CLEAN :: bleach : whiten

Actor : Acted Upon

The word pair includes a person or thing and another person or thing that is commonly acted upon or affected by the first. Examples:

TEACHER : CLASS :: orator : audience

NET : FISH :: trap : game

Action : Acted Upon

Here, an action is paired with the person or thing that commonly receives or is affected by the action. Examples:

ALPHABETIZE : FILES :: catalog : books

RAZE : BUILDING :: fell : tree

Action : Emotion

One of the words describes an action, the other an emotion commonly associated with it. Examples:

LOSS : MOURN :: triumph : celebrate

TREMBLE : FEAR :: shiver : cold

Thing : Description

This kind of word pair includes one word that names a person or thing, another that describes it. Examples:

MISER : STINGY :: spendthrift : wasteful

GLADE : SHADY :: clearing : open

Description : Quality

Here, an adjective that describes a particular quality is paired with a noun that names the quality. Examples:

> LIFELIKE : VIVIDNESS :: truthful : honesty
> ARROGANT : PRIDE :: modest : humility

Differing Connotations

TIP

More students hurt themselves on the SAT by shunning the "obvious" than by taking it for granted. Don't be shy about guessing at word relationships! The test-makers are predictable, and the obvious connection is usually the right one.

In this kind of analogy, two words are linked that have similar meanings but different feelings, moods, or nuances—in other words, different connotations. Examples:

> CAR : JALOPY :: house : shanty
> HIGH : SHRILL :: bright : blinding

Not every analogy on your exam will fit into one of these nine categories, but three quarters of them will. Those that don't will embody "miscellaneous" relationships of their own, like these examples:

> MUSICIAN : CONCERT :: poet : reading

Here, a type of artist is paired with an event at which he or she might perform.

> BOTANY : PLANT :: astronomy : star

A field of science is paired with a typical object that is studied in that field.

> GAUNTLET : HAND :: helmet : head

A gauntlet is an armored glove worn, of course, on the hand; a helmet is an armored hat worn on the head.

SOLVING ANALOGIES: THE BEST TIPS

Use the Analogy Structure to Guess Words You Don't Know

On some analogies, you may encounter words whose meaning you aren't sure of. Don't worry. You can use the analogy structure to help you guess the meaning of the unknown words. First, realize that all the word pairs contain words that are the same parts of speech. For example, if the stem pair contains a noun and a verb, like this:

> TYRANT : OPPRESS

then each of the other word pairs will also contain a noun and a verb, in that order. So in any analogy with an unknown word, by looking at any of the other word pairs, you can tell whether the unknown word is a noun, verb, adjective, or any other part of speech—which in itself can be helpful in guessing its meaning.

Next, try using what you know about analogy relationships—and the words in the question that you *do* understand—to make a smart guess as to the meaning of the unknown word. Look at this example:

ETYMOLOGY : WORD ::

(A) etiology : disease

(B) history : event

(C) literature : author

(D) microscopy : microbe

(E) psychology : insanity

(We've deliberately included some difficult, specialized words in this analogy to illustrate a point; actually, a word like *etiology* is unlikely to be used in an analogy on the real SAT.) You may or may not know what ETYMOLOGY means in the stem pair, but you can tell by glancing at the other word pairs that it must be a noun, since the first word in every pair is a noun. And you can probably guess, from the way the word looks, that it refers to a study or science of some kind. (Words that end in *-ology*, like *biology* and *anthropology*, usually do.)

Now, ETYMOLOGY is paired with WORD. From what you know of analogy relationships, you obviously know that ETYMOLOGY has something to do with a word or words. Given that fact, what's a possible meaning of ETYMOLOGY? Your first guess is likely to be that ETYMOLOGY is "the science or study of words." As it happens, that's not quite correct; but never mind. This guess is probably close enough to enable you to eliminate answers (B), (C), and (E) as clearly wrong. History can't be defined as "the science of events"; it's the study of the past, including events, people, forces, trends, and so on. Literature isn't "the science of authors"; it's the study of what authors produce, namely books and other writings. And psychology isn't "the science of insanity"; psychology studies the mind and human behavior, including both sane and insane subjects. So by sheer guesswork—and a modicum of word-sense—you can narrow your choices to two, giving you great odds for guessing, even if you have little or no idea what *etiology* and *microscopy* mean.

The correct answer, by the way, is (A). ETYMOLOGY is actually the study of word origins—where words come from. Similarly, *etiology* is the study of the origins of disease—where particular illnesses come from. So the analogy is close. (Microscopy has nothing to do with the origin of microbes, if you're wondering.)

Not every obscure word in an analogy may be positioned quite so well for guessing. But many will be. Don't let one or more unknown words in a question alarm you; work from what you do know to make reasonable guesses as to the meaning of the new words, and don't be afraid to base your answer choice on these guesses.

TIP

On some analogies, you may find that your bridge enables you to eliminate two or three answer choices, leaving two or three possible answers. If that happens, try working backward from each of the live possibilities. Look at each word pair, build a bridge that defines their relationship, and then try to plug the stem pair into that bridge. It'll probably work with only one of the answer pairs—and that, of course, is the correct answer.

Don't Fear the Flip-Flop

The logical relationship in the stem pair will "run" a certain way; the relationships in the answer choices will run the same way. For example, suppose you face this stem pair:

PROLIFIC : CREATOR

The relationship here is "Description : Thing," and it might be summarized by the bridge "A PROLIFIC CREATOR is one that produces a lot (of offspring, ideas, artworks, or whatever)." Your job would be to find the answer choice with the same "Description : Thing" relationship, preferably using words that fit nicely into the same bridge. Choosing the right answer, as you've already seen, may at times be subtle, even tricky. But one kind of trick you *don't* have to worry about is the "flip-flop." The test-makers *do not* try to trick you by giving you a correct word pair in reverse order, like this:

SOURCE : ABUNDANT

As we said before, on the SAT, you'll find that all the answer choices match the stem pair in their parts of speech. Similarly, you'll find that relationship reversals are not used to try to trick you. So don't worry about flip-flops—they don't turn up on the SAT.

When All Else Fails . . .

Sometimes, you won't be able to find the one best answer for an analogy question. Remember, the questions get harder as you move through a batch; so in a batch of 13 analogies, you're likely to find the last three or four to be quite hard. And you may encounter words whose meaning you don't know, and can't guess, even using the clues provided by the analogy structure. When this happens, work by elimination. Build the best bridge you can and plug in the answer choices. Eliminate any answer pairs that don't seem to fit, and guess from among the remaining answers.

Occasionally you may find that you've eliminated all the answers you understand, leaving only an answer that contains words you don't know. Don't be afraid—choose it!

TIP

Test-makers call wrong answers "distractors." You can see why. The wrong answers are deliberately designed to "distract" the unwary test-taker from the correct answer—which, on its surface, may appear far-fetched. Don't focus on the surface. Go deeper, focusing on the logical relationship between the words. That's what counts.

SOLVING ANALOGIES: THE MOST IMPORTANT WARNINGS

Ignore the Topics of the Word Pairs

It's easy to go wrong by focusing on the surface meanings of the words in the word pairs rather than on their underlying relationship. Consider this example:

WING : FEATHER ::
- **(A)** turtle : shell
- **(B)** eagle : talon
- **(C)** fish : fin
- **(D)** roof : shingle
- **(E)** bird : flight

The words in the stem pair refer to parts of a bird, of course. A hasty glance at the answer choices shows that four of them also refer to animals of one kind or another, and two (answers B and E) refer specifically to birds. So you might be tempted to pick one of these answers, misled by the surface similarity.

The correct answer, however, is choice (D). A well-thought-out bridge will tell you why. The relationship between the words in the stem pair might be described this way: "The WING of a bird is covered by many small, overlapping segments, each called a FEATHER." Only choice (D) fits the same bridge: "The ROOF of a house is [or may be] covered by many small, overlapping segments, each called a SHINGLE." Can you picture the similarity? No such similarity exists when you picture the turtle and its shell, the eagle and its talon (or claw), or any of the other items named in the answer choices.

Be Prepared to Jump from the Concrete to the Abstract

The test-makers sometimes like to make you connect a pair of words that is concrete—related to the physical world—with a pair that is abstract—related to the world of ideas. Practice recognizing such analogies. Here are a couple of examples:

SPARK : FIRE :: inspiration : invention

SPARK and FIRE are concrete, physical things; a SPARK is a small thing that helps to create a larger, more powerful force, a FIRE. *Inspiration* and *invention* are abstract ideas that have much the same relationship.

RETRACE : PATH :: reiterate : argument

When you RETRACE a PATH, you are walking over the same steps you took before, in a physical sense. When you *reiterate* an *argument*, you are repeating the same ideas you stated before, in an abstract sense.

The following exercise gives you an opportunity to practice identifying answers that *could* be right. As you've just learned, this skill can help you solve SAT analogies—even when you don't know the meaning of the capitalized words.

EXERCISE: IDENTIFYING POSSIBLE RIGHT ANSWERS

Directions: Of the 30 pairs of words below, only 10 are possible correct answers because they exhibit a clear-cut connection. The other pairs are NOT possible right answers. Place a checkmark by those that could be correct answers and an "X" by those that could not be correct.

1. DISTRACT : IGNORANCE
2. STOMACH : FLU
3. COURTESY : CHILD
4. PROSECUTION : DIRECTOR
5. SHOVEL : EXCAVATE
6. PENCIL : POCKET
7. SCALES : JUSTICE
8. CANDLE : POVERTY
9. SIMPLIFY : VALUABLE
10. NULLIFY : VALIDITY
11. SNIP : SCISSORS
12. PRECIOUS : WORRIED
13. TIME : CLOCK
14. ACCESSIBLE : VOYAGE
15. CONTRITE : FAVORITE
16. WHISPER : SHOUT
17. TOTAL : APPLICATION
18. AIR : SUFFOCATION
19. ROMANTIC : INTEREST
20. ILLUMINATE : PALE
21. SHREWD : RESENT
22. PARAGRAPH : ESSAY
23. QUIET : DESPERATION
24. UNIFORM : ERRONEOUS
25. ANTHOLOGY : DESCRIPTIVE
26. ILLNESS : VISION
27. DESTITUTE : MONEY
28. RANDOM : SINCERE
29. CREDULOUS : TRUST
30. PREPARE : DELIGHT

EXERCISE ANSWERS

The following list shows the "possible" right answers from the preceding exercise—and explains the relationship between the paired words.

5. A *shovel* is a tool used to *excavate*.

7. *Scales* are the symbols of *justice*.

10. To *nullify* something is to take away its *validity*.

11. *Scissors* are a tool used to *snip*.

13. A *clock* is a device used to measure *time*.

16. A *shout* is a louder form of communication than a *whisper*.

18. *Suffocation* occurs from lack of *air*.

22. A *paragraph* is a part of an *essay*.

27. To be *destitute* is to lack *money*.

29. To be *credulous* is more extreme than to be *trusting*.

Let's try one more SAT analogy to practice using the "clear-cut connection" test and to fine-tune our guessing strategy:

ICONOCLAST : TRADITION ::

(A) science : fiction

(B) impostor : identity

(C) libertarian : tyranny

(D) stranger : domination

(E) soldier : satisfaction

Chances are good that you know the meaning of the word TRADITION. However, even if you have heard of the word ICONOCLAST (or icon), you probably cannot form a satisfactory sentence between the two words. Don't make up a random sentence because the wrong relationship will do you no good. Instead, work backwards by using the clear-cut connection test.

In this question, three choices drop out because they lack strong relationships. So you should be down to choices (B) and (C). You probably don't know exactly what a *libertarian* is, so you should probably focus your attention on choice (B). By definition, an impostor is someone who fakes his identity. If you think that an ICONOCLAST is someone who fakes his TRADITION, pick choice (B). That does not seem highly likely, though. How does a person fake his tradition, anyway? So if you doubt the likelihood of choice (B), you have to guess choice (C), even if it contains words whose meanings you don't know! As it turns out, choice (C) is correct. An ICONOCLAST is someone who strongly opposes TRADITION and a *libertarian* is someone who strongly opposes *tyranny*.

So what's our guessing strategy on difficult analogies? If you like the relationship between words you know, pick that choice. But if the relationship seems unlikely, you have to have the guts to choose the choice that contains the most difficult vocabulary. Statistically speaking, this will be to your benefit.

SUMMARY

What You Need to Know about Analogies

- Analogies test your ability to find the relationship between paired words.

- The 19 analogy questions on the scored portion of the SAT count for about one quarter of your verbal score.

- When you don't know the capitalized words, work backward:

  1. Use the clear-cut connection test to rule out answer choices.

  2. Guess from the remaining choices. If easy words appear to work, select that choice. If easy words do not appear to fit exactly, guess the choice with the hardest words.

EXERCISES: ANALOGIES

Exercise 1

35 Questions • Time—25 Minutes

Directions: Each of the following questions consists of a capitalized pair of words followed by five pairs of words lettered (A) to (E). The capitalized words bear some meaningful relationship to each other. Choose the lettered pair of words whose relationship is most similar to that expressed by the capitalized pair. Circle the letter that appears before your answer.

Example:

Q DAY : SUN ::

  (A) sunlight : daylight

  (B) ray : sun

  (C) night : moon

  (D) heat : cold

  (E) moon : star

A (A) (B) ● (D) (E)

1. HAIR : BALD ::
   (A) wig : curly
   (B) egg : cooked
   (C) rain : arid
   (D) skin : scarred
   (E) medicine : healthy

2. DINGHY : BOAT ::
   (A) novel : book
   (B) canoe : paddle
   (C) oar : water
   (D) deck : stern
   (E) land : sea

3. APPLE : TREE ::
   (A) silver : ore
   (B) bronze : copper
   (C) plank : wood
   (D) glass : sand
   (E) pearl : oyster

4. CARNIVORE : MEAT ::
   (A) carnivore : vegetables
   (B) herbivore : plants
   (C) vegetarian : vitamins
   (D) botanist : herbs
   (E) pollinator : plants

5. MAUVE : COLOR ::
   (A) basil : spice
   (B) salt : sugar
   (C) light : dark
   (D) tan : brown
   (E) blue : rainbow

6. MUFFLE : SILENCE ::
   (A) cover : report
   (B) sound : alarm
   (C) cry : hear
   (D) stymie : defeat
   (E) glimpse : look

7. DEARTH : PAUCITY ::
   (A) individual : person
   (B) scarcity : shortage
   (C) shortage : plethora
   (D) prairie : forest
   (E) commodity : expectation

8. WATERMARK : PAPER ::
   (A) landmark : monument
   (B) birthmark : person
   (C) tide : character
   (D) line : signal
   (E) signature : author

9. BRIGHT : BRILLIANT ::
   (A) orange : red
   (B) tall : high
   (C) warm : light
   (D) white : cold
   (E) happy : ecstatic

10. DISCIPLINE : ORDER ::
    (A) military : rank
    (B) authority : follower
    (C) parent : child
    (D) teacher : student
    (E) training : preparation

11. NEWS REPORT : DESCRIPTIVE ::
    (A) weather report : unpredictable
    (B) editorial : one-sided
    (C) feature story : newsworthy
    (D) commercial : prescriptive
    (E) joke : funny

12. AGREEMENT : CONSENSUS ::
    (A) discord : harmony
    (B) pleasure : hatred
    (C) tranquility : peace
    (D) argument : solution
    (E) action : conclusion

13. WATER : HYDRAULIC ::
    (A) energy : atomic
    (B) power : electric
    (C) gasoline : inflammable
    (D) pressure : compressible
    (E) air : pneumatic

14. STABLE : HORSE ::
    (A) pond : duck
    (B) sty : pig
    (C) fold : ram
    (D) coop : hen
    (E) zoo : lioness

15. ROLE : ACTOR ::
    (A) aria : soprano
    (B) private : soldier
    (C) melody : singer
    (D) position : ballplayer
    (E) character : part

16. PROW : SHIP ::
    (A) snout : hog
    (B) nose : airplane
    (C) bird : beak
    (D) wheel : car
    (E) point : shaft

17. MAXIMUM : MINIMUM ::
   (A) pessimistic : chauvinistic
   (B) minimum : optimum
   (C) best : good
   (D) most : least
   (E) waning : less

18. SENSATION : ANESTHETIC ::
   (A) breath : lung
   (B) drug : reaction
   (C) satisfaction : disappointment
   (D) poison : antidote
   (E) observation : sight

19. DISEMBARK : SHIP ::
   (A) board : train
   (B) dismount : horse
   (C) intern : jail
   (D) discharge : navy
   (E) dismantle : clock

20. PROTEIN : MEAT ::
   (A) calories : cream
   (B) energy : sugar
   (C) cyclamates : diet
   (D) starch : potatoes
   (E) fat : cholesterol

21. NECK : NAPE ::
   (A) foot : heel
   (B) head : forehead
   (C) arm : wrist
   (D) stomach : back
   (E) eye : lid

22. GRIPPING : PLIERS ::
   (A) appealing : picture
   (B) breaking : hammer
   (C) elevating : jack
   (D) killing : knife
   (E) fastening : screwdriver

23. RADIUS : CIRCLE ::
   (A) rubber : tire
   (B) bisector : angle
   (C) equator : earth
   (D) cord : circumference
   (E) spoke : wheel

24. MISDEMEANOR : FELONY ::
   (A) police : prison
   (B) thief : burglar
   (C) murder : manslaughter
   (D) mishap : catastrophe
   (E) crime : degree

25. HYGROMETER : HUMIDITY ::
   (A) clock : second
   (B) gauge : air
   (C) odometer : speed
   (D) barometer : weather
   (E) thermometer : temperature

26. ASTUTE : STUPID ::
   (A) pedantic : idiotic
   (B) agile : clumsy
   (C) lonely : wary
   (D) dull : ignorant
   (E) intelligent : smart

27. WHALE : FISH ::
   (A) collie : dog
   (B) fly : insect
   (C) bat : bird
   (D) alligator : crocodile
   (E) mako : shark

28. GOLD : PROSPECTOR ::
   (A) medicine : doctor
   (B) prayer : preacher
   (C) wood : carpenter
   (D) clue : detective
   (E) iron : machinist

exercises

29. COUPLET : POEM ::
   (A) letter : page
   (B) sentence : paragraph
   (C) address : house
   (D) epic : poetry
   (E) biography : novel

30. ENTREPRENEUR : PROFIT ::
   (A) interloper : trade
   (B) business : monopoly
   (C) miner : ore
   (D) nemesis : peace
   (E) captain : boat

31. RUDDER : SHIP ::
   (A) wheel : car
   (B) motor : truck
   (C) oar : boat
   (D) string : kite
   (E) wing : plane

32. STALLION : ROOSTER ::
   (A) buck : doe
   (B) filly : colt
   (C) horse : chicken
   (D) foal : calf
   (E) mare : hen

33. READ : BOOK ::
   (A) taste : salt
   (B) attend : movie
   (C) smell : odor
   (D) listen : record
   (E) touch : paper

34. PARROT : SPARROW ::
   (A) dog : poodle
   (B) elephant : ant
   (C) goldfish : guppy
   (D) lion : cat
   (E) eagle : butterfly

35. BONE : LIGAMENT ::
   (A) fracture : cast
   (B) muscle : tendon
   (C) fat : cell
   (D) knuckle : finger
   (E) knee : joint

Exercise 2

15 Questions • Time—10 Minutes

Directions: Each of the following questions consists of a capitalized pair of words followed by five pairs of words lettered (A) to (E). The capitalized words bear some meaningful relationship to each other. Choose the lettered pair of words whose relationship is most similar to that expressed by the capitalized pair. Circle the letter that appears before your answer.

Example

Q DAY : SUN ::
(A) sunlight : daylight
(B) ray : sun
(C) night : moon
(D) heat : cold
(E) moon : star

1. SPICY : INSIPID ::
   (A) peppery : salty
   (B) hot : creamy
   (C) keen : dull
   (D) pickled : sweet
   (E) bland : chewy

2. SCYTHE : DEATH ::
   (A) fall : winter
   (B) knife : murder
   (C) sickle : grain
   (D) harvest : crops
   (E) arrow : love

3. YEAST : LEAVEN ::
   (A) soda : bubble
   (B) iodine : antiseptic
   (C) aspirin : medicine
   (D) flour : dough
   (E) penicillin : plant

4. POLYGLOT : LANGUAGE ::
   (A) teacher : students
   (B) tourist : countries
   (C) linguist : words
   (D) polygamist : children
   (E) factotum : trades

5. EXPURGATE : PASSAGES ::
   (A) defoliate : leaves
   (B) cancel : checks
   (C) incorporate : ideas
   (D) invade : privacy
   (E) till : fields

6. PHARMACIST : DRUGS ::
   (A) psychiatrist : ideas
   (B) mentor : drills
   (C) mechanic : troubles
   (D) chef : foods
   (E) nurse : diseases

7. CONQUER : SUBJUGATE ::
   (A) esteem : respect
   (B) slander : vilify
   (C) discern : observe
   (D) ponder : deliberate
   (E) free : enslave

8. ENGRAVING : CHISEL ::
   (A) printing : paper
   (B) photography : camera
   (C) lithography : stone
   (D) printing : ink
   (E) etching : acid

9. DECIBEL : SOUND ::
   (A) calorie : weight
   (B) volt : electricity
   (C) temperature : weather
   (D) color : light
   (E) area : distance

10. HOMONYM : SOUND ::
    (A) antonym : confusion
    (B) synonym : meaning
    (C) acronym : ideas
    (D) pseudonym : fake
    (E) synopsis : summary

11. WHET : KNIFE ::
    (A) file : spur
    (B) chop : ax
    (C) hone : razor
    (D) stab : sword
    (E) fence : rapier

12. VALUELESS : INVALUABLE ::
    (A) miserly : philanthropic
    (B) frugal : wealthy
    (C) thrifty : cheap
    (D) costly : cut-rate
    (E) incomprehensible : unreadable

13. TRIANGLE : PRISM ::
    (A) sphere : earth
    (B) square : rhomboid
    (C) rectangle : building
    (D) circle : cylinder
    (E) polygon : diamond

14. YOKE : OX ::
    (A) saddle : stallion
    (B) tether : cow
    (C) herd : sheep
    (D) brand : steer
    (E) harness : horse

15. SYMPHONY : CODA ::
    (A) drama : prologue
    (B) letter : introduction
    (C) music : note
    (D) opera : aria
    (E) novel : epilogue

ANSWER KEYS AND EXPLANATIONS

Exercise 1

1.	C	8.	B	15.	D	22.	C	29.	B
2.	A	9.	E	16.	B	23.	E	30.	C
3.	E	10.	E	17.	D	24.	D	31.	A
4.	B	11.	D	18.	D	25.	E	32.	E
5.	A	12.	C	19.	B	26.	B	33.	D
6.	D	13.	E	20.	D	27.	C	34.	C
7.	B	14.	B	21.	A	28.	D	35.	B

1. **The correct answer is (C).** To be *bald* is to lack *hair*. To be *arid* is to lack *rain*.

2. **The correct answer is (A).** A *dinghy* is a type of *boat*, and a *novel* is a type of *book*.

3. **The correct answer is (E).** An *apple* is produced by a *tree*, and a *pearl* is produced by an *oyster*.

4. **The correct answer is (B).** A *carnivore* eats only *meat*, and an *herbivore* eats only *plants*.

5. **The correct answer is (A).** *Mauve* is a *color*, and *basil* is a *spice*.

6. **The correct answer is (D).** To *muffle* something is almost to *silence* it. To *stymie* something is almost to *defeat* it.

7. **The correct answer is (B).** *Paucity* is a synonym for *dearth*, as is *shortage* for *scarcity*.

8. **The correct answer is (B).** *Paper* is sometimes identified by a *watermark*, and a *person* by a *birthmark*.

9. **The correct answer is (E).** A person who is extremely *bright* is *brilliant*. A person who is extremely *happy* is *ecstatic*.

10. **The correct answer is (E).** *Discipline* brings about order rather than *disorder*. *Training* brings about *preparation* rather than lack of preparation.

11. **The correct answer is (D).** A *news report* is *descriptive* of an event, but a *commercial* is *prescriptive*, recommending rather than describing.

12. **The correct answer is (C).** In a case of *consensus* among individuals, there is necessarily an *agreement*. Where there is *tranquility* among individuals, there is also *peace*.

13. **The correct answer is (E).** *Hydraulic* describes something that is operated by means of *water*; *pneumatic* describes something that is operated by means of *air*.

14. **The correct answer is (B).** A *horse* is usually kept and fed in a *stable*; a *pig* is usually kept and fed in a *sty*.

15. **The correct answer is (D).** The *actor* plays a *role*, as a *ballplayer* plays a *position*.

16. **The correct answer is (B).** The *prow* is the forward part of the *ship*, as the *nose* is the forward part of the *airplane*.

17. **The correct answer is (D).** *Maximum* and *minimum* mark extremes in quantity, as do *most* and *least*.

18. **The correct answer is (D).** One can counteract a *sensation* with an *anesthetic* and a *poison* with an *antidote*.

19. The correct answer is (B). One leaves a *ship* by *disembarking* and a *horse* by *dismounting*.

20. The correct answer is (D). *Meat* is a food that supplies us with *protein*; *potatoes* are a food that supplies us with *starch*.

21. The correct answer is (A). The *nape* is the back of the *neck*, and the *heel* is the back of the *foot*.

22. The correct answer is (C). *Pliers* are designed for *gripping*, as is a *jack* for *elevating*.

23. The correct answer is (E). The *radius* is a line extending from the center of the *circle* to the edge, as the *spoke* is a bar extending from the center of the *wheel* to the edge.

24. The correct answer is (D). A *misdemeanor* is not as serious as a *felony*. A *mishap* is not as serious as a *catastrophe*.

25. The correct answer is (E). A *hygrometer* is used to measure *humidity*, as a *thermometer* measures *temperature*.

26. The correct answer is (B). As *astute* is in emphatic opposition to *stupid*, so is *agile* in opposition to *clumsy*. Both terms go beyond simple denials of the opposing terms.

27. The correct answer is (C). A *whale* is a mammal that is mistakenly thought to be a *fish*, and a *bat* is a mammal that is mistakenly thought to be a *bird*.

28. The correct answer is (D). A *prospector* seeks *gold*, and a *detective* seeks a *clue*.

29. The correct answer is (B). A *couplet* makes up part of a *poem*, and a *sentence* makes up part of a *paragraph*.

30. The correct answer is (C). The goal of an *entrepreneur* is to obtain *profit*, just as the goal of a *miner* is to obtain *ore*.

31. The correct answer is (A). A *rudder* is used in directing a *ship*. A *wheel* is used in directing a *car*.

32. The correct answer is (E). A *stallion* and a *rooster* are two different animals of the same sex, as are a *mare* and a *hen*.

33. The correct answer is (D). We assimilate a *book* through *reading*, and a *record* through *listening*.

34. The correct answer is (C). A *parrot* and a *sparrow* are two different sorts of birds. A *goldfish* and a *guppy* are two different sorts of fish.

35. The correct answer is (B). *Muscles* are connected to bones by *tendons*, just as *bones* are connected to bones by *ligaments*.

Exercise 2

1.	C	4.	E	7.	B	10.	B	13.	D
2.	E	5.	A	8.	E	11.	C	14.	E
3.	B	6.	D	9.	B	12.	A	15.	E

1. The correct answer is (C). *Spicy* is the opposite of *insipid* as *keen* is the opposite of *dull*.

2. The correct answer is (E). A *scythe* is used as a symbol of *death*, and an *arrow* is used as a symbol of *love*.

3. The correct answer is (B). *Yeast* is used as a *leaven* and *iodine* as an *antiseptic*. These functions are more specific than aspirin's function as a medicine.

4. The correct answer is (E). A *polyglot* is adept at many *languages* as a *factotum* is adept at many skilled jobs, or *trades*.

5. **The correct answer is (A).** *Passages* can be eliminated by *expurgation* and *leaves* by *defoliation*.

6. **The correct answer is (D).** The basic materials of a *pharmacist* are *drugs*; the basic materials of a *chef* are *foods*.

7. **The correct answer is (B).** To *conquer* someone else is to *subjugate* that person. To *slander* someone else is to *vilify* him or her. In both cases, the subject is hostile toward the object.

8. **The correct answer is (E).** A *chisel* can be used to cut out an *engraving*. *Acid* can be used to cut through a surface to create an *etching*.

9. **The correct answer is (B).** *Sound* is measured in *decibels*, and *electricity* in *volts*.

10. **The correct answer is (B).** *Sound* determines whether two words are *homonyms*. *Meaning* determines whether two words are *synonyms*.

11. **The correct answer is (C).** One *whets* a *knife* to sharpen it. One *hones* a *razor* to sharpen it.

12. **The correct answer is (A).** At one extreme something can be *valueless*, and at another extreme something can be *invaluable*. At one extreme an individual can be *miserly*, and, at another extreme, *philanthropic*.

13. **The correct answer is (D).** A *triangle* has three sides, and a *prism* is a three-sided solid figure. A *circle* is circular, and a *cylinder* is a solid figure that is circular.

14. **The correct answer is (E).** An *ox* is controlled by means of a *yoke*. A *horse* is controlled by means of a *harness*.

15. **The correct answer is (E).** A *symphony* can end with a *coda*, as can a *novel* with an *epilogue*.

SAT Sentence Completion Strategies

chapter 6

OVERVIEW

- Take a closer look at sentence completions
- Learn the basic steps for solving sentence completions
- Learn the best strategies for tackling difficult sentence completion questions
- Practice your skills in solving sentence completions

A CLOSER LOOK AT SENTENCE COMPLETIONS

Are you drawing a blank? Get used to it, because you'll see a lot of them in the sentence completion questions on the SAT. In this kind of question, you are given a sentence that has one or more blanks. A number of words or pairs of words are suggested to fill in the blank spaces. It's up to you to select the word or pair of words that will best complete the meaning of the sentence. In a typical sentence completion question, several of the choices could be inserted into the blank spaces. However, only one answer will make sense and carry out the full meaning of the sentence.

Sentence Completion Questions and Their Format

Your SAT will probably have a total of 19 sentence completions. In one verbal section, you can expect 9 sentence completions out of 30 total questions; in another verbal section, expect 10 sentence completions out of 35 total questions.

Every section of questions will be preceded by a set of directions and an example for your reference, like the following example:

> **Directions:** Each of the following questions consists of an incomplete sentence followed by five words or pairs of words. Choose the word or pair of words that, when substituted for the blank space or spaces, best completes the meaning of the sentence. Circle the letter that appears before your answer.

Example

> **Q** Medieval kingdoms did not become constitutional republics overnight;
> on the contrary, the change was ____.
>
> **(A)** unpopular
> **(B)** unexpected
> **(C)** advantageous
> **(D)** sufficient
> **(E)** gradual
>
>

NOTE

Don't forget that you're being tested on your ability to find the *best* answer. Though more than one answer may seem to work, only one is correct; be sure to make your choice very carefully.

METHODS AND STRATEGIES FOR SOLVING SENTENCE COMPLETIONS

Are you ready to start filling in some of those blanks? The following steps will help you answer sentence completion questions:

1. Read the sentence carefully.

2. Think of a word or words that will fit the blank(s) appropriately.

3. Look through the five answer choices for that word(s). If it's not there, move on to step 4.

4. Examine the sentence for clues to the missing word.

5. Eliminate any answer choices that are ruled out by the clues.

6. Try the ones that are left and pick whichever is best.

Now that you know how to approach these questions most effectively, try a few sample SAT sentence completion questions:

Those who feel that war is stupid and unnecessary think that to die on the battlefield is ____.

(A) courageous
(B) pretentious
(C) useless
(D) illegal
(E) heroic

Now, follow the steps to find the correct answer:

1 Read the sentence.

2 Think of your own word to fill in the blank. You're looking for a word that completes the logic of the sentence. You might come up with something like "stupid" or "dumb."

3 Look for *dumb* in the answer choices. It's not there, but *useless* is. That's pretty close, so mark it and go on.

4 If you couldn't guess the word, take your clue from the words *stupid* and *unnecessary* in the sentence. They definitely point toward some negative-sounding word.

5 The clues immediately eliminate choice (A) *courageous* and choice (E) *heroic*, which are both positive words.

6 Try the remaining choices in the sentence, and you'll see that *useless* fits best.

Here's another question:

Unruly people may well become ____ if they are treated with ____ by those around them.
- **(A)** angry..kindness
- **(B)** calm..respect
- **(C)** peaceful..abuse
- **(D)** interested..medicine
- **(E)** dangerous..love

Now, here are your steps for finding the right answer:

1 Read the sentence. This time there are two blanks, and the missing words need to have some logical connection.

2 Think of your own words to fill in the blanks. You might guess that the unruly people will become "well-behaved" if they are treated with "consideration."

3 Now look for your guesses in the answer choices. They're not there, but there are some possibilities.

4 Go back to the sentence and look for clues. "Become" signals that the unruly people will change their behavior. How that behavior changes will depend on how they are treated.

5 You can eliminate choices (A) and (E) because a negative behavior change (*angry* and *dangerous*) doesn't logically follow a positive treatment (*kindness* and *love*). Likewise, you can eliminate (C) because a *peaceful* behavior change is not likely to follow from *abuse*. Finally, you can eliminate (D) because *interested* and *medicine* have no logical connection.

6 The only remaining choice is (B), which fits the sentence and must be the correct answer.

Don't let sentence completions hold you up. In the 30-minute SAT verbal sections, sentence completion questions always come first. Try to spend no more than 45 to 50 seconds on any sentence completion, so you have time to get through the rest of the test.

The Best Strategies for Sentence Completion Questions

The six-step method for solving sentence completion questions is a tried-and-true approach to solving these questions on the SAT. But, because you want to move through these questions as quickly as you can (while choosing the right answers, of course), you also need to arm yourself with some basic strategies for tackling even the most difficult sentence completion questions. The following sections offer some very simple—and effective—strategies for quickly and accurately answering sentence completion questions.

Thinking up your own answer is the way to start

If you've thought up the best answer before you even look at the choices, you've started solving the problem in advance and have saved time. To test this theory, look at this typical SAT sentence completion question:

Robert was extremely ____ when he received a B on the exam, for he was almost certain he had gotten an A.

(A) elated

(B) dissatisfied

(C) fulfilled

(D) harmful

(E) victorious

In this example, it is obvious that Robert would be "dissatisfied" with the grade he received. You may have come up with a different word, such as "discouraged" or "frustrated," but you can quickly deduce that (B) is the correct answer by the relationship of the answer choice to the word you guessed.

The surrounding words in the sentence offer clues to the missing word

When it comes to sentence completion questions, the word that does *not* appear is the key to the meaning of the sentence. But by thinking about the words that *do* appear, we can see the connection between the two parts of the sentence. Most sentences contain not only a collection of words but also a number of *ideas* that are connected to one another in various ways. When you understand how these ideas are connected, you can say that you really understand the sentence.

Some blanks go with the flow

The missing word may be one that supports another thought in the sentence, so you need to look for an answer that "goes with the flow."

The service at the restaurant was so slow that by the time the salad had arrived we were ____.

(A) ravenous

(B) excited

(C) incredible

(D) forlorn

(E) victorious

Where is this sentence going? The restaurant service is very slow. That means you have to wait a long time for your food, and the longer you wait, the hungrier you'll get. So the word in the blank should be something that completes this train of thought. Answer choice (A), "ravenous," which means very hungry, is the best answer. It works because it "goes with the flow."

Here's another example:

As a teenager, John was withdrawn, preferring the company of books to that of people; consequently, as a young adult John was socially ____.

(A) successful

(B) uninhibited

(C) intoxicating

(D) inept

(E) tranquil

The word *consequently* signals that the second idea is an outcome of the first, so again, you are looking for a word that completes the train of thought. What might happen if you spent too much time with your nose stuck in a book (except for this one, of course)? Most likely you would be more comfortable with books than with people. Choice (D), "inept," meaning awkward, is a good description of someone who lacks social graces, making this the right answer.

Here's yet another example:

A decision that is made before all of the relevant data are collected can only be called ____.

(A) calculated

(B) insincere

(C) laudable

(D) unbiased

(E) premature

The word *called* tells you that the blank is the word that the rest of the sentence describes. A decision that is made before all the facts are collected can only be described as "premature", choice (E).

Some blanks shift gears

The missing word may be one that reverses a thought in the sentence, so you need to look for an answer that "shifts gears." Try this technique in the following question example:

The advance of science has demonstrated that a fact that appears to contradict a certain theory may actually be ____ a more advanced formulation of that theory.

(A) incompatible with

(B) in opposition to

(C) consistent with

(D) eliminated by

(E) foreclosed by

The correct answer is (C). Look at the logical structure of the sentence. The sentence has set up a contrast between what appears to be and what is actually true. This indicates that the correct answer will "shift gears" and be the opposite of "contradict." The choice "consistent with" provides this meaning. The other choices do not.

Here's another example:

Although she knew that the artist's work was considered by some critics to be ____, the curator of the museum was eager to acquire several of the artist's paintings for the museum's collection.

(A) insignificant

(B) important

(C) desirable

(D) successful

(E) retroactive

The correct answer is (A). The very first word of the sentence, "although," signals that the sentence is setting up a contrast between the critics and the curator. The critics had one opinion, but the curator had a different one. Since the curator liked the artworks well enough to acquire them, you can anticipate that the critics disliked the artworks. So the blank requires a word with negative connotations, and choice (A), "insignificant," is the only one that works.

Here's another example of this type of contrast in a sentence completion question:

After witnessing several violent interactions between the animals, the anthropologist was forced to revise her earlier opinion that the monkeys were ____.

(A) peaceable

(B) quarrelsome

(C) insensitive

(D) prosperous

(E) unfriendly

Where do you begin? The words "forced to revise" clearly signal a shift in the anthropologist's ideas. Her discovery that the monkeys were violent made her abandon an earlier contrasting opinion. Among the answer choices, the only contrast to "violent" is choice (A), "peaceable."

The right answer must be both logical and grammatically correct

When answering sentence completion questions, you can always simply toss out any answer choices that do not make sense in the sentence or that would not be grammatically correct. Try this technique in the following example:

> An advocate of consumer rights, Ralph Nader has spent much of his professional career attempting to ____ the fraudulent claims of American business.
>
> **(A)** expose
> **(B)** immortalize
> **(C)** reprove
> **(D)** construe
> **(E)** import

What would you do with a fraudulent claim? Immortalize it? Import it? Not likely. These choices are not logical. The only logical answer is (A). You would *expose* a fraudulent claim.

Two-blank questions give you two ways to get it right

Most SAT sentence completions—about two thirds—have two blanks rather than one. This provides another way of working by elimination. Sometimes you can guess the meaning of one blank, but not the other. Good! Scan the answer choices, looking only for the word you've guessed. Eliminate the answers that *don't* include it (or a near-synonym). Cross them out with your pencil if you like (this saves time if you look back at the question later). Then guess from what remains.

Difficult questions generally have difficult answers

As with analogy questions, easier sentence completions typically have easier answers and harder sentence completions typically have harder answers. This does not mean that you should always guess the hardest words on the hardest questions. However, if you have absolutely no idea which of the remaining choices is correct, it is to your benefit to select the choice with the most difficult vocabulary.

NOTE

Why do difficult questions typically have difficult answers? Because the test-writers know what they're doing. They know that students prefer to pick answer choices that contain familiar vocabulary. After all, it's human nature to be afraid of words we don't know. So don't fall into their trap. Have the intestinal fortitude to guess the hardest words when all else fails!

SUMMARY

What You Need to Know about Sentence Completions

- The scored portion of the SAT contains 19 sentence completion questions, arranged in order of easiest to most difficult.

- Sentence completion questions test your vocabulary and your reading comprehension skills by presenting sentences with one or two blanks and asking you to choose the best words to fill the blanks.

- In general, you follow these steps to answer sentence completion questions:

  1. Read the sentence carefully.
  2. Think of a word or words that will fit the blank(s) appropriately.
  3. Look through the five answer choices for that word(s). If it's not there, move on to step 4.
  4. Examine the sentence for clues to the missing word.
  5. Eliminate any answer choices that are ruled out by the clues.
  6. Try the ones that are left and pick whichever is best.

- Eliminate choices that are illogical or grammatically incorrect, and use both words within a two-word choice to "test" for the best response.

- Try to spend no more than 45 to 50 seconds on any one sentence completion question.

EXERCISES: SENTENCE COMPLETIONS

Exercise 1

35 Questions • Time—25 Minutes

Directions: Each of the following questions consists of an incomplete sentence followed by five words or pairs of words. Choose that word or pair of words that, when substituted for the blank space or spaces, best completes the meaning of the sentence. Circle the letter that appears before your answer.

Example

Q In view of the extenuating circumstances and the defendant's youth, the judge recommended ____.

(A) conviction

(B) a defense

(C) a mistrial

(D) leniency

(E) life imprisonment

A Ⓐ Ⓑ Ⓒ ● Ⓔ

1. The ____ workroom had not been used in years.

   (A) derelict

   (B) bustling

   (C) bereft

   (D) bereaved

   (E) stricken

2. Tempers ran hot among the old-timers, who ____ the young mayor and his ____ city council.

   (A) despised..attractive

   (B) admired..elite

   (C) resented..reforming

   (D) forgave..activist

   (E) feared..apathetic

3. With the discovery of ____ alternative fuel source, oil prices dropped significantly.

   (A) a potential

   (B) a feasible

   (C) a possible

   (D) a variant

   (E) an inexpensive

4. The product of a ____ religious home, he often found ____ in prayer.

   (A) zealously..distraction

   (B) devoutly..solace

   (C) vigorously..comfort

   (D) fanatically..misgivings

   (E) pious..answers

5. Our ____ objections finally got us thrown out of the stadium.
   (A) hurled
   (B) modest
   (C) wary
   (D) vocal
   (E) pliant

6. We should have ____ trouble ahead when the road ____ into a gravel path.
   (A) interrogated..shrank
   (B) anticipated..dwindled
   (C) expected..grew
   (D) enjoyed..transformed
   (E) seen..collapsed

7. The ____ of the house, fresh lobster, was all gone, so we ____ ourselves with crab.
   (A) suggestion..resolved
   (B) embarrassment..consoled
   (C) recommendation..contented
   (D) specialty..pelted
   (E) regret..relieved

8. ____ mob began to form, full of angry men ____ incoherent threats.
   (A) An excited..whispering
   (B) A listless..shouting
   (C) An ugly..gesturing
   (D) A lynch..muttering
   (E) A huge..waving

9. In the ____ downpour, the women managed to ____ us and disappear.
   (A) ensuing..evade
   (B) incessant..pervade
   (C) uncouth..escape
   (D) torrential..provoke
   (E) insipid..avoid

10. As a staunch ____ of our right to leisure time, Ken had few ____.
    (A) proponent..friends
    (B) advocate..defenders
    (C) disciple..rivals
    (D) defender..equals
    (E) opponent..duties

11. A single wall still stood in mute ____ to Nature's force.
    (A) evidence
    (B) tribute
    (C) remainder
    (D) memory
    (E) testimony

12. With the current wave of crime, tourists are ____ to make sure their passports are secure.
    (A) required
    (B) invited
    (C) permitted
    (D) forbidden
    (E) urged

13. Over the ____ of the sirens, you could still hear the hoarse ____ of his voice.
    (A) babble..roar
    (B) drone..power
    (C) gibbering..cries
    (D) wail..sound
    (E) groaning..whisper

14. Working ____ under the pressure of time, Edmond didn't notice his ____ mistake.
    (A) leisurely..stupid
    (B) frantically..inevitable
    (C) rapidly..careless
    (D) sporadically..simple
    (E) continually..redundant

15. Held up only by a ____ steel cable, the chairlift was ____ to carry only two people.
    (A) slender..instructed
    (B) single..intended
    (C) sturdy..obliged
    (D) massive..designed
    (E) narrow..appointed

16. After completing her usual morning chores, Linda found herself ____ tired.
    (A) surprisingly
    (B) erratically
    (C) buoyantly
    (D) forcibly
    (E) unceasingly

17. With a ____ roar, the Concorde took off from New York on its ____ flight to Europe.
    (A) deafening..subterranean
    (B) thunderous..transoceanic
    (C) sickening..transcontinental
    (D) frightening..perennial
    (E) supersonic..eventual

18. The cheerful, lively sound of dance music ____ almost everyone.
    (A) accosted
    (B) drained
    (C) flaunted
    (D) revived
    (E) expired

19. With ____ grin, Mark quickly ____ his way through the crowd toward us.
    (A) an infectious..demolished
    (B) a sappy..devoured
    (C) an irrepressible..maneuvered
    (D) a surly..crawled
    (E) a hapless..lost

20. Though a ____ of four campaigns, he had never seen action on the front lines.
    (A) veteran
    (B) victim
    (C) volunteer
    (D) reveler
    (E) recruit

21. The ____ of the early morning light ____ the room, making it larger and cozier at once.
    (A) brilliance..shattered
    (B) softness..transformed
    (C) harshness..transfigured
    (D) warmth..disfigured
    (E) glare..annihilated

22. As ____ of the original team, Mickey had free ____ for all their games.
    (A) a survivor..advice
    (B) a scholar..passage
    (C) an institution..admission
    (D) an organizer..submission
    (E) a member..entrance

23. From his ____ manner, we could all tell that he was of ____ birth.
    (A) boorish..noble
    (B) aristocratic..humble
    (C) regal..royal
    (D) refined..common
    (E) courteous..illegitimate

24. The presence of armed guards ____ us from doing anything disruptive.
    (A) defeated
    (B) excited
    (C) irritated
    (D) prevented
    (E) encouraged

25. A careful ____ of the house revealed no clues.
    (A) dissemination
    (B) incineration
    (C) autopsy
    (D) dereliction
    (E) examination

26. For his diligent work in astronomy, Professor Wilson was ____ at the banquet as ____ of the Year.
    (A) taunted..Teacher
    (B) praised..Lobotomist
    (C) lauded..Scientist
    (D) honored..Astrologer
    (E) welcomed..Administrator

27. Because of his ____ sense of his own importance, Larry often tried to ____ our activities.
    (A) exaggerated..monopolize
    (B) inflated..autonomize
    (C) insecure..violate
    (D) modest..dominate
    (E) egotistic..diffuse

28. After such ____ meal, we were all quick to ____ Arlene for her delicious cooking.
    (A) a fearful..congratulate
    (B) an enormous..console
    (C) a delightful..avoid
    (D) a heavy..thank
    (E) a wonderful..applaud

29. If you hear the ____ of a gun, don't worry; it's only my car backfiring.
    (A) burst
    (B) report
    (C) retort
    (D) flash
    (E) volume

30. He demanded ____ obedience from us, and was always telling us we must be ____ subjects.
    (A) total..foolish
    (B) partial..cringing
    (C) formal..rigorous
    (D) complete..compliant
    (E) marginal..loyal

31. The ____ of the *Titanic* could have been avoided if more safety ____ had been taken.
    (A) tragedy..precautions
    (B) embargo..preservers
    (C) disaster..reservations
    (D) crew..measures
    (E) fiasco..inspectors

32. We are ____ going to have to face the reality that the resources of Earth are ____.
    (A) finally..worthless
    (B) gradually..limitless
    (C) eventually..finite
    (D) quickly..unavailable
    (E) seldom..vanished

33. A native wit, Angela never ____ for her words.
    (A) groaned
    (B) breathed
    (C) asked
    (D) groped
    (E) worried

34. With ____ a thought for his own safety, Gene ____ dashed back across the court-yard.

   (A) even..quickly
   (B) scarcely..nimbly
   (C) barely..cautiously
   (D) seldom..swiftly
   (E) hardly..randomly

35. As she ____ retirement, Laura became more thoughtful and withdrawn.

   (A) circled
   (B) sighted
   (C) withdrew
   (D) neared
   (E) derived

Exercise 2

15 Questions • Time—10 Minutes

Directions: Each of the following questions consists of an incomplete sentence followed by five words or pairs of words. Choose that word or pair of words that, when substituted for the blank space or spaces, best completes the meaning of the sentence. Circle the letter that appears before your answer.

Example

Q In view of the extenuating circumstances and the defendant's youth, the judge recommended ____.

(A) conviction

(B) a defense

(C) a mistrial

(D) leniency

(E) life imprisonment

A (A) (B) (C) ● (E)

1. Though many thought him a tedious old man, he had a ____ spirit that delighted his friends.
   (A) perverse
   (B) juvenile
   (C) meek
   (D) leaden
   (E) youthful

2. ____, the factories had not closed, and those who needed work most were given a chance to survive during the economic disaster.
   (A) Unintentionally
   (B) Mercifully
   (C) Blithely
   (D) Importunately
   (E) Tragically

3. There was a ____ all about the estate, and the ____ concerned the guards.
   (A) pall..shroud
   (B) focus..scrutiny
   (C) hush..quiet
   (D) coolness..temper
   (E) talent..genius

4. The stubborn families feuded for generations, and ____ feelings are still fixed in their ____.
   (A) begrudging..acceptance
   (B) bitter..generosity
   (C) inimical..antagonism
   (D) suspicious..relief
   (E) chary..helplessness

5. As the archaeologist expected, living con-
ditions in the ancient culture were ____
worse than those of today.
   (A) awfully
   (B) surprisingly
   (C) significantly
   (D) begrudgingly
   (E) boldly

6. Our reunion was completely ____; who'd
have guessed we would have booked the
same flight?
   (A) illogical
   (B) fortuitous
   (C) expected
   (D) abandoned
   (E) usurped

7. There is one ____ thing about them: they
have nothing in common and never will
have.
   (A) immutable
   (B) atypical
   (C) indiscriminate
   (D) indigenous
   (E) alliterative

8. Always one for a long, pleasant talk, Nancy
went on ____ for hours.
   (A) volubly
   (B) tiresomely
   (C) incessantly
   (D) relentlessly
   (E) articulately

9. He should be ____ to complain, since his
salary is ____ with his productivity.
   (A) right..proportionate
   (B) brought..balanced
   (C) foolish..gratuitous
   (D) loath..commensurate
   (E) entitled..alleviated

10. Paul's ____ at work is a natural product
of his ____ nature.
   (A) wastefulness..unpleasant
   (B) thoughtfulness..rarefied
   (C) diligence..sedulous
   (D) candor..familial
   (E) stubbornness..intrepid

11. Blustery winds knocked off hats and
rattled windows, and the adventurous
children were ____.
   (A) frightened
   (B) terrified
   (C) improved
   (D) anxious
   (E) delighted

12. The ____ youngster thought old people
should be polite to him!
   (A) impertinent
   (B) classless
   (C) cultured
   (D) submissive
   (E) alternate

13. Wild beasts roamed the deserted country,
which had not been ____ for hundreds of
years.
   (A) temperate
   (B) active
   (C) winnowed
   (D) lived in
   (E) civilized

14. At night, the inn turned into a theater, not one of actors and actresses, but one of the ____ of real people.
   (A) sciences
   (B) psychologies
   (C) dramas
   (D) jokes
   (E) novels

15. "He who laughs last laughs ____."
   (A) least
   (B) fast
   (C) best
   (D) never
   (E) softest

ANSWER KEYS AND EXPLANATIONS

Exercise 1

1.	A	8.	D	15.	B	22.	E	29.	B
2.	C	9.	A	16.	A	23.	C	30.	D
3.	E	10.	D	17.	B	24.	D	31.	A
4.	B	11.	E	18.	D	25.	E	32.	C
5.	D	12.	E	19.	C	26.	C	33.	D
6.	B	13.	D	20.	A	27.	A	34.	B
7.	C	14.	C	21.	B	28.	E	35.	D

1. **The correct answer is (A).** *Derelict* in this sense means "empty," or "abandoned." Only people are bereaved or bereft.

2. **The correct answer is (C).** This sentence implies discord between the old-timers and the young mayor. Old-timers are likely to *resent* those officials who are trying to change, or *reform*, things.

3. **The correct answer is (E).** There may be many possible alternative fuel sources, but unless they are *inexpensive*, they won't affect the price of oil.

4. **The correct answer is (B).** To say *a pious religious home* is redundant. Only choice (B) completes the thought and intent of the sentence.

5. **The correct answer is (D).** The objections mentioned must have been vocal to get them thrown out.

6. **The correct answer is (B).** Most people do not enjoy trouble, and you can't interrogate it, but you may logically conclude that they foresaw, or *anticipated*, trouble. A road doesn't grow into a path; nor does it collapse into one.

7. **The correct answer is (C).** No restaurant would advertise an *embarrassment* of the house, but you may logically conclude that lobster was their *recommendation*.

8. **The correct answer is (D).** In this item, the final two words are the key. It is impossible to gesture or wave incoherent threats. An excited mob wouldn't whisper and a listless mob wouldn't shout.

9. **The correct answer is (A).** In this question, only choice (A) logically completes the thought of the sentence.

10. **The correct answer is (D).** This sentence assumes that most people support having leisure time, ruling out choices (A) and (B). A *staunch disciple* is bad usage. That an opponent of leisure would have few duties is illogical.

11. **The correct answer is (E).** "A single wall" implies that, formerly, there were other walls. That only one wall still stood is *testimony*, not a *tribute*, to Nature's power. *Evidence to* is poor diction.

12. **The correct answer is (E).** Checking your passport can only be a suggestion, not an order. As losing your passport can pose serious problems to a tourist, *urged* is a better choice than *invited*.

13. **The correct answer is (D).** Sirens may drone or wail, but they don't babble, gibber, or groan. *Hoarse sound* is a better choice than *hoarse power*.

14. **The correct answer is (C).** The pressure of time indicates a need to work quickly. Assuming that mistakes are not inevitable or redundant, choice (C) is the only logical choice.

15. **The correct answer is (B).** This sentence is concerned with the design of the lift. As it says "held up only by," you may assume that the cable is not large, which eliminates choices (C) and (D). Of the three remaining options, only *intended*, choice (B), completes the sentence logically.

16. **The correct answer is (A).** Assuming that routine activity is not exhausting, it would be surprising to find yourself exhausted by it one day.

17. **The correct answer is (B).** A transoceanic flight is one that goes over an ocean, in this case, the Atlantic.

18. **The correct answer is (D).** This sentence assumes that cheerful, lively music has a positive effect on people.

19. **The correct answer is (C).** As there is no such thing as a surly, or sullen, grin, choice (C) is the only answer that supplies the appropriate words for Mark's expression as well as for the manner in which he made his way through the crowd.

20. **The correct answer is (A).** One may be a veteran without ever having seen action, but a *victim* has to have seen it.

21. **The correct answer is (B).** For the light to make the room cozier, it must be soft, not harsh. This implies that the light enhanced the room, rather than disfigured it.

22. **The correct answer is (E).** A person may be an institution, but not an institution of a team. It is more likely that *a member* of the original team rather than a scholar would have a free pass.

23. **The correct answer is (C).** This is the only answer in which the first and second words are consistent.

24. **The correct answer is (D).** Armed guards are intended to prevent any kind of disruption. Choice (D) is the only logical and grammatical choice.

25. **The correct answer is (E).** The sentence implies that the house was being searched, and since you don't perform an autopsy on a house, choice (E) is the best choice.

26. **The correct answer is (C).** An astronomer would not be honored as an astrologer, much less as an administrator.

27. **The correct answer is (A).** Someone with a high opinion of his own importance tends to try to run others' activities. Choice (A) best reflects this attitude.

28. **The correct answer is (E).** One doesn't generally avoid or console someone else for a tasty meal. Thus, choice (E) is the only logical answer.

29. **The correct answer is (B).** The sound of an explosion, whether from a gun or a car, is called a *report*.

30. **The correct answer is (D).** You may assume that no one demands partial or marginal obedience. *Compliant* is the best adjective for subjects.

31. **The correct answer is (A).** The loss of the *Titanic* is best described as a tragedy or a disaster. *Precautions*, not *reservations*, is the second word that is required, making choice (A) the correct response.

32. **The correct answer is (C).** As the Earth's resources are not limitless, worthless, or unavailable, only choice (C) logically completes this sentence.

33. **The correct answer is (D).** A person may grope for words; to say that he or she worries for them is bad usage.

34. The correct answer is (B). If Gene dashed across the courtyard, he must have run swiftly or *nimbly*. He couldn't have taken time to think of himself.

35. The correct answer is (D). Retirement has no physical presence, so it can't be either circled or sighted. One approaches, or nears, retirement.

Exercise 2

1.	E	4.	C	7.	A	10.	C	13. E
2.	B	5.	C	8.	A	11.	E	14. C
3.	C	6.	B	9.	D	12.	A	15. C

1. **The correct answer is (E).** A meek spirit may comfort or console people, but it won't delight them. A juvenile spirit is immature and thus is also inappropriate. A *youthful* spirit, however, may be mature as well as vigorous.

2. **The correct answer is (B).** According to the sense of this sentence, it was merciful, not unintentional, blithe, importunate, or tragic, that the factories remained open.

3. **The correct answer is (C).** It follows that a *hush* or a quiet about an estate would concern the guards, not a pall, focus, coolness, or talent.

4. **The correct answer is (C).** This sentence describes enmity and a persistence of ill will. Choice (C) best completes the thought of this sentence.

5. **The correct answer is (C).** The archaeologist would expect conditions to be *significantly* worse, not surprisingly, awfully, begrudgingly, or boldly worse.

6. **The correct answer is (B).** The sentence implies that the reunion occurred by chance, so it was *fortuitous*.

7. **The correct answer is (A).** *Immutable* means "unchanging." The second part of the sentence concerns finality; therefore, the other choices are not appropriate.

8. **The correct answer is (A).** According to the sentence, Nancy is "one for a long, pleasant talk." *Voluble* means "garrulous," but does not necessarily imply unpleasantness, while tiresome, incessant, and relentless all imply offense. *Articulate* is simply speaking clearly.

9. **The correct answer is (D).** He should be loath (or reluctant) to complain if his is commensurate with (or equal to) his productivity.

10. **The correct answer is (C).** "Natural product" in this sentence means "logical extension or outgrowth of" and joins like characteristics. *Diligence* and *sedulousness* are synonyms.

11. **The correct answer is (E).** Adventurous children will be *delighted* by blustery winds and rattling windows.

12. **The correct answer is (A).** This sentence describes a rebellious attitude. *Impertinence* means "insolence."

13. **The correct answer is (E).** This sentence concerns a wilderness and an absence of people, or civilization. *Lived in* has a meaning similar to *civilized*, but it implies a home or a town and not a countryside.

14. **The correct answer is (C).** The concept of theater is satisfied by *dramas*, not sciences, psychologies, jokes, or novels.

15. **The correct answer is (C).** The last (i.e., "end-of-line") position in certain activities connotes a positive result or a favored position. Some examples are: having the last word; being assigned the last (closing) spot in a show; being up last in baseball; or having a last (final) rebuttal in a debate. Laughing last, then, could not imply laughing *least, fast, never,* or *softest,* because these are not positive terms. The person who laughs last laughs *best,* because being last by definition precludes any possibility of someone else laughing back.

SAT Critical Reading Strategies

chapter 7

OVERVIEW

- Take a closer look at critical reading
- Learn how to answer critical reading questions
- Learn the most important critical reading strategies
- Learn specific strategies for specific question types
- Review what you need to know about critical reading
- Practice your skills with critical reading exercises

A CLOSER LOOK AT CRITICAL READING

The scored portion of the SAT contains five critical reading passages. Two of the passages appear in one verbal section, one passage appears in another, and the paired passages appear in a third section. Each passage or passage pair is followed by 5 to 13 questions, for a total of 40 scored critical reading questions. That means that critical reading accounts for more than half of your SAT verbal score.

The questions test your ability to quickly read the passage and understand its content. These questions *don't* test your ability to memorize details or become expert in the topics discussed in the passages. And, you don't have to be an expert in the areas of fiction, humanities, social studies, or science—the four subject areas from which the passages are drawn.

SAT Reading Passages

SAT reading passages can be anywhere from 400 to 850 words long. Each one begins with a short introduction that gives you some idea of where the passage came from and, often, when it was written. Each passage contains all the information you need to answer the questions about it.

Once on every test you will see a pair of passages on subjects that relate to each other. These paired passages will be followed by a single set of questions that refer to each passage individually or to the two passages together.

NOTE

Note that the critical reading questions are not arranged in order of difficulty. The questions for each passage are arranged in the order in which the information is presented in the passage. In other words, the first questions deal with the early parts of the passage, and later questions deal with the later parts of the passage.

Question Format

On the SAT, each critical reading passage and question set starts with directions that look like this:

> **Directions:** Each passage below is followed by a set of questions. Read each passage and then answer the accompanying questions, basing your answers on what is stated or implied in the passage and in any introductory material provided. Mark the letter of your choice on your answer sheet.

or

> **Directions:** The two passages given below deal with a related topic. Following the passages are questions about the content of each passage or about the relationship between the two passages. Answer the questions based upon what is stated or implied in the passages and in any introductory material provided. Mark the letter of your choice on your answer sheet.

The questions that follow each passage are in the standard multiple-choice format with five answer choices each. Most often, these questions ask you to do one of the following:

- Identify the main idea or the author's purpose.
- Define a word based on its meaning in the passage.
- Choose a phrase that best restates an idea in the passage.
- Draw inferences from ideas in the passage.
- Identify the author's tone or mood.

BEST STRATEGIES FOR ANSWERING CRITICAL READING QUESTIONS

As you read these passages, notice special things about the words or the information. For instance, keep an eye out for an unfamiliar word that is defined right there in the sentence; you'll probably find a question about it. Also, be alert for similes and metaphors. Those often have questions about them, too. And, notice the line numbers along the left-hand side of the passage. Use them! They'll help you find answers more quickly.

To answer critical reading questions, follow these steps:

1 Read the introduction, if one is provided.

2 Read the passage.

3 Read the questions and their answer choices. Go back into the passage to find answers.

4 For any question you're not sure of, eliminate obviously wrong answers and take your best guess.

Let's look at this process in more detail.

1 You don't want to "blow past" the introductory paragraph because it can be very helpful to you. It might provide some important background information about the passage or it might "set the stage" so you know what you're reading about.

2 Now read the passage pretty quickly. Try to pick up main ideas, but don't get bogged down in the factual trivia. After all, you won't even be asked about most of the material in the passage!

3 Read the questions with their answer choices, and answer every question you can. Remember, all the answers are somewhere in the passage, so go back and reread any sections that will help you!

4 Here's the process of elimination again. If you're still not sure of an answer, toss the ones that are obviously wrong and take your best guess from the choices that are left.

Now that you're familiar with how to approach critical reasoning passages and questions, let's try a few.

Sample Critical Reading Passage

The following is an excerpt from a short story, "Miss Tempy's Watchers," by Sarah Orne Jewett, a novelist and short-story writer who lived from 1849–1909. In the story, two women watch over their deceased friend on the evening before her funeral and share their memories of her.

The time of year was April; the place was a small farming town in New Hampshire, remote from any railroad. One by one the lights had been blown out in the scattered houses near Miss Tempy Dent's, but as her neighbors took a last look out of doors, their eyes turned with instinctive curiosity toward the old house where a lamp
(5) burned steadily. They gave a little sigh. "Poor Miss Tempy!" said more than one bereft acquaintance; for the good woman lay dead in her north chamber, and the lamp was a watcher's light. The funeral was set for the next day at one o'clock.

The watchers were two of her oldest friends. Mrs. Crowe and Sarah Ann Binson. They were sitting in the kitchen because it seemed less awesome than the
(10) unused best room, and they beguiled the long hours by steady conversation. One would think that neither topics nor opinions would hold out, at that rate, all through the long spring night, but there was a certain degree of excitement just then, and the two women had risen to an unusual level of expressiveness and confidence. Each had already told the other more than one fact that she had
(15) determined to keep secret; they were again and again tempted into statements that either would have found impossible by daylight. Mrs. Crowe was knitting a blue yarn stocking for her husband; the foot was already so long that it seemed as if she must have forgotten to narrow it at the proper time. Mrs. Crowe knew exactly what she was about, however; she was of a much cooler disposition than Sister
(20) Binson, who made futile attempts at some sewing, only to drop her work into her lap whenever the talk was most engaging.

Their faces were interesting—of the dry, shrewd, quick-witted New England type, and thin hair twisted neatly back out of the way. Mrs. Crowe could look vague and benignant, and Miss Binson was, to quote her neighbors, a little too sharp-set,

NOTE

Just to give you an idea of the breadth of the subject areas covered within the critical reading portion of the SAT, here are some of the topics that have been the subject of reading passages on recent exams: Chinese-American women writers, the classification of species, pioneer life on the Great Plains, the relationship between plants and their environment, the meaning of *Robinson Crusoe*, and the philosophy of science.

TIP

Never skip the intro-
duction as it is likely to
contain some impor-
tant information
about both the
passage and the
types of questions
that accompany it.
The introduction will
identify the type of
passage being
presented, the source
or author of the
passage, the era in
which the passage
was written, or the
event that the
passage describes. All
of this information will
help you focus your
reading and find the
correct answers to the
questions.

(25) but the world knew that she had need to be, with the load she must carry supporting an inefficient widowed sister and six unpromising and unwilling nieces and nephews. The eldest boy was at last placed with a good man to learn the mason's trade. Sarah Ann Binson, for all her sharp, anxious aspect never defended herself, when her sister whined and fretted. She was told every week of her life that *(30)* the poor children would never have had to lift a finger if their father had lived, and yet she had kept her steadfast way with the little farm, and patiently taught the young people many useful things for which, as everybody said, they would live to thank her. However pleasureless her life appeared to outward view, it was brimful of pleasure to herself.

(35)   Mrs. Crowe, on the contrary, was well-to-do, her husband being a rich farmer and an easy-going man. She was a stingy woman, but for all of that she looked kindly; and when she gave away anything, or lifted a finger to help anybody, it was thought a great piece of beneficence, and a compliment, indeed, which the recipient accepted with twice as much gratitude as double the gift that came from a poorer *(40)* and more generous acquaintance. Everybody liked to be on good terms with Mrs. Crowe. Socially, she stood much higher than Sarah Ann Binson.

1. The word *bereft* (line 6) means

  (A) without hope.

  (B) greedy.

  (C) anxious.

  (D) sad.

  (E) lonesome.

The introduction and the rest of the sentence talk about the death of a well-liked person. Sadness would probably be the first thing you'd feel after someone died, so the best answer is choice (D).

2. The author implies that the two women have divulged secrets to each other because

  (A) they are lonely.

  (B) it is nighttime.

  (C) it is a sad occasion.

  (D) they trust each other.

  (E) it is the only time they talk to each other.

We already know that folks are sad, but the author doesn't say anything about the women being trusting or lonely, or only talking because of the situation. The author does make a specific reference to the time of day. Reread that sentence (lines 11–15) and you'll see why the best answer is choice (B).

3. If Mrs. Crowe were confronted with an emergency, you would expect her to

  (A) remain calm.

  (B) ask Miss Binson for help.

  (C) become distracted.

  (D) panic.

  (E) run away.

The passage has clues to Mrs. Crowe's character, talking about her knowing "exactly what she was about" (lines 18–19) and her "cooler disposition" (line 19). Now you can see that choice (A) is clearly the best answer.

4. The phrase "a little too sharp-set" (line 24) means
   (A) thin.
   (B) stern and anxious-looking.
   (C) strong-featured.
   (D) angular.
   (E) well-defined.

The description of Miss Binson's everyday life with her nieces and nephews illustrates that she runs a tight ship and keeps them all in line. So choice (B) is the best answer.

5. Sarah Ann Binson seems to be a woman who is
   (A) terribly unhappy.
   (B) jealous of Mrs. Crowe.
   (C) disloyal.
   (D) quite wealthy.
   (E) self-contented.

To all outward appearances, Miss Binson seemed to have an especially hard life. However, the author ends that sentence saying that "it was brimful of pleasure to herself." Since Miss Binson was pretty happy with her life, choice (E) is the best answer.

Sample Paired Critical Reading Passages

Among the great loves in history are those of the composer Robert Schumann for his wife, Clara, and of Napoleon Bonaparte for his wife, Josephine. Their love is public knowledge due to the hundreds of love letters they left behind. The excerpts that follow are from letters. The first one is from Schumann to his then-fiancée and the second is from Napoleon on the battlefield to his wife at home.

Passage 1—Robert Schumann to Clara Wieck (1838)

I have a hundred things to write to you, great and small, if only I could do it neatly, but my writing grows more and more indistinct, a sign, I fear, of heart weakness. There are terrible hours when your image forsakes me, when I wonder anxiously whether I have ordered my life as wisely as I might, whether I had any right to bind
(5)   you to me, my angel, or can really make you as happy as I should wish. These doubts all arise, I am inclined to think, from your father's attitude towards me. It is so easy to accept other people's estimate of oneself. Your father's behaviour makes me ask myself if I am really so bad—of such humble standing—as to invite such treatment from anyone. Accustomed to easy victory over difficulties, to the
(10)   smiles of fortune, and to affection, I have been spoiled by having things made too easy for me, and now I have to face refusal, insult, and calumny. I have read of

many such things in novels, but I thought too highly of myself to imagine I could ever be the hero of a family tragedy of the Kotzebue sort myself. If I had ever done your father an injury, he might well hate me; but I cannot see why he should
(15) despise me and, as you say, hate me without any reason. But my turn will come, and I will then show him how I love you and himself; for I will tell you, as a secret, that I really love and respect your father for his many great and fine qualities, as no one but yourself can do. I have a natural inborn devotion and reverence for him, as for all strong characters, and it makes his antipathy for me doubly painful. Well,
(20) he may some time declare peace, and say to us, "Take each other, then."

You cannot think how your letter has raised and strengthened me . . . You are splendid, and I have much more reason to be proud of you than of me. I have made up my mind, though, to read all your wishes in your face. Then you will think, even though you don't say it, that your Robert is a really good sort, that he is entirely
(25) yours, and loves you more than words can say. You shall indeed have cause to think so in the happy future. I still see you as you looked in your little cap that last evening. I still hear you call me *du*. Clara, I heard nothing of what you said but that *du*. Don't you remember?

Passage 2—Napoleon Bonaparte to Josephine Bonaparte (1796)

I have not spent a day without loving you; I have not spent a night without
(30) embracing you; I have not so much as drunk a single cup of tea without cursing the pride and ambition which force me to remain separated from the moving spirit of my life. In the midst of my duties, whether I am at the head of my army or inspecting the camps, my beloved Josephine stands alone in my heart, occupies my mind, fills my thoughts. If I am moving away from you with the speed of the Rhône
(35) torrent, it is only that I may see you again more quickly. If I rise to work in the middle of the night, it is because this may hasten by a matter of days the arrival of my sweet love. Yet in your letter of the 23rd and 26th Ventôse, you call me *vous*. *Vous* yourself! Ah! wretch, how could you have written this letter? How cold it is! And then there are those four days between the 23rd and the 26th; what were you
(40) doing that you failed to write to your husband? . . . Ah, my love, that *vous*, those four days make me long for my former indifference. Woe to the person responsible! May he, as punishment and penalty, experience what my convictions and the evidence (which is in your friend's favour) would make me experience! Hell has no torments great enough! *Vous! Vous!* Ah! How will things stand in two weeks? . . .
(45) My spirit is heavy; my heart is fettered and I am terrified by my fantasies . . . You love me less; but you will get over the loss. One day you will love me no longer; at least tell me; then I shall know how I have come to deserve this misfortune. . . .

1. In Passage 1, the word *calumny* (line 11) means

   (A) remorse.

   (B) chance.

   (C) victory.

   (D) kindness.

   (E) slander.

Here's a prime example of context to the rescue. Take a look at the sentence and then test each choice in place of *calumny*. Basically, Schumann is talking about the hard time he is having with Clara's father, so you would not choose a positive word; eliminate choices (C) and (D). Out goes choice (B) because it makes no sense in the sentence. Choice (A) technically makes sense, but it is not a roadblock to success like insults and refusals are. Therefore, the remaining answer is the best one—choice (E).

2. To what does Napoleon refer in Passage 2 when he writes of "the moving spirit of my life" (lines 31–32)?

   (A) France

   (B) ambition

   (C) the army

   (D) his wife

   (E) the Rhône River

Now you have to do some interpretation using the information in the passage. To do this you must know the author's intent. After you find the phrase, read the sentences around it. They all deal with Napoleon's love for Josephine. Since he curses his pride and ambition, choice (B) is out. He is with his army in France, so you can toss out choices (A) and (C). Choice (E) doesn't make sense, so the only choice is (D), his beloved wife.

3. How do the authors feel about being separated from their lovers?

   (A) Separation raises doubts and fears.

   (B) Separation is due to parental disapproval.

   (C) Separations never last long.

   (D) Separations improve a relationship.

   (E) Separations between lovers are inevitable.

This is where the comparison comes into play. The question asks about both authors, so you have to think about both passages and find the similarities. Let's start eliminating choices. The first to go are (D) and (E), since neither author mentions these at all. Choice (C) goes out because the authors don't tell us anything about the length of their separations. We know that while Robert Schumann has a big problem with Clara's dad, Napoleon doesn't seem to have a parental problem; choice (B) is gone. Why is choice (A) the best answer? Take a look back at both passages. Schumann mentions his doubts, and Napoleon tells Josephine that he is "terrified." Choice (A) is the only answer that fits both authors' thoughts.

4. Why do the writers refer to the words *du* and *vous*?

   (A) To remind their readers of their rank

   (B) To refer to their lovers' intimacy or formality

   (C) To ask their lovers to be faithful

   (D) To demonstrate their knowledge of languages

   (E) To address their unborn children

This is the kind of question that can send you into a panic. Calm down—you don't really have to know what the two words mean, you just have to figure out why the authors put them in. Reread the sentences in which the authors mention these special words. Are both authors happy about hearing the words? Are they both upset? Do they feel differently about hearing their sweethearts use these words? Aha! That's the key; Schumann is pleased that Clara used the word *du* (which is an informal word in German), but Napoleon is insulted and worried because Josephine used *vous* (a formal French word). Only choice (B) indicates that the authors might feel differently; the other choices aren't supported at all by a rereading of the information.

LEARN THE MOST IMPORTANT CRITICAL READING TIPS

Critical reading questions can eat up a lot of your time. But you can use some specific strategies and techniques to move through this portion of the SAT efficiently. Check out these tips for smarter solutions to solving critical reading questions quickly and accurately.

Do the Critical Reading Questions Last

In addition to the critical reading questions, the verbal section of the SAT also contains analogies and sentence completions. Because the critical reading questions require the most time to complete, you should save these questions for last. You've already learned timesaving tips for the analogies and sentence completions, so do those questions first. That way, you'll save extra time for critical reading.

Answer All of the Questions before You Move on to the Next Passage

There won't be time to go back to these passages at the end of this section, so you'll want to answer every question that you can about the passage before moving on. If you skip a question and try to come back to it later, you might have to reread the whole passage to find the answer—and you'll be out of time. Guess if you have to, but finish all the questions that you can before you move on to the next passage.

Remember that the Questions Follow the Order of the Passage

The questions are like a map to the passage; in other words, the order of the questions follows the order of the information in the passage. The first questions refer to the early part of the passage, and later questions refer to later parts of the passage. If there are two passages, the first questions are for Passage 1, the next are for Passage 2, and the end questions refer to both. This helps you locate the information quickly.

Do Double Passages One Passage at a Time

Since the questions are arranged like a map, take advantage! Read Passage 1 and answer the questions that relate to Passage 1. Then read Passage 2 and answer the questions that relate to Passage 2. Finally, answer the comparative questions. In this way, you won't have to read too much at once and you won't confuse the message of Passage 1 with that of Passage 2.

Don't Panic When You Read an Unfamiliar Passage

The passages are supposed to be unfamiliar. In their attempt to be fair, the SAT people purposely choose passages that are from the darkest recesses of the library. This helps make sure that no test-taker has ever seen them before. Remember, you're not being tested on your knowledge of the topic, but on how well you:

- figure out the meaning of an unfamiliar word from its context;
- determine what an author means by noting certain words and phrases;
- understand the author's assumptions, point of view, and main idea; and
- analyze the logical structure of a piece of writing.

Remember that Everything You Need to Know Is Right There in Front of You

The introductory paragraph and the passage have all the information you'll need to answer the questions. Even if the passage is about the price of beans in Bulgaria or the genetic makeup of a wombat, don't worry. It's all right there on the page.

Start with the Passages That Interest You

The passages that interest you are easier to work on. If there's a choice, it's best to start with the passage that's more interesting to you, whether it's fiction, a science article, or whatever. If the style appeals to you, you will probably go through the passage more quickly and find the questions easier to deal with.

Use Your Pencil to Highlight Important Information as You Read the Passage

It pays to be an active reader. When you read, use your pencil actively to highlight important names, dates, and facts. Though you aren't required to memorize specific details, the questions are likely to reference the more important information in the passage. If you've highlighted those pieces of information, you'll be able to find them easily when you need them to answer the questions.

ALERT!

Don't choose answers that only work for one of a pair of passages. When you're working with paired passages, some questions ask you to identify a common idea. When that happens, you can immediately reject any answer choice that only applies to one of the passages.

Don't Get Bogged Down in the Details

Remember, you don't have to understand every bit of information. You just have to find the information you need to answer the questions. Don't waste your time trying to analyze or memorize technical details or information that the questions don't ask for.

Don't Confuse a "True" Answer with a "Correct" Answer

The fact that an answer choice is true doesn't mean it's right. What does that mean? It means that a certain answer choice may be perfectly true—in fact, all of the answer choices may be true. But the *right* answer must be the correct answer to the question that's being asked. Only one of the answer choices will be correct and, therefore, the right choice. Read carefully—and don't be fooled!

STRATEGIES FOR ANSWERING SPECIFIC QUESTION TYPES

As you learned earlier in this chapter, critical reading questions ask you to do one of five things:

- Identify the main idea or the author's purpose.
- Define a word based on its meaning in the passage.
- Choose a phrase that best restates an idea in the passage.
- Draw inferences from ideas in the passage.
- Identify the author's tone or mood.

The next six tips present real strategies for dealing with the specific categories of critical reading questions. Before you move to the strategies, however, read the introductory paragraph and the passage following; the tips and questions that follow relate to this passage.

John Dewey, an American educator and philosopher of education, was a prolific writer on the subject. He was particularly interested in the place of education in a democratic republic.

The place of public education within a democratic society has been widely discussed and debated through the years. Perhaps no one has written more widely on the subject in the United States than John Dewey, sometimes called "the father of public education," whose theories of education have a large social component,
(5)   that is, an emphasis on education as a social act and the classroom or learning environment as a replica of society.

Dewey defined various aspects or characteristics of education. First, it was a necessity of life inasmuch as living beings needed to maintain themselves through a process of renewal. Therefore, just as humans needed sleep, food, water,
(10)   and shelter for physiological renewal, they also needed education to renew their minds, assuring that their socialization kept pace with physiological growth.

A second aspect of education was its social component, which was to be accomplished by providing the young with an environment that would provide a

(15) nurturing atmosphere to encourage the growth of their as yet undeveloped social customs.

A third aspect of public education was the provision of direction to youngsters, who might otherwise be left in uncontrolled situations without the steadying and organizing influences of school. Direction was not to be of an overt nature, but rather indirect through the selection of the school situations in which the
(20) youngster participated.

Finally, Dewey saw public education as a catalyst for growth. Since the young came to school capable of growth, it was the role of education to provide opportunities for that growth to occur. The successful school environment is one in which a desire for continued growth is created—a desire that extends throughout one's
(25) life beyond the end of formal education. In Dewey's model, the role of education in a democratic society is not seen as a preparation for some later stage in life, such as adulthood. Rather, education is seen as a process of growth that never ends, with human beings continuously expanding their capacity for growth. Neither did Dewey's model see education as a means by which the past was recapitulated.
(30) Instead education was a continuous reconstruction of experiences, grounded very much in the present environment.

Since Dewey's model places a heavy emphasis on the social component, the nature of the larger society that supports the educational system is of paramount importance. The ideal larger society, according to Dewey, is one in which the
(35) interests of a group are all shared by all of its members and in which interactions with other groups are free and full. According to Dewey, education in such a society should provide members of the group a stake or interest in social relationships and the ability to negotiate change without compromising the order and stability of the society.
(40) Thus, Dewey's basic concept of education in a democratic society is based on the notion that education contains a large social component designed to provide direction and assure children's development through their participation in the group to which they belong.

Remember that the Answer to a Main Idea Question Is Neither Too General Nor Too Specific

For a question about the main idea or the author's purpose, look for an answer choice that states it. Don't be too general or too specific.

1. The main idea of this passage can best be stated as:

    (A) The role of education is extremely complex.

    (B) Dewey's notion of education contains a significant social component.

    (C) Dewey's model of education is not relevant today.

    (D) Direction provided in education must not be overt.

    (E) Public education should be a catalyst for growth.

Choices (A) and (C) are very general; you'd be hard-pressed to find any supporting information in the passage for those main ideas. Choices (D) and (E) seem as if they were single sentences plucked right out of the passage; too specific! Choice (B)—the correct choice—gives an overall statement and you could find supporting details for it as a main idea.

Check the Introductory and Conclusion Paragraphs for the Main Idea of the Passage

Look in the first or last (or both) paragraphs of the passage for answers to main idea/author's purpose questions. Choice (B) above is stated in the last sentence of the first paragraph and restated in the last paragraph. Remember to mark stuff like this as you read. Though the main idea may occur elsewhere in the passage, most often you'll find it in the first or last paragraph.

Plug in Choices to Solve Vocabulary-in-Context Questions

For vocabulary-in-context questions, plug the choices into the original sentence and don't be fooled by the obvious synonym.

2. The word *nurturing* (line 14) means
    (A) nourishing.
    (B) educational.
    (C) critical.
    (D) supportive.
    (E) motivational.

Take a look at the sentence in the passage—". . . nurturing atmosphere to encourage the growth. . ."—and then try each of the answer choices. You might be tempted to just pick *nourishing*, but (D) is the choice that makes sense and supports the idea of the sentence.

Find the Right Restatement by First Restating an Author's Phrase in Your Own Words

3. The phrase "a continuous reconstruction of experiences" (line 30) used in reference to education means that education is
    (A) based in life experiences.
    (B) a never-ending process.
    (C) a meaning-based endeavor.
    (D) an individual pursuit.
    (E) something unattainable.

Not to put words in your mouth, but if you had stated this phrase in your own words you might have used *ongoing* as a substitute for *continuous*. If you take it one more step, you come to (B), "a never-ending process."

ALERT!

Don't expect the answer to a vocabulary-in-context question to rely upon the most common meaning of a word. More often, you can count on the question to rely upon the most common meaning of a word. More often, you can count on the question revolving around an unusual or uncommon usage of the word.

Read Between the Lines to Draw Inferences from the Passage

4. While not directly stated, the passage suggests that

   (A) true education fosters the desire for lifelong learning.

   (B) a truly educated person has an understanding of physics.

   (C) Dewey was a radical philosopher.

   (D) education must cease at some point.

   (E) Dewey's model has been embraced by all.

When a critical reading question asks for something the author has suggested, implied, or not stated directly, you have to use the information in the passage and draw your own conclusions. Read between the lines to see if the author has given any hints that would lead you to the correct answer. In this question, the correct answer is choice (A) because the author's stated positions, taken together, logically lead to this statement. Choice (B) is a pretty far-fetched conclusion to make, and choices (C), (D), and (E) are not logical extensions of the information in the passage.

Look for Descriptive Words to Clue You in to the Tone or Mood of the Passage

5. The tone of this passage can best be described as

   (A) humorous.

   (B) serious.

   (C) dramatic.

   (D) informal.

   (E) frivolous.

This passage probably did not make you even chuckle, so choice (A) can be eliminated right off the bat. The topic is not frivolous, and the language was quite formal, so you can drop choices (E) and (D). There were no episodes or scenes that could be considered dramatics, choice (C), so the best answer is, of course, choice (B). Take a minute to go back and scan the passage, look at the kind of language you find, and see how it sets the tone.

SUMMARY

What You Need to Know about Critical Reading

- All of the information you need is right in the passage.

- Read the introduction, if one is provided.

- Read the passage without getting bogged down in details.

- Read the questions and their answer choices. Go back into the passage to find answers.

- Critical reading questions follow the order of information in the passage. Unlike other verbal questions, they are not arranged in order of difficulty.

- Answer every question for a passage before starting the next passage.

- For any question you're not sure of, eliminate obviously wrong answers and take your best guess.

EXERCISES: CRITICAL READING

Exercise 1

30 Questions • Time—35 Minutes

Directions: The passage below is followed by questions based on its content. Answer the questions on the basis of what is *stated* or *implied* in the passage and in any introductory material that may be provided.

In the eleventh century, the Muslim empire was taken over by Turks of the Seljuk tribes. The main Seljuk sultan had as his advisor a Persian called Nizam al-Mulk. Nizam al-Mulk took it upon himself to reform the government, writing many of his ideas in a treatise called The Book of Government. *This passage is from a chapter entitled "Advice to Governors."*

When ambassadors come from foreign countries, nobody is aware of their movements until they actually arrive at the city gates; nobody gives any information
(5) [that they are coming] and nobody makes any preparation for them; and they will surely attribute this to our negligence and indifference. So officers at the frontiers must be told that whenever anyone
(10) approaches their stations, they should at once dispatch a rider and find out who it is who is coming, how many men there are with him, mounted and unmounted, how much baggage and equipment he
(15) has, and what is his business. A trustworthy person must be appointed to accompany them and conduct them to the nearest big city; there he will hand them over to another agent who will
(20) likewise go with them to the next city (and district), and so on until they reach the court. Whenever they arrive at a place where there is cultivation, it must be a standing order that officers, tax-
(25) collectors and assignees should give them hospitality and entertain them well so that they depart satisfied. When they return, the same procedure is to be followed. Whatever treatment is given to
(30) an ambassador, whether good or bad, it

is as if it were done to the very king who sent him; and kings have always shown the greatest respect to one another and treated envoys well, for by this their own
(35) dignity has been enhanced. And if at any time there has been disagreement or enmity between kings, and if ambassadors have still come and gone as occasion requires, and discharged their mis-
(40) sions according to their instructions, never have they been molested or treated with less than usual courtesy. Such a thing would be disgraceful, as God (to Him be power and glory) says [in the
(45) Quran 24.53], "The messenger has only to convey the message plainly."

It should also be realized that when kings send ambassadors to one another their purpose is not merely the message
(50) or the letter which they communicate openly, but secretly they have a hundred other points and objects in view. In fact they want to know about the state of roads, mountain passes, rivers and graz-
(55) ing grounds, to see whether an army can pass or not; where fodder is available and where not; who are the officers in every place; what is the size of that king's army and how well it is armed and
(60) equipped; what is the standard of his table and company; what is the organization and etiquette of his court and audience hall; does he play polo and hunt; where are his qualities and man-
(65) ners, his designs and intentions, his appearance and bearing; is he cruel or just, old or young; is his country flourishing or decaying; are the peasants rich or poor: is he avaricious or generous; is
(70) he alert or negligent in affairs. . . .

1. What alarms the author about the way ambassadors are currently treated upon their arrival?

   (A) An ambassador might assume that the natives are discourteous and negligent in regard to foreigners.

   (B) Ambassadors may use the opportunity to spy on the natives.

   (C) Ambassadors are often molested at the border.

   (D) No one checks to see if ambassadors are smuggling arms.

   (E) Ambassadors can easily become lost because no one guides them.

2. The word *stations* (line 10) is used to mean

   (A) levels.

   (B) ranks.

   (C) depots.

   (D) posts.

   (E) postures.

3. Why does Nizam al-Mulk want to hand ambassadors from one agent to the next?

   (A) To watch their every move

   (B) To make sure their needs are met

   (C) To remove them from the country quickly

   (D) To keep them from seeing the king

   (E) To stop their complaints

4. The word *envoys* (line 34) means

   (A) methods.

   (B) heralds.

   (C) substitutes.

   (D) accounts.

   (E) representatives.

5. Which of these phrases best summarizes the main idea of paragraph 1?

   (A) Favor everyone with equal care.

   (B) Never molest an ambassador.

   (C) Kings must respect each other.

   (D) Politeness pays.

   (E) Be sure to treat envoys well.

6. Unlike paragraph 1, paragraph 2 deals with

   (A) ambassadors.

   (B) kings.

   (C) messages.

   (D) intelligence.

   (E) procedures.

7. By "objects in view" (line 52) Nizam al-Mulk means

   (A) goals in mind.

   (B) disagreements with opinions.

   (C) commodities to investigate.

   (D) complaints in mind.

   (E) artwork to see.

8. The word *fodder* (line 56) means

   (A) light.

   (B) animal food.

   (C) armaments.

   (D) trees.

   (E) tobacco.

9. The phrase "standard of his table" (lines 60–61) refers to the king's

   (A) flag.

   (B) requirements.

   (C) hospitality.

   (D) performance.

   (E) language.

10. The word *avaricious* (line 69) means
    (A) savage.
    (B) stingy.
    (C) violent.
    (D) fickle.
    (E) charitable.

"The Goodman Who Saved Another from Drowning" is a French tale from the Middle Ages. In today's litigious times, the lesson it teaches remains relevant.

It happened one day that a fisherman putting out to sea in a boat was just about to cast a net, when right in front of him he saw a man on the point of drown-
(5) ing. Being a stout-hearted and at the same time an agile man, he jumped up and, seizing a boathook, thrust it towards the man's face. It caught him right in the eye and pierced it. The
(10) fisherman hauled the man into the boat and made for the shore without casting any of his nets. He had the man carried to his house and given the best possible attention and treatment, until he had
(15) got over his ordeal.

For a long time, that man thought about the loss of his eye, considering it a great misfortune. "That wretched fellow put my eye out, but I didn't do him any
(20) harm. I'll go and lodge a complaint against him—why, I'll make things really hot for him!" Accordingly he went and complained to the magistrate, who fixed a day for the hearing. They both
(25) waited till the day came round, and then went to the court. The one who had lost an eye spoke first, as was appropriate. "Gentlemen," he said, "I'm bringing a complaint against this worthy, who, only
(30) the other day, savagely struck me with a boathook and knocked my eye out. Now I'm handicapped. Give me justice, that's all I ask. I've nothing more to say."

The other promptly spoke up and
(35) said, "Gentlemen, I cannot deny that I knocked his eye out, but if what I did was wrong, I'd like to explain how it all happened. This man was in mortal danger in the sea, in fact he was on the point
(40) of drowning. I went to his aid. I won't deny I struck him with my boathook, but I did it for his own good: I saved his life on that occasion. I don't know what more I can say. For God's sake, give me
(45) justice!"

The court was quite at a loss when it came to deciding the rights of the case, but a fool who was present at the time said to them, "Why this hesitation? Let
(50) the first speaker be thrown back into the sea on the spot where the other man hit him in the face, and if he can get out again, the defendant shall compensate him for the loss of his eye. That I think,
(55) is a fair judgment." Then they all cried out as one man, "You're absolutely right! That's exactly what we'll do!" Judgment was then pronounced to that effect. When the man heard that he was to be thrown
(60) into the sea, just where he had endured all that cold water before, he wouldn't have gone back there for all the world. He released the goodman from any liability, and his earlier attitude came in
(65) for much criticism.

In the light of this incident, you can take it from me that it's a waste of time to help a scoundrel. Release a guilty thief from the gallows, and he will never
(70) like you for it. A wicked man will never be grateful to anyone who does him a good turn: he'll forget all about it; it will mean nothing to him. On the contrary, he would be only too glad to make trouble
(75) for his benefactor if he ever saw him at a disadvantage.

11. The word *cast* (line 3) is used to mean
    (A) tint.
    (B) perform.
    (C) hurl.
    (D) mold.
    (E) copy.

12. Paragraph 1 makes it clear that the fisherman is

(A) essentially well-meaning.

(B) clumsy and foolish.

(C) fat but nimble.

(D) hard-working and honest.

(E) basically unlucky.

13. The word *fixed* (line 24) is used to mean

(A) corrected.

(B) secured.

(C) set.

(D) mended.

(E) attached.

14. The word *worthy* (line 29) is used to mean

(A) caliber.

(B) significance.

(C) morality.

(D) gentleman.

(E) prize.

15. Paragraph 3 concerns

(A) the narrator's beliefs.

(B) the court's wishes.

(C) the one-eyed man's complaint.

(D) the fisherman's plea.

(E) the magistrate's judgment.

16. The fool's suggested solution to the case was

(A) pitiless and spiteful.

(B) absurd but lawful.

(C) harsh but fair.

(D) just and merciful.

(E) sensible but unjust.

17. The phrase "as one man" (line 56) means

(A) manfully.

(B) as someone once said.

(C) one by one.

(D) together.

(E) as he believed.

18. "In the light of this incident" (line 66) means

(A) "thanks to that event."

(B) "because of this tale."

(C) "without further ado."

(D) "as darkness falls."

(E) "as you can see from this story."

19. The narrator clearly believes that the one-eyed man

(A) showed good sense.

(B) had bad luck.

(C) deserved better.

(D) was a scoundrel.

(E) did the right thing.

20. The moral of this story might be

(A) "Do unto others as you would have them do unto you."

(B) "A wicked man is never satisfied."

(C) "You can only be good so long."

(D) "There is no such thing as justice."

(E) "The one-eyed man is king."

Because of its enormous size, the United States is a country of contrasts. Nowhere are the differences between the eastern and western United States so profound as in terms of climate and availability of water.

The eastern and western United States differ in many ways, but perhaps the most significant difference between the two regions is climate. The East receives
(5)   enough rainfall to sustain agriculture, while the West does not receive adequate rainfall to do so. Additionally, there are widely disparate climatic variations within smaller regions in the West than
(10)   there are in the East. The mountains, the Sierra Nevadas and the Cascades, that impede the Pacific Ocean's ability to cool in the summer and warm in the winter, as well as the fronts that bring
(15)   moisture in the form of rain and snow, have much to do with the extremes of climate found in the West. Elevations in

the interior West also affect climate because even the mountainous flatlands
(20) have elevations higher than a mile.

Because of these extremes, particularly in the area of rainfall (there can be as much as 150 inches of precipitation annually on the western side of
(25) the Sierra-Cascade range as contrasted with as little as four inches annually on the eastern side), irrigation becomes critical if the area is to remain viable for human habitation. Actually, it is so hot
(30) in some portions of the western desert that even when rain clouds form, it does not rain because the Earth's reflected heat dissipates the moisture before it can reach the ground. Any drops that
(35) actually reach the ground quickly evaporate. While the arid Central Plains of the United States can use water for irrigation from the Ogallala Aquifer, a closed-basin aquifer, discovered after
(40) World War I, the western regions are too far away to benefit from this trapped run-off from several Ice Ages that is confined in gravel beds, stretching from South Dakota to West Texas. No wonder
(45) then that water is so precious to the people and farmlands of this area and that the population of this area presses for national, state, and local funding for irrigation projects that will store and
(50) reroute water for them.

The Colorado River, with its various tributaries, including, for example, the Gunnison, the Green, and the Gila, has long been the source of most irriga-
(55) tion projects in the desert areas of the West. Much of the water from the Colorado River goes into the state of California to irrigate the Imperial and San Joaquin Valleys. On its route from high
(60) in the Rockies to the Gulf of California, the river is diverted in many areas to irrigate fields. Unfortunately, when it returns after having passed through deposits of mineral salts in the soil that
(65) was irrigated, the salinity content of the water has increased dramatically. The amount of salt in the water can then have a detrimental effect on the crops if proper drainage systems are not built.

(70) Not only is a proper drainage system exorbitantly expensive, but drainage systems also create a run-off, which must be handled in some efficient way. By the time the water is drained, this run-off
(75) would not only contain salt, but probably pesticides as well, and the question of what to do with the run-off becomes an issue.

Despite the years of better than
(80) average rainfall in the late 70s and early to mid-80s that even caused the Great Salt Lake in Utah to flood, the situation in the western desert areas, particularly California, remains critical. It is not
(85) uncommon for droughts in the state to last several years. Consequently, water, not only for crops, but for human consumption itself, is at stake. Thus, it becomes a serious mandate to solve the
(90) water problem in this area if the area is to survive.

21. The word *disparate* (line 8) means

(A) distinct.

(B) different.

(C) unusual.

(D) analogous.

(E) similar.

22. According to the passage, one of the mountain ranges that affects rainfall in the West is the

(A) Rockies.

(B) Appalachian.

(C) Colorado.

(D) Blue Ridge.

(E) Sierra Nevadas.

23. According to the passage, another factor influencing climate in the West is

(A) desert plants.

(B) the Pacific Ocean.

(C) elevation.

(D) the Colorado River.

(E) plateaus.

24. According to the passage, what has become critical on the eastern side of the Sierra-Cascade range?

    (A) crop rotation

    (B) truck farming

    (C) crop dusting

    (D) irrigation

    (E) drainage

25. In some areas of the arid western desert, the formation of rain clouds doesn't assure rain because

    (A) Earth's reflected heat dissipates moisture.

    (B) mountains are too high.

    (C) desert winds blow clouds away.

    (D) plateaus are too dry.

    (E) riverbeds are too deep.

26. The arid Central Plains are able to irrigate with water from

    (A) the Ogallala Aquifier.

    (B) the Colorado River.

    (C) the Rio Grande River.

    (D) the Dakota River.

    (E) the Green River.

27. Which of the following is a tributary of the Colorado River?

    (A) San Joaquin River

    (B) Aspen River

    (C) Gila River

    (D) Cascade River

    (E) Dakota River

28. Most of the water from the Colorado River goes into the state of

    (A) Nevada.

    (B) New Mexico.

    (C) Arizona.

    (D) California.

    (E) Utah.

29. The word *salinity* (line 65) means

    (A) mineral.

    (B) pesticide.

    (C) oxide.

    (D) salt.

    (E) vegetable.

30. Which of the following statements expresses an opinion the author of this passage might have?

    (A) Irrigation projects are an unnecessary expense.

    (B) The situation in the desert of the West is hopeless.

    (C) If this area is to survive as a viable place of habitation, the water problem must be solved.

    (D) The water supply from the Colorado River is completely adequate to take care of the irrigation needs of the area.

    (E) Only the Imperial and San Joaquin Valleys should be irrigated.

Exercise 2

14 Questions • Time—18 Minutes

The Library of Congress in Washington, D.C., is noteworthy in many ways. In this passage, the history of the Library is traced, and the manner in which the Library evolved is considered.

The Library of Congress is the world's largest and most open library. With collections numbering more than 97 million items, it includes materials in 460
(5) languages; the basic manuscript collections of 23 Presidents of the United States; maps and atlases that have aided explorers and navigators in charting both the world and outer space; and the ear-
(10) liest motion pictures and examples of recorded sound, as well as the latest databases and software packages. The Library's services extend not only to members and committees of Congress,
(15) but to the executive and judicial branches of government, to libraries throughout the nation and the world, and to scholars, researchers, artists, and scientists who use its resources.
(20)   This was not always the case. When President John Adams signed the bill that provided for the removal of the seat of government to the new capital city of Washington in 1800, he created a refer-
(25) ence library for Congress only. The bill provided, among other items, $5,000 "for the purchase of such books as may be necessary for the use of Congress—and for putting up a suitable apartment for
(30) containing them therein . . . ."
    After this small congressional library was destroyed by fire along with the Capitol building in 1814, former President Thomas Jefferson offered
(35) therein. . . ." as a replacement his personal library, accumulated over a span of 50 years. It was considered to be one of the finest in the United States. Congress accepted Jefferson's offer. Thus

(40) the foundation was laid for a great national library.
    By the close of the Civil War, the collections of the Library of Congress had grown to 82,000 volumes and were
(45) still principally used by members of Congress and committees. In 1864 President Lincoln appointed as Librarian of Congress a man who was to transform the Library: Ainsworth Rand Spofford,
(50) who opened the Library to the public and greatly expanded its collections. Spofford successfully advocated a change in the copyright law so that the Library would receive two free copies of every
(55) book, map, chart, dramatic or musical composition, engraving, cut, print, or photograph submitted for copyright. Predictably, Spofford soon filled all the Capitol's library rooms, attics, and hall-
(60) ways. In 1873, he then won another lobbying effort, for a new building to permanently house the nation's growing collection and reading rooms to serve scholars and the reading public. The
(65) result was the Thomas Jefferson Building, completed in 1897. Since then, two more buildings have been constructed to house the Library's ever-expanding collection.
(70)   The first Librarian in the new building was a newspaperman with no previous library experience, John Russell Young. He quickly realized that the Library had to get control of the collections
(75) that had been overflowing the rooms in the Capitol. Young set up organizational units and devised programs that changed the Library from essentially an acquisitions operation into an efficient process-
(80) ing factory that organized the materials and made them useful.
    Young was succeeded after only two years by Herbert Putnam, formerly head of the Boston Public Library, who
(85) served as Librarian of Congress for 40

years. While Librarian Spofford had collected the materials, and Young had organized them, Putnam set out to insure that they would be used. He took
(90) the Library of Congress directly into the national library scene and made its holdings known and available to the smallest community library in the most distant part of the country.

(95)   About 1912 both Librarian Putnam and members of Congress became concerned about the distance that was widening between the Library and its employer, the Congress. Various states had
(100) begun to set up "legislative reference bureaus," which brought together skilled teams of librarians, economists, and political scientists whose purpose was to respond quickly to questions that arose
(105) in the legislative process. Congress wanted the same kind of service for itself, so Putnam designed such a unit for the Library of Congress. Called the Legislative Reference Service, it went
(110) into operation in 1914 to prepare indexes, digests, and compilations of law that the Congress might need, but it quickly became a specialized reference unit for information transfer and re-
(115) search. This service was the forerunner of the Library's current Congressional Research Service.

1. By saying that the Library of Congress is "the world's most open library" (lines 1–2), the author means that

   (A) the Library has branches all over the world.

   (B) anyone who wants to can use any of the resources of the Library.

   (C) the Library maintains hours from very early in the morning to very late at night.

   (D) the Library's services are available to a wide variety of institutions and individuals.

   (E) the Thomas Jefferson Building contains several reading rooms for public use.

2. Which of the following kinds of materials is NOT mentioned in the passage as being part of the collection of the Library of Congress?

   (A) computer software

   (B) every book published in English

   (C) musical recordings

   (D) Congressional research

   (E) every photograph copyrighted in the United States

3. Thomas Jefferson's donation of his personal library to Congress can be seen as

   (A) an attempt to outdo John Adams.

   (B) an indication of Jefferson's disenchantment with the library.

   (C) a well-meant but inadequate effort to replace what had been lost.

   (D) the largest single contribution by an individual to the Library of Congress.

   (E) the seed from which the present Library of Congress grew.

4. Which of the following made the collections of the Library of Congress available to the public?

   (A) Thomas Jefferson

   (B) Ainsworth Rand Spofford

   (C) John Adams

   (D) Herbert Putnam

   (E) John Russell Young

5. Ainsworth Rand Spofford wanted to build a new building for the Library of Congress because

    (A) his efforts to expand the collection were so successful that there was no longer room for it in the Capitol.

    (B) he wanted to leave a lasting legacy of his tenure as Librarian of Congress.

    (C) housing the collection in the Capitol building made the library inaccessible to the public.

    (D) there were no reading rooms in the Capitol.

    (E) there was an overwhelming request from the populace for such a building.

6. According to the passage, the Library of Congress now uses how many buildings?

    (A) three

    (B) two

    (C) one

    (D) five

    (E) four

7. A comparison between Ainsworth Rand Spofford and John Russell Young, as they are described in the passage, shows that

    (A) Young made a greater effort to expand the collection of the Library of Congress than Spofford did.

    (B) Spofford had more library experience at the time of his appointment as Librarian of Congress than Young did.

    (C) Spofford served as Librarian of Congress longer than Young did.

    (D) Young was more concerned with housing the collection of the Library of Congress than Spofford was.

    (E) Spofford was more interested in building a memorial to himself.

8. Herbert Putnam's contributions to the Library of Congress included which of the following?

    I. Giving other libraries access to the Library of Congress's resources

    II. Creating distinct organizational units within the Library

    III. Instigating the Legislative Reference Service

    (A) II only

    (B) III only

    (C) I and II only

    (D) II and III only

    (E) I and III only

9. One difference between John Russell Young and Herbert Putnam is

    (A) their level of personal wealth.

    (B) the extent to which they focused on expanding the Library's collection.

    (C) their ability to lobby Congress on the Library's behalf.

    (D) their interest in making the Library's resources available to the public.

    (E) the kind of experience they brought to the post of Librarian of Congress.

10. The purpose of the Legislative Reference Service was

    (A) to encourage members of Congress to use the Library's collection more fully.

    (B) to replace the states' legislative reference bureaus.

    (C) more broadly defined than that of any other unit of the Library.

    (D) similar to the purpose for which the Library was originally established.

    (E) to assist lawyers in preparing trial briefs.

Directions: The two passages below deal with a related topic. Following the passages are questions about the content of each passage or about the relationship between the two passages. Answer the questions based upon what is stated or implied in the passages and in any introductory material provided.

Fanny Wright was a reformer, author, and orator, unusual occupations for a woman in the early nineteenth century. Young Robert Emmet was condemned to death for treason after organizing a rebellion against the English in Ireland. He, too, had achieved fame as an orator, with speeches decrying tyranny.

Passage 1—Fanny Wright to a Fourth-of-July Audience at New Harmony, Indiana (1828)

In continental Europe, of late years, the words patriotism and patriot have been used in a more enlarged sense than it is usual here to attribute to them, or than
(5) is attached to them in Great Britain. Since the political struggles of France, Italy, Spain, and Greece, the word patriotism has been employed, throughout continental Europe, to express a love of
(10) the public good; a preference for the interests of the many to those of the few; a desire for the emancipation of the human race from the thrall of despotism, religious and civil: in short, patrio-
(15) tism there is used rather to express the interest felt in the human race in general than that felt for any country, or inhabitants of a country, in particular. And patriot, in like manner, is employed
(20) to signify a lover of human liberty and human improvement rather than a mere lover of the country in which he lives, or the tribe to which he belongs. Used in this sense, patriotism is a virtue, and a
(25) patriot is a virtuous man. With such an interpretation, a patriot is a useful member of society capable of enlarging all minds and bettering all hearts with which he comes in contact; a useful mem-
(30) ber of the human family, capable of establishing fundamental principles and

of merging his own interests, those of his associates, and those of his nation in the interests of the human race. Laurels
(35) and statues are vain things, and mischievous as they are childish; but could we imagine them of use, on such a patriot alone could they be with any reason bestowed. . . .

Passage 2—Robert Emmet to the Court That Condemned Him to Death (1803)

(40) I am charged with being an emissary of France. An emissary of France! and for what end? It is alleged that I wish to sell the independence of my country; and for what end? Was this the object of my
(45) ambition? . . . No; I am no emissary; and my ambition was to hold a place among the deliverers of my country, not in power nor in profit, but in the glory of the achievement. Sell my country's inde-
(50) pendence to France! and for what? Was it a change of masters? No, but for ambition. Oh, my country! Was it personal ambition that could influence me? Had it been the soul of my actions, could I not,
(55) by my education and fortune, by the rank and consideration of my family, have placed myself amongst the proudest of your oppressors? My country was my idol! To it I sacrificed every selfish,
(60) every endearing sentiment; and for it I now offer up myself, O God! No, my lords; I acted as an Irishman, determined on delivering my country from the yoke of a foreign and unrelenting
(65) tyranny, and the more galling yoke of a domestic faction, which is its joint partner and perpetrator in the patricide, from the ignominy existing with an exterior of splendor and a conscious deprav-
(70) ity. It was the wish of my heart to extri-

cate my country from this double riveted despotism—I wished to place her independence beyond the reach of any power on earth. I wished to exalt her to that
(75) proud station in the world. Connection with France was, indeed, intended, but only as far as mutual interest would sanction or require. Were the French to assume any authority inconsistent with
(80) the purest independence, it would be the signal for their destruction. . . .

Let no man dare, when I am dead, to charge me with dishonor; let no man attaint my memory by believing that I
(85) could have engaged in any cause but that of my country's liberty and independence; or that I could have become the pliant minion of power in the oppression and misery of my country. The proc-
(90) lamation of the provisional government speaks for our views; no inference can be tortured from it to countenance barbarity or debasement at home, or subjection, humiliation, or treachery from
(95) abroad. I would not have submitted to a foreign oppressor, for the same reason that I would resist the foreign and domestic oppressor. In the dignity of freedom, I would have fought upon the
(100) threshold of my country, and its enemy should enter only by passing over my lifeless corpse. And am I, who lived but for my country, and who have subjected myself to the dangers of the jealous and
(105) watchful oppressor, and the bondage of the grave, only to give my countrymen their rights, and my country its independence—am I to be loaded with calumny, and not suffered to resent it? No;
(110) God forbid!

11. In Passage 1, the word *thrall* (line 13) is used to mean

(A) freedom.

(B) bondage.

(C) tremor.

(D) excitement.

(E) stimulation.

12. How could you restate Wright's last sentence?

(A) Laurels and statues are silly, but if they had any meaning at all, a patriot like the one I describe might deserve them.

(B) Tributes make men vain, but such a man could wear them wisely.

(C) We decorate men in vain, but a useful man could be called a patriot.

(D) A patriot such as the one I have mentioned will have no need for statues and laurels.

(E) In vain do we search for appropriate laurels and statues with which to reward such a patriot.

13. In what way does Emmet fail to fit Wright's definition of a patriot?

(A) He prefers the despotism of France to that of England.

(B) He wants to free his people.

(C) He idolizes his own country over all.

(D) He declares the court's sentence to be unjust.

(E) He sees no dishonor in his actions.

14. Emmet's speech moves from

(A) a plea for mercy to acceptance.

(B) interpretation to description.

(C) polite refusal to calm denial.

(D) impassioned denial to angry challenge.

(E) expressions of remorse to expressions of fear.

ANSWER KEYS AND EXPLANATIONS

Exercise 1

1.	A	7.	A	13.	C	19.	D	25.	A
2.	D	8.	B	14.	D	20.	B	26.	A
3.	B	9.	C	15.	D	21.	B	27.	C
4.	E	10.	B	16.	C	22.	E	28.	D
5.	E	11.	C	17.	D	23.	C	29.	D
6.	D	12.	A	18.	E	24.	D	30.	C

1. **The correct answer is (A).** The answer to this is found in paragraph one, lines 7–8. The author never mentions spying, molestation, or lost ambassadors; he is just worried that the messengers will think his countrymen negligent and indifferent.

2. **The correct answer is (D).** This multiple-meaning word has only one synonym given that fits the context of the sentence. If you plug the choices into the line cited, you will easily make the correct choice.

3. **The correct answer is (B).** The author's concerns have to do with behaving in a dignified and appropriate manner. He apparently wants to make sure the ambassadors are led to their destination courteously and swiftly.

4. **The correct answer is (E).** *Envoy* and *ambassador* are used interchangeably by the author to refer to representatives of foreign lands.

5. **The correct answer is (E).** This is an accurate summing up of paragraph 1. Choice (A) is irrelevant, as is choice (C). Choice (B) is not hinted at here, and choice (D) is never directly stated.

6. **The correct answer is (D).** In the connotation of information gleaned by visiting a foreign land, intelligence is precisely the subject of paragraph 2. Even if you do not know the word, you should be able to eliminate the other choices as irrelevant or incorrect.

7. **The correct answer is (A).** Plug the choices into the context of the sentence to determine the correct response. Only choice (A) makes sense.

8. **The correct answer is (B).** If this is a familiar word, you will have no problem. If not, substitute the choices into the sentence to find the one that makes the most sense.

9. **The correct answer is (C).** The phrase uses *standard* to mean "measure"; the ambassador is interested in gauging the measure of the king's table and company—the extent of his hospitality and the quality of his companions.

10. **The correct answer is (B).** The passage sets up a list of opposites. If you recognize this, it should be easy enough to find the word among the choices that is the opposite of *generous*; that is, *stingy*.

11. **The correct answer is (C).** It is used in relation to nets, so the only appropriate synonym for *cast* is *hurl*, choice (C).

12. **The correct answer is (A).** The fisherman may be choice (D), but that is never made clear. He is certainly not choice (B), and he is stout-hearted, not stout, choice (C). There is no support for choice (E). The only answer possible is choice (A), and, in fact, the narrator makes it clear

that the fisherman has done everything possible to help the drowning man.

13. **The correct answer is (C).** *Fixed* has many meanings, and each choice is a possible synonym. However, in the context of "[fixing] a day for the hearing," only choice (C) makes sense.

14. **The correct answer is (D).** This archaic term means "man of worth," or gentleman. Testing the choices in context should lead you to this conclusion.

15. **The correct answer is (D).** All of paragraph 3 is given over to the fisherman's tale of what happened.

16. **The correct answer is (C).** The fool's suggestion to throw the one-eyed man back into the sea may have been harsh, but it offered a certain rough justice.

17. **The correct answer is (D).** Try the choices in context, and you will find that *together* is the only meaningful substitute.

18. **The correct answer is (E).** Choice (B) is incorrect—the narrator did not draw this conclusion because of the incident, but rather uses the incident to illustrate a moral.

19. **The correct answer is (D).** The scoundrel mentioned in line 68 is a reference to the man helped in the story—the one-eyed man.

20. **The correct answer is (B).** This is a reasonable paraphrase of the final paragraph. When you see the word *moral*, you know that you need to draw conclusions about the theme of what you have read. It may help to look back at the end of the story to see whether the author has done that for you, as in this case.

21. **The correct answer is (B).** The context of the sentence, particularly the use of the word *variations*, supports choice (B).

22. **The correct answer is (E).** The two mountain ranges mentioned in the passage are Sierra Nevadas and the Cascades.

23. **The correct answer is (C).** While the Pacific Ocean, choice (B), is mentioned as a potential source of moisture for the area, *elevation* is the critical factor influencing climate.

24. **The correct answer is (D).** Because of the virtual absence of rainfall on the eastern side, *irrigation,* choice (D), is critical.

25. **The correct answer is (A).** The passage specifically states that moisture is dissipated by the earth's heat.

26. **The correct answer is (A).** The underground aquifer is the source of much of the water used for irrigation in the Central Plains.

27. **The correct answer is (C).** Only the *Gila* is a tributary of the Colorado River, according to the passage.

28. **The correct answer is (D).** The passage specifically states that most of the water for irrigation from the Colorado River is used by the state of *California.*

29. **The correct answer is (D).** The context of the sentence, which indicates that the water passes through deposits of mineral salts, supports the choice of (D), *salt.*

30. **The correct answer is (C).** If you have understood the main idea of the passage, you will know that the author believes that the water problem in the area must be solved if the area is to survive.

answers

Exercise 2

1.	D	4.	B	7.	C	10.	D	13.	C
2.	B	5.	A	8.	E	11.	B	14.	D
3.	E	6.	A	9.	E	12.	A		

1. **The correct answer is (D).** In the last sentence of the first paragraph, the author explains what is meant by an "open library" by describing who can use the Library of Congress's resources.

2. **The correct answer is (B).** Computer software is mentioned in line 12, musical recordings in line 11 combined with line 55, Congressional research in line 108, and copyrighted photographs in line 57. Every book *copyrighted in the United States* is put into the Library's collection, but many books published in English are not copyrighted in the United States.

3. **The correct answer is (E).** This answer uses a different metaphor to say what the author says in lines 40–41: "the foundation was laid for a great national library."

4. **The correct answer is (B).** See lines 49–51.

5. **The correct answer is (A).** This answer can be inferred from the previous sentences, particularly line 51, which say that Spofford "greatly expanded [the Library's] collections," and lines 58–60, which say that all the Capitol's space had been filled.

6. **The correct answer is (A).** The three buildings are the Thomas Jefferson Building (line 65) and "two more" constructed "since then" (lines 66–67).

7. **The correct answer is (C).** Young served as Librarian of Congress for two years (lines 82–83). The length of Spofford's tenure is not mentioned, but

he served at least from 1864 (line 46) to 1873 (line 60).

8. **The correct answer is (E).** Answer I is supported in lines 89–94 and answer III in the last paragraph. Creating distinct organizational units was the work of John Russell Young (lines 76–81).

9. **The correct answer is (E).** Young was a newspaperman (line 71), and Putnam was a librarian (lines 83–84).

10. **The correct answer is (D).** According to the second paragraph, the Library's original purpose was to provide Congress with information necessary to its work. The purpose of the Legislative Reference Service, as described in lines 109–115, is also to provide Congress with reference information.

11. **The correct answer is (B).** This is a vocabulary-in-context question. Replace the word cited with the five choices and choose the word that best fits the context. In this case, only one of the words has the same meaning as the italicized word. At times, all five choices will be synonyms, but only one will fit the shade of meaning in the citation. Here, Wright speaks of emancipating the human race "from the thrall of despotism." If you know that emancipating means "freeing" and that despotism is "dictatorship," you will know to look for a word that implies the opposite of freeing—in this case, choice (B), *bondage*. Even if you do not recognize the words *emancipating* or *despotism*, reading the entire sentence will help you understand the meaning of the italicized word.

12. **The correct answer is (A).** This kind of interpretation question asks you to paraphrase a phrase or sentence. Often the language cited is archaic or difficult because of its use of figures of speech. If you merely read the choices above, (A), (B), (D), and (E) might make some kind of sense to you, in light of the passage you read. In order to choose correctly, you must return to the sentence in question and compare it piece by piece to the choices. Here, "Laurels and statues are vain things. . ." might be paraphrased "Laurels and statues are silly." "Could we imagine them of use" might be paraphrased "if they had any meaning at all," and so on. The choice that is closest to the original meaning is choice (A).

13. **The correct answer is (C).** This evaluation question requires you to use Passage 1 to evaluate Passage 2—in this case, to apply a definition from one passage to something in the other passage. In a science selection, you might be asked to apply one writer's hypothesis to another writer's results or to compare two theories. Here, first you must look at Wright's definition of a patriot. She believes that a patriot is a lover of human liberty in general rather than a lover of country in particular. Next, you must look at the choices in light of what you recall about Passage 2. Choice (A) has nothing to do with Wright's definition, and in terms of Emmet's speech, it is simply wrong. He does not prefer one type of tyranny; he hates all tyranny. Choice (B) is certainly true of Emmet,

but it does not contradict Wright's definition, and you are looking for some aspect of Emmet's speech that does. The answer is choice (C)—Wright does not believe in blind chauvinism, but Emmet continually repeats the point that everything he has done, he has done for his country alone. In fact, Emmet supported the French Revolution and probably would have been admired by Fanny Wright, but you must base your answer solely on the material given in the passages. Neither choice (D) nor choice (E) discusses actions or attitudes that are part of Wright's definition of patriotism.

14. **The correct answer is (D).** This kind of synthesis/analysis question asks you to look at the flow of a passage and analyze the author's intent in light of the structure of the work. Skim the passage and look for a point where the tone or intent of the passage changes. Usually this will happen between paragraphs, so the paragraphing of the passage is a definite clue. Paragraph 1 of Passage 2 begins with a statement of the charge against Emmet and his denial of that charge. The tone is impassioned rather than polite choice (C). He never asks for mercy, choice (A), or expresses remorse, choice (E). Nor could this paragraph be termed "interpretation" (B). To test whether choice (D) is correct, go on to paragraph 2. Here, Emmet begins with the words "Let no man dare," angrily challenging those who might call him a dishonorable man. Choice (D) is the only possible answer.

PART IV

SAT MATH STRATEGIES

SAT Multiple-Choice Math Strategies

OVERVIEW

- Understand why multiple-choice math is easier
- Learn to solve multiple-choice math questions
- Know when to use your calculator
- Learn the most important multiple-choice math tips
- Review what you need to know about multiple-choice math
- Practice your skills with multiple-choice math exercises

WHY MULTIPLE-CHOICE MATH IS EASIER

How can one kind of math possibly be easier than another? Well, SAT multiple-choice math is easier than the math tests you take in school. Why? First of all, SAT math focuses on basic arithmetic, elementary algebra, and basic geometry. You won't have to think about trigonometry, calculus, or any other advanced stuff. Also, because it's multiple-choice, the correct answer is always on the page in front of you. So even if you are estimating, you'll be able to narrow down the choices and improve your guessing odds.

SAT Multiple-Choice Math Questions

The scored portion of the SAT contains 35 standard multiple-choice questions, 25 in one section and 10 in another. Within each question set, the questions are arranged in order from easiest to most difficult. The questions don't stick to one content area. They jump around from arithmetic to algebra to geometry in no particular pattern.

Question Format

On the SAT, each set of multiple-choice math questions starts with directions and a reference section that look like this:

> **Directions:** Solve the following problems using any available space on the page for scratchwork. On your answer sheet fill in the choice that best corresponds to the correct answer.

Notes: The figures accompanying the problems are drawn as accurately as possible unless otherwise stated in specific problems. Again, unless otherwise stated, all figures lie in the same plane. All numbers used in these problems are real numbers. Calculators are permitted for this test.

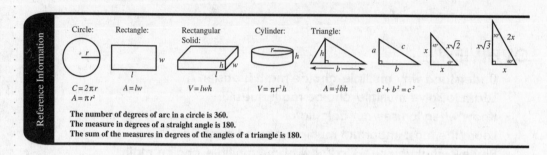

The number of degrees of arc in a circle is 360.
The measure in degrees of a straight angle is 180.
The sum of the measures in degrees of the angles of a triangle is 180.

The information in the reference section should all be familiar to you from your schoolwork. Know that it's there in case you need it. But remember: The formulas themselves aren't the answers to any problems. You have to know when to use them and how to apply them.

Some multiple-choice questions are straight calculations, while others are presented in the form of word problems. Some include graphs, charts, or tables that you will be asked to interpret. All of the questions have five answer choices. These choices are arranged in order by size from smallest to largest or occasionally from largest to smallest.

SOLVING MULTIPLE-CHOICE MATH QUESTIONS

These five steps will help you solve multiple-choice math questions:

MULTIPLE-CHOICE MATH: GETTING IT RIGHT

1. Read the question carefully and determine what's being asked.
2. Decide which math principles apply and use them to solve the problem.
3. Look for your answer among the choices. If it's there, mark it and go on.
4. If the answer you found is not there, recheck the question and your calculations.
5. If you still can't solve the problem, eliminate obviously wrong answers and take your best guess.

Now let's try out these steps on a couple of SAT-type multiple-choice math questions.

NOTE

The answers line up by size. The quantities in math multiple-choice answer choices either go from larger to smaller or the other way around. Remember that when you're trying to eliminate or test answers.

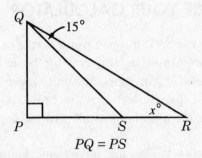

$PQ = PS$

In the figure above, $x =$

(A) 15

(B) 30

(C) 40

(D) 60

(E) 75

1 The problem asks you to find the measure of one angle of right triangle PQR.

2 Two math principles apply: (1) the sum of the measures in degrees of the angles of a triangle is 180, and (2) 45-45-90 right triangles have certain special properties. Since $PQ = PS$, ΔPQS is a 45-45-90 right triangle. Therefore, angle $PQS = 45°$ and angle $PQR = 45 + 15 = 60°$. Therefore, angle $x = 180 - 90 - 60 = 30°$.

3 The correct answer, 30, is choice (B).

If x and y are negative numbers, which of the following is negative?

(A) xy

(B) $(xy)^2$

(C) $(x - y)^2$

(D) $x + y$

(E) $\dfrac{x}{y}$

1 The problem asks you to pick an answer choice that is a negative number.

2 The principles that apply are those governing operations with signed numbers. Since x and y are negative, both choices (A) and (E) must be positive. As for choices (B) and (C), so long as neither x nor y is zero, those expressions must be positive. (Any number other than zero squared gives a positive result.) Choice (D), however, is negative since it represents the sum of two negative numbers.

Therefore, the correct answer must be choice (D). If you have trouble working with letters, try substituting easy numbers for x and y in each choice.

TIP

Remember the Reference Information! The Reference Information at the start of the math section provides valuable information about special right triangles.

KNOW WHEN TO USE YOUR CALCULATOR

Calculators are allowed on the SAT, but you won't *need* a calculator to solve any SAT math questions. Calculators can be helpful in doing basic arithmetic computations, square roots, and percentages, and in comparing and converting fractions. But remember that your calculator is not some sort of magic brain. If you don't understand the questions in the first place, the calculator won't give you some magic solution.

Calculators don't have to be fancy. They just have to add, subtract, multiply, and divide. Actually, the simpler the better, because you're less likely to hit some wacky function key by mistake.

The most important thing to remember is to set up your work on paper first, then plug the info into the calculator. For example, if you have a question that deals with an equation, set up the equation on your scratch paper. Then make your number substitutions on the calculator. This way, you always have something to refer to without having to think, "Oh, nuts, how did I set that up?" as the seconds tick by.

When you use your calculator, check the display each time you enter numbers to make sure you entered them correctly. And make sure to hit the Clear key after each finished operation, otherwise it could get ugly.

LEARN THE MOST IMPORTANT MULTIPLE-CHOICE MATH TIPS

Some of these you've heard before, some will be new to you. Whatever the case, read them, learn them, love them. They will help you.

The Question Number Tells You How Hard the Question Is

Just as in most of the other SAT sections, the questions go from easy to hard as you work toward the end. The first third of the questions are easy, the middle third are average but harder, and the final third get more and more difficult. Take a look at these three examples. Don't solve them yet (you'll be doing that in a couple of minutes), just get an idea of how the level of difficulty changes from Question 1 to Question 12 to Question 25.

1. If $x - 2 = 5$, then $x =$
    (A) -10
    (B) -3
    (C) $\frac{5}{2}$
    (D) 3
    (E) 7

ALERT!

Don't automatically reach for your calculator. If it can't help you solve the problem, you'll just waste time fiddling with it. Save the calculator for what it does best, especially arithmetic calculations, percentages, and square roots.

12. For how many integers x is $-7 < 2x < -5$?

    (A) None
    (B) One
    (C) Two
    (D) Three
    (E) Indefinite number

25. In a set of five books, no two of which have the same number of pages, the longest book has 150 pages and the shortest book has 130 pages. If x pages is the average (arithmetic mean) of the number of pages in the five-book set, which of the following best indicates all possible values of x and only possible values of x?

    (A) $130 < x < 150$
    (B) $131 < x < 149$
    (C) $133 < x < 145$
    (D) $134 < x < 145$
    (E) $135 < x < 145$

TIP

Look for shortcuts. SAT math problems test your math reasoning, not your ability to make endless calculations. If you find yourself calculating too much, you've probably missed a shortcut that would have made your work easier.

Can you see the difference? You can probably do Question 1 with your eyes closed. For Question 12 you probably have to open your eyes and do some calculations on scratch paper. Question 25 may cause you to wince a little, and then get started on some heavy-duty thinking.

Easy Questions Have Easy Answers—Difficult Questions Don't

The easy questions are straightforward and don't have any hidden tricks. The obvious answer is almost always the correct answer. So for Question 1 the answer is indeed choice (E).

When you hit the difficult stuff, you have to think harder. The information is not straightforward and the answers aren't obvious. You can bet that your first-choice, easy answer will be wrong. If you don't believe it, let's take a look at the solution for difficult Question 25.

25. In a set of five books, no two of which have the same number of pages, the longest book has 150 pages and the shortest book has 130 pages. If x pages is the average (arithmetic mean) of the number of pages in the five-book set, which of the following best indicates all possible values of x and only possible values of x?

    (A) $130 < x < 150$
    (B) $131 < x < 149$
    (C) $133 < x < 145$
    (D) $134 < x < 145$
    (E) $135 < x < 145$

Yes, it's difficult mostly because the process you have to use to find the solution is difficult. Let's start by eliminating answer choices. Choice (A) is for suckers. You see the same information as you see in the word problem so you figure it's got to be right. Wrong. All it does is say that the shortest book is 130 pages, the longest book is 150 pages, and the average is between 130 and 150. Simple and wrong.

Choice (B) illustrates the reasoning that "no two books have the same number of pages, so the average must be one page more than the shortest book and one page less than the longest." Remember, it's a difficult question, it's just not that easy an answer.

OK then, let's skip to the correct answer, which is (E), and find out how we got there. First, you want to find the minimum value for x so you assume that the other three books contain 131, 132, and 133 pages. So the average would be:

$$\frac{130+131+132+133+150}{5} = \frac{676}{5} = 135.2$$

So x must be more than 135. Now assume that the other three books contain 149, 148, and 147 pages. Then the average length of all five books would be:

$$\frac{150+149+148+147+130}{5} = \frac{724}{5} = 144.8$$

Then x would be greater than 135 but less than 145.

When Guessing at Hard Questions, You Can Toss Out Easy Answers

Now that you know the difficult questions won't have easy or obvious answers, use a guessing strategy. (Use all the help you can get!) When you have less than a clue about a difficult question, scan the answer choices and eliminate the ones that seem easy or obvious, such as any that just restate the information in the question. Then take your best guess.

Questions of Average Difficulty Won't Have Trick Answers

Let's look again at Question 12:

12. For how many integers x is $-7 < 2x < -5$?
   (A) None
   (B) One
   (C) Two
   (D) Three
   (E) Indefinite number

This is a bit more difficult than Question 1, but it's still pretty straightforward. There is only one integer between −7 and −5, and that's −6. There's also only one value for integer x so that $2x$ equals −6, and that is −3. Get it? $2(-3) = -6$. So, choice (B) is the correct answer. Trust your judgment and your reasoning; no tricks here.

It's Smart to Work Backward

Every standard multiple-choice math problem includes five answer choices. One of them has to be correct; the other four are wrong. This means that it's always possible to solve a problem by testing each of the answer choices. Just plug each choice into the problem and sooner or later you'll find the one that works! Testing answer choices can often be a much easier and surer way of solving a problem than attempting a lengthy calculation.

When Working Backward, Always Start from the Middle

When working on multiple-choice math questions, remember that all of the answer choices are presented in order—either smallest to largest, or vice-versa. As a result, it's always best to begin with the middle option, or choice (C). This way, if you start with choice (C) and it's too large, you'll only have to concentrate on the smaller choices. There, you've just knocked off at least three choices in a heartbeat! Now let's give it a test-run!

If a rectangle has sides of $2x$ and $3x$ and an area of 24, what is the value of x?

(A) 2

(B) 3

(C) 4

(D) 5

(E) 6

You know that one of these is right. Get started by testing choice (C), and assume that $x = 4$. Then the sides would have lengths $2(4) = 8$ and $3(4) = 12$ and the rectangle would have an area of $8 \times 12 = 96$. Since 96 is larger than 24 (the area in the question), start working with the smaller answer choices. (Which means, of course, that you can immediately forget about choices (D) and (E). Great!) When you plug 3 into the figuring, you get $2(3) = 6$ and $3(3)$ 9 and $6 \times 9 = 54$; still too large. The only choice left is (A), and it works.

Now try this testing business with a more difficult question:

A farmer raises chickens and cows. If his animals have a total of 120 heads and a total of 300 feet, how many chickens does the farmer have?

(A) 50

(B) 60

(C) 70

(D) 80

(E) 90

Here goes—starting with choice (C). If the farmer has 70 chickens, he has 50 cows. (You know the farmer has 120 animals, because they each have only one head, right?) So now you're talking about $70 \times 2 = 140$ chicken feet and $50 \times 4 = 200$ cow feet, for a grand total of 340 animal feet. Well, that's more than the 300 animal feet in the question. How will you lose some of those feet? First, assume that the farmer has more chickens and fewer cows (cows have more feet than chickens do). Give choice (D)—80—a try. Test $80 \times 2 = 160$ and $40 \times 4 = 160$; your total is 320 feet, which is closer but not quite right. The only answer left is choice (E), and that's the correct one. Check it out: $90 \times 2 = 180$ and $30 \times 4 = 120$ and the total is . . . 300!

It's Easier to Work with Numbers than with Letters

Because numbers are more meaningful than letters, try plugging them into equations and formulas in place of variables. This technique can make problems much easier to solve. Here are some examples:

If $x - 4$ is 2 greater than y, then $x + 5$ is how much greater than y?

(A) 1

(B) 3

(C) 7

(D) 9

(E) 11

Choose any value for x. Let's say you decide to make $x = 4$. All right, $4 - 4 = 0$, and 0 is 2 greater than y. So $y = -2$. If $x = 4$, then $x + 5 = 4 + 5 = 9$, and so $x + 5$ is 11 more than y. Therefore, the correct answer is choice (E).

TIP

Leave a paper trail! If you need to set up an equation, jot it down in your test booklet. That way, if you come back to recheck your work, you'll know what you were originally thinking.

The unit cost of pens is the same regardless of how many pens are purchased. If the cost of p pens is d dollars, what is the cost, in dollars, of x pens?

(A) xd

(B) xpd

(C) $\dfrac{xd}{p}$

(D) $\dfrac{xp}{d}$

(E) $\dfrac{pd}{x}$

Time to plug in some real numbers, since you need real money to buy anything, including pens. Say that four pens (p) cost $2.00 ($d$), so each pen ($x$) would cost 50 cents. And say that you really only need one pen, so you're spending only $0.50. Then $p = 4$, $d = 2$, and $x = 1$, and the right answer would be 0.5. Now, start using these numbers with the answer choices:

(A) $xd = (1)(2) = 2$ (Nope.)

(B) $xpd = (1)(4)(2) = 8$ (Nope, again.)

(C) $\dfrac{xd}{p} = \dfrac{(1)(2)}{4} = 0.5$ (Yes, there it is.)

(D) $\dfrac{xp}{d} = \dfrac{(1)(4)}{2} = 2$ (Nope.)

(E) $\dfrac{pd}{x} = \dfrac{(4)(2)}{1} = 8$ (Nope.)

If a question asks for an odd integer or an even integer, go ahead and pick any odd or even integer you like.

It's OK to Write in Your Test Booklet, So Use it for Scratchwork

The test booklet is yours, so feel free to use it for your scratchwork. Also, go ahead and mark up any diagrams with length or angle information; it helps. But don't waste time trying to redraw diagrams; it's just not worth it.

Questions in the Three-Statement Format Can be Solved by the Process of Elimination

You may find a three-statement format in certain questions in the multiple-choice math section. The best way to answer this kind of question is to tackle one statement at a time, marking it as either true or false. Here is an example:

If $x - y$ is positive, which of the following statements is true?

 I. $0 > x > y$

 II. $x > 0 > y$

 III. $y > x > 0$

(A) I only

(B) II only

(C) III only

(D) I and II only

(E) II and III only

The answer choices all refer to the three statements. Let's start by checking statement I. If x and y are negative numbers so that x is greater than y, then y has a greater absolute value than x. Since both are negative numbers, $x - y$ is positive. For example, $-3 > -4$ and $-3 - (-4) = -3 + 4 = 1$, and $1 > 0$. Therefore, statement I will appear in the correct answer choice. Now, since choices (B), (C), and (E) don't contain statement I, you can eliminate them.

Now let's check out statement II. If x is positive and y is negative, then $x - y$ would be subtracting a negative number from a positive number, which will give you a positive number. (Subtracting a negative number is really adding a positive number.) Because statement II must appear in the correct answer, you can now eliminate answer choice (A). So, by the process of elimination, you know that choice (D) is correct, and you don't even have to test statement III.

The Area of an Unusual Shape Is Really the Difference Between the Areas of Two Regular Figures

Here's a visual example that might help:

In the figure below, what is the area of the shaded region?

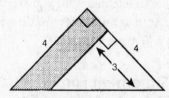

(A) $2\frac{1}{2}$

(B) 4

(C) $3\frac{1}{2}$

(D) 6

(E) 8

Try to isolate the shaded portion of the figure. When you do, you'll see it's a trapezoid. Now, you could try to remember the formula for the area of a trapezoid, but look at the figure you have left after you pull out the trapezoid. It's another, smaller triangle. What you really need to do is figure out the areas of the original large triangle and the smaller triangle and find the difference.

You know that the larger triangle has a right angle and two equal sides, so it's an isosceles right triangle. The smaller triangle has a right angle and its side is parallel to the side of the larger triangle, so it too is an isosceles triangle. Now use the information in the figure to find the areas and then subtract.

Area of smaller triangle $= \dfrac{1}{2}(3)(3) = \dfrac{9}{2}$

Area of larger triangle $= \dfrac{1}{2}(4)(4) = 8$

$8 - \dfrac{9}{2} = 3\dfrac{1}{2}$

Using the Measure of an Angle or a Side of Another Shape Can Help You Find a Measure You Need

In the figure, what is the length of *NP*?

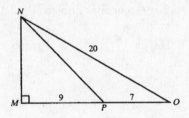

(A) 3

(B) 8

(C) 9

(D) 12

(E) 15

This figure is really two right triangles, *NMO* and *NMP*. Since *NM* is a side of both triangles, once you find the length of that, you can find the length of *NP*. The Pythagorean theorem is what you need:

$NM^2 + MO^2 = NO^2$

$NM^2 + (16)^2 = (20)^2$

Note that 16 and 20 are multiples of 4 and 5, respectively, so you now know that this is a 3-4-5 right triangle, which means that *NM* = 12.

Since you just found out that triangle *NMP* has sides of 9 and 12, it's also a 3-4-5 right triangle, so *NP* must be 15.

A Reality Check Can Help You Eliminate Answers That Can't Possibly Be Right

Knowing whether your calculations should produce a number that's larger or smaller than the quantity you started with can point you toward the right answer. It's also an effective way of eliminating wrong answers. Here's an example:

Using his bike, Daryl can complete a paper route in 20 minutes. Francisco, who walks the route, can complete it in 30 minutes. How long will it take the two boys to complete the route if they work together, one starting at each end of the route?

(A) 8 minutes
(B) 12 minutes
(C) 20 minutes
(D) 30 minutes
(E) 45 minutes

Immediately you can see that choices (C), (D), and (E) are impossible because the two boys working together will have to complete the job in less time than either one of them working alone. In fact, the correct answer is choice (B), 12 minutes.

	Daryl	Francisco
$\dfrac{\text{Time actually spent}}{\text{Time needed to do entire job}}$	$\dfrac{x}{20}$	$\dfrac{x}{30}$

$$\frac{x}{20} + \frac{x}{30} = 1$$

Multiply by 60 to clear fractions:

$$3x + 2x = 60$$
$$5x = 60$$
$$x = 12$$

Your Eye Is a Good Estimator

Figures in the standard multiple-choice math section are always drawn to scale unless you see the warning "Note: Figure not drawn to scale." That means you can sometimes solve a problem just by looking at the picture and estimating the answer. Here's how this works:

In the rectangle $PQRS$ shown, $\overline{TU}$ and $\overline{WV}$ are parallel to $\overline{SR}$. If $PS = 6$, $UV = 1$, and PR (not shown) = 10, what is the area of rectangle $TUVW$?

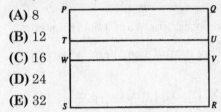

(A) 8

(B) 12

(C) 16

(D) 24

(E) 32

To solve the problem, you will need to find the length of TU. You can do this by using the Pythagorean theorem. The triangle PSR has sides of 6 and 10, so $SR = 8$. Since $TU = SR$, $TU = 8$, so the area of the small rectangle is equal to $1 \times 8 = 8$.

As an alternative, you could simply estimate the length of TU. TU appears to be longer than PS (6), and TU must be shorter than PR (10). Therefore, TU appears to be approximately 8. And the area must be approximately $1 \times 8 = 8$. Is that sufficiently accurate to get the right answer? Look at the choices. (A) is 8, and it's the only choice that is even close to 8.

If Some Questions Always Give You Trouble, Save Them for Last

You know which little demons haunt your math skills. If you find questions that you know will give you nightmares, save them for last. They will take up a lot of your time, especially if you're panicking, and you can use that time to do more of the easier questions.

SUMMARY

What You Need to Know about Multiple-Choice Math

- Follow the five-step plan for answering basic multiple-choice math questions:

  1. Read the question carefully and determine what's being asked.

  2. Decide which math principles apply and use them to solve the problem.

  3. Look for your answer among the choices. If it's there, mark it and go on.

  4. If the answer you found is not there, recheck the question and your calculations.

  5. If you still can't solve the problem, eliminate obviously wrong answers and take your best guess.

- Use a calculator where it can help the most: on basic arithmetic calculations, when calculating square roots and percentages, and in comparing and converting fractions.

- Always set up your work on paper, then enter the numbers in your calculator; that way, if your calculation becomes confused, you don't have to try to replicate your setup from memory.

- The question number tells you how hard the question will be (on a 1 to 25 scale).

- Work backward from the answer choices. When you do, start with choice (C).

- Try to work with numbers instead of letters. This will help you avoid unnecessary algebraic calculations.

- Figures in the math section are always drawn to scale unless you see a warning. So use your eye as an estimator if you need to.

EXERCISES: MULTIPLE-CHOICE MATH
Exercise 1

15 Questions • Time—18 Minutes

Directions: Solve the following problems using any available space on the page for scratchwork. Circle the letter that appears before your answer.

Notes: The figures accompanying the problems are drawn as accurately as possible unless otherwise stated in specific problems. Again, unless otherwise stated, all figures lie in the same plane. All numbers used in these problems are real numbers. Calculators are permitted for this test.

Reference Information

 Circle: Rectangle: 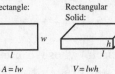 Rectangular Solid: Cylinder: Triangle:

$C = 2\pi r$ $A = lw$ $V = lwh$ $V = \pi r^2 h$ $A = \frac{1}{2}bh$ $a^2 + b^2 = c^2$

$A = \pi r^2$

The number of degrees of arc in a circle is 360.
The measure in degrees of a straight angle is 180.
The sum of the measures in degrees of the angles of a triangle is 180.

1. If $8 \times 8 = 4x$, what is x?
   - **(A)** 2
   - **(B)** 3
   - **(C)** 4
   - **(D)** 5
   - **(E)** 6

2. If $a > 2$, which of the following is the smallest?
   - **(A)** $\frac{2}{a}$
   - **(B)** $\frac{a}{2}$
   - **(C)** $a + \frac{1}{2}$
   - **(D)** $\frac{2}{a+1}$
   - **(E)** $\frac{2}{a-1}$

3. Which of the following has the greatest value?
   - **(A)** $\frac{1}{2}$
   - **(B)** $\sqrt{.2}$
   - **(C)** $.2$
   - **(D)** $(.2)^2$
   - **(E)** $(.02)^3$

4. If $\frac{a}{b} = \frac{3}{4}$, then $12a =$
   - **(A)** b
   - **(B)** $3b$
   - **(C)** $9b$
   - **(D)** $12b$
   - **(E)** $16b$

5. If $a = b$ and $\dfrac{1}{c} = b$, then $c =$

   (A) a

   (B) $-a$

   (C) b

   (D) $\dfrac{1}{a}$

   (E) $-b$

6. If a building B feet high casts a shadow F feet long, then at the same time of day, a tree T feet high will cast a shadow how many feet long?

   (A) $\dfrac{FT}{B}$

   (B) $\dfrac{FB}{T}$

   (C) $\dfrac{B}{FT}$

   (D) $\dfrac{TB}{F}$

   (E) $\dfrac{T}{FB}$

7. The vertices of a triangle are (3, 1), (8, 1), and (8, 3). What is the area of this triangle?

   (A) 5

   (B) 10

   (C) 12

   (D) 14

   (E) 20

8. Of 60 employees at the Star Manufacturing Company, x employees are female. If $\dfrac{2}{3}$ of the remainder are married, how many unmarried men work for this company?

   (A) $40 - \dfrac{2}{3}x$

   (B) $40 - \dfrac{1}{3}x$

   (C) $40 + \dfrac{1}{3}x$

   (D) $20 - \dfrac{2}{3}x$

   (E) $20 - \dfrac{1}{3}x$

9. A circle whose center is at the origin passes through the point whose coordinates are (1, 1). What is the area of this circle?

   (A) π

   (B) 2π

   (C) $\sqrt{2\pi}$

   (D) $2\sqrt{2\pi}$

   (E) 4π

10. In triangle ABC, $AB = BC$ and AC is extended to D. If angle BCD contains 100°, find the number of degrees in angle B.

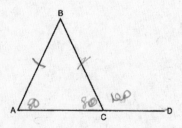

    (A) 20

    (B) 40

    (C) 50

    (D) 60

    (E) 80

11. $\dfrac{4\frac{1}{2}}{10\frac{1}{8}} =$

   (A) $\dfrac{2}{5}$

   (B) $\dfrac{4}{9}$

   (C) $\dfrac{4}{81}$

   (D) $\dfrac{3}{7}$

   (E) $\dfrac{15}{23}$

12. Which of the following is greater than $\dfrac{1}{3}$?

   (A) $.33$

   (B) $\left(\dfrac{1}{3}\right)^2$

   (C) $\dfrac{1}{4}$

   (D) $\dfrac{1}{.3}$

   (E) $\dfrac{.3}{2}$

13. What percent of a half dollar is a penny, a nickel, and a dime?

   (A) 8

   (B) 16

   (C) 20

   (D) 25

   (E) 32

14. If $\dfrac{1}{a} + \dfrac{1}{b} = \dfrac{1}{c}$, then $c =$

   (A) $a + b$

   (B) ab

   (C) $\dfrac{a+b}{ab}$

   (D) $\dfrac{ab}{a+b}$

   (E) $\dfrac{1}{2}ab$

15. What percent of a is b?

   (A) $\dfrac{100b}{a}$

   (B) $\dfrac{a}{b}$

   (C) $\dfrac{b}{100a}$

   (D) $\dfrac{b}{a}$

   (E) $\dfrac{100a}{b}$

Exercise 2

10 Questions • Time—12 Minutes

Directions: Solve the following problems using any available space on the page for scratchwork. Circle the letter that appears before your answer.

Notes: The figures accompanying the problems are drawn as accurately as possible unless otherwise stated in specific problems. Again, unless otherwise stated, all figures lie in the same plane. All numbers used in these problems are real numbers. Calculators are permitted for this test.

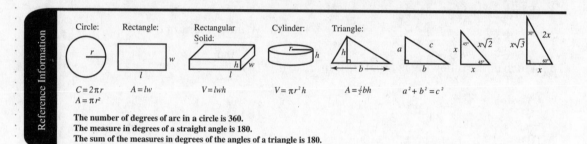

$C = 2\pi r$
$A = \pi r^2$

$A = lw$

$V = lwh$

$V = \pi r^2 h$

$A = \frac{1}{2}bh$

$a^2 + b^2 = c^2$

The number of degrees of arc in a circle is 360.
The measure in degrees of a straight angle is 180.
The sum of the measures in degrees of the angles of a triangle is 180.

1. The average of two numbers is A. If one of the numbers is x, what is the other number?

   (A) $A - x$

   (B) $\dfrac{A}{2} - x$

   (C) $2A - x$

   (D) $\dfrac{A + x}{2}$

   (E) $x - A$

2. If $a = 5b$, then $\dfrac{3}{5}a =$

   (A) $\dfrac{5b}{3}$

   (B) $3b$

   (C) $\dfrac{3b}{5}$

   (D) $\dfrac{b}{3}$

   (E) $\dfrac{b}{5}$

3. A rectangular door measures 5 feet by 6 feet 8 inches. What is the distance from one corner of the door to the diagonally opposite corner?

   (A) 8'2"

   (B) 8'4"

   (C) 8'8"

   (D) 9'

   (E) 9'6"

4. Two ships leave from the same port at 11:30 a.m. If one sails due east at 20 miles per hour and the other due south at 15 miles per hour, how many miles apart are the ships at 2:30 p.m.?

   (A) 25
   (B) 50
   (C) 75
   (D) 80
   (E) 85

5. If m men can paint a house in d days, how many days will it take $m + 2$ men to paint the same house?

   (A) $d + 2$
   (B) $d - 2$
   (C) $\dfrac{m+2}{md}$
   (D) $\dfrac{md}{m+2}$
   (E) $\dfrac{md+2d}{m}$

6. Ken received grades of 90, 88, and 75 on three tests. What grade must he receive on the next test so that his average for these four tests is 85?

   (A) 87
   (B) 89
   (C) 90
   (D) 92
   (E) 95

7. There is enough food at a picnic to feed 20 adults or 32 children. If there are 15 adults at the picnic, how many children can still be fed?

   (A) 6
   (B) 8
   (C) 12
   (D) 16
   (E) 18

8. In parallelogram $ABCD$, angle A contains 60°. What is the sum of angle B and angle D?

   (A) 60°
   (B) 180°
   (C) 240°
   (D) 280°
   (E) 300°

9. The area of circle O is 64π. What is the perimeter of square $ABCD$?

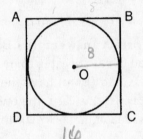

   (A) 32
   (B) 32π
   (C) 64
   (D) 16
   (E) 64π

10. If a train covers 14 miles in 10 minutes, what is the rate of the train in miles per hour?

    (A) 64
    (B) 76
    (C) 84
    (D) 90
    (E) 98

ANSWER KEYS AND EXPLANATIONS

Exercise 1

1.	B	4.	C	7.	A	10.	A	13.	E
2.	D	5.	D	8.	E	11.	B	14.	D
3.	A	6.	A	9.	B	12.	D	15.	A

1. **The correct answer is (B).**

    $$64 = 4x$$

    $$x = 3 \ (4 \times 4 \times 4 = 64)$$

2. **The correct answer is (D).** Both choices (B) and (C) are greater than 1. Choices (A), (D), and (E) all have the same numerator. In this case, the one with the largest denominator will be the smallest fraction.

3. **The correct answer is (A).**

    $$\frac{1}{2} = .5$$

    $$\sqrt{.20} \approx .447$$

    $$(.2)^2 = .04$$

    $$(.2)^3 = .000008$$

4. **The correct answer is (C).** Cross-multiply.

    $$4a = 3b$$

    Multiply by 3.

    $$12a = 9b$$

5. **The correct answer is (D).**

    $$a = b = \frac{1}{c}$$

    $$a = \frac{1}{c}$$

    $$ac = 1$$

    $$c = \frac{1}{a}$$

6. **The correct answer is (A).** The ratio of height to shadow is constant.

    $$\frac{B}{F} = \frac{T}{x}$$

    $$Bx = FT$$

    $$x = \frac{FT}{B}$$

7. **The correct answer is (A).**

    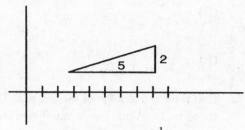

    Right triangle area $= \dfrac{1}{2} \times 5 \times 2 = 5$

8. **The correct answer is (E).**

    $60 - x$ employees are male.

    $\dfrac{1}{3}$ of these are unmarried.

    $$\frac{1}{3}(60 - x) = 20 - \frac{1}{3}x$$

9.   The correct answer is (B).

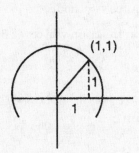

$$1^2 + 1^2 = r^2$$
$$2 = r^2$$
$$\text{Area} = \pi r^2 = 2\pi$$

10. The correct answer is (A).

Angle BCA = Angle BAC = 80°

There are 20° left for angle B.

11. The correct answer is (B).

$$\frac{9}{2} \div \frac{81}{8} = \frac{9}{2} \times \frac{8}{81} = \frac{4}{9}$$

12. The correct answer is (D).

$$\frac{1}{.3} = \frac{10}{3} = 3\frac{1}{3}$$

13. The correct answer is (E).

$$\frac{16}{50} = \frac{32}{100} = 32\%$$

14. The correct answer is (D). Multiply by abc.

$$bc + ac = ab$$
$$c(b + a) = ab$$
$$c = \frac{ab}{b + a}$$

15. The correct answer is (A).

$$\frac{b}{a} \times 100 = \frac{100b}{a}$$

Exercise 2

1. C	3. B	5. D	7. B	9. C
2. B	4. C	6. A	8. C	10. C

1. The correct answer is (C).

$$\frac{x + y}{2} = A$$
$$x + y = 2A$$
$$y = 2A - x$$

2. The correct answer is (B).

$$\frac{3}{\cancel{8}} \times \cancel{8}\, b = 3b$$

3. The correct answer is (B).

5 feet = 60 inches

6 feet 8 inches = 80 inches

This is a 6-8-10 triangle, making the diagonal 100 inches, which is 8 feet 4 inches.

4. The correct answer is (C). In 3 hours, one ship went 60 miles, the other 45 miles. This is a 3-4-5 triangle as 45 = 3(15), 60 = 4(15). The hypotenuse will be 5(15), or 75.

5. The correct answer is (D). This is inverse variation.

$$m \times d = (m + 2) \times x$$
$$\frac{md}{m + 2} = x$$

6. The correct answer is (A). He must score as many points above 85 as below. So far he has 8 above and 10 below. He needs another 2 above.

7. The correct answer is (B). If 15 adults are fed, $\frac{3}{4}$ of the food is gone. $\frac{1}{4}$ of the food will feed $\frac{1}{4} \times 32$, or 8 children.

8. The correct answer is (C). If angle A = 60°, then angle B = 120°.

Angle B = Angle D. Their sum is 240°.

9. **The correct answer is (C).**

    Area of circle $= 64\pi = \pi r^2$

    Radius of circle $= 8$

    Side of square $= 16$

    Perimeter of square $= 64$

10. **The correct answer is (C).**

    $10 \text{ minutes} = \dfrac{1}{6} \text{ hour}$

    In one hour, the train will cover 6(14), or 84 miles.

SAT Quantitative Comparison Strategies

OVERVIEW

- Get to know the quantitative comparison format
- Learn to solve quantitative comparisons
- Learn the most important quantitative comparison tips
- Review what you need to know about quantitative comparisons
- Practice your skills with quantitative comparison exercises

GET TO KNOW THE QUANTITATIVE COMPARISON FORMAT

You picked up this book. You flipped through some pages. You got to this chapter and thought, "What the heck am I supposed to do with these weird questions? What do they want from me now?" Well, quantitative comparisons are not quite as wacky as they look. You can recognize quantitative comparison questions easily because they look very different from other math questions. Each one has two side-by-side boxes containing quantities that you must compare. Then you choose the correct answers from choices (A) through (D).

There are some good things to remember about these. First, the choices are always the same (check out the sample directions on page 182). Second, you don't actually have to solve a problem. The questions are really testing knowledge of mathematical principles rather than your calculating skills. Third, sometimes the SAT folks give you a little help and provide a diagram or other information centered above the boxes with the information you are comparing. Oh, you can use a calculator, too, if you want.

SAT Quantitative Comparison Questions

The scored portion of the SAT contains 15 quantitative comparisons, all grouped in a single section. Within each question set, the questions are arranged in order from easiest to most difficult. The questions cover the same mix of arithmetic, algebra, and geometry that appears in the multiple-choice math section.

Question Format

Each set of quantitative comparisons starts with directions that look like this:

> **Directions:** For each of the following questions, two quantities are given—one in Column A, the other in Column B. Compare the two quantities and mark your answer sheet as follows:
>
> **(A)** if the quantity in Column A is greater
>
> **(B)** if the quantity in Column B is greater
>
> **(C)** if the quantities are equal
>
> **(D)** if the relationship cannot be determined from the information given
>
> **Notes:**
>
> **(1)** Information concerning one or both of the compared quantities will be centered above the two columns for some items.
>
> **(2)** Symbols that appear in both columns represent the same thing in Column A as in Column B.
>
> **(3)** Letters such as x, n, and k are symbols for real numbers.

TIP

Memorize the directions and the answer choices. Remember that the four answer choices for quantitative comparisons are always the same.

SOLVING QUANTITATIVE COMPARISONS

Your estimating and comparison skills, as well as the five steps shown below, will help you cope with these questions. Once you get used to the choices, things can move pretty quickly.

QUANTITATIVE COMPARISONS: GETTING IT RIGHT

1 Try to remember all of the available answers.

2 For each question, compare the boxed quantities.

3 Consider all possibilities for any variables.

4 Decide which answer choice is best.

5 Carefully fill in the answer on the answer sheet.

Now let's look at these steps in more detail.

1 Don't just learn the directions, try to memorize the answer choices. (Remember, they are always the same.) Then you can save time because you won't need to refer to them for every question.

2 Even though there are two quantities in each question, deal with one at a time. If there is extra information above the boxes, see how each quantity relates to it. Then do any figuring you need to do. (There won't be much.)

NOTE

Variables stay constant. A variable that appears in both columns means the same thing in each column.

③ Consider all possibilities for any unknowns. Think what would happen if special numbers such as 0, negative numbers, or fractions were put into play.

④ Choose your answer. You shouldn't have to do involved calculations to get to the answer. If you're calculating endlessly, you've probably missed the mathematical principle the question is asking about.

⑤ Mark your answer sheet CAREFULLY! Did you notice that quantitative comparisons have only *four* answer choices? There is no choice (E), so don't mark (E) by mistake.

<u>Column A</u>	<u>Column B</u>

The price of a pound of cheese
increased from $2.00 to $2.50.

The percent increase in the price of cheese	25%

① You already know the answer choices.

② The centered information tells you that cheese increased in price from $2.00 to $2.50 per pound. Column A asks for the percent increase, which is $\frac{\$0.50}{\$2.00} = 25\%$. Column B requires no calculation, and it's equal to Column A.

③ There are no variables, so go on to step 4.

④ Since the two columns are equal, the answer is choice (C).

⑤ Mark choice (C) on the answer sheet.

<u>Column A</u>	<u>Column B</u>
$x^2 + y^2$	$(x + y)^2$

① You already know the answer choices.

② The expression in Column B is $(x + y)^2 = x^2 + 2xy + y^2$. This is the same as the expression in Column A with the addition of the middle term $2xy$.

③ The terms x and y are variables that can be positive or negative or zero. For example, if x were 1 and y were 2, Column A would be $1^2 + 2^2 = 5$ and Column B would be $(1 + 2)^2 = 9$. The correct answer would then be choice (B). But if x were -1 and y were 2, Column A would be $-1^2 + 2^2 = 5$ and Column B would be $(-1 + 2)^2 = 1^2 = 1$. This time the correct answer would be choice (A).

④ Any time more than one answer can be true for a comparison—as is the case here—then the answer to that question must be choice (D), "the relationship cannot be determined from the information given."

⑤ Mark choice (D) on the answer sheet.

ALERT!

Figures can be deceiving. If a figure carries a warning that it is not drawn to scale, don't depend on estimating or measuring to help you solve the question.

Remember that many quantitative comparisons can be solved without doing any calculating at all. In many cases, you should be able to arrive at the correct answer simply by applying your knowledge of basic math rules and principles. Look at these examples:

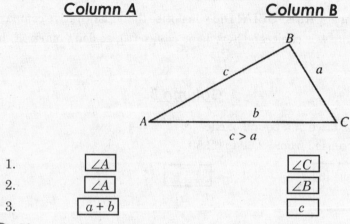

	Column A	_Column B_
1.	$\angle A$	$\angle C$
2.	$\angle A$	$\angle B$
3.	$a + b$	c

1 If two sides of a triangle are unequal, the angles opposite them are unequal, and the larger angle is opposite the longer side. So, the answer for this question is choice (B).

2 Since we can't really tell whether a or b is greater, we can't tell which angle is greater, so choice (D) is the correct answer.

3 The sum of any two sides of a triangle must always be greater than the length of the third side. The only answer for this question is choice (A).

LEARN THE MOST IMPORTANT QUANTITATIVE COMPARISON TIPS

Quantitative comparisons may look complex, but if you come at them from the right angle (pardon the pun), you can streamline the answering process.

Make the Columns Look Alike

Start by doing whatever it takes to make the columns resemble each other. Only when the columns look alike—and therefore are comparable—can you easily tell which is greater. Here's a simple example:

Column A	_Column B_

a is 30% of b
b is 40% of c

Percent that a is of c	11

TIP

When in doubt, try something! It may not be obvious what the test-makers want you to do with either quantity. If so, start messing around with the quantities, using whatever mathematical techniques strike you as natural or logical. Chances are good that some method you've used dozens of times in math class will yield the result the test-makers are looking for.

First, let's be clear what you're looking at. This question starts with two lines of information that are centered between Columns A/B. This information isn't part of either column; instead, it is provided to help you interpret the values given in the columns. You're to assume that this information is true and that it applies to whatever quantities appear in the columns underneath.

Now look at the two quantities that you're supposed to compare. Column A *describes* a quantity: the "percent that *a* is of *c*." Column B, by contrast, *states* a quantity, in the simplest possible form: it's the integer 11. Can you tell, at a glance, which is greater? Probably not. The reason is that the two quantities are named in terms so different that they're not readily comparable.

To compare them, you need to make them look alike. Since Column B is already stated in the simplest possible form, your plan should be to make Column A look like Column B—that is, turn it into a simple number as well. To do that, you'll have to use your math skills. Since the shared information tells you that *a* is 30% of *b* and *b* is 40% of *c*, you can tell that *a* must be 30% of 40% of *c*. What is 30% of 40%? Multiply it out, using your calculator if you like:

$$.30 \times .40 = .12$$

So you can tell from the information given that *a* is 12% of *c*. Now we have a quantity for Column A—12—that can easily be compared with the quantity in Column B. Since 12 is greater than 11, Column A is greater, and choice (A) is the answer for this question.

Here's another example:

Column A   Column B

x and *y* are negative

| $(x + y)(x + y)$ | $x^2 + y^2$ |

In this question, neither column contains a quantity that's easy to measure—especially since we don't know the value of either unknown, *x* or *y*. But don't despair! It may still be possible to figure out how the two quantities compare, if we can make them appear similar and therefore comparable.

Which column can more easily be made to resemble the other? In this case, you can probably see how Column A can be made to look something like Column B. Two quantities contained in parentheses, like those in Column A, are practically crying out to be multiplied together. And you can probably tell that, when you multiply them out, you'll end up with a quantity that includes x^2 and y^2, not unlike Column B. Here's what happens to the comparison when the multiplication in Column A is carried out:

Column A	Column B
$x^2 + 2xy + y^2$	$x^2 + y^2$

We've used a basic algebra process here: when you multiply two binomials, like those in Column A, you end up with a trinomial like the one we've now created. See Chapter 14 if this procedure seems unfamiliar.

Now the two columns resemble each other, and we can compare them more easily. But, in this case, to determine which is greater, we need to use the second basic strategy for quantitative comparisons. . . .

Eliminate Whatever the Columns Share

Remember, you're interested in figuring out the *difference* between the two quantities. That means that anything that the two quantities have in common—anything they share—is *irrelevant*.

Here's an analogy. Suppose you're trying to decide which of two used cars to buy. Also suppose that both cars are four-door models, about the same size, made in the same model year, with roughly the same amount of mileage on them. Since all of those factors are the *same*, they are all *irrelevant* to your choice—none of these will help you decide which car is better. Instead, you'll have to choose based on ways in which the two cars *differ*—price, for example, or appearance.

In the same way, when comparing two mathematical quantities on the SAT, you can eliminate as irrelevant anything both quantities share. Let's go back to the item we've been considering, with Column A transformed by having been multiplied out:

Making the two columns resemble each other often requires you to simplify one or both quantities—for example, by simplifying a fraction to simplest form. It may also require you to translate one quantity so that both quantities are expressed in the same terms. For example, you might have to translate pounds into ounces, a fraction into a percentage, or minutes into hours.

Column A	Column B
$x^2 + 2xy + y^2$	$x^2 + y^2$

At a glance, you can see that both columns now have two terms in common: x^2 and y^2. We don't know the numeric value of either of these terms, since we don't know the value of either x or y. Nonetheless, we can eliminate both x^2 and y^2 from the comparison, since they appear in both columns. The *difference* between the columns can't be contained in what they have in common!

Once we eliminate—remove—these two terms from both sides of the comparison, we can compare what remains:

Column A	Column B
$2xy$	0

Having eliminated x^2 and y^2 from Column A, all that's left there is $2xy$. And having made the same elimination from Column B, all that's left there is nothing—zero! So to answer the question, we simply have to decide whether $2xy$ is greater than, less than, or equal to zero.

By using the information given above the two quantities, you can determine this. If both unknowns are negative, then when the two are multiplied together, the result is positive. (A negative times a negative is always a positive—a basic algebra principle you need to remember.) So xy is positive, and $2xy$, of course, will also be positive—which means it is greater than zero. So the answer to this question is (A): Column A is greater than Column B. The quickest way to determine this is to eliminate what both columns have in common and then compare what's left—which is easy.

Here's another example of the principle of eliminating what the columns share:

Column A	_Column B_
$35 \times 112 \times 76$	$78 \times 56 \times 2 \times 35$

Whatever you do, *don't* start multiplying. It's time-consuming and may lead to a careless mistake—especially if you start rushing. Quantitative comparison items are generally written to minimize calculations, and this question is no exception; you can answer it with no figuring whatsoever. Here's how.

First, notice that both "multiplication chains" have one factor in common—35. Eliminate it from both sides, either mentally or (better still) by physically crossing it out with your pencil. Now the comparison looks like this:

Column A	_Column B_
112×76	$78 \times 56 \times 2$

Now what? Do you have to start multiplying after all? Not if you're observant. The two columns now have something else in common. The term 112 in Column A is exactly the same in value as the two terms 56×2 in Column B! (You can probably "see" this even without calculating it.) So these values can be eliminated from the two columns as well. All that's left to compare now is:

Column A	_Column B_
76	78

ALERT!

In many quantitative comparison items, it's impossible to determine the precise value of one or both quantities. This may tempt you to opt for choice (D), "the relationship cannot be determined." Not necessarily! Even imprecise or vague quantities can sometimes be compared. (You know the Sears Tower is taller than your local post office, even if you don't know the actual height of either building.)

Obviously, Column B is greater. Not a single multiplication is required.

One more example:

Column A	**Column B**
The number of prime numbers between 10 and 30	The number of prime numbers between 20 and 40

To answer this question, you need to figure out how many prime numbers there are between 10 and 30 and how many there are between 20 and 40—right? Not quite. Notice that there is an area of overlap between the range of numbers included in these two groups. Primes between 20 and 30 would fall into *both* categories. Therefore, they can be ignored! All you really need to consider are the primes between 10 and 20 (Column A) and the primes between 30 and 40 (Column B).

If you know the definition of a prime number—a number that can be evenly divided only by itself and 1—enumerating them isn't too difficult. The primes between 10 and 20 are 11, 13, 17, and 19. (Primes greater than 2 must be odd, of course, since all even numbers are divisible by two.) The primes between 30 and 40 are 31 and 37. There are more primes between 10 and 20, so the answer to this item is (A). Notice the time we saved by, in effect, ignoring half of the question—the half that covered the overlap!

Plug in Values for *X*

Many quantitative comparisons include algebra-style unknowns: x, y, a, n, and so on. Often the quantitative comparison item itself will naturally suggest some algebraic operation; we saw an example in the second problem above, where it seemed natural to multiply out the binomials so as to produce a quantity that would be easier to compare with its counterpart.

Once you've taken all the obvious steps, however—multiplying to remove parentheses, simplifying fractions, consolidating like terms, and so on—you will usually still have the mysterious unknown quantity to reckon with. When this happens, take a few seconds to try plugging in a couple of possible values for the unknown and see what happens. Often the correct answer will jump out at you as a result.

Here's an example:

Column A	**Column B**
$3r - 4 > 11$	
5	r

Of course, you need to understand the inequality sign here: it means "is greater than," since it points toward the right side. If $3r - 4$ is greater than 11, what is a possible value of r? Could it be greater than the quantity you're supposed to compare it to, which is 5? Try plugging in an arbitrary value—6, for example—in place of r in the original inequality, and see whether it works:

$$3(6) - 4 > 11$$
$$18 - 4 > 11$$
$$14 > 11$$

Yes, that's correct—14 is greater than 11; so r could equal 6. But to make sure choice (B) is the right answer, also try plugging in a value of r that is less than 5:

$$3(4) - 4 > 11$$
$$12 - 4 > 11$$
$$8 > 11 \quad ? \quad \text{No Way}$$

Or try making r equal to 5 itself:

$$3(5) - 4 > 11$$
$$15 - 4 > 11$$
$$11 > 11 \quad ? \quad \text{No}$$

The value 11 is not greater than *itself*, obviously. So by plugging in three possible values for the unknown—one greater than, one less than, and one equal to the quantity given in the "opposite" column—you can determine that the answer to this question is choice (B).

Note: We've printed out the steps in our calculations here just for clarity's sake, to make it easy for you to follow. But notice how easy the calculations are. Most likely, you won't have to write anything on the test paper at all.

Here's one more example of plugging in numbers:

Column A	*Column B*
	$0 < m < 1$	
$\boxed{m^2}$	$\boxed{m^3}$

NOTE

On the real exam, you *will* have time to plug in possible values on most quantitative comparison items. The math calculations are deliberately kept simple, because the test-makers are more concerned with whether you grasp the underlying arithmetic concepts rather than your ability to carry out the additions, subtractions, multiplications, and divisions. So unless you encounter an unusually complicated problem, don't hesitate to plug in numbers—on most quantitative comparison items you can do the figuring in your head within a few seconds.

Again, we don't know the precise value of the unknown m. It doesn't matter. If you're not sure which of the two comparable quantities is greater, plug in a possible value and see what happens. In this case, we know that m is a positive fraction less than 1. Let's plug in the simplest possible value for m, $\frac{1}{2}$. (That will make the calculations a breeze.) If m is $\frac{1}{2}$, then $m^2 = \left(\frac{1}{2}\right)\left(\frac{1}{2}\right) = \frac{1}{4}$, and $m^3 = \left(\frac{1}{2}\right)\left(\frac{1}{2}\right)\left(\frac{1}{2}\right) = \frac{1}{8}$. Since $\frac{1}{4}$ is greater than $\frac{1}{8}$, Column A is greater.

But before filling in the answer space, stop and ask: Will the answer be different if the value of m is different? In this case, no. If m is $\frac{1}{4}$, $\frac{3}{5}$, $\frac{11}{26}$, or any other positive fraction less than 1, the same relationship will exist—the value continues to go down as the fraction is multiplied repeatedly by itself. (That fact is what the question is designed to test.) But always ask that crucial question, "Will the answer be different if the value of the unknown is different?" when you plug in a number. That way, you won't be misled by an answer that just *happens* to be true with a particular value for x.

THE BEST TIPS
Memorize the Answer System

You should practice quantitative comparisons enough before the day of the test so that the weird multiple-choice answer system begins to feel like second nature. You shouldn't have to read the directions or spend any time during the section thinking about what choices (A), (B), (C), and (D) stand for. And be sure never to absentmindedly fill in choice (E) for any quantitative comparison item! That's an automatic wrong answer.

Look for Math Shortcuts

We've already seen that most quantitative comparisons require few calculations and simple ones. This is deliberate: The test-makers are eager to measure your understanding of the underlying concepts rather than your ability to handle the calculations. (And keeping the math simple allows them to throw more questions at you in the same amount of time!) So avoid lengthy or complicated figuring; if a question seems to require it, you've probably overlooked a built-in shortcut.

Here's an example:

<table>
<tr><td><u>*Column A*</u></td><td><u>*Column B*</u></td></tr>
</table>

The average (arithmetic mean)
of 5 integers *m*, *n*, *o*, *p*, and *q* is 19.

| The average (arithmetic mean) of *m*, *n*, *o*, *p*, *q*, and 17.5 | 19 |

On the principle of "When in doubt, try something," your first instinct may be to start working with the definition of "average." As you know, an average is calculated by taking the sum of a set of numbers and dividing it by the number of numbers in the set. In this case, if five integers have an average of 19, it would be possible to calculate the sum of those integers by multiplying the average by the number of numbers ($19 \times 5 = 95$). Then you could go ahead and calculate the sum of the set of six numbers shown in Column A, with the sixth number 17.5 thrown in, and finally divide that new sum by 6 to come up with the new average.

But stop! None of this is necessary. Look at the quantities being compared. All you need to figure out is whether the new average is more than or less than 19—the old average. Now, what makes the new average different from the old average? It's simply the new member of the set, the sixth number 17.5. And will that new member raise or lower the overall average? Since 17.5 is below the old average, it will drag the average down—it will lower it. Therefore, *with no calculations at all*, you can see that the answer will be choice (B): The old average, 19, is greater than the new average, *whatever it is*.

THE MOST IMPORTANT WARNINGS
Assume Nothing!

Quantitative comparisons are designed to test how quickly, creatively, and accurately you can think about a wide range of what might be called "math situations." As you've seen, these situations can be drawn from every area of math: arithmetic, algebra, geometry, word problems, etc., enabling the test-makers to test your knowledge of techniques in all of these areas. One key aspect of accuracy under these conditions is the ability to separate the *facts* you've been given from the *assumptions* you might make— which may or may not be correct.

Let's consider a few examples.

Column A	Column B

In 1990, the price of
a certain item was $50.00.

The price of the same item in 1998	$50.00

It's tempting to answer this question based on what you know about the real world. Because of the economic phenomenon known as inflation, prices of most things tend to go up over time (though this is not true of everything: computers, for example, have consistently fallen in price during the 1980s and 1990s). Therefore, it's extremely likely that the "certain item" that cost $50.00 in 1990 cost more than that in 1998. The right answer, in that case, would be choice (A).

The logic is tempting—and wrong. You can't assume that inflation applies to this item *because you haven't been told to assume it*. We're not in the "real world" now but rather in SAT territory, where only the facts as stated in the question can be assumed to be true. The correct answer for this item is choice (D)—the relationship can't be determined.

Column A	Column B

Parking is legal on Pine Street only
on even-numbered calendar days.

Number of legal parking days in a calendar month	15

Obviously, the number of legal parking days in a calendar month will be somewhere around 15—since half the days are even-numbered days, and most months have around 30 days. But which month are we talking about? The question doesn't specify, so let's think it through. The month could be January or July, with 31 days, of which 15 are even-numbered (the 2nd, the 4th, the 6th, . . . the 30th); it could be June or September, with 30 days, of which the same 15 are even-numbered. The correct answer then would be choice (C): the number of legal parking days (Column A) would be equal to the number 15 (Column B). But the month could also be February, which has only 28 days (except in leap year), of which just 14 are even-numbered. In that case, the correct answer would be choice (B).

So there are two possible answers—choices (C) and (B)—and we don't know which is correct, because the question doesn't tell us. Sure, there are 11 chances out of 12 that the month is *not* February, but we can't make that assumption. Since choice (C) is correct under one possible assumption and choice (B) is correct under another, the correct answer is choice (D)—it cannot be determined.

One more example of the danger of making assumptions:

Column A	Column B

On a certain day, 30 percent of the girls were absent and 50 percent of the boys were present in a history class.

Number of girls present	Number of boys present

From the information given, you can tell that the percentage of girls present was greater than the percentage of boys present (70 versus 50). But notice what you are being asked to compare, not the percentage of girls and boys present, but the *number* present. We know nothing about this, because we don't know *how many* girls or boys were enrolled in the history class. You might, without much thought, assume that the number of girls and boys is approximately equal—but that's simply an assumption, with no special validity. The correct answer for this item is choice (D)—it cannot be determined.

Strictly speaking, there *are* a few—a very few—facts you can safely assume on quantitative comparison items:

- Everyday facts like the number of inches in a foot and the number of days in a week are fair game.

- The basic formulas from geometry (for calculating the area of a circle or a triangle, for example) are not only assumed but provided as "Reference Information" at the start of each SAT math section. (You should know them by heart, however.)

- And you can assume, as the test-makers state, that all unknowns (like *x*) stand for "real numbers" (as opposed to "imaginary numbers," a special kind of number used only in certain quite specialized and advanced math operations).

Other than these facts, however, you should avoid assuming anything—as you've seen, it's dangerous.

When There's No Unknown, Don't Guess (D)

On quantitative comparison items, as on every other kind of question, there may be times when you have to guess. Perhaps you will find yourself running out of time but with several questions left to answer, or perhaps a couple of items will call for math skills you just can't recall. General guessing strategies for quantitative comparisons should be much the same as for other question types: follow a hunch, if you have one; when you can, eliminate answers and guess from what remains.

NOTE

The real meaning of answer choice (D) is slightly hidden by its wording ("the relationship cannot be determined"). Don't think of it as meaning, "I don't know what the answer is." Instead, think of it as meaning, "More than one answer could be true." If any two answers—(A) and (B), (A) and (C), or (B) and (C)—are both possible, then the correct answer for the item is (D).

However, there's one special rule about guessing that applies only to quantitative comparisons. On about one third of quantitative comparison items, no unknown quantity is involved: there is no algebraic x or n, nor is there any geometric quantity (the degree measure of an angle or the length of a line segment, say) that is unknowable. Whenever this is true, the answer cannot be choice (D). Even if you, for whatever reason, can't figure out which quantity is greater, it is theoretically *possible* to figure it out—so choice (D) is an incorrect option.

Here's an example:

Column A	Column B
Price of a $320 stereo after a discount of 15%	$275

If you've run out of time, or forgotten how to multiply by a percentage, you may not be able to answer this question. (Since $320 × 85% = $272, the answer is choice (B).) However, the question itself does not contain any unknown quantity. Therefore, if you have to guess on a question like this, don't guess, choice (D). Since there is no unknown, only choices (A), (B), and (C) are possible.

What You Need to Know about
Quantitative Comparisons

- Memorize the directions and the answer choices—they are identical for all quantitative comparison questions.

- For each question, compare the boxed quantities.

- Consider all possibilities for any variables.

- Remember that you don't need to do all of the calculations—for most of these questions, you can estimate or use your knowledge of basic mathematical principles.

- Remember that like the rest of the test, quantitative comparisons go from easy to hard.

EXERCISES: QUANTITATIVE COMPARISONS

Exercise 1

35 Questions • Time—35 Minutes

Directions: For each of the following questions, two quantities are given—one in Column A, the other in Column B. Compare the two quantities and mark your answer sheet as follows:

(A) if the quantity in Column A is greater

(B) if the quantity in Column B is greater

(C) if the quantities are equal

(D) if the relationship cannot be determined from the information given

Notes:

(1) Information concerning one or both of the compared quantities will be centered above the two columns for some items.

(2) Symbols that appear in both columns represent the same thing in Column A as in Column B.

(3) Letters such as x, n, and k are symbols for real numbers.

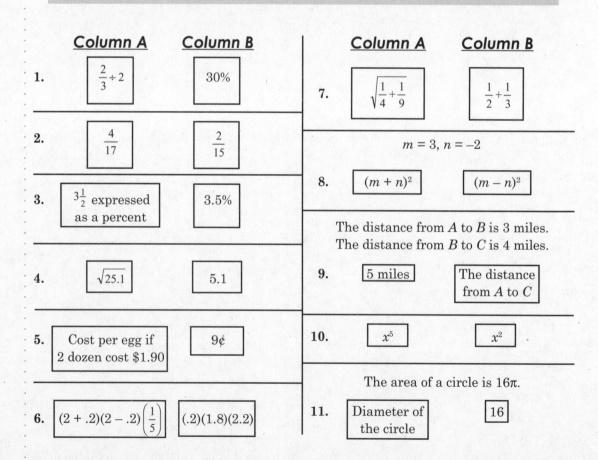

	Column A	Column B
1.	$\frac{2}{3} \div 2$	30%
2.	$\frac{4}{17}$	$\frac{2}{15}$
3.	$3\frac{1}{2}$ expressed as a percent	3.5%
4.	$\sqrt{25.1}$	5.1
5.	Cost per egg if 2 dozen cost $1.90	9¢
6.	$(2 + .2)(2 - .2)\left(\frac{1}{5}\right)$	$(.2)(1.8)(2.2)$

	Column A	Column B
7.	$\sqrt{\frac{1}{4} + \frac{1}{9}}$	$\frac{1}{2} + \frac{1}{3}$

$m = 3, n = -2$

	Column A	Column B
8.	$(m + n)^2$	$(m - n)^2$

The distance from A to B is 3 miles.
The distance from B to C is 4 miles.

	Column A	Column B
9.	5 miles	The distance from A to C
10.	x^5	x^2

The area of a circle is 16π.

	Column A	Column B
11.	Diameter of the circle	16

Column A	Column B

The average of 5 numbers is 20.

12. The sum of the 5 numbers | 110

13. $\dfrac{1}{.5}$ | $\dfrac{1}{.05}$

14. $.1\pi$ | $\sqrt{.9}$

15. Area of a square having perimeter 32 | Area of a circle having radius 5

$x = 8 = y^2 - 1$

16. x | y

$a^2 = 49$

17. a | 7

$a > b > 0$

18. $\dfrac{1}{a}$ | $\dfrac{1}{b}$

$(2)(2)(a) = (3)(3)(3)$

19. a | 2

$-4 < x < -2$

20. $\dfrac{1}{x^4}$ | $\dfrac{1}{x^5}$

21. $(16)(351)(10)$ | $(15)(351)(11)$

$a^2 > 0$

22. a | 0

Column A	Column B

23. A single discount of 10% | Two successive discounts of 5% and 5%

24. 50% | $\dfrac{1}{.02}$

25. Time elapsed from 11:50 p.m. to 12:02 a.m. | $\dfrac{1}{3}$ hour

The diagram below applies to problems 26–29.

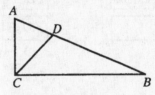

$\overline{AC} \cong \overline{CD} \cong \overline{AD}; \quad \overline{AC} \perp \overline{CB}$

26. CD | DB

27. $\angle A$ | $\angle B$

28. CD | CB

29. AD | DB

Questions 30–31 refer to the figure below.

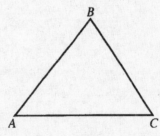

$\overline{AB} \cong \overline{BC}$ Angle B < Angle A

30. $\angle B$ | $\angle C$

31. AB | AC

Column A   **Column B**   **Column A**   **Column B**

Questions 32–34 refer to the figure below.

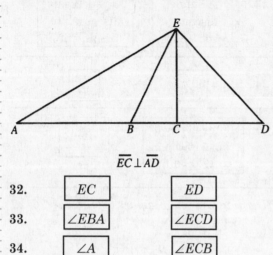

$$\overline{EC} \perp \overline{AD}$$

32. | EC | | ED |

33. | $\angle EBA$ | | $\angle ECD$ |

34. | $\angle A$ | | $\angle ECB$ |

$$a > 0, \, b > 0, \, \frac{a}{b} < 1$$

35. | a | | b |

Exercise 2

15 Questions • Time—15 Minutes

Directions: For each of the following questions, two quantities are given—one in Column A, the other in Column B. Compare the two quantities and mark your answer sheet as follows:

(A) if the quantity in Column A is greater

(B) if the quantity in Column B is greater

(C) if the quantities are equal

(D) if the relationship cannot be determined from the information given

Notes:

(1) Information concerning one or both of the compared quantities will be centered above the two columns for some items.

(2) Symbols that appear in both columns represent the same thing in Column A as in Column B.

(3) Letters such as x, n, and k are symbols for real numbers.

Column A	Column B		Column A	Column B

Questions 1–3 apply to the figure below.

Questions 4–6 apply to the figure below.

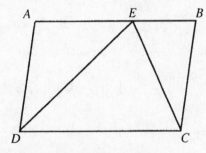

ABCD is a parallelogram.
E is any point on $\overline{AB}$.

Radius of outer circle = 10
Radius of inner circle = 5

	Column A	Column B
1.	Twice the area of triangle *DEC*	Area of parallelogram *ABCD*
2.	$\angle A$	$\angle B$
3.	*AD*	*DC*

	Column A	Column B
4.	Twice area of inner circle	Area of shaded portion
5.	Area of inner circle	75
6.	Circumference of inner circle	50% of circumference of outer circle

	Column A	Column B
7.	105% of 200	50% of 400
8.	35%	$\dfrac{0.7}{2}$

$6x = 3y = 2z$

	Column A	Column B
9.	x	z

$a > b > c$

	Column A	Column B
10.	$2a$	$b + c$

$\dfrac{1}{x} > 1$

	Column A	Column B
11.	x	1

	Column A	Column B
	$\dfrac{1}{x} < 0$	
12.	x	0
13.	The percent of increase from $10 to $12	The percent of increase from $20 to $22
14.	Sylvia's average rate if she drives 100 miles in 2 hours 30 minutes	Gloria's average rate if she drives 20 miles in 30 minutes

$m > 0, n > 0$

	Column A	Column B
15.	$(m + n)^2$	$m^2 + n^2$

ANSWER KEYS AND EXPLANATIONS

Exercise 1

1.	A	8.	B	15.	B	22.	D	29.	C
2.	A	9.	D	16.	A	23.	A	30.	B
3.	A	10.	D	17.	D	24.	B	31.	A
4.	B	11.	B	18.	B	25.	B	32.	B
5.	B	12.	B	19.	A	26.	C	33.	A
6.	C	13.	B	20.	A	27.	A	34.	B
7.	B	14.	B	21.	B	28.	B	35.	B

1. **The correct answer is (A).**

$$\frac{2}{3} \div 2 = \frac{2}{3} \cdot \frac{1}{2} = \frac{1}{3} = 33\frac{1}{3}\%$$

2. **The correct answer is (A).** To compare $\frac{a}{b}$ with $\frac{c}{d}$, compare ad with bc. If $ad < bc$, then the first fraction is smaller. If $ad = bc$, the fractions are equal. If $ad > bc$, then the first fraction is larger. 4 times 15 is greater than 17 times 2. Therefore, the first fraction is greater.

3. **The correct answer is (A).**

$$3\frac{1}{2} = 3.5 = 350\%$$

4. **The correct answer is (B).**

$$(5.1)^2 = 26.01$$
$$(\sqrt{25.1})^2 = 25.1$$

5. **The correct answer is (B).** There are 24 eggs in 2 dozen.

$$24\overline{)1.90} \quad .079$$
$$\underline{1\ 68}$$
$$220$$

Each egg costs almost 8 cents.

6. **The correct answer is (C).**

$$2 + .2 = 2.2$$
$$2 - .2 = 1.8$$
$$\frac{1}{5} = .2$$

Factors on both sides are the same.

7. **The correct answer is (B).**

$$\sqrt{\frac{1}{4} + \frac{1}{9}} = \sqrt{\frac{13}{36}} = \frac{\sqrt{13}}{6}$$
$$\frac{1}{2} + \frac{1}{3} = \frac{5}{6}$$

8. **The correct answer is (B).**

$$(m+n)^2 = (1)^2 = 1$$
$$(m-n)^2 = (5)^2 = 25$$

9. **The correct answer is (D).** There is no indication as to the direction from B to C.

10. **The correct answer is (D).** If $x > 1$, A is bigger. If $x = 1$, A and B are equal. If $x < 0$, B is bigger.

11. **The correct answer is (B).**

$$\text{Area of a circle} = \pi r^2$$
$$16\pi = \pi r^2$$
$$16 = r^2$$
$$r = 4$$
$$\text{diameter} = 8$$

12. **The correct answer is (B).** If the average is 20, then the 5 numbers were added and the sum divided by 5 to give 20. The sum of these numbers must be 100.

13. **The correct answer is (B).**

$$\frac{1}{.5} = \frac{10}{5} = 2$$
$$\frac{1}{.05} = \frac{100}{5} = 20$$

14. The correct answer is (B).

$$.1(3.14) = .314$$

$$\sqrt{9} \approx .949$$

15. The correct answer is (B). Each side of the square is 8. Area of the square is 64. Area of the circle is 25π. $25(3.14)$ is greater than 64.

16. The correct answer is (A).

$$8 = y^2 - 1$$

$$9 = y^2$$

$$y = 3 \text{ or } -3$$

Since $x = 8$, x is greater for either value of y.

17. The correct answer is (D). a may be either 7 or −7.

18. The correct answer is (B). When fractions have equal numerators, the fraction having the smaller denominator has the greater value.

19. The correct answer is (A).

$$4a = 27 \quad a = 6\frac{3}{4}$$

20. The correct answer is (A). Since x is negative, any even power of x is positive, while any odd power of x is negative.

21. The correct answer is (B). Because it is true that $(16)(10)$ is less than $(15)(11)$.

22. The correct answer is (D). If a^2 is positive, a can be either negative or positive.

23. The correct answer is (A). Consider a marked price of $100. A single discount of 10% gives $10 off. An initial discount of 5% gives $5 off, making the new price $95. The second 5% discount is 5% of $95 or $4.75, making the total discount only $5 + $4.75 or $9.75.

24. The correct answer is (B).

$$50\% = \frac{1}{2}$$

$$\frac{1}{.02} = \frac{100}{2} = 50$$

25. The correct answer is (B). From 11:50 p.m. to 12:02 a.m. is 12 minutes. One third of an hour is 20 minutes.

26. The correct answer is (C).

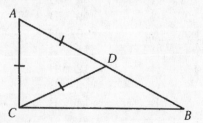

Triangle ACD is equilateral, making each angle 60°. Angle DCB is then 30°, and angle CDB is 120°, leaving 30° for angle B. Therefore, triangle DCB is isosceles.

27. The correct answer is (A). Angle A is 60° and angle B is 30°.

28. The correct answer is (B). In triangle CDB, CD is opposite a 30° angle, while CB is opposite 120°.

29. The correct answer is (C). Both of these segments are equal to CD.

30. The correct answer is (B). Since $\angle A$ and $\angle C$ must be equal, because the sides opposite are congruent, $\angle B$ is also less than $\angle C$.

31. The correct answer is (A). Since $\angle B$ is less than $\angle C$, AC will be less than AB.

32. The correct answer is (B). The shortest distance from a point to a line is the perpendicular.

33. The correct answer is (A). Angle EBA is an exterior angle of triangle EBC and is therefore greater than angle ECB. Since angle ECD is also a right angle, angle EBA will be greater than angle ECD.

34. The correct answer is (B). Triangle ECA has a right angle. Since there will be 90° left to divide between the two remaining angles, angle A must be less than 90°.

35. The correct answer is (B). If $\frac{a}{b} < 1$, the denominator must be greater than the numerator.

Exercise 2

1. C	4. B	7. A	10. A	13. A	
2. D	5. A	8. C	11. B	14. C	
3. D	6. C	9. D	12. B	15. A	

1. **The correct answer is (C).** The altitude of triangle EDC is equal to the altitude of the parallelogram. Both the triangle and the parallelogram have the same base. Since the area of a triangle is $\frac{1}{2}bh$ and the area of a parallelogram is bh, these quantities are equal.

2. **The correct answer is (D).** There is no way to tell which is greater.

3. **The correct answer is (D).** There is no way to tell which is greater.

4. **The correct answer is (B).**

   Area of outer circle = $\pi r^2 = 100\pi$

   Area of inner circle = 25π

   Shaded portion is outer circle minus inner circle, or 75π.

5. **The correct answer is (A).** Area of inner circle = $\pi r^2 = 25\pi$. 25(3.14) is more than 75π.

6. **The correct answer is (C).**

   Circumference = πd

   Circumference of outer circle = $\pi (20)$

   Circumference of inner circle = $\pi (10)$

   $50\% = \frac{1}{2}$

   $\frac{1}{2}$ of outer circumference = 10π

7. **The correct answer is (A).** 105% of 200 is more than 200.

   50% or $\frac{1}{2}$ of 400 is 200.

8. **The correct answer is (C).**

   $35\% = .35$

   $\frac{0.7}{2} = .35$

9. **The correct answer is (D).** If $6x = 2z$,

then $3x = z$, or $x = \frac{1}{3}z$. If either x or z is zero, both quantities are equal; if both are positive, z is larger. If both are negative, x is larger.

10. **The correct answer is (A).**

    $a > b$

    $\underline{a > c}$

    $2a > b + c$

11. **The correct answer is (B).** If $\frac{1}{x} > 1$, multiply each side by x to get $1 > x$. There should be no concern about reversing the inequality, as x must be positive if $\frac{1}{x} > 1$.

12. **The correct answer is (B).** If $\frac{1}{x}$ is to be negative, x must be negative, since a positive number divided by a negative number gives a negative quotient. 0 is larger than any negative number.

13. **The correct answer is (A).**

    Percent of increase = $\frac{\text{Amount of increase}}{\text{Original}} \bullet 100$

    The percent of increase in A is $\frac{2}{10} \bullet 100$.

    The percent of increase in B is $\frac{2}{10}$, or $\frac{1}{10} \bullet 100$.

14. **The correct answer is (C).**

    Average rate = $\frac{\text{Total distance}}{\text{Total time}}$

    Sylvia's average rate = $\frac{100}{2.5} = 40$

    Gloria's average rate = $\frac{20}{.5} = 40$

15. **The correct answer is (A).** $(m + n)^2 = m^2 + 2mn + n^2$. Since m and n are both positive, $2mn$ is positive.

SAT Grid-In Strategies

OVERVIEW
- Understand why grid-ins are easier than you think
- Know how to record your answers
- Understand why guessing on grid-ins can't hurt you
- Review what you need to know about grid-ins
- Practice your skills with grid-in exercises

WHY GRID-INS ARE EASIER THAN YOU THINK

You should be pretty good at filling in ovals by now, right? Here comes a new angle—grid-ins. These are officially named "student-produced responses," because you have to do the calculations and find the answer on your own; there are no multiple-choice answers to choose from. These special grids are the way to let the SAT people know which answer you came up with.

Many students get intimidated by grid-ins. Don't be! Grid-in questions test the exact same mathematical concepts as multiple-choice math. And there are only 10 of them to deal with, arranged in order from easy to hard. So you should only expect to have difficulty with a couple of questions.

SAT Grid-In Questions

As we indicated, the scored portion of the SAT contains 10 grid-in questions. They are all grouped together in a single math section, where they are numbered from 16 through 25 (Questions 1 through 15 are quantitative comparisons).

Grid-ins test the same mix of arithmetic, algebra, and geometry concepts that are tested by multiple-choice math questions. The only difference is that there are no answer choices.

TAKE A LOOK AT A GRID

The special answer grid has some very different sections. There are blank boxes at the top so you can actually write in your answer. Below the boxes are some ovals that have fraction slashes and decimal points. You fill these in if your answer needs them. The largest section has ovals with numbers in them. You have to fill in the ovals to correspond to the answer you have written in the boxes.

Yes, it's a lot to think about, but once you understand how to use them it's not a big deal. Here is a sample grid:

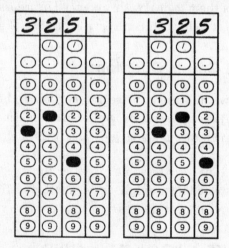

HOW TO RECORD YOUR ANSWERS

On the SAT, each set of grid-in questions starts with directions that look approximately like this:

> **Directions:** Solve each of these problems. Write the answer in the corresponding grid on the answer sheet and fill in the ovals beneath each answer you write. Here are some examples.

Note: A mixed number such as $3\frac{1}{2}$ must be gridded as 7/2 or as 3.5. If gridded as "3 1/2," it will read as "thirty-one halves."

Note: Either position is correct.

Once you get these rules down pat, you can concentrate just on solving the math problems in this section.

GRIDDING: GETTING IT RIGHT

1. Write your answer in the boxes at the top of the grid.

2. Mark the corresponding ovals, one per column.

3. Start in any column.

4. Work with decimals or fractions.

5. Express mixed numbers as decimals or improper fractions.

6. If more than one answer is possible, grid any one.

Now let's look at these rules in more detail:

1. Write your answer in the boxes at the top of the grid. Technically, this isn't required by the SAT. Realistically, it gives you something to follow as you fill in the ovals. Do it—it will help you.

2. Make sure to mark the ovals that correspond to the answer you entered in the boxes, one per column. The machine that scores the test can only read the ovals, so if you don't fill them in, you won't get credit. Just entering your answer in the boxes is not enough!

3. You can start entering your answer in any column, if space permits. Unused columns should be left blank; don't put in zeroes. Look at this example:

Here are two ways to enter an answer of "150."

4. You can write your answer as a decimal or as a fraction. In other words, an answer can be expressed as $\frac{3}{4}$ or as .75. You don't have to put a zero in front of a decimal that is less than 1. Just remember that you have only four spaces to work with and that a decimal point or a fraction slash uses up one of the spaces.

NOTE

Don't use a comma in a number larger than 999. Just fill in the four digits and the corresponding ovals. You only have ovals for numbers, decimal points, and fraction slashes; there aren't any for commas.

For decimal answers, be as accurate as possible but keep it within four spaces. Say you get an answer of .1777; here are your options:

Answers .177 and .178 would both be marked as correct.

 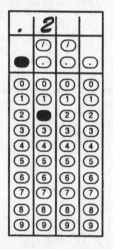

Answers .18 or .2 would be marked wrong because they could have been written more accurately in the space provided.

Fractions do not have to be simplified to simplest form unless they don't fit in the answer grid. For example, you can grid $\frac{4}{10}$, but you can't grid $\frac{12}{16}$ because you'd need five spaces. So, you would simplify it and grid $\frac{3}{4}$.

5 A mixed number has to be expressed as a decimal or as an improper fraction. If you tried to grid $1\frac{3}{4}$, it would be scored as $\frac{13}{4}$, which would give you a wrong answer. Instead, you could grid the answer as 1.75 or as $\frac{7}{4}$.

The above answers are acceptable.

The above answer is unacceptable.

6 Sometimes the problems in this section will have more than one correct answer. Choose one and grid it.

For example, if a question asks for a prime number between 5 and 13, the answer could be 7 or 11. Grid 7 or grid 11, but don't put in both answers.

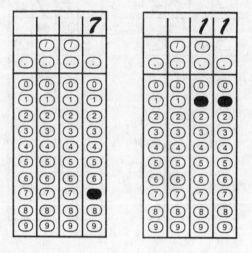

Either answer is acceptable, but not both.

GUESSING ON GRID-INS CAN'T HURT YOU

Unfortunately, you cannot receive partial credit for grid-ins. Your answers are either completely correct or completely wrong. But no points are deducted for incorrect responses, so guessing is better than leaving a question blank.

What You Need to Know about Grid-Ins

- When you grid answers to student-produced response questions, follow these rules:

    1. Write your answer in the boxes at the top of the grid.

    2. Mark the corresponding ovals, one per column.

    3. Start in any column.

    4. Work with decimals or fractions.

    5. Express mixed numbers as decimals or improper fractions.

    6. If more than one answer is possible, grid any one.

- Remember that grid-ins test the same concepts as multiple-choice math.

- Because there are only 10 grid-ins per test, you should be able to answer almost all of them correctly.

- The most important advice for grid-ins? Don't be intimidated.

EXERCISES: GRID-INS

Exercise 1

10 Questions • Time—15 Minutes

Directions: Solve each of these problems. Write the answer in the corresponding grid on the answer sheet and fill in the ovals beneath each answer you write. Here are some examples.

Answer: $\frac{3}{4}$ (=.75; show answer either way)　　　**Answer:** 325

Note: A mixed number such as $3\frac{1}{2}$ must be gridded as 7/2 or as 3.5. If gridded as "3 1/2," it will be read as "thirty-one halves."

Note: Either position is correct.

1. Simplified to a simplest fraction, what part of a dime is a quarter?

2. Marion is paid $24 for 5 hours of work in the school office. Janet works 3 hours and makes $10.95. How much more per hour does Marion make than Janet? (Ignore the dollar sign in gridding your answer.)

3. If the outer diameter of a cylindrical oil tank is 54.28 inches and the inner diameter is 48.7 inches, what is the thickness of the wall of the tank, in inches?

4. What number added to 40% of itself is equal to 84?

5. If $r = 25 - s$, what is the value of $4(r + s)$?

exercises

214

PART IV: SAT Math Strategies

6. A plane flies over Denver at 11:20 a.m. It passes over Coolidge, 120 miles from Denver, at 11:32 a.m. Find the rate of the plane in miles per hour.

7. 53% of the 1,000 students at Jackson High are girls. How many boys are there in the school?

8. How many digits are there in the square root of a perfect square of 12 digits?

9. In May, Carter's Appliances sold 40 washing machines. In June, because of a special promotion, the store sold 80 washing machines. What is the percent of increase in the number of washing machines sold?

10. Find the value of $(3\sqrt{2})^2$.

www.petersons.com/arco

Master the SAT

Exercise 2

6 Questions • Time—8 Minutes

> **Directions:** Solve each of these problems. Write the answer in the corresponding grid on the answer sheet and fill in the ovals beneath each answer you write. Here are some examples.

Answer: $\frac{3}{4}$ (=.75; show answer either way)   **Answer: 325**

Note: A mixed number such as $3\frac{1}{2}$ must be gridded as 7/2 or as 3.5. If gridded as "3 1/2", it will be read as "thirty-one halves."

Note: Either position is correct.

1. If $\frac{3}{8}$ is added to $\frac{3}{8}$, what is the result?

2. If $2^{n-3} = 32$, what is the value of n?

3. In a group of 40 students, 25 applied to Columbia and 30 applied to Cornell. If 3 students applied to neither Columbia nor Cornell, how many students applied to both schools?

4. If $x^2 - y^2 = 100$ and $x - y = 20$, what is the value of $x + y$?

5. A gallon of water is added to 6 quarts of a solution that is 50% acid. What percent of the new solution is acid?

6. A gasoline tank is $\frac{1}{4}$ full. After adding 10 gallons of gasoline, the gauge indicates that the tank is $\frac{2}{3}$ full. Find the capacity of the tank in gallons.

ANSWER EXPLANATIONS

Exercise 1

1. $\frac{25}{10} = \frac{5}{2}$ **(answer)**

2. Marion's hourly wage is $\frac{\$24}{5}$ or $4.80.

   Janet's hourly wage is $\frac{\$10.95}{3}$ or $3.65.

   $4.80 − $3.65 = $1.15 **(answer)**

3. The difference of 5.58 must be divided between both ends. The thickness on each side is 2.79 **(answer)**.

4. $x + .40x = 84$
   $1.40x = 84$
   $14x = 840$
   $x = 60$ **(answer)**

5. $r + s = 25$
   $4(r + s) = 4(25) = 100$ **(answer)**

6. The plane covers 120 miles in 12 minutes or $\frac{1}{5}$ hour. In $\frac{5}{5}$ or 1 hour, it covers $5(120)$, or 600 miles. 600 **(answer)**

7. 47% of 1000 are boys.

   $(.47)(1000) = 470$ boys **(answer)**

8. For every pair of digits in a number, there will be one digit in the square root.

   6 **(answer)**

9. Increase of 40

   Percent of Increase =

   [Amount of Increase/Original] × 100%

   $\frac{40}{40} \times 100\% = 100\%$ **(answer)**

10. $(3\sqrt{2})(3\sqrt{2}) = 9 \times 2 = 18$ **(answer)**

Exercise 2

1. $\frac{3}{8} + \frac{3}{8} = \frac{6}{8}$ or $\frac{3}{4}$ **(answers; both acceptable)**

2. $2^{n-3} = 2^5$
   $n - 3 = 5$
   $n = 8$ **(answer)**

3.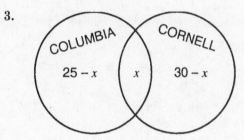

   $25 - x + x + 30 - x = 37$
   $55 - x = 37$
   $18 = x$
   18 **(answer)**

4. $x^2 - y^2 = (x - y)(x + y)$
   $100 = 20(x + y)$
   $5 = (x + y)$
   5 **(answer)**

5.

	No. of quarts	% acid	Amount = of acid
Original	6	.50	3
Added	4	0	0
New	10		3

   $\frac{3}{10} = 30\%$ **(answer)**

6. 10 gallons is $\frac{2}{3} - \frac{1}{4}$ of the tank.

   $\frac{2}{3} - \frac{1}{4} = \frac{8-3}{12} = \frac{5}{12}$
   $\frac{5}{12}x = 10$
   $5x = 120$
   $x = 24$ **(answer)**

PART V

SAT VOCABULARY PREP COURSE

How Word Parts Work

OVERVIEW

- **Learn how words are built**
- **Learn how word parts work**
- **Learn common word parts to boost your SAT vocabulary**
- **Practice your skills with word parts exercises**

The SAT isn't a spelling test, and it isn't a "vocabulary bee." It is, however, a test of how much you *know* about vocabulary—how words are formed and the meanings of their parts. If you want to increase that knowledge (and increase your score), you'll want to learn about the structure of words. This will help you figure out the meanings of unfamiliar words you come across in the verbal section of the SAT. In this chapter, you learn the basics of how words are built, what word parts mean, and how they work together. You'll also get a crash-course list of common word parts that will help you understand the meanings of words you may encounter (maybe for the first time) on the SAT. The exercises at the end of this chapter help you practice your vocabulary skills, so you'll be ready to score high on the verbal sections of the SAT.

HOW WORDS ARE BUILT

Knowing what the parts of words mean is the key to deciphering words you've never seen before. Let's take a look at the word *biography* and its parts. You know that a biography is something written about a person's life. How do the word parts tell you this? Well, the second part of the word, *graphy*, comes from a Greek word that means "writing." The first part of the word, *bio*, is also from Greek and it means "life." Put them both together and you get . . . *biography*, the story of a person's life. If you add the Latin word for "self"—*auto*—you get . . . *autobiography*, a story you write about your own life. Think about some other words that use one or more of these parts, like *automobile*, *biochemistry*, and *autograph*. Can you see how the meaning fits the word parts?

chapter 11

THE THREE BASIC WORD PARTS AND HOW THEY WORK

Different kinds of word parts work together to make a fully functioning word. Think about it: If your car is going to do more than just sit there, it needs a collection of parts put together in the right way. Two steering wheels won't do you any good if you don't have a gas tank.

Each kind of word part has a specific purpose. There are three basic types of word parts:

1 **Prefixes**—These parts attach to the beginning of a root word to alter its meaning or create a new word.

2 **Suffixes**—These parts attach to the end of a root word to change its meaning, help make it grammatically correct in context, or form a new word.

3 **Roots**—The basic element of a word that determines its meaning. Groups of words from the same root word are called word families.

A word can have a root, a prefix, and a suffix; it can have a root and two suffixes or a root and one prefix. The possibilities are endless (almost), but you must always have a root.

Use the word list that follows to expand your word horizons. Once you begin to learn the word parts on the list, you'll be able to take apart unfamiliar words like a master mechanic. As you make your way through the list, try to think of other words with the same parts. If you have time, check their meanings in a dictionary and take a look at the word origins in the entry.

When you know some common word parts and how they work, you have a formula for deciphering unfamiliar words. Just divide the word into its parts, then use the information you learn in this chapter to determine what the parts mean and how they work. Then, you're well on your way to recognizing the meaning of the word.

LIST OF COMMON WORD PARTS
Prefixes

Prefix	Meaning	Example
a-	in, on, of, to	*abed*—in bed
a-, ab-, abs-	from, away	*abrade*—wear off
		absent—away, not present
a-, an-	lacking, not	*asymptomatic*—showing no symptoms
		anaerobic—able to live without air
ac-, ad-, af-, ag-, al-, an-, ap-, ar-, as-, at-	to, toward	*accost*—approach and speak to
		adjunct—something added to
		aggregate—bring together
ambi-, amphi-	around, both	*ambidextrous*—using both hands equally
		amphibious—living both in water and on land
ana-	up, again, anew, throughout	*analyze*—loosen up, break up into parts
		anagram—word spelled by mixing up letters of another word
ante-	before	*antediluvian*—before the flood
anti-	against	*antiwar*—against war
arch-	first, chief	*archetype*—first model
auto-	self	*automobile*—self-moving vehicle
bene-, ben-	good, well	*benefactor*—one who does good deeds
bi-	two	*bilateral*—two-sided
circum-	around	*circumnavigate*—sail around
com-, co-, col-, con-, cor-	with, together	*concentrate*—bring closer together
		cooperate—work with
		collapse—fall together

Prefix	Meaning	Example
contra-, contro-, counter-	against	*contradict*—speak against *counterclockwise*—against the clock
de-	away from, down, opposite of	*detract*—draw away from
demi-	half	*demitasse*—half cup
di-	twice, double	*dichromatic*—having two colors
dia-	across, through	*diameter*—measurement across
dis-, di-	not, away from	*dislike*—to not like *digress*—turn away from the subject
dys-	bad, poor	*dyslexia*—poor reading
equi-	equal	*equivalent*—of equal value
ex-, e-, ef-	from, out	*expatriate*—one who lives outside his or her native country *emit*—send out
extra-	outside, beyond	*extraterrestrial*—from beyond the earth
fore-	in front of, previous	*forecast*—tell ahead of time *foreleg*—front leg
geo-	earth	*geography*—science of the earth's surface
homo-	same, like	*homophonic*—sounding the same
hyper-	too much, over	*hyperactive*—overly active
hypo-	too little, under	*hypothermia*—state of having too little body heat
in-, il-, ig-, im-, ir-	not	*innocent*—not guilty *ignorant*—not knowing *illogical*—not logical *irresponsible*—not responsible
in-, il-, im-, ir-	on, into, in	*impose*—place on *invade*—go into

Prefix	Meaning	Example
inter-	between, among	*interplanetary*—between planets
intra-, intro-	within, inside	*intrastate*—within a state
mal-, male-	bad, wrong, poor	*maladjusted*—adjust poorly *malevolent*—ill-wishing
mis-	badly, wrongly	*misunderstand*—understand wrongly
mis-, miso-	hatred	*misogyny*—hatred of women
mono-	single, one	*monorail*—train that runs on a single rail
neo-	new	*neolithic*—of the New Stone Age
non-	not	*nonentity*—a nobody
ob-	over, against, toward	*obstruct*—stand against
omni-	all	*omnipresent*—present in all places
pan-	all	*panorama*—a complete view
peri-	around, near	*periscope*—device for seeing all around
poly-	many	*polygonal*—many-sided
post-	after	*postmortem*—after death
pre-	before, earlier than	*prejudice*—judgment in advance
pro-	in favor of, forward, in front of	*proceed*—go forward *prowar*—in favor of war
re-	back, again	*rethink*—think again *reimburse*—pay back
retro-	backward	*retrospective*—looking backward
se-	apart, away	*seclude*—keep away
semi-	half	*semiconscious*—half conscious
sub-, suc-, suf-, sug-, sus-	under, beneath	*subscribe*—write underneath *suspend*—hang down *suffer*—undergo
super-	above, greater	*superfluous*—overflowing, beyond what is needed

Prefix	Meaning	Example
syn-, sym-, syl-, sys-	with, at the same time	*synthesis*—a putting together *sympathy*—a feeling with
tele-	far	*television*—machine for seeing far
trans-	across	*transport*—carry across a distance
un-	not	*uninformed*—not informed
vice-	acting for, next in rank to	*viceroy*—one acting for the king

Suffixes

Suffix	Meaning	Example
-able, -ble	able, capable	*acceptable*—able to be accepted
-acious, -cious	characterized by, having quality of the	*fallacious*—having the quality of a fallacy
-age	sum, total	*mileage*—total number of miles
-al	of, like, suitable for	*theatrical*—suitable for theater
-ance, -ancy	act or state of	*disturbance*—act of disturbing
-ant, -ent	one who	*defendant*—one who defends him- or herself
-ary, -ar	having the nature of, concerning	*military*—relating to soldiers *polar*—concerning the pole
-cy	act, state, or position of	*presidency*—position of president *ascendancy*—state of being raised up
-dom	state, rank, that which belongs to	*wisdom*—state of being wise
-ence	act, state, or quality of	*dependence*—state of depending
-er, -or	one who, that which	*doer*—one who does *conductor*—that which conducts

Suffix	Meaning	Example
-escent	becoming	*obsolescent*—becoming obsolete
-fy	to make	*pacify*—make peaceful
-hood	state, condition	*adulthood*—state of being adult
-ic, -ac	of, like	*demonic*—of or like a demon
-il, -ile	having to do with, like, suitable for	*civil*—having to do with citizens *tactile*—having to do with touch
-ion	act or condition of	*operation*—act of operating
-ious	having, characterized by	*anxious*—characterized by anxiety
-ish	like, somewhat	*foolish*—like a fool
-ism	belief or practice of	*racism*—belief in racial superiority
-ist	one who does, makes, or is concerned with	*scientist*—one concerned with science
-ity, -ty, -y	character or state of being	*amity*—friendship *jealousy*—state of being jealous
-ive	of, relating to, tending to	*destructive*—tending to destroy
-logue, -loquy	speech or writing	*monologue*—speech by one person *colloquy*—conversation
-logy	speech, study of	*geology*—study of the Earth
-ment	act or state of	*abandonment*—act of abandoning
-mony	a resulting thing, condition, or state	*patrimony*—property inherited from one's father
-ness	act or quality	*kindness*—quality of being kind
-ory	having the quality of	*compensatory*—having the quality of a place or thing for compensation *lavatory*—place for washing

Suffix	Meaning	Example
-ous, -ose	full of, having	*glamorous*—full of glamour
-ship	skill, state of being	*horsemanship*—skill in riding
		ownership—state of being an owner
-some	full of, like	*frolicsome*—playful
-tude	state or quality of	*rectitude*—state of being morally upright
-ward	in the direction of	*homeward*—in the direction of home
-y	full of, like, somewhat	*wily*—full of wiles

Roots

Root	Meaning	Examples
acr	bitter	*acrid, acrimony*
act, ag	do, act, drive	*action, react, agitate*
acu	sharp, keen	*acute, acumen*
agog	leader	*pedagogue, demagogic*
agr	field	*agronomy, agriculture*
ali	other	*alias, alienate, inalienable*
alt	high	*altitude, contralto*
alter, altr	other, change	*alternative, altercation, altruism*
am, amic	love, friend	*amorous, amiable*
anim	mind, life, spirit	*animism, animate, animosity*
annu, enni	year	*annual, superannuated, biennial*
anthrop	man	*anthropoid, misanthropy*
apt, ept	fit	*apt, adapt, ineptitude*
aqu	water	*aquatic, aquamarine*
arbit	judge	*arbiter, arbitrary*
arch	chief	*anarchy, matriarch*
arm	arm, weapon	*army, armature, disarm*
art	skill, a fitting together	*artisan, artifact, articulate*
aster, astr	star	*asteroid, disaster, astral*
aud, audit, aur	hear	*auditorium, audition, auricle*
aur	gold	*aureate, Aureomycin*

Root	Meaning	Examples
aut	self	*autism, autograph*
bell	war	*antebellum, belligerent*
ben, bene	well, good	*benevolent, benefit*
bibli	book	*bibliography, bibliophile*
bio	life	*biosphere, amphibious*
brev	short	*brevity, abbreviation*
cad, cas, cid	fall	*cadence, casualty, occasion, accident*
cand	white, shining	*candid, candle, incandescent*
cant, chant	sing, charm	*cantor, recant, enchant*
cap, capt, cept, cip	take, seize, hold	*capable, captive, accept, incipient*
capit	head	*capital, decapitate, recapitulate*
carn	flesh	*carnal, incarnate*
cede, ceed, cess	go, yield	*secede, exceed, process, intercession*
cent	hundred	*percentage, centimeter*
cern, cert	perceive, make certain, decide	*concern, certificate, certain*
chrom	color	*monochrome, chromatic*
chron	time	*chronometer, anachronism*
cide, cis	cut, kill	*genocide, incision*
cit	summon, impel	*cite, excite, incitement*
civ	citizen	*uncivil, civilization*
clam, claim	shout	*clamorous, proclaim, claimant*
clar	clear	*clarity, clarion, declare*
clin	slope, lean	*inclination, recline*
clud, clus, clos	close, shut	*seclude, recluse, closet*
cogn	know	*recognize, incognito*
col, cul	till	*colony, cultivate, agriculture*
corp	body	*incorporate, corpse*
cosm	order, world	*cosmetic, cosmos, cosmopolitan*
crac, crat	power, rule	*democrat, theocracy*
cre, cresc, cret	grow	*increase, crescent, accretion*
cred	trust, believe	*credit, incredible*

Root	Meaning	Examples
crux, cruc	cross	crux, crucial, crucifix
crypt	hidden	cryptic, cryptography
culp	blame	culprit, culpability
cur, curr, curs	run, course	occur, current, incursion
cura	care	curator, accurate
cycl	wheel, circle	bicycle, cyclone
dec	ten	decade, decimal
dem	people	demographic, demagogue
dent	tooth	dental, indentation
derm	skin	dermatitis, pachyderm
di, dia	day	diary, quotidian
dic, dict	say, speak	indicative, edict, dictation
dign	worthy	dignified, dignitary
doc, doct	teach, prove	indoctrinate, docile, doctor
domin	rule	predominate, domineer, dominion
dorm	sleep	dormitory, dormant
du	two	duo, duplicity, dual
duc, duct	lead	educate, abduct, ductile
dur	hard, lasting	endure, obdurate, duration
dyn	force, power	dynamo, dynamite
ego	I	egomania, egotist
equ	equal	equation, equitable
erg, urg	work, power	energetic, metallurgy, demiurge
err	wander	error, aberrant
ev	time, age	coeval, longevity
fac, fact, fect, fic	do, make	facility, factual, perfect, artifice
fer	bear, carry	prefer, refer, conifer, fertility
ferv	boil	fervid, effervesce
fid	belief, faith	infidelity, confidant, perfidious
fin	end, limit	finite, confine
firm	strong	reaffirm, infirmity
flect, flex	bend	reflex, inflection
flor	flower	florescent, floral
flu, fluct, flux	flow	fluid, fluctuation, influx

Root	Meaning	Examples
form	shape	*formative, reform, formation*
fort	strong	*effort, fortitude*
frag, fract	break	*fragility, infraction*
fug	flee	*refuge, fugitive*
fus	pour, join	*infuse, transfusion*
gam	marry	*exogamy, polygamous*
ge, geo	earth	*geology, geode, perigee*
gen	birth, kind, race	*engender, general, generation*
gest	carry, bear	*gestation, ingest, digest*
gon	angle	*hexagonal, trigonometry*
grad, gress	step, go	*regress, gradation*
gram	writing	*grammar, cryptogram*
graph	writing	*telegraph, graphics*
grat	pleasing, agreeable	*congratulate, gratuitous*
grav	weight, heavy	*gravamen, gravity*
greg	flock, crowd	*gregarious, segregate*
habit, hibit	have, hold	*habitation, inhibit, habitual*
heli	sun	*helium, heliocentric, aphelion*
hem	blood	*hemoglobin, hemorrhage*
her, hes	stick, cling	*adherent, cohesive*
hydr	water	*dehydration, hydrofoil*
iatr	heal, cure	*pediatrics, psychiatry*
iso	same, equal	*isotope, isometric*
it	journey, go	*itinerary, exit*
ject	throw	*reject, subjective, projection*
jud	judge	*judicial, adjudicate*
jug, junct	join	*conjugal, juncture, conjunction*
jur	swear	*perjure, jurisprudence*
labor	work	*laborious, belabor*
leg	law	*legal, illegitimate*
leg, lig, lect	choose, gather, read	*illegible, eligible, select, lecture*
lev	light, rise	*levity, alleviate*
liber	free	*liberal, libertine*
liter	letter	*literate, alliterative*
lith	rock, stone	*Eolithic, lithograph*

Root	Meaning	Examples
loc	place	*locale, locus, allocate*
log	word, study	*logic, biology, dialogue*
loqu, locut	talk, speech	*colloquial, loquacious, interlocutor*
luc, lum	light	*translucent, pellucid, illumine, luminous*
lud, lus	play	*allusion, ludicrous, interlude*
magn	large, great	*magnificent, magnitude*
mal	bad, ill	*malodorous, malinger*
man, manu	hand	*manifest, manicure, manuscript*
mar	sea	*maritime, submarine*
mater, matr	mother	*matriarchal, maternal*
medi	middle	*intermediary, medieval*
mega	large, million	*megaphone, megacycle*
ment	mind	*demented, mental*
merg, mers	plunge, dip	*emerge, submersion*
meter, metr, mens	measure	*chronometer, metronome, geometry, commensurate*
micr	small	*microfilm, micron*
min	little	*minimum, minute*
mit, miss	send	*remit, admission, missive*
mon, monit	warn	*admonish, monument, monitor*
mor	custom	*mores, immoral*
mor, mort	death	*mortify, mortician*
morph	shape	*amorphous, anthropomorphic*
mov, mob, mot	move	*removal, automobile, motility*
multi	many	*multiply, multinational*
mut	change	*mutable, transmute*
nasc, nat	born	*native, natural, nascent, innate*
nav	ship, sail	*navy, navigable*
necr	dead, die	*necropolis, necrosis*
neg	deny	*renege, negative*
neo	new	*neologism, neoclassical*

Root	Meaning	Examples
nomen, nomin	name	*nomenclature, cognomen, nominate*
nomy	law, rule	*astronomy, antinomy*
nov	new	*novice, innovation*
ocul	eye	*binocular, oculist*
omni	all	*omniscient, omnibus*
onym	name	*pseudonym, eponymous*
oper	work	*operate, cooperation, inoperable*
ora	speak, pray	*oracle, oratory*
orn	decorate	*adorn, ornate*
orth	straight, correct	*orthodox, orthopedic*
pan	all	*panacea, pantheon*
pater, patr	father	*patriot, paternity*
path, pat, pass	feel, suffer	*telepathy, patient, compassion, passion*
ped	child	*pedagogue, pediatrics*
ped, pod	foot	*pedestrian, impede, tripod*
pel, puls	drive, push	*impel, propulsion*
pend, pens	hang	*pendulous, suspense*
pet, peat	seek	*petition, impetus, repeat*
phil	love	*philosopher, Anglophile*
phob	fear	*phobic, agoraphobia*
phon	sound	*phonograph, symphony*
phor	bearing	*semaphore, metaphor*
phot	light	*photograph, photoelectric*
pon, pos	place, put	*component, repose, postpone*
port	carry	*report, portable, deportation*
pot	power	*potency, potential*
press	press	*pressure, impression*
prim	first	*primal, primordial*
proto, prot	first	*proton, protagonist*
psych	mind	*psychic, metempsychosis*
pyr	fire	*pyrite, pyrophobia*
quer, quir, quis, ques	ask, seek	*query, inquiry, inquisitive, quest*
reg, rig, rect	straight, rule	*regulate, dirigible, corrective*
rid, ris	laugh	*deride, risible, ridiculous*

Root	Meaning	Examples
rog	ask	rogation, interrogate
rupt	break	erupt, interruption, rupture
sanct	holy	sacrosanct, sanctify, sanction
sci, scio	know	nescient, conscious, omniscience
scop	watch, view	horoscope, telescopic
scrib, script	write	scribble, proscribe, description
sed, sid, sess	sit, seat	sedate, residence, session
seg, sect	cut	segment, section, intersect
sent, sens	feel, think	nonsense, sensitive, sentient, dissent
sequ, secut	follow	sequel, consequence, consecutive
sign	sign, mark	signature, designate, assign
sol	alone	solitary, solo, desolate
solv, solu, solut	loosen	dissolve, soluble, absolution
somn	sleep	insomnia, somnolent
son	sound	sonorous, unison
soph	wise, wisdom	philosophy, sophisticated
spec, spic, spect	look	specimen, conspicuous, spectacle
spir	breathe	spirit, conspire, respiration
stab, stat	stand	unstable, status, station, establish
stead	place	instead, steadfast
string, strict	bind	astringent, stricture, restrict
stru, struct	build	construe, structure, destructive
sum, sumpt	take	presume, consumer, assumption
tang, ting, tact, tig	touch	tangent, contingency, contact, tactile, contiguous
tax, tac	arrange, arrangement	taxonomy, tactic
techn	skill, art	technique, technician

Root	Meaning	Examples
tele	far	*teletype, telekinesis*
tempor	time	*temporize, extemporaneous*
ten, tain, tent	hold	*tenant, tenacity, reten-tion, contain*
tend, tens, tent	stretch	*contend, extensive, intent*
tenu	thin	*tenuous, attenuate*
term	end	*terminal, terminate*
terr, ter	land, earth	*inter, terrain*
test	witness	*attest, testify*
the	god	*polytheism, theologizer*
therm	heat	*thermos, isotherm*
tom	cut	*atomic, appendectomy*
tort, tors	twist	*tortuous, torsion, contort*
tract	pull, draw	*traction, attract, protract*
trib	assign, pay	*attribute, tribute, retri-bution*
trud, trus	thrust	*obtrude, intrusive*
turb	agitate	*perturb, turbulent, disturb*
umbr	shade	*umbrella, penumbra, umbrage*
uni	one	*unify, disunity, union*
urb	city	*urbane, suburb*
vac	empty	*vacuous, evacuation*
vad, vas	go	*invade, evasive*
val, vail	strength, worth	*valid, avail, prevalent*
ven, vent	come	*advent, convene, preven-tion*
ver	true	*aver, veracity, verity*
verb	word	*verbose, adverb, verbatim*
vert, vers	turn	*revert, perversion*
vest	dress	*vestment*
vid, vis	see	*video, evidence, vision, re-vise*
vinc, vict	conquer	*evince, convict, victim*
viv, vit	life	*vivid, revive, vital*
voc, vok	call	*vociferous, provocative, revoke*
vol	wish	*involuntary, volition*
voly, volut	roll, turn	*involve, convoluted, revo-lution*
vulg	common	*divulge, vulgarity*
zo	animal	*zoologist, Paleozoic*

SUMMARY

What You Need to Know about Word Parts

- Words have three basic parts: *prefixes, suffixes,* and *roots.*

- Each word part has a specific purpose.

- Word parts work together to form the meaning and function of the word in which they occur.

EXERCISES: WORD PARTS

Directions: In each of the following exercises, the words in the left-hand column are built on roots given in the word-part list. Match each word with its definition from the right-hand column. Refer to the list if necessary. Can you identify the roots of each word? If you can't figure out a word, look it up in a dictionary.

Exercise 1

1.	mutable	A.	able to be touched
2.	culpable	B.	laughable
3.	interminable	C.	empty of meaning or interest
4.	amiable	D.	of the first age
5.	vacuous	E.	holding firmly
6.	vital	F.	necessary to life
7.	primeval	G.	unending
8.	tenacious	H.	stable, not able to be loosened or broken up
9.	tangible	I.	changeable
10.	inoperable	J.	friendly
11.	risible	K.	blameworthy
12.	indissoluble	L.	not working, out of order

Exercise 2

1. infinity	A.	list of things to be done
2. duplicity	B.	sum paid yearly
3. levity	C.	a throwing out or from
4. brevity	D.	shortness
5. ejection	E.	endlessness
6. edict	F.	body of teachings
7. infraction	G.	killing of a race
8. genocide	H.	lightness of spirit
9. agenda	I.	a breaking
10. annuity	J.	double-dealing
11. microcosm	K.	official decree; literally, a speaking out
12. doctrine	L.	world in miniature

Exercise 3

1. recede	A.	state as the truth
2. abdicate	B.	throw light on
3. homogenize	C.	forswear, give up a power
4. illuminate	D.	put into words
5. supervise	E.	make freer
6. verbalize	F.	go away
7. liberalize	G.	bury
8. legislate	H.	oversee
9. intervene	I.	make laws
10. inter	J.	draw out
11. aver	K.	make the same throughout
12. protract	L.	come between

Exercise 4

1.	abduction	A.	arrival, a coming to
2.	fortitude	B.	a pressing together
3.	consequence	C.	a flowing together
4.	confluence	D.	something added to
5.	compression	E.	a coming back to life
6.	locus	F.	place
7.	status	G.	truthfulness
8.	disunity	H.	that which follows as a result
9.	veracity	I.	strength
10.	revival	J.	lack of oneness
11.	advent	K.	a leading away, kidnapping
12.	adjunct	L.	standing, position

Exercise 5

1.	nascent	A.	being born
2.	centennial	B.	before the war
3.	prospective	C.	believing easily
4.	circumspect	D.	going against
5.	multinational	E.	in name only
6.	clamorous	F.	hard, unyielding
7.	antebellum	G.	looking, forward
8.	contrary	H.	careful, looking in all directions
9.	impassioned	I.	hundred-year anniversary
10.	credulous	J.	have interests in many countries
11.	obdurate	K.	full of strong feeling
12.	nominal	L.	shouting

ANSWER KEYS

Exercise 1

1.	I	4.	J	7.	D	9.	A	11.	B
2.	K	5.	C	8.	E	10.	L	12.	H
3.	G	6.	F						

Exercise 2

1.	E	4.	D	7.	I	9.	A	11.	L
2.	J	5.	C	8.	G	10.	B	12.	F
3.	H	6.	K						

Exercise 3

1.	F	4.	B	7.	E	9.	L	11.	A
2.	C	5.	H	8.	I	10.	G	12.	J
3.	K	6.	D						

Exercise 4

1.	K	4.	C	7.	L	9.	G	11.	A
2.	I	5.	B	8.	J	10.	E	12.	D
3.	H	6.	F						

Exercise 5

1.	A	4.	H	7.	B	9.	K	11.	F
2.	I	5.	J	8.	D	10.	C	12.	E
3.	G	6.	L						

The SAT "Top 500" Word List

chapter 12

OVERVIEW

- **Master the best ways to learn new words**
- **Hit list: Learn the top 500 SAT words**
- **Review a summary of everything you need to know about SAT words**
- **Practice your skills on SAT word exercises**

As you learned in Chapter 11, a good vocabulary goes a long way in preparing you for success on the SAT. But that doesn't mean you have to memorize the dictionary before the test. This chapter lists and defines some of the words most commonly used on the SAT. It also shows you some of the best strategies for learning the words—and for choosing *which* words to learn. You also get an opportunity to practice your newly upgraded vocabulary skills in the exercises at the end of this chapter.

THE BEST WAYS TO LEARN NEW WORDS

Before you jump in headfirst, make sure you're taking a realistic approach to upgrading your vocabulary for the SAT. Let's face it—this chapter contains a lot of vocabulary words. You won't be able to learn all of these words, or all of the word parts, all at once. If you do want to try to learn the complete lists, give yourself plenty of time before the test date and break them down into manageable chunks. If you've decided to just concentrate on the words that seem most unfamiliar to you, it's still a good idea to work in smaller chunks to avoid information overload.

The following are a few techniques for designing a successful (and manageable) program for building your SAT vocabulary.

Make Some Portable Lists

Take a look at the "Top 500 SAT Words" and choose 15 to 20 words that are new to you. Copy those words and their definitions on a separate sheet of paper. Now you've got a very portable list of words to learn. Once these words are comfortably lodged in your brain, make another list of new words.

241

Tip

Make Flash Cards

Gather up a batch of index cards and search the word list for words you don't know. Write one word on each index card. Then, write the definition on the back of the card. Study the words and their meanings—in small batches, of course—and then test yourself. Look at a word on one of your cards and write the definition on a separate sheet of paper. Then turn the card over and see if you're correct. If you have a study partner (or a friend who is also starting to sweat about the SAT), you can test each other.

THE TOP 500 SAT WORDS

There has to be a kazillion words in the English language, right? (And by the way, *kazillion* isn't one of them.) How could you ever figure out which words would be on the SAT? You can use the handy-dandy word list that follows. It doesn't contain every word you'll encounter on the exam, but it does represent the top 500 SAT words from recent tests.

It's also not a bad idea to start reading some newspapers such as *The New York Times* or the *Washington Post*. They use the kind of vocabulary that you'll find on the SAT, and these newspapers are usually available in the library.

You might also do some random thesaurus searching. Think of a word and then find it in the thesaurus. See what some of the synonyms are and how their construction corresponds in word parts and meaning to the word you know.

-A-

aberration *(noun)* Deviation from what is correct or right.

abeyance *(noun)* Suspension of an activity; postponement.

abstemious *(adj)* Sparing in use of food or drink; moderate.

abstruse *(adj)* Concealed; difficult to comprehend; obscure.

accolade *(noun)* Embrace; award; commendation.

acerbic *(adj)* Bitter; harsh; caustic.

acrimonious *(adj)* Sarcastic; caustic; angry; mordant.

acuity *(noun)* Sharpness; acuteness; keenness.

acute *(adj)* 1. Perceptive. 2. Excruciating.

adept *(adj)* Proficient; masterful; expert.

adherent *(noun)* Believer; supporter; devotee.

adjunct *(noun)* 1. Attachment; appendage. 2. Subordinate or auxiliary capacity.

admonish *(verb)* Caution; reprove mildly; reprimand.

adroit *(adj)* Dexterous; proficient; skillful.

adulation *(noun)* Excessive flattery; adoration; idolization.

adulterate *(verb)* Make impure or inferior by adding improper ingredients; contaminate; pollute.

advocate *(verb)* 1. Argue for a cause; defend. 2. Support; uphold.

aesthete *(noun)* Person who cultivates beauty or art; connoisseur.

aggrandize *(verb)* Make more powerful; amplify; increase.

alacrity *(noun)* Eagerness; zeal; speed.

altruistic *(adj)* Concerned about the general welfare of others; charitable; generous.

ambivalence *(noun)* Uncertainty; doubt; indecisiveness.

ambulatory *(adj)* Able to walk; not stationary.

ameliorate *(verb)* Make better; improve.

amiable *(adj)* Cordial; of pleasant disposition; friendly.

amorphous *(adj)* Without structure; shapeless; nebulous.

animate *(verb)* Energize; enliven.

anomaly *(noun)* Abnormality; deviation from the general rule; irregularity.

antediluvian *(adj)* Ancient; antiquated; obsolete.

antipathy *(noun)* Feeling of opposition or repugnance; aversion; dislike.

apathy *(noun)* Lack of concern, emotion or interest; indifference.

aperture *(noun)* Gap; opening; orifice.

apocryphal *(adj)* False; unauthenticated; disputed.

apotheosis *(noun)* 1. Essence; epitome. 2. Canonization.

appease *(verb)* Satisfy; make peace; placate.

approbatory *(adj)* Expressing approval.

arable *(adj)* Suitable for cultivation or plowing.

arrogant *(adj)* Feeling superior to other people; egotistical.

ascetic *(adj)* Strict; austere.

assuage *(verb)* Ease; make less burdensome; mitigate.

atrophy *(verb)* Waste away from lack of use; degenerate.

audacity *(noun)* Boldness or adventurousness; gall.

authoritarian *(noun)* 1. Person who acts like a dictator; tyrant. 2. Disciplinarian.

avarice *(noun)* Extreme desire for wealth; greed; acquisitiveness.

aviary *(noun)* Large enclosure confining birds.

avouch *(verb)* Guarantee; take responsibility for; affirm.

avow *(verb)* Affirm; assert; declare; acknowledge.

-B-

baleful (adj) Sorrowful; sinister; evil.

balm *(noun)* Soothing ointment for pain or healing; salve.

banal *(adj)* Trite; insipid; ordinary.

bane *(noun)* Deadly affliction; curse; plague.

barbarity *(noun)* Cruel action; inhuman act; harsh conduct.

barren *(adj)* 1. Infertile; impotent. 2. Arid; unproductive.

befuddle *(verb)* Stupefy or confuse; misconstrue.

belated *(adj)* Tardy; overdue.

beleaguer *(verb)* Besiege; surround.

belittle *(verb)* Humiliate; tease; diminish in importance.

bemoan *(verb)* 1. Experience pain or distress. 2. Express pity for; mourn.

bemused *(adj)* Preoccupied by thought; bewildered; perplexed.

bilk *(verb)* Defraud; deceive; hoodwink.

blandishment *(noun)* Cajolery; enticement.

bliss *(noun)* Gaiety; happiness; enjoyment.

blithe *(adj)* Happy; pleased; delighted.

boisterous *(adj)* Noisy; loud; violent; rowdy.

boorish *(adj)* Ill-mannered; rude; gauche.

brevity *(noun)* Briefness; succinctness; terseness.

broach *(verb)* Introduce; bring up; mention.

browbeat *(verb)* Intimidate; harass; dominate.

bungle *(verb)* Botch; mismanage; spoil.

buttress *(noun)* Truss; foundation; support.

-C-

cacophonous *(adj)* Discordant; dissident; harsh.

callow *(adj)* Inexperienced; immature; naive.

candid *(adj)* Frank; blunt; open.

carouse *(verb)* Drink to excess; live it up.

cease *(verb)* Stop; end; halt.

celerity *(noun)* Swift motion; speed; alacrity.

censorious *(adj)* Critical; attacking; denouncing.

charlatan *(noun)* Fraud; person claiming knowledge he/she does not have; humbug; fake; hustler.

chary *(adj)* Careful; cautious.

chasten *(verb)* Castigate; punish; reprove.

cherubic *(adj)* Sweet; kind; innocent.

chimerical *(adj)* Fanciful; whimsical; playful.

chronic *(adj)* Compulsive; typical; habitual; inveterate.

churlish *(adj)* Selfish; rancorous; surly.

circuitous *(adj)* Indirect; roundabout; rambling.

clamor *(noun)* Loud noise or complaint; commotion; din.

clandestine *(adj)* Furtive; surreptitious; secret.

clemency *(noun)* Lenience; mercy; compassion.

cloister *(noun)* Convent; monastery; religious place.

coagulate *(verb)* Congeal; curdle; clot.

coalesce *(verb)* Combine; incorporate; merge.

coddle *(verb)* Pamper; overindulge; baby; spoil.

coercion *(noun)* Intimidation; duress; force; compulsion.

cognate *(adj)* Related by blood; having the same origin.

commensurate *(adj)* Equal in measure; of the same duration or size.

compile *(verb)* Collect data; accumulate; amass.

concomitant *(adj)* Concurrent; attendant; occurring with something else.

concordance *(noun)* Agreement; treaty; accord.

confluence *(noun)* Nexus; union; meeting; conflux.

confound *(verb)* Perplex; baffle; confuse.

conglomerate *(noun)* Corporation; partnership; firm.

conjugal *(adj)* Matrimonial; nuptial; marital.

constrict *(verb)* Squeeze; pinch; obstruct; block.

contentious *(adj)* Argumentative; pugnacious; quarrelsome.

contrite *(adj)* Penitent; apologetic; remorseful.

conundrum *(noun)* Mystery; puzzle.

convoke *(verb)* Convene; assemble.

copious *(adj)* Plentiful; ample; profuse.

corpulence *(noun)* Stoutness; obesity.

coterie *(noun)* Small group of people who share interests and meet frequently.

crass *(adj)* Vulgar, grossly ignorant; indelicate.

credulous *(adj)* Gullible; unsuspecting; naive.

cryptic *(adj)* Enigmatic; obscure; secret; puzzling.

ctenoid *(adj)* Comblike; having narrow segments.

cuboid *(adj)* Having the shape of a cube.

cucullate *(adj)* Hood-shaped.

curmudgeon *(noun)* Cantankerous person.

-D-

daub *(verb)* Blur; smear; spread.

dawdle *(verb)* Procrastinate; loiter; idle; dally.

dearth *(noun)* Paucity; shortage; deficiency.

debased *(adj)* Lowered in status or character; degenerate.

decipher *(verb)* Solve or figure out a puzzle; translate; untangle.

declivity *(noun)* Downward slope.

decorum *(noun)* Appropriate conduct; polite or proper behavior, protocol.

delectable *(adj)* Delicious; delightful; savory.

deleterious *(adj)* Destructive; poisonous; unhealthy.

delineate *(verb)* Describe; outline; depict.

delusion *(noun)* Untrue belief; hallucination; fallacy; misconception.

demagogue *(noun)* Incendiary; agitator; opportunist.

denounce *(verb)* Reprove; accuse; condemn.

depravity *(noun)* Perverted disposition; wickedness; vileness; corruption.

deprecatory *(adj)* Disapproving; belittling.

desecrate *(verb)* Contaminate; profane; defile.

desist *(verb)* Discontinue or stop; cease; renounce.

desolate *(adj)* Alone; without hope or comfort; forsaken.

despoil *(verb)* Ravage; rob; loot.

despot *(noun)* Dictator; tyrant; totalitarian.

diatribe *(noun)* Extreme, bitter, and abusive speech; vituperation; tirade.

didactic *(adj)* Pedantic; academic; for teaching.

diffidence *(noun)* Self-doubt; timidity; shyness.

dilatory *(adj)* Lackadaisical; lazy; remiss.

diligent *(adj)* Assiduous; studious; hard-working.

diminution *(noun)* Decrease; reduction.

disaffected *(adj)* Disillusioned; dissatisfied; discontented.

disapprobation *(noun)* Dislike; reservation; denunciation.

disband *(verb)* Disperse; dissipate; scatter; dispel.

discontent *(adj)* Unhappy; displeased; miserable.

discursive *(adj)* Circuitous; digressive; rambling.

dishearten *(verb)* Dismay; daunt; depress.

disinterment *(noun)* Exhumation; removal of a body from a grave.

disoblige *(verb)* Slight or offend.

disparage *(verb)* Deprecate; belittle or abuse.

dispassionate *(adj)* Imperturbable; unemotional; calm; composed.

disputatious *(adj)* Quarrelsome; contentious; argumentative.

dissemble *(verb)* Disguise; conceal; mask; camouflage.

dissension *(noun)* Conflict; disagreement; strife.

dissonant *(adj)* Cacophonous; inharmonious; discordant; strident.

dissuade *(verb)* Obstruct; hinder; deter.

distend *(verb)* Bloat, bulge; swell; stretch.

dither *(noun)* Commotion; turmoil.

divination *(noun)* Prediction; prophecy; forecast.

dolt *(noun)* Cretin; fool; dimwit; idiot.

dotard *(noun)* Senile person.

dubious *(adj)* Irresolute; uncertain; moot.

duplicity *(noun)* Cunning; fraud; trickery; deception.

-E-

edify *(verb)* Instruct; enlighten; educate.

efface *(verb)* Cancel; delete; obliterate.

effervescent *(adj)* Lively; volatile.

effigy *(noun)* Mannequin; likeness; image.

effrontery *(noun)* Impudence; nerve; gall.

egregious *(adj)* Flagrant; glaring; outrageous.

elegiac *(adj)* Mournful; sorrowful; sad.

elucidate *(verb)* Interpret; define; clarify; explain.

emanate *(verb)* Radiate; flow from; emit.

emasculate *(verb)* Deprive of strength.

embroil *(verb)* Implicate; enmesh; involve.

emcee *(noun)* Master of ceremonies.

empathize *(verb)* Identify with; understand.

emulate *(verb)* Model; pattern.

enervate *(verb)* Exhaust or weaken; debilitate.

engender *(verb)* Generate; produce; cause.

enigmatic *(adj)* Cryptic; baffling; mysterious.

enmesh *(verb)* Tangle or involve.

ennui *(noun)* Dullness; boredom; monotony.

enthrall *(verb)* Mesmerize; captivate; thrill.

entrench *(verb)* Fortify; reinforce; secure.

ephemeral *(adj)* Transitory; fleeting; passing; temporary.

epicure *(noun)* Person devoted to luxurious living; person with refined tastes.

epithet *(noun)* Word used to describe or characterize a person or thing.

equilibrium *(noun)* Balance; stability; poise.

equivocate *(verb)* Prevaricate; dodge; evade; hedge.

erudition *(noun)* Learning; knowledge; enlightenment.

escapade *(noun)* Adventurous conduct; unusual behavior.

esoteric *(adj)* Confidential; personal; private; privileged.

espouse *(verb)* Embrace; defend; support.

ethereal *(adj)* Incorporeal; intangible; airy.

eulogy *(noun)* Commendation; speech giving great tribute.

euphonic *(adj)* Agreeable to the ear.

evanescent *(adj)* Ephemeral; fading; brief.

exigent *(adj)* Pressing; insistent; urgent.

exonerate *(verb)* Acquit; vindicate; free from responsibility.

exorcise *(verb)* Cast out evil spirits; expel demons.

expatriate *(verb)* Send into exile; renounce one's own country.

expedite *(verb)* Speed up matters; accelerate; quicken.

expunge *(verb)* Obliterate; remove; erase; exterminate.

expurgate *(verb)* Remove erroneous or objectionable material; delete; edit.

extemporaneous *(adj)* Spontaneous; impromptu.

extol *(verb)* Praise; laud; hail; glorify.

extradite *(verb)* Transfer a person to another jurisdiction for possible prosecution for an alleged offense.

extricate *(verb)* Remove; loosen; untie.

-F-

fallible *(adj)* Faulty; imperfect.

fallow *(adj)* Idle; dormant.

fastidious *(adj)* Meticulous; exacting.

fathom *(verb)* Measure; discover; perceive.

fatuous *(adj)* Ludicrous; inane; idiotic; silly.

fecund *(adj)* Prolific; productive; fruitful.

felicity *(noun)* Great happiness; bliss.

fetid *(adj)* Possessing an offensive smell; malodorous; foul; gamey.

fetter *(verb)* Restrain; restrict; curb.

fickle *(adj)* Capricious; erratic; spasmodic.

fledgling *(noun)* Young or inexperienced person; young bird.

flippant *(adj)* Nonchalant; frivolous, superficial; light.

florid *(adj)* Ornate; flushed with rosy color; ruddy.

flout *(verb)* Ridicule; scoff; mock; scorn.

foible *(noun)* Frailty; imperfection; weakness.

forswear *(verb)* Repudiate; forsake; eschew.

fulsome *(adj)* Loathsome; excessive.

fume *(noun)* Gas; vapor; harmful or irritating smoke.

furtive *(adj)* Clandestine; secretive; surreptitious; covert.

-G-

gambol *(verb)* Play; frolic; romp.

garble *(verb)* Confuse; scramble; distort.

garish *(adj)* Gaudy; ostentatious; excessive.

garner *(verb)* Collect; receive; attain; acquire.

giddy *(adj)* Scatterbrained; silly; frivolous.

goad *(verb)* Incite; pressure; irk; arouse; awaken.

grandiloquence *(noun)* Pompous or bombastic speech; lofty, welling language.

grisly *(adj)* Frightening; ghastly; gory; hideous.

grovel *(verb)* Act in a servile way; cringe; kneel.

guile *(noun)* Wiliness; deceit; cunning.

guzzle *(verb)* Gulp; swill; consume to excess.

-H-

hackneyed *(adj)* Trite; common; overdone; banal.

haggle *(verb)* Dicker; barter; make a deal.

hallow *(verb)* Make holy; consecrate; sanctify.

hamper *(verb)* Hinder; frustrate; impede.

harbor *(verb)* Preserve; conceal; secure; shelter.

hardy *(adj)* Stalwart; robust; sturdy.

haughty *(adj)* Arrogant; disdainful; blatantly proud; contemptuous.

hearten *(verb)* Encourage; give strength.

hedge *(verb)* Enclose; surround; fence.

hedonism *(noun)* Intemperance; self-indulgence; excess.

herald *(verb)* Announce; broadcast; report.

heretic *(noun)* Nihilist; infidel; radical; dissenter.

hiatus *(noun)* Interruption; pause; gap.

hilarity *(noun)* Boisterous merriment; enjoyment.

histrionic *(adj)* Pertaining to actors; melodramatic.

hoary *(adj)* Frosted; grey; grizzled.

hyperbole *(noun)* Exaggeration; fanciful statement; enhancement.

-I-

iconoclasm *(noun)* Attack on religious values or symbols.

ignoramus *(noun)* Moron; fool; dimwit.

immutable *(adj)* Incorruptible; enduring; unchanging.

impecunious *(adj)* Poor; destitute; penniless.

imperturbable *(adj)* Even-tempered; level-headed; calm.

impervious *(adj)* Airtight; sealed; impenetrable.

impetuous *(adj)* Hasty; rash; impulsive.

impregnable *(adj)* Invincible; invulnerable; unable to be captured or entered.

impromptu *(adj)* Makeshift; spontaneous.

improvident *(adj)* Reckless; rash.

impugn *(verb)* Denounce; censor; attack.

inaudible *(adj)* Faint; soft; hard to hear.

inauspicious *(adj)* Unfavorable.

incipient *(adj)* Embryonic; developing; in the beginning stages.

incisive *(adj)* Perceptive; astute.

inclusive *(adj)* All-encompassing; broad in scope; comprehensive.

incoherent *(adj)* Illogical; inconsistent.

incongruous *(adj)* Inconsistent; unsuitable; contradictory.

incorrigible *(adj)* Unruly; delinquent; incapable of reform.

indecorous *(adj)* Inappropriate; indelicate; unseemly.

indefatigable *(adj)* Diligent; persistent; inexhaustible.

indenture *(noun)* Contract binding a person to work for another.

indolence *(noun)* Lethargy; idleness; sloth.

inebriation *(noun)* Drunkenness; intoxication.

ingenuous *(adj)* Genuine; open; candid; frank.

inimical *(adj)* Antagonistic; hurtful; harmful; adverse.

innocuous *(adj)* Dull; harmless; innocent.

inscrutable *(adj)* Mysterious; perplexing.

insipid *(adj)* Dull; banal; tasteless.

insolvent *(adj)* Bankrupt; unable to pay debts.

intercede *(verb)* Intervene; negotiate.

intonate *(verb)* Speak or utter with a particular tone.

intractable *(adj)* Unruly; disobedient.

intrinsic *(adj)* Inherent; natural; innate.

inveigh *(verb)* Abuse; criticize; rebuke.

inveterate *(adj)* Habitual; chronic.

irascible *(adj)* Testy; touchy; irritable.

issue *(verb)* Discharge; emerge; emanate.

-J-

jettison *(verb)* Eliminate; discharge.

jollity *(noun)* Gaiety; merriment.

judicious *(adj)* Logical; reasonable; clever.

juncture *(noun)* Joint; seam; intersection; joining.

juxtapose *(verb)* Place side by side.

-K-

kinetic *(adj)* Caused by motion; dynamic.

kiosk *(noun)* A small structure used as a newsstand, bandstand, etc.

kitsch *(noun)* Popular art or writing of a shallow nature.

knave *(noun)* A dishonest, deceitful person; a rogue.

knoll *(noun)* Hillock; mound.

knotty *(adj)* Snarled; tangled.

kudos *(noun)* Credit or praise for an achievement; glory.

-L-

labyrinth *(noun)* Maze; network; puzzle.

lachrymose *(adj)* Weepy; tearful.

laconic *(adj)* Concise; terse; curt.

lamentation *(noun)* Complaint; moan.

lampoon *(verb)* Mock; ridicule.

languish *(verb)* Decline; diminish; weaken.

largess *(noun)* Charity; philanthropy; gift.

lassitude *(noun)* Fatigue; weariness; debility.

laudable *(adj)* Commendable; admirable; exemplary.

laxity *(noun)* Carelessness; indifference.

lethargy *(noun)* Idleness; listlessness; passivity.

levity *(noun)* Lightness; frivolity.

linger *(verb)* Loiter; remain; hesitate.

lithe *(adj)* Flexible; agile; mobile; bendable.

loutish *(adj)* Clumsy; idiotic; buffoonlike.

ludicrous *(adj)* Outlandish; silly; ridiculous.

lurid *(adj)* Shockingly vivid; horrifying; sensational.

-M-

maladroit *(adj)* Clumsy; unskilled.

malapropism *(noun)* Inappropriate or ludicrous use of a word.

malevolent *(adj)* Venomous; spiteful; malignant.

malinger *(verb)* Feign illness to escape work; shirk.

marred *(adj)* Having blemishes; damaged; defaced.

maudlin *(adj)* Overemotional; mushy.

meander *(verb)* Twist; bend; zigzag.

mendicant *(noun)* Almsman; beggar; leech; parasite.

meticulous *(adj)* Precise; scrupulous; particular.

mettle *(noun)* Stamina; bravery; courage.

mince *(verb)* Chop; mitigate.

mire *(noun)* Mud; slime; muck.

moribund *(adj)* Failing; waning; ailing.

motley *(adj)* Multicolored; spotted; mixed.

multifarious *(adj)* Diverse; many-sided; multiple.

mundane *(adj)* Boring; ordinary; typical; tedious.

munificent *(adj)* Generous; extravagant; philanthropic.

-N-

nadir *(noun)* Lowest point.

naive *(adj)* Foolishly simple; childlike.

nascent *(adj)* Beginning; embryonic; incipient.

nebulous *(adj)* Unclear; vague; indefinite.

needle *(verb)* Provoke.

nefarious *(adj)* Evil; vile; sinister; wicked.

nemesis *(noun)* Just punishment; retribution.

neologism *(noun)* Newly coined phrase or expression.

noisome *(adj)* Noxious to health.

noxious *(adj)* Harmful; malignant.

-O-

obdurate *(adj)* Stubborn; intractable.

obsequious *(adj)* Servile; groveling.

obviate *(verb)* Make unnecessary.

odious *(adj)* Detestable; loathsome; revolting; sickening.

officious *(adj)* Meddlesome.

opaque *(adj)* Impenetrable by light; dull; dark; obscure.

optimum *(noun)* Peak or prime; ideal.

opulent *(adj)* Affluent; well-to-do; plentiful.

ostentatious *(adj)* Conspicuous; showy.

ostracize *(verb)* Exclude; isolate; bar; shun.

-P-

palpable *(adj)* Noticeable; obvious; apparent.

paltry *(adj)* Minor; petty; insignificant.

panegyric *(noun)* Elaborate praise, public compliment.

paragon *(noun)* Model or standard of excellence.

pariah *(noun)* Outcast; misfit; refugee.

parochial *(adj)* Religious; restricted.

parsimony *(noun)* Miserliness; unusually excessive frugality.

partisan *(noun)* Fan or supporter; enthusiast supporting a particular cause or issue.

pastiche *(noun)* Hodgepodge; literary or musical piece imitating other works.

paucity *(noun)* Scarcity; shortage; dearth.

peccadillo *(noun)* Small sin or fault.

pedantic *(adj)* Stuffy or dogmatic; meticulous; academic.

peevish *(adj)* Irritable; grouchy; ill-tempered.

pejorative *(adj)* Degrading; derogatory; negative.

percipient *(adj)* Able to perceive or see things as they actually are.

perfidy *(noun)* Deliberate breach of faith or trust; treachery.

peripheral *(adj)* Marginal; outer; surrounding.

perspicacious *(adj)* Astute; keen; perceptive.

philistine *(noun)* Barbarian; person lacking artistic judgment.

pique *(verb)* Irritate; miff; offend.

pithy *(adj)* 1. Substantial; profound. 2. Brief; concise.

placid *(adj)* Sincere; tranquil; composed; sedate.

plaintive *(adj)* Sad; mournful; pathetic.

platitude *(noun)* 1. Triteness. 2. Cliché; trivial remark.

plaudit *(noun)* Enthusiastic expression.

pliable *(adj)* Limber; malleable; flexible.

poignant *(adj)* Intense; powerful; biting; piercing.

polemical *(adj)* Controversial; argumentative; debatable.

polyphony *(noun)* Music with two or more melodies blended together.

porous *(adj)* Permeable; absorbent; having holes.

posthumous *(adj)* Arising or continuing after someone's death.

potable *(adj)* Drinkable.

prattle *(verb)* Gab; babble.

precocious *(adj)* Showing premature development.

precursor *(noun)* Forerunner.

prescient *(adj)* Showing foresight; predicting events before they occur.

primeval *(adj)* Belonging to a primitive age.

primordial *(adj)* Belonging to a primitive age; first in time.

proclivity *(noun)* Tendency; inclination; propensity.

procrastinate *(verb)* Postpone; stall; defer.

prodigious *(adj)* Exceptional; impressive; of huge quantity; immense.

proficient *(adj)* Skillful; masterful; expert.

progeny *(noun)* Heir; descendant; offspring.

prolific *(adj)* Fruitful; abundant; fertile.

prosaic *(adj)* Common; routine; ordinary.

protean *(adj)* Taking many forms; changeable; variable.

protract *(verb)* Elongate; lengthen; prolong.

prudent *(adj)* Careful; cautious; judicious.

puerile *(adj)* Juvenile; immature; childish.

pugilism *(noun)* Boxing.

pugnacity *(noun)* Eagerness to fight; belligerence.

pulchritude *(noun)* Beauty; physical appeal.

pulverize *(verb)* Grind; crush; smash.

-Q-

quagmire *(noun)* Marsh; quicksand; swamp.

quandary *(noun)* Dilemma; mire; entanglement.

querulous *(adj)* Difficult; testy; disagreeable.

quibble *(verb)* Argue or bicker.

quixotic *(adj)* Romantic; whimsical; unrealistic.

-R-

rabid *(adj)* Berserk; diseased; sick.

ramble *(verb)* Meander; roam.

rancorous *(adj)* Antagonistic; hostile; spiteful.

rarefy *(verb)* Make thin; purify; make less dense.

raucous *(adj)* Harsh; annoying; piercing; shrill.

raze *(verb)* Demolish; level; topple.

reactionary *(adj)* Opposing progress; characterized by reaction.

recalcitrant *(adj)* Headstrong; disobedient; stubborn.

recant *(verb)* Rescind; retract; take back.

reconciliation *(noun)* Settlement or resolution.

redundant *(adj)* Excessive; repetitious; unnecessary.

refractory *(adj)* Unmanageable; obstinate; not responsive to treatment.

refurbish *(verb)* Overhaul; remodel.

regimen *(noun)* Administration; government; system.

remedial *(adj)* Restorative; corrective; healing.

remuneration *(noun)* Compensation; wages.

rend *(verb)* Rip; tear; splinter.

reprobate *(noun)* Degenerate; person without morals.

repudiate *(verb)* Recant; disclaim; reject; disavow.

rescind *(verb)* Cancel; repeal; veto.

resilient *(adj)* Elastic; stretchy; rebounding.

resonant *(adj)* Reverberant; ringing.

resplendent *(adj)* Dazzling; glorious; intense.

restive *(adj)* Nervous; restless; uneasy.

retrospection *(noun)* Contemplation of past things.

reverent *(adj)* Devout; solemn; worshipful.

ribald *(adj)* Lewd; obscene; irreverent.

rudiment *(noun)* Beginning; foundation or source.

ruffian *(noun)* Brutal person; cruel and sadistic person.

ruminate *(verb)* Contemplate; think about.

-S-

saccharine *(adj)* Sugary; syrupy.

savant *(noun)* Intellectual; scholar; philosopher.

scanty *(adj)* Meager; scarce.

scoff *(verb)* Mock; ridicule.

sequester *(verb)* Separate; isolate; segregate.

soporific *(adj)* Hypnotic; lethargic; causing sleep.

spurious *(adj)* Bogus; false.

spurn *(verb)* Defy; reject.

squalor *(noun)* 1. Severe poverty. 2. Filthiness.

stratagem *(noun)* Plot; tactic; deception.

strident *(adj)* Discordant; harsh; piercing.

strife *(noun)* Conflict; turmoil; struggle.

stultify *(verb)* Inhibit; make ineffective; cripple.

supercilious *(adj)* Egotistic; proud; arrogant.

surfeit *(noun)* Overabundance; excess; surplus.

surly *(adj)* Choleric; rude; sullen.

surreptitious *(adj)* Covert; furtive; acquired by stealthy means.

svelte *(adj)* Graceful; slim.

sybarite *(noun)* Someone devoted to luxury; pleasure-seeker.

sycophant *(noun)* Flatterer.

-T-

taciturn *(adj)* Reserved; shy; uncommunicative.

tantamount *(adj)* Indistinguishable; equivalent.

taper *(verb)* Diminish; thin; narrow.

tawdry *(adj)* Gaudy; showy; loud.

temerity *(noun)* Rashness; audacity; recklessness.

tensile *(adj)* Pertaining to tension; stretchable; ductile.

tenuous *(adj)* Attenuated; flimsy; thin.

tirade *(noun)* Diatribe; angry speech.

torpor *(noun)* Lethargy; apathy; dormancy.

trepidation *(noun)* Anxiety; alarm; apprehension.

truant *(adj)* Indolent; absent; idle.

turgid *(adj)* Swollen; bombastic; distended.

turpitude *(noun)* Depravity; baseness; shamefulness.

-U-

undulate *(verb)* Move in a wavy manner.

unfathomable *(adj)* Baffling; puzzling; incomprehensible.

unkempt *(adj)* Uncombed; messy; untidy.

unscathed *(adj)* Unhurt; uninjured.

unwieldy *(adj)* Clumsy; awkward; unmanageable.

upbraid *(verb)* Rebuke; scold; criticize.

upshot *(noun)* Final result; conclusion; end.

-V-

vacillate *(verb)* Hedge; waver; fluctuate.

variegated *(adj)* Multicolored; polychromatic; varied.

vehement *(adj)* Fierce; emphatic; intense.

venerate *(verb)* Admire; show respect.

veracity *(noun)* Truth; sincerity; honesty; candor.

verbose *(adj)* Wordy; talkative; profuse.

verdant *(adj)* Lush; thick with vegetation; leafy.

viable *(adj)* Living; alive; feasible.

vigilance *(noun)* Attentiveness; prudence; care.

vilify *(verb)* Defame; denigrate.

virulent *(adj)* Fatal; lethal; toxic.

vitriolic *(adj)* Scathing; caustic.

vociferous *(adj)* Clamorous; outspoken; noisy; vocal.

voluble *(adj)* Verbose; wordy; garrulous.

voluminous *(adj)* Huge; immense; bulky.

voracious *(adj)* 1. Enthusiastic; overly eager. 2. Starving.

vouchsafe *(verb)* Confer; grant; permit.

-W-

wan *(adj)* Anemic; colorless; pale.

waver *(verb)* Totter; fluctuate.

whet *(verb)* Stimulate; sharpen; intensify.

wistful *(adj)* Yearning; pensive; sad.

woe *(noun)* Anguish; grief; affliction.

writhe *(verb)* Squirm; twist.

-X-

xenophobe *(noun)* One who dislikes strangers or foreigners.

-Y-

yeoman *(noun)* Peasant; ordinary person.

yore *(noun)* Time long past.

yowl *(noun)* Long, mournful cry or howl.

-Z-

zealot *(noun)* Fanatic; radical; enthusiast.

zenith *(noun)* Apex; summit; peak.

What You Need to Know about SAT Words

- Whether you attempt to learn the entire "Top 500 SAT Words" or just parts of the list, break the words into manageable groups of 15 to 20 words, and study one group at a time.

- Portable lists and flash cards can help you study word groups—wherever you are.

- Use the word skills you learned in Chapter 11 to try to define unfamiliar words.

- Read good newspapers and other well-written books and periodicals to help broaden your vocabulary. Keep a dictionary or thesaurus nearby, so you can look up unfamiliar words.

EXERCISES: SAT WORDS

Exercise 1

35 Questions • Time—15 Minutes

Directions: For each of the following questions, select the one word that has most nearly the same meaning as the italicized word in the context of the sentence. Circle the letter that precedes your answer choice. Stop working at the end of the allotted time, then score your work. Afterward, return to the exercises and complete those questions you didn't finish.

1. The young girl listened to her grandfather's endless and repetitious stories with *laudable* patience.
   - (A) exorbitant
   - (B) meticulous
   - (C) unwavering
   - (D) exemplary
   - (E) intractable

2. When the right job comes along, act with *celerity* to take advantage of the opportunity.
   - (A) alacrity
   - (B) resourcefulness
   - (C) pragmatism
   - (D) compunction
   - (E) diligence

3. His *diffidence* caused him to miss many opportunities.
   - (A) ignorance
   - (B) timidity
   - (C) indifference
   - (D) indolence
   - (E) arrogance

4. The business survived on a *tenuous* relationship with one customer.
   - (A) tentative
   - (B) insubstantial
   - (C) lucrative
   - (D) salient
   - (E) amatory

5. He asked for compensation *commensurate* to his work.
   - (A) approximate
   - (B) previous
   - (C) equal
   - (D) appropriate
   - (E) incongruous

6. Visitors to impoverished countries are often shocked at the number of *mendicants* in the streets.
   - (A) beggars
   - (B) criminals
   - (C) vendors
   - (D) drunkards
   - (E) soldiers

7. It will take more than good intentions to *ameliorate* the conditions in the schools.

   (A) understand
   (B) counteract
   (C) eliminate
   (D) camouflage
   (E) improve

8. *Ephemeral* pleasures may leave long-lasting memories.

   (A) enervated
   (B) irresolute
   (C) frivolous
   (D) adventurous
   (E) transitory

9. The critic *belittled* her talent by suggesting that her beauty, rather than her acting ability, was responsible for her success.

   (A) illuminated
   (B) disparaged
   (C) declared
   (D) diminished
   (E) inveighed

10. The father *upbraided* his children for their extravagance.

    (A) scolded
    (B) scorned
    (C) advocated
    (D) bolstered
    (E) flouted

11. Imagination and curiosity are the antidotes for *ennui*.

    (A) inactivity
    (B) indolence
    (C) boredom
    (D) jollity
    (E) woe

12. His friends *dissuaded* him from that unwise course of action.

    (A) protected
    (B) ostracized
    (C) deterred
    (D) sequestered
    (E) enmeshed

13. They *rescinded* their offer of aid when they became disillusioned with the project.

    (A) renegotiated
    (B) withdrew
    (C) reinstated
    (D) rethought
    (E) validated

14. The novel told a *lurid* tale of murder and lust.

    (A) sensational
    (B) nonsensical
    (C) esoteric
    (D) unrealistic
    (E) dubious

15. She made many enemies because of her *acerbic* wit.

    (A) boorish
    (B) caustic
    (C) inane
    (D) ingratiating
    (E) magnanimous

16. The ancient town was a *labyrinth* of narrow, winding streets.

    (A) confusion
    (B) model
    (C) maze
    (D) collection
    (E) path

17. I will *ruminate* on your proposal and let you know my decision next week.

(A) ameliorate

(B) linger

(C) report

(D) procrastinate

(E) contemplate

18. One *contentious* student can disrupt an entire class.

(A) rambunctious

(B) vociferous

(C) quarrelsome

(D) humorous

(E) garrulous

19. The hot, humid weather can *enervate* even hearty souls.

(A) intimidate

(B) invigorate

(C) weaken

(D) incite

(E) impugn

20. Insisting on a luxury car you cannot afford is *fatuous*.

(A) inane

(B) avarice

(C) nefarious

(D) impetuous

(E) pretentious

21. They had to *jettison* the cargo to lighten the plane.

(A) relocate

(B) divide

(C) eject

(D) disregard

(E) consume

22. His ideas were *quixotic* and thoroughly useless.

(A) erroneous

(B) dubious

(C) incomprehensible

(D) unrealistic

(E) incoherent

23. He was *candid* about his financial difficulties.

(A) incredulous

(B) apprehensive

(C) enigmatic

(D) blunt

(E) ambiguous

24. Because of the drug's *soporific* effect, you should not drive after taking it.

(A) noxious

(B) sedative

(C) inimical

(D) poignant

(E) incongruous

25. He is always *chary* with a new acquaintance.

(A) eager

(B) amiable

(C) impudent

(D) baleful

(E) cautious

26. An *intractable* person is slow to adapt to a new way of life.

(A) timid

(B) bemused

(C) ascetic

(D) stubborn

(E) antediluvian

exercises

27. She responded with *alacrity* to every customer request.

(A) indignation

(B) aggression

(C) laxity

(D) diffidence

(E) zeal

28. Knowing how sensitive she was about money, he did not *broach* the subject of who should pay for the ticket.

(A) introduce

(B) avoid

(C) postpone

(D) prolong

(E) bemoan

29. United States law *emanates* from English common law.

(A) fluctuates

(B) merges

(C) mitigates

(D) originates

(E) amasses

30. He was expelled from the club because of his *nefarious* activities.

(A) unsolicited

(B) questionable

(C) sinister

(D) unauthorized

(E) pejorative

31. They met *surreptitiously* in the night to exchange information.

(A) clandestinely

(B) egregiously

(C) punctiliously

(D) exigently

(E) indecorously

32. Only a personal apology will *appease* his rage at having been slighted.

(A) control

(B) entrench

(C) placate

(D) obviate

(E) modify

33. Health benefits are part of the *remuneration* that goes with the position.

(A) paucity

(B) surfeit

(C) pay

(D) advantages

(E) package

34. The band of terrorists threatened to *despoil* the town unless it surrendered.

(A) infiltrate

(B) ravage

(C) scoff

(D) browbeat

(E) stultify

35. She was surprised to find that the *callow* youth had grown into a sophisticated man.

(A) awkward

(B) immature

(C) banal

(D) gauche

(E) coddled

Exercise 2

15 Questions • Time—7 Minutes

Directions: For each of the following questions, select the one word that has most nearly the same meaning as the italicized word in the context of the sentence. Circle the letter that precedes your answer choice. Stop working at the end of the allotted time, then score your work. Afterward, return to the exercises and complete those questions you didn't finish.

1. *Impetuous* actions often lead to trouble.
   - (A) contentious
   - (B) malicious
   - (C) irrational
   - (D) dilatory
   - (E) impulsive

2. A *recalcitrant* child is a difficult pupil.
   - (A) indefatigable
   - (B) churlish
   - (C) unfocused
   - (D) impudent
   - (E) obdurate

3. *Brevity* is the essence of journalistic writing.
   - (A) continuity
   - (B) opacity
   - (C) succinctness
   - (D) incisiveness
   - (E) hedonism

4. Supporting her *impecunious* aunt was a drain on her resources.
   - (A) extravagant
   - (B) thrifty
   - (C) munificent
   - (D) eccentric
   - (E) destitute

5. The silly costumes and party hats epitomized the *levity* of the occasion.
   - (A) inebriation
   - (B) frivolity
   - (C) emotion
   - (D) banality
   - (E) mettle

6. The jury's deliberation was *protracted* because of their confusion over a point of law.
   - (A) lengthened
   - (B) befuddled
   - (C) decided
   - (D) illuminated
   - (E) distended

7. She had a *proclivity* for getting into trouble.
   - (A) compulsion
   - (B) propensity
   - (C) guile
   - (D) antipathy
   - (E) vulnerability

8. Only a few scrubby trees clung to the rocky soil of that *barren* landscape.
   - (A) verdant
   - (B) undesirable
   - (C) odious
   - (D) arid
   - (E) insolvent

9. The *dearth* of rain can create a desert in a few years.
    (A) contamination
    (B) deficiency
    (C) hiatus
    (D) equilibrium
    (E) abundance

10. The rock sample was a *conglomerate* of quartz pebbles.
    (A) mixture
    (B) collusion
    (C) emulation
    (D) paragon
    (E) apotheosis

11. Squeezing through the *aperture* between the rocks, she found herself in a cool, dark cave.
    (A) chasm
    (B) confluence
    (C) path
    (D) orifice
    (E) anomaly

12. Sometimes a *circuitous* route is the best way to reach your destination.
    (A) scenic
    (B) alternative
    (C) roundabout
    (D) audacious
    (E) desolate

13. To *expedite* delivery of the letter, he sent it by overnight mail.
    (A) accelerate
    (B) assure
    (C) efface
    (D) extradite
    (E) secure

14. The *adroit* juggler held the attention of the crowd.
    (A) inept
    (B) stunning
    (C) magnificent
    (D) confident
    (E) skillful

15. The confession of one prisoner *exonerated* the other suspects.
    (A) infuriated
    (B) acquitted
    (C) condemned
    (D) implicated
    (E) denounced

answers

ANSWER KEYS

Exercise 1

1. D	8. E	15. B	22. D	29. D
2. A	9. B	16. C	23. D	30. C
3. B	10. A	17. E	24. B	31. A
4. B	11. C	18. C	25. E	32. C
5. C	12. C	19. C	26. D	33. C
6. A	13. B	20. A	27. E	34. B
7. E	14. A	21. C	28. A	35. B

Exercise 2

1. E	4. E	7. B	10. A	13. A
2. E	5. B	8. D	11. D	14. E
3. C	6. A	9. B	12. C	15. B

PART VI

SAT MATH REVIEW

SAT Arithmetic Review

OVERVIEW

- Operations with whole numbers and decimals
- Operations with fractions
- Verbal problems involving fractions
- Variation
- Finding percents
- Verbal problems involving percents
- Averages

OPERATIONS WITH WHOLE NUMBERS AND DECIMALS

The four basic arithmetic operations are addition, subtraction, multiplication, and division. The results of these operations are called *sum, difference, product,* and *quotient,* respectively. Because these words are often used in problems, you should be thoroughly familiar with them.

ADDING. When adding whole numbers and decimals, remember to keep your columns straight and to write all digits in their proper columns, according to place value.

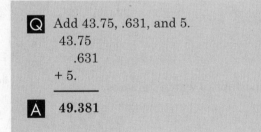

Q Add 43.75, .631, and 5.

```
  43.75
   .631
+ 5.
_____
```

A 49.381

SUBTRACTING. When subtracting whole numbers and decimals, it is likewise important to put numbers in their proper columns. Be particularly careful in subtracting a decimal with more place values after the decimal from a decimal with less.

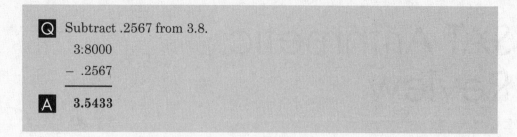

Q Subtract .2567 from 3.8.

$$3.8000$$
$$-\ .2567$$

A **3.5433**

In order to perform this subtraction, zeros must be attached to the top numeral to extend it to equal length with the bottom number. The zeros in this case are only placeholders and in no way change the value of the number.

MULTIPLYING. When multiplying whole numbers, pay particular attention to zeros.

Q Find the product of 403 and 30.

$$403$$
$$\times\ 30$$

A **12,090**

When multiplying decimals, remember that the number of decimal places in the product must be equal to the sum of the number of decimal places in the numbers being mutiplied.

Q Find the product of 4.03 and .3.

$$4.03$$
$$\times\ .3$$

A **1.209**

DIVIDING. When dividing, it is also important to watch for zeros.

Q Divide 4935 by 7.

A
$$\begin{array}{r} 705 \\ 7)\overline{4935} \\ \underline{49} \\ 3 \\ \underline{0} \\ 35 \end{array}$$

Since 49 is divisible by 7, there is no remainder to carry to the next digit. However, 3 is not divisible by 7, so you must put a 0 into the quotient. Carrying the 3, you can then divide 35 by 7.

When dividing by a decimal, always rename the decimal to a whole number by moving the decimal point to the end of the divisor. To do this, multiply the divisor by a power of 10. (Multiplying by 10 moves a decimal point one place to the right. Multiplying by 100 moves it two places to the right, and so forth.) Then multiply the number being divided by the same power of 10. Since division can always be written as a fraction in which the divisor is the denominator and the number being divided is the numerator, when you remove a decimal point from the divisor, you are really multiplying both parts of the fraction by the same number, which changes its form, but not its value.

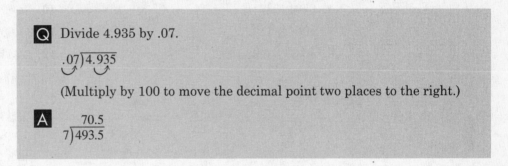

Q Divide 4.935 by .07.

$$.07\overline{)4.935}$$

(Multiply by 100 to move the decimal point two places to the right.)

A $$\frac{70.5}{7\overline{)493.5}}$$

Exercise: Operations with Whole Numbers and Decimals

> **Directions:** Work out each problem on scratch paper.

Add:

1. 6 + 37 + 42,083 + 125
2. .007 + 32.4 + 1.234 + 7.3
3. .37 + .037 + .0037 + 37

Subtract:

4. 3701 − 371
5. 1000 − 112
6. 40.37 − 6.983

Multiply:

7. 3147 by 206
8. 2.137 by .11
9. .45 by .06

Divide:

10. 12,894 by 42
11. 34.68 by 3.4
12. .175 by 25

Solutions

1.
$$\begin{array}{r} 6 \\ 37 \\ 42083 \\ +\ 125 \\ \hline 42251 \end{array}$$

2.
$$\begin{array}{r} .007 \\ 32.4 \\ 1.234 \\ +\ 7.3 \\ \hline 40.941 \end{array}$$

3.
$$\begin{array}{r} .37 \\ .037 \\ .0037 \\ +\ 37. \\ \hline 37.4107 \end{array}$$

4.
$$\begin{array}{r} 3701 \\ -\ 371 \\ \hline 3330 \end{array}$$

5.
$$\begin{array}{r} 1000 \\ -\ 112 \\ \hline 888 \end{array}$$

6.
$$\begin{array}{r} 40.370 \\ -\ 6.983 \\ \hline 33.387 \end{array}$$

7.
$$\begin{array}{r} 3147 \\ \times\ 206 \\ \hline 18882 \\ 629400 \\ \hline 648282 \end{array}$$

8.
$$\begin{array}{r} 2.137 \\ \times\ .11 \\ \hline 2137 \\ 2137 \\ \hline .23507 \end{array}$$

9.
$$\begin{array}{r} .45 \\ \times\ .06 \\ \hline .0270 \end{array}$$

10.
$$\begin{array}{r} 307 \\ 42\overline{)12894} \\ \underline{126} \\ 294 \\ \underline{294} \end{array}$$

11.
$$\begin{array}{r} 10.2 \\ 3.4\overline{)34.68} \\ \underline{34} \\ 68 \\ \underline{68} \end{array}$$

12.
$$\begin{array}{r} .007 \\ 25\overline{)175} \\ 175 \end{array}$$

OPERATIONS WITH FRACTIONS

ADDING AND SUBTRACTING. In adding or subtracting fractions, you must remember that the numbers must have the same (common) denominator.

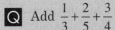 Add $\dfrac{1}{3}+\dfrac{2}{5}+\dfrac{3}{4}$

The least number which is divisible by 3, 5, and 4 is 60. Therefore, use 60 as the common denominator. To add the fractions, divide 60 by each denominator and multiply the result by the given numerator.

A $\dfrac{20+24+45}{60}=\dfrac{89}{60}$, or $1\dfrac{29}{60}$

$$\frac{a}{b}\times\frac{c}{d}=\frac{ad+bc}{bd}$$

A similar shortcut applies to subtraction.

$$\frac{a}{b}\times\frac{c}{d}=\frac{ad-bc}{bd}$$

$$\frac{3}{4}\times\frac{5}{7}=\frac{21-20}{28}=\frac{1}{28}$$

All fractions should be left in their simplest form. That is, there should be no factor common to both numerator and denominator. Often in multiple-choice questions you may find that the answer you have correctly computed is not among the choices but an equivalent fraction is. Be careful!

In simplifying fractions involving large numbers, it is helpful to be able to tell whether a factor is common to both numerator and denominator before a lengthy trial division. Certain tests for divisibility help with this.

TIP

To add or subtract fractions quickly, remember that a sum can be found by adding the two cross-products and putting this answer over the denominator product.

TESTS FOR DIVISIBILITY

To test if a number is divisible by:	Check to see:
2	if it is even
3	if the sum of the digits is divisible by 3
4	if the number formed by the last two digits is divisible by 4
5	if its last digit is a 5 or 0
6	if it is even and the sum of the digits is divisible by 3
8	if the number formed by the last three digits is divisible by 8
9	if the sum of the digits is divisible by 9
10	if its last digit is 0

Q Simplify $\dfrac{3525}{4341}$

This fraction can be simplified by dividing 3, since the sum of the digits of the numerator is 15 and those of the denominator add up to 12, both divisible by 3.

A $\dfrac{3525}{4341} = \dfrac{1175}{1447}$

The resulting fraction meets no further divisibility tests and therefore has no common factor listed above. Larger divisors would be unlikely on an SAT test.

To add or subtract mixed numbers, it is again important to remember common denominators. In subtraction, you must borrow in terms of the common denominator.

Addition:
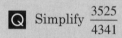
$$43\frac{2}{5} \quad = \quad 43\frac{6}{15}$$
$$+\ 8\frac{1}{3} \quad = \quad +\ 8\frac{5}{15}$$
$$51\frac{11}{15}$$

Subtraction:
$$43\frac{2}{5} \quad = \quad 43\frac{6}{15} \quad = \quad 42\frac{21}{15}$$
$$-\ 6\frac{2}{3} \quad = \quad -\ 6\frac{10}{15} \quad = \quad -\ 6\frac{10}{15}$$
$$36\frac{11}{15}$$

MULTIPLYING. To multiply fractions, always try to divide common factors where possible before actually multiplying. In multiplying mixed numbers, always rename them as improper fractions first.

Multiply: $\dfrac{\cancel{2}}{\cancel{5}} \cdot \dfrac{\overset{2}{\cancel{10}}}{\cancel{11}} \cdot \dfrac{\overset{9}{\cancel{99}}}{\underset{55}{\cancel{110}}} = \dfrac{18}{55}$

Multiply: $4\dfrac{1}{2} \cdot 1\dfrac{2}{3} \cdot 5\dfrac{1}{5}$

$\dfrac{\overset{3}{\cancel{9}}}{\cancel{2}} \cdot \dfrac{\cancel{5}}{\cancel{3}} \cdot \dfrac{\overset{13}{\cancel{26}}}{\cancel{5}} = 39$

DIVIDING. To divide fractions or mixed numbers, remember to multiply by the reciprocal of the divisor (the number after the division sign).

Divide: $4\dfrac{1}{2} \div \dfrac{3}{4} = \dfrac{\overset{3}{\cancel{9}}}{\cancel{2}} \cdot \dfrac{\overset{2}{\cancel{4}}}{\cancel{3}} = 6$

Divide: $62\dfrac{1}{2} \div 5 = \dfrac{\overset{25}{\cancel{125}}}{2} \cdot \dfrac{1}{\cancel{5}} = 12\dfrac{1}{2}$

To simplify complex fractions (fractions within fractions), multiply every term by the least common multiple of all denominators in order to clear all fractions in the given numerator and denominator.

Q $\dfrac{\dfrac{1}{2} + \dfrac{1}{3}}{\dfrac{1}{4} + \dfrac{1}{6}}$

A The least number that can be used to clear all fractions is 12. Multiplying each term by 12 yields

$\dfrac{6+4}{3+2} = \dfrac{10}{5} = 2$

Q $\dfrac{\dfrac{3}{4} + \dfrac{2}{3}}{1 - \dfrac{1}{2}}$

A Again, multiply by 12.

$\dfrac{9+8}{12-6} = \dfrac{17}{6} = 2\dfrac{5}{6}$

Exercise: Operations with Fractions

Directions: Work out each problem in the space provided.

Add:

1. $12\frac{5}{6} + 2\frac{3}{8} + 21\frac{1}{4}$

2. $\frac{1}{2} + \frac{1}{3} + \frac{1}{4} + \frac{1}{5} + \frac{1}{6}$

Subtract:

3. $5\frac{3}{4}$ from $10\frac{1}{2}$

4. $17\frac{2}{3}$ from 50

5. $25\frac{3}{5}$ from $30\frac{9}{10}$

Multiply:

6. $5\frac{1}{4} \cdot 1\frac{5}{7}$

7. $\frac{3}{4} \cdot \frac{3}{4} \cdot \frac{3}{4}$

8. $12\frac{1}{2} \cdot 16$

Divide:

9. $\frac{1}{5} \div 5$

10. $5 \div \frac{1}{5}$

11. $3\frac{2}{3} \div 1\frac{5}{6}$

Simplify:

12. $\dfrac{\frac{5}{6} - \frac{1}{3}}{2 + \frac{1}{5}}$

13. $\dfrac{3 + \frac{1}{4}}{5 - \frac{1}{2}}$

Solutions

1.
$$12\frac{5}{6} = \frac{20}{24}$$
$$2\frac{3}{8} = \frac{9}{24}$$
$$+\ 21\frac{1}{4} = \frac{6}{24}$$
$$35 + \frac{35}{24} = 36\frac{11}{24}$$

2.
$$\frac{1}{2} = \frac{30}{60}$$
$$\frac{1}{3} = \frac{20}{60}$$
$$\frac{1}{4} = \frac{15}{60}$$
$$\frac{1}{5} = \frac{12}{60}$$
$$+\ \frac{1}{6} = \frac{10}{60}$$
$$\frac{87}{60} = 1\frac{27}{60} = 1\frac{9}{20}$$

3.
$$10\frac{1}{2} = 9\frac{3}{2} = 9\frac{6}{4}$$
$$-\ 5\frac{3}{4}$$
$$4\frac{3}{4}$$

4.
$$\overset{493}{\cancel{50}}\frac{3}{3}$$
$$-\ 17\frac{2}{3}$$
$$32\frac{1}{3}$$

5.
$$30\frac{9}{10} = 30\frac{9}{10}$$
$$-\ 25\frac{3}{5} = 25\frac{6}{10}$$
$$5\frac{3}{10}$$

6.
$$\frac{\overset{3}{\cancel{21}}}{\cancel{4}} \cdot \frac{\overset{3}{\cancel{12}}}{\cancel{1}} = 9$$

7.
$$\frac{3}{4} \cdot \frac{3}{4} \cdot \frac{3}{4} = \frac{27}{64}$$

8.
$$\frac{25}{\cancel{2}} \cdot \overset{8}{\cancel{16}} = 200$$

9.
$$\frac{1}{5} \cdot \frac{1}{5} = \frac{1}{25}$$

10. $5 \cdot 5 = 25$

11.
$$\frac{\cancel{11}}{\cancel{3}} \cdot \frac{\overset{2}{\cancel{6}}}{\cancel{11}} = 2$$

12.
$$\frac{25-10}{60+6} = \frac{15}{66} = \frac{5}{22}$$
Each term was multiplied by 30.

13.
$$\frac{12+1}{20-2} = \frac{13}{18}$$
Each term was multiplied by 4.

VERBAL PROBLEMS INVOLVING FRACTIONS

Fraction problems deal with parts of a whole.

Q If a class consists of 12 boys and 18 girls, what part of the class is boys?

A 12 out of 30 students, or $\frac{12}{30} = \frac{2}{5}$

Read all the questions carefully. Often a problem may require more than one calculation.

Q $\frac{1}{4}$ of this year's seniors have averages above 90. $\frac{1}{2}$ of the remainder have averages between 80 and 90. What part of the senior class have averages below 80?

A $\frac{1}{4}$ have averages above 90.

$\frac{1}{2}$ of $\frac{3}{4}$ or $\frac{3}{8}$ have averages between 80 and 90.

$\frac{1}{4} + \frac{3}{8} = \frac{2}{8} + \frac{3}{8} = \frac{5}{8}$ have averages above 80.

Therefore, $\frac{3}{8}$ of the class have averages below 80.

Q 14 is $\frac{2}{3}$ of what number?

A $14 = \frac{2}{3}x$

Multiply each side by $\frac{3}{2}$

$21 = x$

Q If John has p hours of homework and has worked for r hours, what part of his homework is yet to be done?

A If John had 5 hours of homework and had worked for 3 hours, you would first find he had $5 - 3$ hours, or 2 hours, yet to do. This represents $\frac{2}{5}$ of his work. Using letters, his remaining work is represented by $\frac{p-r}{p}$.

EXERCISE: VERBAL PROBLEMS INVOLVING FRACTIONS

Directions: Work out each problem. Circle the letter next to your choice.

1. A team played 30 games of which it won 24. What part of the games played did the team lose?

   (A) $\frac{4}{5}$

   (B) $\frac{1}{4}$

   (C) $\frac{1}{5}$

   (D) $\frac{3}{4}$

   (E) $\frac{2}{3}$

2. If a man's weekly salary is X and he saves Y, what part of his weekly salary does he spend?

   (A) $\frac{X}{Y}$

   (B) $\frac{X-Y}{X}$

   (C) $\frac{X-Y}{Y}$

   (D) $\frac{Y-X}{X}$

   (E) $\frac{Y-X}{Y}$

3. What part of an hour elapses between 11:50 a.m. and 12:14 p.m.?

   (A) $\frac{2}{5}$

   (B) $\frac{7}{30}$

   (C) $\frac{17}{30}$

   (D) $\frac{1}{6}$

   (E) $\frac{1}{4}$

4. One half of the employees of Acme Co. earn salaries above $18,000 annually. One third of the remainder earn salaries between $15,000 and $18,000. What part of the staff earns below $15,000?

   (A) $\frac{1}{6}$

   (B) $\frac{2}{3}$

   (C) $\frac{1}{2}$

   (D) $\frac{1}{10}$

   (E) $\frac{1}{3}$

5. David received his allowance on Sunday. He spends $\frac{1}{4}$ of his allowance on Monday and $\frac{2}{3}$ of the remainder on Tuesday. What part of his allowance is left for the rest of the week?

   (A) $\frac{1}{3}$

   (B) $\frac{1}{12}$

   (C) $\frac{1}{4}$

   (D) $\frac{1}{2}$

   (E) $\frac{4}{7}$

6. 12 is $\frac{3}{4}$ of what number?

   (A) 16

   (B) 9

   (C) 36

   (D) 20

   (E) 15

7. A piece of fabric is cut into three sections so that the first is three times as long as the second and the second section is three times as long as the third. What part of the entire piece is the smallest section?

(A) $\dfrac{1}{12}$

(B) $\dfrac{1}{9}$

(C) $\dfrac{1}{3}$

(D) $\dfrac{1}{7}$

(E) $\dfrac{1}{13}$

8. What part of a gallon is one quart?

(A) $\dfrac{1}{2}$

(B) $\dfrac{1}{4}$

(C) $\dfrac{2}{3}$

(D) $\dfrac{1}{3}$

(E) $\dfrac{1}{5}$

9. A factory employs M men and W women. What part of its employees are women?

(A) $\dfrac{W}{M}$

(B) $\dfrac{M+W}{W}$

(C) $\dfrac{W}{M-W}$

(D) $\dfrac{W}{M+W}$

(E) W

10. A motion was passed by a vote of 5:3. What part of the votes cast were in favor of the motion?

(A) $\dfrac{5}{8}$

(B) $\dfrac{5}{3}$

(C) $\dfrac{3}{5}$

(D) $\dfrac{2}{5}$

(E) $\dfrac{3}{8}$

11. If the ratio of $x : y$ is 9:7, what is the value of $x + y$?

(A) 2

(B) 14

(C) 16

(D) 63

(E) It cannot be determined from the information.

12. In a certain class the ratio of men to women is 3:5. If the class has 24 people in it, how many are women?

(A) 9

(B) 12

(C) 15

(D) 18

(E) 21

13. If the ratio of men to women in a class is 3:5 and the class contains 24 people, how many additional men would have to enroll to make the ratio of men to women 1:1?

(A) 3

(B) 6

(C) 9

(D) 12

(E) 15

14. If x is $\frac{2}{3}$ of y and y is $\frac{3}{4}$ of z, what is the ratio of $z:x$?

(A) 1:2

(B) 1:1

(C) 2:1

(D) 3:2

(E) 4:3

15. What fraction of 8 tons is 1,000 lbs?

(A) $\frac{1}{32}$

(B) $\frac{1}{16}$

(C) $\frac{1}{8}$

(D) $\frac{8}{1}$

(E) $\frac{16}{1}$

Solutions

1. **The correct answer is (C).** The team lost 6 games out of 30. $\frac{6}{30} = \frac{1}{5}$

2. **The correct answer is (B).** The man spends $X - Y$ out of X. $\frac{X-Y}{X}$

3. **The correct answer is (A).** 10 minutes elapse by noon, and another 14 after noon, making a total of 24 minutes. There are 60 minutes in an hour. $\frac{24}{60} = \frac{2}{5}$

4. **The correct answer is (E).** One half earn over $18,000. One third of the other $\frac{1}{2}$, or $\frac{1}{6}$, earn between $15,000 and $18,000. This accounts for $\frac{1}{2} + \frac{1}{6}$, or $\frac{3}{6} + \frac{1}{6} = \frac{4}{6} = \frac{2}{3}$ of the staff, leaving $\frac{1}{3}$ to earn below $15,000.

5. **The correct answer is (C).** David spends $\frac{1}{4}$ on Monday and $\frac{2}{3}$ of the other $\frac{3}{4}$, or $\frac{1}{2}$, on Tuesday, leaving only $\frac{1}{4}$ for the rest of the week.

6. **The correct answer is (A).** $12 = \frac{3}{4}x$. Multiply each side by $\frac{4}{3}$. $16 = x$

7. **The correct answer is (E).** Let the third or shortest section $= x$. Then the second section $= 3x$, and the first section $= 9x$. The entire piece of fabric is then $13x$, and the shortest piece represents $\frac{x}{13x}$ or $\frac{1}{13}$ of the entire piece.

8. **The correct answer is (B).** There are four quarts in one gallon.

9. **The correct answer is (D).** The factory employs $M + W$ people, out of which W are women.

10. **The correct answer is (A).** For every 5 votes in favor, 3 were cast against. 5 out of every 8 votes cast were in favor of the motion.

11. **The correct answer is (E).** Remember, a ratio is a fraction. If x is 18 and y is 14, the ratio $x:y$ is 9:7, but $x + y$ is 32. The point of this problem is that x and y can take on *many* possible values, just as long as the ratio 9:7 is preserved. Given the multiplicity of possible values, it is not possible here to establish *one* definite value for the sum of x and y.

12. **The correct answer is (C).** The ratio of women to the total number of people is 5:8. We can set up a proportion. If $\frac{5}{8} = \frac{x}{24}$, then $x = 15$.

13. **The correct answer is (B).** From the previous problem we know that the class contains 15 women and 9 men. In order to have the same number of men and women, 6 additional men would have to enroll.

14. **The correct answer is (C).** There are several ways to attack this problem. If x is $\frac{2}{3}$ of y, then y is $\frac{3}{2}$ of x. If y is $\frac{3}{4}$ of z, then z is $\frac{4}{3}$ of y. Therefore, y is $\frac{3}{2}x$ and $z = 2x$. The ratio of $z:x$ is 2:1. You could also plug in a real number and solve. If x is 2, figure out what y and z would be. Therefore, y would be 3 and z would be 4, so the ratio of z to x is 2:1.

15. **The correct answer is (B).** A ton contains 2,000 pounds. So the fraction would be $\frac{1,000}{16,000}$, which is $\frac{1}{16}$.

VARIATION

DIRECT VARIATION. Two quantities are said to vary directly if they change in the same direction. As one increases, the other increases.

For example, the amount owed to the milkman varies directly with the number of quarts of milk purchased. The amount of sugar needed in a recipe varies directly with the amount of butter used. The number of inches between two cities on a map varies directly with the number of miles between the cities.

> **Q** If a two-ounce package of peanuts costs 20¢, what is the cost of a pound of peanuts?
>
> **A** Here you are comparing cents with ounces, so $\dfrac{20}{2} = \dfrac{x}{16}$
>
> In solving a proportion, it is easiest to cross-multiply, remembering that the product of the means (the second and third terms of a proportion) is equal to the product of the extremes (the first and last terms of a proportion).
>
> $2x = 320$
>
> $x = 160$
>
> Remember that the original units were cents, so the cost is $1.60.

When two fractions are equal, as in a proportion, it is sometimes easier to see what change has taken place in the given numerator or denominator and then to apply the same change to the missing term. In keeping fractions equal, the change will always involve multiplying or dividing by a constant. In the previous example, the denominator was changed from 2 to 16. This involved multiplication by 8; therefore, the numerator (20) must also be multiplied by 8, giving 160 as an answer without any written work necessary. Since time is a very important factor in this type of examination, shortcuts such as this could be critical.

> **Q** If a truck can carry m pounds of coal, how many trucks are needed to carry p pounds of coal?
>
> **A** You are comparing trucks with pounds. This again is a direct variation, because the number of trucks increases as the number of pounds increases.
>
> $\dfrac{1}{m} = \dfrac{x}{p}$
>
> $mx = p$
>
> $x = \dfrac{p}{m}$

TIP

Whenever two quantities vary directly, you can find a missing term by setting up a proportion. However, be very careful to compare the same units, in the same order, on each side of the equal sign.

INVERSE VARIATION. Two quantities are said to vary inversely if they change in opposite directions. As one increases, the other decreases.

For example, the number of workers hired to paint a house varies inversely with the number of days the job will take. A doctor's stock of flu vaccine varies inversely with the number of patients injected. The number of days a given supply of cat food lasts varies inversely with the number of cats being fed.

Q   If a case of cat food can feed 5 cats for 4 days, how long would it feed 8 cats?

A   Since this is a case of inverse variation (the more cats, the fewer days), multiply the number of cats by the number of days in each instance and set them equal.

$$5 \times 4 = 8 \times x$$
$$20 = 8x$$
$$2\frac{1}{2} = x$$

Exercise: Variation

Directions: Work out each problem. Circle the letter next to your choice.

1. If 60 feet of uniform wire weighs 80 pounds, what is the weight of 2 yards of the same wire?

   (A) $2\frac{2}{3}$

   (B) 6

   (C) 2400

   (D) 120

   (E) 8

2. A gear 50 inches in diameter turns a smaller gear 30 inches in diameter. If the larger gear makes 15 revolutions, how many revolutions does the smaller gear make in that time?

   (A) 9

   (B) 12

   (C) 20

   (D) 25

   (E) 30

3. If x men can do a job in h days, how long would y men take to do the same job?

(A) $\dfrac{x}{h}$

(B) $\dfrac{xh}{y}$

(C) $\dfrac{hy}{x}$

(D) $\dfrac{xy}{h}$

(E) $\dfrac{x}{y}$

4. If a furnace uses 40 gallons of oil in a week, how many gallons, to the nearest gallon, does it use in 10 days?

(A) 57

(B) 4

(C) 28

(D) 400

(E) 58

5. A recipe requires 13 ounces of sugar and 18 ounces of flour. If only 10 ounces of sugar are used, how much flour, to the nearest ounce, should be used?

(A) 13

(B) 23

(C) 24

(D) 14

(E) 15

6. If a car can drive 25 miles on two gallons of gasoline, how many gallons will be needed for a trip of 150 miles?

(A) 12

(B) 3

(C) 6

(D) 7

(E) 10

7. A school has enough bread to feed 30 children for 4 days. If 10 more children are added, how many days will the bread last?

(A) $5\dfrac{1}{3}$

(B) $1\dfrac{1}{3}$

(C) $2\dfrac{2}{3}$

(D) 12

(E) 3

8. At c cents per pound, what is the cost of a ounces of salami?

(A) $\dfrac{c}{a}$

(B) $\dfrac{a}{c}$

(C) ac

(D) $\dfrac{ac}{16}$

(E) $\dfrac{16c}{a}$

9. If 3 miles are equivalent to 4.83 kilometers, then 11.27 kilometers are equivalent to how many miles?

(A) $7\dfrac{1}{3}$

(B) $2\dfrac{1}{3}$

(C) 7

(D) 5

(E) $6\dfrac{1}{2}$

10. If p pencils cost d dollars, how many pencils can be bought for c cents?

(A) $\dfrac{100pc}{d}$

(B) $\dfrac{pc}{100d}$

(C) $\dfrac{pd}{c}$

(D) $\dfrac{pc}{d}$

(E) $\dfrac{cd}{p}$

Solutions

1. The correct answer is (E). You are comparing feet with pounds. The more feet, the more pounds. This is DIRECT. Remember to rename yards as feet:

$$\frac{60}{80} = \frac{6}{x}$$
$$60x = 480$$
$$x = 8$$

2. The correct answer is (D). The larger a gear, the fewer times it revolves in a given period of time. This is INVERSE.

$$50 \cdot 15 = 30 \cdot x$$
$$750 = 30x$$
$$25 = x$$

3. The correct answer is (B). The more men, the fewer days. This is INVERSE.

$$x \cdot h = y \cdot ?$$
$$\frac{xh}{y} = ?$$

4. The correct answer is (A). The more days, the more oil. This is DIRECT. Remember to rename the week as 7 days.

$$\frac{40}{7} = \frac{x}{10}$$
$$7x = 400$$
$$x = 57\frac{1}{7}$$

5. The correct answer is (D). The more sugar, the more flour. This is DIRECT.

$$\frac{13}{18} = \frac{10}{x}$$
$$13x = 180$$
$$x = 13\frac{11}{13}$$

6. The correct answer is (A). The more miles, the more gasoline. This is DIRECT.

$$\frac{25}{2} = \frac{150}{x}$$
$$25x = 300$$
$$x = 12$$

7. The correct answer is (E). The more children, the fewer days. This is INVERSE.

$$30 \cdot 4 = 40 \cdot x$$
$$120 = 40x$$
$$3 = x$$

8. The correct answer is (D). The more salami, the more it will cost. This is DIRECT. Remember to rename the pound as 16 ounces.

$$\frac{c}{16} = \frac{x}{a}$$
$$x = \frac{ac}{16}$$

9. The correct answer is (C). The more miles, the more kilometers. This is DIRECT.

$$\frac{3}{4.83} = \frac{x}{11.27}$$
$$4.83x = 33.81$$
$$x = 7$$

10. The correct answer is (B). The more pencils, the more cost. This is DIRECT. Remember to rename dollars as cents.

$$\frac{p}{100d} = \frac{x}{c}$$
$$x = \frac{pc}{100d}$$

TIP

To change a % to a decimal, remove the % sign and divide by 100. This has the effect of moving the deci-mal point two places to the LEFT.

TIP

To change a decimal to a %, add the % sign and multiply by 100. This has the effect of moving the decimal point two places to the RIGHT.

TIP

To change a % to a fraction, remove the % sign and divide by 100. This has the effect of putting the % over 100 and simplifying the resulting fraction.

FINDING PERCENTS

PERCENT EQUIVALENTS. "Percent" means "out of 100." If you understand this concept, it becomes very easy to rename a percent as an equivalent decimal or fraction.

$$5\% = \frac{5}{100} = .05$$

$$2.6\% = \frac{2.6}{100} = .026$$

$$c\% = \frac{c}{100} = \frac{1}{100} \cdot c = .01c$$

$$\frac{1}{2}\% = \frac{\frac{1}{2}}{100} = \frac{1}{100} \cdot \frac{1}{2} = \frac{1}{100} \cdot .5 = .005$$

Certain fractional equivalents of common percents occur frequently enough that they should be memorized. Learning the values in the following table will make your work with percent problems much easier.

PERCENT–FRACTION EQUIVALENT TABLE

$50\% = \frac{1}{2}$	$33\frac{1}{3}\% = \frac{1}{3}$	$12\frac{1}{2}\% = \frac{1}{8}$
$25\% = \frac{1}{4}$	$66\frac{2}{3}\% = \frac{2}{3}$	$37\frac{1}{2}\% = \frac{3}{8}$
$75\% = \frac{3}{4}$	$20\% = \frac{1}{5}$	$62\frac{1}{2}\% = \frac{5}{8}$
$10\% = \frac{1}{10}$	$40\% = \frac{2}{5}$	$87\frac{1}{2}\% = \frac{7}{8}$
$30\% = \frac{3}{10}$	$60\% = \frac{3}{5}$	$16\frac{2}{3}\% = \frac{1}{6}$
$70\% = \frac{7}{10}$	$80\% = \frac{4}{5}$	$83\frac{1}{3}\% = \frac{5}{6}$
$90\% = \frac{9}{10}$		

Most percentage problems can be solved by using the following proportion:

$$\frac{\%}{100} = \frac{\text{part}}{\text{whole}}$$

Although this method works, it often yields unnecessarily large numbers that are difficult to compute. Following are examples of the three basic types of percent problems and different methods for solving them.

To Find a Percent of a Number

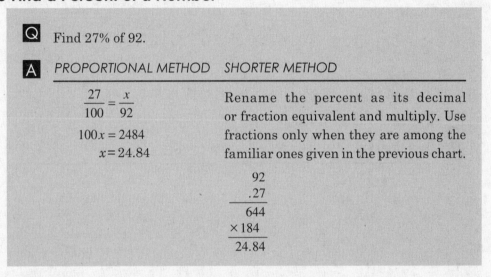

Q Find 27% of 92.

A PROPORTIONAL METHOD   SHORTER METHOD

$$\frac{27}{100} = \frac{x}{92}$$

$$100x = 2484$$

$$x = 24.84$$

Rename the percent as its decimal or fraction equivalent and multiply. Use fractions only when they are among the familiar ones given in the previous chart.

$$\begin{array}{r} 92 \\ .27 \\ \hline 644 \\ \times 184 \\ \hline 24.84 \end{array}$$

Q Find $12\frac{1}{2}$% of 96.

A PROPORTIONAL METHOD   DECIMAL METHOD   FRACTIONAL METHOD

$$\frac{12\frac{1}{2}}{100} = \frac{x}{96}$$

$$100x = 1200$$

$$x = 12$$

$$\begin{array}{r} .125 \\ \times 96 \\ \hline 750 \\ 1125 \\ \hline 12.000 \end{array}$$

$$\frac{1}{8} \cdot 96 = 12$$

Which method is easiest? It really pays to memorize those fractional equivalents.

To Find a Number When a Percent of It Is Given

Q Seven is 5% of what number?

A *PROPORTIONAL METHOD*   *SHORTER METHOD*

$$\frac{5}{100} = \frac{7}{x}$$
$$5x = 700$$
$$x = 140$$

Translate the problem into an algebraic equation. In doing this, the percent must be written as a fraction or decimal.

$$7 = .05x$$
$$700 = 5x$$
$$140 = x$$

Q 20 is $33\frac{1}{3}$% of what number?

A *PROPORTIONAL METHOD*   *SHORTER METHOD*

$$\frac{33\frac{1}{3}}{100} = \frac{20}{x}$$
$$33\frac{1}{3}x = 2000$$
$$\frac{100}{3}x = 2000$$
$$100x = 6000$$
$$x = 60$$

$$20 = \frac{1}{3}x$$
$$60 = x$$

Just think of the time you will save and the number of extra problems you will solve if you know that $33\frac{1}{3}\% = \frac{1}{3}$.

To Find What Percent One Number Is of Another

Q 90 is what percent of 1500?

A *PROPORTIONAL METHOD*   *SHORTER METHOD*

$$\frac{x}{100} = \frac{90}{1500}$$
$$1500x = 9000$$
$$15x = 90$$
$$x = 6$$

Put the part over the whole. Simplify the fraction and multiply by 100.

$$\frac{90}{1500} = \frac{9}{150} = \frac{3}{50} \cdot 100 = 6$$

Q 7 is what percent of 35?

A *PROPORTIONAL METHOD* *SHORTER METHOD*

$$\frac{x}{100} = \frac{7}{35}$$

$$35x = 700$$

$$x = 20$$

$$\frac{7}{35} = \frac{1}{5} = 20\%$$

Q 18 is what percent of 108?

A *PROPORTIONAL METHOD* *SHORTER METHOD*

$$\frac{x}{100} = \frac{18}{108}$$

$$108x = 1800$$

$$\frac{18}{108} = \frac{9}{54} = \frac{1}{6} = 16\frac{2}{3}\%$$

Time-consuming long division is necessary to get: $x = 16\frac{2}{3}$

Once again, if you know the fraction equi-equivalents of common percents, computation can be done in a few seconds.

To Find a Percent Over 100

Q Find 125% of 64.

A *PROPORTIONAL METHOD* *DECIMAL METHOD* *FRACTIONAL METHOD*

$$1\frac{1}{4} \cdot 64$$

$$\frac{5}{4} \cdot 64 = 80$$

$$\frac{125}{100} = \frac{x}{64}$$

$$100x = 8,000$$

$$x = 80$$

$$\begin{array}{r} 64 \\ \underline{1.25} \\ 320 \\ 128 \\ \underline{64} \\ 80.00 \end{array}$$

Q 36 is 150% of what number?

A *PROPORTIONAL*
METHOD   *DECIMAL METHOD*   *FRACTIONAL METHOD*

$36 = 1\frac{1}{2}x$

$$\frac{150}{100} = \frac{36}{x}$$

$36 = 1.50x$

$150x = 3600$

$360 = 15x$

$36 = \frac{3}{2}x$

$15x = 360$

$24 = x$

$x = 24$

$72 = 3x$

$24 = x$

Q 60 is what percent of 50?

A *PROPORTIONAL METHOD*   *FRACTIONAL METHOD*

$$\frac{x}{100} = \frac{60}{50}$$

$$\frac{60}{50} = \frac{6}{5} = 1\frac{1}{5} = 120\%$$

$50x = 6000$

$5x = 600$

$x = 120$

Exercise: Finding Percents

Directions: Work out each problem. Circle the letter next to your choice.

1. Write .2% as a decimal.

    (A) .2

    (B) .02

    (C) .002

    (D) 2

    (E) 20

2. Write 3.4% as a fraction.

    (A) $\frac{34}{1000}$

    (B) $\frac{34}{10}$

    (C) $\frac{34}{100}$

    (D) $\frac{340}{100}$

    (E) $\frac{34}{10,000}$

3. Write $\frac{3}{4}$% as a decimal.

    (A) .75

    (B) .075

    (C) .0075

    (D) .00075

    (E) 7.5

4. Find 60% of 70.

    (A) 420

    (B) 4.2

    (C) $116\frac{2}{3}$

    (D) 4,200

    (E) 42

5. What is 175% of 16?

    (A) $9\frac{1}{7}$

    (B) 28

    (C) 24

    (D) 12

    (E) 22

6. What percent of 40 is 16?

    (A) 20

    (B) $2\frac{1}{2}$

    (C) $33\frac{1}{3}$

    (D) 250

    (E) 40

7. What percent of 16 is 40?

    (A) 20

    (B) $2\frac{1}{2}$

    (C) 200

    (D) 250

    (E) 40

8. $4 is 20% of what?

    (A) $5

    (B) $20

    (C) $200

    (D) $5

    (E) $10

9. 12 is 150% of what number?

(A) 18

(B) 15

(C) 6

(D) 9

(E) 8

10. How many sixteenths are there in $87\frac{1}{2}\%$?

(A) 7

(B) 14

(C) 3.5

(D) 13

(E) 15

Solutions

1. The correct answer is (C).

.2% = .002 The decimal point moves to the LEFT two places.

2. The correct answer is (A).

$3.4\% = \dfrac{3.4}{100} = \dfrac{34}{1000}$

3. The correct answer is (C).

$\dfrac{3}{4}\% = .75\% = .0075$

4. The correct answer is (E).

$60\% = \dfrac{3}{5} \quad \dfrac{3}{5} \cdot 70 = 42$

5. The correct answer is (B).

$175\% = 1\dfrac{3}{4} \quad \dfrac{7}{4} \cdot 16 = 28$

6. The correct answer is (E).

$\dfrac{16}{40} = \dfrac{2}{5} = 40\%$

7. The correct answer is (D).

$\dfrac{40}{16} = \dfrac{5}{2} = 2\dfrac{1}{2} = 250\%$

8. The correct answer is (B).

$20\% = \dfrac{1}{5}$, so $4 = \dfrac{1}{5}x \quad 20 = x$

9. The correct answer is (E).

$150\% = 1\dfrac{1}{2} \quad \dfrac{3}{2}x = 12 \quad 3x = 24 \quad x = 8$

10. The correct answer is (B).

$87\dfrac{1}{2}\% = \dfrac{7}{8} = \dfrac{14}{16}$

VERBAL PROBLEMS INVOLVING PERCENT

Certain types of business situations are excellent applications of percent.

Percent of Increase or Decrease

The percent of increase or decrease is found by putting the amount of increase or decrease over the original amount and renaming this fraction as a percent, as explained in a previous section.

> **Q** Over a five-year period, the enrollment at South High dropped from 1,000 students to 800. Find the percent of decrease.
>
> **A** $\dfrac{200}{1000} = \dfrac{20}{100} = 20\%$

> **Q** A company normally employs 100 people. During a slow spell, it fired 20% of its employees. By what percent must it now increase its staff to return to full capacity?
>
> **A** 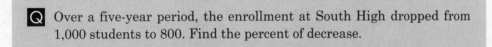 $20\% = \dfrac{1}{5} \quad \dfrac{1}{5} \cdot 100 = 20$
>
> The company now has $100 - 20 = 80$ employees. If it then increases by 20, the percent of increase is $\frac{20}{80} = \frac{1}{4}$, or 25%.

TIP

In word problems, *of* can usually be interpreted to mean *times* (in other words, *multiply*).

Discount

A discount is usually expressed as a percent of the marked price that will be deducted from the marked price to determine the sale price.

> **Q** Bill's Hardware offers a 20% discount on all appliances during a sale week. If they take advantage of the sale, how much must the Russells pay for a washing machine marked at $280?
>
> **A**
>
> | LONG METHOD | SHORTCUT METHOD |
> |---|---|
> | $20\% = \dfrac{1}{5}$ $\dfrac{1}{5} \cdot 280 = \$56$ discount $\$280 - \$56 = \$224$ sale price | If there is a 20% discount, the Russells will pay 80% of the marked price. |
> | The danger inherent in this method is that $56 is sure to be among the multiple-choice answers. | $80\% = \dfrac{4}{5}$ $\dfrac{4}{5} \cdot 280 = \$224$ sale price |

> **Q** A store offers a television set marked at $340 less discounts of 10% and 5%. Another store offers the same set with a single discount of 15%. How much does the buyer save by buying at the better price?
>
> **A** In the first store, the initial discount means the buyer pays 90% or $\frac{9}{10}$ of 340, which is $306. The additional 5% discount means the buyer pays 95% of $306, or $290.70. Note that the second discount must be figured on the first sale price. Taking 5% off $306 is a smaller amount than taking the additional 5% off $340. The second store will therefore have a lower sale price. In the second store, the buyer will pay 85% of $340, or $289, making the price $1.70 less than in the first store.

Commission

Many salespeople earn money on a commission basis. In order to encourage sales, they are paid a percentage of the value of goods sold. This amount is called a commission.

Q A salesperson at Brown's Department Store is paid $80 per week in salary plus a 4% commission on all her sales. How much will that salesperson earn in a week in which she sells $4,032 worth of merchandise?

A Find 4% of $4,032 and add this amount to $80.

4032
×.04
$161.28 + $80 = $241.28

Q Bill Olson delivers newspapers for a dealer and keeps 8% of all money collected. One month he was able to keep $16. How much did he forward to the newspaper?

A First, determine how much he collected by finding the number that 16 is 8% of.

$16 = .08x$

$1600 = 8x$

$200 = x$

If Bill collected $200 and kept $16, he gave the dealer $200 − $16, or $184.

Taxes

Taxes are a percent of money spent or money earned.

Q Noname County collects a 7% sales tax on automobiles. If the price of a car is $8,532 before taxes, what will this car cost once sales tax is added in?

A Find 7% of $8,532 to determine tax and then add it to $8,532. This can be done in one step by finding 107% of $8,532.

8532
× 1.07
59724
85320
$9129.24

Q If the tax rate in Anytown is $3.10 per $100, what is the annual real estate tax on a house assessed at $47,200?

A Annual tax = Tax rate × Assessed value

= ($3.10/$100)($47,200)

= (.031)(47,200)

= $1,463.20

ALERT!

Watch out! You should think of zero as an even number.

Exercise: Verbal Problems Involving Percent

Directions: Work out each problem. Circle the letter next to your choice.

1. A suit marked at $80 is sold for $68. What is the rate of discount?

    (A) 15%

    (B) 12%

    (C) $17\frac{11}{17}$%

    (D) 20%

    (E) 24%

2. What was the original price of a radio that sold for $70 during a 20%-off sale?

    (A) $84

    (B) $56

    (C) $87.50

    (D) $92

    (E) $90

3. How many dollars does a salesperson earn on a sale of s dollars at a commission of r%?

    (A) rs

    (B) $\frac{r}{s}$

    (C) $100rs$

    (D) $\frac{r}{100s}$

    (E) $\frac{rs}{100}$

4. At a selling price of $273, a refrigerator yields a 30% profit on the cost. What selling price will yield a 10% profit on the cost?

    (A) $210

    (B) $231

    (C) $221

    (D) $235

    (E) $240

5. What single discount is equivalent to two successive discounts of 10% and 15%?

    (A) 25%

    (B) 24%

    (C) 24.5%

    (D) 23.5%

    (E) 22%

6. The net price of a certain article is $306 after successive discounts of 15% and 10% off the marked price. What is the marked price?

    (A) $234.09

    (B) $400

    (C) $382.50

    (D) $408

    (E) None of these

7. If a merchant makes a profit of 20% based on the selling price of an article, what percent does the merchant make on the cost?

    (A) 20

    (B) 40

    (C) 25

    (D) 80

    (E) None of these

8. A certain radio costs a merchant $72. At what price must the merchant sell this radio in order to make a profit of 20% of the selling price?

   (A) $86.40

   (B) $92

   (C) $90

   (D) $144

   (E) $148

9. A baseball team has won 40 games out of 60 played. It has 32 more games to play. How many of these must the team win to make its record 75% for the season?

   (A) 26

   (B) 29

   (C) 28

   (D) 30

   (E) 32

10. If prices are reduced 25% and sales increase 20%, what is the net effect on gross receipts?

    (A) They increase by 5%.

    (B) They decrease by 5%.

    (C) They remain the same.

    (D) They increase by 10%.

    (E) They decrease by 10%.

11. A salesperson earns 5% on all sales between $200 and $600, and 8% on the part of the sales over $600. What is her commission in a week in which her sales total $800?

    (A) $20

    (B) $46

    (C) $88

    (D) $36

    (E) $78

12. If the enrollment at State U. was 3,000 in 1975 and 12,000 in 2000, what was the percent of increase in enrollment?

    (A) 125%

    (B) 25%

    (C) 300%

    (D) 400%

    (E) 3%

13. If 6 students, representing $16\frac{2}{3}$% of the class, failed algebra, how many students passed the course?

    (A) 48

    (B) 36

    (C) 42

    (D) 30

    (E) 32

14. If 95% of the residents of Coral Estates live in private homes and 40% of these live in air-conditioned homes, what percent of the residents of Coral Estates live in air-conditioned homes?

    (A) 3%

    (B) 30%

    (C) 3.8%

    (D) 40%

    (E) 38%

15. A salesperson receives a salary of $100 a week and a commission of 5% on all sales. What must be the amount of sales for a week in which the salesperson's total weekly income is $360?

    (A) $6,200

    (B) $5,200

    (C) $2,600

    (D) $720

    (E) $560

Solutions

1. **The correct answer is (A).** The amount of discount is $12. Rate of discount is figured on the original price.

$$\frac{12}{80} = \frac{3}{20} \quad \frac{3}{20} \cdot 100 = 15\%$$

2. **The correct answer is (C).** $70 represents 80% of the original price.

$$70 = .80x$$
$$700 = 8x$$
$$\$87.50 = x$$

3. **The correct answer is (E).** $r\% = \frac{r}{100}$

The commission is $\frac{r}{100} \cdot s = \frac{rs}{100}$

4. **The correct answer is (B).**

$$1.30x = 273$$
$$13x = 2730$$
$$x = \$210 = \text{cost}$$

$273 represents 130% of the cost.

The new price will add 10% of cost, or $21, for profit.

New price = $231

5. **The correct answer is (D).** Work with a simple figure, such as 100.

First sale price is 90% of $100, or $90.

Final sale price is 85% of $90, or $76.50

Total discount is $100 − $76.50 = $23.50

Percent of discount = $\frac{23.50}{100}$ or 23.5%

6. **The correct answer is (B).** If marked price = m, first sale price = $.85m$ and net price = $.90(.85m) = .765m$

$$.765m = 306$$
$$m = 400$$

In this case, it would be easy to work from the answer choices.

15% of $400 is $60, making a first sale price of $340.

10% of this price is $34, making the net price $306.

Choices (A), (C), and (D) would not give a final answer in whole dollars.

7. **The correct answer is (C).** Use an easy amount of $100 for the selling price. If the profit is 20% of the selling price, or $20, the cost is $80. Profit based on cost is

$$\frac{20}{80} = \frac{1}{4} = 25\%$$

8. **The correct answer is (C).** If the profit is to be 20% of the selling price, the cost must be 80% of the selling price.

$$72 = .80x$$
$$720 = 8x$$
$$90 = x$$

9. **The correct answer is (B).** The team must win 75%, or $\frac{3}{4}$, of the games played during the entire season. With 60 games played and 32 more to play, the team must win $\frac{3}{4}$ of 92 games in all. $\frac{3}{4} \cdot 92 = 69$. Since 40 games have already been won, the team must win 29 additional games.

10. **The correct answer is (E).** Let original price = p, and original sales = s. Therefore, original gross receipts = ps. Let new price = $.75p$, and new sales = $1.20s$. Therefore, new gross receipts = $.90ps$. Gross receipts are only 90% of what they were.

11. **The correct answer is (B).** Five percent of sales between $200 and $600 is $.05(600) = 30. 8% of sales over $600 is $.08(200) = 16. Total commission = $30 + $16 = $46.

12. **The correct answer is (C).** Increase is 9,000. Percent of increase is figured on original. $\frac{9000}{3000} = 3 = 300\%$

13. **The correct answer is (D).** $16\frac{2}{3}\% = \frac{1}{6}$

$$6 = \frac{1}{6}x$$
$$36 = x$$

36 students in class: 6 failed, 30 passed

14. The correct answer is (E). $40\% = \dfrac{2}{5}$

$\dfrac{2}{5}$ of $95\% = 38\%$

15. The correct answer is (B).

Let s = sales

$$\$100 + .05s = 360$$
$$.05s = 260$$
$$5s = 26,000$$
$$s = \$5,200$$

AVERAGES

ADD, THEN DIVIDE. The concept of average is familiar to most students. To find the average of n numbers, simply add the numbers and divide by n.

> **Q** Find the average of 32, 50, and 47.
>
> **A**
> $$\begin{array}{r} 32 \\ 50 \\ +\ 47 \\ \hline 129 \end{array} \qquad 3\overline{)129}\,^{43}$$

A more frequently encountered type of average problem will give the average and ask you to find a missing term.

> **Q** The average of three numbers is 43. If two of the numbers are 32 and 50, find the third number.
>
> **A** Using the definition of average, write the equation:
>
> $$\dfrac{32 + 50 + x}{3} = 43$$
> $$32 + 50 + x = 129$$
> $$82 + x = 129$$
> $$x = 47$$

WEIGHTED AVERAGE. Another concept to understand is the weighted average.

> **Q** Andrea has four grades of 90 and two grades of 80 during the spring semester of calculus. What is her average in the course for this semester?
>
> **A** 90   or
>
>   90
>
>   90 $90 \cdot 4 = 360$
>
>   90 $80 \cdot 2 = \underline{160}$
>
>   80 $6\overline{)520}$
>
> $+ \ \underline{80}$ $86\dfrac{2}{3}$
>
> $6\overline{)\ 520}$
>
> $86\dfrac{2}{3}$

Be sure to understand that you cannot simply average 90 and 80, since there are more grades of 90 than 80.

AVERAGE RATE. The final concept of average that you should master is average rate. The average rate for a trip is the total distance covered, divided by the total time spent.

> **Q** In driving from New York to Boston, Mr. Portney drove for 3 hours at 40 miles per hour and 1 hour at 48 miles per hour. What was his average rate for this portion of the trip?
>
> **A** Average rate $= \dfrac{\text{Total distance}}{\text{Total time}}$
>
> Average rate $= \dfrac{3(40) + 1(48)}{3 + 1}$
>
> Average rate $= \dfrac{168}{4} = 42$ miles per hour

Since more of the trip was driven at 40 mph than at 48 mph, the average should be closer to 40 than to 48, which it is. This will help you to check your answer, or to pick out the correct choice in a multiple-choice question.

Exercise: Averages

Directions: Work out each problem. Circle the letter next to your choice.

1. Dan had an average of 72 on his first four math tests. After taking the next test, his average dropped to 70. Which of the following is his most recent test grade?

    (A) 60

    (B) 62

    (C) 64

    (D) 66

    (E) 68

2. What is the average of $\sqrt{.64}$, .85, and $\frac{9}{10}$?

    (A) $\frac{21}{25}$

    (B) 3.25

    (C) 2.55

    (D) 85%

    (E) $\frac{4}{5}$

3. The average of two numbers is XY. If the first number is Y, what is the other number?

    (A) $2XY-Y$

    (B) $XY-2Y$

    (C) $2XY-X$

    (D) X

    (E) $XY-Y$

4. 30 students had an average of X, while 20 students had an average of 80. What is the average for the entire group?

    (A) $\dfrac{X+80}{50}$

    (B) $\dfrac{X+80}{2}$

    (C) $\dfrac{50}{X+80}$

    (D) $\dfrac{3}{5}X+32$

    (E) $\dfrac{30X+80}{50}$

5. What is the average of the first 15 positive integers?

    (A) 7

    (B) 7.5

    (C) 8

    (D) 8.5

    (E) 9

6. A man travels a distance of 20 miles at 60 miles per hour and then returns over the same route at 40 miles per hour. What is his average rate for the round trip in miles per hour?

    (A) 50

    (B) 48

    (C) 47

    (D) 46

    (E) 45

7. A number p equals $\frac{3}{2}$ the average of 10, 12, and q. What is q in terms of p?

    (A) $\frac{2}{3}p - 22$

    (B) $\frac{4}{3}p - 22$

    (C) $2p - 22$

    (D) $\frac{1}{2}p + 11$

    (E) $\frac{9}{2}p - 22$

8. Susan has an average of 86 in three examinations. What grade must she receive on her next test to raise her average to 88?

    (A) 94

    (B) 90

    (C) 92

    (D) 100

    (E) 96

9. The heights of the five starters on Redwood High's basketball team are 5'11", 6'3", 6', 6'6", and 6'2". The average height of these players is

    (A) 6'1"

    (B) 6'2"

    (C) 6'3"

    (D) 6'4"

    (E) 6'5"

10. What is the average of all numbers from 1 to 100 that end in 2?

    (A) 46

    (B) 47

    (C) 48

    (D) 50

    (E) None of these

Solutions

1. **The correct answer is (B).**

$$\frac{4(72)+x}{5}=70$$
$$288+x=350$$
$$x=62$$

2. **The correct answer is (D).** In order to average these three numbers, they should all be expressed as decimals.

$$\sqrt{.64}=.8$$
$$.85=.85$$
$$\frac{9}{10}=.9$$

$$\text{Average}=\frac{.8+.85+.9}{3}=\frac{2.55}{3}=.85$$

This is equal to 85%.

3. **The correct answer is (A).**

$$\frac{Y+x}{2}=XY$$
$$Y+x=2XY$$
$$x=2XY-Y$$

4. **The correct answer is (D).**

$$\frac{30(X)+20(80)}{50}=\text{Average}$$
$$\frac{30(X)+1600}{50}=\frac{3X+160}{5}=\frac{3}{5}X+32$$

5. **The correct answer is (C).** Positive integers begin with 1.

$$\frac{1+2+3+4+5+6+7+8+9+10+11+12+13+14+15}{15}$$

Since these numbers are evenly spaced, the average will be the middle number, 8.

6. **The correct answer is (B).**

$$\text{Average rate}=\frac{\text{Total distance}}{\text{Total time}}$$

Total distance = 20 + 20 = 40

Since time = $\frac{\text{distance}}{\text{time}}$, time for first part of trip is $\frac{20}{60}$, or $\frac{1}{3}$ hour, while time for the second part of trip is $\frac{20}{40}$, or $\frac{1}{2}$ hour.

Total time = $\frac{1}{3}+\frac{1}{2}$, or $\frac{5}{6}$ hour

Average rate = $\frac{40}{\frac{5}{6}}=40\cdot\frac{6}{5}=48$ mph

7. **The correct answer is (C).**

$$p=\frac{3}{2}\left(\frac{10+12+q}{3}\right)$$
$$p=\frac{10+12+q}{2}$$
$$2p=22+q$$
$$2p-22=q$$

8. **The correct answer is (A).**

$$\frac{3(86)+x}{4}=88$$
$$258+x=352$$
$$x=94$$

9. **The correct answer is (B).**

$$
\begin{array}{r}
5'11'' \\
6'3'' \\
6' \\
6'6'' \\
6'2'' \\
\hline
\end{array}
$$

$$29'22''=5)\overline{30'10''}$$
$$6'2''$$

10. **The correct answer is (B).**

$$\frac{2+12+22+32+42+52+62+72+82+92}{10}$$

Since these numbers are equally spaced, the average is the middle number. However, since there is an even number of addends, the average will be halfway between the middle two. Halfway between 42 and 52 is 47.

SAT Algebra Review

OVERVIEW

- Signed numbers
- Linear equations
- Exponents
- Quadratic equations
- Literal expressions
- Roots and radicals
- Factoring and algebraic fractions
- Problem solving in algebra
- Inequalities
- Defined operation problems

SIGNED NUMBERS

To solve algebra problems, you must be able to compute accurately with signed numbers.

Addition: To add signed numbers with the same sign, add the magnitudes of the numbers and keep the same sign. To add signed numbers with different signs, subtract the magnitudes of the numbers and use the sign of the number with the greater magnitude.

Subtraction: Change the sign of the number being subtracted and follow the rules for addition.

Multiplication: If there are an odd number of negative signs, the product is negative. An even number of negative signs gives a positive product.

Division: If the signs are the same, the quotient is positive. If the signs are different, the quotient is negative.

chapter 14

Exercise: Signed Numbers

Directions: Work out each problem. Circle the letter next to your choice.

1. When +3 is added to –5, the sum is
    (A) –8
    (B) +8
    (C) –2
    (D) +2
    (E) –15

2. When –4 and –5 are added, the sum is
    (A) –9
    (B) +9
    (C) –1
    (D) +1
    (E) +20

3. Subtract +3
               – 6
    (A) –3
    (B) +3
    (C) +18
    (D) –9
    (E) +9

4. When –5 is subtracted from +10, the result is
    (A) +5
    (B) +15
    (C) –5
    (D) –15
    (E) –50

5. (–6)(–3) equals
    (A) –18
    (B) +18
    (C) +2
    (D) –9
    (E) +9

6. The product of $(-6)(+\frac{1}{2})(-10)$ is
    (A) $-15\frac{1}{2}$
    (B) $+15\frac{1}{2}$
    (C) –30
    (D) +30
    (E) +120

7. When the product of (–4) and (+3) is divided by (–2), the quotient is
    (A) $\frac{1}{2}$
    (B) $3\frac{1}{2}$
    (C) 6
    (D) $-\frac{1}{2}$
    (E) – 6

Solutions

1. **The correct answer is (C).** In adding numbers with opposite signs, subtract their magnitudes $(5 - 3 = 2)$ and use the sign of the number with the greater magnitude (negative).

2. **The correct answer is (A).** In adding numbers with the same sign, add their magnitudes $(4 + 5 = 9)$ and keep the same sign.

3. **The correct answer is (E).** Change the sign of the second number and follow the rules for addition.

$$
\begin{array}{r}
+ \quad 3 \\
+ \ominus 6 \\
\hline
+ \quad 9
\end{array}
$$

4. **The correct answer is (B).** Change the sign of the second number and follow the rules for addition.

$$
\begin{array}{r}
+ \quad 10 \\
+ \ominus 5 \\
\hline
+ \quad 15
\end{array}
$$

5. **The correct answer is (B).** The product of two negative numbers is a positive number.

6. **The correct answer is (D).** The product of an even number of negative numbers is positive.

$$(\overset{3}{\cancel{6}})\left(\frac{1}{\cancel{2}}\right)(10) = 30$$

7. **The correct answer is (C).**

$$(-4)(+3) = -12$$

Dividing a negative number by a negative number gives a positive quotient.

$$\frac{-12}{-2} = +6$$

TIP

If you have a string of multiplications and divisions to do and the number of negative factors is *even*, the result will be positive; if the number of negative factors is *odd*, the result will be negative.

LINEAR EQUATIONS

The next step in solving algebra problems is mastering linear equations. Whether an equation involves numbers or only variables, the basic steps are the same.

Strategy:

1 If there are fractions or decimals, remove them by multiplication.

2 Collect all terms containing the unknown for which you are solving on the same side of the equation. Remember that whenever a term crosses the equal sign from one side of the equation to the other, it must pay a toll. That is, it must change its sign.

3 Determine the coefficient of the unknown by combining similar terms or factoring when terms cannot be combined.

4 Divide both sides of the equation by this coefficient.

Q Solve for x: $5x - 3 = 3x + 5$

A $2x = 8$
$x = 4$

Q Solve for x: $ax - b = cx + d$

A $ax - cx = b + d$
$x(a - c) = b + d$
$x = \dfrac{b + d}{a - c}$

Q Solve for x: $\frac{3}{4}x + 2 = \frac{2}{3}x + 3$

A Multiply by 12: $9x + 24 = 8x + 36$
$x = 12$

Q Solve for x: $.7x + .04 = 2.49$

A Multiply by 100: $70x + 4 = 249$
$70x = 245$
$x = 3.5$

SIMULTANEOUS EQUATIONS. In solving equations with two unknowns, you must work with two equations simultaneously. The object is to eliminate one of the two unknowns, and solve for the resulting single unknown.

Q Solve for x: $2x - 4y = 2$

$\qquad$ $3x + 5y = 14$

A Multiply the first equation by 5:

$10x - 20y = 10$

Multiply the second equation by 4:

$12x + 20y = 56$

Since the y terms now have the same numerical coefficients, but with opposite signs, you can eliminate them by adding the two equations. If they had the same signs, you would eliminate them by subtracting the equations.

Add the equations:

$10x - 20y = 10$

$12x + 20y = 56$

$\underline{22x \qquad = 66}$

$\qquad x = 3$

Since you were only asked to solve for x, stop here. If you were asked to solve for both x and y, you would now substitute 3 for x in either equation and solve the resulting equation for y.

$3(3) + 5y = 14$

$\quad 9 + 5y = 14$

$\qquad 5y = 5$

$\qquad y = 1$

Q Solve for x:

$ax + by = c$

$dx + ey = f$

A Multiply the first equation by e:

$aex + bey = ce$

Multiply the second equation by b:

$bdx + bey = bf$

Since the y terms now have the same coefficient, with the same sign, eliminate these terms by subtracting the two equations.

$$aex + bey = ce$$
$$- (bdx + bey = bf)$$
$$\overline{aex - bdx = ce - bf}$$

Factor to determine the coefficient of x:
$$x(ae - bd) = ce - bf$$

Divide by the coefficient of x:

$$x = \frac{ce - bf}{ae - bd}$$

Exercise: Linear Equations

Directions: Work out each problem. Circle the letter next to your choice.

1. If $5x + 6 = 10$, then x equals
   - (A) $\frac{16}{5}$
   - (B) $\frac{5}{16}$
   - (C) $-\frac{5}{4}$
   - (D) $\frac{4}{5}$
   - (E) $\frac{5}{4}$

2. Solve for x: $ax = bx + c, a \neq b$
   - (A) $\frac{b+c}{a}$
   - (B) $\frac{c}{a-b}$
   - (C) $\frac{c}{b-a}$
   - (D) $\frac{a-b}{c}$
   - (E) $\frac{c}{a+b}$

3. Solve for k: $\frac{k}{3} + \frac{k}{4} = 1$
   - (A) $\frac{11}{8}$
   - (B) $\frac{8}{11}$
   - (C) $\frac{7}{12}$
   - (D) $\frac{12}{7}$
   - (E) $\frac{1}{7}$

4. If $x + y = 8p$ and $x - y = 6q$, then x is
   - (A) $7pq$
   - (B) $4p + 3q$
   - (C) pq
   - (D) $4p - 3q$
   - (E) $8p + 6q$

5. If $7x = 3x + 12$, then $2x + 5 =$
   - **(A)** 10
   - **(B)** 11
   - **(C)** 12
   - **(D)** 13
   - **(E)** 14

6. In the equation $y = x^2 + rx - 3$, for what value of r will $y = 11$ when $x = 2$?
   - **(A)** 6
   - **(B)** 5
   - **(C)** 4
   - **(D)** $3\frac{1}{2}$
   - **(E)** 0

7. If $1 + \frac{1}{t} = \frac{t+1}{t}$, what does t equal?
   - **(A)** +1 only
   - **(B)** +1 or –1 only
   - **(C)** +1 or +2 only
   - **(D)** No values
   - **(E)** All values except 0

8. If $.23m = .069$, then $m =$
   - **(A)** .003
   - **(B)** .03
   - **(C)** .3
   - **(D)** 3
   - **(E)** 30

9. If $35rt + 8 = 42rt$, then $rt =$
   - **(A)** $\frac{8}{7}$
   - **(B)** $\frac{8}{87}$
   - **(C)** $\frac{7}{8}$
   - **(D)** $\frac{87}{8}$
   - **(E)** $-\frac{8}{7}$

10. For what values of n is $n + 5$ equal to $n - 5$?
   - **(A)** No value
   - **(B)** 0
   - **(C)** All negative values
   - **(D)** All positive values
   - **(E)** All values

exercises

Solutions

1. **The correct answer is (D).**

   $$5x = 4$$

   $$x = \frac{4}{5}$$

2. **The correct answer is (B).**

   $$ax - bx = c \quad x(a - b) = c \quad x = \frac{c}{a - b}$$

3. **The correct answer is (D).** Multiply by 12:

   $$4k + 3k = 12$$

   $$7k = 12$$

   $$k = \frac{12}{7}$$

4. **The correct answer is (B).** Add equations to eliminate y:

   $$x + y = 8p$$
   $$\underline{x - y = 6q}$$
   $$2x \quad = 8p + 6q$$

   Divide by 2: $x = 4p + 3q$

5. **The correct answer is (B).** Solve for x:

   $$4x = 12$$

   $$x = 3$$

   $$2x + 5 = 2(3) + 5 = 11$$

6. **The correct answer is (B).** Substitute given values:

   $$11 = 4 + 2r - 3$$
   $$10 = 2r$$
   $$r = 5$$

7. **The correct answer is (E).**

   Multiply by t: $t + 1 = t + 1$

   This is an identity and is therefore true for all values. However, since t was a denominator in the given equation, t may not equal 0, because you can never divide by 0.

8. **The correct answer is (C).** Multiply by 100 to make coefficient an integer.

   $$23x = 6.9$$

   $$x = .3$$

9. **The correct answer is (A).** Even though this equation has two unknowns, you are asked to solve for rt, which may be treated as a single unknown.

   $$8 = 7rt$$

   $$\frac{8}{7} = rt$$

10. **The correct answer is (A).** There is no number such that, when 5 is added, you get the same result as when 5 is subtracted. Do not confuse choices (A) and (B). Choice (B) would mean that the number 0 satisfies the equation, which it does not.

EXPONENTS

DEFINITIONS. An *exponent* is a mathematical notation indicating that a number, called the *base*, has been multiplied one or more times by itself. For example, in the term 2^3, the 2 is the base and the ^{3} is the exponent. This term means "two times two times two" and is read "two to the third power." The word *power* tells how many times the base number appears in the multiplication.

$x^3 = x$ times x times x

$x^2 = x$ times x

$x^1 = x$

$x^0 = 1$

The Rules of Exponents

❶ To multiply powers of the same base, add the exponents.

x^2 times $x^3 = x^{2+3} = x^5$

x^5 times $x^4 = x^{5+4} = x^9$

❷ To divide powers of the same base, subtract the exponent of the divisor from the exponent of the dividend.

$$\frac{x^6}{x^2} = x^{6-2} = x^4$$

$$\frac{x^{10}}{x^3} = x^{10-3} = x^7$$

❸ To find the power of a power, multiply the exponents.

$(x^2)^3 = x^{(2)(3)} = x^6$

$(x^3y^5)^2 = x^{(3)(2)}y^{(5)(2)} = x^6y^{10}$

A variable base with an even exponent has two values, one positive and one negative.

$x^2 = 25$; x could be positive 5 or negative 5.

A variable base can be zero (unless otherwise stated in the problem). In that case, no matter what the exponent, the value of the term is zero.

Is x^4 always greater than x^2? No; if x is zero, then x^4 and x^2 are equal.

When the base is a fraction between 0 and 1, the larger the exponent, the smaller the value of the term.

Which is greater, $\left(\frac{37}{73}\right)$ or $\left(\frac{37}{73}\right)^2$? The correct answer is $\left(\frac{37}{73}\right)$ because $\left(\frac{37}{73}\right)$ is almost $\frac{1}{2}$, while $\left(\frac{37}{73}\right)^2$ is about $\frac{1}{4}$.

TIP

Commit to memory small powers of small numbers that come up in many questions. For example, the powers of 2: 2, 4, 8, 16, 32, . . . ; the powers of 3: 3, 9, 27, 81, . . . and so on.

Exercise: Exponents

Directions: Work out each problem. Circle the letter next to your choice.

1. If x and y are not equal to 0, then $x^{12}y^6$ must be

   I. Positive

   II. Negative

   III. An integer

   IV. A mixed fraction

   (A) I only

   (B) II only

   (C) III only

   (D) IV only

   (E) I and III only

2. $(x^2y^3)^4 =$

   (A) x^6y^7

   (B) x^8y^{12}

   (C) $x^{12}y^8$

   (D) x^2y

   (E) x^6y^9

3. $\dfrac{x^{16}y^6}{x^4y^2} =$

   (A) $x^{20}y^8$

   (B) x^4y^3

   (C) x^5y^6

   (D) $x^{12}y^3$

   (E) $x^{12}y^4$

4. If $x^4 = 16$ and $y^2 = 36$, then the *maximum* possible value for $x - y$ is

   (A) −20

   (B) 20

   (C) −4

   (D) 6

   (E) 8

5. $p^8 \times q^4 \times p^4 \times q^8 =$

   (A) $p^{12}q^{12}$

   (B) p^4q^4

   (C) $p^{32}q^{32}$

   (D) $p^{64}q^{64}$

   (E) $p^{16}q^{16}$

Solutions

1. **The correct answer is (A).** If x and y are not 0, then the even exponents would force x^{12} and y^6 to be positive.

2. **The correct answer is (B).** To raise a power to a power, multiply the exponents. $x^{(2)(4)}y^{(3)(4)} = x^8y^{12}$

3. **The correct answer is (E).** All fractions are implied division. When dividing terms with a common base and different exponents, subtract the exponents. Therefore, $16 - 4 = 12$ and $6 - 2 = 4$.

4. **The correct answer is (E).** x could be positive 2 or negative 2. y could be positive 6 or negative 6. The four possible values for $x - y$ are as follows:

    $$2 - 6 = -4$$
    $$2 - (-6) = 8$$
    $$-2 - 6 = -8$$
    $$-2 - (-6) = 4$$

    The maximum value would be 8.

5. **The correct answer is (A).** The multiplication signs do not change the fact that this is the multiplication of terms with a common base and different exponents. Solve this kind of problem by adding the exponents.

    $$p^{8+4} \times q^{4+8} = p^{12}q^{12}$$

QUADRATIC EQUATIONS

ROOTS AND FACTORING. In solving quadratic equations, remember that there will always be two roots, even though these roots may be equal. A complete quadratic equation is of the form $ax^2 + bx + c = 0$ and, in the SAT, can always be solved by factoring.

Q   Factor: $x^2 + 7x + 12 = 0$

A $(x \quad)(x \quad) = 0$.

The last term of the equation is positive; therefore, both factors must have the same sign, since the last two terms multiply to a positive product. The middle term is also positive; therefore, both factors must be positive, since they also add to a positive sum.

$(x + 4)(x + 3) = 0$

If the product of two factors is 0, each factor may be set equal to 0, yielding the values for x of -4 or -3.

Q   Factor: $x^2 + 7x - 18 = 0$.

A $(x \quad)(x \quad) = 0$

Now you are looking for two numbers with a product of -18; therefore, they must have opposite signs. To yield $+7$ as a middle coefficient, the numbers must be $+9$ and -2.

$(x + 9)(x - 2) = 0$

This equation gives the roots -9 and $+2$.

Incomplete quadratic equations are those in which b or c is equal to 0.

Q   Solve for x: $x^2 - 16 = 0$

A $x^2 = 16$

   $x = \pm 4$ Remember, there must be two roots.

Q   Solve for x: $4x^2 - 9 = 0$

A $4x^2 = 9$

   $x^2 = \dfrac{9}{4}$

   $x = \pm \dfrac{3}{2}$

Q Solve for x: $x^2 + 4x = 0$

A Never divide through an equation by the unknown, as this would yield an equation of lower degree having fewer roots than the original equation. Always factor this type of equation.

$x(x + 4) = 0$

The roots are 0 and −4.

Q Solve for x: $4x^2 - 9x = 0$

A $x(4x - 9) = 0$

The roots are 0 and $\dfrac{9}{4}$.

RADICALS. In solving equations containing radicals, always get the radical alone on one side of the equation; then square both sides to remove the radical and solve. Remember that all solutions to radical equations must be checked, as squaring both sides may sometimes result in extraneous roots.

Q Solve for x: $\sqrt{x + 5} = 7$

A $x + 5 = 49$
   $x = 44$
Checking, we have $\sqrt{49} = 7$, which is true.

Q Solve for x: $\sqrt{x} = -6$

A $x = 36$
Checking, we have $\sqrt{36} = -6$, which is not true, as the radical sign means the positive, or principal, square root only. This equation has no solution because $\sqrt{36} = 6$, not −6,

ALERT!

Don't forget: In working with any equation, if you move a term from one side of the equal sign to the other, you must change its sign.

Q Solve for x: $\sqrt{x^2+6}-3=x$

$$\sqrt{x^2+6}=x+3$$

$$x^2+6=x^2+6x+9$$

$$6=6x+9$$

$$-3=6x$$

$$-\frac{1}{2}=x$$

Checking, we have $\sqrt{6\frac{1}{4}}-3=-\frac{1}{2}$

$$\sqrt{\frac{25}{4}}-3=-\frac{1}{2}$$

$$\frac{5}{2}-3=-\frac{1}{2}$$

$$2\frac{1}{2}-3=-\frac{1}{2}$$

$$-\frac{1}{2}=-\frac{1}{2}$$

This is a true statement. Therefore, $-\frac{1}{2}$ is a true root.

Exercise: Quadratic Equations

Directions: Work out each problem. Circle the letter next to your choice.

1. Solve for x: $x^2 - 2x - 15 = 0$

   (A) +5 or –3

   (B) –5 or +3

   (C) –5 or –3

   (D) +5 or +3

   (E) None of these

2. Solve for x: $x^2 + 12 = 8x$

   (A) +6 or –2

   (B) –6 or +2

   (C) –6 or –2

   (D) +6 or +2

   (E) None of these

3. Solve for x: $4x^2 = 12$

   (A) $\sqrt{3}$

   (B) 3 or –3

   (C) $\sqrt{3}$ or $-\sqrt{3}$

   (D) $\sqrt{3}$ or $\sqrt{-3}$

   (E) 9 or –9

4. Solve for x: $3x^2 = 4x$

   (A) $\dfrac{4}{3}$

   (B) 0 or $\dfrac{4}{3}$

   (C) $-\dfrac{4}{3}$ or 0

   (D) $\dfrac{4}{3}$ or $-\dfrac{4}{3}$

   (E) None of these

5. Solve for x: $\sqrt{x^2 + 7} - 2 = x - 1$

   (A) No values

   (B) $\dfrac{1}{3}$

   (C) $-\dfrac{1}{3}$

   (D) –3

   (E) 3

Solutions

1. **The correct answer is (A).**

   $$(x-5)(x+3)=0$$

   $$x = 5 \text{ or } -3$$

2. **The correct answer is (D).**

   $$x^2 - 8x + 12 = 0$$

   $$(x-6)(x-2)=0$$

   $$x = 6 \text{ or } 2$$

3. **The correct answer is (C).**

   $$x^2 = 3$$

   $$x = \pm\sqrt{3}$$

4. **The correct answer is (B).**

   $$3x^2 - 4x = 0$$

   $$x(3x-4)=0$$

   $$x = 0 \text{ or } \frac{4}{3}$$

5. **The correct answer is (E).**

   $$\sqrt{x^2 + 7} = x + 1$$

   $$x^2 + 7 = x^2 + 2x + 1$$

   $$6 = 2x$$

   $$x = 3$$

   Checking: $\sqrt{16} - 2 = 3 - 1$

   $$4 - 2 = 3 - 1$$

   $$2 = 2$$

LITERAL EXPRESSIONS

If you can compute with numbers, working with variables should be easy. The computational processes are exactly the same. Just think of how you would do the problem with numbers and do exactly the same thing with letters.

Q Find the number of inches in 2 feet 5 inches.

A Since there are 12 inches in a foot, multiply 2 feet by 12 to change it to 24 inches and then add 5 more inches, giving an answer of 29 inches.

Q Find the number of inches in f feet and i inches.

A Doing exactly as you did above, multiply f by 12, giving $12f$ inches, and add i more inches, giving an answer of $12f + i$ inches.

Q A telephone call from New York to Chicago costs 85 cents for the first three minutes and 21 cents for each additional minute. Find the cost of an eight-minute call at this rate.

A The first three minutes cost 85 cents. There are five additional minutes above the first three. These five are billed at 21 cents each, for a cost of $1.05. The total cost is $1.90.

Q A telephone call costs c cents for the first three minutes and d cents for each additional minute. Find the cost of a call that lasts m minutes if $m > 3$.

A The first three minutes cost c cents. The number of *additional* minutes is $(m-3)$. These are billed at d cents each, for a cost of $d(m-3)$ or $dm - 3d$. Thus, the total cost is $c + dm - 3d$. Remember that the first three minutes have been paid for in the basic charge; therefore, you must subtract from the total number of minutes to find the *additional* minutes.

Exercise: Literal Expressions

Directions: Work out each problem. Circle the letter next to your choice.

1. David had d dollars. After a shopping trip, he returned with c cents. How many cents did he spend?

   (A) $d - c$

   (B) $c - d$

   (C) $100d - c$

   (D) $100c - d$

   (E) $d - 100c$

2. How many ounces are there in p pounds and q ounces?

   (A) $\dfrac{p}{16} + q$

   (B) pq

   (C) $p + 16q$

   (D) $p + q$

   (E) $16p + q$

3. How many passengers can be seated on a plane with r rows, if each row consists of d double seats and t triple seats?

   (A) rdt

   (B) $rd + rt$

   (C) $2dr + 3tr$

   (D) $3dr + 2tr$

   (E) $rd + t$

4. How many dimes are there in $4x - 1$ cents?

   (A) $40x - 10$

   (B) $\dfrac{2}{5}x - \dfrac{1}{10}$

   (C) $40x - 1$

   (D) $4x - 1$

   (E) $20x - 5$

5. If u represents the tens' digit of a certain number and t represents the units' digit, then the number with the digits reversed can be represented by

   (A) $10t + u$

   (B) $10u + t$

   (C) tu

   (D) ut

   (E) $t + u$

6. Joe spent k cents of his allowance and has r cents left. What was his allowance in dollars?

   (A) $k + r$

   (B) $k - r$

   (C) $100(k + r)$

   (D) $\dfrac{k + r}{100}$

   (E) $100kr$

7. If p pounds of potatoes cost \$$k$, find the cost (in cents) of one pound of potatoes.

   (A) $\dfrac{k}{p}$

   (B) $\dfrac{k}{100p}$

   (C) $\dfrac{p}{k}$

   (D) $\dfrac{100k}{p}$

   (E) $\dfrac{100p}{k}$

8. Mr. Rabner rents a car for d days. He pays m dollars per day for each of the first 7 days, and half that rate for each additional day. Find the total charge if $d > 7$.

   (A) $m + 2m(d - 7)$

   (B) $m + \dfrac{m}{2}(d - 7)$

   (C) $7m + \dfrac{m}{2}(d - 7)$

   (D) $7m + \dfrac{md}{2}$

   (E) $7m + 2md$

9. A salesperson earns 900 dollars per month plus a 10% commission on all sales over 1,000 dollars. One month she sells r dollars' worth of merchandise where $r > \$1,000$. How many dollars does she earn that month?

   (A) $800 + .1r$

   (B) $800 - .1r$

   (C) $900 + 1r$

   (D) $900 - .1r$

   (E) $810 + .1r$

10. Elliot's allowance was just raised to k dollars per week. He gets a raise of c dollars per week every 2 years. How much will his allowance be per week y years from now?

    (A) $k + cy$

    (B) $k + 2cy$

    (C) $k + \dfrac{1}{2}cy$

    (D) $k + 2c$

    (E) $ky + 2c$

exercises

Solutions

1. **The correct answer is (C).** Since the answer is to be in cents, change d dollars to cents by multiplying it by 100 and subtract from that the c cents he spent.

2. **The correct answer is (E).** There are 16 ounces in a pound. Therefore, you must multiply p pounds by 16 to change it to ounces and then add q more ounces.

3. **The correct answer is (C).** Each double seat holds 2 people, so d double seats hold $2d$ people. Each triple seat holds 3 people, so t triple seats hold $3t$ people. Therefore, each row holds $2d + 3t$ people. There are r rows, so multiply the number of people in each row by r.

4. **The correct answer is (B).** To change cents to dimes, divide by 10.

$$\frac{4x-1}{10} = \frac{4}{10}x - \frac{1}{10} = \frac{2}{5}x - \frac{1}{10}$$

5. **The correct answer is (A).** The original number would be $10u + t$. The number with the digits reversed would be $10t + u$.

6. **The correct answer is (D).** Joe's allowance was $k + r$ cents. To change this to dollars, divide by 100.

7. **The correct answer is (D).** This can be solved by using a proportion. Remember to change \$$k$ to $100k$ cents.

$$\frac{p}{100k} = \frac{1}{x}$$
$$px = 100k$$
$$x = \frac{100k}{p}$$

8. **The correct answer is (C).** He pays m dollars for each of 7 days, for a total of $7m$ dollars. Then he pays $\frac{1}{2}m$ dollars for $(d - 7)$ days, for a cost of $\frac{m}{2}(d - 7)$.

   The total charge is $7m + \frac{m}{2}(d - 7)$.

9. **The correct answer is (A).**

   She gets a commission of 10% of $(r - 1000)$, or $.1(r - 1000)$, which is $.1r - 100$. Adding this to 900 yields $800 + .1r$.

10. **The correct answer is (C).** Since he gets a raise only every 2 years, in y years, he will get $\frac{1}{2}y$ raises. Each raise is c dollars, so with $\frac{1}{2}y$ raises, his present allowance will be increased by $c(\frac{1}{2}y)$.

ROOTS AND RADICALS

ADDING AND SUBTRACTING. Rules for adding and subtracting radicals are much the same as for adding and subtracting variables. Radicals must be exactly the same if they are to be added or subtracted, and they merely serve as a label that does not change.

$$4\sqrt{2} + 3\sqrt{2} = 7\sqrt{2}$$
$$\sqrt{2} + 2\sqrt{3} \text{ cannot be added}$$
$$\sqrt{2} + \sqrt{3} \text{ cannot be added}$$

Sometimes, when radicals are not the same, simplification of one or more radicals will make them the same. Remember that radicals are simplified by factoring out any perfect square factors.

$$\sqrt{27} + \sqrt{75}$$
$$\sqrt{9 \cdot 3} + \sqrt{25 \cdot 3}$$
$$3\sqrt{3} + 5\sqrt{3} = 8\sqrt{3}$$

MULTIPLYING AND DIVIDING. In multiplying and dividing, treat radicals in the same way as you treat variables. They are factors and must be handled as such.

$$\sqrt{2} \cdot \sqrt{3} = \sqrt{6}$$
$$2\sqrt{5} \cdot 3\sqrt{7} = 6\sqrt{35}$$
$$(2\sqrt{3})^2 = 2\sqrt{3} \cdot 2\sqrt{3} = 4 \cdot 3 = 12$$
$$\frac{\sqrt{75}}{\sqrt{3}} = \sqrt{25} = 5$$
$$\frac{10\sqrt{3}}{5\sqrt{3}} = 2$$

SIMPLIFYING. To simplify radicals that contain a sum or difference under the radical sign, add or subtract first, then take the square root.

$$\sqrt{\frac{x^2}{9} + \frac{x^2}{16}}$$
$$\sqrt{\frac{16x^2 + 9x^2}{144}} = \sqrt{\frac{25x^2}{144}} = \frac{5x}{12}$$

If you take the square root of each term before combining, you would have $\frac{x}{3} + \frac{x}{4}$, or $\frac{7x}{12}$, which is clearly not the same answer. Remember that $\sqrt{25}$ is 5. However, if you write that $\sqrt{25}$ as $\sqrt{16 + 9}$, you cannot say it is 4 + 3 or 7. *Always* combine the quantities within a radical sign into a single term before taking the square root.

If a number ends in 9, such as in the example right, its square root would have to end in a digit that, when multiplied by itself, would end in 9. This might be either 3 or 7. Only one of these would probably be among the choices; very few SAT problems call for much computation.

FINDING SQUARE ROOTS. To find the number of digits in the square root of a number, remember that the first step in the procedure for finding a square root is to pair off the numbers in the radical sign on either side of the decimal point. Every pair of numbers under the radical gives one number in the answer.

$\sqrt{32\ 14\ 89}$ will have 3 digits.

Q The square root of 61504 is exactly

(A) 245

(B) 246

(C) 247

(D) 248

(E) 249

A The only answer among the choices that will end in 4 when squared is choice (D).

Exercise: Roots and Radicals

Directions: Work out each problem. Circle the letter next to your choice.

1. What is the sum of $\sqrt{12} + \sqrt{27}$?
   (A) $\sqrt{29}$
   (B) $3\sqrt{5}$
   (C) $13\sqrt{3}$
   (D) $5\sqrt{3}$
   (E) $7\sqrt{3}$

2. What is the difference between $\sqrt{150}$ and $\sqrt{54}$?
   (A) $2\sqrt{6}$
   (B) $16\sqrt{6}$
   (C) $\sqrt{96}$
   (D) $6\sqrt{2}$
   (E) $8\sqrt{6}$

3. What is the product of $\sqrt{18x}$ and $\sqrt{2x}$?
   (A) $6x^2$
   (B) $6x$
   (C) $36x$
   (D) $36x^2$
   (E) $6\sqrt{x}$

4. If $\frac{1}{x} = \sqrt{.25}$, what does x equal?
   (A) 2
   (B) .5
   (C) .2
   (D) 20
   (E) 5

5. If $n = 3.14$, find n^3 to the nearest hundredth.
   (A) 3.10
   (B) 30.96
   (C) 309.59
   (D) 3,095.91
   (E) 30,959.14

6. The square root of 24,336 is exactly
   (A) 152
   (B) 153
   (C) 155
   (D) 156
   (E) 158

7. The square root of 306.25 is exactly
   (A) .175
   (B) 1.75
   (C) 17.5
   (D) 175
   (E) 1750

8. Divide $6\sqrt{45}$ by $3\sqrt{5}$.
   (A) 9
   (B) 4
   (C) 54
   (D) 15
   (E) 6

9. $\sqrt{\dfrac{y^2}{25} + \dfrac{y^2}{16}} =$
   (A) $\dfrac{2y}{9}$
   (B) $\dfrac{9y}{20}$
   (C) $\dfrac{y}{9}$
   (D) $\dfrac{y\sqrt{41}}{20}$
   (E) $\dfrac{41y}{20}$

10. $\sqrt{a^2 + b^2}$ is equal to
    (A) $a + b$
    (B) $a - b$
    (C) $(a+b)(a-b)$
    (D) $\sqrt{a^2} + \sqrt{b^2}$
    (E) None of these

Solutions

1. **The correct answer is (D).**

$$\sqrt{12} = \sqrt{4}\sqrt{3} = 2\sqrt{3}$$
$$\sqrt{27} = \sqrt{9}\sqrt{3} = 3\sqrt{3}$$
$$2\sqrt{3} + 3\sqrt{3} = 5\sqrt{3}$$

2. **The correct answer is (A).**

$$\sqrt{150} = \sqrt{25}\sqrt{6} = 5\sqrt{6}$$
$$\sqrt{54} = \sqrt{9}\sqrt{6} = 3\sqrt{6}$$
$$5\sqrt{6} - 3\sqrt{6} = 2\sqrt{6}$$

3. **The correct answer is (B).**

$$\sqrt{18x} \cdot \sqrt{2x} = \sqrt{36x^2} = 6x$$

4. **The correct answer is (A).**

$$\sqrt{.25} = .5$$
$$\frac{1}{x} = .5$$
$$1 = .5x$$
$$10 = 5x$$
$$2 = x$$

5. **The correct answer is (B).** $(3)^3$ would be 27, so the answer should be a little larger than 27.

6. **The correct answer is (D).** The only answer that will end in 6 when squared is choice (D).

7. **The correct answer is (C).** The square root of this number must have two digits before the decimal point.

8. **The correct answer is (E).**

$$\frac{6\sqrt{45}}{3\sqrt{5}} = 2\sqrt{9} = 2 \cdot 3 = 6$$

9. **The correct answer is (D).**

$$\sqrt{\frac{y^2}{25} + \frac{y^2}{16}} = \sqrt{\frac{16y^2 + 25y^2}{400}}$$
$$= \sqrt{\frac{41y^2}{400}} = \frac{y\sqrt{41}}{20}$$

10. **The correct answer is (E).** Never take the square root of a sum separately. There is no way to simplify $\sqrt{a^2 + b^2}$.

MONOMIALS AND POLYNOMIALS

When we add a collection of expressions together, each expression is called a *term*. *Monomial* means one term. For example, we might say that $2x + 3y^2 + 7$ is the sum of three terms or three monomials. When we talk about a monomial, we generally mean a term that is just the product of constants and variables, possibly raised to various powers. Examples might be 7, $2x$, $-3y^2$, and $4x^2z^5$. The constant factor is called the *coefficient* of the variable factor. Thus, in $-3y^2$, -3 is the coefficient of y^2.

If we restrict our attention to monomials of the form Axn, the sums of such terms are called *polynomials* (in one variable). Expressions like $3x + 5$, $2x^2 - 5x + 8$, and $x^4 - 7x^5 - 11$, are all examples of polynomials. The highest power of the variable that appears is called the *degree* of the polynomial. The three examples just given are of degree 1, 2, and 5, respectively.

In evaluating monomials and polynomials for negative values of the variable, the greatest pitfall is keeping track of the minus signs. Always remember that in an expression like $-x^2$, the power 2 is applied to the x, and the minus sign in front should be thought of as (-1) times the expression. If you want to have the power apply to $-x$, you must write $(-x)^2$.

Q Find the value of $3x - x^3 - x^2$, when $x = -2$.

A Substitute -2 every place you see an x, thus:
$3(-2) - (-2)^3 - (-2)^2 = -6 - (-8) - (+4) = -6 + 8 - 4 = -2$.

Combining Monomials

Monomials with identical variable factors can be added together by adding their coefficients. So $3x^2 + 4x^2 = 7x^2$. Of course, subtraction is handled the same way, thus:

$$3x^4 - 9x^4 = -6x^4$$

Monomials are multiplied by taking the product of their coefficients and taking the product of the variable part by adding exponents of factors with like bases. So $(3xy^2)(2xy^3) = 6x^2y^5$.

Monomial fractions can be simplified to simplest form by dividing out common factors of the coefficients and then using the usual rules for subtraction of exponents in division. An example might be:

$$\frac{6x^3y^5}{2x^4y^3} = \frac{3y^2}{x}$$

Combine into a single monomial: $\dfrac{8x^3}{4x^2} - 6x$.

The fraction simplifies to $2x$, and $2x - 6x = -4x$.

Combining Polynomials and Monomials

Polynomials are added or subtracted by just combining like monomial terms in the appropriate manner. Thus,

$$(3x^2 - 3x - 4) + (2x^2 + 5x - 11)$$

is summed by removing the parentheses and combining like terms, to yield

$$5x^2 + 2x - 15$$

In subtraction, when you remove the parentheses with a minus sign in front, be careful to change the signs of *all* the terms within the parentheses. So:

$$(3x^2 - 3x - 4) - (2x^2 + 5x - 11)$$
$$= 3x^2 - 3x - 4 - 2x^2 - 5x + 11$$
$$= x^2 - 8x + 7$$

(Did you notice that $3x^2 - 2x^2 = 1x^2$ but the "1" is not shown?)

To multiply a polynomial by a monomial, use the distributive law to multiply each term in the polynomial by the monomial factor. For example, $2x(2x^2 + 5x - 11) = 4x^3 + 10x^2 - 22x$.

When multiplying a polynomial by a polynomial, you are actually repeatedly applying the distributive law to form all possible products of the terms in the first polynomial with the terms in the second polynomial. The most common use of this is in multiplying two *binomials* (polynomials with two terms), such as $(x + 3)(x - 5)$. In this case, there are four terms in the result, $x \times x = x^2$; $x(-5) = -5x$; $3 \times x = 3x$; and, $3 \times (-5) = -15$; but the two middle terms are added together to give $-2x$. Thus, the product is $x^2 - 2x - 15$.

This process is usually remembered as the FOIL method. That is, form the products of First, Outer, Inner, Last, as shown in the figure below.

$$(x + 3)(x - 5) = x^2 + (-5x + 3x) - 15$$

> **Q** If d is an integer, and $(x + 2)(x + d) = x^2 - kx - 10$, what is the value of $k + d$?
>
> **A** The product of the two last terms, $2d$, must be -10. Therefore, $d = -5$. If $d = -5$, then the sum of the outer and inner products becomes $-5x + 2x = -3x$, which equals $-kx$. Hence, $k = 3$, and $k + d = 3 + (-5) = -2$.

Factoring Monomials

Factoring a monomial simply involves reversing the distributive law. For example, if you are looking at $4x^2 + 12xy$, you should see that $4x$ is a factor of both terms. Hence, you could just as well write this as $4x(x + 3y)$. Multiplication using the distributive law will restore the original formulation.

> **Q** If $3x - 4y = -2$, what is the value of $9x - 12y$?
>
> **A** Although you seem to have one equation in two unknowns, you can still solve the problem, because you do not need to know the values of the individual variables. Just rewrite: $9x - 12y = 3(3x - 4y)$. Since $3x - 4y = -2$, $9x - 12y$ is 3 times -2, or -6.

Exercise: Monomials and Polynomials

Directions: Circle the letter next to your choice.

1. $6x^3(x^2)^3 =$
   (A) $6x^7$
   (B) $6x^8$
   (C) $6x^9$
   (D) $6x^{10}$
   (E) $6x^{12}$

2. $(3w^2y^3)^4 =$
   (A) $18w^8y^{12}$
   (B) $18w^6y^7$
   (C) $81w^6y^7$
   (D) $81w^8y^{12}$
   (E) $81w^8y^7$

3. $5x^3(-3x^8) =$

(A) $15x^{11}$

(B) $-15x^{11}$

(C) $-15x^{24}$

(D) $15x^{24}$

(E) $15x^5$

4. $\left(\dfrac{2}{3}\right)^3 =$

(A) $\dfrac{8}{27}$

(B) $\dfrac{6}{9}$

(C) $\dfrac{4}{9}$

(D) $\dfrac{16}{27}$

(E) $\dfrac{16}{9}$

Solutions

1. The correct answer is (C).

$$6x^3(x^2)^3 = 6 \times x^3 \times (x^2)^3$$
$$= 6 \times x^3 \times x^{(2 \times 3)}$$
$$= 6 \times x^3 \times x^6$$
$$= 6 \times x^9$$
$$= 6x^9$$

2. The correct answer is (D).

$$(3w^2y^3)^4 = (3)^4 \times w^{(2 \times 4)} \times y^{(3 \times 4)}$$
$$= 81 \times w^8 \times y^{12}$$
$$= 81\,w^8y^{12}$$

3. The correct answer is (B).

$$5x^3(-3x^8) = 5 \times x^3 \times (-3) \times x^8$$
$$= 5 \times (-3) \times x^3 \times x^8$$
$$= -15 \times x^{3+8}$$
$$= -15x^{11}$$

4. The correct answer is (A).

$$\left(\frac{2}{3}\right)^3 = \frac{2}{3} \times \frac{2}{3} \times \frac{2}{3}$$
$$= \frac{2 \times 2 \times 2}{3 \times 3 \times 3}$$
$$= \frac{2^3}{3^3}$$
$$= \frac{8}{27}$$

PROBLEM-SOLVING IN ALGEBRA

When you are working with algebraic word problems, remember that before you begin working you should be absolutely certain that you understand precisely what you are to answer. Once this is done, represent what you are looking for algebraically. Write an equation that translates the words of the problem to the symbols of mathematics. Then solve that equation by the techniques reviewed previously.

This section reviews the types of algebra problems most frequently encountered on the SAT. Thoroughly familiarizing yourself with the problems that follow will help you to translate and solve all kinds of verbal problems.

Solving Two Linear Equations in Two Unknowns

Many word problems lead to equations in two unknowns. Usually, one needs two equations to solve for both unknowns, although there are exceptions. There are two generally used methods to solve two equations in two unknowns. They are the method of *substitution* and the method of *elimination by addition and subtraction*.

We'll illustrate both methods via example. Here is one that uses the method of substitution.

Q Mr. Green took his four children to the local craft fair. The total cost of their admission tickets was $14. Mr. and Mrs. Molina and their six children had to pay $23. What was the cost of an adult ticket to the craft fair, and what was the cost of a child's ticket?

A Expressing all amounts in dollars, let x = cost of an adult ticket and let y = cost of a child's ticket.

For the Greens:

$x + 4y = 14$

For the Molinas:

$2x + 6y = 23$

The idea of the method of substitution is to solve one equation for one variable in terms of the other and then substitute that solution into the second equation. So we solve the first equation for x, because that is the simplest one to isolate:

$x = 14 - 4y$,

and substitute into the second equation:

$2(14 - 4y) + 6y = 23$.

This gives us one equation in one unknown that we can solve:

$28 - 8y + 6y = 23$

$-2y = -5; y = 2.5$.

Now that we know $y = 2.5$, we substitute this into $x = 14 - 4y$ to get:

$x = 14 - 4(2.5) = 4$.

Thus, the adult tickets were $4.00 each, and the children's tickets were $2.50 each.

Here is an example using the method of elimination.

Q Paul and Denise both have after-school jobs. Two weeks ago, Paul worked 6 hours, Denise worked 3 hours, and they earned a total of $39. Last week, Paul worked 12 hours, Denise worked 5 hours, and they earned a total of $75. What is each one's hourly wage?

A Again, let us express all amounts in dollars. Let x = Paul's hourly wage, and let y = Denise's hourly wage.

For the first week:

$6x + 3y = 39$.

For the second week:

$12x + 5y = 75$.

The idea of the method of elimination is that adding equal quantities to equal quantities gives a true result. So we want to add some multiple of one equation to the other one so that *if we add the two equations together*, one variable will be eliminated. In this case, it is not hard to see that if we multiply the first equation by -2, the coefficient of x will become -12. Now when we add the two equations, x will be eliminated. Hence,

$$-12x - 6y = -78$$
$$\underline{12x + 5y = 75}$$
$$-y = -3$$

Thus, $y = 3$. We now substitute this into either of the two equations. Let's use the first:

$6x + (3)(3) = 39$; $x = 5$.

Thus, Denise makes only $3 per hour, while Paul gets $5.

Word Problems in One or Two Unknowns

Word problems can be broken down into a number of categories. To do *consecutive integer* problems, you need to remember that consecutive integers differ by 1, so a string of such numbers can be represented as $n, n + 1, n + 2, \ldots$

Consecutive even integers differ by 2, so a string of such numbers can be represented as $n, n+2, n+4, \ldots$ Consecutive odd integers also differ by 2! So a string of such numbers can also be represented as $n, n+2, n+4, \ldots$

Rate-time-distance problems require you to know the formula $d = rt$. That is, distance equals rate times time.

Here are some examples of several types of word problems.

Q Sibyl is 5 years older than Moira. Three years ago, Sibyl was twice as old as Moira. How old is Sibyl?

A If you have trouble setting up the equations, try using numbers. Suppose that Moira is 11. If Sibyl is 5 years older than Moira, how old is Sibyl? She is 16. You got from 11 to 16 by *adding* 5. So, if S is Sibyl's age and M is Moira's age, $S = M + 5$. Three years ago, Sibyl was $S - 3$, and Moira was $M - 3$. So, from the second sentence, $S - 3 = 2(M - 3)$ or $S - 3 = 2M - 6$; or, adding 3 to both sides,

$S = 2M - 3$.

Now, substituting $S = M + 5$,

$M + 5 = 2M - 3$

$M = 8$.

Which means Sybil is $8 + 5 = 13$.

Q Three consecutive integers are written in increasing order. If the sum of the first and second and twice the third is 93, what is the second number?

A Calling the smallest number x, the second is $x + 1$, and the third is $x + 2$. Therefore,

$$x + (x + 1) + 2(x + 2) = 93$$
$$x + x + 1 + 2x + 4 = 93$$
$$4x + 5 = 93$$
$$4x = 88; x = 22.$$

Hence the middle number is $22 + 1 = 23$.

> **Q** It took Andrew 15 minutes to drive downtown at 28 miles per hour to get a pizza. How fast did he have to drive back in order to be home in ten minutes?
>
> **A** 15 minutes is $\frac{1}{4}$ of an hour. Hence, going 28 miles per hour, the distance to the pizza parlor can be computed using the formula $d = rt$; $d = (28)(\frac{1}{4})$ = 7 miles. Since ten minutes is $\frac{1}{6}$ of an hour, we have the equation $7 = r(\frac{1}{6})$ and multiplying by 6, $r = 42$ mph.

Fraction Problems

A fraction is a ratio between two numbers. If the value of a fraction is $\frac{2}{3}$, it does not mean the numerator must be 2 and the denominator 3. The numerator and denominator could be 4 and 6, respectively, or 1 and 1.5, or 30 and 45, or any of infinitely many other combinations. All you know is that the ratio of numerator to denominator will be 2:3. Therefore, the numerator may be represented by $2x$, the denominator by $3x$, and the fraction by $\frac{2x}{3x}$.

> **Q** The value of a fraction is $\frac{3}{4}$. If 3 is subtracted from the numerator and added to the denominator, the value of the fraction is $\frac{2}{5}$. Find the original fraction.
>
> **A** Let the original fraction be represented by $\frac{3x}{4x}$. If 3 is subtracted from the numerator and added to the denominator, the new fraction becomes $\frac{3x-3}{4x+3}$. The value of the new fraction is $\frac{2}{5}$.
>
> $$\frac{3x-3}{4x+3} = \frac{2}{5}$$
>
> Cross-multiply to eliminate fractions.
>
> $$15x - 15 = 8x + 6$$
> $$7x = 21$$
> $$x = 3$$
>
> Therefore, the original fraction is
>
> $$\frac{3x}{4x} = \frac{9}{12}$$

Exercise: Problem-Solving in Algebra

Directions: Circle the letter next to your choice.

1. A box contains five blocks numbered 1, 2, 3, 4, and 5. Johnnie picks a block and replaces it. Lisa then picks a block. What is the probability that the sum of the numbers they picked is even?

   (A) $\dfrac{9}{25}$

   (B) $\dfrac{2}{5}$

   (C) $\dfrac{1}{2}$

   (D) $\dfrac{13}{25}$

   (E) $\dfrac{3}{5}$

2. If a fleet of m buses uses g gallons of gasoline every two days, how many gallons of gasoline will be used by 4 buses every 5 days?

   (A) $\dfrac{10g}{m}$

   (B) $10gm$

   (C) $\dfrac{10m}{g}$

   (D) $\dfrac{20g}{m}$

   (E) $\dfrac{5g}{4m}$

3. A faucet is dripping at a constant rate. If, at noon on Sunday, 3 ounces of water have dripped from the faucet into a holding tank and, at 5 p.m. on Sunday, a total of 7 ounces have dripped into the tank, how many ounces will have dripped into the tank by 2:00 a.m. on Monday?

   (A) 10

   (B) $\dfrac{51}{5}$

   (C) 12

   (D) $\dfrac{71}{5}$

   (E) $\dfrac{81}{5}$

4. If A and B are positive integers and $24AB$ is a perfect square, then which of the following *cannot* be possible?

   I. Both A and B are odd.

   II. AB is a perfect square

   III. Both A and B are divisible by 6

   (A) I only

   (B) II only

   (C) III only

   (D) I and II only

   (E) I, II, and III

Solutions

1. **The correct answer is (D).** Since each person had 5 choices, there are 25 possible pairs of numbers. The only way the sum could be odd is if one person picked an odd number and the other picked an even number. Suppose that Johnnie chose the odd number and Lisa, the even one. Johnnie had 3 possible even numbers to select from, and for each of these, Lisa had 2 possible choices, for a total of $(3)(2)=6$ possibilities. However, you could have had Johnnie pick an even number and Lisa pick an odd one, and there are also 6 ways to do that. Hence, out of 25 possibilities, 12 have an odd total, and 13 have an even total. The probability of an even total, then, is choice (D) $\frac{13}{25}$.

2. **The correct answer is (A).** Running m buses for 2 days is the same as running one bus for $2m$ days. If we use g gallons of gasoline, each bus uses $\frac{g}{2m}$ gallons each day. So if you multiply the number of gallons per day used by each bus by the number of buses and the number of days, you should get total gasoline usage. That is, $\frac{g}{2m}\times(4)(5)=\frac{10g}{m}$.

3. **The correct answer is (D).** In 5 hours, 4 ounces $(7-3)$ have dripped. Therefore, the "drip rate" is $\frac{4}{5}$ of an ounce per hour. From 5:00 p.m. on Sunday until 2:00 a.m. on Monday is 9 hours, causing the total to be:

$$7+\frac{4}{5}\times9=7+\frac{36}{5}=\frac{71}{5}$$

4. **The correct answer is (D).** The prime factorization of 24 is $2^3 3$; hence, if $24AB$ is a perfect square, then AB must have a factor of 2 and a factor of 3. This means, first of all, that both A and B cannot be odd. So I cannot be possible. II also cannot be possible, because if AB were a perfect square and $24AB$ were also a perfect square, then 24 would be a perfect square, which it is not. Of course, if, for example, A were 6 and B were 36, $24AB$ would be a perfect square with both A and B divisible by 6, so III is possible. Hence, the correct choice is (D).

INEQUALITIES

Algebraic inequality statements are solved just as equations are solved. However, you must remember that whenever you multiply or divide by a negative number, the order of the inequality, that is, the inequality symbol, must be reversed.

> **Q** Solve for x: $3 - 5x > 18$
>
> **A** Add −3 to both sides:
>
> $-5x > 15$
>
> Divide by −5, remembering to reverse the inequality:
>
> $x < -3$

> **Q** $5x - 4 > 6x - 6$
>
> **A** Collect all x terms on the left and numerical terms on the right. As with equations, remember that if a term crosses the inequality symbol, the term changes sign.
>
> $-x > -2$
>
> Divide (or multiply) by −1:
>
> $x < 2$

Postulates and Theorems

In working with geometric inequalities, certain postulates and theorems should be reviewed. The list follows:

1 If unequal quantities are added to unequal quantities of the same order, the result is unequal quantities in the same order.

2 If equal quantities are added to, or subtracted from, unequal quantities, the results are unequal in the same order.

3 If unequal quantities are subtracted from equal quantities, the results are unequal in the opposite order.

4 Doubles or halves of unequals are unequal in the same order.

5 If the first of three quantities is greater than the second, and the second is greater than the third, then the first is greater than the third.

6 The sum of two sides of a triangle must be greater than the third side.

7 If two sides of a triangle are unequal, the angles opposite these sides are unequal, with the greater angle opposite the greater side.

8 If two angles of a triangle are unequal, the sides opposite these angles are unequal, with the greater side opposite the greater angle.

9 An exterior angle of a triangle is greater than either remote interior angle.

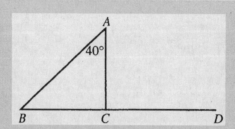

Q If *BCD* is a straight line and $m \angle A = 40°$, then angle *ACD* contains

    (A) 40°

    (B) 140°

    (C) less than 40°

    (D) more than 40°

    (E) 100°

A The correct answer is (D), since an exterior angle of a triangle is always greater than either of the remote interior angles.

Q Which of the following statements is true regarding the triangle?

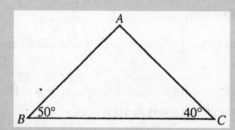

    (A) $AB > AC$

    (B) $AC > BC$

    (C) $AB > BC$

    (D) $AC > AB$

    (E) $BC > AB + AC$

A The correct answer is (D), since a comparison between two sides of a triangle depends upon the angles opposite these sides. The greater side is always opposite the greater angle. Since angle *A* contains 90°, the greatest side of this triangle is $\overline{BC}$, followed by $\overline{AC}$ and then $\overline{AB}$.

Exercise: Inequalities

Directions: Work out each problem. Circle the letter next to your choice.

1. If $x < y$, $2x = A$, and $2y = B$, then
   (A) $A = B$
   (B) $A < B$
   (C) $A > B$
   (D) $A < x$
   (E) $B < y$

2. If $a > b$ and $c > d$, then
   (A) $a = c$
   (B) $a < d$
   (C) $a + d = b + c$
   (D) $a + c < b + d$
   (E) $a + c > b + d$

3. If $ab > 0$ and $a < 0$, which of the following is negative?
   (A) b
   (B) $-b$
   (C) $-a$
   (D) $(a - b)$
   (E) $-(a + b)$

4. If $4 - x > 5$, then
   (A) $x > 1$
   (B) $x > -1$
   (C) $x < 1$
   (D) $x < -1$
   (E) $x = -1$

5. Point X is located on line segment $\overline{AB}$ and point Y is located on line segment $\overline{CD}$. If $AB = CD$ and $AX > CY$, then
   (A) $XB > YD$
   (B) $XB < YD$
   (C) $AX > XB$
   (D) $AX < XB$
   (E) $AX > AB$

6. If $w > x$, $y < z$, and $x > z$, then which of the following must be true?
   (A) $w > x > y > z$
   (B) $w > x > z > y$
   (C) $x > z > y > w$
   (D) $z < y < x < w$
   (E) $z < x < y < w$

7. If x and y are positive integers such that $0 < (x + y) < 10$, then which of the following must be true?
   (A) $x < 8$
   (B) $x > 3$
   (C) $x > y$
   (D) $x + y = 5$
   (E) $x - y \leq 7$

8. In the diagram below, which of the following is always true?

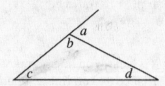

   I. $a > b$
  II. $c > a$
 III. $d > a$

(A) I only

(B) II and III only

(C) I, II, and III

(D) II only

(E) None of these

9. If point X is on line segment $\overline{AB}$, all of the following may be true EXCEPT

(A) $AX = XB$

(B) $AX > XB$

(C) $AX < XB$

(D) $AB > XB$

(E) $AX + XB < AB$

10. If $x > 0$, $y > 0$, and $x - y < 0$, then

(A) $x > y$

(B) $x < y$

(C) $x + y < 0$

(D) $y - x < 0$

(E) $x = -y$

Solutions

1. **The correct answer is (B).** Doubles of unequals are unequal in the same order.

2. **The correct answer is (E).** If unequal quantities are added to unequal quantities of the same order, the results are unequal in the same order.

3. **The correct answer is (A).** If the product of two numbers is > 0 (positive), then either both numbers are positive or both are negative. Since $a < 0$ (negative), b must also be negative.

4. **The correct answer is (D).**

   $$4 - x > 5$$
   $$-x > 1$$

   Divide by -1 and change the inequality sign.

   $$x < -1$$

5. **The correct answer is (B).**

   If unequal quantities are subtracted from equal quantities, the results are unequal in the same order.

6. **The correct answer is (B).** The first and third statements assert:

   $w > x$ and $x > z$, therefore $w > x > z$.

   The second statement says that y is less than z, therefore:

   $w > x > z > y$.

7. **The correct answer is (E).** Perhaps using numbers is the easiest way to explain this item:

   (A) x could be 8 and y could be 1:

   $0 < (8 + 1) < 10$

   (B) x could be 3 and y could be 6:

   $0 < (3 + 6) < 10$

   (C) This is wrong as just shown above.

   (D) This too is wrong as shown above.

   (E) The largest possible value for x is 8, and the smallest possible value for y is 1. So the greatest possible value for $x - y$ is 7.

8. **The correct answer is (E).** An exterior angle of a triangle must be greater than either remote interior angle. There is no fixed relationship between an exterior angle and its adjacent interior angle.

9. **The correct answer is (E).** Point X could be so located to make each of the other choices true, but the whole segment $\overline{AB}$ will always be equal to the sum of its parts $\overline{AX}$ and $\overline{XB}$.

10. **The correct answer is (B).** If x and y are both positive, but $x - y$ is negative, then y must be a greater number than x.

DEFINED OPERATION PROBLEMS

"Defined operation" is another name for "function." A function problem might look like this: The function of x is obtained by squaring x and then multiplying the result by 3. If you wanted to know $f(4)$, you would square 4 and multiply that product by 3; the answer would be 48. On the SAT the $f(x)$ symbol is not normally used. Instead the test-makers use arbitrary symbols and define what function they represent. You approach these symbols as you would a function: talk to yourself about what the function does. In math you usually change words into mathematical notation, but with functions you change mathematical notation into words.

$$!x = 2x + 4$$

What does the "!" do in this problem? It takes x and doubles it and then adds four.

Q   What is the value of !6?

A   !6 = 2(6) + 4 = 16

Exercise: Defined Operation Problems

Directions: Work out each problem. Circle the letter next to your choice.

1. $\&x$ is such that $\&x = \frac{x^3}{2}$. What is the value of $\&4$?

   (A) 8

   (B) 16

   (C) 32

   (D) 40

   (E) 64

2. $\$x$ is such that $\$x$ is equal to the largest integer less than x. What is the value of $\$6.99$ times $\$-2.01$?

   (A) 18

   (B) 12

   (C) −12

   (D) −18

   (E) −21

3. The operation # is defined in the following way for any two numbers:

   $$p \# q = (p - q) \text{ times } (q - p).$$

   If $p \# q = -1$, then which of the following are true:

   I. p could equal 5 and q could equal 4

   II. p could equal 4 and q could equal 5

   III. p could equal 1 and q could equal −1

   IV. p could equal −1 and q could equal 1

   (A) I and II only

   (B) I and III only

   (C) II and IV only

   (D) III and IV only

   (E) I, II, III, IV

4. Every letter in the alphabet has a number value that is equal to its place in the alphabet; the letter A has a value of 1 and C a value of 3. The number value of a word is obtained by adding up the value of the letters in the word and then multiplying that sum by the length of the word. The word "DFGH" would have a number value of

   (A) 22

   (B) 44

   (C) 66

   (D) 100

   (E) 108

5. Let $\wedge x \wedge$ be defined such that $\wedge x \wedge = x + \frac{1}{x}$. The value of $\wedge 6\wedge + \wedge 4\wedge + \wedge 2\wedge$ is

   (A) 12

   (B) $12\frac{7}{12}$

   (C) $12\frac{11}{12}$

   (D) $13\frac{1}{12}$

   (E) $13\frac{5}{12}$

Solutions

1. **The correct answer is (C).**

$$4^3 = 64$$

$$64 \div 2 = 32$$

2. **The correct answer is (D).** The key phrase in the problem is "the largest integer." The largest integer less than 6.99 is 6 (not 7, this problem does not say to round the numbers) and the largest integer less than –2.01 is –3 (not –2 as –2 is greater than –2.01).

3. **The correct answer is (A).** The best way to solve this is to plug the values into the equation:

$$(5 - 4) \times (4 - 5) = -1$$

$$(4 - 5) \times (5 - 4) = -1$$

$$(1 - -1) \times (-1 - 1) = -4$$

$$(-1 - 1) \times (1 - -1) = -4$$

Statements I and II give the stated value, –1.

4. **The correct answer is (D).**

D = 4, F = 6, G = 7, H = 8

So the sum of the letters would be 25. 25 multiplied by 4 (the length of the word) is 100.

5. **The correct answer is (C).** The work of this problem is adding up the reciprocals of the numbers.

$$6 + 4 + 2 = 12$$

$$\frac{1}{6} + \frac{1}{4} + \frac{1}{2} = \frac{2}{12} + \frac{3}{12} + \frac{6}{12} = \frac{11}{12}$$

SAT Geometry Review

OVERVIEW

- **Area**
- **Perimeter**
- **Circles**
- **Volume**
- **Triangles**
- **Right triangles**
- **Parallel lines**
- **Polygons**
- **Similar polygons**
- **Coordinate geometry**

Here are some of the most important geometry formulas that you should know for the SAT.

AREA

① Rectangle = bh

Area = $6 \cdot 3 = 18$

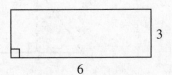

② Parallelogram = bh

Area = $8 \cdot 4 = 32$

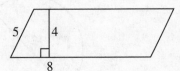

③ Rhombus = $\dfrac{1}{2} d_1 d_2$

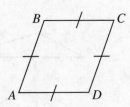

If $AC = 10$ and $BD = 8$, then area is $\dfrac{1}{2}(10)(8) = 40$.

chapter 15

④ Square = s^2 or $\frac{1}{2}d^2$

Area = 6^2 = 36

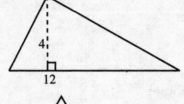

Area = $\frac{1}{2}(10)(10)$ = 50

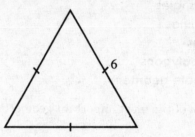

⑤ Triangle = $\frac{1}{2}bh$

Area = $\frac{1}{2}(12)(4)$ = 24

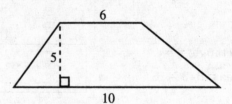

⑥ Equilateral triangle = $\frac{s^2}{4}\sqrt{3}$

Area = $\frac{36}{4}\sqrt{3} = 9\sqrt{3}$

⑦ Trapezoid = $\frac{1}{2}h(b_1 + b_2)$

Area = (5)(16) = 40

⑧ Circle = πr^2

Area = $\pi(6)^2 = 36\pi$

ALERT!

Don't confuse the two formulas for calculating the circumference and area of circles. A good way to keep them straight is to remember the *square* in r^2. It should remind you that area must be in square units.

PERIMETER

① Any polygon = sum of all sides

$P = 5 + 8 + 11 = 24$

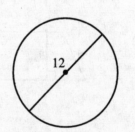

② Circle = πd

(called circumference)

Circle = $\pi(12) = 12\pi$

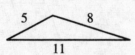
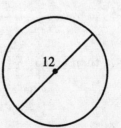

3 The distance covered by a wheel in one revolution is equal to the circumference of the wheel.

In one revolution, this wheel covers $\pi \cdot \frac{14}{\pi}$, or 14 feet.

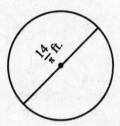

CIRCLES

1 A central angle is equal in degrees to its intercepted arc.

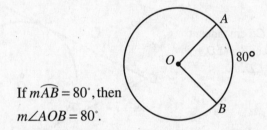

If $m\widehat{AB} = 80°$, then
$m\angle AOB = 80°$.

2 An inscribed angle is equal in degrees to one half its intercepted arc.

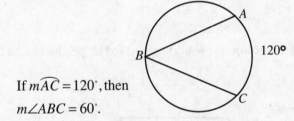

If $m\widehat{AC} = 120°$, then
$m\angle ABC = 60°$.

3 An angle formed by two chords intersecting in a circle is equal in degrees to one half the sum of its intercepted arcs.

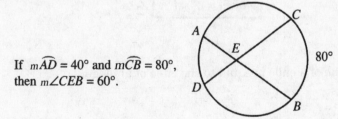

If $m\widehat{AD} = 40°$ and $m\widehat{CB} = 80°$,
then $m\angle CEB = 60°$.

4 An angle formed outside a circle by two secants, a secant and a tangent, or two tangents is equal in degrees to one half the difference of its intercepted arcs.

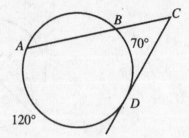

If $m\widehat{AD} = 120°$ and $m\widehat{BD} = 70°$, then $m\angle ACD = 25°$.

5 Two tangent segments drawn to a circle from the same external point are congruent.

If AC and CE are tangent to circle O at B and D, then $CB = CD$.

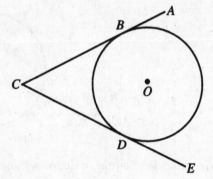

VOLUME

1 The volume of a rectangular solid is equal to the product of its length, width, and height.

$V = lwh$

$V = (6)(2)(4) = 48$

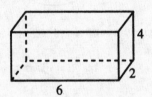

2 The volume of a cube is equal to the cube of an edge.

$V = e^3$

$V = (5)^3 = 125$

3 The volume of a cylinder is equal to π times the square of the radius of the base times the height.

$V = \pi r^2 h$

$V = \pi(5)^2(3) = 75\pi$

TRIANGLES

1 If two sides of a triangle are congruent, the angles opposite these sides are congruent.

If $AB \cong AC$, then
$\angle B \cong \angle C$.

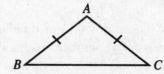

2 If two angles of a triangle are congruent, the sides opposite these angles are congruent.

If $\angle B \cong \angle C$, then
$AB \cong AC$.

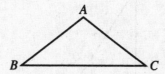

3 The sum of the measures of the angles of a triangle is 180°.

4 The measure of an exterior angle of a triangle is equal to the sum of the measures of the two remote interior angles.

$m\angle 1 = 130°$

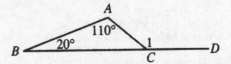

5 If two angles of one triangle are congruent to two angles of a second triangle, the third angles are congruent.

$\angle D \cong \angle A$

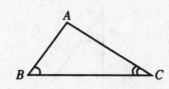 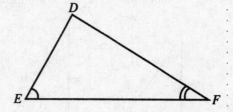

RIGHT TRIANGLES

❶ Pythagorean theorem

$$(\text{leg})^2 + (\text{leg})^2 = (\text{hypotenuse})^2$$
$$4^2 + 5^2 = x^2$$
$$16 + 25 = x^2$$
$$41 = x^2$$
$$\sqrt{41} = x$$

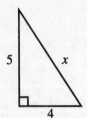

❷ Pythagorean triples: These are sets of numbers that satisfy the Pythagorean theorem. When a given set of numbers such as 3-4-5 forms a Pythagorean triple ($3^2 + 4^2 = 5^2$), any multiples of this set such as 6, 8, 10 or 15, 20, 25 also form a Pythagorean triple. The most common Pythagorean triples that should be memorized are:

3-4-5

5-12-13

8-15-17

7-24-25

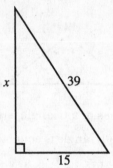

Squaring these numbers in order to apply the Pythagorean theorem would take too much time. Instead, recognize the hypotenuse as 3(13). Suspect a 5-12-13 triangle. Since the given leg is 3(5), the missing leg must be 3(12), or 36, with no computation and a great saving of time.

❸ The 30°-60°-90° triangle

a) The leg opposite the 30° angle is $\frac{1}{2}$ hypotenuse.

b) The leg opposite the 60° angle is $\frac{1}{2}$ hypotenuse $\cdot \sqrt{3}$.

c) An altitude in an equilateral triangle forms a 30°-60°-90° triangle and is therefore equal to $\frac{1}{2}$ hypotenuse $\cdot \sqrt{3}$.

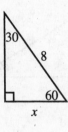
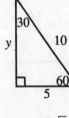
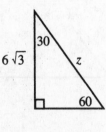
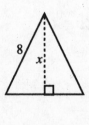

$x = 4$ $y = 5\sqrt{3}$ $z = 12$ $x = 4\sqrt{3}$

4 The 45°-45°-90° triangle (isosceles right triangle)

a) Each leg is $\frac{1}{2}$ · hypotenuse · $\sqrt{2}$.

b) Hypotenuse is leg · $\sqrt{2}$.

c) The diagonal in a square forms a 45°-45°-90° triangle and is therefore equal to a side · $\sqrt{2}$.

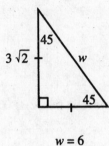 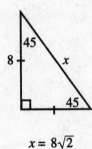 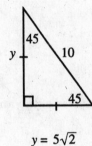 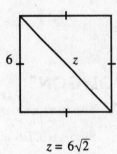

$w = 6$ $x = 8\sqrt{2}$ $y = 5\sqrt{2}$ $z = 6\sqrt{2}$

PARALLEL LINES

1 If two parallel lines are cut by a transversal, the alternate interior angles are congruent.

If *AB*∥*CD*, then
∠1 ≅ ∠3 and
∠2 ≅ ∠4.

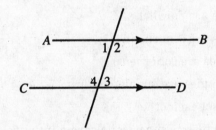

2 If two parallel lines are cut by a transversal, the corresponding angles are congruent.

If *AB*∥*CD*, then
∠1 ≅ ∠5,
∠2 ≅ ∠6,
∠3 ≅ ∠7, and
∠4 ≅ ∠8.

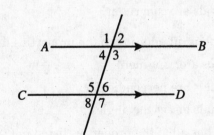

❸ If two parallel lines are cut by a transversal, interior angles on the same side of the transversal are supplementary.

If $AB \| CD$, then
∠1 is supplementary to ∠4 and
∠2 is supplementary to ∠3.

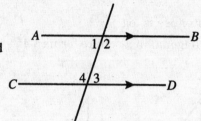

POLYGONS

❶ The sum of the measures of the angles of a polygon of n sides is $(n-2)180°$.

Since $ABCDE$ has 5 sides,

$m\angle A + m\angle B + m\angle C +$

$m\angle D + m\angle E = (5-2)180 = 3(180) = 540°.$

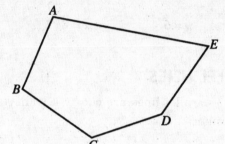

❷ In a parallelogram

a) Opposite sides are parallel.

b) Opposite sides are congruent.

c) Opposite angles are congruent.

d) Consecutive angles are supplementary.

e) Diagonals bisect each other.

f) Each diagonal bisects the parallelogram into two congruent triangles.

❸ In a rectangle, in addition to the properties listed in (2), above,

a) All angles are right angles.

b) Diagonals are congruent.

❹ In a rhombus, in addition to the properties listed in (2), above,

a) All sides are congruent.

b) Diagonals are perpendicular.

c) Diagonals bisect the angles.

❺ A square has all of the properties listed in (2), (3), and (4), above.

6 The apothem of a regular polygon is perpendicular to a side, bisects that side, and also bisects a central angle.

OX is an apothem.

It bisects *AB*, is perpendicular to *AB*, and bisects ∠*AOB*.

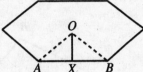

7 The area of a regular polygon is equal to one half the product of its apothem and perimeter.

$$A = \frac{1}{2}(3)(30) = 45$$

SIMILAR POLYGONS

1 Corresponding angles of similar polygons are congruent.

2 Corresponding sides of similar polygons are in proportion.

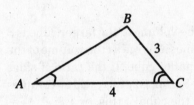

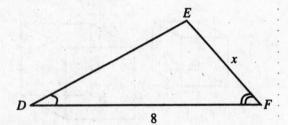

If triangle *ABC* is similar to triangle *DEF*,
and the sides are given as marked, then
EF must be equal to 6, as the ratio
between corresponding sides is 4:8 or 1:2.

3 When figures are similar, all corresponding linear ratios are equal. The ratio of one side to its corresponding side is the same as perimeter to perimeter, apothem to apothem, altitude to altitude, etc.

④ When figures are similar, the ratio of their areas is equal to the square of the ratio between two corresponding linear quantities.

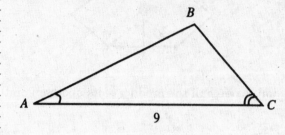

If triangle *ABC* is similar to triangle *DEF*, the area of triangle *ABC* will be 9 times as great as that of triangle *DEF*. The ratio of sides is 9:3, or 3:1. The ratio of areas will be the square of 3:1, or 9:1.

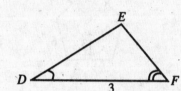

⑤ When figures are similar, the ratio of their volumes is equal to the cube of the ratio between two corresponding linear quantities.

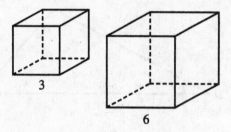

The volume of the larger cube is 8 times as large as the volume of the smaller cube. If the ratio of sides is 3:6, or 1:2, the ratio of volumes is the cube of this, or 1:8.

COORDINATE GEOMETRY

① Distance between two points:

$$\sqrt{(x_2 - x_1)^2 + (y_2 - y_1)^2}$$

The distance from (–2, 3) to (4, –1) is:

$$\sqrt{[4 - (-2)]^2 + [-1 - (3)]^2}$$
$$\sqrt{(6)^2 + (-4)^2} = \sqrt{36 + 16} = \sqrt{52}$$

2 The midpoint of a line segment:

$$\left(\frac{x_1+x_2}{2}, \frac{y_1+y_2}{2}\right)$$

The midpoint of the segment joining $(-2, 3)$ to $(4, -1)$ is:

$$\left(\frac{-2+4}{2}, \frac{3+(-1)}{2}\right) = \left(\frac{2}{2}, \frac{2}{2}\right) = (1,1)$$

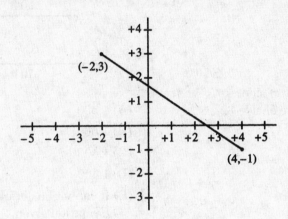

Exercise: Geometry

Directions: Work out each problem. Circle the letter next to your choice.

1. If the angles of a triangle are in the ratio 2:3:7, the triangle is

   (A) acute.

   (B) isosceles.

   (C) obtuse.

   (D) right.

   (E) equilateral.

2. If the area of a square of side x is 5, what is the area of a square of side $3x$?

   (A) 15

   (B) 45

   (C) 95

   (D) 75

   (E) 225

3. If the radius of a circle is decreased by 10%, by what percent is its area decreased?

   (A) 10

   (B) 19

   (C) 21

   (D) 79

   (E) 81

4. A spotlight is mounted on the ceiling 5 feet from one wall of a room and 10 feet from the adjacent wall. How many feet is it from the intersection of the two walls?

   (A) 15

   (B) $5\sqrt{2}$

   (C) $5\sqrt{5}$

   (D) $10\sqrt{2}$

   (E) $10\sqrt{5}$

5. A dam has the dimensions indicated in the figure. Find the area of this isosceles trapezoid.

   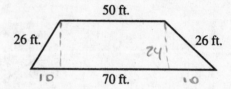

   (A) 1,300

   (B) 1,560

   (C) 1,400

   (D) 1,440

   (E) It cannot be determined from the information given.

6. In parallelogram $PQRS$, angle P is four times angle Q. What is the measure in degrees of angle P?

   (A) 36

   (B) 72

   (C) 125

   (D) 144

   (E) 150

7. If $\overline{PQ} \cong \overline{QS}$, $\overline{QR} \cong \overline{RS}$ and the measure of angle $PRS = 100°$, what is the measure, in degrees, of angle QPS?

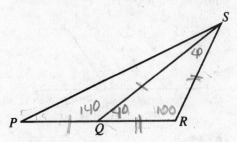

(A) 10

(B) 15

(C) 20

(D) 25

(E) 30

8. A line segment is drawn from the point (3, 5) to the point (9, 13). What are the coordinates of the midpoint of this line segment?

(A) (3, 4)

(B) (12, 18)

(C) (6, 8)

(D) (9, 6)

(E) (6, 9)

9. A rectangular box with a square base contains 6 cubic feet. If the height of the box is 18 inches, how many feet are there in each side of the base?

(A) 1

(B) 2

(C) $\sqrt{3}$

(D) $\dfrac{\sqrt{3}}{3}$

(E) 4

10. The surface area of a cube is 150 square feet. How many cubic feet are there in the volume of the cube?

(A) 30

(B) 50

(C) 100

(D) 125

(E) 150

11. Peter lives 12 miles west of school and Bill lives north of the school. Peter finds that the direct distance from his house to Bill's is 6 miles shorter than the distance by way of school. How many miles north of the school does Bill live?

(A) 6

(B) 9

(C) 10

(D) $6\sqrt{2}$

(E) None of these

12. A square is inscribed in a circle of area 18π. Find a side of the square.

(A) 3

(B) 6

(C) $3\sqrt{2}$

(D) $6\sqrt{2}$

(E) It cannot be determined from the information given.

13. A carpet is y yards long and f feet wide. How many dollars will it cost if the carpet sells for x cents per square foot?

(A) xyf

(B) $3xyf$

(C) $\dfrac{xyf}{3}$

(D) $\dfrac{.03yf}{x}$

(E) $.03xyf$

14. If a triangle of base 6 has the same area as a circle of radius 6, what is the altitude of the triangle?

(A) 6π

(B) 8π

(C) 10π

(D) 12π

(E) 14π

15. The vertex angle of an isosceles triangle is p degrees. How many degrees are there in one of the base angles?

(A) $180 - p$

(B) $90 - p$

(C) $180 - 2p$

(D) $180 - \dfrac{p}{2}$

(E) $90 - \dfrac{p}{2}$

16. In a circle with center O, the measure of arc $RS = 132$ degrees. How many degrees are there in angle RSO?

(A) $66°$

(B) $20°$

(C) $22°$

(D) $24°$

(E) $48°$

17. The ice compartment of a refrigerator is 8 inches long, 4 inches wide, and 5 inches high. How many ice cubes will it hold if each cube is 2 inches on an edge?

(A) 8

(B) 10

(C) 12

(D) 16

(E) 20

18. In the figure, PSQ is a straight line and RS is perpendicular to ST. If the measure of angle $RSQ = 48°$, how many degrees are there in angle PST?

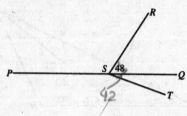

(A) $48°$

(B) $132°$

(C) $90°$

(D) $136°$

(E) $138°$

19. A cylindrical pail has a radius of 7 inches and a height of 9 inches. If there are 231 cubic inches to a gallon, approximately how many gallons will this pail hold?

(A) 6

(B) $\dfrac{12}{7}$

(C) 7.5

(D) 8.2

(E) 9

20. In triangle PQR, $\overline{QS}$ and $\overline{SR}$ are angle bisectors and the measure of angle $P = 80°$. How many degrees are there in angle QSR?

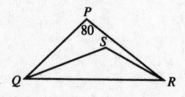

(A) $115°$

(B) $120°$

(C) $125°$

(D) $130°$

(E) $135°$

Solutions

1. **The correct answer is (C).** Represent the angles as $2x$, $3x$, and $7x$.

   $2x + 3x + 7x = 180°$

   $\qquad\quad 12x = 180°$

   $\qquad\qquad x = 15°$

   The angles are 30°, 45°, and 105°. Since one angle is between 90° and 180°, the triangle is called an obtuse triangle.

2. **The correct answer is (B).** If the sides have a ratio 1:3, the areas have a ratio 1:9. Therefore, the area of the large square is 9(5), or 45.

3. **The correct answer is (B).** If the radii of the two circles have a ratio of 10:9, the areas have a ratio of 100:81. Therefore, the decrease is 19 out of 100, or 19%.

4. **The correct answer is (C).**

   $5^2 + 10^2 = x^2$

   $25 + 100 = x^2$

   $\qquad x^2 = 125$

   $\qquad x = \sqrt{125} = \sqrt{25}\sqrt{5} = 5\sqrt{5}$

5. **The correct answer is (D).**

   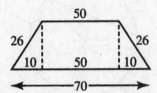

   When altitudes are drawn from both ends of the upper base in an isosceles trapezoid, the figure is divided into a rectangle and two congruent right triangles. The center section of the lower base is equal to the upper base, and the remainder of the lower base is divided equally between both ends. The altitude can then be found using the Pythagorean theorem. In this case, we have a 5-12-13 triangle with all measures doubled, so the altitude is 24.

   The area is $\frac{1}{2}(24)(120)$, or 1,440.

6. **The correct answer is (D).** The consecutive angles of a parallelogram are supplementary, so

   $x + 4x = 180°$

   $\quad\; 5x = 180°$

   $\qquad x = 36°$

   Angle P is 4(36), or 144°.

7. **The correct answer is (C).**

   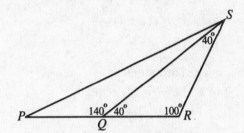

   Since $\overline{QR} \cong \overline{RS}$, $\angle RQS \cong \angle RSQ$. There are 80° left in the triangle, so each of these angles is 40°. $\angle SQP$ is supplementary to $\angle SQR$, making it 140°. Since $\overline{QP} \cong \overline{QS}$, $\angle QPS \cong \angle QSP$. There are 40° left in the triangle, so each of these angles is 20°.

8. **The correct answer is (E).** Add the x values and divide by 2. Add the y values and divide by 2.

9. **The correct answer is (B).** Change 18 inches to 1.5 feet. Letting each side of the base be x, the volume is $1.5x^2$.

   $1.5x^2 = 6$

   $\;15x^2 = 60$

   $\quad\; x^2 = 4$

   $\qquad x = 2$

10. **The correct answer is (D).** The surface area of a cube is made up of 6 equal squares. If each edge of the cube is x, then

    $6x^2 = 150$

    $\;\; x^2 = 25$

    $\quad\; x = 5$

    Volume = $(\text{edge})^3 = 5^3 = 125$

11. The correct answer is (B).

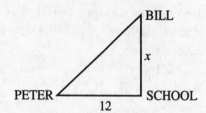

The direct distance from Peter's house to Bill's can be represented by means of the Pythagorean theorem as $\sqrt{144 + x^2}$. Then

$$\sqrt{144 + x^2} = (12 + x) - 6$$

$$\sqrt{144 + x^2} = x + 6$$

Square both sides.

$$144 + x^2 = x^2 + 12x + 36$$

$$144 = 12x + 36$$

$$108 = 12x$$

$$9 = x$$

12. The correct answer is (B).

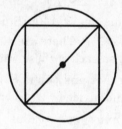

The diagonal of the square will be a diameter of the circle.

$$\pi r^2 = 18\pi$$

$$r^2 = 18$$

$$r = \sqrt{18} = \sqrt{9}\sqrt{2} = 3\sqrt{2}$$

The diameter is $6\sqrt{2}$ and, since the triangles are 45°-45°-90°, a side of the square is 6.

13. The correct answer is (E). To find the area in square feet, change y yards to $3y$ feet. The area is then $(3y)(f)$, or $3yf$ square feet. If each square foot costs x cents, change this to dollars by dividing x by 100. Thus, each square foot costs $\frac{x}{100}$ dollars.

The cost of $3yf$ square feet will be $(3yf)\left(\frac{x}{100}\right)$, or $\frac{3xyf}{100}$.

Since $\frac{3}{100} = .03$, the correct answer is (E).

14. The correct answer is (D). The area of the circle is $(6)^2p$, or 36π. In the triangle

$$\frac{1}{2}(6)(h) = 36\pi$$

$$3h = 36\pi$$

$$h = 12\pi$$

15. The correct answer is (E). There are $(180 - p)$ degrees left, which must be divided between 2 congruent angles. Each angle will contain $\frac{(180-p)}{2}$, or $90 - \frac{p}{2}$ degrees.

16. The correct answer is (D).

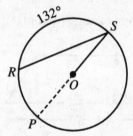

By extending SO until it hits the circle at P, arc PRS is a semicircle. Therefore, the measure of arc $PR = 48°$, and the measure of the inscribed angle $RSO = 24°$.

17. **The correct answer is (D).**

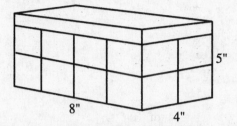

The compartment will hold 2 layers, each of which contains 2 rows of 4 cubes each. This leaves a height of 1 inch on top empty. Therefore, the compartment can hold 16 cubes.

18. **The correct answer is (E).**

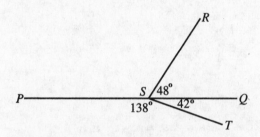

Since ∠*RST* is a right angle, 42° are left for ∠*QST*. Since *PSQ* is a straight angle of 180°, ∠*PST* contains 138°.

19. **The correct answer is (A).** The volume of the pail is found using the formula $V = \pi r^2 h$. Since the answers are not in terms of π, it is best to use $\frac{22}{7}$ as a value for π because the 7 will divide out r^2: $V = \frac{22}{7} \cdot 49^7 \cdot 9$. Rather than multiply this out, which will take unnecessary time, divide by 231 and divide wherever possible.

$$\frac{\overset{2}{\cancel{22}} \cdot \cancel{7} \cdot \overset{3}{\cancel{9}}}{\underset{\underset{\cancel{3}}{\cancel{33}}}{231}} = 6$$

20. **The correct answer is (D).** If $m\angle P = 80°$, there are 100° left between −*PQR* and ∠*PRQ*. If they are both bisected, there will be 50° between ∠*SQR* and ∠*SRQ*, leaving 130° in triangle *SRQ* for ∠*QSR*.

PART VII
PRACTICE TESTS

CHAPTER 16   Five Practice Tests

Five Practice Tests

The practice tests in this book make up one of the most important parts of your SAT and PSAT preparation program. Use them as benchmarks as you work through the other chapters in this book. Each test gives you a great opportunity to gauge your progress and focus your ongoing study. Together, the tests map the growth of your skills and demonstrate your SAT "readiness." And, when you take the practice exams under simulated SAT test-taking conditions, they give you a wonderful opportunity to adjust to the test-taking environment. When you enter the SAT testing room, you'll know what to expect—and you'll be ready to score high on the exam.

SIMULATE TEST-TAKING CONDITIONS

Above and beyond everything else, the five practice exams in this part of the book help you prepare for the experience of taking a timed, standardized test. Taking these tests will improve your familiarity with the SAT, reduce your number of careless errors, and increase your overall level of confidence. To make sure that you get the most out of this practice, you should do everything in your power to simulate actual test-taking conditions. The following sections outline the best methods for simulating SAT testing conditions when you work through the practice exams.

Find 3 Quiet Hours

Because the SAT is administered in one long block of time, the best way to simulate test-taking conditions is to take an entire practice exam in one sitting. This means that you should set aside 3 consecutive hours to take a test. If you find it difficult to find 3 quiet hours at home, maybe take the test in the library. If you decide to take a test at home, take precautions. Turn off the ringer on all nearby telephones, ask your parents to hold your calls, and convince siblings to stay out of your room. Easier said than done, right? Although infrequent interruptions won't completely invalidate your testing experience, you should try to avoid them.

chapter 16

TIP

If you are taking the practice tests at home, try to schedule them during your home's typical "quiet times." If your home doesn't have any "typical quiet times," maybe you can arrange some with your family. Be as resourceful as you can in finding a quiet space where you can spend 3 hours simulating a full-length SAT. It's one of the best ways you can prepare for the real test.

Work at a Desk and Wear a Watch

Don't take a practice test while you are lounging on your bed. After all, the SAT people won't let you take the test lying down! Clear off sufficient space on a desk or table to work comfortably. Wear a watch to properly administer the sections under timed conditions. Remember that every section on the SAT takes 30 minutes with the exception of the two 15-minute "mini-sections." You are not allowed to explore other sections of the test while you are assigned to a particular section. So don't look back or press on. Take the full time to complete each individual section.

Practice on a Weekend Morning

Since the SAT is typically administered at 8:30 a.m. on Saturday (or Sunday for religious observers), why not take the exam at the exact same time on a weekend morning? You should be most energetic in the morning anyway. If you are not a morning person, now is a good time to become one since that's when you'll have to take the actual SAT! When you take the practice test, allow yourself two breaks. Give yourself a 5-minute break after Section 2 to run to the bathroom, scoff down a snack, and resharpen your pencils. After Section 4, give yourself a 1-minute stretch break. During this time on SAT day, you are not allowed to leave the room or speak with anyone. To simulate this, stand up after Section 4, take a minute to collect your thoughts, and then proceed to Section 5.

TIMING DRILLS CAN HELP WHEN YOU ARE SHORT ON TIME

We know that it will be extremely difficult for you to find 3 consecutive hours during which to take full practice examinations. You have a life, after all—homework, social commitments, family responsibilities, etc. Maybe you'll only be able to take one or two complete examinations under simulated testing conditions. But you can do *timing drills* to get valuable practice in shorter periods of time. Timing drills are short groups of questions that allow you to work on your weaknesses under timed conditions.

TIP

If your watch has a beeper, it can help you keep track of the time during your practice test. But remember, your watch can't beep during the real SAT or PSAT. You'll have to turn the beeper off, or wear a non-beeping watch.

Math Timing Drills

If you feel that you need work on a particular type of math question, the first thing you should do is revisit earlier portions of the book for review. For example, if multiple-choice math gives you difficulty, read Chapter 8 to review strategies and do exercises. The same can be said if you have difficulty with quantitative comparisons or grid-ins. Once you have done this, you can get extra valuable review by doing specific timing drills out of the practice tests.

If you want a good review of multiple-choice problems, find a 25-question section out of a practice test and give yourself a timing drill. Approach the section as you would approach the actual SAT. Allow exactly 30 minutes. Then check your answers, review your results, and look for patterns among your answers. (Try to determine whether you need to review your arithmetic, algebra, or geometry and revisit those chapters as necessary.) If you need to practice quantitative comparisons, find the section that contains the 15 quantitative comparisons and allow 15 minutes to do them. If grid-ins intimidate you, take 15 minutes to tackle the 10 of them.

Verbal Timing Drills

You should also revisit earlier chapters to combat your verbal weaknesses. Once you have, you can do the same kind of timing drills. If you feel that you need work on every type of verbal question and you don't have time to take an entire practice test, take a full 30-minute section. This will give you a chance to practice sentence completions, analogies, and critical reading questions in a timed format. If you find sentence completions particularly troubling, allow 7 minutes to answer a drill of 9 or 10 questions. If you want to review analogies, give yourself 9 minutes to do a group of 13 questions. And if critical reading is your stumbling block, allow 15 minutes to answer either a lengthy passage (10 or more questions) or a double passage.

We see timing drills sort of like exercise. You know how people say that if you exercise just 20 minutes per day, three times per week, you can stay in shape? Well, if you do timing drills with regularity, it works the same way. In just 15 to 30 minutes per sitting, you can keep mentally fit for the SAT. Try 'em. They're relatively painless and extraordinarily effective.

A Table of Timing Drills

The following table puts all of the timing drill information in a "one-stop" format, so you can refer to it often when planning your SAT study time.

Type of Question	Number of Questions	Time to Allot
Full Section Multiple-Choice Math	25	30 minutes
Quantitative Comparisons	15	15 minutes
Grid-Ins	10	15 minutes
Full Section Verbal	35 or 30	30 minutes
Sentence Completions	9 or 10	7 minutes
Analogies	13	9 minutes
Critical Reading	10 to 13	15 minutes

ALERT!

If you're worried that you won't be able to resist the temptation of checking the answer keys during the practice tests, rip out the keys and put them in a safe place. Don't allow yourself to become dependent upon a "sneak" look now and then. You won't have answer keys available on test day, and the main purpose of the practice tests is to prepare you for the real experience.

NOTE

We know that doing all of this might appear to be excessive. But remember that your goal is to take these practice tests in as true an environment as possible so that you're prepared to take the real SAT. You will be accustomed to sitting for 3 hours and you will know when to take breaks. This knowledge will make you considerably less anxious on test day.

SUMMARY

What You Need to Know to Take Practice Tests and Do Timing Drills

If you are going to take a full practice examination, try to simulate test-taking conditions by doing the following:

- To take a full-length practice test, you'll need 3 quiet hours.

- Work at a desk and wear a watch when you take the practice exams.

- If temptation may lead you to "sneak a peak" at the answers during the exam, rip out the answer keys and put them in a safe place.

- Whenever possible, take the practice tests on weekend mornings.

- If you don't have the time to take a full test, or you need work on a specific type of question, take the appropriate timing drills.

PRACTICE TEST 1

Answer Sheet

If a section has fewer questions than answer ovals, leave the extra ovals blank.

SECTION 1

1 Ⓐ Ⓑ Ⓒ Ⓓ Ⓔ   11 Ⓐ Ⓑ Ⓒ Ⓓ Ⓔ   21 Ⓐ Ⓑ Ⓒ Ⓓ Ⓔ   31 Ⓐ Ⓑ Ⓒ Ⓓ Ⓔ
2 Ⓐ Ⓑ Ⓒ Ⓓ Ⓔ   12 Ⓐ Ⓑ Ⓒ Ⓓ Ⓔ   22 Ⓐ Ⓑ Ⓒ Ⓓ Ⓔ   32 Ⓐ Ⓑ Ⓒ Ⓓ Ⓔ
3 Ⓐ Ⓑ Ⓒ Ⓓ Ⓔ   13 Ⓐ Ⓑ Ⓒ Ⓓ Ⓔ   23 Ⓐ Ⓑ Ⓒ Ⓓ Ⓔ   33 Ⓐ Ⓑ Ⓒ Ⓓ Ⓔ
4 Ⓐ Ⓑ Ⓒ Ⓓ Ⓔ   14 Ⓐ Ⓑ Ⓒ Ⓓ Ⓔ   24 Ⓐ Ⓑ Ⓒ Ⓓ Ⓔ   34 Ⓐ Ⓑ Ⓒ Ⓓ Ⓔ
5 Ⓐ Ⓑ Ⓒ Ⓓ Ⓔ   15 Ⓐ Ⓑ Ⓒ Ⓓ Ⓔ   25 Ⓐ Ⓑ Ⓒ Ⓓ Ⓔ   35 Ⓐ Ⓑ Ⓒ Ⓓ Ⓔ
6 Ⓐ Ⓑ Ⓒ Ⓓ Ⓔ   16 Ⓐ Ⓑ Ⓒ Ⓓ Ⓔ   26 Ⓐ Ⓑ Ⓒ Ⓓ Ⓔ   36 Ⓐ Ⓑ Ⓒ Ⓓ Ⓔ
7 Ⓐ Ⓑ Ⓒ Ⓓ Ⓔ   17 Ⓐ Ⓑ Ⓒ Ⓓ Ⓔ   27 Ⓐ Ⓑ Ⓒ Ⓓ Ⓔ   37 Ⓐ Ⓑ Ⓒ Ⓓ Ⓔ
8 Ⓐ Ⓑ Ⓒ Ⓓ Ⓔ   18 Ⓐ Ⓑ Ⓒ Ⓓ Ⓔ   28 Ⓐ Ⓑ Ⓒ Ⓓ Ⓔ   38 Ⓐ Ⓑ Ⓒ Ⓓ Ⓔ
9 Ⓐ Ⓑ Ⓒ Ⓓ Ⓔ   19 Ⓐ Ⓑ Ⓒ Ⓓ Ⓔ   29 Ⓐ Ⓑ Ⓒ Ⓓ Ⓔ   39 Ⓐ Ⓑ Ⓒ Ⓓ Ⓔ
10 Ⓐ Ⓑ Ⓒ Ⓓ Ⓔ   20 Ⓐ Ⓑ Ⓒ Ⓓ Ⓔ   30 Ⓐ Ⓑ Ⓒ Ⓓ Ⓔ   40 Ⓐ Ⓑ Ⓒ Ⓓ Ⓔ

SECTION 2

1 Ⓐ Ⓑ Ⓒ Ⓓ Ⓔ   11 Ⓐ Ⓑ Ⓒ Ⓓ Ⓔ   21 Ⓐ Ⓑ Ⓒ Ⓓ Ⓔ   31 Ⓐ Ⓑ Ⓒ Ⓓ Ⓔ
2 Ⓐ Ⓑ Ⓒ Ⓓ Ⓔ   12 Ⓐ Ⓑ Ⓒ Ⓓ Ⓔ   22 Ⓐ Ⓑ Ⓒ Ⓓ Ⓔ   32 Ⓐ Ⓑ Ⓒ Ⓓ Ⓔ
3 Ⓐ Ⓑ Ⓒ Ⓓ Ⓔ   13 Ⓐ Ⓑ Ⓒ Ⓓ Ⓔ   23 Ⓐ Ⓑ Ⓒ Ⓓ Ⓔ   33 Ⓐ Ⓑ Ⓒ Ⓓ Ⓔ
4 Ⓐ Ⓑ Ⓒ Ⓓ Ⓔ   14 Ⓐ Ⓑ Ⓒ Ⓓ Ⓔ   24 Ⓐ Ⓑ Ⓒ Ⓓ Ⓔ   34 Ⓐ Ⓑ Ⓒ Ⓓ Ⓔ
5 Ⓐ Ⓑ Ⓒ Ⓓ Ⓔ   15 Ⓐ Ⓑ Ⓒ Ⓓ Ⓔ   25 Ⓐ Ⓑ Ⓒ Ⓓ Ⓔ   35 Ⓐ Ⓑ Ⓒ Ⓓ Ⓔ
6 Ⓐ Ⓑ Ⓒ Ⓓ Ⓔ   16 Ⓐ Ⓑ Ⓒ Ⓓ Ⓔ   26 Ⓐ Ⓑ Ⓒ Ⓓ Ⓔ   36 Ⓐ Ⓑ Ⓒ Ⓓ Ⓔ
7 Ⓐ Ⓑ Ⓒ Ⓓ Ⓔ   17 Ⓐ Ⓑ Ⓒ Ⓓ Ⓔ   27 Ⓐ Ⓑ Ⓒ Ⓓ Ⓔ   37 Ⓐ Ⓑ Ⓒ Ⓓ Ⓔ
8 Ⓐ Ⓑ Ⓒ Ⓓ Ⓔ   18 Ⓐ Ⓑ Ⓒ Ⓓ Ⓔ   28 Ⓐ Ⓑ Ⓒ Ⓓ Ⓔ   38 Ⓐ Ⓑ Ⓒ Ⓓ Ⓔ
9 Ⓐ Ⓑ Ⓒ Ⓓ Ⓔ   19 Ⓐ Ⓑ Ⓒ Ⓓ Ⓔ   29 Ⓐ Ⓑ Ⓒ Ⓓ Ⓔ   39 Ⓐ Ⓑ Ⓒ Ⓓ Ⓔ
10 Ⓐ Ⓑ Ⓒ Ⓓ Ⓔ   20 Ⓐ Ⓑ Ⓒ Ⓓ Ⓔ   30 Ⓐ Ⓑ Ⓒ Ⓓ Ⓔ   40 Ⓐ Ⓑ Ⓒ Ⓓ Ⓔ

SECTION 3

Answer spaces for Section 3 are on the back of this Answer Sheet.

SECTION 4

1 Ⓐ Ⓑ Ⓒ Ⓓ Ⓔ   11 Ⓐ Ⓑ Ⓒ Ⓓ Ⓔ   21 Ⓐ Ⓑ Ⓒ Ⓓ Ⓔ   31 Ⓐ Ⓑ Ⓒ Ⓓ Ⓔ
2 Ⓐ Ⓑ Ⓒ Ⓓ Ⓔ   12 Ⓐ Ⓑ Ⓒ Ⓓ Ⓔ   22 Ⓐ Ⓑ Ⓒ Ⓓ Ⓔ   32 Ⓐ Ⓑ Ⓒ Ⓓ Ⓔ
3 Ⓐ Ⓑ Ⓒ Ⓓ Ⓔ   13 Ⓐ Ⓑ Ⓒ Ⓓ Ⓔ   23 Ⓐ Ⓑ Ⓒ Ⓓ Ⓔ   33 Ⓐ Ⓑ Ⓒ Ⓓ Ⓔ
4 Ⓐ Ⓑ Ⓒ Ⓓ Ⓔ   14 Ⓐ Ⓑ Ⓒ Ⓓ Ⓔ   24 Ⓐ Ⓑ Ⓒ Ⓓ Ⓔ   34 Ⓐ Ⓑ Ⓒ Ⓓ Ⓔ
5 Ⓐ Ⓑ Ⓒ Ⓓ Ⓔ   15 Ⓐ Ⓑ Ⓒ Ⓓ Ⓔ   25 Ⓐ Ⓑ Ⓒ Ⓓ Ⓔ   35 Ⓐ Ⓑ Ⓒ Ⓓ Ⓔ
6 Ⓐ Ⓑ Ⓒ Ⓓ Ⓔ   16 Ⓐ Ⓑ Ⓒ Ⓓ Ⓔ   26 Ⓐ Ⓑ Ⓒ Ⓓ Ⓔ   36 Ⓐ Ⓑ Ⓒ Ⓓ Ⓔ
7 Ⓐ Ⓑ Ⓒ Ⓓ Ⓔ   17 Ⓐ Ⓑ Ⓒ Ⓓ Ⓔ   27 Ⓐ Ⓑ Ⓒ Ⓓ Ⓔ   37 Ⓐ Ⓑ Ⓒ Ⓓ Ⓔ
8 Ⓐ Ⓑ Ⓒ Ⓓ Ⓔ   18 Ⓐ Ⓑ Ⓒ Ⓓ Ⓔ   28 Ⓐ Ⓑ Ⓒ Ⓓ Ⓔ   38 Ⓐ Ⓑ Ⓒ Ⓓ Ⓔ
9 Ⓐ Ⓑ Ⓒ Ⓓ Ⓔ   19 Ⓐ Ⓑ Ⓒ Ⓓ Ⓔ   29 Ⓐ Ⓑ Ⓒ Ⓓ Ⓔ   39 Ⓐ Ⓑ Ⓒ Ⓓ Ⓔ
10 Ⓐ Ⓑ Ⓒ Ⓓ Ⓔ   20 Ⓐ Ⓑ Ⓒ Ⓓ Ⓔ   30 Ⓐ Ⓑ Ⓒ Ⓓ Ⓔ   40 Ⓐ Ⓑ Ⓒ Ⓓ Ⓔ

TEAR HERE

SECTION 5

1 (A) (B) (C) (D) (E)   6 (A) (B) (C) (D) (E)   11 (A) (B) (C) (D) (E)
2 (A) (B) (C) (D) (E)   7 (A) (B) (C) (D) (E)   12 (A) (B) (C) (D) (E)
3 (A) (B) (C) (D) (E)   8 (A) (B) (C) (D) (E)   13 (A) (B) (C) (D) (E)
4 (A) (B) (C) (D) (E)   9 (A) (B) (C) (D) (E)   14 (A) (B) (C) (D) (E)
5 (A) (B) (C) (D) (E)   10 (A) (B) (C) (D) (E)   15 (A) (B) (C) (D) (E)

SECTION 6

1 (A) (B) (C) (D) (E)   6 (A) (B) (C) (D) (E)   11 (A) (B) (C) (D) (E)
2 (A) (B) (C) (D) (E)   7 (A) (B) (C) (D) (E)   12 (A) (B) (C) (D) (E)
3 (A) (B) (C) (D) (E)   8 (A) (B) (C) (D) (E)   13 (A) (B) (C) (D) (E)
4 (A) (B) (C) (D) (E)   9 (A) (B) (C) (D) (E)   14 (A) (B) (C) (D) (E)
5 (A) (B) (C) (D) (E)   10 (A) (B) (C) (D) (E)   15 (A) (B) (C) (D) (E)

SECTION 3

Note: ONLY the answers entered on the grid are scored. Handwritten answers at the top of the column are NOT scored.

1 (A) (B) (C) (D) (E)   6 (A) (B) (C) (D) (E)   11 (A) (B) (C) (D) (E)
2 (A) (B) (C) (D) (E)   7 (A) (B) (C) (D) (E)   12 (A) (B) (C) (D) (E)
3 (A) (B) (C) (D) (E)   8 (A) (B) (C) (D) (E)   13 (A) (B) (C) (D) (E)
4 (A) (B) (C) (D) (E)   9 (A) (B) (C) (D) (E)   14 (A) (B) (C) (D) (E)
5 (A) (B) (C) (D) (E)   10 (A) (B) (C) (D) (E)   15 (A) (B) (C) (D) (E)

16. 17. 18. 19. 20.

21. 22. 23. 24. 25.

(Grid-in answer boxes numbered 16–25, each with digit bubbles 0–9 and fraction/decimal markers)

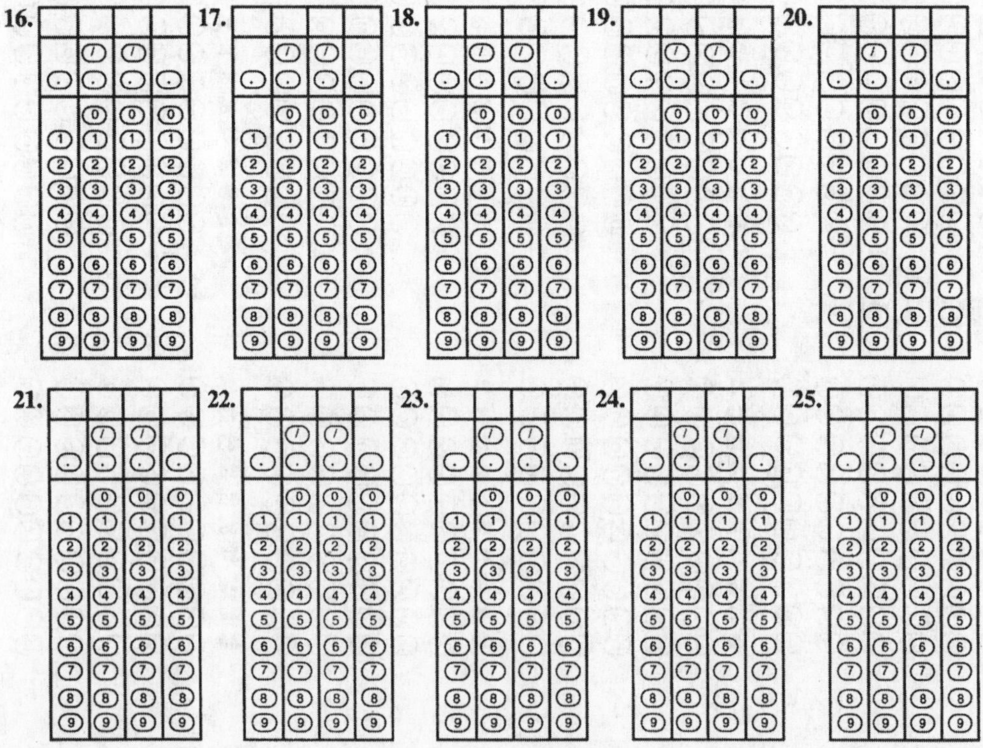

TEAR HERE

PRACTICE TEST 1

Section 1

25 Questions • Time—30 Minutes

Directions: Solve the following problems using any available space on the page for scratchwork. On your answer sheet fill in the choice that best corresponds to the correct answer.

Notes: The figures accompanying the problems are drawn as accurately as possible unless otherwise stated in specific problems. Again, unless otherwise stated, all figures lie in the same plane. All numbers used in these problems are real numbers. Calculators are permitted for this test.

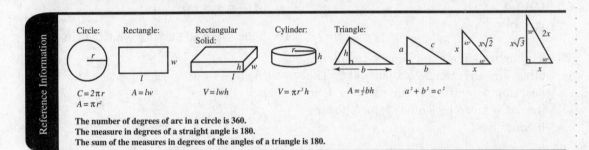

Reference Information

Circle: $C = 2\pi r$, $A = \pi r^2$ Rectangle: $A = lw$ Rectangular Solid: $V = lwh$ Cylinder: $V = \pi r^2 h$ Triangle: $A = \frac{1}{2}bh$ $a^2 + b^2 = c^2$

The number of degrees of arc in a circle is 360.
The measure in degrees of a straight angle is 180.
The sum of the measures in degrees of the angles of a triangle is 180.

1. $0.2 \times 0.02 \times 0.002 =$
   (A) .08
   (B) .008
   (C) .0008
   (D) .00008
   (E) .000008

2. If it costs $1.30 a square foot to lay linoleum, what will be the cost of laying 20 square yards of linoleum? (3 ft. = 1 yd.)
   (A) $47.50
   (B) $49.80
   (C) $150.95
   (D) $249.00
   (E) $234.00

3. In a family of five, the heights of the members are 5 feet 1 inch, 5 feet 7 inches, 5 feet 2 inches, 5 feet, and 4 feet 7 inches. The average height is
   (A) 4 feet $4\frac{1}{5}$ inches.
   (B) 5 feet.
   (C) 5 feet 1 inch.
   (D) 5 feet 2 inches.
   (E) 5 feet 3 inches.

4. Three times the first of three consecutive odd integers is 3 more than twice the third. Find the third integer.
   (A) 7
   (B) 9
   (C) 11
   (D) 13
   (E) 15

5. In the figure below, the largest possible circle is cut out of a square piece of tin. The area, in square inches, of the remaining piece of tin is approximately

   (A) .14
   (B) .75
   (C) .86
   (D) 1.0
   (E) 3.14

6. The figure shows one square inside another and a rectangle of diagonal T. The best approximation to the value of T, in inches, is given by which of the following inequalities?

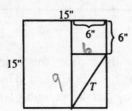

   (A) $8 < T < 9$
   (B) $9 < T < 10$
   (C) $10 < T < 11$
   (D) $11 < T < 12$
   (E) $12 < T < 13$

7. If nails are bought at 35 cents per dozen and sold at 3 for 10 cents, the total profits on $5\frac{1}{2}$ dozen is
   (A) 25 cents.
   (B) $27\frac{1}{2}$ cents.
   (C) $28\frac{1}{2}$ cents.
   (D) $31\frac{1}{2}$ cents.
   (E) 35 cents.

8. The total number of eighths in $2\frac{3}{4}$ is:
   (A) 11
   (B) 14
   (C) 19
   (D) 22
   (E) 24

9. What is the difference when $-x-y$ is subtracted from $-x^2 + 2y$?
   (A) $x^2 - x - 3y$
   (B) $-3x + y$
   (C) $x^2 + 3y$
   (D) $-x^2 + x - 3y$
   (E) $-x^2 + x + 3y$

10. If $2m = 4x$ and $2w = 8x$, what is m in terms of w?
   (A) $w - 1$
   (B) $w + 1$
   (C) $2w - 1$
   (D) $2w + 1$
   (E) w^2

11. $1\frac{1}{4}$ subtracted from its reciprocal is:
   (A) $\dfrac{9}{20}$
   (B) $\dfrac{1}{5}$
   (C) $-\dfrac{1}{20}$
   (D) $-\dfrac{1}{5}$
   (E) $-\dfrac{9}{20}$

12. The total number of feet in x yards, y feet, and z inches is:
   (A) $3x + y + \dfrac{z}{12}$
   (B) $12(x + y + z)$
   (C) $x + y + z$
   (D) $\dfrac{x}{36} + \dfrac{y}{12} + z$
   (E) $x + 3y + 36z$

13. If five triangles are constructed having sides of the lengths indicated below, the triangle that will NOT be a right triangle is:

    (A) 5-12-13
    (B) 3-4-5
    (C) 8-15-17
    (D) 9-40-41
    (E) 12-15-18

14. Of the following, the one that may be used correctly to compute $26 \times 3\frac{1}{2}$ is:

    (A) $(26 \times 30) + (26 \times \frac{1}{2})$
    (B) $(20 \times 3) + (6 \times 3\frac{1}{2})$
    (C) $(20 \times 3\frac{1}{2}) + (6 \times 3)$
    (D) $(20 \times 3) + (26 \times \frac{1}{2}) + (6 \times 3\frac{1}{2})$
    (E) $(26 \times \frac{1}{2}) + (20 \times 3) + (6 \times 3)$

15. In the figure, ST is tangent to the circle at T. RT is a diameter. If $RS = 12$, and $ST = 8$, what is the area of the circle?

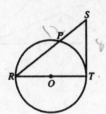

    (A) 5p
    (B) 8p
    (C) 9p
    (D) 20p
    (E) 40p

16. What would be the marked price of an article if the cost was $12.60 and the gain was 10% of the selling price?

    (A) $11.34
    (B) $12.48
    (C) $13.66
    (D) $13.86
    (E) $14.00

17. If the average weight of boys who are John's age and height is 105 lbs., and if John weighs 110% of the average, then how many pounds does John weigh?

    (A) 110
    (B) 110.5
    (C) 112
    (D) 114.5
    (E) 115.5

18. The radius of a circle that has a circumference equal to the perimeter of a hexagon whose sides are each 22 inches long is closest in length to which of the following?

    (A) 7
    (B) 14
    (C) 21
    (D) 24
    (E) 28

19. In the first year of the U.S. Stickball League, the Bayonne Bombers won 50% of their games. During the second season of the league, the Bombers won 65% of their games. If there were twice as many games played in the second season as in the first, what percentage of the games did the Bombers win in the first two years of the league?

    (A) 115%
    (B) 60%
    (C) 57.5%
    (D) 55%
    (E) It cannot be determined from the information given.

20. If the total weight of an apple is $\frac{4}{5}$ of its weight plus $\frac{4}{5}$ of an ounce, what is its weight in ounces?

(A) $1\frac{3}{5}$

(B) $3\frac{1}{2}$

(C) 4

(D) $4\frac{4}{5}$

(E) 5

21. Nine playing cards from the same deck are placed as shown in the figure below to form a large rectangle of area 180 sq. in. How many inches are there in the perimeter of this large rectangle?

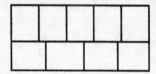

(A) 29

(B) 58

(C) 64

(D) 116

(E) 210

22. If each of the dimensions of a rectangle is increased 100%, the area is increased:

(A) 100%

(B) 200%

(C) 300%

(D) 400%

(E) 500%

23. A recipe for a cake calls for $2\frac{1}{2}$ cups of milk and 3 cups of flour. With this recipe, a cake was baked using 14 cups of flour. How many cups of milk were required?

(A) $10\frac{1}{3}$

(B) $10\frac{3}{4}$

(C) 11

(D) $11\frac{3}{5}$

(E) $11\frac{2}{3}$

24. In the figure below, M and N are midpoints of the sides PR and PQ, respectively, of $\triangle PQR$. What is the ratio of the area of $\triangle MNS$ to that of $\triangle PQR$?

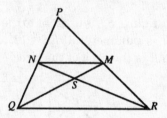

(A) 2:5

(B) 2:9

(C) 1:4

(D) 1:8

(E) 1:12

25. What is 10% of $\frac{1}{3}x$ if $\frac{2}{3}x$ is 10% of 60?

(A) .1

(B) .2

(C) .3

(D) .4

(E) .5

STOP

END OF SECTION 1. IF YOU HAVE ANY TIME LEFT, GO OVER YOUR WORK IN THIS SECTION ONLY. DO NOT WORK IN ANY OTHER SECTION OF THE TEST.

Section 2

31 Questions • Time—30 Minutes

> **Directions:** Each of the following questions consists of an incomplete sentence followed by five words or pairs of words. Choose that word or pair of words that, when substituted for the blank space or spaces, best completes the meaning of the sentence and mark the letter of your choice on your answer sheet.

Example

Q In view of the extenuating circumstances and the defendant's youth, the judge recommended ____.
(A) conviction
(B) a defense
(C) a mistrial
(D) leniency
(E) life imprisonment

A Ⓐ Ⓑ Ⓒ ● Ⓔ

1. Because the elder Johnson was regarded with much ____ by an appreciative public, the younger quite naturally received ____.
   (A) disdain..kudos
   (B) awe..respect
   (C) curiosity..familiarity
   (D) contemplation..abandonment
   (E) pleasantry..laughs

2. Her temperament was exceedingly ____, angry one minute but serene the next.
   (A) mercurial
   (B) steadfast
   (C) distraught
   (D) archetypal
   (E) circumspect

3. Traveling by automobile was ____ to him, but he thought nothing of bobsledding, which had been his ____ for many years.
   (A) tiresome..profession
   (B) tiring..outlet
   (C) harrowing..hobby
   (D) a threat..relief
   (E) exciting..fun

4. Perennial flowers, such as irises, remain ____ every winter, but they ____ in the spring.
   (A) fertile..wither
   (B) arable..congeal
   (C) dormant..burgeon
   (D) distended..contract
   (E) attenuated..rebound

5. The ____ customer was ____ by the manager's prompt action and apology.
   (A) pecuniary..appalled
   (B) weary..enervated
   (C) sedulous..consoled
   (D) intrepid..mortified
   (E) irate..mollified

6. His ____ manner served to hide the fact that he secretly indulged in the very vices he publicly ____.

   (A) sedulous..dispelled
   (B) sanctimonious..condemned
   (C) dogmatic..espoused
   (D) stentorian..prescribed
   (E) candid..promulgated

7. Because of the ____ caused by the flood, living conditions in the area have ____; many people have lost all their belongings.

   (A) trepidation..augmented
   (B) morass..careened
   (C) censure..abated
   (D) devastation..deteriorated
   (E) vertigo..ameliorated

8. Propaganda is a(n) ____ of truth, a mixture of half-truths and half-lies calculated to deceive.

   (A) revision
   (B) perversion
   (C) dissension
   (D) perception
   (E) invasion

9. Though brilliantly presented, the report was ____ since the information on which it was based was erroneous.

   (A) informative
   (B) erudite
   (C) laudable
   (D) worthless
   (E) verbose

Directions: Each of the following questions consists of a capitalized pair of words followed by five pairs of words lettered (A) to (E). The capitalized words bear some meaningful relationship to each other. Choose the lettered pair of words whose relationship is most similar to that expressed by the capitalized pair and mark its letter on your answer sheet.

Example

Q DAY : SUN ::

   (A) sunlight : daylight
   (B) ray : sun
   (C) night : moon
   (D) heat : cold
   (E) moon : star

A Ⓐ Ⓑ ● Ⓓ Ⓔ

10. NOSE : HEAD ::

    (A) hand : arm
    (B) foot : toe
    (C) eye : lid
    (D) wrist : finger
    (E) teeth : gums

11. WHEAT : GRAIN ::

    (A) cow : beef
    (B) orange : lime
    (C) carrot : vegetable
    (D) coconut : palm
    (E) hamburger : steak

12. COTTAGE : CASTLE ::

    (A) house : apartment
    (B) puppy : dog
    (C) dory : liner
    (D) man : family
    (E) poet : gentleman

13. OLD : ANTIQUE ::
    (A) new : modern
    (B) cheap : expensive
    (C) useless : useful
    (D) wanted : needed
    (E) rich : valuable

14. POSSIBLE : PROBABLE ::
    (A) likely : unlikely
    (B) best : better
    (C) willing : eager
    (D) quick : fast
    (E) frightened : worried

15. DIGRESS : RAMBLE ::
    (A) muffle : stifle
    (B) rust : weld
    (C) introduce : conclude
    (D) rest : stir
    (E) find : explain

Directions: Each passage below is followed by a set of questions. Read each passage, then answer the accompanying questions, basing your answers on what is stated or implied in the passage and in any introductory material provided. Mark the letter of your choice on your answer sheet.

Questions 16–22 are based on the following passage.

This passage is taken from the first book of short stories published by Willa Cather (1873–1947), better known for her novels of the western past such as O Pioneers! *For obvious reasons, "Paul's Case" is subtitled "A Study in Temperament."*

It was Paul's afternoon to appear before the faculty of the Pittsburgh High School to account for his various misdemeanors. He had been suspended a week ago,
(5) and his father had called at the Principal's office and confessed his perplexity about his son. Paul entered the faculty room suave and smiling. His clothes were a trifle outgrown, and the
(10) tan velvet on the collar of his open overcoat was frayed and worn; but for all that there was something of the dandy in him, and he wore an opal pin in his neatly knotted black four-in-hand, and
(15) a red carnation in his buttonhole. This latter adornment the faculty somehow felt was not properly significant of the contrite spirit befitting a boy under the ban of suspension.
(20) Paul was tall for his age and very thin, with high, cramped shoulders and a narrow chest. His eyes were remarkable for a certain hysterical brilliancy, and he continually used them in a con-
(25) scious, theatrical sort of way, peculiarly offensive in a boy. The pupils were abnormally large, as though he was addicted to belladonna, but there was a glassy glitter about them which that
(30) drug does not produce.
When questioned by the Principal as to why he was there Paul stated, politely enough, that he wanted to come back to school. This was a lie, but Paul
(35) was quite accustomed to lying; found it, indeed, indispensable for overcoming friction. His teachers were asked to state their respective charges against him, which they did with such a rancor and
(40) aggrievedness as evinced that this was not a usual case. Disorder and impertinence were among the offenses named, yet each of his instructors felt that it was scarcely possible to put into words
(45) the cause of the trouble, which lay in a sort of hysterically defiant manner of the boy's; in the contempt which they all knew he felt for them, and which he seemingly made not the least effort to
(50) conceal. Once, when he had been making a synopsis of a paragraph at the blackboard, his English teacher had stepped to his side and attempted to guide his hand. Paul had started back
(55) with a shudder and thrust his hands violently behind him. The astonished woman could scarcely have been more hurt and embarrassed had he struck at her. The insult was so involuntary and
(60) definitely personal as to be unforgettable. In one way and another he had made all of his teachers, men and women alike, conscious of the same feeling of physical aversion. In one class he ha-
(65) bitually sat with his hand shading his eyes; in another he always looked out the window during the recitation; in another he made a running commentary on the lecture, with humorous in-
(70) tention.
His teachers felt this afternoon that his whole attitude was symbolized by his shrug and his flippantly red carnation flower, and they fell upon him with-
(75) out mercy, his English teacher leading the pack. He stood through it smiling, his pale lips parted over his white teeth. (His lips were constantly twitching, and

(80) he had a habit of raising his eyebrows that was contemptuous and irritating to the last degree.) Older boys than Paul had broken down and shed tears under that baptism of fire, but his set smile did not once desert him, and his only sign of *(85)* discomfort was the nervous trembling of the fingers that toyed with the buttons of his overcoat, and an occasional jerking of the other hand that held his hat. Paul was always smiling, always glanc- *(90)* ing about him, seeming to feel that people might be watching him and trying to detect something. This conscious expression, since it was as far as possible from boyish mirthfulness, was usually attrib- *(95)* uted to insolence or "smartness."

16. The subtitle "A Study in Temperament" suggests that Cather wants to examine

(A) a certain type of character.

(B) reactions under pressure.

(C) how people change over time.

(D) people and their settings.

(E) inner rage.

17. Cather makes it clear in the first paragraph that the faculty of the high school

(A) are perplexed by Paul's actions.

(B) find Paul's demeanor inappropriate.

(C) cannot understand Paul's words.

(D) want only the best for Paul.

(E) are annoyed at Paul's disruption of their day.

18. As it is used in lines 23 and 46, *hysterical* seems to imply

(A) hilarious.

(B) raving.

(C) uncontrolled.

(D) frothing.

(E) delirious.

19. To keep the reader from sympathizing with the faculty, Cather compares them metaphorically to

(A) rabbits.

(B) wolves.

(C) dictators.

(D) comedians.

(E) warships.

20. The word *smartness* (line 95) is used to mean

(A) wit.

(B) intelligence.

(C) impudence.

(D) reasonableness.

(E) resoucefulness.

21. Which adjective does NOT describe Paul as Cather presents him here?

(A) paranoid

(B) defiant

(C) proud

(D) flippant

(E) candid

22. By the end of the selection, we find that the faculty

(A) resents and loathes Paul.

(B) admires and trusts Paul.

(C) struggles to understand Paul.

(D) are physically revolted by Paul.

(E) may learn to get along with Paul.

Questions 23–31 are based on the following passage.

Thomas Jefferson wrote in 1787 to his nephew, Peter Carr, a student at the College of William and Mary. Here, Jefferson gives advice about Peter's proposed course of study.

Paris, August 10, 1787
Dear Peter, _____ I have received your two letters of Decemb. 30 and April 18 and am very happy to find by them, as
(5) well as by letters from Mr. Wythe, that you have been so fortunate as to attract his notice and good will: I am sure you will find this to have been one of the more fortunate events of your life, as I
(10) have ever been sensible it was of mine. I inclose you a sketch of the sciences to which I would wish you to apply in such order as Mr. Wythe shall advise: I mention also the books in them worth your
(15) reading, which submit to his correction. Many of these are among your father's books, which you should have brought to you. As I do not recollect those of them not in his library, you must write to me
(20) for them, making out a catalogue of such as you think you shall have occasion for in 18 months from the date of your letter, and consulting Mr. Wythe on the subject. To this sketch I will add a few
(25) particular observations.
1. Italian. I fear the learning of this language will confound your French and Spanish. Being all of them degenerated dialects of the Latin, they are apt to mix
(30) in conversation. I have never seen a person speaking the three languages who did not mix them. It is a delightful language, but late events having rendered the Spanish more useful, lay it
(35) aside to prosecute that.
2. Spanish. Bestow great attention on this, and endeavor to acquire an accurate knowledge of it. Our future connections with Spain and Spanish America
(40) will render that language a valuable acquisition. The ancient history of a great part of America too is written in that language. I send you a dictionary.

3. Moral philosophy. I think it lost time to attend lectures in this branch.
(45) He who made us would have been a pitiful bungler if he had made the rules of our moral conduct a matter of science. For one man of science, there are thousands who are not. What would
(50) have become of them? Man was destined for society. His morality therefore was to be formed to this object. He was endowed with a sense of right and wrong merely relative to this. This sense is as
(55) much a part of his nature as the sense of hearing, seeing, feeling; it is the true foundation of morality. . . . The moral sense, or conscience, is as much a part of man as his leg or arm. It is given to all
(60) human beings in a stronger or weaker degree, as force of members is given them in a greater or less degree. . . . State a moral case to a ploughman and a professor. The former will decide it as
(65) well, and often better than the latter, because he has not been led astray by artificial rules. . . .

23. As he refers to Mr. Wythe, Jefferson seems to

(A) affect an air of condescension.

(B) reject many of that man's opinions.

(C) warn his nephew not to repeat his mistakes.

(D) relive pleasant memories from his youth.

(E) dispute his nephew's preconceived notions.

24. Jefferson uses the word *sciences* (line 11) to mean

(A) Italian and Spanish only.

(B) moral philosophy and the physical sciences.

(C) school subjects in general.

(D) the subjects treated in his father's books.

(E) biology and chemistry.

25. Jefferson's numbered points refer to
    (A) subjects in order of importance.
    (B) academic courses.
    (C) languages of the world.
    (D) topics discussed in an earlier letter.
    (E) items from a catalogue.

26. Jefferson uses the word *confound* (line 27) to mean
    (A) fluster.
    (B) misunderstand.
    (C) curse.
    (D) muddle.
    (E) clarify.

27. Jefferson encourages his nephew to study Spanish because
    (A) it is related to Latin.
    (B) it will prove useful in international relations.
    (C) there are many good dictionaries available.
    (D) it will prove helpful in learning Italian.
    (E) it is the language of history.

28. By "lost time" (lines 44–45), Jefferson means
    (A) wasted time.
    (B) the past.
    (C) missing time.
    (D) youth.

    (E) about time.

29. Jefferson's main objection to attending lectures in moral philosophy is that
    (A) it could be taught as well by farmers.
    (B) it is innate and cannot be taught.
    (C) it is better practiced outside school.
    (D) very few people understand what it means.
    (E) parents, not professors, should be the instructors.

30. The example of the ploughman and the professor is used to
    (A) illustrate the uselessness of education.
    (B) demonstrate the path to true knowledge.
    (C) explain the universality of morality.
    (D) define the nature of conscience.
    (E) disprove Mr. Wythe's theory of moral conduct.

31. Jefferson compares conscience to a physical limb of the body to show
    (A) that it is natural and present in all human beings.
    (B) how easily we take it for granted.
    (C) that without it, men are powerless.
    (D) how mental and physical states are integrated.
    (E) what is meant by "the arm of the law."

STOP

END OF SECTION 2. IF YOU HAVE ANY TIME LEFT, GO OVER YOUR WORK IN THIS SECTION ONLY. DO NOT WORK IN ANY OTHER SECTION OF THE TEST.

Section 3

25 Questions • Time—30 Minutes

Directions: Solve the following problems using any available space on the page for scratchwork. On your answer sheet fill in the choice that best corresponds to the correct answer.

Notes: The figures accompanying the problems are drawn as accurately as possible unless otherwise stated in specific problems. Again, unless otherwise stated, all figures lie in the same plane. All numbers used in these problems are real numbers. Calculators are permitted for this test.

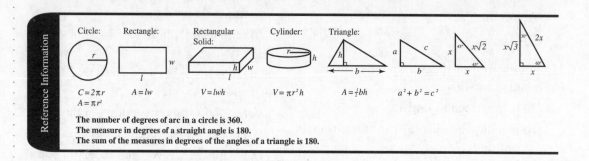

The number of degrees of arc in a circle is 360.
The measure in degrees of a straight angle is 180.
The sum of the measures in degrees of the angles of a triangle is 180.

Part 1: Quantitative Comparison Questions

Directions: For each of the following questions, two quantities are given—one in Column A, and the other in Column B. Compare the two quantities and mark your answer sheet as follows:

(A) if the quantity in Column A is greater

(B) if the quantity in Column B is greater

(C) if the two quantities are equal

(D) if the relationship cannot be determined from the information given

Notes:

(1) Information concerning one or both of the compared quantities will be centered above the two columns for some items.

(2) Symbols that appear in both columns represent the same thing in Column A as in Column B.

(3) Letters such as x, n, and k are symbols for real numbers.

Examples

Column A	Column B

$$a > 0$$

$$x > 0$$

E1. $\boxed{a - x}$ $\qquad$ $\boxed{a + x}$

E2. $\boxed{\begin{array}{c}\text{The average of} \\ \text{17, 19, 21, 23}\end{array}}$ $\boxed{\begin{array}{c}\text{The average of} \\ \text{16, 18, 20, 22}\end{array}}$

Answers

E1. Ⓐ ● Ⓒ Ⓓ   DO NOT MARK
CHOICE (E) FOR
THESE QUESTIONS.

E2. ● Ⓑ Ⓒ Ⓓ   THERE ARE ONLY
FOUR ANSWER
CHOICES.

Column A	Column B
1. The number of sides in a polygon	The number of sides in a quadrilateral

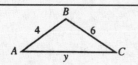

2. Length of side AC	10

$$x(y + z) = 0$$
$$y = -z$$

3. x	$y + z$

4. Area of a circle with a radius of $\frac{2r}{3}$	Area of a circle with a diameter of $\frac{4r}{3}$

$$a \phi b = (a + b)(a - b)$$

5. $2 \phi 2$	$-2 \phi -2$

p is an integer

6. The ratio of p to $(p + 1)$ if $5 < p < 10$	The ratio of p to $(p + 1)$ if $10 < p < 15$

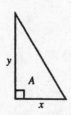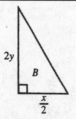

7. Area of triangle A	Area of triangle B

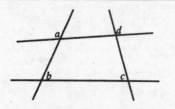

8. $\dfrac{a+b+c+d}{4}$	90

Column A	Column B

Questions 9 and 10 refer to the statement below.

In a sequence of N numbers the first is −1, the second is 1, the third is −2, the fourth is 2, and so on.

9. The ninth number times the eleventh number	The tenth number times the twelfth number

10. The sum of the first through the fifth numbers	The sum of the sixth through the tenth numbers

$$0 < k < 1$$

11. $2k$	$k2$

p is a positive integer

12. The remainder when $3p + 5$ is divided by 3	The remainder when $7p + 8$ is divided by 7

13. The number of prime numbers between 1 and 25	9

$$\frac{m^4}{3} = 27$$

14. m	4

$$s > 1$$

15. The volume of a cube with a side of s	The volume of a rectangular solid with sides of s, $s + 1$, and $s - 1$

Part 2: Student-Produced Response Questions

Directions: Solve each of these problems. Write the answer in the corresponding grid on the answer sheet and fill in the ovals beneath each answer you write. Here are some examples.

Answer: $\frac{3}{4}$ (=.75; show answer either way)   **Answer: 325**

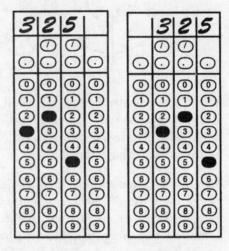

Note: A mixed number such as $3\frac{1}{2}$ must be gridded as 7/2 or as 3.5. If gridded as "3 1/2," it will be read as "thirty-one halves."

Note: Either position is correct.

16. The average temperatures for five days were 82°, 86°, 91°, 79°, and 91°. What is the mode for these temperatures?

17. If $-2x + 5 = 2 - (5 - 2x)$, what is the value of x?

18. In the figure below, $BA \perp AD$ and $CD \perp AD$. Using the values indicated in the figure, what is the area of polygon $ABCD$?

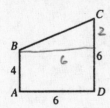

19. In the figure below, $AC = BC$. If m$\angle B = 50°$, what is the measure of $\angle ECD$? (Do not grid the degree symbol.)

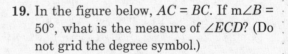
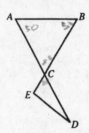

20. What is the value of $-m^2n^3$, when $m = -2$ and $n = -1$?

21. Given a square, a rectangle, a trapezoid, and a circle, if one of these figures is selected at random, what is the probability that the figure has four right angles?

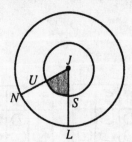

22. Given the concentric circles above, if radius JN is 3 times JU, then the ratio of the shaded area to the area of sector NJL is $1:b$. What is the value of b?

23. In a three-hour examination of 350 questions, there are 50 mathematical problems. If twice as much time should be allowed for each mathematical problem as for each of the other questions, how many minutes should be spent on the mathematical problems?

24. In a pantry there are 28 cans of vegetables. Eight of these have labels with white lettering, 18 have labels with green lettering, and 8 have labels with neither white nor green lettering. How many cans have both white and green lettering?

25. B, C, and D divide AE into 4 equal parts. AB, BC, and CD are divided into 4 equal parts as shown. DE is divided into 3 equal parts as shown.

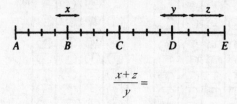

$$\frac{x+z}{y} =$$

STOP

END OF SECTION 3. IF YOU HAVE ANY TIME LEFT, GO OVER YOUR WORK IN THIS SECTION ONLY. DO NOT WORK IN ANY OTHER SECTION OF THE TEST.

Section 4

35 Questions • Time—30 Minutes

Directions: Each of the following questions consists of an incomplete sentence followed by five words or pairs of words. Choose that word or pair of words that, when substituted for the blank space or spaces, best completes the meaning of the sentence and mark the letter of your choice on your answer sheet.

Example

Q In view of the extenuating circumstances and the defendant's youth, the judge recommended ____.
   (A) conviction
   (B) a defense
   (C) a mistrial
   (D) leniency
   (E) life imprisonment

1. He dashed into the house, ran for the phone, and answered ____, tripping over the cord.
   (A) hesitantly
   (B) nobly
   (C) soothingly
   (D) distantly
   (E) breathlessly

2. The criminal record of the witness caused the jury to ____ his testimony.
   (A) affirm
   (B) belie
   (C) retract
   (D) acquit
   (E) discredit

3. Although the storm left the family ____, it could not ____ their spirits.
   (A) discordant..raise
   (B) moribund..drench
   (C) destitute..dampen
   (D) sodden..excite
   (E) indolent..inhibit

4. By a stroke of luck the troops ____, avoiding a crushing ____.
   (A) converged..blow
   (B) prevailed..defeat
   (C) diverged..siege
   (D) retrenched..retreat
   (E) interceded..assault

5. You must act with ____ if you want to buy your airline ticket before tomorrow's price increase.
   (A) celerity
   (B) clemency
   (C) facility
   (D) lassitude
   (E) laxity

6. The ____ background music hinted of the dangers threatening the movie's heroine.
   (A) trenchant
   (B) ebullient
   (C) sardonic
   (D) portentous
   (E) precocious

7. Nineteenth-century advances in women's rights were gradual and ____; years might separate one advance from the next.

   (A) reticent

   (B) onerous

   (C) incumbent

   (D) docile

   (E) sporadic

8. Since several offices have been ____ across the street, the old directory is now ____.

   (A) refurbished..adequate

   (B) relocated..obsolete

   (C) deployed..reserved

   (D) transmuted..oblivious

   (E) removed..upgraded

9. The junta's promise of free elections was ____, a mere sop to world opinion.

   (A) spurious

   (B) contentious

   (C) unctuous

   (D) lucid

   (E) presumptuous

10. The woman acted in a ____ manner, pretending not to notice the nearby celebrities.

    (A) convivial

    (B) doleful

    (C) nonchalant

    (D) cogent

    (E) vicarious

Directions: Each of the following questions consists of a capitalized pair of words followed by five pairs of words lettered (A) to (E). The capitalized words bear some meaningful relationship to each other. Choose the lettered pair of words whose relationship is most similar to that expressed by the capitalized pair and mark its letter on your answer sheet.

Example

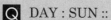 DAY : SUN ::

   (A) sunlight : daylight

   (B) ray : sun

   (C) night : moon

   (D) heat : cold

   (E) moon : star

11. LIBRARY : BOOKS ::

    (A) hotel : children

    (B) zoo : animals

    (C) office : sales

    (D) park : cars

    (E) school : buses

12. TINY : HUGE ::

    (A) small : little

    (B) great : grand

    (C) weak : strong

    (D) sad : gloomy

    (E) chaotic : confused

13. FRIGHTEN : SCARE ::

    (A) question : ask

    (B) look : see

    (C) terrorize : startle

    (D) brave : fear

    (E) upset : calm

14. SEARCH : FIND ::
   (A) fight : win
   (B) obey : believe
   (C) look : seek
   (D) write : read
   (E) listen : talk

15. DOOR : OPEN ::
   (A) cap : remove
   (B) knife : cut
   (C) blackboard : erase
   (D) gift : take
   (E) car : speed

16. DASTARD : COWARDICE ::
   (A) cipher : importance
   (B) scoundrel : immorality
   (C) native : intimacy
   (D) refugee : nationality
   (E) client : independence

17. TOE : FOOT ::
   (A) elbow : wrist
   (B) fist : hand
   (C) shoe : sock
   (D) pupil : eye
   (E) arm : leg

18. STRUM : GUITAR ::
   (A) tune : instrument
   (B) tighten : drum
   (C) polish : bugle
   (D) pedal : organ
   (E) hum : song

19. PUERILE : MATURITY ::
   (A) pungent : poignancy
   (B) poised : serenity
   (C) obscure : clarity
   (D) ostentatious : pretension
   (E) profuse : extravagance

20. HURTLE : TOSS ::
   (A) strike : tap
   (B) throw : bite
   (C) squelch : crush
   (D) quarrel : squabble
   (E) murmur : mumble

21. INFINITE : BOUNDS ::
   (A) intangible : property
   (B) kinetic : motion
   (C) nebulous : clarity
   (D) ponderous : bulk
   (E) propitious : favor

22. TIME : MINUTES ::
   (A) month : calendar
   (B) clock : faces
   (C) race : laps
   (D) yard : square
   (E) arms : legs

23. MOUNTAIN : TUNNEL ::
   (A) window : frame
   (B) river : bridge
   (C) door : handle
   (D) charcoal : fire
   (E) wall : window

practice test

Directions: The reading passage below is followed by a set of questions. Read the passage and answer the accompanying questions, basing your answers on what is stated or implied in the passage. Mark the letter of your choice on your answer sheet.

Questions 24–35 are based on the following passage.

A major step forward in the history of the novel, Don Quixote, *was penned by Miguel de Cervantes and first published in Spain in 1605. Driven mad by his constant perusal of tales of chivalry, Alonso Quijano changes his name to Don Quixote and rides off to seek adventure. This passage describes his first expedition.*

Once these preparations were completed, he was anxious to wait no longer before putting his ideas into effect, impelled to this by the thought of the loss the world
(5) suffered by his delay, seeing the grievances there were to redress, the wrongs to right, the injuries to amend, and the debts to discharge. So, telling nobody of his intentions, and quite unobserved,
(10) one morning before dawn—it was on one of those sweltering July days—he armed himself completely, mounted Rocinante, put on his badly-mended headpiece, slung on his shield, seized his lance and
(15) went out into the plain through the back gate of his yard, pleased and delighted to see with what ease he had started on his fair design. But scarcely was he in open country when he was assailed by a
(20) thought so terrible that it almost made him abandon the enterprise he had just begun. For he suddenly remembered that he had never received the honor of knighthood, and so, according to the
(25) laws of chivalry, he neither could nor should take arms against any knight, and even if he had been knighted he was bound, as a novice, to wear plain armour without a device on his shield until he
(30) should gain one by his prowess. These reflections made him waver in his resolve, but as his madness outweighed

any other argument, he made up his mind to have himself knighted by the
(35) first man he met, in imitation of many who had done the same, as he had read in the books which had so influenced him. As to plain armor, he decided to clean his own, when he had time, till it
(40) was whiter than ermine. With this he quieted his mind and went on his way, taking whatever road his horse chose, in the belief that in this lay the essence of adventure.

(45)   As our brand-new adventurer journeyed along, he talked to himself, saying: "Who can doubt that in ages to come, when the authentic story of my famous deeds comes to light, the sage who writes
(50) of them will say, when he comes to tell of my first expedition so early in the morning: 'Scarce had the ruddy Apollo spread the golden threads of his lovely hair over the broad and spacious face of the earth,
(55) and scarcely had the forked tongues of the little painted birds greeted with mellifluous harmony the coming of the rosy Aurora who, leaving the soft bed of her jealous husband, showed herself at the
(60) doors and balconies of the Manchegan horizon, when the famous knight, Don Quixote de la Mancha, quitting the slothful down, mounted his famous steed Rocinante and began to journey across
(65) the ancient and celebrated plain of Montiel'?" That was, in fact, the road that our knight actually took, as he went on: "Fortunate the age and fortunate the times in which my famous deeds will
(70) come to light, deeds worthy to be engraved in bronze, carved in marble and painted on wood, as a memorial for posterity. And you, sage enchanter, whoever you may be, to whose lot it falls to be
(75) the chronicler of this strange history, I beg you not to forget my good Rocinante,

my constant companion on all my rides and journeys!" And presently he cried again, as if he had really been in love: "O
(80) Princess Dulcinea, mistress of this captive heart! You did me great injury in dismissing me and inflicting on me the cruel rigour of your command not to appear in your beauteous presence.
(85) Deign, lady, to be mindful of your captive heart, which suffers such griefs for love of you."

He went on stringing other nonsense on to this, all after the fashion he
(90) had learnt in his reading, and imitating the language of his books as best he could. And all the while he rode so slowly and the sun's heat increased so fast that it would have been enough to turn his
(95) brain, if he had had any.

24. The word *redress* in line 6 most nearly means to

(A) locate a residence.

(B) put on clothes.

(C) downplay.

(D) correct.

(E) confuse.

25. As described in lines 23–31, Don Quixote was hesitant to fight because he

(A) was afraid for his life.

(B) didn't believe in violence.

(C) would break the established code of chivalry.

(D) would lose his wife if he fought for what he truly believed.

(E) was indifferent to the cause.

26. The word *device* in line 29 probably means

(A) emblem.

(B) tool.

(C) gadget.

(D) trick.

(E) metal.

27. The words that best describe the first speech Cervantes has Don Quixote make (lines 47–66) might be

(A) informative and deliberate.

(B) profound and resolute.

(C) dull and ill-conceived.

(D) shocking and defamatory.

(E) flowery and overwrought.

28. What does Don Quixote mean when he says "quitting the slothful down" (lines 62–63)?

(A) leaving the farm

(B) climbing into the saddle

(C) feeling happier and more energetic

(D) recovering from illness

(E) getting out of bed

29. The phrase "as if he had really been in love" (line 79) is used to illuminate Don Quixote's

(A) need for attention.

(B) starved spirit.

(C) dementia.

(D) unhappy childhood.

(E) inability to emote.

30. Cervantes has his hero address his remarks to

(A) God.

(B) the reader.

(C) his horse.

(D) a mythical historian and a princess.

(E) an unknown knight.

31. The last line of the selection reminds us that

(A) the story takes place in Spain.

(B) Don Quixote is mad.

(C) Rocinante has no destination in mind.

(D) other knights have taken this same route.

(E) the long day is about to end.

32. We first suspect that Don Quixote is not quite the hero he seems when he recalls that

(A) he left his armor at home.

(B) his horse is named Rocinante.

(C) he is not a real knight.

(D) Dulcinea holds him captive.

(E) he started his journey with ease.

33. According to the author, Don Quixote's speech is affected by

(A) romantic books he has read.

(B) the language of seventeenth-century Spain.

(C) letters received from Dulcinea.

(D) the speeches of Alfonso X.

(E) his night visions.

34. Cervantes's opinion of the literature of his day seems to be that it is

(A) written by madmen.

(B) argumentative and controversial.

(C) not up to the standards of the previous century.

(D) sentimental drivel.

(E) derivative.

35. The best word to describe Cervantes's feeling toward his hero might be

(A) disdainful.

(B) revolted.

(C) indifferent.

(D) mocking.

(E) appreciative.

STOP

END OF SECTION 4. IF YOU HAVE ANY TIME LEFT, GO OVER YOUR WORK IN THIS SECTION ONLY. DO NOT WORK IN ANY OTHER SECTION OF THE TEST.

Section 5

10 Questions • Time—15 Minutes

Directions: Solve the following problems using any available space on the page for scratchwork. On your answer sheet fill in the choice that best corresponds to the correct answer.

Notes: The figures accompanying the problems are drawn as accurately as possible unless otherwise stated in specific problems. Again, unless otherwise stated, all figures lie in the same plane. All numbers used in these problems are real numbers. Calculators are permitted for this test.

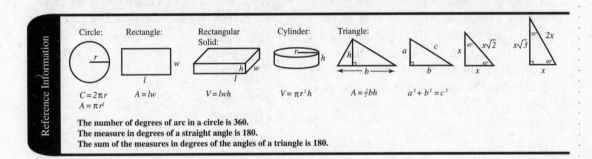

The number of degrees of arc in a circle is 360.
The measure in degrees of a straight angle is 180.
The sum of the measures in degrees of the angles of a triangle is 180.

1. The total savings in purchasing thirty 13-cent lollipops for a class party at a reduced rate of $1.38 per dozen is:

   (A) $.35
   (B) $.38
   (C) $.40
   (D) $.45
   (E) $.50

2. A gallon of water is equal to 231 cubic inches. How many gallons of water are needed to fill a fish tank that measures 11" high, 14" long, and 9" wide?

   (A) 6
   (B) 8
   (C) 9
   (D) 14
   (E) 16

3. The area of a right triangle is 12 square inches. The ratio of its legs is 2:3. Find the number of inches in the hypotenuse of this triangle.

   (A) $\sqrt{13}$
   (B) $\sqrt{26}$
   (C) $3\sqrt{13}$
   (D) $\sqrt{52}$
   (E) $4\sqrt{13}$

4. A rectangular block of metal weighs 3 ounces. How many pounds will a similar block of the same metal weigh if the edges are twice as large?

(A) $\frac{3}{8}$

(B) $\frac{3}{4}$

(C) $1\frac{1}{2}$

(D) 3

(E) 24

5. A college graduate goes to work for x dollars per week. After several months the company gives all the employees a 10% pay cut. A few months later the company gives all the employees a 10% raise. What is the college graduate's new salary?

(A) $.90x$

(B) $.99x$

(C) x

(D) $1.01x$

(E) $1.11x$

6. What is the net amount of a bill of $428.00 after a discount of 6% has been allowed?

(A) $432.62

(B) $430.88

(C) $414.85

(D) $412.19

(E) $402.32

7. A certain type of board is sold only in lengths of multiples of 2 feet, from 6 feet to 24 feet. A builder needs a larger quantity of this type of board in $5\frac{1}{2}$-foot lengths. For minimum waste, the lengths in feet to be ordered should be:

(A) 6

(B) 12

(C) 18

(D) 22

(E) 24

8. A cube has an edge that is four inches long. If the edge is increased by 25%, then the volume is increased by approximately:

(A) 25%

(B) 48%

(C) 73%

(D) 95%

(E) 122%

9. The ratio of $\frac{1}{4}$ to $\frac{3}{5}$ is:

(A) 1 to 3

(B) 3 to 20

(C) 5 to 12

(D) 3 to 4

(E) 5 to 4

10. Which of the following numbers is the smallest?

(A) $\sqrt{3}$

(B) $\frac{1}{\sqrt{3}}$

(C) $\frac{\sqrt{3}}{3}$

(D) $\frac{1}{3}$

(E) $\frac{1}{3\sqrt{3}}$

STOP

END OF SECTION 5. IF YOU HAVE ANY TIME LEFT, GO OVER YOUR WORK IN THIS SECTION ONLY. DO NOT WORK IN ANY OTHER SECTION OF THE TEST.

Section 6

12 Questions • Time—15 Minutes

Directions: The two passages given below deal with a related topic. Following the passages are questions about the content of each passage or about the relationship between the two passages. Answer the questions based upon what is stated or implied in the passages and in any introductory material provided. Mark the letter of your choice on your answer sheet.

Questions 1–12 are based on the following passages:

The struggle of African Americans to make economic and political progress within the socioeconomic structure of the United States has been long and filled with setbacks. These two passages document some of the events in that long struggle and seek to explain why the struggle was so difficult.

PASSAGE 1—The Economic Scene

Because of slavery, which lasted until 1865, and undereducation, African Americans have been at a disadvantage in terms of socioeconomic progress until
(5) well into the twentieth century. Segregated schools were often not on a par with the schools in which whites were educated; consequently, when African Americans competed for jobs with whites,
(10) they often found they could not.

Increased opportunities for African Americans followed in the wake of the civil rights movement, and as a result, African Americans were able to
(15) gain higher levels of education and achieve more managerial positions within the various professions. In the 1980s, African Americans moved into the upper middle class in large num-
(20) bers.

Consistently in the last five decades, African Americans have moved into higher-status jobs, have opened their own businesses, and have increased their
(25) levels of education. Because of such progress, it is safe to assume that those African Americans who have become upwardly mobile would not be able to tolerate racial discrimination as it ex-
(30) isted prior to the civil rights movement.

While progress has been made in some segments of the African-American population, less progress has occurred among low-income African Americans.
(35) Many low-income African Americans do not have a place in the class structure because of racial segregation and poverty, particularly in urban areas. When segregation and poverty prevail, urban
(40) neighborhoods become places of high crime, poor schools, and poorly maintained homes.

Thus, what has emerged in the 1990s is a widening socioeconomic gap
(45) between low-income African Americans and the African Americans who have been able to improve their socioeconomic status.

PASSAGE 2—The Political Scene

Only with the enforcement of the Recon-
(50) struction Act of 1867 and the ratification of the Fifteenth Amendment to the Constitution did African Americans first win seats in Congress. Hiram Revels of Mississippi became the first African
(55) American to serve in Congress when he took his seat in the Senate on February 25, 1870. Joseph Rainey of South Carolina became the first African-American member of the House of Representa-
(60) tives later in 1870.

African Americans throughout the South became politically active soon after emancipation and the close of the Civil War. A generation of African-
(65) American leaders emerged who nearly

unanimously adhered to the Republican Party because it had championed the rights of African Americans. African Americans elected to Congress during *(70)* Reconstruction found the national legislature an effective forum for the advocacy of political equality. Following the end of federal Reconstruction in 1877, African Americans continued to win elec- *(75)* tion to Congress, and carried on the struggle for civil rights and economic opportunity.

During the 1890s and early 1900s, no African American won election to *(80)* Congress, in part because of restrictive state election codes in some southern states. During World War I and in the following decade, however, African-American migration to northern cities *(85)* established the foundations for political organization in urban centers. Over the next three decades African Americans won congressional seats in New York City, Detroit, and Philadelphia. In the *(90)* wake of the civil rights movement and the enforcement of the Voting Rights Act of 1965, African Americans regained seats in the South. Since the 1930s, nearly all African-American represen- *(95)* tatives have been Democrats.

Since the nineteenth century, African-American members of Congress have served as advocates for all African Americans as well as representatives *(100)* for their constituencies. During Reconstruction and the late nineteenth century, African-American representatives called on their colleagues to protect the voting rights of African Americans. They *(105)* also called for expanded educational opportunities and land grants for freed African Americans. In the mid-twentieth century, African-American representatives turned to the needs of urban *(110)* communities and urged federal programs for improved housing and job training. These representatives served as defenders of the civil rights movement and proponents of legislation to *(115)* end segregation. The Congressional Black Caucus demonstrated a special concern for the protection of civil rights;

the guarantee of equal opportunity in education, employment, and housing; *(120)* and a broad array of foreign and domestic policy issues.

Since the victories of the civil rights movement in the 1960s, African-American men and women have won election *(125)* to Congress from increasingly diverse regions of the country. Whether from largely urban districts, suburban areas, or more recently from rural Mississippi, these members of Congress have main- *(130)* tained their common concern with economic issues that affect African Americans with the protection of civil rights.

The collected biographies of African Americans who served in the House *(135)* and Senate provide an important perspective on the history of the Congress and the role of African Americans in American politics. Their stories offer eloquent testimony to the long struggle *(140)* to extend the ideals of the founders to encompass all citizens of the United States.

1. The author's attitude in Passage 1 is primarily one of

   (A) complete detachment.

   (B) unbridled outrage.

   (C) indifference.

   (D) disinterest.

   (E) objectivity.

2. Passage 1 indicates that socioeconomic progress for African Americans has been slow because of

   (A) prejudice.

   (B) insurmountable poverty.

   (C) slavery and undereducation.

   (D) generally slow economic progress in the United States.

   (E) immigrants from Central America.

3. The phrase "on a par" (line 6) means
   (A) in the same location.
   (B) at odds with.
   (C) in competition with.
   (D) on the same level.
   (E) on a different level.

4. According to the passage, African Americans have done all of the following in the last five decades EXCEPT
   (A) move into higher-status jobs.
   (B) open their own businesses.
   (C) tolerate more racial discrimination.
   (D) achieve more managerial positions.
   (E) increase their level of education.

5. While not directly stated, the passage implies that the civil rights movement
   (A) had no effect on African-American upward mobility.
   (B) caused a setback for African-American socioeconomic progress.
   (C) was not supported by African Americans.
   (D) had very little strong leadership.
   (E) helped African Americans in their struggle to achieve economic goals.

6. The conclusion that the author ultimately reaches in Passage 1 is that
   (A) all African Americans have made socioeconomic progress.
   (B) upward mobility is no longer an issue with African Americans.
   (C) the civil rights movement was not a success as far as most African Americans are concerned.
   (D) poverty in the inner cities of the United States is insurmountable.
   (E) the 1990s have seen a widening of the gap between low-income African Americans and those who have made economic progress.

7. According to Passage 2, the first African American to serve in the House of Representatives was
   (A) a former slave.
   (B) Hiram Revels.
   (C) from Chicago.
   (D) Joseph Rainey.
   (E) Oscar DePriest.

8. One difference between African-American congressional representatives in the nineteenth century and those in the mid-twentieth century was
   (A) their commitment to education for African Americans.
   (B) the political party to which they were likely to belong.
   (C) the strength of their ties to the African-American community as a whole.
   (D) the extent to which they represented *all* African Americans.
   (E) their ability to influence other congressional members.

9. When the African-American representatives "turned to" certain issues in the mid-twentieth century (line 109), they
   (A) became antagonistic toward those issues.
   (B) reversed their positions on those issues.
   (C) referred to those issues.
   (D) devoted themselves to those issues.
   (E) listened to criticisms of those issues.

10. One reason cited in the passage for the election of African Americans to Congress from both southern states after Reconstruction and northern states after World War I is the

    (A) strength of local African-American political organizations.

    (B) success of the civil rights movement.

    (C) passage and enforcement of the Fifteenth Amendment.

    (D) predominance of African Americans in certain districts.

    (E) elimination of regional differences.

11. The author expresses admiration for the African-American congressional representatives discussed in the passage for their

    (A) political acumen.

    (B) attempts to ensure the rights of all Americans.

    (C) single-minded devotion to the struggle for civil rights.

    (D) focus on providing economic opportunity for African Americans.

    (E) ability to regularly secure re-election.

12. The author of Passage 1 connects increased opportunity for African Americans with the civil rights movement of the 1960s while the author of Passage 2

    (A) believes that African-American empowerment didn't occur until the 1980s.

    (B) argues that since the American revolution blacks have had significant political opportunities.

    (C) states that since the end of the Civil War, African Americans have enjoyed a steady rise in political power.

    (D) points out that although political empowerment started in 1867, there have been bumps in the road to progress.

    (E) claims that not until World War I did African Americans come to power.

STOP

END OF SECTION 6. IF YOU HAVE ANY TIME LEFT, GO OVER YOUR WORK IN THIS SECTION ONLY. DO NOT WORK IN ANY OTHER SECTION OF THE TEST.

ANSWERS AND EXPLANATIONS

Section 1: Math

1. E	6. C	11. E	16. E	21. B
2. E	7. B	12. A	17. E	22. C
3. C	8. D	13. E	18. C	23. E
4. E	9. E	14. E	19. B	24. E
5. C	10. A	15. D	20. C	25. C

Section 2: Verbal

1. B	8. B	14. C	20. C	26. D
2. A	9. D	15. A	21. E	27. B
3. C	10. A	16. A	22. A	28. A
4. C	11. C	17. B	23. D	29. B
5. E	12. C	18. C	24. C	30. C
6. B	13. A	19. B	25. B	31. A
7. D				

Section 3: Math

Part 1

1. D	4. C	7. C	10. B	13. C
2. B	5. C	8. C	11. A	14. B
3. D	6. B	9. C	12. A	15. A

Part 2

16. 91	18. 30	20. 4	22. 9	24. 6
17. 2	19. 80	21. $\frac{1}{2}=.5$	23. 45	25. 2

Section 4: Verbal

1. E	8. B	15. B	22. C	29. C
2. E	9. A	16. B	23. B	30. D
3. C	10. C	17. D	24. D	31. B
4. B	11. B	18. D	25. C	32. C
5. A	12. C	19. C	26. A	33. A
6. D	13. A	20. A	27. E	34. D
7. E	14. A	21. C	28. E	35. D

Section 5: Math

1. D	3. D	5. B	7. D	9. C
2. A	4. C	6. E	8. D	10. E

Section 6: Verbal

1. E	4. C	7. D	9. D	11. B
2. C	5. E	8. B	10. A	12. D
3. D	6. E			

> **Note:** A 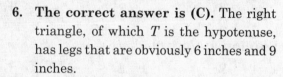 following a math answer explanation indicates that a calculator could be helpful in solving that particular problem.

Section 1

1. **The correct answer is (E).** Count the number of decimal places in the terms to be multiplied; this adds up to 6. It should be clear that the last number must be 8. There must be six decimal places accounted for and thus there must be five zeros in front of the 8.

2. **The correct answer is (E).** 20 square yards = 180 square feet. At $1.30 per square foot, it will cost $234.00.

3. **The correct answer is (C).**

    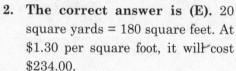

    5 ft.1 in.
    5 ft.7 in.
    5 ft.2 in.
    5 ft.
    4 ft.7 in.
    24 ft.17 in., or 25 ft. 5 in.

    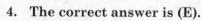

    Average = $\dfrac{25 \text{ ft. 5 in.}}{5}$ = 5 ft. 1 in.

4. **The correct answer is (E).**

    Let x = first integer

    $x + 2$ = second integer

    $x + 4$ = third integer

    $3(x) = 3 + 2(x+4)$

    $3x = 3 + 2x + 8$

    $x = +11$

    The third integer is 15.

5. **The correct answer is (C).**

    Area of square = $2^2 = 4$

    Area of circle = $\pi \cdot 1^2 = \pi$

    Difference = $4 - \pi = 4 - 3.14 = .86$

6. **The correct answer is (C).** The right triangle, of which T is the hypotenuse, has legs that are obviously 6 inches and 9 inches.

    Hence, $T^2 = 6^2 + 9^2$

    $T^2 = 36 + 81 = 117$

    $T = \sqrt{117}$

    or $10 < T < 11$.

7. **The correct answer is (B).** $5\frac{1}{2}$ dozen nails are bought for $5\frac{1}{2}$ dozen × 35 cents per dozen = 192.5 cents. There are 66 nails in $5\frac{1}{2}$ dozen and 66 ÷ 3 = 22 sets sold at 10 cents per set, so 22 sets × 10 cents per set = 220 cents. The profit is $220 - 192.5 = 27\frac{1}{2}$ cents.

8. **The correct answer is (D).**

    $2\dfrac{3}{4} \div \dfrac{1}{8} = \dfrac{11}{4} \div \dfrac{1}{8} = \dfrac{11}{4} \times 8 = 22$

9. **The correct answer is (E).**

    $-x^2 + 2y - (-x-y)$

    $= -x^2 + 2y + x + y$

    $= -x^2 + x + 3y$

10. **The correct answer is (A).**

    Multiply the equation $2m = 4x$ by 2

    $2(2^m) = 2(4x)$

    $2^{m+1} = 8x = 2^w$

    $\therefore w = m+1$ and $m = w-1$

11. **The correct answer is (E).** The reciprocal of $1\frac{1}{4}$ is $\frac{4}{5}$. $\frac{4}{5} - \frac{5}{4} = \frac{16}{20} - \frac{25}{20} = -\frac{9}{20}$.

12. **The correct answer is (A).** x yards = $3x$ feet; y feet = y feet; z inches = $\frac{z}{12}$ feet. Therefore, x yards + y feet + z inches = $3x$ feet + y feet + $\frac{z}{12}$ feet, or $3x + y + \frac{z}{12}$ feet.

13. **The correct answer is (E).** If a triangle is a right triangle, then the squares of two sides will add up to the square of the hypotenuse. $12^2 = 144. 15^2 = 225. 18^2 = 324$. $144 + 225 \neq 324$.

14. **The correct answer is (E).** By the distributive law, $26 \times 3\frac{1}{2} = (26 \times 3) + (26 \times \frac{1}{2})$. By the distributive law, $26 \times 3 = (20 \times 3) + (6 \times 3)$. Therefore, $26 \times 3\frac{1}{2} = (26 \times \frac{1}{2}) + (20 \times 3) + (6 \times 3)$.

15. **The correct answer is (D).** Angle T is a right angle. By the Pythagorean theorem, $RT^2 + ST^2 = RS^2$. Since $RS = 12$ and $ST = 8$, RT must equal $\sqrt{80}$ so, $OT = \frac{1}{2}\sqrt{80}$. By the formula for the area of a circle $(A = \pi r^2)$, area equals $(\pi)\left(\frac{1}{2}\right)^2\left(\sqrt{80}\right)^2$, or $(\pi)\left(\frac{1}{4}\right)(80)$, which equals 20π.

16. **The correct answer is (E).** If the gain was 10% of the selling price, then $12.60 was 90%. Therefore, 100% was equal to $14.00.

17. **The correct answer is (E).** If John weighs 110% of the average, he weighs 10% more than the average weight of 105 lbs., or $.10 \times 105 = 10.5$ lbs. John weighs $105 + 10.5 = 115.5$ lbs.

18. **The correct answer is (C).** A hexagon with 22-inch sides has a perimeter of 6×22, or 132 inches.

$$C = 2\pi r$$
$$132 = 2\pi r$$
$$132 = 2(3.14)r$$
$$132 = 6.28r$$
$$21.02 = r$$

19. **The correct answer is (B).** We are not told how many games the Bombers played, but we know that the ratio of the number of games played in the second year to that in the first is 2:1. Problems like this can be

solved by plugging in real numbers. Let's say that there were 50 games in the first year, so they won 25. In the second year there were 100 games, so they won 65 games. Altogether they won 90 out of 150 games, and this fraction can be simplified to 3 out of 5, or 60%.

20. **The correct answer is (C).** Let $x =$ weight in ounces of the apple. Then,

$$x = \frac{4}{5}x + \frac{4}{5}$$
$$5x = 4x + 4$$
$$x = 4$$

21. **The correct answer is (B).** Let $L =$ length of each card and $W =$ width of each card. Then $5W =$ length of large rectangle and $L + W =$ width of large rectangle. Length of large rectangle $= 4L$. Thus, $5W = 4L$.

$$5W(L+W) = 180, \text{ also}$$
$$9LW = 180 \text{ or } LW = 20$$
$$5LW + 5W^2 = 180$$
$$LW + W^2 = 36$$
$$20 + W^2 = 36$$
$$W^2 = 16$$
$$W = 4 \text{ and } L = 5$$

Thus, perimeter $= 2[5W + (L + W)]$
$$= 2(20 + 9) = 58.$$

22. **The correct answer is (C).** If each of the dimensions is doubled, the area of the new rectangle is four times the size of the original one. The increase is three times, or 300%.

23. **The correct answer is (E).** This is a proportion of $2\frac{1}{2}:3 = x:14; x = \frac{35}{3}$, or $11\frac{2}{3}$.

24. **The correct answer is (E).** $MN = \frac{1}{2}QR$ and MN is parallel to QR. Since $\triangle MNS - \triangle QSR$, it follows that the altitude from S to $NM = \frac{1}{2}$ the altitude from S to QR. Hence, the altitude from S to $NM = \frac{1}{3}$ of $\frac{1}{2}$ the altitude from P to QR, or $\frac{1}{6}$ of this altitude (h).

Thus, the area of $\triangle NMS = \frac{1}{2} \cdot MN \cdot$ alt. from S to MN.

$$= \frac{1}{2}\left(\frac{1}{2}QR\right)\left(\frac{1}{6}h\right)$$

$$= \frac{1}{2}\left(\frac{1}{2}QR \cdot h\right) = \frac{1}{12}\left(\frac{1}{2} \cdot QR \cdot h\right).$$

But $\frac{1}{2} \cdot QR \cdot h = \triangle PQR$.

Hence, $\triangle NMS = \frac{1}{12} \cdot \triangle PQR$.

Ratio is 1:12.

25. **The correct answer is (C).**

$$\text{Given } \frac{2}{3}x = \frac{1}{10}(60) = 6$$

$$\therefore x = 9$$

$$\text{Find } \frac{1}{10}\left(\frac{1}{3}x\right) = \frac{1}{30}(9) = \frac{3}{10} = .3$$

Section 2

1. **The correct answer is (B).** An "appreciative public" is likely to give the elder Johnson's son *respect*.

2. **The correct answer is (A).** A person who is angry one minute but serene the next is said to be *mercurial* (changeable).

3. **The correct answer is (C).** Irony or paradox is indicated by the phrase "but he thought nothing of." It is ironic that automobile travel should be *harrowing*, or frightening, to someone used to bobsledding, a dangerous sport.

4. **The correct answer is (C).** A perennial flower is one that blooms every year. In the winter it lies *dormant* (inactive), but the following spring it *burgeons* (sprouts) anew.

5. **The correct answer is (E).** A manager who apologizes must be dealing with an *irate* (angry) customer. As a result of the apology, the customer was *mollified* (soothed and pacified).

6. **The correct answer is (B).** Normally, vices are publicly *condemned*. Secret indulgence in them might, however, be hidden by a *sanctimonious* (excessively righteous) manner.

7. **The correct answer is (D).** A flood that destroys people's belongings causes *devastation*. Living conditions in the area can be said to have *deteriorated* (worsened).

8. **The correct answer is (B).** A *perversion* of the truth is a deviation from the truth, or the half-truths and half-lies mentioned in the second half of the sentence.

9. **The correct answer is (D).** As indicated by the word *though*, the sentence requires a contrast. Since the presentation was positive, the blank should be filled by a negative; *worthless* is the best choice to describe a report full of errors.

10. **The correct answer is (A).** The *nose* is part of the *head*, and the *hand* is part of the *arm*.

11. **The correct answer is (C).** *Wheat* is a type of *grain*; *carrot* is a type of *vegetable*. Both are foodstuffs.

12. **The correct answer is (C).** A *cottage* is a small house; a *castle* is a large and luxurious one. A *dory* is a modest rowboat; a *liner* is a large and luxurious passenger ship.

13. **The correct answer is (A).** Something *antique* is necessarily *old*, and something *modern* is necessarily *new*.

14. **The correct answer is (C).** Something that is *possible* might be, but is not necessarily, *probable*. Someone who is *willing* might be, but is not necessarily, *eager*.

15. **The correct answer is (A).** To *digress* from a topic is to *ramble*, and to *muffle* a sound is to *stifle* it. The relationship is one of synonyms.

16. **The correct answer is (A).** Only the first choice explains the subtitle. The other choices may be included under the idea "A Study in Temperament," but they are not the main idea.

17. **The correct answer is (B).** The faculty may be perplexed (A), but the first paragraph focuses on their feeling that Paul's dress and behavior are not properly contrite.

18. **The correct answer is (C).** Paul seems to be unable to control his odd mannerisms, but he is not actually frenzied, as (B), (D), or (E) would suggest.

19. **The correct answer is (B).** The faculty "fell upon him without mercy, his English teacher leading the pack" (lines 74–76). The comparison is to a pack of wolves.

20. **The correct answer is (C).** All of these choices could mean "smartness," but only *impudence* makes sense in context.

21. **The correct answer is (E).** There is evidence for every other choice in the descriptions of Paul's actions. The point is made in lines 34–37 that Paul often lies; he cannot be called "candid."

22. **The correct answer is (A).** Paul is physically revolted by the faculty, not vice versa (D). The faculty's attack on Paul indicates their hatred for him.

23. **The correct answer is (D).** Jefferson is "ever sensible" that meeting and attracting the good will of Mr. Wythe was "one of the most fortunate events" of his life (lines 8–9).

24. **The correct answer is (C).** Jefferson uses the word *sciences* as a general term covering Italian, Spanish, and moral philosophy. Clearly, he is referring to school subjects in general.

25. **The correct answer is (B).** The numbered points are (1) Italian, (2) Spanish, and (3) Moral philosophy—courses that Peter proposes taking.

26. **The correct answer is (D).** This is part of Jefferson's argument that, since Italian, French, and Spanish are related, people mix or muddle them in conversation.

27. **The correct answer is (B).** Jefferson says "Our future connections with Spain and Spanish America will render that language a valuable acquisition."

28. **The correct answer is (A).** Point 3 is all about the fact that no one needs to study moral philosophy. In other words, to study it is a waste of time.

29. **The correct answer is (B).** Lines 44–49 explain this reasoning.

30. **The correct answer is (C).** Jefferson's point is that either one is as likely to decide a moral argument fairly; morality is bred into everyone and does not require an advanced degree.

31. **The correct answer is (A).** Choices (B), (C), and (D) may be true, but Jefferson only covers the first point, that morality is as natural as an arm or leg, and is given to all "in a stronger or weaker degree" (lines 61–62).

Section 3

Part 1

1. **The correct answer is (D).** Since a polygon can have three or more sides, an answer is not possible.

2. **The correct answer is (B).** No one side of a triangle can be greater than or equal to the sum of the other two sides.

3. **The correct answer is (D).** If y is the opposite of z, then we know that $y + z$ is equal to 0. We do not, however, know the value of x.

4. **The correct answer is (C).** The radius is equal to one half the diameter. The circle in Column B has a diameter of $\frac{4r}{3}$, and $\frac{1}{2}$ of that is $\frac{2r}{3}$. Therefore, the columns are equal.

5. **The correct answer is (C).** Both columns are equal to 0.

6. **The correct answer is (B).** The largest fraction that Column A could be is $\frac{9}{10}$. The smallest fraction that Column B could be is $\frac{11}{12}$. Thus, Column B is always bigger.

7. **The correct answer is (C).** Triangle B has a height that is double that of Triangle A; it has a base that is half that of Triangle A. This will result in the two triangles having the same area.

8. **The correct answer is (C).** Since the vertical angles are equal, angles a and d can be moved inside the quadrilateral. All quadrilaterals contain 360 degrees: 360 divided by 4 is 90.

9. **The correct answer is (C).** In this problem it is easy to figure out that the ninth through twelfth numbers would be $-5, 5, -6$, and 6. $(-5) \times (-6) = 30$ and $5 \times 6 = 30$.

10. **The correct answer is (B).** Column A would equal -3. Column B would equal 3.

11. **The correct answer is (A).** If a fraction between 0 and 1 is squared, the result is always smaller than the original number.

12. **The correct answer is (A).** The question can be simplified. When you divide 5 by 3, the remainder is 2. When you divide 8 by 7, the remainder is 1.

13. **The correct answer is (C).** The prime numbers would be 2, 3, 5, 7, 11, 13, 17, 19, and 23.

14. **The correct answer is (B).** If you multiply both sides by 3, you find that $m^4 = 81$. Therefore, m can equal 3 or -3. In either case, m is less than 4.

15. **The correct answer is (A).** This is easily solved by substitution. Make s equal to 2. The volume of a cube with a side of 2 is 8. The volume of the rectangular block in Column B is $2 \times 1 \times 3 = 6$.

Part 2

16. The mode is the data element with the greatest frequency.

Mode = 91

17.
$$-2x+5 = 2-(5-2x)$$
$$= 2-5+2x$$
$$= -3+2x$$
$$-2x+5 = -3+2x$$
$$\underline{+2x \quad = \quad +2x}$$
$$5 = -3+4x$$
$$\underline{+3 = +3}$$
$$8 = 4x$$
$$x = 2$$

18.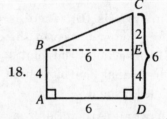

Area of rectangle $ABED$:
$$bh = 6(4) = 24$$
Area of $\triangle BEC = \frac{1}{2}bh = \frac{1}{2}(6)(2) = 6$
Area of polygon $= 24 + 6 = 30$

19.

If $AC = BC$,
then $m\angle A = m\angle B = 50°$.
In $\triangle ABC$:

$\angle ACB = 180° - (\angle A + \angle B)$
$\angle ACB = 80°$

$m\angle ACB = m\angle ECD$ (vertical angles)
$m\angle ECD = 80°$

20. $-m^2n^3 = -(-2)^2(-1)^3$
$= -(4)(-1) = 4$

21.

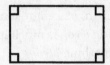

The square has four right angles.

The rectangle has four right angles.

The trapezoid does not have four right angles.

The circle does not have four right angles.
Probability of four right angles

$= \dfrac{\text{number of successes}}{\text{number of possibilities}} = \dfrac{2}{4} = \dfrac{1}{2} = .5.$

22.

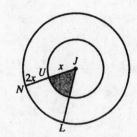

If $JU = x$, then $JN = 3x$ ∴ $NU = 2x$. The area of the smaller circle $= \pi(x)2 = \pi x 2$. The area of the larger circle =

$\pi(3x)^2 = 9x^2(\pi)$
$= 9\pi x^2$

$\dfrac{\text{Area } JUS}{\text{Area } NJL} = \dfrac{\pi x^2}{9\pi x^2} = \dfrac{1}{9} = 1:b$

∴ $b = 9$

23. Letting m be the time per regular question, $2m$ is the time per math problem. The total time for all the regular questions is $300m$ and $50(2m)$ is the total time for all the math problems. Since the exam is 3 hours, or 180 minutes, $300m + 100m = 180$ minutes, $400m = 180$, and $m = \dfrac{180}{400} = \dfrac{9}{20}$. The time to do a math problem is $2\left(\dfrac{9}{20}\right) = \left(\dfrac{9}{10}\right)$. All 50 math problems can be done in $50\left(\dfrac{9}{10}\right) = 45$ minutes.

24.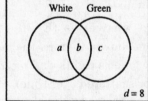

$a + b = 8$, $b + c = 18$, $d = 8$

$\underbrace{\text{Total}}_{28} = \underbrace{a + b}_{8} + c + \underbrace{d}_{8}$

$28 = 8 + c + 8$

∴ $c = 12$

Since $b + c = 18$ and $c = 12$

∴ $b = 6$

25. $x=\dfrac{2}{4}, \; y=\dfrac{1}{4}+\dfrac{1}{3}, \; z=\dfrac{2}{3}$

$$\frac{x+z}{y}=\frac{\left(\dfrac{2}{4}\right)+\left(\dfrac{2}{3}\right)}{\dfrac{1}{4}+\dfrac{1}{3}}=\frac{2\left(\dfrac{1}{4}+\dfrac{1}{3}\right)}{\left(\dfrac{1}{4}+\dfrac{1}{3}\right)}=2$$

Section 4

1. **The correct answer is (E).** If he "dashed into the house," then he was in a hurry and probably out of breath.

2. **The correct answer is (E).** A criminal record may indeed cause a jury to *discredit* (disbelieve) a witness's testimony.

3. **The correct answer is (C).** A catastrophic storm might leave a family *destitute* (living in poverty). For the second blank, the word *although* indicates a shift in mood from negative to positive; poverty could not *dampen* (depress) the family's spirits.

4. **The correct answer is (B).** "By a stroke of luck" implies good fortune; the troops likely *prevailed* (were victorious), thereby avoiding a crushing *defeat*.

5. **The correct answer is (A).** If the price is going up tomorrow, you must do your buying with *celerity* (swiftness).

6. **The correct answer is (D).** If danger threatens, the music would likely be *portentous* (ominous).

7. **The correct answer is (E).** If years separated one advance from the next, progress in women's rights was *sporadic* (occasional or scattered over time).

8. **The correct answer is (B).** Offices that are now across the street have been *relocated* (moved). As a result, the directory is *obsolete* (out of date).

9. **The correct answer is (A).** Since the promise—a mere sop to world opinion—was unlikely to be kept, it was *spurious* (false).

10. **The correct answer is (C).** Pretending not to notice nearby celebrities is acting in a *nonchalant* (casually indifferent) manner.

11. **The correct answer is (B).** A *library* is a place for *books*, just as a *zoo* is a place for *animals*.

12. **The correct answer is (C).** Something *tiny* is much smaller in size than something *huge*. Something *weak* is much less in strength than something *strong*.

13. **The correct answer is (A).** To *frighten* someone is to *scare* that person; to *question* someone is to *ask* that person.

14. **The correct answer is (A).** *Finding* is a result of *searching*, and *winning* is a result of *fighting*.

15. **The correct answer is (B).** By means of a *door*, we can *open* something. By means of a *knife*, we can *cut* into something.

16. **The correct answer is (B).** A *dastard* is characterized by *cowardice*, just as a *scoundrel* is characterized by *immorality*.

17. **The correct answer is (D).** A *toe* is part of the *foot*, and the *pupil* is part of the eye.

18. **The correct answer is (D).** *Strumming* and *pedaling* are methods of playing an instrument. We strum the *guitar* and pedal the *organ*.

19. **The correct answer is (C).** *Puerile* means childish or lacking in *maturity*. *Obscure* means vague or lacking in *clarity*.

20. **The correct answer is (A).** To *hurtle* is to throw with force; to *toss* is to throw lightly. Similarly, to *strike* is to hit with force and to *tap* is to hit lightly.

21. **The correct answer is (C).** Something *infinite* (endless) lacks *limits* or bounds, just as something *nebulous* (vague) lacks *clarity*.

22. **The correct answer is (C).** *Time* is measured in *minutes* as a *race* is measured in *laps.*

23. **The correct answer is (B).** A *tunnel* is a roadway through a *mountain,* and a *bridge* is a roadway over a *river.*

24. **The correct answer is (D).** In the text, the author discusses Quixote's desire to change wrongs to right and redress grievances. In this context, *redress* means to fix, change, or correct for the better.

25. **The correct answer is (C).** Because Don Quixote is not a knight, to take up arms against another knight would be a breach in the code of chivalry.

26. **The correct answer is (A).** Don Quixote is worried that he cannot wear armor with a *device* on his shield that denotes his knighthood. The only appropriate choice is (A).

27. **The correct answer is (E).** With such malapropisms as "forked tongues" of birds, Cervantes imbues his hero with language that mimics the flowery language of the romances he reads.

28. **The correct answer is (E).** In his florid, overblown language, Don Quixote tells of getting out of bed to ride off on his adventure. "The slothful down" seems to refer to the down mattress on which he sleeps.

29. **The correct answer is (C).** Don Quixote is talking to himself and calling on a woman who may or may not exist. His speech cries out for his love for Dulcinea, but Cervantes pulls the reader back with this line to show that Quixote is mad.

30. **The correct answer is (D).** Don Quixote speaks first to the "sage enchanter" who might chronicle his tale (lines 73–75) and then to Dulcinea, "mistress of this captive heart" (lines 80–81).

31. **The correct answer is (B).** The sun's heat "would have been enough to turn his brain, if he had had any." Cervantes is again reminding the reader that Don Quixote is out of his mind.

32. **The correct answer is (C).** The story up to this point might be the tale of any knight somewhat down on his luck, but in lines 33–36, Cervantes jolts the reader into realizing that Don Quixote is out of his mind—he is not even a real knight.

33. **The correct answer is (A).** Cervantes refers to the romantic books that fill Don Quixote's head in lines 37–38 and 89–92.

34. **The correct answer is (D).** Although he never comes right out and says so, Cervantes's mocking reproduction of the language of romantic books makes it clear that he does not think much of the writing styles he imitates. The fact that the hero who speaks the way such writers write is completely mad is another ironic twist that reveals Cervantes's opinion.

35. **The correct answer is (D).** Throughout, Cervantes uses a gently mocking tone to show Don Quixote's ridiculousness.

Section 5

1. **The correct answer is (D).** Buying the lollipops singly would cost: 30 pops × $.13 per pop = $3.90. The reduced rate is $1.38 per dozen. Thirty pops is $2\frac{1}{2}$ dozen, so the cost for 30 pops is $1.38 × 2.5 = $3.45. The savings with this reduced rate is $3.90 − $3.45 = $.45.

2. **The correct answer is (A).** The volume of the fish tank is 11" × 14" × 9" = 1,386 cu. in. The amount needed to fill the tank is 1,386 cu. in. ÷ 231 cu. in./gal. = 6 gallons.

3. **The correct answer is (D).** Let legs be $2x$ and $3x$. Then,

$$(2x)^2 + (3x)^2 = (\text{hypotenuse})^2,$$

and

$$\frac{1}{2} \cdot 2x \cdot 3x = 12$$
$$3x^2 = 12$$
$$x^2 = 4$$
$$x = 2$$

Thus, $4^2 + 6^2 = (\text{hypotenuse})^2$

$$16 + 36 = 52$$
$$\text{hypotenuse} = \sqrt{52}$$

4. **The correct answer is (C).** The weights are proportional to the volumes, and the volumes vary as the cubes of their dimensions. If the edges are doubled, the volume becomes $2^3 = 8$ times as large. Hence, the weight $= 8 \times 3 = 24$ ounces $= 1\frac{1}{2}$ lbs.

5. **The correct answer is (B).** The graduate starts at x dollars per week. After the pay cut, the graduate receives 90% of the original salary. The 10% raise adds 9% to the salary (10% of 90%), so the new salary is $.99x$.

6. **The correct answer is (E).** $428.00 $- (.06)$ $428.00 = $402.32

7. **The correct answer is (D).** There will be no waste if the lengths are multiples of $5\frac{1}{2}$ feet. This occurs between 6 and 24 feet only for 22 feet.

8. **The correct answer is (D).** A cube with an edge of 4 has a volume of 64 cubic inches. A cube with an edge of 5 has a volume of 125 cubic inches. The percentage increase is $\frac{61}{64}$ or approximately 95%.

9. **The correct answer is (C).**

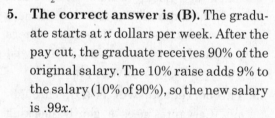

$$\frac{1}{4} : \frac{3}{5} = \frac{1}{4} \div \frac{3}{5}$$
$$= \frac{1}{4} \div \frac{5}{3}$$
$$= \frac{5}{12}$$
$$= 5 : 12$$

10. **The correct answer is (E).**

$$\sqrt{3} = 1.73 \text{ (approx.)}$$

$$\frac{1}{\sqrt{3}} = \frac{\sqrt{3}}{3} = \frac{1.73}{3} = .57$$
$$\frac{\sqrt{3}}{3} = \frac{1.73}{3} = .57$$
$$\frac{1}{3} = .333.....$$
$$\frac{1}{3\sqrt{3}} = \frac{\sqrt{3}}{3 \times 3} = \frac{\sqrt{3}}{9} = \frac{1.73}{9} = .19$$

Thus, the smallest is $\dfrac{1}{3\sqrt{3}}$.

Section 6

1. **The correct answer is (E).** Most of the choices are extremes, either extreme outrage or extreme lack of interest. The author takes more of an objective middle ground in outlining the history of African-American economics.

2. **The correct answer is (C).** In the first sentence of the passage, the author indicates that slavery and undereducation hindered economic progress for African Americans until well into the twentieth century.

3. **The correct answer is (D).** The context of the sentence indicates that the best answer is "on the same level."

4. **The correct answer is (C).** On the contrary, in the last five decades African Americans have become much less tolerant of racial discrimination.

5. **The correct answer is (E).** The passage generally implies that the civil rights movement did help African Americans in their quest for economic and political equality.

6. **The correct answer is (E).** The passage acknowledges that progress has been made in some segments of the African-American population, but that the gap is widening between lower-income and higher-income African Americans.

7. **The correct answer is (D).** See lines 53–56. Hiram Revels was the first African American in Congress, but he was elected to the Senate. Answer (A) may be true, but it is not mentioned in the passage.

8. **The correct answer is (B).** Compare lines 64–68 and 93–95.

9. **The correct answer is (D).** The context makes it clear that "turned to" means "concentrated on" or "devoted themselves to."

10. **The correct answer is (A).** Political organizations in southern states in the nineteenth century are mentioned in lines 61–64; political organizations in northern states in the twentieth century are cited in lines 82–86.

11. **The correct answer is (B).** In this passage, the author expresses admiration only in the last paragraph, where the representatives' "long struggle to extend the ideals of the founders to encompass all citizens of the United States" is cited.

12. **The correct answer is (D).** Although the author of Passage 2 points out that political gain occurred immediately following the Civil War, he also indicates that African Americans suffered political powerlessness from 1890–1900. Therefore, there were bumps in the road.

COMPUTING YOUR SCORES

To get a sense of your progress in preparing for the SAT, you need to compute individual verbal and mathematical raw scores for this first practice test. Once you have computed these, use the conversion scales on the next page to compute your SAT scaled scores (200–800). Keep in mind that these formulas have been simplified to give you a "quick and dirty" sense of where you are scoring, not a perfectly precise score.

To Compute Your Raw Scores

1. Enter the number of correct answers for each verbal and mathematical reasoning section into the boxes marked Number of Questions Correct.

2. Enter the number of incorrect answers (not blanks) for each verbal and mathematical reasoning section into the boxes marked Number of Questions Incorrect.

3. Total the number correct and number incorrect.

4. Follow this formula: Take the total correct and minus one quarter of the total incorrect. Round up in your favor to compute your raw score.

Verbal Section	Total Number of Questions	Number of Questions Correct	Number of Questions Incorrect
2	31		
4	35		
6	12		
Totals	78	Total Correct:	Total Incorrect:

Verbal Raw Score = Total Correct – ($\frac{1}{4}$ × Total Incorrect) = _____

Math Section	Total Number of Questions	Number of Questions Correct	Number of Questions Incorrect
1	25		
3	25		
5	10		
Totals	60	Total Correct:	Total Incorrect:

Math Raw Score = Total Correct – ($\frac{1}{4}$ × Total Incorrect) = _____

Conversion Scales

VERBAL REASONING

Raw Score	Scaled Score	Raw Score	Scaled Score
75	800	35	520
70	800	30	480
65	760	25	440
60	710	20	410
55	670	15	370
50	620	10	340
45	590	5	290
40	550	0	230

MATHEMATICAL REASONING

Raw Score	Scaled Score	Raw Score	Scaled Score
60	800	25	510
55	760	20	480
50	690	15	440
45	650	10	410
40	610	5	340
35	580	0	280
30	550		

Although you now have some idea of what your scores would look like had they been scaled according to unofficial ETS standards, you will probably want to know how to interpret your raw scores in more familiar terms. If so, use the following Self-Evaluation Charts to see what your raw scores actually mean.

SELF-EVALUATION CHARTS

VERBAL REASONING: Raw Score		MATHEMATICAL REASONING: Raw Score	
Excellent	60–75	Excellent	50–60
Good	50–59	Good	40–49
Average	30–49	Average	20–39
Fair	20–29	Fair	10–19
Poor	0–19	Poor	0–9

PRACTICE TEST 2

Answer Sheet

If a section has fewer questions than answer ovals, leave the extra ovals blank.

SECTION 1

1 Ⓐ Ⓑ Ⓒ Ⓓ Ⓔ	11 Ⓐ Ⓑ Ⓒ Ⓓ Ⓔ	21 Ⓐ Ⓑ Ⓒ Ⓓ Ⓔ	31 Ⓐ Ⓑ Ⓒ Ⓓ Ⓔ
2 Ⓐ Ⓑ Ⓒ Ⓓ Ⓔ	12 Ⓐ Ⓑ Ⓒ Ⓓ Ⓔ	22 Ⓐ Ⓑ Ⓒ Ⓓ Ⓔ	32 Ⓐ Ⓑ Ⓒ Ⓓ Ⓔ
3 Ⓐ Ⓑ Ⓒ Ⓓ Ⓔ	13 Ⓐ Ⓑ Ⓒ Ⓓ Ⓔ	23 Ⓐ Ⓑ Ⓒ Ⓓ Ⓔ	33 Ⓐ Ⓑ Ⓒ Ⓓ Ⓔ
4 Ⓐ Ⓑ Ⓒ Ⓓ Ⓔ	14 Ⓐ Ⓑ Ⓒ Ⓓ Ⓔ	24 Ⓐ Ⓑ Ⓒ Ⓓ Ⓔ	34 Ⓐ Ⓑ Ⓒ Ⓓ Ⓔ
5 Ⓐ Ⓑ Ⓒ Ⓓ Ⓔ	15 Ⓐ Ⓑ Ⓒ Ⓓ Ⓔ	25 Ⓐ Ⓑ Ⓒ Ⓓ Ⓔ	35 Ⓐ Ⓑ Ⓒ Ⓓ Ⓔ
6 Ⓐ Ⓑ Ⓒ Ⓓ Ⓔ	16 Ⓐ Ⓑ Ⓒ Ⓓ Ⓔ	26 Ⓐ Ⓑ Ⓒ Ⓓ Ⓔ	36 Ⓐ Ⓑ Ⓒ Ⓓ Ⓔ
7 Ⓐ Ⓑ Ⓒ Ⓓ Ⓔ	17 Ⓐ Ⓑ Ⓒ Ⓓ Ⓔ	27 Ⓐ Ⓑ Ⓒ Ⓓ Ⓔ	37 Ⓐ Ⓑ Ⓒ Ⓓ Ⓔ
8 Ⓐ Ⓑ Ⓒ Ⓓ Ⓔ	18 Ⓐ Ⓑ Ⓒ Ⓓ Ⓔ	28 Ⓐ Ⓑ Ⓒ Ⓓ Ⓔ	38 Ⓐ Ⓑ Ⓒ Ⓓ Ⓔ
9 Ⓐ Ⓑ Ⓒ Ⓓ Ⓔ	19 Ⓐ Ⓑ Ⓒ Ⓓ Ⓔ	29 Ⓐ Ⓑ Ⓒ Ⓓ Ⓔ	39 Ⓐ Ⓑ Ⓒ Ⓓ Ⓔ
10 Ⓐ Ⓑ Ⓒ Ⓓ Ⓔ	20 Ⓐ Ⓑ Ⓒ Ⓓ Ⓔ	30 Ⓐ Ⓑ Ⓒ Ⓓ Ⓔ	40 Ⓐ Ⓑ Ⓒ Ⓓ Ⓔ

SECTION 2

1 Ⓐ Ⓑ Ⓒ Ⓓ Ⓔ	11 Ⓐ Ⓑ Ⓒ Ⓓ Ⓔ	21 Ⓐ Ⓑ Ⓒ Ⓓ Ⓔ	31 Ⓐ Ⓑ Ⓒ Ⓓ Ⓔ
2 Ⓐ Ⓑ Ⓒ Ⓓ Ⓔ	12 Ⓐ Ⓑ Ⓒ Ⓓ Ⓔ	22 Ⓐ Ⓑ Ⓒ Ⓓ Ⓔ	32 Ⓐ Ⓑ Ⓒ Ⓓ Ⓔ
3 Ⓐ Ⓑ Ⓒ Ⓓ Ⓔ	13 Ⓐ Ⓑ Ⓒ Ⓓ Ⓔ	23 Ⓐ Ⓑ Ⓒ Ⓓ Ⓔ	33 Ⓐ Ⓑ Ⓒ Ⓓ Ⓔ
4 Ⓐ Ⓑ Ⓒ Ⓓ Ⓔ	14 Ⓐ Ⓑ Ⓒ Ⓓ Ⓔ	24 Ⓐ Ⓑ Ⓒ Ⓓ Ⓔ	34 Ⓐ Ⓑ Ⓒ Ⓓ Ⓔ
5 Ⓐ Ⓑ Ⓒ Ⓓ Ⓔ	15 Ⓐ Ⓑ Ⓒ Ⓓ Ⓔ	25 Ⓐ Ⓑ Ⓒ Ⓓ Ⓔ	35 Ⓐ Ⓑ Ⓒ Ⓓ Ⓔ
6 Ⓐ Ⓑ Ⓒ Ⓓ Ⓔ	16 Ⓐ Ⓑ Ⓒ Ⓓ Ⓔ	26 Ⓐ Ⓑ Ⓒ Ⓓ Ⓔ	36 Ⓐ Ⓑ Ⓒ Ⓓ Ⓔ
7 Ⓐ Ⓑ Ⓒ Ⓓ Ⓔ	17 Ⓐ Ⓑ Ⓒ Ⓓ Ⓔ	27 Ⓐ Ⓑ Ⓒ Ⓓ Ⓔ	37 Ⓐ Ⓑ Ⓒ Ⓓ Ⓔ
8 Ⓐ Ⓑ Ⓒ Ⓓ Ⓔ	18 Ⓐ Ⓑ Ⓒ Ⓓ Ⓔ	28 Ⓐ Ⓑ Ⓒ Ⓓ Ⓔ	38 Ⓐ Ⓑ Ⓒ Ⓓ Ⓔ
9 Ⓐ Ⓑ Ⓒ Ⓓ Ⓔ	19 Ⓐ Ⓑ Ⓒ Ⓓ Ⓔ	29 Ⓐ Ⓑ Ⓒ Ⓓ Ⓔ	39 Ⓐ Ⓑ Ⓒ Ⓓ Ⓔ
10 Ⓐ Ⓑ Ⓒ Ⓓ Ⓔ	20 Ⓐ Ⓑ Ⓒ Ⓓ Ⓔ	30 Ⓐ Ⓑ Ⓒ Ⓓ Ⓔ	40 Ⓐ Ⓑ Ⓒ Ⓓ Ⓔ

SECTION 3

1 Ⓐ Ⓑ Ⓒ Ⓓ Ⓔ	11 Ⓐ Ⓑ Ⓒ Ⓓ Ⓔ	21 Ⓐ Ⓑ Ⓒ Ⓓ Ⓔ	31 Ⓐ Ⓑ Ⓒ Ⓓ Ⓔ
2 Ⓐ Ⓑ Ⓒ Ⓓ Ⓔ	12 Ⓐ Ⓑ Ⓒ Ⓓ Ⓔ	22 Ⓐ Ⓑ Ⓒ Ⓓ Ⓔ	32 Ⓐ Ⓑ Ⓒ Ⓓ Ⓔ
3 Ⓐ Ⓑ Ⓒ Ⓓ Ⓔ	13 Ⓐ Ⓑ Ⓒ Ⓓ Ⓔ	23 Ⓐ Ⓑ Ⓒ Ⓓ Ⓔ	33 Ⓐ Ⓑ Ⓒ Ⓓ Ⓔ
4 Ⓐ Ⓑ Ⓒ Ⓓ Ⓔ	14 Ⓐ Ⓑ Ⓒ Ⓓ Ⓔ	24 Ⓐ Ⓑ Ⓒ Ⓓ Ⓔ	34 Ⓐ Ⓑ Ⓒ Ⓓ Ⓔ
5 Ⓐ Ⓑ Ⓒ Ⓓ Ⓔ	15 Ⓐ Ⓑ Ⓒ Ⓓ Ⓔ	25 Ⓐ Ⓑ Ⓒ Ⓓ Ⓔ	35 Ⓐ Ⓑ Ⓒ Ⓓ Ⓔ
6 Ⓐ Ⓑ Ⓒ Ⓓ Ⓔ	16 Ⓐ Ⓑ Ⓒ Ⓓ Ⓔ	26 Ⓐ Ⓑ Ⓒ Ⓓ Ⓔ	36 Ⓐ Ⓑ Ⓒ Ⓓ Ⓔ
7 Ⓐ Ⓑ Ⓒ Ⓓ Ⓔ	17 Ⓐ Ⓑ Ⓒ Ⓓ Ⓔ	27 Ⓐ Ⓑ Ⓒ Ⓓ Ⓔ	37 Ⓐ Ⓑ Ⓒ Ⓓ Ⓔ
8 Ⓐ Ⓑ Ⓒ Ⓓ Ⓔ	18 Ⓐ Ⓑ Ⓒ Ⓓ Ⓔ	28 Ⓐ Ⓑ Ⓒ Ⓓ Ⓔ	38 Ⓐ Ⓑ Ⓒ Ⓓ Ⓔ
9 Ⓐ Ⓑ Ⓒ Ⓓ Ⓔ	19 Ⓐ Ⓑ Ⓒ Ⓓ Ⓔ	29 Ⓐ Ⓑ Ⓒ Ⓓ Ⓔ	39 Ⓐ Ⓑ Ⓒ Ⓓ Ⓔ
10 Ⓐ Ⓑ Ⓒ Ⓓ Ⓔ	20 Ⓐ Ⓑ Ⓒ Ⓓ Ⓔ	30 Ⓐ Ⓑ Ⓒ Ⓓ Ⓔ	40 Ⓐ Ⓑ Ⓒ Ⓓ Ⓔ

SECTION 4

1 Ⓐ Ⓑ Ⓒ Ⓓ Ⓔ	6 Ⓐ Ⓑ Ⓒ Ⓓ Ⓔ	11 Ⓐ Ⓑ Ⓒ Ⓓ Ⓔ
2 Ⓐ Ⓑ Ⓒ Ⓓ Ⓔ	7 Ⓐ Ⓑ Ⓒ Ⓓ Ⓔ	12 Ⓐ Ⓑ Ⓒ Ⓓ Ⓔ
3 Ⓐ Ⓑ Ⓒ Ⓓ Ⓔ	8 Ⓐ Ⓑ Ⓒ Ⓓ Ⓔ	13 Ⓐ Ⓑ Ⓒ Ⓓ Ⓔ
4 Ⓐ Ⓑ Ⓒ Ⓓ Ⓔ	9 Ⓐ Ⓑ Ⓒ Ⓓ Ⓔ	14 Ⓐ Ⓑ Ⓒ Ⓓ Ⓔ
5 Ⓐ Ⓑ Ⓒ Ⓓ Ⓔ	10 Ⓐ Ⓑ Ⓒ Ⓓ Ⓔ	15 Ⓐ Ⓑ Ⓒ Ⓓ Ⓔ

TEAR HERE

Note: ONLY the answers entered on the grid are scored.

Handwritten answers at the top of the column are NOT scored.

16. 17. 18. 19. 20.

21. 22. 23. 24. 25.

SECTION 5

1 (A) (B) (C) (D) (E)   6 (A) (B) (C) (D) (E)   11 (A) (B) (C) (D) (E)   16 (A) (B) (C) (D) (E)
2 (A) (B) (C) (D) (E)   7 (A) (B) (C) (D) (E)   12 (A) (B) (C) (D) (E)   17 (A) (B) (C) (D) (E)
3 (A) (B) (C) (D) (E)   8 (A) (B) (C) (D) (E)   13 (A) (B) (C) (D) (E)   18 (A) (B) (C) (D) (E)
4 (A) (B) (C) (D) (E)   9 (A) (B) (C) (D) (E)   14 (A) (B) (C) (D) (E)   19 (A) (B) (C) (D) (E)
5 (A) (B) (C) (D) (E)   10 (A) (B) (C) (D) (E) 15 (A) (B) (C) (D) (E)   20 (A) (B) (C) (D) (E)

SECTION 6

1 (A) (B) (C) (D) (E)   6 (A) (B) (C) (D) (E)   11 (A) (B) (C) (D) (E)
2 (A) (B) (C) (D) (E)   7 (A) (B) (C) (D) (E)   12 (A) (B) (C) (D) (E)
3 (A) (B) (C) (D) (E)   8 (A) (B) (C) (D) (E)   13 (A) (B) (C) (D) (E)
4 (A) (B) (C) (D) (E)   9 (A) (B) (C) (D) (E)   14 (A) (B) (C) (D) (E)
5 (A) (B) (C) (D) (E)   10 (A) (B) (C) (D) (E) 15 (A) (B) (C) (D) (E)

PRACTICE TEST 2
Section 1

31 Questions • Time—30 Minutes

Directions: Each of the following questions consists of an incomplete sentence followed by five words or pairs of words. Choose that word or pair of words that when substituted for the blank space or spaces, best completes the meaning of the sentence and mark the letter of your choice on your answer sheet.

Example

Q In view of the extenuating circumstances and the defendant's youth, the judge recommended ____.
(A) conviction
(B) a defense
(C) a mistrial
(D) leniency
(E) life imprisonment

A Ⓐ Ⓑ Ⓒ ● Ⓔ

1. An audience that laughs in all the wrong places can ____ even the most experienced actor.
(A) disparage
(B) allay
(C) disconcert
(D) upbraid
(E) satiate

2. Their assurances of good faith were hollow; they ____ on the agreement almost at once.
(A) conferred
(B) expiated
(C) recapitulated
(D) obtruded
(E) reneged

3. If we ____ our different factions, then together we can gain the majority in their legislature.
(A) amalgamate
(B) manifest
(C) preclude
(D) alienate
(E) deviate

4. The Eighteenth Amendment, often called the Prohibition Act, ____ the sale of alcoholic beverages.
(A) prolonged
(B) preempted
(C) sanctioned
(D) proscribed
(E) encouraged

5. The police received a(n) ____ call giving them valuable information, but the caller would not give his name out of fear of ____.
(A) private..impunity
(B) anonymous..reprisals
(C) professional..dissension
(D) enigmatic..refusal
(E) adamant..transgression

6. A person who is ____ is slow to adapt to a new way of life.

   (A) nonchalant
   (B) intractable
   (C) rabid
   (D) insolent
   (E) doughty

7. Though they came from ____ social backgrounds, the newly married couple shared numerous interests and feelings.

   (A) desultory
   (B) obsolete
   (C) malleable
   (D) disparate
   (E) deleterious

8. The ____ was a ____ of gastronomic delights.

   (A) internist..progeny
   (B) gourmet..connoisseur
   (C) scientist..facilitator
   (D) xenophobe..promotor
   (E) tyro..master

9. Mrs. Jenkins, upon hearing that her arm was broken, looked ____ at the doctor.

   (A) jovially
   (B) plaintively
   (C) fortuitously
   (D) serendipitously
   (E) opportunely

Directions: Each of the following questions consists of a capitalized pair of words followed by five pairs of words lettered (A) to (E). The capitalized words bear some meaningful relationship to each other. Choose the lettered pair of words whose relationship is most similar to that expressed by the capitalized pair and mark its letter on your answer sheet.

Example

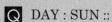 DAY : SUN ::

   (A) sunlight : daylight
   (B) ray : sun
   (C) night : moon
   (D) heat : cold
   (E) moon : star

10. THROAT : SWALLOW ::

   (A) teeth : chew
   (B) eyelid : wink
   (C) nose : point
   (D) ear : absorb
   (E) mouth : smile

11. GARNET : RED ::

   (A) pearl : round
   (B) diamond : solid
   (C) emerald : green
   (D) ivory : living
   (E) silver : shining

12. PATIENCE : VIRTUES ::

   (A) prudence : skills
   (B) sailing : crafts
   (C) grief : traits
   (D) temerity : vices
   (E) literature : arts

13. SOAR : ALIGHT ::

   (A) hop : stumble
   (B) crawl : run
   (C) lift : carry
   (D) walk : hike
   (E) sail : moor

14. OASIS : DESERT ::

(A) canyon : gorge

(B) savanna : steppe

(C) island : ocean

(D) tundra : icecap

(E) channel : reef

15. COTTON : SOFT ::

(A) wool : warm

(B) iron : hard

(C) nylon : strong

(D) wood : polished

(E) silk : expensive

Directions: Each passage below is followed by a set of questions. Read each passage, then answer the accompanying questions, basing your answers on what is stated or implied in the passage and in any introductory material provided. Mark the letter of your choice on your answer sheet.

Questions 16–23 are based on the following passage.

The Great Famine, which occurred in Ireland between 1845–1848, affected the country so profoundly that today, more than 100 years later, it is still discussed both in Irish–American communities in the United States and in Ireland. The passage presents a timeline of the famine and some of the events leading up to it.

During the mid-1840s, from 1845–1848, the potato crop in Ireland failed, creating a famine that ravaged the population. This event, the Great Famine, was

(5) one of the most significant events in the 8,000-year history of this island nation, and the effects of it continue to haunt the Irish, both those who still live in Ireland and those who live in the United

(10) States. The most immediate effect of the famine was the dramatic decline in the Irish population—either through death from starvation and disease or through emigration to other countries.

(15) In Ireland, the potato had historically been the mainstay of the diet of a large proportion of the rural population. Highly nutritional, the potato was easy to plant and easy to harvest. If a family

(20) of six had one acre of land, it could grow a potato crop that would feed them for almost a year. However, dependence on one crop had its downside as well. Pota-

toes could not be stored for long, and

(25) farmers who had grown so accustomed to dealing with this one crop neglected to plant other crops as a hedge against possible failures.

Rapid population increases in the

(30) years preceding the Great Famine had created a country whose expanding population was often poverty-stricken. Expanding population, coupled with landowners' lack of responsibility to-

(35) ward tenant–farmers, led to a system where tenant–farmers frequently subdivided their land so that they could gain a bit of rent themselves. Consequently, the rural areas were dotted

(40) with small plots of land, most of which were used for potato farming. Prior to the famine, urban areas in Ireland were also experiencing economic distress because of a decline in Irish industry that

(45) resulted in unemployment and poverty in cities such as Dublin.

In 1845, the year the famine began, a good potato crop was expected, so it came as a great surprise when nearly

(50) half of the crop of the country failed because of a blight that had come from North America. This particular blight was unusual inasmuch as when the potato was dug from the ground, it ap-

(55) peared to be healthy; it was only after a day or two that the potato began to rot.

Despite the fact that only half the crop failed in 1845, starvation and disease plagued the entire country because

(60) many starving people, some of whom were infected with contagious diseases, roamed the countryside looking for food and spreading disease. Then, in 1846, the crop failed completely. In 1847, there
(65) was another partial failure, but because people had eaten their seed potatoes in 1846, the crop was much smaller in 1847. Then again in 1848, the crop failed completely.

(70)   As if the crop failures were not enough, other factors affected the seriousness of the situation. Various contagious diseases such as typhus, dysentery, and several different types
(75) of fever spread rapidly. Landlords evicted tenant–farmers, and the government did very little to provide relief. Nor did it help that the winter of 1846–1847 was one of the coldest on record.

(80)   When the famine was over in 1849, a cholera epidemic struck Ireland, so that by 1850 the country found its population reduced from 8.5 million to 6.5 million. One million people had died
(85) from disease and starvation, and one million had left Ireland for Britain, Europe, or North America.

    The results of the Great Famine were profound. Farming in Ireland
(90) changed from a one-crop economy to an agricultural economy that included livestock and other crops, such as grains. The seeds of animosity toward Great Britain, which had not helped the Irish
(95) in their time of need, were sown. And a pattern of emigration was established that lasts until today.

16. The word *ravaged* (line 3) means

(A) pillaged.

(B) devastated.

(C) wasted.

(D) sacked.

(E) assisted.

17. According to the passage, the potato became a staple of the Irish diet for all of the following reasons EXCEPT

(A) it was filled with nutrients.

(B) it was easy to plant.

(C) it was easy to harvest.

(D) the soil was good for potatoes.

(E) one acre could support a whole family.

18. The passage implies that

(A) dependence on one crop was sensible.

(B) the potato was not the only crop in Ireland.

(C) the dependence on one crop had no downside.

(D) the Irish were a happy people.

(E) dependence on one crop was dangerous.

19. According to the passage, rural life in the years before the Great Famine can best be described as

(A) prosperous.

(B) declining in population.

(C) harsh.

(D) decreasing in tenant–farmers.

(E) expanding in farm size.

20. Irish farmers tended to subdivide their farms repeatedly because

(A) the farms were getting too large.

(B) they had big families.

(C) it was easier to farm a smaller plot.

(D) they needed rent payments.

(E) they wanted to diversify their crops.

21. The word *blight* (line 52) means

(A) curse.

(B) disease.

(C) injury.

(D) omen.

(E) impairment.

22. Disease plagued the Irish during the famine because

(A) the potato was diseased.

(B) immigrants brought disease.

(C) starving Irish carried disease from place to place.

(D) living conditions were not sanitary.

(E) they were not prepared.

23. All of the following were results of the famine EXCEPT

(A) the Irish emigrated to new lands.

(B) the Irish began to raise livestock.

(C) the Irish were no longer dependent on one crop.

(D) the Irish became independent from Great Britain.

(E) the Irish became angered at the British

Questions 24–31 are based on the following passage.

Thomas Bulfinch (1796–1867) was a teacher and writer known for his popularization of myths and legends. In this excerpt from Bulfinch's Mythology, *he tells the story behind the Trojan War.*

Minerva was the goddess of wisdom, but on one occasion she did a very foolish thing; she entered into competition with Juno and Venus for the prize of beauty.
(5) It happened thus: At the nuptials of Peleus and Thetis all the gods were invited with the exception of Eris, or Discord. Enraged at her exclusion, the goddess threw a golden apple among the
(10) guests, with the inscription, "For the fairest." Thereupon Juno, Venus, and Minerva each claimed the apple. Jupiter, not willing to decide in so delicate a matter, sent the goddesses to Mount
(15) Ida, where the beautiful shepherd Paris was tending his flocks, and to him was committed the decision. The goddesses accordingly appeared before him. Juno promised him power and riches, Minerva
(20) glory and renown in war, and Venus the fairest of women for his wife, each attempting to bias his decision in her own favor. Paris decided in favour of Venus and gave her the golden apple, thus
(25) making the two other goddesses his enemies. Under the protection of Venus, Paris sailed to Greece, and was hospitably received by Menelaus, king of Sparta. Now Helen, the wife of Menelaus, was
(30) the very woman whom Venus had destined for Paris, the fairest of her sex. She had been sought as a bride by numerous suitors, and before her decision was made known, they all, at the suggestion of
(35) Ulysses, one of their number, took an oath that they would defend her from all injury and avenge her cause if necessary. She chose Menelaus, and was living with him happily when Paris became
(40) their guest. Paris, aided by Venus, persuaded her to elope with him, and carried her to Troy, whence arose the famous Trojan war, the theme of the greatest poems of antiquity, those of Homer and
(45) Virgil.
Menelaus called upon his brother chieftains of Greece to fulfill their pledge, and join him in his efforts to recover his wife. They generally came forward, but
(50) Ulysses, who had married Penelope, and was very happy in his wife and child, had no disposition to embark in such a troublesome affair. He therefore hung back and Palamedes was sent to urge
(55) him. When Palamedes arrived at Ithaca, Ulysses pretended to be mad. He yoked an ass and an ox together to the plough and began to sow salt. Palamedes, to try him, placed the infant Telemachus be-
(60) fore the plough, whereupon the father turned the plough aside, showing plainly that he was no madman, and after that

could no longer refuse to fulfill his promise. Being now himself gained for the
(65) undertaking, he lent his aid to bring in
other reluctant chiefs, especially Achilles. This hero was the son of that Thetis
at whose marriage the apple of Discord
had been thrown among the goddesses.
(70) Thetis was herself one of the immortals,
a sea-nymph, and knowing that her son
was fated to perish before Troy if he
went on the expedition, she endeavoured
to prevent his going. She sent him away
(75) to the court of King Lycomedes, and
induced him to conceal himself in the
disguise of a maiden among the daughters of the king. Ulysses, hearing he was
there, went disguised as a merchant to
(80) the palace and offered for sale female
ornaments, among which he had placed
some arms. While the king's daughters
were engrossed with the other contents
of the merchant's pack, Achilles handled
(85) the weapons and thereby betrayed himself to the keen eye of Ulysses, who
found no great difficulty in persuading
him to disregard his mother's prudent
counsels and join his countrymen in the
(90) war.

24. Bulfinch describes Jupiter as unwilling
to "decide in so delicate a matter" (lines
13–14), implying that

(A) Jupiter is usually heavy-handed.

(B) any decision is bound to offend someone.

(C) Jupiter is overly sensitive.

(D) the problems are so obscure that no
one can judge them.

(E) all three goddesses are fragile and
dainty.

25. The word *disposition* (line 52) is used to
mean

(A) inclination.

(B) nature.

(C) integrity.

(D) value.

(E) habit.

26. The sowing of salt is used by Bulfinch to
show

(A) Ulysses's attempt to be found insane.

(B) the difficulty of cultivating in rocky
soil.

(C) how the tears of the gods created the
sea.

(D) the gods' punishment of those who
disobey them.

(E) Ulysses's talent as a soldier rather
than a farmer.

27. When Palamedes "tries" Ulysses (line 58),
he

(A) finds him guilty.

(B) judges him.

(C) tests him.

(D) attempts to help him.

(E) taxes his patience.

28. Bulfinch reveals that Thetis is a sea-
nymph in order to explain

(A) why she married Peleus.

(B) why she dislikes the idea of war.

(C) the effect of the apple of Discord.

(D) her love for Achilles.

(E) her ability to predict the future.

29. Among the chieftains of Greece apparently are

 (A) Juno, Venus, and Minerva.

 (B) Paris and Lycomedes.

 (C) Ulysses, Achilles, and Menelaus.

 (D) Eris and Thetis.

 (E) Homer and Virgil.

30. Why does Ulysses display arms among the ornaments?

 (A) To test Achilles into revealing himself

 (B) As a declaration of war

 (C) To mislead the daughters of the king

 (D) To complete his disguise as a merchant

 (E) Because he wants to start an altercation

31. A reasonable title for this narrative might be

 (A) "Disputes and Deceit."

 (B) "Achilles and Ulysses."

 (C) "Beauty and the Beast."

 (D) "The Pettiness of the Gods."

 (E) "The Apple of Discord Leads to War."

STOP

END OF SECTION 1. IF YOU HAVE ANY TIME LEFT, GO OVER YOUR WORK IN THIS SECTION ONLY. DO NOT WORK IN ANY OTHER SECTION OF THE TEST.

Section 2

25 Questions • Time—30 Minutes

Directions: Solve the following problems using any available space on the page for scratchwork. On your answer sheet fill in the choice that best corresponds to the correct answer.

Notes: The figures accompanying the problems are drawn as accurately as possible unless otherwise stated in specific problems. Again, unless otherwise stated, all figures lie in the same plane. All numbers used in these problems are real numbers. Calculators are permitted for this test.

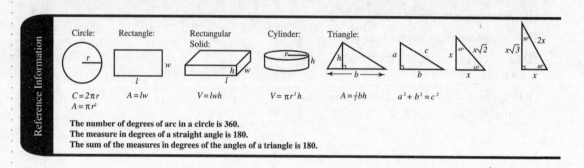

The number of degrees of arc in a circle is 360.
The measure in degrees of a straight angle is 180.
The sum of the measures in degrees of the angles of a triangle is 180.

1. One angle of a triangle is 82°. The other two angles are in the ratio 2:5. Find the number of degrees in the smallest angle of the triangle.

    (A) 14
    (B) 25
    (C) 28
    (D) 38
    (E) 82

2. Village A has a population of 6,800, which is decreasing at a rate of 120 per year. Village B has a population of 4,200, which is increasing at a rate of 80 per year. In how many years will the population of the two villages be equal?

    (A) 9
    (B) 11
    (C) 13
    (D) 14
    (E) 16

3. If $*x$ is defined such that $*x = x^2 - 2x$, the value of $*2 - *1$ is

    (A) −1
    (B) 0
    (C) 1
    (D) 2
    (E) 4

4. In a right triangle, the ratio of the legs is 1:2. If the area of the triangle is 25 square units, what is the length of the hypotenuse?

    (A) $\sqrt{5}$
    (B) $5\sqrt{5}$
    (C) $5\sqrt{3}$
    (D) $10\sqrt{3}$
    (E) $25\sqrt{5}$

5. In the graph below, the axes and the origin are not shown. If point P has coordinates (3, 7), what are the coordinates of point Q, assuming each box is one unit?

   (A) (5, 6)
   (B) (1, 10)
   (C) (6, 9)
   (D) (6, 5)
   (E) (5, 10)

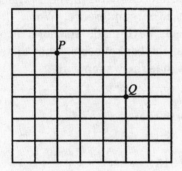

6. If $r = 5x$, how many tenths of r does $\frac{1}{2}$ of x equal?

   (A) 1
   (B) 2
   (C) 3
   (D) 4
   (E) 5

7. ABCD is a parallelogram, and $DE = EC$.

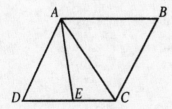

   What is the ratio of the area of triangle ADE to the area of the parallelogram?

   (A) 2:5
   (B) 1:2
   (C) 1:3
   (D) 1:4
   (E) It cannot be determined from the information given.

8. In any square, the length of one side is
   (A) one half the diagonal of the square.
   (B) the square root of the perimeter of the square.
   (C) about .7 the length of the diagonal of the square.
   (D) the square root of the diagonal.
   (E) one fourth the area.

9. A pulley having a 9-inch diameter is belted to a pulley having a 6-inch diameter, as shown in the figure. If the large pulley runs at 120 rpm, how fast does the small pulley run, in revolutions per minute?

   (A) 80
   (B) 100
   (C) 160
   (D) 180
   (E) 240

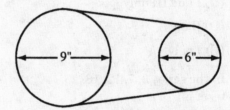

10. The number of degrees through which the hour hand of a clock moves in 2 hours and 12 minutes is
   (A) 66
   (B) 72
   (C) 126
   (D) 732
   (E) 792

11. The average of 8 numbers is 6; the average of 6 other numbers is 8. What is the average of all 14 numbers?

    (A) 6
    (B) $6\frac{6}{7}$
    (C) 7
    (D) $7\frac{2}{7}$
    (E) $8\frac{1}{7}$

12. If x is between 0 and 1, which of the following increases as x increases?

    I. $1 - x^2$

    II. $x - 1$

    III. $\frac{1}{x^2}$

    (A) I and II only
    (B) II and III only
    (C) I and III only
    (D) II only
    (E) I only

13. In the series 3, 7, 12, 18, 25, ... the 9th term is

    (A) 50
    (B) 63
    (C) 75
    (D) 86
    (E) 88

14. Simplify $\frac{x^2 - y^2}{x - y}$

    (A) $\frac{xy}{x + y}$
    (B) $\frac{x + y}{xy}$
    (C) $x + y$
    (D) xy
    (E) $x^2 + y^2 - 1$

15. The front wheels of a wagon are 7 feet in circumference and the back wheels are 9 feet in circumference. When the front wheels have made 10 more revolutions than the back wheels, what distance, in feet, has the wagon gone?

    (A) 126
    (B) 180
    (C) 189
    (D) 315
    (E) 630

16. A rectangular flower bed, dimensions 16 yards by 12 yards, is surrounded by a walk 3 yards wide. The area of the walk in square yards is

    (A) 78
    (B) 93
    (C) 132
    (D) 204
    (E) 396

17. Doreen can wash her car in 15 minutes, while her younger brother Dave takes twice as long to do the same job. If they work together, how many minutes will the job take them?

    (A) 5
    (B) $7\frac{1}{2}$
    (C) 10
    (D) $22\frac{1}{2}$
    (E) 30

18. A circle is inscribed in a given square and another circle is circumscribed about the same square. What is the ratio of the area of the inscribed to the area of the circumscribed circle?

    (A) 1:4
    (B) 4:9
    (C) 1:2
    (D) 2:3
    (E) 3:4

19. If $\frac{3}{7}$ of a bucket can be filled in 1 minute, how many minutes will it take to fill the rest of the bucket?

    (A) $\frac{7}{3}$
    (B) $\frac{4}{3}$
    (C) 1
    (D) $\frac{3}{4}$
    (E) $\frac{4}{7}$

20. In the figure below, the side of the large square is 14. The four smaller squares are formed by joining the midpoints of opposite sides. Find the value of Y.

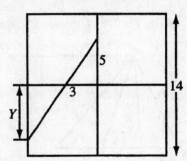

    (A) 5
    (B) 6
    (C) $6\frac{5}{8}$
    (D) $6\frac{2}{3}$
    (E) 6.8

21. If the base of a rectangle is increased by 30% and the altitude is decreased by 20%, the area is increased by

    (A) 4%
    (B) 5%
    (C) 10%
    (D) 25%
    (E) 104%

22. Using a 9×12-inch sheet of paper lengthwise, a typist leaves a 1-inch margin on each side and a $1\frac{1}{2}$-inch margin on top and bottom. What fractional part of the page is used for typing?

    (A) $\frac{5}{12}$
    (B) $\frac{7}{12}$
    (C) $\frac{5}{9}$
    (D) $\frac{3}{4}$
    (E) $\frac{21}{22}$

23. In the figure, *PQRS* is a parallelogram, and *ST* = *TV* = *VR*. What is the ratio of the area of triangle *SPT* to the area of the parallelogram?

Note: Figure is not drawn to scale.

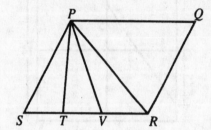

(A) $\frac{1}{6}$

(B) $\frac{1}{5}$

(C) $\frac{2}{7}$

(D) $\frac{1}{3}$

(E) It cannot be determined from the information given.

24. Given formula $A = P(1 + rt)$, then $t =$

(A) $A - P - Pr$

(B) $\frac{A+P}{Pr}$

(C) $\frac{A}{P} - r$

(D) $\frac{A-P}{Pr}$

(E) $\frac{A-r}{Pr}$

25. If $p > q$ and $r < 0$, which of the following is (are) true?

　I. $pr < qr$

　II. $p + r > q + r$

　III. $p - r < q - r$

(A) I only

(B) II only

(C) I and III only

(D) I and II only

(E) I, II, and III

STOP

END OF SECTION 2. IF YOU HAVE ANY TIME LEFT, GO OVER YOUR WORK IN THIS SECTION ONLY. DO NOT WORK IN ANY OTHER SECTION OF THE TEST.

Section 3

35 Questions • Time—30 Minutes

> **Directions:** Each of the following questions consists of an incomplete sentence followed by five words or pairs of words. Choose that word or pair of words that, when substituted for the blank space or spaces, best completes the meaning of the sentence and mark the letter of your choice on your answer sheet.

Example

> **Q** In view of the extenuating circumstances and the defendant's youth, the judge recommended ____.
> **(A)** conviction
> **(B)** a defense
> **(C)** a mistrial
> **(D)** leniency
> **(E)** life imprisonment
>
> **A** Ⓐ Ⓑ Ⓒ ● Ⓔ

1. The ____ was greatest when the pitcher paused before delivering the last strike.
   (A) game
   (B) crowd
   (C) cheering
   (D) sportsmanship
   (E) tension

2. Her ____ instincts led her to fund the construction of a hospital for the poor.
   (A) far-ranging
   (B) humanitarian
   (C) humble
   (D) popular
   (E) eclectic

3. After years of ____ war, the Great Wall was constructed to ____ the Chinese people.
   (A) internecine…instigate
   (B) destructive…resurrect
   (C) unceasing…protect
   (D) amicable…unite
   (E) pitiable…win

4. His remarks were so ____ that we could not decide which of the possible meanings was correct.
   (A) facetious
   (B) ambiguous
   (C) cogent
   (D) impalpable
   (E) congruent

5. In an attempt to ____ a strike, the two sides agreed to negotiate through the night.
   (A) arbitrate
   (B) herald
   (C) trigger
   (D) transmute
   (E) avert

6. Elder statesmen used to be ____ for their wisdom when respect for age was part of every person's upbringing.

   (A) deplored
   (B) exonerated
   (C) rebuked
   (D) venerated
   (E) exiled

7. Being less than perfectly prepared, she approached the exam with ____.

   (A) aplomb
   (B) trepidation
   (C) indifference
   (D) confidence
   (E) duplicity

8. As citizens, we would be ____ if we did not make these facts public.

   (A) derelict
   (B) pejorative
   (C) impersonal
   (D) private
   (E) derogatory

9. She was usually a model of ____, so her sudden burst of temper was atypical.

   (A) veracity
   (B) lucidity
   (C) facility
   (D) equanimity
   (E) hostility

10. The ____ attitudes politicians have today cause them to ____ at the slightest hint of controversy.

   (A) dauntless..recoil
   (B) craven..cower
   (C) pusillanimous..prevail
   (D) undaunted..quail
   (E) fractious..grovel

Directions: Each of the following questions consists of a capitalized pair of words followed by five pairs of words lettered (A) to (E). The capitalized words bear some meaningful relationship to each other. Choose the lettered pair of words whose relationship is most similar to that expressed by the capitalized pair and mark its letter on your answer sheet.

Example

 DAY : SUN ::
   (A) sunlight : daylight
   (B) ray : sun
   (C) night : moon
   (D) heat : cold
   (E) moon : star

11. FEEL : TOUCH ::
   (A) tickle : hurt
   (B) see : look
   (C) sprint : lift
   (D) giggle : laugh
   (E) shed : grow

12. CIRCLE : SQUARE ::

(A) ball : bat

(B) oval : rectangle

(C) sphere : globe

(D) angular : straight

(E) volume : area

13. CHICKEN : ROOSTER ::

(A) deer : doe

(B) duck : drake

(C) flock : hen

(D) ewe : ram

(E) pig : piglet

14. TRIGGER : PISTOL ::

(A) bullet : gun

(B) rifle : revolver

(C) guard : police

(D) switch : motor

(E) fire : shoot

15. GOOD : ANGELIC ::

(A) bad : poor

(B) glad : joyous

(C) mean : human

(D) sweet : musty

(E) correct : incorrect

16. CLARINET : WOODWIND ::

(A) piano : key

(B) symphony : composer

(C) banjo : guitar

(D) trumpet : brass

(E) horn : tuba

17. GRIEF : DOLEFUL ::

(A) melancholy : hopeful

(B) greed : successful

(C) anger : wrathful

(D) fear : unintentional

(E) reaction : involuntary

18. PAIL : WATER ::

(A) milk : quart

(B) eggs : dozen

(C) gallon : container

(D) river : ocean

(E) shaker : salt

19. FISH : AQUARIUM ::

(A) birds : aviary

(B) car : garage

(C) insects : ground

(D) lightning : sky

(E) dogs : pets

20. DISAGREEMENT : CONCORD ::

(A) limitation : restriction

(B) impartiality : bias

(C) advantage : agreement

(D) predicament : dilemma

(E) predictability : routine

21. YEAR : CENTURY ::

(A) inch : yard

(B) mile : speed

(C) week : month

(D) cent : dollar

(E) day : year

22. MULE : INTRACTABLE ::

(A) horse : turbulent

(B) fox : wily

(C) dog : candid

(D) wolf : fickle

(E) tiger : inexorable

23. STUMBLE : WALK ::

(A) creep : run

(B) pain : hurt

(C) stammer : speak

(D) pitch : throw

(E) smile : frown

practice test

Questions 24–35 are based on the following passage.

Louisa May Alcott (1832–1888) was a beloved author of books for children, but she also wrote gothic tales and short stories for adults. This excerpt is from "Mrs. Gay's Prescription."

The poor little woman looked as if she
needed rest but was not likely to get it;
for the room was in a chaotic state, the
breakfast table presented the appear-
(5) ance of having been devastated by a
swarm of locusts, the baby began to fret,
little Polly set up her usual whine of "I
want sumpin to do," and a pile of work
loomed in the corner waiting to be done.
(10)   "I don't see how I ever shall get
through it all," sighed the despondent
matron as she hastily drank a last cup of
tea, while two great tears rolled down
her cheeks, as she looked from one puny
(15) child to the other, and felt the weariness
of her own tired soul and body more
oppressive than ever.
    "A good cry" was impending, when
there came a brisk ring at the door, a step
(20) in the hall, and a large, rosy woman
came bustling in, saying in a cheery voice
as she set a flower pot down upon the
table, "Good morning! Nice day, isn't it?
Came in early on business and brought
(25) you one of my Lady Washingtons, you
are so fond of flowers."
    "Oh, it's lovely! How kind you are.
Do sit down if you can find a chair; we are
all behind hand today, for I was up half
(30) the night with poor baby, and haven't
energy enough to go to work yet," answered Mrs. Bennet, with a sudden smile
that changed her whole face, while baby
stopped fretting to stare at the rosy clus-
(35) ters, and Polly found employment in ex-
ploring the pocket of the new comer, as if
she knew her way there.

"Let me put the pot on your stand
first, girls are so careless, and I'm proud
(40) of this. It will be an ornament to your
parlor for a week," and opening a door
Mrs. Gay carried the plant to a sunny
bay window where many others were
blooming beautifully.
(45)   Mrs. Bennet and the children followed to talk and admire, while the
servant leisurely cleared the table.
    "Now give me that baby, put your-
self in the easy chair, and tell me all
(50) about your worries," said Mrs. Gay, in
the brisk, commanding way which few
people could resist.
    "I'm sure I don't know where to
begin," sighed Mrs. Bennet, dropping
(55) into the comfortable seat while baby
changed bearers with great composure.
    "I met your husband and he said
the doctor had ordered you and these
chicks off to Florida for the winter. John
(60) said he didn't know how he should man-
age it, but he meant to try."
    "Isn't it dreadful? He can't leave
his business to go with me, and we shall
have to get Aunt Miranda to come and
(65) see to him and the boys while I'm gone,
and the boys can't bear her strict, old-
fashioned ways, and I've got to go that
long journey all alone and stay among
strangers, and these heaps of fall work
(70) to do first, and it will cost an immense
sum to send us, and I don't know what
is to become of me."
    Here Mrs. Bennet stopped for
breath, and Mrs. Gay asked briskly,
(75) "What is the matter with you and the
children?"
    "Well, baby is having a hard time
with his teeth and is croupy, Polly doesn't
get over scarlet fever well, and I'm used
(80) up; no strength or appetite, pain in my
side and low spirits. Entire change of
scene, milder climate, and less work for

me, is what we want, the doctor says. John is very anxious about us, and I feel (85) regularly discouraged."

"I'll spend the day and cheer you up a bit. You just rest and get ready for a new start tomorrow; it is a saving of time to stop short now and then and see (90) where to begin next. Bring me the most pressing job of work. I can sew and see to this little rascal at the same time."

24. The "little woman" referred to in line 1 is

 (A) Lady Washington.

 (B) Alcott's mother.

 (C) a servant.

 (D) Mrs. Bennet.

 (E) Mrs. Gay.

25. When Alcott compares the breakfast table to something "devastated by a swarm of locusts" (lines 5–6), she means

 (A) that it is a mess left by an uncaring mob.

 (B) that children are no more meaningful than insects to Mrs. Bennet.

 (C) to indicate Mrs. Bennet's flightiness.

 (D) to illustrate the horror of Mrs. Bennet's life.

 (E) that the Bennets are pests.

26. All of the following contribute to the Bennets' "chaotic state" of affairs EXCEPT

 (A) the overall appearance of the breakfast table.

 (B) the fretting of the baby.

 (C) the contribution of Polly.

 (D) the uncompleted pile of work.

 (E) the optimism of Mrs. Gay.

27. The word *despondent* in line 11 most nearly means

 (A) different.

 (B) daring.

 (C) excited.

 (D) exasperated.

 (E) dilapidated.

28. Had Mrs. Gay not arrived when she did, Alcott leads us to suspect that

 (A) Mrs. Bennet would have gone back to bed.

 (B) the children would have continued to cry.

 (C) Mrs. Bennet would have accomplished little all day.

 (D) sickness would have overtaken the entire family.

 (E) the servant would have left the dishes untended.

29. The "rosy clusters" in lines 34–35 are

 (A) Mrs. Gay's cheeks.

 (B) Mrs. Bennet's cheeks.

 (C) flowers.

 (D) candies from Mrs. Gay's pockets.

 (E) embroidered pockets.

30. In lines 41–44 Alcott

 (A) reveals Mrs. Bennet's only talent.

 (B) uses the sunny parlor as a symbol of hope.

 (C) contrasts Mrs. Gay's sunniness with Mrs. Bennet's dullness.

 (D) contrasts Mrs. Bennet's plants with her children.

 (E) opens the door to Mrs. Bennet's despair.

31. When Mrs. Bennet says that she's "used up" (line 79–80), she means that she

 (A) has no energy.

 (B) is abused.

 (C) is exploited.

 (D) has spent all her money.

 (E) has given up.

32. The word *pressing* (line 91) means

(A) heavy.

(B) ardent.

(C) forceful.

(D) important.

(E) concentrated.

33. Mrs. Bennet's friend's disposition is indicated by

(A) her name.

(B) her speech.

(C) her clothing.

(D) both A and B.

(E) both B and C.

34. Alcott implies that Mrs. Bennet's real problem is

(A) her inability to cope.

(B) a touch of fever.

(C) the cold winter weather.

(D) unsympathetic children.

(E) a lack of common sense.

35. Mrs. Gay's primary quality seems to be her

(A) lethargy.

(B) obliviousness.

(C) anxiety.

(D) dignity.

(E) practical nature.

STOP

END OF SECTION 3. IF YOU HAVE ANY TIME LEFT, GO
OVER YOUR WORK IN THIS SECTION ONLY. DO NOT
WORK IN ANY OTHER SECTION OF THE TEST.

Section 4

25 Questions • Time—30 Minutes

Directions: Solve the following problems using any available space on the page for scratchwork. On your answer sheet fill in the choice that best corresponds to the correct answer.

Notes: The figures accompanying the problems are drawn as accurately as possible unless otherwise stated in specific problems. Again, unless otherwise stated, all figures lie in the same plane. All numbers used in these problems are real numbers. Calculators are permitted for this test.

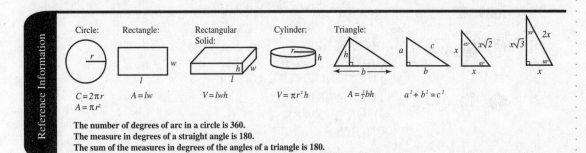

The number of degrees of arc in a circle is 360.
The measure in degrees of a straight angle is 180.
The sum of the measures in degrees of the angles of a triangle is 180.

Part 1: Quantitative Comparison Questions

Directions: For each of the following questions, two quantities are given—one in Column A, the other in Column B. Compare the two quantities and mark your answer sheet as follows:

(A) if the quantity in Column A is greater

(B) if the quantity in Column B is greater

(C) if the quantities are equal

(D) if the relationship cannot be determined from the information given

Notes:

(1) Information concerning one or both of the compared quantities will be centered above the two columns for some items.

(2) Symbols that appear in both columns represent the same thing in Column A as in Column B.

(3) Letters such as x, n, and k are symbols for real numbers.

Examples

	Column A	Column B
	$a > 0$	
	$x > 0$	
E1.	$a - x$	$a + x$
E2.	The average of 17, 19, 21, 23	The average of 16, 18, 20, 22

Answers

E1. Ⓐ ● Ⓒ Ⓓ   DO NOT MARK CHOICE (E) FOR THESE QUESTIONS.

E2. ● Ⓑ Ⓒ Ⓓ   THERE ARE ONLY FOUR ANSWER CHOICES.

Column A	Column B
1. $\dfrac{a^2 + b}{2}$	$.5(a^2 + b)$

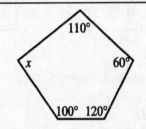

Column A	Column B
2. x	$90°$

$$\dfrac{m}{n} = \dfrac{7}{10}$$

Column A	Column B
3. mn	70

For all real numbers x and y,
let Δ be defined as $x \Delta y = \dfrac{xy}{x-y}$.

Column A	Column B
4. $-3\Delta - 2$	$-2\Delta - 3$

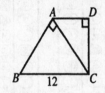

Column A	Column B
5. 12	CD

$\ell_1 \| \ell_2 \| \ell_3$

Column A	Column B
6. $x + y$	$y + z$

Column A	Column B
7. 3% of 4%	$.0012$

Column A	Column B

A two-pound box of Brand A costs $7.88.

A three-pound box of Brand B costs $11.79.

	Column A	Column B
8.	Cost per pound of Brand A	Cost per pound of Brand B

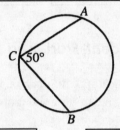

	Column A	Column B
9.	90	Degree measure of arc AB

	Column A	Column B
10.	$\sqrt{8} + \sqrt{24}$	$\sqrt{32}$

Box A   **Box B**

	Column A	Column B
11.	Number of different two-digit numbers that can be constructed using the digits in Box A	Number of different two-digit numbers that can be constructed using the digits in Box B

	Column A	Column B
12.	$a(b + c)$	$\dfrac{b+c}{a}$

$$p^2 - q^2 = 4$$
$$p - q = -1$$

	Column A	Column B
13.	$p + q$	4

Column A	Column B	Column A	Column B

40% of the boys in a class are in the band.

60% of the girls in the same class are in the band.

p, q, and r are positive

14.

Number of boys not in band	Number of girls not in band

15.

$p \times q \times r$	$p + q + r$

Part 2: Student-Produced Response Questions

Directions: Solve each of these problems. Write the answer in the corresponding grid on the answer sheet and fill in the ovals beneath each answer you write. Here are some examples.

Answer: $\frac{3}{4}$ (=.75; show answer either way)   Answer: 325

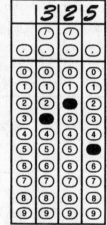

Note: A mixed number such as $3\frac{1}{2}$ must be gridded as 7/2 or as 3.5. If gridded as "3 1/2," it will be read as "thirty-one halves."

Note: Either position is correct.

16. $\left(\sqrt{18} - \sqrt{8}\right)^2 =$

17. The distance from the center of a circle to a chord is 5. If the length of the chord is 24, what is the length of the radius of the circle?

18. If the cost of a party is to be split equally among 11 friends, each would pay $15.00. If 20 persons equally split the same cost, how much would each person pay?

19. In the figure below, $\angle N = (9x - 40)°$, $\angle J = (4x + 30)°$ and $\angle JLR = (8x + 40)°$. What is the measure of $\angle J$? (Do not grid the degree symbol.)

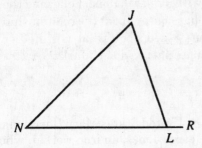

20. $\dfrac{2^2 + 3^2}{5^2} + \dfrac{1}{10} =$

21. In the figure below, two circles are tangent to each other and each is tangent to three sides of the rectangle. If the radius of each circle is 3, then the area of the shaded portion is $a - b\pi$. What is the value of a?

22. The measures of the angles of a triangle are in the ratio of 3:5:7. What is the measure, in degrees, of the smallest angle? (Do not grid the degree symbol.)

23. The length of the line segment whose end points are $(3, -2)$ and $(-4, 5)$ is $b\sqrt{2}$. What is the value of b?

24. Jessica caught five fish with an average weight of 10 pounds. If three of the fish weigh 9, 9, and 10 pounds, respectively, what is the average (arithmetic mean) weight of the other two fish?

25. In the figure below, what is the area of $\triangle NKL$?

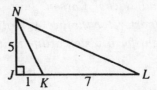

STOP

END OF SECTION 4. IF YOU HAVE ANY TIME LEFT, GO OVER YOUR WORK IN THIS SECTION ONLY. DO NOT WORK IN ANY OTHER SECTION OF THE TEST.

Section 5

12 Questions • Time—15 Minutes

Directions: The two passages given below deal with a related topic. Following the passages are questions about the content of each passage or about the relationship between the two passages. Answer the questions based upon what is stated or implied in the passages and in any introductory material provided. Mark the letter of your choice on your answer sheet.

Questions 1–12 are based on the following passages.

The two American women described in the following passages, Mary Harris (Mother Jones) and Rachel Carson, lived almost a century apart, yet in the face of great obstacles both fought for a vision of life that they believed in.

PASSAGE 1—Mother Jones, the Miners' Angel

Mary Harris (Mother Jones) was born in County Cork, Ireland, in the late 1830s, and came to be known in the United States as the "miner's angel" for the
(5) work that she did on behalf of coal miners from West Virginia to Colorado. Working at a time when very few women were active in the public arena, Harris worked tirelessly on behalf of workers,
(10) who were often mistreated during that part of the nineteenth century. She helped to organize unions among the textile workers, steel workers, brewery workers, and coal miners.

(15) And who was this woman? Born in Ireland during a time of Irish rebellion against the British, Mary Harris was quite familiar with unrest and violence. The Irish at that point in their troubled
(20) history could not vote, hold office, or buy land, and Mary's family was known in County Cork as dissident rebels who fought the British oppressors. Forced to leave Ireland for political reasons, the
(25) Harris family fled to the United States with waves of other Irish immigrants. In

the United States Mary Harris married George Jones, an iron worker, who was a member of a trade union in Chicago. It
(30) was in Chicago that Mary Jones, after the untimely loss of her husband and young family to yellow fever, began her early union work. Finding herself homeless after the Chicago fire in 1871, Mary
(35) began to spend time at the hall where the Knights of Labor held their meetings. It was through what she learned at these meetings that she became a radical union organizer. Remaining loyal to
(40) the Knights of Labor through its growing pains of the 1870s and 1880s, she continued to fight for the rights of working people who suffered greatly due to the capriciousness of employers, who
(45) could reduce their wages at the first sign of economic difficulty. Railroad workers were particularly oppressed, and it was to their cause that Mary Jones first gave her support, working with Eugene V.
(50) Debs, who had organized the American Railway Union. But it was in the coal fields of Pennsylvania during the 1890s that Mary made her most significant contributions. It was here that she re-
(55) ceived the name "Mother Jones" from the miners because she called them "her boys." She convinced the miners she was willing to risk her life for them, and earned their undying love and grati-
(60) tude. Although she organized textile workers, fought for child labor laws, and spent time with Colorado miners, her heart was always with the miners of West Virginia; she returned time after
(65) time to help them organize, often placing her own life in danger.

Mother Jones lived to be 100 years old, and during her lifetime, she crossed the country time and again to fight (70) battles for fair labor laws. A woman of vision with a clear understanding of the rights of workers, she was buried in Mt. Olive, Illinois, in a union cemetery next to miners who were killed in an 1898 (75) labor dispute.

PASSAGE 2—Rachel Carson, Protector of the Environment

Today we can hardly imagine a world without newspapers and magazines that express deep concern about the environment; without Earth Day speeches and (80) marches, and without elected officials assuring their constituencies that they will do everything in their power to assure that the ecological balance is preserved in their areas. But in 1962, when (85) Rachel Carson's *Silent Spring* was first published, this was not the case. Carson, a former marine biologist for the Fish and Game Service, disturbed many who had a vested interest in maintaining the (90) status quo as far as the environment was concerned. Her credibility as a scientist and her deep and abiding personal courage enabled Carson to withstand the steady onslaught of criti- (95) cism heaped on her during her lifetime. This criticism seemed to be directed at her on several levels—as a woman whose emotional response to the situation was getting in the way of scientific accuracy (100) and as a scientist who believed that man should accommodate to nature rather than try to control it.

And what exactly was it that Rachel Carson did that was so disturbing? She (105) pointed out the dangers of pesticides, DDT in particular, to the environment. Designed to contain insect pests in gardens and on farmland, the pesticides were permeating the soil, the rivers, and (110) adhering to tree leaves and branches that were the home for various birds and unharmful insects.

Carson contended that the levels of chemical pesticides in major rivers, (115) ground water, wildlife, soil, fish, earth-

worms, and humans, for example, were at levels that were alarming. The synthetic insecticides, according to Carson, were so potent that they were able to (120) penetrate systems and remain there for years, perhaps leading to a breakdown in tissue and immune systems, and possibly causing malignancies.

Arsenic, the chief ingredient in in- (125) secticides and pesticides at the time of Carson's writing, is extremely toxic, causing reactions in livestock near areas dusted with arsenic sprays. Arsenic absorbed in the soil has even been found in (130) plant tissues, thereby causing unsprayed plants to take up toxicity from the soil. As residue from the pesticides continues to build up in the soil over the years, more and more plant life is contami- (135) nated.

The furor caused by Carson's writing was mostly felt by the chemical companies that produced pesticides. Not willing to acknowledge the potential haz- (140) ards of their products, they resisted by seeking to discredit Carson. And despite her credentials, Carson was discredited for a period of time. However, in 1970 with the establishment of the Environ- (145) mental Protection Agency, the nation became more concerned with issues that Carson had raised. Even though not as much progress has been made as Carson might have wished, DDT has been (150) banned in the United States.

Rachel Carson, a scientist of vision and determination, was able to change the course of history and bring environmental issues to the attention of the (155) world.

1. According to Passage 1, the work of Mary Harris was particularly noteworthy because

    (A) she was an Irish immigrant.

    (B) she fought for workers' rights.

    (C) everyone was sure that she would fail.

    (D) no one was supporting workers at that time.

    (E) very few women worked in the public sector.

2. The author implies that Mother Jones became a champion of workers' rights because

    (A) she experienced injustices in her native Ireland.

    (B) no other work was open to her.

    (C) the workers prevailed upon her to take up their cause.

    (D) she knew how hard life in the textile mills was.

    (E) workers were so mistreated in the mid-nineteenth century.

3. Mother Jones's family responded to the oppression of the British by

    (A) joining the rebels.

    (B) emigrating to Australia.

    (C) becoming involved in local government.

    (D) joining the Labor Party.

    (E) establishing large land holdings.

4. Mother Jones learned to become a radical union organizer through her association with

    (A) Irish rebels.

    (B) the Knights of Labor.

    (C) West Virginia coal miners.

    (D) textile workers.

    (E) County Cork Association.

5. When the passage refers to the *capriciousness of employers*, it means

    (A) employers were subject to no rules.

    (B) employers were generous.

    (C) employers were interested in profits.

    (D) employers hired only nonunion workers.

    (E) employers were not interested in workers' problems.

6. According to Passage 1, Eugene V. Debs organized the

    (A) Knights of Labor.

    (B) Textile Workers' Union.

    (C) American Railway Union.

    (D) Coal Miners' Union.

    (E) Steel Workers' Union.

7. In Passage 2, the word *constituencies* (line 81) means

    (A) an advisory committee.

    (B) financial contributors.

    (C) campaign workers.

    (D) legislative body.

    (E) a group of citizens.

8. According to Passage 2, the reaction to Carson's findings and recommendations during her lifetime was

    (A) completely indifferent.

    (B) highly supportive.

    (C) somewhat critical.

    (D) negative and hostile.

    (E) positive and accepting.

9. Rachel Carson pointed out the hazards to the environment associated with

    (A) pesticides.

    (B) acid rain.

    (C) smog.

    (D) destruction of the rain forest.

    (E) noise pollution.

10. According to the passage, Carson maintained that the use of insecticides was responsible for all of the following EXCEPT

    (A) human tissue breakdown.

    (B) breakdown of the immune system.

    (C) breathing difficulties.

    (D) malignancies.

    (E) plant tissue contamination.

11. One of the most toxic ingredients in insecticides, according to the passage, is

    (A) synthetic toxins.

    (B) DDT.

    (C) arsenic.

    (D) Agent Orange.

    (E) poisonous herbs.

12. The authors of the two passages would agree that a quality shared by Mother Jones and Rachel Carson was

    (A) need for power.

    (B) desire for the limelight.

    (C) belief in a cause.

    (D) understanding of the media.

    (E) interest in monetary reward.

STOP

END OF SECTION 5. IF YOU HAVE ANY TIME LEFT, GO OVER YOUR WORK IN THIS SECTION ONLY. DO NOT WORK IN ANY OTHER SECTION OF THE TEST.

Section 6

10 Questions • Time—15 Minutes

> **Directions:** Solve the following problems using any available space on the page for scratchwork. On your answer sheet fill in the choice that best corresponds to the correct answer.
>
> **Notes:** The figures accompanying the problems are drawn as accurately as possible unless otherwise stated in specific problems. Again, unless otherwise stated, all figures lie in the same plane. All numbers used in these problems are real numbers. Calculators are permitted for this test.

Reference Information

Circle: $C = 2\pi r$, $A = \pi r^2$
Rectangle: $A = lw$
Rectangular Solid: $V = lwh$
Cylinder: $V = \pi r^2 h$
Triangle: $A = \frac{1}{2}bh$, $a^2 + b^2 = c^2$

The number of degrees of arc in a circle is 360.
The measure in degrees of a straight angle is 180.
The sum of the measures in degrees of the angles of a triangle is 180.

1. Which one of the following quantities has the least value?

   (A) $\frac{4}{5}$

   (B) $\frac{7}{9}$

   (C) .76

   (D) $\frac{5}{7}$

   (E) $\frac{9}{11}$

2. A salesperson earns twice as much in December as in each of the other months of a year. What part of this salesperson's entire year's earnings is earned in December?

   (A) $\frac{1}{7}$

   (B) $\frac{2}{13}$

   (C) $\frac{1}{6}$

   (D) $\frac{2}{11}$

   (E) $\frac{3}{14}$

3. If $x = -1$, then $3x^3 + 2x^2 + x + 1 =$
   (A) –5
   (B) –1
   (C) 1
   (D) 2
   (E) 5

4. $.03\% \times .21 =$
   (A) .63
   (B) .063
   (C) .0063
   (D) .00063
   (E) .000063

5. An equilateral triangle 3 inches on a side is cut up into smaller equilateral triangles 1 inch on a side. What is the greatest number of such triangles that can be formed?
   (A) 3
   (B) 6
   (C) 9
   (D) 12
   (E) 15

6. A square 5 units on a side has one vertex at the point (1, 1). Which one of the following points *cannot* be diagonally opposite that vertex?
   (A) (6, 6)
   (B) (–4, 6)
   (C) (–4, –4)
   (D) (6, –4)
   (E) (4, –6)

7. Five equal squares are placed side by side to make a single rectangle whose perimeter is 372 inches. Find the number of square inches in the area of one of these squares.
   (A) 72
   (B) 324
   (C) 900
   (D) 961
   (E) 984

8. The water level of a swimming pool, 75 feet by 42 feet, is to be raised four inches. How many gallons of water must be added to accomplish this? (7.48 gal. = 1 cubic ft.)
   (A) 140
   (B) 7,854
   (C) 31,500
   (D) 94,500
   (E) 727,650

9. What part of the total quantity is represented by a 24-degree sector of a circle graph?
   (A) $6\frac{2}{3}\%$
   (B) 12%
   (C) $13\frac{1}{3}\%$
   (D) 15%
   (E) 24%

10. The square of a fraction between 0 and 1 is
    (A) less than the original fraction.
    (B) greater than the original fraction.
    (C) twice the original fraction.
    (D) less than the cube of the fraction.
    (E) not necessarily any of the preceding.

STOP

END OF SECTION 6. IF YOU HAVE ANY TIME LEFT, GO OVER YOUR WORK IN THIS SECTION ONLY. DO NOT WORK IN ANY OTHER SECTION OF THE TEST.

ANSWERS AND EXPLANATIONS

Section 1: Verbal

1.	C	8.	B	14.	C	20.	D	26.	A
2.	E	9.	B	15.	B	21.	B	27.	C
3.	A	10.	A	16.	B	22.	C	28.	E
4.	D	11.	C	17.	D	23.	D	29.	C
5.	B	12.	E	18.	E	24.	B	30.	A
6.	B	13.	E	19.	C	25.	A	31.	E
7.	D								

Section 2: Math

1.	C	6.	A	11.	B	16.	D	21.	A
2.	C	7.	D	12.	D	17.	C	22.	B
3.	C	8.	C	13.	B	18.	C	23.	A
4.	B	9.	D	14.	C	19.	B	24.	D
5.	D	10.	A	15.	D	20.	D	25.	D

Section 3: Verbal

1.	E	8.	A	15.	B	22.	B	29.	C
2.	B	9.	D	16.	D	23.	C	30.	B
3.	C	10.	B	17.	C	24.	D	31.	A
4.	B	11.	B	18.	E	25.	A	32.	D
5.	E	12.	B	19.	A	26.	E	33.	D
6.	D	13.	B	20.	B	27.	D	34.	A
7.	B	14.	D	21.	D	28.	C	35.	E

Section 4: Math

Part 1

1.	C	4.	B	7.	C	10.	A	13.	B
2.	A	5.	A	8.	A	11.	B	14.	D
3.	D	6.	C	9.	B	12.	D	15.	D

Part 2

16.	2	18.	8.25	20.	$\frac{31}{50} = .62$	22.	36	24.	11
17.	13	19.	70	21.	72	23.	7	25.	$17.5 = \frac{35}{2}$

Section 5: Verbal

1.	E	4.	B	7.	E	9.	A	11.	C
2.	A	5.	A	8.	D	10.	C	12.	C
3.	A	6.	C						

Section 6: Math

1.	D	3.	B	5.	C	7.	D	9.	A
2.	B	4.	E	6.	E	8.	B	10.	A

Note: A [calculator icon] following a math answer explanation indicates that a calculator could be helpful in solving that particular problem.

Section 1

1. **The correct answer is (C).** Audience laughter at the wrong moment can easily *disconcert* (upset or confuse) an actor.

2. **The correct answer is (E).** Since the assurances of good faith were "hollow," it is not surprising that those who made them *reneged* on (went back on) their agreement.

3. **The correct answer is (A).** To win the majority, we must unite, or *amalgamate*, the different factions.

4. **The correct answer is (D).** A law known as the Prohibition Act would naturally be expected to *proscribe* (outlaw) something.

5. **The correct answer is (B).** A caller who will not give his name is by definition *anonymous*. Since he is giving information to the police, he may well fear *reprisals* (retaliation) by a criminal.

6. **The correct answer is (B).** An *intractable*, or stubborn, individual is likely to have trouble adapting to a new way of life. Choice (A), *nonchalant*, means unconcerned. Choice (C), *rabid*, means furious. Choice (D), *insolent*, means rude. And choice (E), *doughty*, means valiant.

7. **The correct answer is (D).** The key word *though* indicates that the word in the blank should be opposite in meaning from *shared*. The only choice that satisfies this condition is *disparate* (very different; having nothing in common).

8. **The correct answer is (B).** If you understand that *gastronomic* is an adjective having to do with eating, the only possible choice is (B). A *gourmet* (person who appreciates good food) is a *connoisseur*, or expert, in food.

9. **The correct answer is (B).** The phrase "her arm was broken" points to a negative word choice for this sentence. The only negative word is *plaintively*, which means *sadly*. All other choices are positive.

10. **The correct answer is (A).** A primary function of the *throat* is to *swallow*, and a primary function of the *teeth* is to *chew*.

11. **The correct answer is (C).** A *garnet* has the color *red*, and an *emerald* has the color *green*.

12. **The correct answer is (E).** *Patience* is considered one of the virtues, just as *literature* is considered one of the *arts*.

13. **The correct answer is (E).** An airplane that can *soar* will eventually *alight* on the ground. A boat that can *sail* will eventually *moor* at a dock.

14. **The correct answer is (C).** An *oasis* is a place of refuge in the middle of the *desert*. An *island* is a place of refuge in the middle of the *ocean*.

15. **The correct answer is (B).** *Cotton* is *soft* to the touch, as an *iron* is *hard* to the touch.

16. **The correct answer is (B).** While answers (A), (C), and (D) are all synonyms for *ravaged*, the context of the sentence supports the choice of *devastated*.

17. **The correct answer is (D).** Nowhere in the passage is the quality of the soil mentioned as a reason for the dependence on the potato as a staple.

18. **The correct answer is (E).** While not directly stated in the passage, the author certainly implies that the dependence on one crop was dangerous.

19. **The correct answer is (C).** The passage certainly describes Irish life as characterized by poverty and oppression from landlords, so *harsh* is the correct answer.

20. **The correct answer is (D).** The passage states that farmers were compelled to subdivide in order to make rent payments to their landlords.

21. **The correct answer is (B).** The best answer according to the context of the sentence is *disease*, particularly since in the sentence the word applies to the crop.

22. **The correct answer is (C).** While some of the other responses may be true, they are not stated in the passage.

23. **The correct answer is (D).** The Irish did not gain their independence during this period; no reference to Irish independence is made in the passage.

24. **The correct answer is (B).** Jupiter is being asked to decide which of three goddesses is the fairest—it is a no-win decision, since it is bound to anger two of the three.

25. **The correct answer is (A).** Ulysses has no inclination to embark on the adventure, since he is happy at home with his family.

26. **The correct answer is (A).** "Ulysses pretended to be mad" (line 56), and one of the methods he chose was to hitch up a mismatched team and sow something that could not grow.

27. **The correct answer is (C).** Palamedes doesn't buy Ulysses' mad act, and he thinks up a way to test him. Since Ulysses is unwilling to run over his own son, he is obviously not as mad as he pretends to be.

28. **The correct answer is (E).** Rather than say that Thetis, being a sea-nymph, can read the future, Bulfinch merely mentions her immortal status and expects the reader to understand that this means that she knows "her son was fated to perish."

29. **The correct answer is (C).** The names in (A) are those of goddesses. Paris is a "beautiful shepherd" (line 15). Eris is a goddess (line 9). Thetis is a sea-nymph (line 71). Homer and Virgil are poets (lines 44–45). Only choice (C) names three chieftains of Greece.

30. **The correct answer is (A).** Again Bulfinch expects his readers to understand Ulysses' clever ploy without its being spelled out. Achilles is disguised as a woman, but he is inappropriately interested in manly objects.

31. **The correct answer is (E).** This is an accurate summary of the main themes in the passage.

Section 2

1. **The correct answer is (C).** Let the other two angles be $2x$ and $5x$. Thus,

$$2x + 5x + 82 = 180$$
$$7x = 98$$
$$x = 14$$
$$2x = 28$$
$$5x = 70$$

Smallest angle = 28°

2. **The correct answer is (C).** Let x = number of years for two populations to be equal. Then,

$$6800 - 120x = 4200 + 80x$$
$$2600 = 200x$$
$$x = 13$$

3. **The correct answer is (C).** Simply plug the two values into the formula.

$$2^2 - 2(2) = 0 \text{ and } 1^2 - 2(1) = -1$$

$$*2 - *1 = 0 - (-1) = 1.$$

4. **The correct answer is (B).**

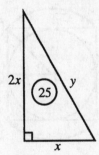

$$\frac{1}{2} \bullet x \bullet 2x = 25$$
$$x^2 = 25$$
$$x = 5$$
$$2x = 10$$
$$y^2 = 5^2 + 10^2$$
$$y^2 = 25 + 100$$
$$y^2 = 125$$
$$y = \sqrt{125} = \sqrt{25 \times 5}$$
$$y = 5\sqrt{5}$$

5. **The correct answer is (D).** The abscissa of Q is 3 more than that of P. The ordinate of Q is 2 less than that of P. Hence, coordinates of Q are $(3 + 3, 7 - 2) = (6, 5)$.

6. **The correct answer is (A).** $r = 5x$

Divide both sides by 10.

$$\frac{r}{10} = \frac{5}{10}x$$
$$\text{or } \frac{1}{10}r = \frac{1}{2}x$$

Hence, 1 is the answer.

7. **The correct answer is (D).** The area of triangle ADE equals the area of triangle AEC, since they have the same base and altitude. The area of triangle ABC equals that of triangle ADC, since the diagonal of a parallelogram divides it equally.

8. **The correct answer is (C).** If the side of a square is s, its diagonal is the hypotenuse of a right triangle with two sides as its legs. The length of the diagonal is

$$\sqrt{s^2 + s^2} = \sqrt{2}s$$

$$0.7\left(\sqrt{2}s\right) \approx (0.7)(1.4)s \approx 1s = s.$$

9. **The correct answer is (D).** This is an inverse proportion; that is:

$$\frac{9}{6} = \frac{x}{120}$$
$$6x = 1080$$
$$x = 180$$

10. **The correct answer is (A).** Thinking of a clock in terms of degrees, there are 360 degrees from 12 noon to 12 midnight. In one hour there are 360 degrees ÷ 12 hours = 30 degrees per hour. In two hours the hour hand moves 2 hours × 30 degrees per hour = 60 degrees. Therefore, in 2 hours and 12 minutes the hour hand moves 66 degrees.

11. **The correct answer is (B).**

$$8 \times 6 = 48$$
$$6 \times 8 = 48$$
$$48 + 48 = 96 \text{ (sum of all 14 numbers)}$$
$$\text{Average} = \frac{96}{14} = 6\frac{6}{7}$$

12. **The correct answer is (D).**

   I. As x increases, $(1 - x^2)$ decreases.

   II. As x increases, $(x - 1)$ increases.

   III. As x increases, $\frac{1}{x^2}$ decreases.

   Hence, only II increases.

13. **The correct answer is (B).** In the 3, 7, 12, 18, 25, differences are 4, 5, 6, 7, 8, . . . etc.

   Thus, the series progresses as follows: 3, 7, 12, 18, 25, 33, 42, 52, 63.

14. **The correct answer is (C).** The numerator is the difference between perfect squares; $x^2 - y^2$ is equal to the product of $(x + y)$ and $(x - y)$. Therefore,

$$\frac{x^2 + y^2}{x - y} = \frac{(x + y)(x - y)}{x - y} = x + y$$

15. **The correct answer is (D).** The distance traveled is the circumference of the wheel times the number of revolutions. If r is the number of revolutions of the back wheel, $r + 10$ will be the number of revolutions of the front wheel. They will have traveled the same distance, so 7 ft. $\times$ $(r + 10) = 9$ ft. $\times r$, and $r = 35$. The wagon has gone 9 ft. $\times$ 35 revolutions = 315 ft.

16. **The correct answer is (D).** The dimensions of the flower bed including the walk are (12 + 6) and (16 + 6). Thus, the area is 18 yds. $\times$ 22 yds = 396 square yds. The area of the flower bed alone is 12 $\times$ 16 = 192 square yds. Therefore, the area of the walk is 396 square yds. $-$ 192 square yds. = 204 square yds.

17. **The correct answer is (C).** Dave takes 30 minutes to wash the car alone.

$$\frac{x}{15} + \frac{x}{30} = 1$$
$$2x + x = 30$$
$$3x = 30$$
$$x = 10$$

18. **The correct answer is (C).** Let r = radius of inscribed circle and s = radius of circumscribed circle. Then, in right triangle OPQ, $PQ = OQ = r$ and $s = OP = r\sqrt{2}$.

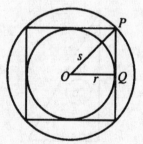

Area of inscribed circle = πr^2

Area of circumscribed circle = $\pi s^2 = \pi\left(r\sqrt{2}\right)^2 = 2\pi r^2$

Ratio = $\dfrac{\pi r^2}{2\pi r^2} = 1{:}2$

19. The correct answer is (B). Let $x =$ number of minutes to fill $\frac{4}{7}$ of bucket. Then,

$$\frac{\frac{3}{7}}{1} = \frac{\frac{4}{7}}{x}, \text{ or } \frac{3}{1} = \frac{4}{x}$$

$$3x = 4 \qquad x = \frac{4}{3}$$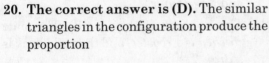

20. The correct answer is (D). The similar triangles in the configuration produce the proportion

$$\frac{3}{5} = \frac{4}{Y}$$

$$3Y = 20$$

$$Y = 6\frac{2}{3}$$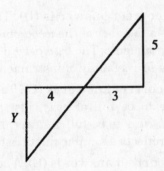

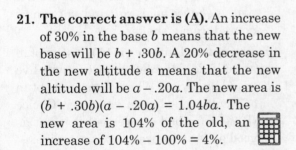

21. The correct answer is (A). An increase of 30% in the base b means that the new base will be $b + .30b$. A 20% decrease in the new altitude a means that the new altitude will be $a - .20a$. The new area is $(b + .30b)(a - .20a) = 1.04ba$. The new area is 104% of the old, an increase of 104% − 100% = 4%.

22. The correct answer is (B). Typing space is $12 - 3 = 9$ inches long and $9 - 2 = 7$ inches wide.

Part used $= \frac{9 \times 7}{9 \times 12} = \frac{7}{12}$.

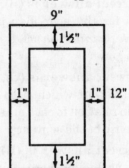

23. The correct answer is (A). Triangle $SPT = \frac{1}{3}\Delta PSR$ since they have common altitude and the base $ST = \frac{1}{3}SR$.

But, $\Delta PSR = \frac{1}{2} \cdot PQRS$.

Hence, $\Delta SPT = \frac{1}{3} \times \frac{1}{2} \times PQRS = \frac{1}{6} \times PQRS$.

24. The correct answer is (D).

$$A = P(1 + rt)$$
$$A = P + Prt$$
$$A - P = Prt$$

Divide both sides by Pr. $t = \frac{A - P}{Pr}$

25. The correct answer is (D).

I. If $p > q$ and $r < 0$, multiplying both sides by r reverses the inequality $pr < qr$.

II. Also, $p + r > q + r$.

III. However, subtracting r from both sides leaves inequality in same order.

Hence, I and II only.

Section 3

1. **The correct answer is (E).** *Tension* is likely to mount before a pitcher delivers the last strike of a game—especially during a pause.

2. **The correct answer is (B).** Funding a hospital for the poor may properly be called a *humanitarian* act. It may or may not be popular.

3. **The correct answer is (C).** This is the only answer in which both words are correct in relation to each other as well as to the sense of the sentence.

4. **The correct answer is (B).** The word that means "having more than one meaning" is *ambiguous*.

5. **The correct answer is (E).** The two sides might negotiate, or bargain, through the night in an attempt to *avert*, or prevent, a strike.

6. **The correct answer is (D).** The missing word must mean the same as "respect for age." The correct choice is *venerated*.

7. **The correct answer is (B).** It is likely that someone who is unprepared would approach an exam with *trepidation*, or apprehension, not with *aplomb* (self-assurance), *indifference* (lack of concern), *confidence*, or *duplicity* (hypocrisy).

8. **The correct answer is (A).** The only word that makes sense in this context is *derelict*, meaning neglectful of duty, or remiss.

9. **The correct answer is (D).** If a show of temper is atypical or unusual, she must be something opposite in meaning. *Equanimity*, or calmness, is the correct choice.

10. **The correct answer is (B).** In this sentence, two negative words are needed, thus eliminating choices (A), (C), and (D), which have at least one positive response. Choice (E) makes no sense. The correct answer is (B), which includes two evidently negative responses. The *craven*, or cowardly, attitudes of politicians may cause them to *cower*, or shrink back, when there is controversy.

11. **The correct answer is (B).** When you *touch* something, you *feel* it. Similarly, when you *look* at something, you *see* it.

12. **The correct answer is (B).** The contrast in shape between a *circle* and a *square* is not unlike that between an *oval* and a *rectangle*.

13. **The correct answer is (B).** The male *chicken* is a *rooster*, and the male *duck* is a *drake*.

14. **The correct answer is (D).** A *trigger* activates a *pistol* and a *switch,* a *motor*.

15. **The correct answer is (B).** *Angelic* is a greater degree of *good*, just as *joyous* is a greater degree of *glad*.

16. **The correct answer is (D).** The *clarinet* is a member of the *woodwind* family of instruments. The *trumpet* is a member of the *brass* family of instruments.

17. **The correct answer is (C).** To be *doleful* is to be full of *grief*, just as to be *wrathful* is to be full of *anger*. No other pair reflects a similar relationship.

18. **The correct answer is (E).** A *pail* holds *water* and water can be poured from a pail. A *shaker* holds *salt* and salt can be poured from a shaker.

19. **The correct answer is (A).** *Fish* kept in an artificial environment in captivity live in an *aquarium*. When *birds* are kept in captivity, they live in an *aviary*. Choice (B) is not a bad answer but it is not as good as (A) because a car is not alive.

20. **The correct answer is (B).** *Disagreement* is characterized by a lack of *concord* (harmony). Similarly, *impartiality* is characterized by a lack of *bias* (prejudice).

21. **The correct answer is (D).** A *year* is a hundredth of a *century*, and a *cent* is a hundredth of a *dollar*.

22. **The correct answer is (B).** A well-known characteristic of a *mule* is that it

is *intractable* (stubborn). Likewise, the *fox* is known for being *wily* (sly and crafty).

23. **The correct answer is (C).** If we *stumble*, our *walking* is impeded, and if we *stammer*, our *speaking* is impeded.

24. **The correct answer is (D).** Introduced as the "little woman" and "despondent matron," Mrs. Bennet is named in paragraph 4. Alcott's epithets for Mrs. Bennet emphasize her weakness.

25. **The correct answer is (A).** Mrs. Bennet's family has left her this mess with as little concern as a swarm of insects might have. Locusts are not particularly horrible; had Alcott used a more potent simile, (D) might be correct.

26. **The correct answer is (E).** Mrs. Gay's presence has a beneficial effect on the chaotic Bennet. All of the other items either directly contribute to the chaos or are by-products of it.

27. **The correct answer is (D).** In this context, *despondent* most nearly means sad, frustrated, or exasperated. This is explained in the context of lines 13–14 during which the reader learns that Mrs. Bennett is crying.

28. **The correct answer is (C).** Before Mrs. Gay's arrival, Mrs. Bennet was about to have "a good cry" (line 18). There is no indication that she would have been able to cope with her household duties.

29. **The correct answer is (C).** The flowers Mrs. Gay brings echo the rosiness of Mrs. Gay herself—she is earlier described as "a large, rosy woman" (line 20).

30. **The correct answer is (B).** In contrast to Mrs. Bennet's disorderly breakfast room, her front parlor is sunny and filled with blooming flowers, which contrast with her sickly children (D). Choice (D) is not the correct response, however, because it only tells part of the story.

31. **The correct answer is (A).** Mrs. Bennet's lack of energy is her primary quality.

32. **The correct answer is (D).** Mrs. Gay, in her practical way, requests the job that is most vital, knowing that to get that job out of the way will improve Mrs. Bennet's spirits.

33. **The correct answer is (D).** Mrs. Gay has a name that suits her, and every speech she makes reveals her good humor and energy.

34. **The correct answer is (A).** Mrs. Bennet seems paralyzed by her situation. The "weariness of her own tired soul and body" oppresses her (lines 15–16), and she surveys her household with despair.

35. **The correct answer is (E).** The last paragraph of the passage best expresses this quality. Mrs. Gay's get-things-done attitude is contrasted with Mrs. Bennet's ineffectiveness.

Section 4
Part 1

1. **The correct answer is (C).** Since dividing by 2 and multiplying by .5 have the same results, the quantities must be equal.

2. **The correct answer is (A).** Since the figure has 5 sides, it contains

   $180(5 - 2) = 540$ degrees

   $540 = x + 110 + 60 + 120 + 100$

   $540 = x + 390$

   $150 = x$

3. **The correct answer is (D).** The problem tells us only that the ratio of m to n is 7 to 10. It is possible, for example, that m is 700 and n is 1000.

4. **The correct answer is (B).** Simply plug the values into the formula.

   Column A $= \dfrac{(-3)(-2)}{-3-(-2)} = \dfrac{6}{-1} = -6$

   Column B $= \dfrac{(-2)(-3)}{-2-(-3)} = \dfrac{6}{1} = 6$

5. **The correct answer is (A).** Notice the right angle at $\angle BAC$. Side BC must be the longest side since it is opposite the largest angle. Since $\angle ADC$ is also a right angle, side AC must be longer than CD.

6. **The correct answer is (C).** Since there are three parallel lines, the corresponding angles are equal. If x, y, and z are all the same, then $x + y$ must equal $y + z$.

7. **The correct answer is (C).** Since $3\% = .03$ and $4\% = .04$, then $.03 \times .04 = .0012$.

8. **The correct answer is (A).** $7.88 divided by 2 equals $3.94. $11.79 divided by 3 equals $3.93.

9. **The correct answer is (B).** When an angle is inscribed in a circle, the arc is twice the angle. AB equals 2 times 50, which is 100.

10. **The correct answer is (A).** $\sqrt{8}$ is almost 3. $\sqrt{24}$ is almost 5. Thus, Column A is close to 8. This is larger than $\sqrt{32}$, which is less than 6.

11. **The correct answer is (B).** Since there are more digits in Box B, it must contain more possibilities.

12. **The correct answer is (D).** There is no way to determine the relative values of a, b, and c.

13. **The correct answer is (B).**

    We can substitute -1 for $(p - q)$.

    $p^2 - q^2 = (p + q)(p - q) = 4$. 1 for $(p - q)$.

    $(p + q)(-1) = 4$

    $(p + q) = -4$

14. **The correct answer is (D).** The information tells us about percents only. We do not know how many boys or girls are in the class.

15. **The correct answer is (D).** While p, q, and r are positive, we do not know whether they are fractions. If the three variables were $\frac{1}{2}$, $\frac{1}{3}$, and $\frac{1}{4}$, the sum of the variables would be greater than the product.

Part 2

16. $\left(\sqrt{18} - \sqrt{8}\right)^2$

    $= \left(3\sqrt{2} - 2\sqrt{2}\right)^2$

    $= \left(\sqrt{2}\right)^2 = 2$

17.

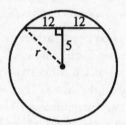

A radius drawn perpendicular to a chord bisects the chord. Construct the radius as shown above.

$5^2 + 12^2 = r^2$

$25 + 144 = r^2$

$r^2 = 169$

$r = 13$

18. $\dfrac{x}{11} = 15$

    $x = 165$

    $\dfrac{165}{20} = 8.25$

19.

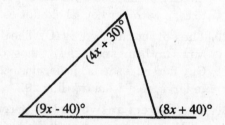

An exterior angle of a triangle is equal to the sum of the two remote interior angles.

$8x + 40 = (9x - 40) + (4x + 30)$

$8x + 40 = 13 - 10$

$5x = 50$

$x = 10$

$\angle J = (4x + 30)° = (40 + 30)° = 70°$

20. $\dfrac{2^2+3^2}{5^2}+\dfrac{1}{10}=\dfrac{4+9}{25}+\dfrac{1}{10}$

$\qquad\qquad\qquad =\dfrac{13}{25}+\dfrac{1}{10}$

The least common denominator is 50.

$=\dfrac{26}{50}+\dfrac{5}{50}=\dfrac{31}{50}=.62$

21. The shaded area is the area of the rect-angle minus the area of the two circles.

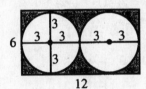

Area of the rectangle $= 6(12) = 72$

Area of circle $= \pi r^2 = 9\pi$

Shaded area $= 72 - 2(9\pi)$

$\qquad\qquad\quad = 72 - 18\pi$

$\qquad\qquad\quad = a - b\pi$

$\therefore a = 72$ and $b = 18$

22.

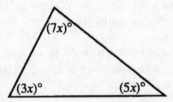

Let $3x =$ the measure of one of the angles

$5x =$ the measure of the 2nd angle

$7x =$ the measure of the 3rd angle

$3x+5x+7x = 180$

$\qquad\quad 15x = 180$

$\qquad\qquad x = 12$

The smallest angle $= 3x = 36°$.

23. $d=\sqrt{\left(x_2-x_1\right)^2+\left(y_2-y_1\right)^2}$

$\quad =\sqrt{\left(3-(-4)\right)^2+\left(-2-5\right)^2}$

$\quad =\sqrt{7^2+(-7)^2}$

$\quad =\sqrt{49+49}=\sqrt{98}=\sqrt{49}\sqrt{2}$

$\quad =7\sqrt{2}=b\sqrt{2}$

$\therefore b = 7$

24. $\dfrac{9+9+10+x+y}{5}=10$

$\qquad 28+x+y = 50$

$\qquad\qquad x+y = 22$

The average of x and y is

$\dfrac{x+y}{2}=\dfrac{22}{2}=11$

25.

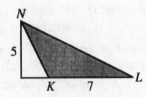

Area $\triangle NKL = \dfrac{1}{2}(b)(h)$

$\qquad\qquad\quad = \dfrac{1}{2}(7)(5) = 17.5 = \dfrac{35}{2}$

Section 5

1. **The correct answer is (E).** The author makes the point that Mary's work was most unusual because women did not work in the public arena during the mid-nineteenth century.

2. **The correct answer is (A).** The passage, with its emphasis on Mary's history of standing up for human rights, certainly implies that previous injustices influenced her later work with workers.

3. **The correct answer is (A).** The passage clearly states that Mary's family joined the Irish rebels.

4. **The correct answer is (B).** When Mary found herself homeless (lines 33–34), she lived at the union hall and became involved with the Knights of Labor.

5. **The correct answer is (A).** The context of the sentence that mentions that employers could reduce wages whenever they wished supports the choice of (A).

6. **The correct answer is (C).** The passage clearly states (lines 50–51) that Debs founded the American Railway Union.

7. **The correct answer is (E).** The context of the sentence indicates that "a group of citizens" is the best choice.

8. **The correct answer is (D).** During Carson's lifetime, the response to her work was negative and hostile; it was only later that her work was appreciated for its vision.

9. **The correct answer is (A).** Carson's work concerned the effect of pesticides on the environment (lines 106–107).

10. **The correct answer is (C).** Nowhere in the passage are breathing difficulties mentioned as a side effect of using insecticides.

11. **The correct answer is (C).** The passage mentions arsenic (lines 125–127) as the most toxic ingredient.

12. **The correct answer is (C).** The choice must be "belief in a cause," as the other choices are contrary to the picture painted of each woman in the passages.

Section 6

1. **The correct answer is (D).**

$$\frac{4}{5} = .8$$

$$\frac{7}{9} = 9\overline{)7.00} \quad .78$$

$$\frac{5}{7} = 7\overline{)5.00} \quad .71$$

$$\frac{9}{11} = 11\overline{)9.00} \quad .82$$

Thus, $\frac{5}{7}$ is the smallest quantity.

2. **The correct answer is (B).** Let $x =$ amount earned each month. $2x =$ amount earned in December. Then,

$$11x + 2x = 13x \text{ (entire earnings).}$$

$$\frac{2x}{13x} = \frac{2}{13}$$

3. **The correct answer is (B).**

$$3x^3 + 2x^2 + x + 1$$

$$= 3(-1)^3 + 2(-1)^2 + (-1) + 1$$

$$= 3(-1) + 2(1) - 1 + 1$$

$$= -3 + 2 + 0$$

$$= -1$$

4. **The correct answer is (E).** Convert the percent to decimal form before multiplying.

$$.03\% = .0003$$

$$.0003 \times .21 = .000063$$

The number of decimal places in the product must be equal to the sum of the number of decimal places in the terms to be multiplied.

5. **The correct answer is (C).** Since the ratio of the sides is 3:1, the ratio of the areas is 9:1.

The subdivision into 9Δ is shown.

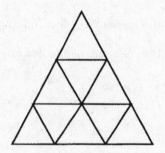

6. **The correct answer is (E).** The opposite vertices may be any of the number pairs (1±5, 1±5), or (6, 6), (−4, −4), (−4, 6), and (6, −4).

   Thus, (4, −6) is not possible.

7. **The correct answer is (D).**

   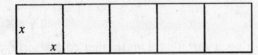

   Perimeter of rectangle $= x+5x+x+5x$

   Thus, $12x = 372$

   $x = 31$

   Area of square $= 31^2 = 961$

8. **The correct answer is (B).** Four inches is $\frac{1}{3}$ ft. The volume of the added level is $75 \times 42 \times \frac{1}{3} = 1,050$ cubic ft. There are 7.48 gallons in 1 cubic ft., so 1050 cubic ft. × 7.48 gal./cubic ft. = 7,854 gallons.

9. **The correct answer is (A).** There are 360 degrees in a circle. A 24-degree sector is $\frac{24}{360} = .067$, or about $6\frac{2}{3}\%$ of a circle.

10. **The correct answer is (A).** In these fractions the numerator n is always less than the denominator d. After squaring the fraction $\left(\frac{n}{d}\right)^2 = \frac{n^2}{d^2}$, the new fraction is less than the original since the denominator is getting larger faster than the numerator.

Computing Your Scores

To check your progress in preparing for the SAT, you need to compute individual verbal and mathematical raw scores for this practice test. Once you have computed these, use the conversion scales in the section that follows to compute your SAT scaled scores (200–800). Keep in mind that these formulas have been simplified to give you a "quick and dirty" sense of where you are scoring, not a perfectly precise score.

To Compute Your Raw Scores

1 Enter the number of correct answers for each verbal and mathematical reasoning section into the boxes marked Number of Questions Correct.

2 Enter the number of incorrect answers (not blanks) for each verbal and mathematical reasoning section into the boxes marked Number of Questions Incorrect.

3 Total the number correct and number incorrect.

4 Follow this formula: Take the total correct and minus one quarter of the total incorrect. Round up in your favor to compute your raw score.

Verbal Section	Total Number of Questions	Number of Questions Correct	Number of Questions Incorrect
1	31		
3	35		
5	12		
Totals	78	Total Correct:	Total Incorrect:

Verbal Raw Score = Total Correct – ($\frac{1}{4}$ × Total Incorrect) = _____

Math Section	Total Number of Questions	Number of Questions Correct	Number of Questions Incorrect
2	25		
4	25		
6	10		
Totals	60	Total Correct:	Total Incorrect:

Math Raw Score = Total Correct – ($\frac{1}{4}$ × Total Incorrect) = _____

CONVERSION SCALES

VERBAL REASONING

Raw Score	Scaled Score	Raw Score	Scaled Score
75	800	35	520
70	800	30	480
65	760	25	440
60	650	20	410
55	670	15	370
50	620	10	340
45	590	5	290
40	550	0	230

MATHEMATICAL REASONING

Raw Score	Scaled Score	Raw Score	Scaled Score
60	800	25	510
55	760	20	480
50	690	15	440
45	650	10	410
40	610	5	340
35	580	0	280
30	550		

Although you now have some idea of what your scores would look like had they been scaled according to unofficial ETS standards, you will probably want to know how to interpret your raw scores in more familiar terms. If so, use the following Self-Evaluation Charts to see what your raw scores actually mean.

SELF–EVALUATION CHARTS

VERBAL REASONING: Raw Score		MATHEMATICAL REASONING: Raw Score	
Excellent	60–75	Excellent	50–60
Good	50–59	Good	40–49
Average	30–49	Average	20–39
Fair	20–29	Fair	10–19
Poor	0–19	Poor	0–9

PRACTICE TEST 3

Answer Sheet

If a section has fewer questions than answer ovals, leave the extra ovals blank.

SECTION 1

1 (A) (B) (C) (D) (E)   11 (A) (B) (C) (D) (E)   21 (A) (B) (C) (D) (E)   31 (A) (B) (C) (D) (E)
2 (A) (B) (C) (D) (E)   12 (A) (B) (C) (D) (E)   22 (A) (B) (C) (D) (E)   32 (A) (B) (C) (D) (E)
3 (A) (B) (C) (D) (E)   13 (A) (B) (C) (D) (E)   23 (A) (B) (C) (D) (E)   33 (A) (B) (C) (D) (E)
4 (A) (B) (C) (D) (E)   14 (A) (B) (C) (D) (E)   24 (A) (B) (C) (D) (E)   34 (A) (B) (C) (D) (E)
5 (A) (B) (C) (D) (E)   15 (A) (B) (C) (D) (E)   25 (A) (B) (C) (D) (E)   35 (A) (B) (C) (D) (E)
6 (A) (B) (C) (D) (E)   16 (A) (B) (C) (D) (E)   26 (A) (B) (C) (D) (E)   36 (A) (B) (C) (D) (E)
7 (A) (B) (C) (D) (E)   17 (A) (B) (C) (D) (E)   27 (A) (B) (C) (D) (E)   37 (A) (B) (C) (D) (E)
8 (A) (B) (C) (D) (E)   18 (A) (B) (C) (D) (E)   28 (A) (B) (C) (D) (E)   38 (A) (B) (C) (D) (E)
9 (A) (B) (C) (D) (E)   19 (A) (B) (C) (D) (E)   29 (A) (B) (C) (D) (E)   39 (A) (B) (C) (D) (E)
10 (A) (B) (C) (D) (E)   20 (A) (B) (C) (D) (E)   30 (A) (B) (C) (D) (E)   40 (A) (B) (C) (D) (E)

SECTION 2

1 (A) (B) (C) (D) (E)   11 (A) (B) (C) (D) (E)   21 (A) (B) (C) (D) (E)   31 (A) (B) (C) (D) (E)
2 (A) (B) (C) (D) (E)   12 (A) (B) (C) (D) (E)   22 (A) (B) (C) (D) (E)   32 (A) (B) (C) (D) (E)
3 (A) (B) (C) (D) (E)   13 (A) (B) (C) (D) (E)   23 (A) (B) (C) (D) (E)   33 (A) (B) (C) (D) (E)
4 (A) (B) (C) (D) (E)   14 (A) (B) (C) (D) (E)   24 (A) (B) (C) (D) (E)   34 (A) (B) (C) (D) (E)
5 (A) (B) (C) (D) (E)   15 (A) (B) (C) (D) (E)   25 (A) (B) (C) (D) (E)   35 (A) (B) (C) (D) (E)
6 (A) (B) (C) (D) (E)   16 (A) (B) (C) (D) (E)   26 (A) (B) (C) (D) (E)   36 (A) (B) (C) (D) (E)
7 (A) (B) (C) (D) (E)   17 (A) (B) (C) (D) (E)   27 (A) (B) (C) (D) (E)   37 (A) (B) (C) (D) (E)
8 (A) (B) (C) (D) (E)   18 (A) (B) (C) (D) (E)   28 (A) (B) (C) (D) (E)   38 (A) (B) (C) (D) (E)
9 (A) (B) (C) (D) (E)   19 (A) (B) (C) (D) (E)   29 (A) (B) (C) (D) (E)   39 (A) (B) (C) (D) (E)
10 (A) (B) (C) (D) (E)   20 (A) (B) (C) (D) (E)   30 (A) (B) (C) (D) (E)   40 (A) (B) (C) (D) (E)

SECTION 3

Answer spaces for Section 3 are on the back of this Answer Sheet.

SECTION 4

1 (A) (B) (C) (D) (E)   11 (A) (B) (C) (D) (E)   21 (A) (B) (C) (D) (E)   31 (A) (B) (C) (D) (E)
2 (A) (B) (C) (D) (E)   12 (A) (B) (C) (D) (E)   22 (A) (B) (C) (D) (E)   32 (A) (B) (C) (D) (E)
3 (A) (B) (C) (D) (E)   13 (A) (B) (C) (D) (E)   23 (A) (B) (C) (D) (E)   33 (A) (B) (C) (D) (E)
4 (A) (B) (C) (D) (E)   14 (A) (B) (C) (D) (E)   24 (A) (B) (C) (D) (E)   34 (A) (B) (C) (D) (E)
5 (A) (B) (C) (D) (E)   15 (A) (B) (C) (D) (E)   25 (A) (B) (C) (D) (E)   35 (A) (B) (C) (D) (E)
6 (A) (B) (C) (D) (E)   16 (A) (B) (C) (D) (E)   26 (A) (B) (C) (D) (E)   36 (A) (B) (C) (D) (E)
7 (A) (B) (C) (D) (E)   17 (A) (B) (C) (D) (E)   27 (A) (B) (C) (D) (E)   37 (A) (B) (C) (D) (E)
8 (A) (B) (C) (D) (E)   18 (A) (B) (C) (D) (E)   28 (A) (B) (C) (D) (E)   38 (A) (B) (C) (D) (E)
9 (A) (B) (C) (D) (E)   19 (A) (B) (C) (D) (E)   29 (A) (B) (C) (D) (E)   39 (A) (B) (C) (D) (E)
10 (A) (B) (C) (D) (E)   20 (A) (B) (C) (D) (E)   30 (A) (B) (C) (D) (E)   40 (A) (B) (C) (D) (E)

SECTION 5

1 (A) (B) (C) (D) (E)   6 (A) (B) (C) (D) (E)   11 (A) (B) (C) (D) (E)
2 (A) (B) (C) (D) (E)   7 (A) (B) (C) (D) (E)   12 (A) (B) (C) (D) (E)
3 (A) (B) (C) (D) (E)   8 (A) (B) (C) (D) (E)   13 (A) (B) (C) (D) (E)
4 (A) (B) (C) (D) (E)   9 (A) (B) (C) (D) (E)   14 (A) (B) (C) (D) (E)
5 (A) (B) (C) (D) (E)   10 (A) (B) (C) (D) (E)   15 (A) (B) (C) (D) (E)

TEAR HERE

SECTION 6

1 Ⓐ Ⓑ Ⓒ Ⓓ Ⓔ   6 Ⓐ Ⓑ Ⓒ Ⓓ Ⓔ   11 Ⓐ Ⓑ Ⓒ Ⓓ Ⓔ
2 Ⓐ Ⓑ Ⓒ Ⓓ Ⓔ   7 Ⓐ Ⓑ Ⓒ Ⓓ Ⓔ   12 Ⓐ Ⓑ Ⓒ Ⓓ Ⓔ
3 Ⓐ Ⓑ Ⓒ Ⓓ Ⓔ   8 Ⓐ Ⓑ Ⓒ Ⓓ Ⓔ   13 Ⓐ Ⓑ Ⓒ Ⓓ Ⓔ
4 Ⓐ Ⓑ Ⓒ Ⓓ Ⓔ   9 Ⓐ Ⓑ Ⓒ Ⓓ Ⓔ   14 Ⓐ Ⓑ Ⓒ Ⓓ Ⓔ
5 Ⓐ Ⓑ Ⓒ Ⓓ Ⓔ   10 Ⓐ Ⓑ Ⓒ Ⓓ Ⓔ   15 Ⓐ Ⓑ Ⓒ Ⓓ Ⓔ

SECTION 3

1 Ⓐ Ⓑ Ⓒ Ⓓ Ⓔ   6 Ⓐ Ⓑ Ⓒ Ⓓ Ⓔ   11 Ⓐ Ⓑ Ⓒ Ⓓ Ⓔ
2 Ⓐ Ⓑ Ⓒ Ⓓ Ⓔ   7 Ⓐ Ⓑ Ⓒ Ⓓ Ⓔ   12 Ⓐ Ⓑ Ⓒ Ⓓ Ⓔ
3 Ⓐ Ⓑ Ⓒ Ⓓ Ⓔ   8 Ⓐ Ⓑ Ⓒ Ⓓ Ⓔ   13 Ⓐ Ⓑ Ⓒ Ⓓ Ⓔ
4 Ⓐ Ⓑ Ⓒ Ⓓ Ⓔ   9 Ⓐ Ⓑ Ⓒ Ⓓ Ⓔ   14 Ⓐ Ⓑ Ⓒ Ⓓ Ⓔ
5 Ⓐ Ⓑ Ⓒ Ⓓ Ⓔ   10 Ⓐ Ⓑ Ⓒ Ⓓ Ⓔ   15 Ⓐ Ⓑ Ⓒ Ⓓ Ⓔ

Note: ONLY the answers entered on the grid are scored.

Handwritten answers at the top of the column are NOT scored.

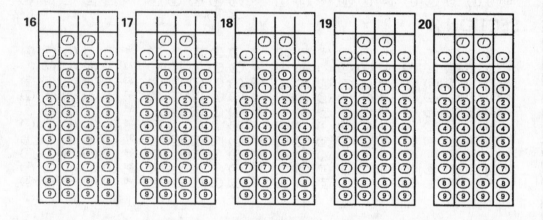

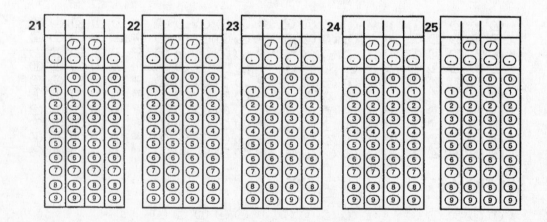

TEAR HERE

PRACTICE TEST 3
Section 1

25 Questions • Time—30 Minutes

> **Directions:** Solve the following problems using any available space on the page for scratchwork. On your answer sheet fill in the choice that best corresponds to the correct answer.
>
> **Notes:** The figures accompanying the problems are drawn as accurately as possible unless otherwise stated in specific problems. Again, unless otherwise stated, all figures lie in the same plane. All numbers used in these problems are real numbers. Calculators are permitted for this test.

Circle: Rectangle: Rectangular Solid: Cylinder: Triangle:

$C = 2\pi r$ $A = lw$ $V = lwh$ $V = \pi r^2 h$ $A = \frac{1}{2}bh$ $a^2 + b^2 = c^2$
$A = \pi r^2$

The number of degrees of arc in a circle is 360.
The measure in degrees of a straight angle is 180.
The sum of the measures in degrees of the angles of a triangle is 180.

1. If $9x + 5 = 23$, what is the numerical value of $18x + 5$?

   (A) 46

   (B) 41

   (C) 36

   (D) 32

   (E) It cannot be determined from the information given.

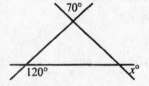

2. In the figure above, $x =$

   (A) 35

   (B) 50

   (C) 70

   (D) 90

   (E) 110

3. If $2y = \dfrac{1}{3}$, then $\dfrac{1}{4y} =$

   (A) $\dfrac{3}{2}$

   (B) $\dfrac{3}{4}$

   (C) $\dfrac{2}{5}$

   (D) $\dfrac{1}{5}$

   (E) $\dfrac{4}{3}$

4. Pieces of wire are soldered together so as to form the edges of a cube, whose volume is 64 cubic inches. The number of inches of wire used is

   (A) 24

   (B) 48

   (C) 64

   (D) 96

   (E) 120

5. If a box of notepaper costs \$4.20 after a 40% discount, what was its original price?

   (A) \$2.52

   (B) \$4.60

   (C) \$5.33

   (D) \$7.00

   (E) \$10.50

6. *A* is 15 years old. *B* is one-third older. How many years ago was *B* twice as old as *A*?

   (A) 3

   (B) 5

   (C) 7.5

   (D) 8

   (E) 10

7. The distance, *s*, in feet that an object falls in *t* seconds when dropped from a height is obtained by use of the formula $s = 16t^2$. How many feet will an object fall in 8 seconds?

   (A) 256

   (B) 1,024

   (C) 2,048

   (D) 15,384

   (E) 16,000

8. Three circles are tangent externally to each other and have radii of 2 inches, 3 inches, and 4 inches, respectively. How many inches are in the perimeter of the triangle formed by joining the centers of the three circles?

   (A) 9

   (B) 12

   (C) 15

   (D) 18

   (E) 21

9. One tenth is what part of three fourths?

   (A) $\dfrac{3}{40}$

   (B) $\dfrac{1}{8}$

   (C) $\dfrac{2}{15}$

   (D) $\dfrac{15}{2}$

   (E) $\dfrac{40}{3}$

10. The area of square *PQRS* is 49. What are the coordinates of *Q*?

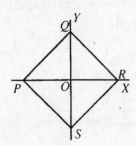

(A) $(\frac{7}{2}\sqrt{2}, 0)$

(B) $(0, \frac{7}{2}\sqrt{2})$

(C) $(0, 7)$

(D) $(7, 0)$

(E) $(0, 7\sqrt{2})$

11. If one half of the female students in a certain college eat in the cafeteria and one third of the male students eat there, what fractional part of the student body eats in the cafeteria?

(A) $\frac{5}{12}$

(B) $\frac{2}{5}$

(C) $\frac{3}{4}$

(D) $\frac{5}{6}$

(E) It cannot be determined from the information given.

12. A recent report states that if you were to eat each meal in a different restaurant in New York City, it would take you more than 19 years to cover all of New York City's eating places, assuming that you eat three meals a day. On the basis of this information, the number of restaurants in New York City

(A) exceeds 20,500.

(B) is closer to 20,000 than 21,000.

(C) exceeds 21,000.

(D) exceeds 21,000 but does not exceed 21,500.

(E) is less than 20,500.

13. In the figure below, *AB = BC* and angle *BEA* is a right angle. If the length of *DE* is four times the length of *BE*, then what is the ratio of the area of Δ*ACD* to the area of Δ*ABC*?

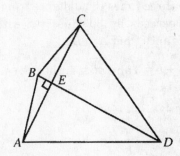

(A) 1:4

(B) 1:2

(C) 2:1

(D) 4:1

(E) It cannot be determined from the information given.

14. A pound of water is evaporated from 6 pounds of seawater containing 4% salt. The percentage of salt in the remaining solution is

(A) 3.6%

(B) 4%

(C) 4.8%

(D) 5.2%

(E) 6%

15. The product of 75^3 and 75^7 is

    (A) $(75)^5$

    (B) $(75)^{10}$

    (C) $(150)^{10}$

    (D) $(5625)^{10}$

    (E) $(75)^{21}$

16. The distance from City A to City B is 150 miles and the distance from City A to City C is 90 miles. Therefore, it is necessarily true that

    (A) the distance between B to C is 60 miles.

    (B) six times the distance from A to B equals 10 times the distance from A to C.

    (C) the distance from B to C is 240 miles.

    (D) the distance from A to B exceeds by 30 miles twice the distance from A to C.

    (E) three times the distance from A to C exceeds by 30 miles twice the distance from A to B.

17. If $a + b = 3$ and $ab = 4$, then $\frac{1}{a} + \frac{1}{b}$

    (A) $\frac{3}{4}$

    (B) $\frac{3}{7}$

    (C) $\frac{4}{7}$

    (D) $\frac{1}{7}$

    (E) $\frac{1}{12}$

18. $(x)^6 + (2x^2)^3 + (3x^3)^2 =$

    (A) $5x^5 + x^6$

    (B) $17x^5 + x^6$

    (C) $6x^6$

    (D) $18x^6$

    (E) $6x^{18}$

19. The scale of a map is $\frac{3}{4}$ inch = 10 miles. If the distance on the map between two towns is 6 inches, the actual distance in miles is

    (A) 45

    (B) 60

    (C) 75

    (D) 80

    (E) 90

20. If $d = m - \frac{50}{m}$, and m is a positive number, then as m increases in value, d

    (A) increases in value.

    (B) decreases in value.

    (C) remains unchanged.

    (D) increases, then decreases.

    (E) decreases, then increases.

21. If a cubic inch of metal weighs 2 pounds, a cubic foot of the same metal weighs how many pounds?

    (A) 8

    (B) 24

    (C) 96

    (D) 288

    (E) 3,456

22. If the number of square inches in the area of a circle is equal to the number of inches in its circumference, the diameter of the circle in inches is

    (A) 4

    (B) π

    (C) 2

    (D) $\frac{\pi}{2}$

    (E) 1

23. John is now three times Pat's age. Four years from now John will be x years old. In terms of x, how old is Pat now?

   (A) $\dfrac{x+4}{3}$

   (B) $3x$

   (C) $x + 4$

   (D) $x - 4$

   (E) $\dfrac{x-4}{3}$

24. When the fractions $\frac{2}{3}$, $\frac{5}{7}$, $\frac{8}{11}$, and $\frac{9}{13}$ are arranged in ascending order of size, the result is

   (A) $\dfrac{8}{11}, \dfrac{5}{7}, \dfrac{9}{13}, \dfrac{2}{3}$

   (B) $\dfrac{5}{7}, \dfrac{8}{11}, \dfrac{2}{3}, \dfrac{9}{13}$

   (C) $\dfrac{2}{3}, \dfrac{8}{11}, \dfrac{5}{7}, \dfrac{9}{13}$

   (D) $\dfrac{2}{3}, \dfrac{9}{13}, \dfrac{5}{7}, \dfrac{8}{11}$

   (E) $\dfrac{9}{13}, \dfrac{2}{3}, \dfrac{8}{11}, \dfrac{5}{7}$

25. In a certain course, a student takes eight tests, all of which count equally. When figuring out the final grade, the instructor drops the best and the worst grades and averages the other six. The student calculates that his average for all eight tests is 84%. After dropping the best and the worst grades the student averages 86%. What was the average of the best and the worst test?

   (A) 68

   (B) 72

   (C) 78

   (D) 88

   (E) It cannot be determined from the information given.

STOP

END OF SECTION 1. IF YOU HAVE ANY TIME LEFT, GO OVER YOUR WORK IN THIS SECTION ONLY. DO NOT WORK IN ANY OTHER SECTION OF THE TEST.

Section 2

31 Questions • Time—30 Minutes

> **Directions:** Each of the following questions consists of an incomplete sentence followed by five words or pairs of words. Choose that word or pair of words that, when substituted for the blank space or spaces, best completes the meaning of the sentence and mark the letter of your choice on your answer sheet.

Example

> **Q** In view of the extenuating circumstances and the defendant's youth, the judge recommended ____.
>
> (A) conviction
> (B) a defense
> (C) a mistrial
> (D) leniency
> (E) life imprisonment
>
> **A**

1. Unsure of her skills in English, the young girl was ____ when called on to speak in class.

    (A) remunerative
    (B) transient
    (C) reticent
    (D) sartorial
    (E) resilient

2. Anyone familiar with the facts could ____ his arguments, which seemed logical but were actually ____ .

    (A) refute..specious
    (B) support..protracted
    (C) repeat..recumbent
    (D) review..cogent
    (E) elicit..prodigious

3. Each spring the ____ tree put out fewer and fewer leaves.

    (A) ambient
    (B) malignant
    (C) desultory
    (D) moribund
    (E) reclusive

4. The building had been ____ ; she could not even be sure exactly where it had stood.

    (A) jettisoned
    (B) debilitated
    (C) mitigated
    (D) berated
    (E) obliterated

5. The bully's menacing, ____ manner was actually just for show; in reality it was entirely ____ .

    (A) imperturbable..vapid
    (B) truculent..affected
    (C) stringent..credulous
    (D) supercilious..blatant
    (E) parsimonious..contentious

6. The municipality attracted the country's scientific elite and ____ them, insulating them entirely from the problems of ordinary civilian life.

   (A) cajoled
   (B) muted
   (C) mused
   (D) cosseted
   (E) impeded

7. Although the bank executive gave the appearance of a ____ businessman, he was really a ____.

   (A) dedicated..capitalist
   (B) respectable..reprobate
   (C) depraved..profligate
   (D) empathetic..philanthropist
   (E) churlish..miscreant

8. During a campaign, politicians often engage in ____ debate, attacking each other's proposals in a torrent of ____ words.

   (A) acerbic..amiable
   (B) acrimonious..angry
   (C) intensive..nebulous
   (D) garrulous..inarticulate
   (E) impassioned..vapid

9. He was uneven in his approach to the problem, at once ____ and ____.

   (A) surly..unwilling
   (B) sincere..well-meaning
   (C) harmonious..foolhardy
   (D) conscientious..frivolous
   (E) careless..insouciant

Directions: Each of the following questions consists of a capitalized pair of words followed by five pairs of words lettered (A) to (E). The capitalized words bear some meaningful relationship to each other. Choose the lettered pair of words whose relationship is most similar to that expressed by the capitalized pair and mark its letter on your answer sheet.

Example:

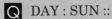 DAY : SUN ::

   (A) sunlight : daylight
   (B) ray: sun
   (C) night : moon
   (D) heat : cold
   (E) moon : star

10. PEEL : APPLE ::

   (A) skin : knee
   (B) sail : boat
   (C) shell : lobster
   (D) pit : grape
   (E) coat : fur

11. FINGER : RING ::

   (A) neck : necklace
   (B) bandage : wound
   (C) bracelet : wrist
   (D) glove : hand
   (E) lip : tune

12. ADULT : CHILD ::

   (A) mother : baby
   (B) sheep : lamb
   (C) cow : calf
   (D) puppy : baby
   (E) buck : fawn

13. PEPPER : SEASON ::
   (A) cinnamon : prepare
   (B) sugar : sweeten
   (C) celery : plant
   (D) accent : cook
   (E) salt : taste

14. BEEF : JERKY ::
   (A) corn : flake
   (B) ham : pork
   (C) grape : raisin
   (D) meat : sausage
   (E) flesh : bone

15. SCHOOL : FISH ::
   (A) herd : cows
   (B) cars : traffic
   (C) dog : puppy
   (D) bird : wing
   (E) pig : barn

Directions: Each passage below is followed by a set of questions. Read each passage, then answer the accompanying questions, basing your answers on what is stated or implied in the passage and any introductory material provided. Mark the letter of your choice on your answer sheet.

Questions 16–23 are based on the following passage.

The following speech was delivered at the height of the 1960s civil rights movement by Dr. Martin Luther King, head of the Southern Christian Leadership Conference and the movement's most eloquent spokesperson.

We have come to this hallowed spot to remind America of the fierce urgency of now. This is no time to engage in the luxury of cooling off or to take the tran-
(5) quilizing drug of gradualism. Now is the time to make real the promises of democracy. Now is the time to rise from the dark and desolate valley of segregation to the sunlit path of racial justice. Now
(10) is the time to lift our nation from the quicksand of racial injustice to the solid rock of brotherhood. Now is the time to make justice a reality for all of God's children.
(15)   It would be fatal for the nation to overlook the urgency of the moment. This sweltering summer of the Negro's legitimate discontent will not pass until there is an invigorating autumn of free-
(20) dom and equality. Those who hope that the Negro needed to blow off steam and will now be content will have a rude awakening if the nation returns to business as usual. There will be neither rest
(25) nor tranquility in America until the Negro is granted his citizenship rights. The whirlwinds of revolt will continue to shake the foundations of our nation until the bright day of justice emerges.
(30)   But that is something that I must say to my people who stand on the warm threshold which leads into the palace of justice. In the process of gaining our rightful place we must not be guilty of
(35) wrongful deeds. Let us not seek to satisfy our thirst for freedom by drinking from the cup of bitterness and hatred.
     We must forever conduct our struggle on the high plane of dignity and
(40) discipline. We must not allow our creative protest to degenerate into physical violence. Again and again we must rise to the majestic heights of meeting physi-

cal force with soul force. The marvelous
(45) new militancy which has engulfed the
Negro community must not lead us to a
distrust of all white people, for many of
our white brothers, as evidenced by their
presence here today, have come to real-
(50) ize that their destiny is tied up with our
destiny. And they have come to realize
that their freedom is inextricably bound
to our freedom. We cannot walk alone.

As we walk, we must make the
(55) pledge that we shall always march ahead.
We cannot turn back. There are those
who are asking the devotees of civil
rights, "When will you be satisfied?" We
can never be satisfied as long as the
(60) Negro is the victim of the unspeakable
horrors of police brutality. We can never
be satisfied as long as the Negro's basic
mobility is from a smaller ghetto to a
larger one. We can never be satisfied as
(65) long as our children are stripped of their
selfhood and robbed of their dignity by
signs stating "For Whites Only." We
cannot be satisfied as long as a Negro in
Mississippi cannot vote and a Negro in
(70) New York believes he has nothing for
which to vote. No, no, we are not satisfied, and we will not be satisfied until
justice rolls down like waters and righteousness like a mighty stream.

(75) I am not unmindful that some of
you have come out of great trials and
tribulations. Some of you have come
fresh from narrow jail cells. Some of you
have come from areas where your quest
(80) for freedom left you battered by the
storms of persecution and staggered by
the winds of police brutality. You have
been the veterans of creative suffering.
Continue to work with the faith that
(85) unearned suffering is redemptive.

Go back to Mississippi, go back to
Alabama, go back to South Carolina, go
back to Louisiana, go back to the slums
and ghettos of our Northern cities, know-
(90) ing that somehow this situation can and
will be changed. Let us not wallow in the
valley of despair.

16. When King says in line 85 that "unearned suffering is redemptive," he means that it
   (A) provokes police brutality.
   (B) confers sanctity, or holiness, upon the sufferer.
   (C) is bound to continue forever.
   (D) strips children of their dignity or self-worth.
   (E) will never be repaid.

17. In the passage, King's attitude is generally
   (A) prejudiced.
   (B) cynical.
   (C) fearful.
   (D) optimistic.
   (E) neutral.

18. Which quotation best suggests the main idea of the speech?
   (A) ". . . we must not be guilty of wrongful deeds."
   (B) "We cannot walk alone."
   (C) "We can never be satisfied as long as the Negro's basic mobility is from a smaller ghetto to a larger one."
   (D) ". . . to remind America of the fierce urgency of now."
   (E) ". . . this situation can and will be changed."

19. The tone of this speech can best be described as
   (A) inspirational.
   (B) boastful.
   (C) defiant.
   (D) sad.
   (E) buoyant.

20. King's attitude toward white Americans appears to be based on
   (A) noncommitment.
   (B) contempt for authority.
   (C) mutual distrust.
   (D) mutual respect.
   (E) negativism.

21. King's remarks indicate that he considers the racial problem a national problem because
   (A) all white Americans are prejudiced.
   (B) African Americans are moving to the suburbs.
   (C) all areas of American life are affected.
   (D) the United States Constitution supports segregation.
   (E) laws will be broken if the problem is left unattended.

22. In the passage, King implies that the struggle for racial justice can be best won through
   (A) marching on Washington.
   (B) civil disorder.
   (C) creative protest.
   (D) challenging unjust laws.
   (E) doing nothing.

23. In this speech, King specifically recommends
   (A) nonviolent resistance.
   (B) faith in God.
   (C) Communist ideas.
   (D) social turmoil.
   (E) turbulent revolt.

Questions 24–31 are based on the following passage.

Agustín Yáñez was the author of many short stories, most of them based in or around Guadalajara, Mexico, his hometown. "Alda," from which this passage is excerpted, is from a collection entitled Archipiélago de Mujeres.

I never met my first love. She must have been a sweet and sad child. Her photographs inspire my imagination to reconstruct the outlines of her soul, simple and
(5) austere as a primitive church, extensive as a castle, stately as a tower, deep as a well. Purity of brow, which, like the throat, the hands, the entire body, must have been carved in crystal or marble; the very
(10) soft lines of the face; the deep-set eyes with a look of surprise, sweet and sad, beneath the veil of the eyelashes; a brief mouth with fine lips, immune to sensuality; docile hair, harmonious and still;
(15) simply dressed in harmony with the obvious distinction and nobility of her bearing; all of her, aglow with innocence and a certain gravity in which are mixed the delights of childhood and the reverie of
(20) first youth. Her photographs invite one to try to imagine the timbre and rhythm of her voice, the ring of her laughter, the depth of her silences, the cadence of her movements, the direction and intensity
(25) of her glances. Her arms must have moved like the wings of a musical and tranquil bird; her figure must have yielded with the gentleness of a lily in an April garden. How many times her translucent hands
(30) must have trimmed the lamps of the vigilant virgins who know not the day or the hour; in what moments of rapture did her mouth and eyes accentuate their sadness? When did they emphasize her sweet
(35) smile?
   No, I never met her. And yet, even her pictures were with me for a long time after she died. Long before then, my life was filled with her presence, fashioned
(40) of unreal images, devoid of all sensation; perhaps more faithful, certainly more vivid, than these almost faded photo-

graphs. Hers was a presence without volume, line or color; an elusive phan-
(45) tom, which epitomized the beauty of all faces without limiting itself to any one, and embodied the delicacy of the best and loftiest spirits, indefinitely.

I now believe that an obscure feel-
(50) ing, a fear of reality, was the cause of my refusal to exchange the formless images for a direct knowledge of her who inspired them. How many times, just when the senses might have put a limit to
(55) fancy did I avoid meeting her; and how many others did Fate intervene! On one of the many occasions that I watched the house in which my phantom lived, I decided to knock; but the family was out.

24. What does Yáñez mean when he says "I never met my first love" (line 1)?

(A) He loved unconditionally.

(B) His first love died young.

(C) He never fell in love.

(D) He fell in love with someone he never really knew.

(E) His first love was not a human being.

25. The description in the first paragraph moves from

(A) sound to sight.

(B) smell to sight to sound.

(C) sight to touch.

(D) sight to sound to movement.

(E) touch to sound to sight.

26. The word *docile* (line 14) is used to imply

(A) wildness.

(B) conformity.

(C) manageability.

(D) indifference.

(E) willingness.

27. In the first paragraph, to what does Yáñez compare Alda's soul?

(A) A series of buildings

(B) Crystal and marble

(C) The wings of a bird

(D) A flower in a garden

(E) A photograph

28. When Yáñez says he is "devoid of all sensation" (line 40), he means that he

(A) has no sense of who Alda might be.

(B) does not see, hear, or touch Alda.

(C) cannot be sensible where Alda is concerned.

(D) has little judgment.

(E) feels nothing for Alda.

29. The word *faithful* (line 41) is used to mean

(A) loyal.

(B) constant.

(C) devoted.

(D) firm.

(E) reliable.

30. Unlike the previous paragraphs, the third paragraph

(A) suggests an explanation for the author's behavior.

(B) describes the author's photographs of Alda.

(C) mentions the elusive qualities of Alda.

(D) compares Alda to someone else the author loved later.

(E) expresses regret for losing Alda's love.

31. How might you reword the phrase "the senses might have put a limit to fancy" (lines 54–55)?

(A) If I were sensible, I would not have fantasized.

(B) My good taste enabled me to dream without limits.

(C) Good sense would have made things plainer.

(D) I could sense that she wanted to end my dreams.

(E) Seeing her might have stopped my fantasies.

STOP

END OF SECTION 2. IF YOU HAVE ANY TIME LEFT, GO OVER YOUR WORK IN THIS SECTION ONLY. DO NOT WORK IN ANY OTHER SECTION OF THE TEST.

Section 3

25 Questions • Time—30 Minutes

Directions: Solve the following problems using any available space on the page for scratchwork. On your answer sheet fill in the choice that best corresponds to the correct answer.

Notes: The figures accompanying the problems are drawn as accurately as possible unless otherwise stated in specific problems. Again, unless otherwise stated, all figures lie in the same plane. All numbers used in these problems are real numbers. Calculators are permitted for this test.

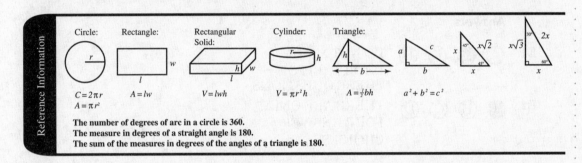

The number of degrees of arc in a circle is 360.
The measure in degrees of a straight angle is 180.
The sum of the measures in degrees of the angles of a triangle is 180.

Part 1: Quantitative Comparison Questions

Directions: For each of the following questions two quantities are given—one in Column A, the other in Column B. Compare the two quantities and mark your answer sheet as follows:

(A) if the quantity in Column A is greater

(B) if the quantity in Column B is greater

(C) if the quantities are equal

(D) if the relationship cannot be determined from the information given

Notes:

(1) Information concerning one or both of the compared quantities will be centered above the two columns for some items.

(2) Symbols that appear in both columns represent the same thing in Column A as in Column B.

(3) Letters such as x, n, and k are symbols for real numbers.

Examples

	Column A	Column B

$$a > 0$$

$$x > 0$$

E1. $\boxed{a - x}$ $\boxed{a + x}$

E2. $\boxed{\begin{array}{c}\text{The average of}\\ 17, 19, 21, 23\end{array}}$ $\boxed{\begin{array}{c}\text{The average of}\\ 16, 18, 20, 22\end{array}}$

Answers

E1.   (A) ● (C) (D)   DO NOT MARK CHOICE (E) FOR THESE QUESTIONS.

E2.   ● (B) (C) (D)   THERE ARE ONLY FOUR ANSWER CHOICES.

Column A	Column B

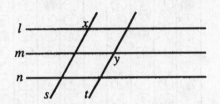

1. $a - y$ | x

Questions 2–3 refer to the following definition.

$$\boxed{u} = u^2 - u$$

2. $\boxed{3}$ | $\boxed{-3}$

3. $\boxed{u+1}$ | $\boxed{u-1}$

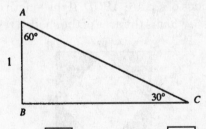

4. $\angle x$ | $\angle y$

5. Area of square with side 4 | Twice the area of a triangle with base 4 and height 4

6. $\sqrt{3}$ | BC

$3x + 4 = y$; x is a positive integer less than or equal to 7.

7. The number of values for y that are prime numbers | 2

Column A	Column B

r is the radius of a given circle.

8. r^2 | r^3

9. $\dfrac{9 + 3(-2)}{(4-5)+1}$ | $\dfrac{(3-6)}{[2-5(3-4)]}$

10. The average of the degrees in all the angles in a quadrilateral | The average of the degrees in all the angles of two triangles

$$s = 1$$
$$t = 4$$
$$r = -3$$

11. $4s + 3t$ | $2t - 2r$

12. 12% of 72,000 | 7% of 37,000

13. The average of 17, 19, 21, 23, 25, 27 | The average of 18, 20, 22, 24, 26

14. Area of circle A | 12

15. $\dfrac{1}{6}\left(\dfrac{3}{8}+\dfrac{9}{24}\right)$ | $\left(\dfrac{1}{6}\right)\left(\dfrac{3}{8}\right)+\left(\dfrac{9}{24}\right)\left(\dfrac{1}{6}\right)$

Part 2: Student-Produced Response Questions

Directions: Solve each of these problems. Write the answer in the corresponding grid on the answer sheet and fill in the ovals beneath each answer you write. Here are some examples.

Answer: $\frac{3}{4}$ (= .75; show answer either way)   Answer: 325

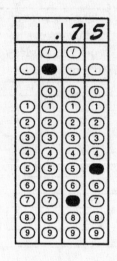

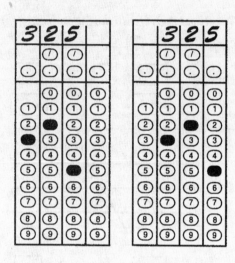

Note: A mixed number such as $3\frac{1}{2}$ must be gridded as 7/2 or as 3.5. If gridded as "3 1/2," it will be read as "thirty-one halves."

Note: Either position is correct

16. Joshua bought two dozen apples for 3 dollars. At this rate, how much will 18 apples cost? (Do not grid the dollar sign.)

17. What is $\frac{1}{10}$% of $\frac{1}{10}$ of 10?

18. $\dfrac{\frac{-1}{3}}{3} - \dfrac{3}{\frac{-1}{3}} =$

19. Dawn's average for four math tests is 80. What score must she receive on her next exam to increase her average by three points?

20. In the figure below, square *WXYZ* is formed by connecting the midpoints of the sides of square *ABCD*. If the length of *AB* = 6, what is the area of the shaded region?

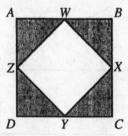

21. Thirty-thousand two hundred forty minutes is equivalent to how many weeks?

22. In the figure below, line l_1 is parallel to l_2. Transversals t_1 and t_2 are drawn. What is the value of $a + b + c + d$? (Do not grid the degree symbol.)

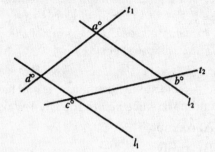

23. A car travels from town A to town B, a distance of 360 miles, in 9 hours. How many hours would the same trip have taken had the car traveled 5 mph faster?

24. In the figure below, *KJ* bisects $\angle J$. The measure of $\angle K$ is 40° and the measure of $\angle L$ is 20°. What is the measure of $\angle N$? (Do not grid the degree symbol.)

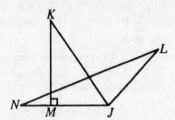

25. The area of a circle that is inscribed in a square with a diagonal of 8 is $a\pi$. What is the value of a?

STOP

END OF SECTION 3. IF YOU HAVE ANY TIME LEFT, GO OVER YOUR WORK IN THIS SECTION ONLY. DO NOT WORK IN ANY OTHER SECTION OF THE TEST.

Section 4

35 Questions • Time—30 minutes

Directions: Each of the following questions consists of an incomplete sentence followed by five words or pairs of words. Choose that word or pair of words that, when substituted for the blank space or spaces, *best* completes the meaning of the sentence and mark the letter of your choice on your answer sheet

Example

Q In view of the extenuating circumstances and the defendant's youth, the judge recommended ____.

(A) conviction

(B) a defense

(C) a mistrial

(D) leniency

(E) life imprisonment

A

1. Her clear ____ of the situation kept the meeting from breaking up into ____.

    (A) grasp..chaos

    (B) vision..anarchy

    (C) knowledge..uproar

    (D) control..harmony

    (E) idea..laughter

2. The mayor remained ____ in her commitment to ____ the rise of unemployment among her constituents.

    (A) firm..uphold

    (B) wavering..identify

    (C) steadfast..stem

    (D) uncertain..staunch

    (E) alone..approach

3. A ____ old stone farmhouse, it had been a landmark since before the Civil War.

    (A) corrupt

    (B) sturdy

    (C) rickety

    (D) ramshackle

    (E) vital

4. Because she thought her hateful cousin's behavior was ____, it ____ her to hear the adults praise him.

    (A) intangible..thrilled

    (B) putative..baffled

    (C) laconic..encouraged

    (D) insipid..demeaned

    (E) obnoxious..galled

5. A public official must be ____ in all his or her actions to avoid even the appearance of impropriety.

    (A) redolent

    (B) unctuous

    (C) baleful

    (D) circumspect

    (E) propitious

6. So many people turned out for the meeting that there were not enough seats to ____ them all.

    (A) count

    (B) ascertain

    (C) accommodate

    (D) delineate

    (E) delegate

7. The editorial accused the mayor of ____ for making promises he knew he could not ____.
   (A) hypocrisy..fulfill
   (B) revulsion..condone
   (C) impunity..reprise
   (D) liability..improve
   (E) petulance..verify

8. She was ____ as a child, accepting without question everything she was told.
   (A) obstreperous
   (B) recalcitrant
   (C) credulous
   (D) truculent
   (E) tearful

9. Warned by an anonymous phone call that an explosion was ____, the police ____ the building immediately.
   (A) expected..filled
   (B) ubiquitous..purged
   (C) eminent..checked
   (D) imminent..evacuated
   (E) insidious..obviated

10. Route 71 has always been known to wind its ____ way through steep mountain passes and coarse terrain.
    (A) neat
    (B) indirect
    (C) evasive
    (D) tortuous
    (E) deceitful

Directions: Each of the following questions consists of a capitalized pair of words followed by five pairs of words lettered (A) to (E). The capitalized words bear some meaningful relationship to each other. Choose the lettered pair of words whose relationship is most similar to that expressed by the capitalized pair and mark its letter on your answer sheet.

Example

Q DAY : SUN ::
   (A) sunlight : daylight
   (B) ray : sun
   (C) night : moon
   (D) heat : cold
   (E) moon : star

A

11. CRACK : SMASH ::
    (A) merge : break
    (B) run : hover
    (C) whisper : scream
    (D) play : work
    (E) tattle : tell

12. SURGEON : DEXTEROUS ::
    (A) clown : fat
    (B) actress : beautiful
    (C) athlete : tall
    (D) acrobat : agile
    (E) man : strong

13. SPECTATOR : SPORT ::
    (A) jury : trial
    (B) witness : crime
    (C) soloist : music
    (D) player : team
    (E) fan : grandstand

14. WALK : AMBLE ::
- **(A)** work : tinker
- **(B)** play : rest
- **(C)** run : jump
- **(D)** jog : trot
- **(E)** go : come

15. HILT : BLADE ::
- **(A)** holster : gun
- **(B)** sheath : knife
- **(C)** leash : dog
- **(D)** stem : leaf
- **(E)** petal : branch

16. RULER : DISTANCE ::
- **(A)** king : country
- **(B)** yardstick : dimension
- **(C)** barometer : weather
- **(D)** microscope : size
- **(E)** thermometer : temperature

17. HAMMER : TOOL ::
- **(A)** tire : wheel
- **(B)** wagon : vehicle
- **(C)** nail : screw
- **(D)** stick : drum
- **(E)** saw : wood

18. FLIPPERS : DIVER ::
- **(A)** baton : runner
- **(B)** cap : ballplayer
- **(C)** gloves : skater
- **(D)** tights : dancer
- **(E)** spikes : golfer

19. BRAGGART : DIFFIDENCE ::
- **(A)** benefactor : generosity
- **(B)** pariah : esteem
- **(C)** partisan : partiality
- **(D)** savant : wisdom
- **(E)** sycophant : flattery

20. DIATRIBE : BITTERNESS ::
- **(A)** dictum : injury
- **(B)** critique : even-handedness
- **(C)** polemic : consonance
- **(D)** encomium : praise
- **(E)** concordance : disagreement

21. TRAVESTY : RIDICULE ::
- **(A)** reproduction : provoke
- **(B)** forgery : deceive
- **(C)** imitation : feign
- **(D)** treachery : reprieve
- **(E)** poetry : comprehend

22. AUTHOR : NOVEL ::
- **(A)** composer : piano
- **(B)** artist : easel
- **(C)** sculptor : statue
- **(D)** painter : color
- **(E)** mechanic : oil

23. MAGNANIMOUS : PETTY ::
- **(A)** arrogant : insolent
- **(B)** valiant : belligerent
- **(C)** passionate : blasé
- **(D)** munificent : generous
- **(E)** circumspect : prudent

Directions: The reading passage below is followed by a set of questions. Read the passage and answer the accompanying questions, basing your answers on what is stated or implied in the passage. Mark the letter of your choice on your answer sheet.

Questions 24–35 are based on the following passage.

Alexander Wilson was a poet and a naturalist. Born in Scotland in 1766, he emigrated to Pennsylvania in 1794 and soon became a full-time naturalist. This excerpt on hummingbird nests is from a nine-volume work titled American Ornithology, *published in 1808–1814.*

About the twenty-fifth of April the Hummingbird usually arrives in Pennsylvania; and about the tenth of May begins to build its nest. This is generally fixed on
(5) the upper side of a horizontal branch, not among the twigs, but on the body of the branch itself. Yet I have known instances where it was attached by the side to an old moss-grown trunk; and
(10) others where it was fastened on a strong rank stalk, or weed, in the garden; but these cases are rare. In the woods it very often chooses a white oak sapling to build on; and in the orchard, or garden,
(15) selects a pear tree for that purpose. The branch is seldom more than ten feet from the ground. The nest is about an inch in diameter, and as much in depth. A very complete one is now lying before
(20) me, and the materials of which it is composed are as follows: —The outward coat is formed of small pieces of bluish grey lichen that vegetates on old trees and fences, thickly glued on with the
(25) saliva of the bird, giving firmness and consistency to the whole, as well as keeping out moisture. Within this are thick matted layers of the fine wings of certain flying seeds, closely laid together; and
(30) lastly, the downy substance from the great mullein, and from the stalks of the common fern, lines the whole. The base of the nest is continued round the stem of the branch, to which it closely ad-
(35) heres; and, when viewed from below,

appears a mere mossy knot or accidental protuberance. The eggs are two, pure white, and of equal thickness at both ends. . . . On a person's approaching
(40) their nest, the little proprietors dart around with a humming sound, passing frequently within a few inches of one's head; and should the young be newly hatched, the female will resume her
(45) place on the nest even while you stand within a yard or two of the spot. The precise period of incubation I am unable to give; but the young are in the habit, a short time before they leave the nest, of
(50) thrusting their bills into the mouths of their parents, and sucking what they have brought them. I never could perceive that they carried them any animal food; tho, from circumstances that will
(55) presently be mentioned, I think it highly probable they do. As I have found their nest with eggs so late as the twelfth of July, I do not doubt but that they frequently, and perhaps usually, raise two
(60) broods in the same season.

24. In line 4, the word "fixed" most nearly means
(A) changed.
(B) improved.
(C) found.
(D) understood.
(E) undermined.

25. According to the author, all of the following are places where one could find a hummingbird EXCEPT
(A) on the upper side of a branch.
(B) on a moss grown trunk.
(C) on a white oak sapling.
(D) on a pear tree.
(E) in the meadow.

26. Why does Wilson mention the "old moss-grown trunk" and "strong rank stalk" (lines 9 and 11)?

(A) To compare relative sizes of birds

(B) To establish the birds' eating patterns

(C) To illustrate nontypical nesting behaviors

(D) To delineate plant life in Pennsylvania

(E) To complete a list of related flora

27. When Wilson remarks that the birds' nests resemble an "accidental protuberance" (lines 36–37), he implies that

(A) the nests are messily constructed.

(B) nests may be destroyed accidently.

(C) the nests are usually invisible.

(D) the nests are designed to blend into their surroundings.

(E) most nests resemble the beak of the bird itself.

28. The phrase "little proprietors" (line 40) refers to

(A) children in the orchard.

(B) eggs.

(C) naturalists.

(D) shopowners.

(E) nesting pairs of hummingbirds.

29. When Wilson remarks that he "never could perceive" hummingbirds feeding their nestlings animal food (lines 52–53), he is suggesting

(A) that his eyesight is failing.

(B) his limitations as an observer.

(C) that animal food may, in fact, be eaten.

(D) that no animal food is eaten.

(E) that hummingbirds eat only at night.

30. The fact that Wilson has found nests with eggs "so late as the twelfth of July" indicates that

(A) birds do not lay eggs before June.

(B) most eggs are found earlier than July 12.

(C) the eggs are not likely to hatch.

(D) the birds began nesting late in the season.

(E) some birds abandon their nests.

31. The hummingbirds' nest is composed of all of the following EXCEPT

(A) moss.

(B) lichen.

(C) the wings of flying seeds.

(D) a downy substance from fern stalks.

(E) hummingbird saliva.

32. How does Wilson reconstruct the makeup of the nest?

(A) By taking apart a nest that hangs in the orchard

(B) By watching a hummingbird build a nest in the stable

(C) By reading a report by John Audubon

(D) By inspecting a nest that lies on his desk

(E) By making a copy of a nest he has observed

33. Which of the following can be inferred about the hummingbirds' habits?

(A) They flourish only in Pennsylvania.

(B) Their broods each consist of a single egg.

(C) They migrate in the spring.

(D) They always raise two broods in a season.

(E) They spend the winter in Pennsylvania.

34. The main purpose of this passage is to describe

(A) the nesting behavior of the hummingbird.

(B) the mating behavior of the hummingbird.

(C) the relative size of the hummingbird.

(D) hummingbirds in Pennsylvania.

(E) young hummingbird fledglings.

35. If Wilson were to study crows, he would be likely to

(A) stuff and mount them.

(B) observe them in the wild.

(C) read all about them.

(D) mate them in a laboratory.

(E) dissect them.

STOP

END OF SECTION 4. IF YOU HAVE ANY TIME LEFT, GO OVER YOUR WORK IN THIS SECTION ONLY. DO NOT WORK IN ANY OTHER SECTION OF THE TEST.

practice test

Section 5

10 Questions • Time—15 Minutes

Directions: Solve the following problems using any available space on the page for scratchwork. On your answer sheet fill in the choice that best corresponds to the correct answer.

Notes: The figures accompanying the problems are drawn as accurately as possible unless otherwise stated in specific problems. Again, unless otherwise stated, all figures lie in the same plane. All numbers used in these problems are real numbers. Calculators are permitted for this test.

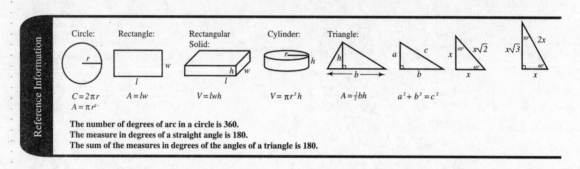

Circle: $C = 2\pi r$ $A = \pi r^2$

Rectangle: $A = lw$

Rectangular Solid: $V = lwh$

Cylinder: $V = \pi r^2 h$

Triangle: $A = \frac{1}{2}bh$ $a^2 + b^2 = c^2$

The number of degrees of arc in a circle is 360.
The measure in degrees of a straight angle is 180.
The sum of the measures in degrees of the angles of a triangle is 180.

1. In the figure, what percent of the area of rectangle *PQRS* is shaded?

   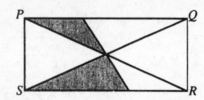

   (A) 20
   (B) 25
   (C) 30
   (D) $33\frac{1}{3}$
   (E) 35

2. One wheel has a diameter of 30 inches and a second wheel has a diameter of 20 inches. The first wheel traveled a certain distance in 240 revolutions. In how many revolutions did the second wheel travel the same distance?

   (A) 120
   (B) 160
   (C) 360
   (D) 420
   (E) 480

3. The one of the following to which 1.86×10^5 is equivalent is:

   (A) 18,600
   (B) 186,000
   (C) 18,600,000
   (D) $186 \times 500,000$
   (E) 1,860,000

4. How many of the numbers between 100 and 300 begin or end with 2?

    (A) 20
    (B) 40
    (C) 100
    (D) 110
    (E) 180

5. The area of a square is $49x^2$. What is the length of a diagonal of the square?

    (A) $7x$
    (B) $7x\sqrt{2}$
    (C) $14x$
    (D) $7x2$
    (E) $\dfrac{7x}{\sqrt{2}}$

6. If shipping charges to a certain point are 62 cents for the first five ounces and 8 cents for each additional ounce, the weight of a package, in pounds, for which the charges are $1.66 is

    (A) $\dfrac{7}{8}$
    (B) 1
    (C) $1\dfrac{1}{8}$
    (D) $1\dfrac{1}{4}$
    (E) $1\dfrac{1}{2}$

7. If 15 cans of food are needed for seven adults for two days, the number of cans needed to feed four adults for seven days is

    (A) 15
    (B) 20
    (C) 25

    (D) 30
    (E) 35

8. A rectangular sign is cut down by 10% of its height and 30% of its width. What percent of the original area remains?

    (A) 30
    (B) 37
    (C) 57
    (D) 63
    (E) 70

9. If the average (arithmetic mean) of a series of numbers is 20 and their sum is 160, how many numbers are in the series?

    (A) 8
    (B) 16
    (C) 32
    (D) 48
    (E) 80

10. If the result of squaring a number is less than the number, the number is

    (A) negative and greater than –1.
    (B) negative and less than –1.
    (C) a positive fraction greater than 1.
    (D) positive and less than 1.
    (E) 1 and only 1.

STOP

END OF SECTION 5. IF YOU HAVE ANY TIME LEFT, GO OVER YOUR WORK IN THIS SECTION ONLY. DO NOT WORK IN ANY OTHER SECTION OF THE TEST.

Section 6

12 Questions • Time—15 Minutes

> **Directions:** The two passages below deal with a related topic. Following the passages are questions about the content of each passage or about the relationship between the two passages. Answer the questions based upon what is stated or implied in the passages and in any introductory material provided. Mark the letter of your choice on your answer sheet.

Questions 1–12 are based on the following passages.

Achilles, the Greek hero, and Cuchulain, the Champion of Ireland, achieved mythical status because of their acts of courage. The following passages compare the two heroes and their heroic feats.

Passage 1—Achilles, Defender of Honor

When Achilles heard that his friend Patroclus had been killed in battle, he became so despondent that his friends feared he might end his own life. When
(5) word of his complete and agonizing distress reached his mother, Thetis, in the depths of the ocean where she resided, she raced to his side. She found him in a highly distraught state, feeling guilty
(10) that he, in some way, might have been responsible for his friend's demise. His only consolation were thoughts of revenge for which he needed the help of Hector. However, his mother reminded
(15) him that he was without armor, having lost his recently in battle. His mother, however, promised him that she would procure for him a suit of armor from Vulcan far superior to the one he had
(20) lost. Achilles agreed and Thetis immediately repaired to Vulcan's palace. Thetis found Vulcan busy at his forge making magical tripods that moved forward when they were wanted, and retreated
(25) when dismissed. Vulcan immediately honored Thetis's request for a set of armor for her son, and ceasing his own work, hastened to meet her demands.

Vulcan created a magnificent suit of
(30) armor for Achilles. The shield was adorned with elaborate ornaments. The helmet had a gold crest, and the body of the armor was perfectly suited to his body and of the very finest workman-
(35) ship. The armor was completed in one night. When Thetis received it, she descended to earth, and laid it down at Achilles' feet at the first dawn of day.

Seeing the armor brought the first
(40) signs of life to Achilles that he had felt since the death of his friend Patroclus. The armor was so splendid that Achilles was stunned at the sight of it. Achilles went into battle with his new armor,
(45) consumed with rage and thirst for vengeance that made him an unbeatable foe. The bravest warriors fled from him or were killed by his lance.

Passage 2—Cuchulain, Champion of Ireland

In days of yore, the men of Ulster sought
(50) to choose a champion. They enlisted the help of Curoi of Kerry, a wise man, to help them reach their decision. Three brave men, Laegire, Connall Cearnach, and Cuchulain indicated that they
(55) wished to be considered. Each was told that he would have to meet the challenge of a terrible stranger. When the stranger arrived, all were in awe of him. "Behold my axe," the stranger said. "My
(60) challenge is this. Whoever will take the axe today may cut my head off with it, provided that I may, in like manner, cut off his head tomorrow. If you have no champions who dare face me, I will say
(65) that the men of Ulster have lost their courage and should be ashamed."

Laegire was the first to accept the challenge. The giant laid his head on a block. With one blow the hero severed it (70) from the body. Thereupon the giant arose, took the head and the axe, and headless, walked slowly from the hall. The following night the giant returned, sound as ever, to claim the fulfillment of (75) Laegires' promise. However, Laegire did not come forward. The stranger scoffed at the men of Ulster because their great champion showed no courage. He could not face the blow he should receive in (80) return for the one he gave.

The men from Ulster were sorely ashamed, but Conall Cearnach, the second aspiring champion, made another pact with the stranger. He, too, gave a (85) blow which beheaded the giant. But again, when the giant returned whole and sound on the following evening, the champion was not there.

Now it was the turn of Cuchulain, (90) who as the others had done, cut off the giant's head at one stroke. The next day everyone watched Cuchulain to see what he would do. They would not have been surprised if he had not appeared. This (95) champion, however, was there. He was not going to disgrace Ulster. Instead, he sat with great sadness in his place. "Do not leave this place till all is over," he said to his king. "Death is coming to me (100) soon, but I must honor my promise, for I would rather die than break my word."

At the end of the day the giant appeared.

"Where is Cuchulain?' he cried.
(105)   "Here I am," answered Cuchulain.
"Cuchulain, your speech is morose, and the fear of death is obviously foremost in your thoughts, but at least you have honored your promise."
(110)   Cuchulain went towards the giant, as he stood with his great axe ready, and knelt to receive the blow.

The would-be champion of Ulster laid his head on the block.
(115)   When the giant did not immediately use his axe, Cuchulain said, "Slay me now with haste, for I did not keep you waiting last night."

The stranger raised his axe so high (120) that it crashed upwards through the rafters of the hall, like the crash of trees falling in a storm. When the axe came down with a sound that shook the room, all men looked fearfully at Cuchulain. (125) But to the surprise of all, the descending axe had not even touched him; it had come down with the blunt side on the ground, and Cuchulain knelt there unharmed. Smiling at him and leaning on (130) his axe, stood no terrible and hideous stranger, but Curoi of Kerry, who had taken on the form of the giant to test the champions. He was now there to give his decision.
(135)   "Rise up, Cuchulain," said Curoi. "There is none among all the heroes of Ulster to equal you in courage and loyalty and truth. The Championship is yours." Thereupon Curoi vanished. The (140) assembled warriors gathered around Cuchulain, and all with one voice acclaimed him the champion.

1. The word *despondent* in Passage 1 (line 3) means

   (A) very depressed.

   (B) in need of food.

   (C) angry.

   (D) embarrassed.

   (E) belligerent.

2. Achilles' feelings of guilt were related to

   (A) the loss of his armor.

   (B) the loss of his last battle.

   (C) his estrangement from his mother.

   (D) the death of his friend.

   (E) his relationship with Vulcan.

3. In line 21, the word *repaired* means

   (A) glazed.

   (B) retired.

   (C) replenished.

   (D) returned.

   (E) untouched.

4. Although not stated directly in the passage, it is obvious that Vulcan

   (A) blames Achilles for his friend's death.

   (B) is a lower-level god.

   (C) is extremely powerful.

   (D) loves Thetis.

   (E) does not wish to help Achilles.

5. Achilles' feeling as he went into battle can best be described as

   (A) guilty.

   (B) nervous.

   (C) confident.

   (D) depressed.

   (E) arrogant.

6. According to Passage 2, when the men of Ulster wished to select a champion they enlisted the help of

   (A) Curoi.

   (B) the king.

   (C) Laegire.

   (D) Connall.

   (E) Cearnach.

7. The challenge that the would-be champion had to meet involved

   (A) fighting a giant with an axe.

   (B) beheading a giant.

   (C) competing against other men of Ulster.

   (D) winning a match with the king.

   (E) fighting Curoi of Kerry.

8. According to the passage, the giant was unusual because

   (A) he was so tall.

   (B) he was so huge.

   (C) he defeated all his opponents.

   (D) he remained alive while headless.

   (E) he had three eyes.

9. The word *sorely* (line 81) means

   (A) feverishly.

   (B) utterly.

   (C) angrily.

   (D) bitterly.

   (E) pitifully.

10. Cuchulain appeared as promised to meet the giant because

    (A) he was afraid.

    (B) he knew the giant would not kill him.

    (C) he knew the giant was Curoi.

    (D) he did not wish to fail his king.

    (E) he gave his word.

11. In line 106, the word *morose* most nearly means

(A) serious and somber.

(B) riotous and humorous.

(C) indifferent and detached.

(D) informed and knowledgeable.

(E) satisfied.

12. Cuchulain is sometimes called the "Irish Achilles," probably because of his

(A) honesty.

(B) bravery.

(C) strength.

(D) wisdom.

(E) intelligence.

STOP

END OF SECTION 6. IF YOU HAVE ANY TIME LEFT, GO OVER YOUR WORK IN THIS SECTION ONLY. DO NOT WORK IN ANY OTHER SECTION OF THE TEST.

ANSWERS AND EXPLANATIONS

Section 1: Math

1.	B	6.	E	11.	E	16.	B	21.	E
2.	B	7.	B	12.	A	17.	A	22.	A
3.	A	8.	D	13.	D	18.	D	23.	E
4.	B	9.	C	14.	C	19.	D	24.	D
5.	D	10.	B	15.	B	20.	A	25.	C

Section 2: Verbal

1.	C	8.	B	15.	A	22.	C	29.	E
2.	A	9.	D	16.	B	23.	A	30.	A
3.	D	10.	C	17.	D	24.	D	31.	E
4.	E	11.	A	18.	E	25.	D		
5.	B	12.	B	19.	A	26.	C		
6.	D	13.	B	20.	D	27.	A		
7.	B	14.	C	21.	C	28.	B		

Section 3: Math

Part 1

1.	C	4.	C	7.	A	10.	A	13.	C
2.	B	5.	C	8.	D	11.	A	14.	A
3.	D	6.	C	9.	A	12.	A	15.	C

Part 2

16.	$2.25 = \frac{9}{4}$	18.	$\frac{80}{9} = 8.89$	20.	18	22.	360	24.	60
17.	.001	19.	95	21.	3	23.	8	25.	8

Section 4: Verbal

1.	A	8.	C	15.	D	22.	C	29.	C
2.	C	9.	D	16.	E	23.	C	30.	B
3.	B	10.	D	17.	B	24.	C	31.	A
4.	E	11.	C	18.	E	25.	E	32.	D
5.	D	12.	D	19.	B	26.	C	33.	C
6.	C	13.	B	20.	D	27.	D	34.	A
7.	A	14.	A	21.	B	28.	E	35.	B

Section 5: Math

1.	B	3.	B	5.	B	7.	D	9.	A
2.	C	4.	D	6.	C	8.	D	10.	D

Section 6: Verbal

1.	A	4.	C	7.	B	9.	B	11.	A
2.	D	5.	C	8.	D	10.	E	12.	B
3.	D	6.	A						

Note: A ⊞ following a math answer explanation indicates that a calculator could be helpful in solving that particular problem.

Section 1

1. **The correct answer is (B).** If $9x + 5 = 23$, $9x = 18$, or $x = 2$. Thus, $18x + 5 = 36 + 5 = 41$. ⊞

2. **The correct answer is (B).**

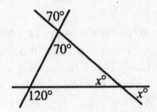

$$120 = 70 + x$$

$$x = 50$$

3. **The correct answer is (A).**

$$2y = \frac{1}{3}$$

$$6y = 1$$

$$y = \frac{1}{6}$$ ⊞

$$\frac{1}{4y} = \frac{1}{4\left(\frac{1}{6}\right)} = \frac{1}{\frac{2}{3}} = \frac{3}{2}$$

4. **The correct answer is (B).** The volume of a cube is $V = s^3$. The sides of this cube is $\sqrt[3]{64} = 4$ in. Since there are 12 edges to a cube, the amount of wire needed is 12×4 in., or 48 inches.

5. **The correct answer is (D).**

$$\text{Let } x = \text{ original price}$$
$$\text{Then } .60x = \$4.20$$
$$\text{or } 6x = \$42.00$$
$$x = \$7.00$$

6. **The correct answer is (E).**

$$A = 15$$

$$B = 15 + \frac{1}{3}(15) = 20$$

$15 - n$ is A's age n years ago

$20 - n$ is B's age n years ago

$$(20 - n) = 2(15 - n)$$

$$20 - n = 30 - 2n$$

$$n = 10$$

7. **The correct answer is (B).** By simple substitutions,

$$s = 16 \times 8 \times 8, \text{ or } 1,024.$$ ⊞

8. **The correct answer is (D).** The line of center of two tangent circles passes through the point of tangency. Hence, perimeter of $\Delta = (2 + 3) + (3 + 4) + (4 + 2) = 5 + 7 + 6 = 18$. ⊞

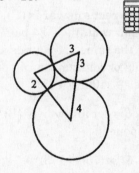

9. **The correct answer is (C).**

$$\frac{1}{10} = x \bullet \frac{3}{4} = \frac{3x}{4}$$

$$30x = 4$$ ⊞

$$x = \frac{2}{15}$$

10. **The correct answer is (B).** Since $QR = 7$, and triangle QOR is a right isosceles triangle, $OQ = \frac{7}{\sqrt{2}} = \frac{7\sqrt{2}}{2}$.

Hence, coordinates of Q are $(0, \frac{7}{2}\sqrt{2})$.

11. **The correct answer is (E).** There is no indication as to the exact percentage of students who eat in the cafeteria, since we do not know how many boys or girls there are.

12. **The correct answer is (A).** Three meals a day times 365 days per year means there are $3 \times 365 = 1,095$ meals in one year. Over 19 years there are $1,095 \times 19 = 20,805$ meals. Therefore, the number of restaurants in New York City exceeds 20,500.

13. **The correct answer is (D).** Both of the triangles share a common base, AC. The difference in their area is accounted for by the difference in their altitudes. Since we are given a right angle we know that DE is the altitude of the larger triangle and BE is the altitude of the smaller triangle. Since the ratio of those two segments is 4:1, then the areas must be in the ratio of 4:1.

14. **The correct answer is (C).** The original 6 pounds contained .24 pounds of salt. Now, the same .24 pounds are in 5 pounds of solution, so the percentage is $\frac{.24}{5}(100) = 4.8\%$.

15. **The correct answer is (B).** By the Law of Exponents:

$$(75)^3 \times (75)^7 = (75)^{3+7} = (75)^{10}$$

16. **The correct answer is (B).** Cities A, B, and C need not be on a straight line; therefore, one cannot add or subtract miles. Six times the distance between A and B is $150 \times 6 = 900$, which is 10 times the distance between A and C, or $10 \times 90 = 900$.

17. **The correct answer is (A).**

$$\frac{1}{a} + \frac{1}{b} = \frac{b+a}{ab} = \frac{3}{4}$$

18. **The correct answer is (D).**

$$x^6 + (2x^2)^3 + (3x^3)^2 = x^6 + 8x^6 + 9x^6 = 18x^6$$

19. **The correct answer is (D).** Set up a proportion and solve for x:

$$\frac{\frac{3}{4} \text{ in.}}{6 \text{ in.}} = \frac{10 \text{ mi.}}{x \text{ mi.}}$$

$$\frac{3}{4}x = 60$$

$$x = 80$$

20. **The correct answer is (A).** If h is any positive quantity, then letting $d = (m+h) - \frac{50}{m+h}$, we can see that d is greater than d, since h is greater than zero, and $\frac{50}{m}$ is greater than $\frac{50}{m+h}$. Therefore, d increases as m does.

21. **The correct answer is (E).** One cubic foot equals 12^3 cubic inches, or 1,728. Thus, one cubic foot of the metal would weigh 3,456 pounds.

22. **The correct answer is (A).** The area of the circle is πr^2 and the circumference is $2\pi r$. If the area equals the circumference, solve the equation $\pi r^2 = 2\pi r$, or $r = 2$. The diameter is $2r$, or 4 inches.

23. **The correct answer is (E).** Let's substitute J for John and P for Pat.

(J is 3 times P) $J = 3P$

(J in four years) $x = J + 4$

(substitute $3P$ for J) $x = 3P + 4$

$$x - 4 = 3P$$

$$\frac{x-4}{3} = P$$

You can also reason this way: If John will be x years old in 4 years, then he is $x - 4$ years old now. Since Pat's age is now one third of John's, Pat is now $\frac{x-4}{3}$ years old.

24. **The correct answer is (D).** Renaming as decimals, $\frac{2}{3}$=.666. . ., $\frac{5}{7}$=.7142. . ., $\frac{8}{11}$=.7272. . ., $\frac{9}{13}$=.6923. . ., so the order is $\frac{2}{3}, \frac{9}{13}, \frac{5}{7}, \frac{8}{11}$.

25. **The correct answer is (C).** If the average for the eight tests is 84%, then the sum of the eight tests must be 8 times 84, or 672. For the six tests the sum must be 6 times 86, or 516. The two dropped tests must have accounted for 156 points. 156 divided by 2 is 78.

Section 2

1. **The correct answer is (C).** If the young girl was unsure of her English skills, she was likely to be *reticent* (shy and restrained) when asked to speak.

2. **The correct answer is (A).** Arguments that only seemed logical were likely to be *specious* (false), and anyone familiar with the facts could *refute* (disprove) them.

3. **The correct answer is (D).** A tree that puts out fewer and fewer leaves is probably *moribund* (dying).

4. **The correct answer is (E).** If no trace of the building remained, it had been *obliterated* (destroyed completely).

5. **The correct answer is (B).** A manner that is menacing or threatening is said to be *truculent*. If, however, it is put on only for show, it is merely *affected*.

6. **The correct answer is (D).** Those who are protected from the harsh world around them are pampered, or *cosseted*. The other choices make no sense.

7. **The correct answer is (B).** The transitional word *although* sets up a contrast suggesting that one choice will be positive and one choice will be negative. The only possible choice is (B). Someone only appearing to be a *respectable* businessman may in reality be a *reprobate*, or a scoundrel.

8. **The correct answer is (B).** The word *attacking* indicates the need for two strong negative words. Only choice (B) satisfies this requirement with *acrimonious*, meaning harsh or bitter, and *angry*.

9. **The correct answer is (D).** *Conscientious* (extremely careful) and *frivolous* (silly) are opposing characteristics.

10. **The correct answer is (C).** The *peel* is the outer layer of an *apple*, just as the *shell* is the outer covering of a *lobster*.

11. **The correct answer is (A).** A *ring* is worn around the *finger* and a *necklace* is worn around the *neck*.

12. **The correct answer is (B).** A *child*, on becoming a fully mature person, is an *adult*. A *lamb* becomes a *sheep* on reaching full maturity. (*Cow* and *buck*, other mature animals, are specifically female and male, respectively.)

13. **The correct answer is (B).** *Pepper* is added to food to *season* it, and *sugar* to *sweeten* it.

14. **The correct answer is (C).** *Beef* can be dried to make *jerky*, and *grapes* can be dried to make *raisins*.

15. **The correct answer is (A).** A group of *fish* is called a *school* and a group of *cows* is called a *herd*.

16. **The correct answer is (B).** King urges his listeners to "continue to work with the faith that unearned suffering is redemptive." Even if you did not know the meaning of *redemptive*, you could infer that it promised something positive. Of the choices only (B) satisfies this condition.

17. **The correct answer is (D).** The last paragraph gives King's belief that ". . .this situation can and will be changed."

18. **The correct answer is (E).** This is stated in the last paragraph and sums up the point of the entire speech.

19. **The correct answer is (A).** King is attempting to inspire his listeners.

20. The correct answer is (D). Lines 46–50 state that this new attitude "...must not lead us to a distrust of all white people, for many of our white brothers ... have come to realize that their destiny is tied up with our destiny."

21. The correct answer is (C). King states in lines 24–26: "There will be neither rest nor tranquility in America until the Negro is granted his citizenship rights."

22. The correct answer is (C). Paragraph four specifically mentions creative protest.

23. The correct answer is (A). The second paragraph discusses "the whirlwinds of revolt" that will continue until justice prevails; the third paragraph urges listeners to obey the law, as "...we must not be guilty of wrongful deeds." Thus "non-violent resistance" is the best response.

24. The correct answer is (D). This is a completely literal statement. As the rest of the passage makes clear, the narrator never really knew Alda.

25. The correct answer is (D). To answer this synthesis/analysis question will require looking back at the paragraph and tracing its structure. The narrator describes what Alda looked like, speculates on what she sounded like, and guesses what she moved like, in that order.

26. The correct answer is (C). *Docile* has several connotations, but a look back at the citation in question will tell you that only two of the choices could easily be applied to hair, and (A) is exactly opposite to the meaning the narrator intends.

27. The correct answer is (A). He compares her brow to (B) and he speaks of a flower (D) and a photograph (E). However, he compares her soul to a church, castle, and tower as well as to a well (see lines 5–7).

28. The correct answer is (B). Reread the surrounding text to remind yourself of the author's main point. Her presence has no sensation for him, because he has not really met her.

29. The correct answer is (E). Each choice is a possible synonym, but only choice (E) suits the idea of memory being more faithful than faded photographs.

30. The correct answer is (A). In the first sentence of paragraph 3, the author suggests that his fear of reality was the reason he failed to meet Alda. This is the first time he has made such a suggestion. Paragraph 3 might also be said to support (C), but so do paragraphs 1 and 2. Choices (D) and (E) are not supported anywhere in the passages.

31. The correct answer is (E). Here is an example of an oddly worded phrase that cannot be easily deciphered. By testing the choices in place of the phrase in context, however, the reasonable translation is clear.

Section 3
Part 1

1. **The correct answer is (C).** The exterior angle of a triangle is equal to the sum of the two interior nonadjacent angles. Thus, $x+y=a$ and $\therefore x=a-y$. Therefore, Column A and Column B are equal.

2. **The correct answer is (B).** $3^2 - 3 = 6$. $(-3)^2 - (-3) = 12$

3. **The correct answer is (D).** This type of problem is most easily solved by plugging in small values.

   If $u = 0$, then $1^2 - 1 = 0$, while $(-1)^2 - (-1) = 2$.

   If $u = 1$, then $2^2 - 2 = 2$, while $(0)^2 - 0 = 0$. Since Column B is larger than Column A when $u = 0$, but smaller when $u = 1$, the answer must be (D).

4. **The correct answer is (C).** An alternate exterior angle of $\angle x$ is a vertical angle to an alternate exterior angle of $\angle y$. Since alternate exterior angles of two parallel lines cut by a transversal are equal, and vertical angles are always equal, $\angle x = \angle y$. Thus, the two columns are equal.

5. **The correct answer is (C).** The area of a square with side 4 is $4^2 = 16$. The area of the triangle in Column B is $(\frac{1}{2})(4)(4) = 8$. Twice this area is 16. Thus, the two areas are equal.

6. **The correct answer is (C).** Since two of the angles of this triangle total 90°, and there are 180° in a triangle, angle B must equal 90°, and this is a right triangle. In a right triangle in which the angles are 90°, 60°, and 30°, the length of the side opposite the 30° angle is one half the length of the hypotenuse, and the length of the side opposite the 60° angle is one half the length of the hypotenuse times $\sqrt{3}$. Side AB is opposite the 30° angle, and so must be one half the hypotenuse. AB is 1; therefore, AC must be 2. BC, then, will be one half the length of the hypotenuse times $\sqrt{3}$. So BC will be $\sqrt{3}$. Thus, the two columns are equal.

7. **The correct answer is (A).** x can range in value from 1 to 7. Plugging in each of those values, y can be 7, 10, 13, 16, 19, 22, and 25. Of these, 7, 13, and 19 are prime numbers.

8. **The correct answer is (D).** Since r is the radius of a circle, r cannot be negative. Thus $r^3 > r^2$. But, if $0 < r < 1$, $r^2 > r^3$. Hence, it cannot be determined which is larger.

9. **The correct answer is (A).** The values of Column A and Column B are 16 and −21, respectively. Therefore, Column A is greater than Column B.

10. **The correct answer is (A).** There are 360 degrees and 4 angles in all quadrilaterals and 360 divided by 4 is 90. A triangle contains 180 degrees and 3 angles. For two triangles the average would be 360 divided by 6, or 60.

11. **The correct answer is (A).** Substituting for s and t in Column A, $4(1) + 3(4) = 16$. Substituting t and r in Column B, $2(4) - 2(-3) = 14$. Therefore, Column A is larger than Column B.

12. **The correct answer is (A).** In Column A, 12% of 72,000 is $(.12)(72,000) = 8,640$. In Column B, 7% of 37,000 is $(.07)(37,000) = 2,590$. Therefore, Column A is greater than Column B.

13. **The correct answer is (C).** The average can be found by totaling the numbers in each column and dividing that sum by the number of terms.

$$\text{Column A } \frac{132}{6} = 22.$$
$$\text{Column B } \frac{110}{5} = 22.$$

14. **The correct answer is (A).** The area of circle A with radius 2 is $\pi r^2 = 4\pi$. 4π is approximately 12.56, so Column A is bigger.

15. **The correct answer is (C).** The values of Column A and Column B are both $\frac{1}{8}$. Using the distributive law of multiplication over addition, this is obviously equal.

Part 2

16. Use a ratio of apples to dollars.

$$\frac{\text{apples}}{\text{dollars}} \rightarrow \frac{24}{3} = \frac{18}{x}$$
$$8 = \frac{18}{x}$$
$$8x = 18$$
$$x = 2.25 = \frac{9}{4}$$

17. $\dfrac{1}{10}\% = \dfrac{1}{1000}$

$\dfrac{1}{1000} \cdot \dfrac{1}{10} \cdot \dfrac{10}{1} = \dfrac{1}{1000} = .001$

18. $\dfrac{-\dfrac{1}{3}}{3} - \dfrac{\dfrac{3}{1}}{-\dfrac{1}{3}} = \dfrac{-\dfrac{1}{3}}{\dfrac{3}{1}} - \dfrac{\dfrac{3}{1}}{-\dfrac{1}{3}}$

$= -\dfrac{1}{3}\left(\dfrac{1}{3}\right) - \dfrac{3}{1}\left(-\dfrac{3}{1}\right)$

$= -\dfrac{1}{9} + 9$

$= 8\dfrac{8}{9} = \dfrac{80}{9} = 8.89$

19. The sum of Dawn's scores for the first four tests is $80(4) = 320$.

$\dfrac{320 + x}{5} = 83$

$320 + x = 415$

$x = 95$

20.

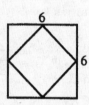

Area of a square $=$ (side)^2

or

$= \dfrac{(\text{diagonal})^2}{2}$

Area of $\square ABCD = (\text{side})^2 = 6^2 = 36$

Area of $\square WXYZ = \dfrac{(\text{diagonal})^2}{2} = \dfrac{6^2}{2} = 18$

Shaded area $= 36 - 18 = 18$

21. 1 week $=$ 7 days

1 day $=$ 24 hours

1 hour $=$ 60 minutes

$\dfrac{30,240}{7(24)(60)} = 3$

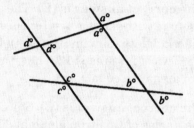

22. The sum of the interior angles of a quadrilateral is $360°$.

$\therefore a + b + c + d = 360$

23.   Distance $=$ rate $\times$ time

$360 = r(9)$

$40 = r$

If r were $40 + 5 = 45$

$d = rt$

$360 = 45t$

$t = 8$

24.

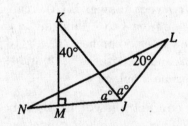

$40 + 90 + a = 180$

$a = 50$

$\angle J = 2(50) = 100°$

$\angle N + \angle J + \angle L = 180°$

$\angle N + 100° + 20° = 180°$

$\angle N = 60°$

25.

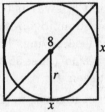

$$x^2 + x^2 = 8^2$$
$$2x^2 = 64$$
$$x = 4\sqrt{2}$$

The side of the square = $4\sqrt{2}$.

The radius of the circle = $\frac{1}{2}\left(4\sqrt{2}\right) = 2\sqrt{2}$.

$$A = \pi r^2$$
$$= \pi(2\sqrt{2})^2 = 8\pi = a\pi \therefore a = 8$$

Section 4

1. **The correct answer is (A).** Keeping a meeting from breaking up requires more than a clear *idea* or *vision*; it requires control, or a *grasp* of the situation.

2. **The correct answer is (C).** The word *commitment* signals the appropriate actions of the mayor; to be *steadfast* in her commitment, she must *stem*, or check, the increase of economic problems for the people who voted her into office.

3. **The correct answer is (B).** For the farmhouse to have been a landmark since before the Civil War, it must have been well built, or *sturdy*.

4. **The correct answer is (E).** If she thought her cousin was hateful, it is most likely that she found his behavior *obnoxious* (offensive) and that she was *galled*, or irritated, to hear him praised.

5. **The correct answer is (D).** *Circumspect*, meaning "watchful or wary," is the only choice that makes sense.

6. **The correct answer is (C).** *Accomodate*, meaning "to provide space for," is the only answer that makes sense.

7. **The correct answer is (A).** To make promises you know you cannot *fulfill* is

hypocrisy. No other choice correctly fills both blanks.

8. **The correct answer is (C).** One who accepts without question is *credulous* (tending to believe readily).

9. **The correct answer is (D).** If the police know an explosion is *imminent* (about to happen), they are likely to *evacuate* (empty) the building quickly.

10. **The correct answer is (D).** The key word is *wind*. A road that winds is *tortuous* (D). Choices (C) and (E) are wrong because they refer to other meanings of *tortuous*. Choices (A) and (B) make no sense.

11. **The correct answer is (C).** To *smash* something is to do much greater damage than merely *crack* it. To *scream* is to make a much greater noise than to *whisper*.

12. **The correct answer is (D).** A *surgeon* is necessarily *dexterous* (skillful in using the hands), and an *acrobat* is necessarily *agile*.

13. **The correct answer is (B).** A *sport* is viewed by a *spectator*, and a *crime* is viewed by a *witness*.

14. **The correct answer is (A).** To *amble* is to *walk* unhurriedly without a predetermined destination. To *tinker* is to *work* aimlessly without a predetermined direction.

15. **The correct answer is (D).** A *hilt* (handle) is the part of a sword to which the *blade* is attached. Similarly, the *stem* is part of a plant to which a *leaf* is attached.

16. **The correct answer is (E).** A *ruler* is used to measure *distance*, and a *thermometer* is used to measure *temperature*.

17. **The correct answer is (B).** A *hammer* is a *tool*, and a *wagon* is a *vehicle*.

18. **The correct answer is (E).** *Flippers* and *spikes* are each footgear for a sport: *flippers* for the *diver* and *spikes* for the *golfer*.

19. The correct answer is (B). A *braggart* (offensively boastful person) lacks *diffidence* (modesty), just as a *pariah* (outcast) lacks *esteem* (regard).

20. The correct answer is (D). A *diatribe* is a speech full of *bitterness*. An *encomium* is a speech full of *praise*.

21. The correct answer is (B). A *travesty* is an imitation intended to *ridicule*. A *forgery* is an imitation intended to *deceive*.

22. The correct answer is (C). An *author* produces a *novel* while a *sculptor* makes a *statue*.

23. The correct answer is (C). One who is *magnanimous* (generous) is not *petty* (mean-spirited), just as one who is *passionate* (ardent) is not *blasé* (bored).

24. The correct answer is (C). In this context, the word *fixed* means situated or found, not its more common meaning—changed or altered.

25. The correct answer is (E). All of the other choices are explicitly mentioned by the author as the resting places of the hummingbird.

26. The correct answer is (C). Wilson states that nests are sometimes attached to such objects, but "these cases are rare" (line 12).

27. The correct answer is (D). The nest is not easily seen, but it is not invisible, as (C) suggests. Wilson describes seeing it from below (lines 35–36).

28. The correct answer is (E). Wilson refers to the proprietors darting around to protect the nest (lines 40–42).

29. The correct answer is (C). Wilson believes that hummingbirds *do* feed their young such food, saying, "I think it highly probable they do" (lines 55–56). However, he has not seen it.

30. The correct answer is (B). Since Wilson takes this to mean that hummingbirds may raise two broods (lines 59–60), the only possible answer here is (B).

31. The correct answer is (A). According to the passage (lines 18–27), the nest is composed of bluish-grey lichen glued on with hummingbird saliva, the wings of flying seeds, and downy substances from fern stalks and from the great mullein (another kind of plant).

32. The correct answer is (D). Lines 19–20 show that Wilson is looking at something that "is now lying before me."

33. The correct answer is (C). It can be inferred from the sentence that the hummingbirds migrate into Pennsylvania (presumably from the south) "about the twenty-fifth of April." None of the other choices is supported by the passage.

34. The correct answer is (A). Although other details about the hummingbird are included, the passage focuses on hummingbirds' nesting.

35. The correct answer is (B). Most of Wilson's observations in this piece happen in the wild; it is safe to assume that he would study crows the same way.

Section 5

1. **The correct answer is (B).**

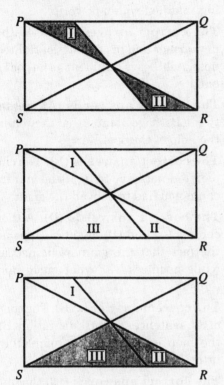

PR and *SQ* are diagonals of rectangle *PQRS*.

The diagonals of a rectangle divide the rectangle into four triangles of equal area.

∴ΔIII + ΔII = 25% of rectangle *PQRS*

2. **The correct answer is (C).** The number of revolutions is inversely proportional to the size of the wheel. Thus,

$$\frac{30}{20} = \frac{n}{240}.$$

Where n = number of revolutions for second wheel,

$20n = 7200$

$n = 360$

3. **The correct answer is (B).** 1.86 × 10⁵ = 1.86 × 100,000 = 186,000

4. **The correct answer is (D).** All the numbers from 200 to 299 begin with 2. There are 100 of these. Then all numbers like 102, 112, . . ., 192 end with 2. There are 10 of these.

Hence, there are 110 such numbers.

5. **The correct answer is (B).** If the area is $49x^2$, the side of the square is $7x$. Therefore, the diagonal of the square must be the hypotenuse of a right isosceles triangle of leg $7x$.

Hence, diagonal = $7x\sqrt{2}$.

6. **The correct answer is (C).** The amount paid for weight over 5 ounces is $1.66 – $.62 = $1.04. At $.08 for each additional ounce, $\frac{\$1.04}{\$.08}$ = 13 ounces of additional weight. The total weight is 13 ounces + 5 ounces = 18 ounces $x\left(\frac{1\text{ lb.}}{16\text{ oz.}}\right) = 1\frac{1}{8}$ lbs.

7. **The correct answer is (D).** Each adult needs 15 cans/7 adults = $\frac{15}{7}$ cans in two days, or $\left(\frac{1}{2}\right)\left(\frac{15}{7}\right) = \frac{15}{14}$ cans per adult per day. Multiply this by the number of adults and by the number of days:

$\left(\frac{15}{14}\right)$(4 adults)(7 days) = 30 cans of food.

8. **The correct answer is (D).** Let the original sign be 10 by 10.

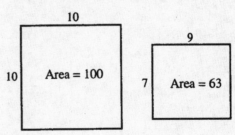

Then, the new sign is 9 by 7.

$\frac{63}{100} = 63\%$

9. The correct answer is (A). The average is found by taking the sum of a list of numbers and dividing the sum by the number in the list. If n is the number of numbers in the series, $160 \div n = 20$, so $n = 8$ numbers.

10. The correct answer is (D). Squaring a negative number will make it positive, so choices (A) and (B) are not true. $1^2 = 1$, so choice (E) is not true. Squaring any number greater than 1 will always be larger than the number itself, but squaring a fraction less than 1, where the denominator is larger than the numerator, will make the denominator much larger than the numerator, thus making the whole fraction smaller.

Section 6

1. The correct answer is (A). The context of the sentence, with its reference to taking his own life, supports this choice.

2. The correct answer is (D). Sentence three specifically cites the cause of Achilles' feelings of guilt.

3. The correct answer is (D). In this context, Thetis is traveling or returning to Vulcan.

4. The correct answer is (C). The passage refers to Vulcan's palace and his ability to create magical tripods, indicating that he is quite powerful.

5. The correct answer is (C). With his new armor and his feelings of righteousness, Achilles is confident as he goes into battle.

6. The correct answer is (A). Sentence two in Passage 2 states that they enlisted the help of Curoi of Kerry.

7. The correct answer is (B). The champion did not have to fight the giant; the champion had to behead the giant.

8. The correct answer is (D). Although choices (A) and (B) might be appealing, the fact that the giant remained alive while headless was what made him so unusual.

9. The correct answer is (B). The context of the sentence supports definition (B), as the men of Ulster were completely or utterly ashamed.

10. The correct answer is (E). Cuchulain is a man to whom his word is his bond; he had to meet the giant because he gave his word.

11. The correct answer is (A). His speech is serious and sad because he is afraid of imminent death.

12. The correct answer is (B). The quality that Achilles and Cuchulain share is courage.

Computing Your Scores

To check your SAT preparation progress at the end of this third practice test, you need to compute individual verbal and mathematical raw scores. Once you have computed these, use the conversion scales in the section that follows to compute your SAT scaled scores (200–800). Keep in mind that these formulas have been simplified to give you a "quick and dirty" sense of where you are scoring, not a perfectly precise score.

To Compute Your Raw Scores:

1 Enter the number of correct answers for each verbal and mathematical reasoning section into the boxes marked Number of Questions Correct.

2 Enter the number of incorrect answers (not blanks) for each verbal and mathematical reasoning section into the boxes marked Number of Questions Incorrect.

3 Total the number correct and number incorrect.

4 Follow this formula: Take the total correct and minus one quarter of the total incorrect. Round up in your favor to compute your raw score.

Verbal Section	Total Number of Questions	Number of Questions Correct	Number of Questions Incorrect
1	31		
3	35		
5	12		
Totals	78	Total Correct:	Total Incorrect:

Verbal Raw Score = Total Correct – ($\frac{1}{4}$ × Total Incorrect) = _____

Math Section	Total Number of Questions	Number of Questions Correct	Number of Questions Incorrect
2	25		
4	25		
6	10		
Totals	60	Total Correct:	Total Incorrect:

Math Raw Score = Total Correct – ($\frac{1}{4}$ × Total Incorrect) = _____

Conversion Scales

VERBAL REASONING

Raw Score	Scaled Score	Raw Score	Scaled Score
75	800	35	520
70	800	30	480
65	760	25	440
60	710	20	410
55	670	15	370
50	620	10	340
45	590	5	290
40	550	0	230

MATHEMATICAL REASONING

Raw Score	Scaled Score	Raw Score	Scaled Score
60	800	25	510
55	760	20	480
50	690	15	440
45	650	10	410
40	610	5	340
35	580	0	200
30	550		

Although you now have some idea of what your scores would look like had they been scaled according to unofficial ETS standards, you will probably want to know how to interpret your raw scores in more familiar terms. If so, use the following Self-Evaluation Charts to see what your raw scores actually mean.

SELF–EVALUATION CHARTS

VERBAL REASONING: Raw Score		MATHEMATICAL REASONING: Raw Score	
Excellent	60–75	Excellent	50–60
Good	50–59	Good	40–49
Average	30–49	Average	20–39
Fair	20–29	Fair	10–19
Poor	0–19	Poor	0–9

PRACTICE TEST 4

Answer Sheet

If a section has fewer questions than answer ovals, leave the extra ovals blank.

SECTION 1

1 (A)(B)(C)(D)(E)	11 (A)(B)(C)(D)(E)	21 (A)(B)(C)(D)(E)	31 (A)(B)(C)(D)(E)
2 (A)(B)(C)(D)(E)	12 (A)(B)(C)(D)(E)	22 (A)(B)(C)(D)(E)	32 (A)(B)(C)(D)(E)
3 (A)(B)(C)(D)(E)	13 (A)(B)(C)(D)(E)	23 (A)(B)(C)(D)(E)	33 (A)(B)(C)(D)(E)
4 (A)(B)(C)(D)(E)	14 (A)(B)(C)(D)(E)	24 (A)(B)(C)(D)(E)	34 (A)(B)(C)(D)(E)
5 (A)(B)(C)(D)(E)	15 (A)(B)(C)(D)(E)	25 (A)(B)(C)(D)(E)	35 (A)(B)(C)(D)(E)
6 (A)(B)(C)(D)(E)	16 (A)(B)(C)(D)(E)	26 (A)(B)(C)(D)(E)	36 (A)(B)(C)(D)(E)
7 (A)(B)(C)(D)(E)	17 (A)(B)(C)(D)(E)	27 (A)(B)(C)(D)(E)	37 (A)(B)(C)(D)(E)
8 (A)(B)(C)(D)(E)	18 (A)(B)(C)(D)(E)	28 (A)(B)(C)(D)(E)	38 (A)(B)(C)(D)(E)
9 (A)(B)(C)(D)(E)	19 (A)(B)(C)(D)(E)	29 (A)(B)(C)(D)(E)	39 (A)(B)(C)(D)(E)
10 (A)(B)(C)(D)(E)	20 (A)(B)(C)(D)(E)	30 (A)(B)(C)(D)(E)	40 (A)(B)(C)(D)(E)

SECTION 2

1 (A)(B)(C)(D)(E)	11 (A)(B)(C)(D)(E)	21 (A)(B)(C)(D)(E)	31 (A)(B)(C)(D)(E)
2 (A)(B)(C)(D)(E)	12 (A)(B)(C)(D)(E)	22 (A)(B)(C)(D)(E)	32 (A)(B)(C)(D)(E)
3 (A)(B)(C)(D)(E)	13 (A)(B)(C)(D)(E)	23 (A)(B)(C)(D)(E)	33 (A)(B)(C)(D)(E)
4 (A)(B)(C)(D)(E)	14 (A)(B)(C)(D)(E)	24 (A)(B)(C)(D)(E)	34 (A)(B)(C)(D)(E)
5 (A)(B)(C)(D)(E)	15 (A)(B)(C)(D)(E)	25 (A)(B)(C)(D)(E)	35 (A)(B)(C)(D)(E)
6 (A)(B)(C)(D)(E)	16 (A)(B)(C)(D)(E)	26 (A)(B)(C)(D)(E)	36 (A)(B)(C)(D)(E)
7 (A)(B)(C)(D)(E)	17 (A)(B)(C)(D)(E)	27 (A)(B)(C)(D)(E)	37 (A)(B)(C)(D)(E)
8 (A)(B)(C)(D)(E)	18 (A)(B)(C)(D)(E)	28 (A)(B)(C)(D)(E)	38 (A)(B)(C)(D)(E)
9 (A)(B)(C)(D)(E)	19 (A)(B)(C)(D)(E)	29 (A)(B)(C)(D)(E)	39 (A)(B)(C)(D)(E)
10 (A)(B)(C)(D)(E)	20 (A)(B)(C)(D)(E)	30 (A)(B)(C)(D)(E)	40 (A)(B)(C)(D)(E)

SECTION 3

1 (A)(B)(C)(D)(E)	11 (A)(B)(C)(D)(E)	21 (A)(B)(C)(D)(E)	31 (A)(B)(C)(D)(E)
2 (A)(B)(C)(D)(E)	12 (A)(B)(C)(D)(E)	22 (A)(B)(C)(D)(E)	32 (A)(B)(C)(D)(E)
3 (A)(B)(C)(D)(E)	13 (A)(B)(C)(D)(E)	23 (A)(B)(C)(D)(E)	33 (A)(B)(C)(D)(E)
4 (A)(B)(C)(D)(E)	14 (A)(B)(C)(D)(E)	24 (A)(B)(C)(D)(E)	34 (A)(B)(C)(D)(E)
5 (A)(B)(C)(D)(E)	15 (A)(B)(C)(D)(E)	25 (A)(B)(C)(D)(E)	35 (A)(B)(C)(D)(E)
6 (A)(B)(C)(D)(E)	16 (A)(B)(C)(D)(E)	26 (A)(B)(C)(D)(E)	36 (A)(B)(C)(D)(E)
7 (A)(B)(C)(D)(E)	17 (A)(B)(C)(D)(E)	27 (A)(B)(C)(D)(E)	37 (A)(B)(C)(D)(E)
8 (A)(B)(C)(D)(E)	18 (A)(B)(C)(D)(E)	28 (A)(B)(C)(D)(E)	38 (A)(B)(C)(D)(E)
9 (A)(B)(C)(D)(E)	19 (A)(B)(C)(D)(E)	29 (A)(B)(C)(D)(E)	39 (A)(B)(C)(D)(E)
10 (A)(B)(C)(D)(E)	20 (A)(B)(C)(D)(E)	30 (A)(B)(C)(D)(E)	40 (A)(B)(C)(D)(E)

TEAR HERE

SECTION 4

1 Ⓐ Ⓑ Ⓒ Ⓓ Ⓔ   6 Ⓐ Ⓑ Ⓒ Ⓓ Ⓔ   11 Ⓐ Ⓑ Ⓒ Ⓓ Ⓔ
2 Ⓐ Ⓑ Ⓒ Ⓓ Ⓔ   7 Ⓐ Ⓑ Ⓒ Ⓓ Ⓔ   12 Ⓐ Ⓑ Ⓒ Ⓓ Ⓔ
3 Ⓐ Ⓑ Ⓒ Ⓓ Ⓔ   8 Ⓐ Ⓑ Ⓒ Ⓓ Ⓔ   13 Ⓐ Ⓑ Ⓒ Ⓓ Ⓔ
4 Ⓐ Ⓑ Ⓒ Ⓓ Ⓔ   9 Ⓐ Ⓑ Ⓒ Ⓓ Ⓔ   14 Ⓐ Ⓑ Ⓒ Ⓓ Ⓔ
5 Ⓐ Ⓑ Ⓒ Ⓓ Ⓔ   10 Ⓐ Ⓑ Ⓒ Ⓓ Ⓔ   15 Ⓐ Ⓑ Ⓒ Ⓓ Ⓔ

Note: ONLY the answers entered on the grid are scored.

Handwritten answers at the top of the column are NOT scored.

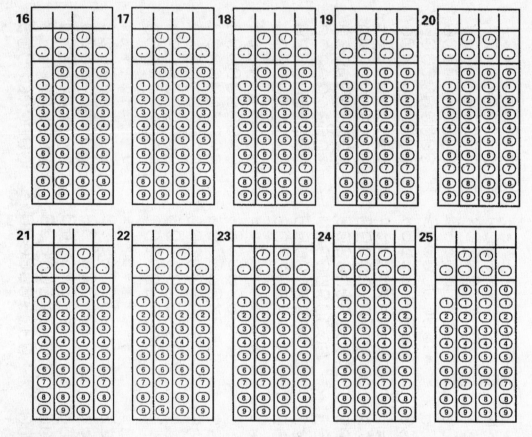

SECTION 5

1 Ⓐ Ⓑ Ⓒ Ⓓ Ⓔ   6 Ⓐ Ⓑ Ⓒ Ⓓ Ⓔ   11 Ⓐ Ⓑ Ⓒ Ⓓ Ⓔ
2 Ⓐ Ⓑ Ⓒ Ⓓ Ⓔ   7 Ⓐ Ⓑ Ⓒ Ⓓ Ⓔ   12 Ⓐ Ⓑ Ⓒ Ⓓ Ⓔ
3 Ⓐ Ⓑ Ⓒ Ⓓ Ⓔ   8 Ⓐ Ⓑ Ⓒ Ⓓ Ⓔ   13 Ⓐ Ⓑ Ⓒ Ⓓ Ⓔ
4 Ⓐ Ⓑ Ⓒ Ⓓ Ⓔ   9 Ⓐ Ⓑ Ⓒ Ⓓ Ⓔ   14 Ⓐ Ⓑ Ⓒ Ⓓ Ⓔ
5 Ⓐ Ⓑ Ⓒ Ⓓ Ⓔ   10 Ⓐ Ⓑ Ⓒ Ⓓ Ⓔ   15 Ⓐ Ⓑ Ⓒ Ⓓ Ⓔ

SECTION 6

1 Ⓐ Ⓑ Ⓒ Ⓓ Ⓔ   6 Ⓐ Ⓑ Ⓒ Ⓓ Ⓔ   11 Ⓐ Ⓑ Ⓒ Ⓓ Ⓔ
2 Ⓐ Ⓑ Ⓒ Ⓓ Ⓔ   7 Ⓐ Ⓑ Ⓒ Ⓓ Ⓔ   12 Ⓐ Ⓑ Ⓒ Ⓓ Ⓔ
3 Ⓐ Ⓑ Ⓒ Ⓓ Ⓔ   8 Ⓐ Ⓑ Ⓒ Ⓓ Ⓔ   13 Ⓐ Ⓑ Ⓒ Ⓓ Ⓔ
4 Ⓐ Ⓑ Ⓒ Ⓓ Ⓔ   9 Ⓐ Ⓑ Ⓒ Ⓓ Ⓔ   14 Ⓐ Ⓑ Ⓒ Ⓓ Ⓔ
5 Ⓐ Ⓑ Ⓒ Ⓓ Ⓔ   10 Ⓐ Ⓑ Ⓒ Ⓓ Ⓔ   15 Ⓐ Ⓑ Ⓒ Ⓓ Ⓔ

TEAR HERE

PRACTICE TEST 4

Section 1

35 Questions • Time—30 Minutes

Directions: Each of the following questions consists of an incomplete sentence followed by five words or pairs of words. Choose that word or pair of words that, when substituted for the blank space or spaces, best completes the meaning of the sentence and mark the letter of your choice on your answer sheet.

Example

Q In view of the extenuating circumstances and the defendant's youth, the judge recommended ____.

(A) conviction

(B) a defense

(C) a mistrial

(D) leniency

(E) life imprisonment

A Ⓐ Ⓑ Ⓒ ⬤ Ⓔ

1. ____ by her family, the woman finally agreed to sell the farm.

(A) Decimated

(B) Importuned

(C) Encumbered

(D) Interpolated

(E) Designated

2. The ghost of his royal father ____ the young Hamlet to avenge his murder.

(A) enervates

(B) parlays

(C) marauds

(D) exhorts

(E) inculcates

3. Concerned for his children's safety, the father tried to ____ in them a(n) ____ attitude toward strangers.

(A) obviate..hospitable

(B) ingratiate..assiduous

(C) insinuate..salubrious

(D) assimilate..benevolent

(E) inculcate..wary

4. A life of hardship and poverty has ____ them to petty physical discomforts.

(A) ascribed

(B) inured

(C) remonstrated

(D) deferred

(E) impugned

5. Displeased with the ____ of his novel, the author withdrew from the television project.

(A) adaptation

(B) compilation

(C) transliteration

(D) transfusion

(E) resurgence

6. Because he changed his mind nearly every day, the governor had a reputation for ____.
    (A) impudence
    (B) impartiality
    (C) perspicuity
    (D) prevarication
    (E) vacillation

7. Her ____ smile ____ all those who saw it.
    (A) devastating..replenished
    (B) penultimate..inured
    (C) radiant..obliged
    (D) sunny..tanned
    (E) bright..dazzled

8. Although he was known as a ____ old miser, his anonymous gifts to charity were always ____.
    (A) grasping..tasteless
    (B) spendthrift..gracious
    (C) gregarious..selfish
    (D) penurious..generous
    (E) stingy..mangy

9. With one ____ motion, Brian disarmed his assailant and gained his freedom.
    (A) maladroit
    (B) deft
    (C) ponderous
    (D) superfluous
    (E) brusque

10. The platypus is a biological ____; although it's classed as a mammal, it has a duck-like bill and lays eggs.
    (A) euphemism
    (B) exemplar
    (C) antidote
    (D) periphery
    (E) anomaly

Directions: Each of the following questions consists of a capitalized pair of words followed by five pairs of words lettered (A) to (E). The capitalized words bear some meaningful relationship to each other. Choose the lettered pair of words whose relationship is most similiar to that expressed by the capitalized pair and mark its letter on your answer sheet.

Example

Q DAY : SUN ::
    (A) sunlight : daylight
    (B) ray : sun
    (C) night : moon
    (D) heat : cold
    (E) moon : star

11. TEACHER : INSTRUCTION ::
    (A) lawyer : crime
    (B) army : regiment
    (C) doctor : disease
    (D) guard : protection
    (E) student : learning

12. USHER : THEATER ::
   (A) conductor : train
   (B) program : movie
   (C) aisle : row
   (D) friend : actor
   (E) pilot : airplane

13. SKATE : RINK ::
   (A) build : arena
   (B) sleep : lecture
   (C) repose : bed
   (D) park : stadium
   (E) draw : circle

14. SAPLING : TREE ::
   (A) weed : plant
   (B) grass : wheat
   (C) puppy : dog
   (D) seed : vegetable
   (E) acorn : oak

15. FRET : RELAX ::
   (A) worry : avoid
   (B) sob : cry
   (C) fight : submit
   (D) sing : laugh
   (E) frolic : play

16. STUTTER : TALK ::
   (A) worry : analyze
   (B) stumble : walk
   (C) walk : run
   (D) hear : understand
   (E) trip : fall

17. DAMAGE : DEMOLISH ::
   (A) whimper : wail
   (B) break : mar
   (C) loosen : cinch
   (D) punish : accept
   (E) plan : act

18. HOSE : WATER ::
   (A) lawn : grass
   (B) speaker : sound
   (C) window : air
   (D) vent : flap
   (E) chimney : smoke

19. EXERCISE : STRENGTH ::
   (A) concern : resource
   (B) practice : skill
   (C) success : loss
   (D) sport : contest
   (E) gym : weight

20. SERGEANT : SOLDIERS ::
   (A) captain : sports
   (B) colonel : tanks
   (C) coach : players
   (D) director : scripts
   (E) teacher : books

21. VOLATILE : STABILITY ::
   (A) spontaneous : enthusiasm
   (B) voluble : glibness
   (C) wanton : restraint
   (D) reverent : respect
   (E) servile : humility

22. SCIENTIST : LABORATORY ::
   (A) chemist : test tube
   (B) lawyer : client
   (C) dentist : drill
   (D) teacher : classroom
   (E) actor : playwright

23. JOCULAR : SOLEMNITY ::
   (A) latent : visibility
   (B) pompous : spectacle
   (C) ruined : demolition
   (D) vindictive : enmity
   (E) lonely : insularity

> **Directions:** The reading passage below is followed by a set of questions. Read the passage and answer the accompanying questions, basing your answers on what is stated or implied in the passage. Mark the letter of your choice on your answer sheet.

Questions 24–35 are based on the following passage.

The history of a place is preserved in various ways, including through its landmarks, historic buildings, and public areas. The following passage discusses Los Angeles, and what is being done there to preserve its place of history.

An outsider approaches the subject gingerly, lest civic feelings be bruised. Los Angeles gives the impression of having erased much of its history by allowing
(5) the city's development to run unchecked. Insiders like Dolores Hayden . . . pull no punches: "It is . . . common," she wrote, "for fond residents to quote Gertrude Stein's sentence about Oakland when
(10) summing up urban design in Los Angeles: 'There's no there, there.'" Hayden has also acknowledged that Los Angeles is generally "the first (American city) singled out as having a problem about
(15) sense of place." Both statements come from a handsome brochure-*cum*-itinerary, drawn up by Hayden, Gail Dubrow, and Carolyn Flynn to introduce The Power of Place, a local nonprofit group
(20) with a mission to retrieve some of the city's misplaced "there."

Founded by Hayden in 1982, The Power of Place lays special emphasis on redressing an imbalance in memory—
(25) and memorials. As Hayden has pointed out, in 1987 less than half the population of Los Angeles was Anglo-American; yet almost 98 percent of the city's cultural historic landmarks were de-
(30) voted to the history and accomplishments of Anglo-Americans. Even these personages come from a narrow spectrum of achievers—in Hayden's phrase, "a small minority of landholders,

(35) bankers, business leaders, and their architects"—almost all of whom were male. . . .

The likeliest explanation for this under-representation may be an urban
(40) variation on the great-man theory of history: History is what public figures do, and by their civic monuments shall ye know them—especially the structures they designed or built. In Hayden's view,
(45) however, "The task of choosing a past for Los Angeles is a political as well as an historic and cultural one," and the unexamined preference for architecture as the focus of historic preservation ef-
(50) forts can slight less conscious but perhaps equally powerful human forces. Hayden's goal has been to supplement the city's ample supply of monocultural landmarks and memorials with others
(55) representing its ethnic and gender-based diversity. Accordingly, some sites need new status as official landmarks, others need reinterpretation. Other sites no longer contain structures emblematic of
(60) their histories or are located in blighted neighborhoods; these do not readily lend themselves to resuscitation through renovation and commercial development, as preservationists have managed
(65) elsewhere.

The Power of Place has identified nine places on which to concentrate in the first phase of its work: development of a walking tour of little-known Los
(70) Angeles sites, for which The Power of Place brochure serves as a guide.

The most ethnically evocative of these sites is probably Vignes Vineyard/Wolfskill Grove, neighboring plots that
(75) once supported a share of the vineyards and citrus groves abounding in early 19th-century Los Angeles. The first cultivators of the wine grapes and citrus were Franciscan missionaries and their

(80) Native American converts. The padres gave way to white entrepreneurs; the Native Americans to various waves of immigrants, including Chinese, then Japanese, and finally, Mexicans. . . .

(85) The Power of Place brochure concludes its summary of what is known about each stop on the walking tour with a postscript called Placemaking, which describes the site's current status and

(90) suggests ways to make it more redolent of its past. For the vineyard/grove complex, the current situation is not atypical: "Present uses . . . are commercial and industrial." Then comes word of

(95) what seems to be a minor miracle: "One tall slender grapefruit tree . . . has been preserved and relocated in the courtyard of the Japanese American Cultural and Community Center. . . ." Sugges-

(100) tions for recapturing more of the past proposed by The Power of Place include returning orange trees to the Wolfskill site and installing historical markers on the Vignes site.

24. Which of the following most accurately summarizes the main idea of the passage?

(A) Multicultural landmarks are better than monocultural ones.

(B) The Power of Place is attempting to correct an imbalance in Los Angeles historical landmarks.

(C) Los Angeles has a limited sense of place because it has not adequately preserved its history.

(D) Dolores Hayden has an iconoclastic viewpoint on the state of historical preservation in Los Angeles.

(E) Los Angelenos do not care about their surroundings.

25. The author uses the phrase "civic feelings" (line 2) to mean the

(A) allegiance of a city's residents to their city.

(B) emotions that breed courtesy and good behavior.

(C) respect for each other shown by people who think of themselves as civilized.

(D) defensiveness that city residents sometimes show toward outsiders.

(E) regularity with which citizens vote.

26. What is the danger of allowing the development of Los Angeles to "run unchecked"? (lines 5–6)

(A) The roadways will become overrun with traffic.

(B) Developers will use up all arable land.

(C) Smog will become an even bigger environmental concern.

(D) Much of the city's cultural history will be lost to modernization.

(E) People will emigrate from Los Angeles in search of more suitable living conditions.

27. In quoting Gertrude Stein's saying, "There's no there, there" (line 11), Dolores Hayden most likely means to say that

(A) the same lack of urban design that characterizes Oakland is also typical of Los Angeles.

(B) a sprawling city like Los Angeles often has no particular center where residents congregate.

(C) Los Angeles's historic monuments focus too exclusively on a particular segment of the population.

(D) Los Angeles is not an old city historically.

(E) Los Angeles seems to have no outstanding characteristics that define it as a place.

28. According to Dolores Hayden, most of the historical landmarks of Los Angeles

    (A) do not enhance a sense of place among the people of Los Angeles.

    (B) have been chosen according to political rather than aesthetic criteria.

    (C) are not representative of the history of all of the people of Los Angeles.

    (D) should be replaced by landmarks that celebrate the accomplishments of minorities and women.

    (E) are not on a par with historical landmarks elsewhere.

29. With which of the following statements about the people memorialized by most existing Los Angeles monuments would Dolores Hayden be most likely to agree?

    I. They were usually of a higher social class than were the people highlighted by The Power of Place.

    II. Their accomplishments are more conspicuous than are those of the people highlighted by The Power of Place.

    III. They made greater contributions to the economic development of Los Angeles than did the people highlighted by The Power of Place.

    (A) I only

    (B) I, II, and III

    (C) I and III only

    (D) I and II only

    (E) II only

30. Which of the following statements most accurately characterizes Hayden's view on historic preservation, as those views are described in the passage?

    (A) Political and economic considerations should have no place in the designation of cultural and historic landmarks.

    (B) Plants and other natural phenomena make better historic landmarks than do buildings and other human artifacts.

    (C) Some parts of history cannot be memorialized in surviving buildings and landmarks, so new ways must be found to more fully recapture the past.

    (D) The homes and workplaces of working people should be preserved whenever possible because the history of working people is more important than that of so-called "great men."

    (E) The past cannot be memorialized in anything but buildings and landmarks so that every care must be taken to preserve them.

31. Which one of the following is cited in the passage as a difficulty The Power of Place faces in preserving the history of women and minorities?

    (A) Most citizens of Los Angeles are uninterested in the preservation effort.

    (B) Few written records of the history of women and minorities have been preserved.

    (C) Women and minorities are not in support of the efforts on their behalf.

    (D) Many of the historical sites have completely changed in the intervening years.

    (E) Funding for historical preservation tends to go to groups that memorialize famous public figures.

32. The author of the passage seems to value the Vignes/Wolfskill site most for

    (A) its well-preserved state.

    (B) the main uses the site has served over the years.

    (C) its evocation of one of the most important industries in nineteenth-century Los Angeles.

    (D) the variety of cultural groups whose history is represented there.

    (E) its connection to the early founders of Los Angeles.

33. For Hayden, "Placemaking" (line 88) most nearly means

    (A) finding ways to overcome urban blight.

    (B) capturing the character of the city by evoking the past of all its people.

    (C) restoring an historic site to its previous condition.

    (D) showing the city's residents how particular sites have been used in the past.

    (E) creating new landmarks.

34. The author most likely refers to the existence of a grapefruit tree at the Vignes/Wolfskill site as "a minor miracle" (line 95) because

    (A) the tree's slenderness indicates that it has survived so far only because of exceptionally good care.

    (B) grapefruit trees grow best in groves rather than singly.

    (C) citrus trees, once common at the site, have been replaced by businesses and factories.

    (D) grapefruit trees are not native to the area and often do not grow well there.

    (E) the area has been so heavily vandalized.

35. In the author's view, all of the following would most likely be *undervalued* cultural landmarks EXCEPT

    (A) indigenous trees.

    (B) endangered species of animal and plant life.

    (C) historic buildings in dilapidated areas.

    (D) city hall.

    (E) china town.

STOP

END OF SECTION 1. IF YOU HAVE ANY TIME LEFT, GO OVER YOUR WORK IN THIS SECTION ONLY. DO NOT WORK IN ANY OTHER SECTION OF THE TEST.

Section 2

25 Questions • Time—30 Minutes

Directions: Solve the following problems using any available space on the page for scratchwork. On your answer sheet fill in the choice that best corresponds to the correct answer.

Notes: The figures accompanying the problems are drawn as accurately as possible unless otherwise stated in specific problems. Again, unless otherwise stated, all figures lie in the same plane. All numbers used in these problems are real numbers. Calculators are permitted for this test.

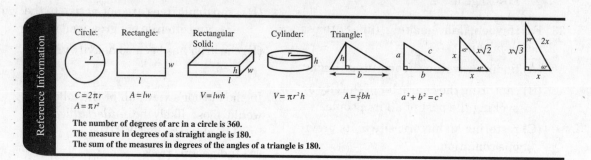

Reference Information

Circle: Rectangle: Rectangular Solid: Cylinder: Triangle:

$C = 2\pi r$
$A = \pi r^2$ $A = lw$ $V = lwh$ $V = \pi r^2 h$ $A = \frac{1}{2}bh$ $a^2 + b^2 = c^2$

The number of degrees of arc in a circle is 360.
The measure in degrees of a straight angle is 180.
The sum of the measures in degrees of the angles of a triangle is 180.

---

1. If for all real numbers (a.b.c. − d.e.f.) = (a − d) × (b − e) × (c − f), then (4.5.6. − 1.2.3.) =

(A) −27

(B) 0

(C) 27

(D) 54

(E) 108

2. The sum of an odd number and an even number is

(A) sometimes an even number.

(B) always divisible by 3 or 5 or 7.

(C) always an odd number.

(D) always a prime number.

(E) always divisible by 2.

3. If $6x + 12 = 9$, $x^2 =$

(A) $\frac{21}{6}$

(B) $-\frac{1}{2}$

(C) $\frac{9}{12}$

(D) $\frac{1}{4}$

(E) $\frac{9}{6}$

4. Under certain conditions, sound travels at about 1,100 ft. per second. If 88 ft. per second is approximately equivalent to 60 miles per hour, the speed of sound in miles per hour under the above conditions is closest to

(A) 730

(B) 740

(C) 750

(D) 760

(E) 780

5. If on a blueprint $\frac{1}{4}$ inch equals 12 inches, what is the actual length in feet of a steel bar that is represented on the blueprint by a line $3\frac{3}{8}$ inches long?

   (A) $2\frac{1}{2}$

   (B) $3\frac{3}{8}$

   (C) $6\frac{3}{4}$

   (D) 9

   (E) $13\frac{1}{2}$

6. If one angle of a triangle is three times a second angle and the third angle is 20 degrees more than the second angle, the second angle, in degrees, is

   (A) 64

   (B) 50

   (C) 40

   (D) 34

   (E) 32

7. If $x = \frac{3}{2}$ and $y = 2$, then $x + y^2 - \frac{1}{2} =$

   (A) 5

   (B) 10

   (C) $11\frac{1}{2}$

   (D) $9\frac{1}{2}$

   (E) $\frac{6}{2}$

8. A math class has 27 students in it. Of those students, 14 are also enrolled in history and 17 are enrolled in English. What is the minimum percentage of the students in the math class who are also enrolled in history *and* English?

   (A) 15%

   (B) 22%

   (C) 49%

   (D) 63%

   (E) 91%

9. A cylindrical container has a diameter of 14 inches and a height of 6 inches. Since one gallon equals 231 cubic inches, the capacity of the tank in gallons is approximately

   (A) $\frac{2}{3}$

   (B) $1\frac{1}{7}$

   (C) $2\frac{2}{7}$

   (D) $2\frac{2}{3}$

   (E) 4

10. If $\frac{1}{x+y} = 6$ and $x = 2$, then $y =$

    (A) $-\frac{11}{6}$

    (B) $-\frac{9}{4}$

    (C) -2

    (D) -1

    (E) 4

11. The number of grams in one ounce is 28.35. The number of grams in a kilogram is 1,000. Therefore the number of kilograms in one pound is approximately

    (A) 0.045

    (B) 0.45

    (C) 1.0

    (D) 2.2

    (E) 4.5

12. Which one of the following numbers is NOT the square of a rational number?

    (A) .0016

    (B) .16

    (C) 1.6

    (D) 16

    (E) 1,600

13. In the figure below, lines l and m are parallel. Which of the following must be equal to 180 degrees?

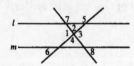

I. 1 plus 3

II. 2 plus 4

III. 5 plus 6

IV. 7 plus 8

V. 8 plus 6

(A) I and II only

(B) III and IV only

(C) V only

(D) I, II, III, IV only

(E) I, II, III, IV, V

14. If x is a fraction that ranges from $\frac{1}{4}$ to $\frac{1}{2}$ and y is a fraction that ranges from $\frac{3}{4}$ to $\frac{11}{12}$, what is the maximum value for $\frac{x}{y}$?

(A) $\frac{3}{16}$

(B) $\frac{11}{48}$

(C) $\frac{3}{8}$

(D) $\frac{11}{24}$

(E) $\frac{2}{3}$

15. These circles share a common center, point O. The smallest circle has a radius of 2; the next circle, a radius of 5; and the largest circle, a radius of 9. What fraction of the area of the largest circle is the area of the shaded region?

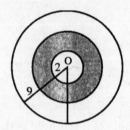

(A) $\frac{7}{27}$

(B) $\frac{25}{81}$

(C) $\frac{1}{3}$

(D) $\frac{7}{11}$

(E) $\frac{12}{17}$

16. If n and d represent positive whole numbers $(n > d > l)$, the fractions

I. $\frac{d}{n}$

II. $\frac{d+1}{n+1}$

III. $\frac{d-1}{n-1}$

IV. $\frac{n}{d}$

V. $\frac{n-1}{d-1}$

arranged in ascending order of magnitude are represented correctly by

(A) III, II, I, V, IV

(B) IV, V, III, I, II

(C) II, I, IV, III, V

(D) III, V, IV, I, II

(E) III, I, II, IV, V

17. A train running between two towns arrives at its destination 10 minutes late when it goes 40 miles per hour and 16 minutes late when it goes 30 miles per hour. The distance in miles between the towns is

    (A) $8\frac{6}{7}$

    (B) 12

    (C) 192

    (D) 560

    (E) 720

18. A square has a diagonal of x units. If the diagonal is increased by 2 units, what is the length of the side of the new square?

    (A) $x + 2$

    (B) $(x+2)\sqrt{2}$

    (C) $\frac{(x+2)\sqrt{2}}{2}$

    (D) $(x + 2)2$

    (E) $\frac{(x+2)\sqrt{2}}{4}$

19. $PQRS$ is a square and triangle PTS is an equilateral triangle. How many degrees are there in angle TRS?

    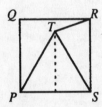

    (A) 60

    (B) 75

    (C) 80

    (D) 90

    (E) It cannot be determined from the information given.

20. In the figure, line PQ is parallel to line RS, angle $y = 60°$, and angle $z = 130°$. How many degrees are there in angle x?

    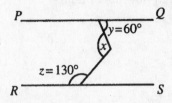

    (A) 90°

    (B) 100°

    (C) 110°

    (D) 120°

    (E) 130°

21. In the figure below, QOR is a quadrant of a circle. $PS = 6$ and $PT = 8$. What is the length of arc QR?

    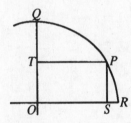

    (A) 5π

    (B) 10π

    (C) 20π

    (D) 24

    (E) It cannot be determined from the information given.

22. The ice compartment in a refrigerator is 8 inches deep, 5 inches high, and 4 inches wide. How many ice cubes will it hold if each cube is 2 inches on each edge?

    (A) 16

    (B) 20

    (C) 24

    (D) 80

    (E) 160

23. If Paul can paint a fence in 2 hours and Fred can paint the same fence in 3 hours, Paul and Fred working together can paint the fence in how many hours?

(A) 2.5

(B) $\frac{5}{6}$

(C) 5

(D) 1

(E) 1.2

24. If one third of the liquid contents of a can evaporates on the first day and three fourths of the remainder evaporates on the second day, the fractional part of the original contents remaining at the close of the second day is

(A) $\frac{1}{6}$

(B) $\frac{1}{4}$

(C) $\frac{5}{12}$

(D) $\frac{1}{2}$

(E) $\frac{7}{12}$

25. A motorist drives 60 miles to her destination at an average speed of 40 miles per hour and makes the return trip at an average rate of 30 miles per hour. Her average speed in miles per hour for the entire trip is

(A) 17

(B) $34\frac{2}{7}$

(C) 35

(D) $43\frac{1}{3}$

(E) 70

STOP

END OF SECTION 2. IF YOU HAVE ANY TIME LEFT, GO OVER YOUR WORK IN THIS SECTION ONLY. DO NOT WORK IN ANY OTHER SECTION OF THE TEST.

Section 3

31 Questions • Time—30 Minutes

> **Directions:** Each of the following questions consists of an incomplete sentence followed by five words or pairs of words. Choose that word or pair of words that, when substituted for the blank space or spaces, best completes the meaning of the sentence and mark the letter of your choice on the answer sheet.

Example

> **Q** In view of the extenuating circumstances and the defendant's youth, the judge recommended ____.
>
> (A) conviction
> (B) a defense
> (C) a mistrial
> (D) leniency
> (E) life imprisonment
>
> **A** Ⓐ Ⓑ Ⓒ ● Ⓔ

1. They acted in concert, each ____ for a(n) ____ of the plot.
   (A) reliable..source
   (B) responsible..element
   (C) unavailable..section
   (D) appointed..article
   (E) agreeable..felony

2. They were unwisely ____ during their education, and ____ was the result.
   (A) neglected..ignorance
   (B) interrupted..consistency
   (C) befriended..alienation
   (D) instructed..genius
   (E) taught..attendance

3. Most young children are highly conformist and will ____ a classmate whose appearance or manners are ____.
   (A) welcome..bizarre
   (B) shun..conventional
   (C) emulate..unusual
   (D) ostracize..different
   (E) deride..ordinary

4. The royal astrologers were commanded to determine the most ____ date for the king's coronation.
   (A) propitious
   (B) ostensible
   (C) aberrant
   (D) resplendent
   (E) obsequious

5. The poem by the great satirist was dripping with venom and was ____ with scorn.
   (A) contentious
   (B) discordant
   (C) redolent
   (D) sardonic
   (E) vicarious

6. The ____ rites of the fraternity were kept secret by the members and were never ____ to outsiders.
   (A) eclectic..delegated
   (B) esoteric..divulged
   (C) dubious..maligned
   (D) inscrutable..traduced
   (E) elusive..proscribed

7. The composer was ____ enough to praise the work of a musician he detested.

   (A) magnanimous
   (B) loquacious
   (C) munificent
   (D) parsimonious
   (E) surreptitious

8. The goodwill of its customers is a genuine but ____ asset for a company.

   (A) insensate
   (B) redolent
   (C) dismissive
   (D) intangible
   (E) vigilant

9. Though the law's ____ purpose was to curtail false advertising, its actual result was to ____ free speech.

   (A) potential..preclude
   (B) mendacious..eschew
   (C) ostensible..circumscribe
   (D) illicit..reconcile
   (E) recalcitrant..repress

Directions: Each of the following questions consists of a capitalized pair of words followed by five pairs of words lettered (A) to (E). The capitalized words bear some meaningful relationship to each other. Choose the lettered pair of words whose relationship is most similar to that expressed by the capitalized pair and mark its letter on your answer sheet.

Example

Q DAY : SUN ::

   (A) sunlight : daylight
   (B) ray : sun
   (C) night : moon
   (D) heat : cold
   (E) moon : star

A (A) (B) ● (D) (E)

10. AWL : PUNCTURE ::

   (A) tire : ride
   (B) cleaver : cut
   (C) plane : soar
   (D) throttle : start
   (E) axle : steer

11. LUSH : JUNGLE ::

   (A) delicious : fruit
   (B) diligent : worker
   (C) barren : desert
   (D) hot : weather
   (E) obvious : wealth

12. HAND : GNARLED ::

   (A) tree : tall
   (B) foot : sore
   (C) flower : crushed
   (D) brow : creased
   (E) tire : round

13. PLANET : ROTATES ::

   (A) top : spins
   (B) star : shines
   (C) moon : glows
   (D) toy : plays
   (E) rocket : fires

14. MILK : SPOIL ::
- **(A)** metal : bend
- **(B)** water : filter
- **(C)** wood : rot
- **(D)** fish : swim
- **(E)** animal : rest

15. MUNIFICENT : GENEROSITY ::
- **(A)** dolorous : sorrow
- **(B)** domineering : timidity
- **(C)** indisputable : doubt
- **(D)** fortunate : haplessness
- **(E)** beguiled : judiciousness

Directions: Each passage below is followed by a set of questions. Read each passage, then answer the accompanying questions, basing your answers on what is stated or implied in the passage and in any introductory material provided. Mark the letter of your choice on your answer sheet.

Questions 16–23 are based on the following passage.

John Adams Audubon (1785–1851) is known primarily for his bird studies, but as this passage from Ornithological Biography *shows, he was fascinated by the behavior of other animals as well.*

The Black Bear (*Ursus ameri-canus*), however clumsy in appearance, is active, vigilant, and persevering; possesses great strength, courage, and address;
(5) and undergoes with little injury the greatest fatigues and hardships in avoiding the pursuit of the hunter. Like the Deer, it changes its haunts with the seasons, and for the same reason,
(10) namely, the desire of obtaining suitable food, or of retiring to the more inaccessible parts, where it can pass the time in security, unobserved by man, the most dangerous of its enemies. During the
(15) spring months, it searches for food in the low rich alluvial lands that border the rivers, or by the margins of such inland lakes as, on account of their small size, are called by us ponds. There it procures
(20) abundance of succulent roots, and of the tender juicy stems of plants, on which it chiefly feeds at that season. During the summer heat, it enters the gloomy swamps, passes much of its time in wal-
(25) lowing in the mud, like a hog, and con-

tents itself with crayfish, roots, and nettles, now and then, when hard pressed by hunger, seizing on a young pig, or perhaps a sow, or even a calf. As soon as
(30) the different kinds of berries which grow on the mountain begin to ripen, the Bears betake themselves to the high grounds, followed by their cubs. In such retired parts of the country where there
(35) are no hilly grounds, it pays visits to the maize fields, which it ravages for a while. After this, the various species of nuts, acorns, grapes, and other forest fruits, that form what in the western country is
(40) called *mast*, attract its attention. The Bear is then seen rambling singly through the woods to gather this harvest, not forgetting to rob every Bee tree it meets with, Bears being, as you well
(45) know, expert at this operation. You also know that they are good climbers, and may have been told, or at least may now be told, that the Black Bear now and then houses itself in the hollow trunks of
(50) the larger trees for weeks together, when it is said to suck its paws. You are probably not aware of a habit in which it indulges, and which, being curious, must be interesting to you.
(55) At one season, the Black Bear may be seen examining the lower part of the trunk of a tree for several minutes with much attention, at the same time looking around, and snuffing the air, to as-

(60) sure itself that no enemy is near. It then raises itself on its hind legs, approaches the trunk, embraces it with its forelegs, and scratches the bark with its teeth and claws for several minutes in con-
(65) tinuance. Its jaws clash against each other, until a mass of foam runs down both sides of the mouth. After this it continues its rambles.

In various portions of our country,
(70) many of our woodsmen and hunters who have seen the Bear performing the singular operation just described, imagine that it does so for the purpose of leaving behind an indication of its size and power.
(75) They measure the height at which the scratches are made, and in this manner, can, in fact, form an estimate of the magnitude of the individual. My own opinion, however, is different. It seems
(80) to me that the Bear scratches on the trees, not for the purpose of showing its size or its strength, but merely for that of sharpening its teeth and claws, to enable it better to encounter a rival of its
(85) own species during the amatory season. The Wild Boar of Europe clashes its tusks and scrapes the earth with its feet, and the Deer rubs its antlers against the lower part of the stems of young trees or
(90) bushes, for the same purpose.

16. The bear migrates from one habitat to another in order to

(A) teach its cubs to climb.

(B) locate a hollow tree.

(C) visit every bee tree.

(D) escape from the wild boar.

(E) find food and security.

17. The fact that Audubon calls man the bear's "most dangerous" enemy (lines 13–14) indicates that he

(A) is himself a hunter.

(B) has some sympathy for hunted bears.

(C) is an animal rights activist.

(D) does not believe that bears are dangerous.

(E) thinks bears are more dangerous than people.

18. The word *alluvial* (line 16) refers to

(A) high grounds.

(B) rocky shorelines.

(C) river-deposited sediment.

(D) thick underbrush.

(E) maize fields.

19. According to the passage, black bears eat all of the following EXCEPT

(A) bark.

(B) maize.

(C) mast.

(D) honey.

(E) crayfish.

20. Audubon believes that bears scratch trees to

(A) show their power.

(B) leave a mark.

(C) sharpen their claws.

(D) navigate.

(E) indicate their size.

21. Audubon assumes that his reader knows about bears'

(A) scratching behavior and threatening manner.

(B) eating of roots and berries.

(C) size and coloring.

(D) fear of man.

(E) climbing expertise and love of honey.

22. Audubon compares the bear with deer twice,

(A) once in relation to its migratory habits, and once in comparing its rubbing behavior.

(B) once in relation to its eating habits, and once in comparing its combative behavior.

(C) both times having to do with its habitat.

(D) both times having to do with hibernation.

(E) both times having to do with size and weight.

23. From his description, it seems that Audubon's attitude toward black bears is one of

(A) fear.

(B) respect.

(C) amusement.

(D) alarm.

(E) bewilderment.

Questions 24–31 are based on the following passage.

The study of plant life is very different from the study of animal life because of unique plant characteristics. The following passage provides an overview of those characteristics along with some plant classifications that are of interest to scientists.

Compared to animals, plants present unique problems in demographic studies. The idea of counting living individuals becomes difficult given perennials
(5) that reproduce vegetatively by sending out runners or rhizomes, by splitting at the stem base, or by producing arching canes that take root where they touch the ground. In these ways some indi-
(10) viduals, given sufficient time, can extend out over a vast area.

There are five typical plant life spans, and each has a basic associated life form. *Annual plants* live for 1 year or
(15) less. Their average life span is 1–8 months, depending on the species and on the environment where they are located (the same desert plant may complete its life cycle in 8 months one year,
(20) and in 1 month the next, depending on the amount of rain it receives). Annuals with extremely short life cycles are classified as *ephemeral* plants. An example of an ephemeral is *Boerrhavia repens* of
(25) the Sahara Desert, which can go from seed to seed in just 10 days. Annuals are herbaceous, which means that they lack a secondary meristem that produces lateral, woody tissue. They complete their
(30) life cycle after seed production for several reasons: nutrient depletion, hormone changes, or inability of nonwoody tissue to withstand unfavorable environmental conditions following the grow-
(35) ing season. A few species can persist for more than a year in uncommonly favorable conditions.

Biennial plants are also herbaceous, but usually live for 2 years. Their
(40) first year is spent in vegetative growth, which generally takes place more below ground than above. Reproduction occurs in the second year, and this is followed by the completion of the life cycle.
(45) Under poor growing conditions, or by experimental manipulation, the vegetative stage can be drawn out for more than 1 year.

Herbaceous perennials typically
(50) live for 20–30 years, although some species have been known to live for 400–800 years. These plants die back to the root system and root crown at the end of each growing season. The root system be-
(55) comes woody, but the above-ground system is herbaceous. They have a juvenile, vegetative stage for the first 2–8 years, then bloom and reproduce yearly. Sometimes they bloom only once at the con-
(60) clusion of their life cycle. Because herbaceous perennials have no growth rings, it is difficult to age them. Methods that have been used to age them include counting leaf scars or estimating the
(65) rate of spread in *tussock* (clumped) forms.

Suffrutescent shrubs (hemixyles) fall somewhere between herbaceous perennials and true shrubs. They develop perennial, woody tissue only near the
(70) base of their stems; the rest of the shoot system is herbaceous and dies back each year. They are small, and are short-lived compared to true shrubs.

Woody perennials (trees and
(75) shrubs) have the longest life spans. Shrubs live on the average 30–50 years. Broadleaf trees (angiosperm) average 200–300 years, and conifer (needles) trees average 500–1000 years. Woody
(80) perennials spend approximately the first 10% of their life span in a juvenile, totally vegetative state before they enter a combined reproductive and vegetative state, achieving a peak of reproduc-
(85) tion several years before the conclusion of their life cycle.

Regardless of the life span, annual or perennial, one can identify about eight important age states in an individual
(90) plant or population. They are: (1) viable seed, (2) seedling, (3) juvenile, (4) immature, (5) mature, (6) initial reproductive, (7) maximum vigor (reproductive and vegetative), and (8) senescent. If a popu-
(95) lation shows all eight states, it is stable and is most likely a part of a *climax* community. If it shows only the last four states, it may not maintain itself and may be part of a *seral* community.

24. The author believes that plants present "unique problems in demographic studies" (lines 2–3) because

(A) they cannot be aged accurately.

(B) it is difficult to define and identify an individual.

(C) many have very short lifespans.

(D) there has been little interest in such studies.

(E) the scientific community is not capable of conducting them.

25. The best definition of *ephemeral* (line 23) might be

(A) resilient.

(B) short-lived.

(C) awkward.

(D) uncomplicated.

(E) shrub-like.

26. Which of these statements is (are) true, according to paragraph 2?

  I. All herbaceous plants are annuals.

 II. All annuals are herbaceous plants.

III. All annuals are ephemeral.

(A) I only

(B) III only

(C) II only

(D) I and III only

(E) I and II only

27. A plant that spends a year growing below ground and a year growing above ground before dying would be called

(A) an angiosperm.

(B) a true shrub.

(C) a meristem.

(D) ephemeral.

(E) a biennial.

28. *Annual* and *perennial* are names of

(A) plant life spans.

(B) plant species.

(C) woody plants.

(D) plant age states.

(E) plant life forms.

29. Paragraph 5 deals mainly with

(A) suffrutescent shrubs.

(B) a form of tree shrub.

(C) a form of herbaceous perennial.

(D) a woody biennial.

(E) none of the above.

30. Which of the following is a woody perennial?

    (A) a tulip
    (B) a fern
    (C) a strawberry
    (D) an oak
    (E) an angiosperm

31. The best definition of *senescent* (line 94) might be

    (A) doddering.
    (B) receptive.
    (C) solitary.
    (D) complicated.
    (E) aged.

STOP

END OF SECTION 3. IF YOU HAVE ANY TIME LEFT, GO
OVER YOUR WORK IN THIS SECTION ONLY. DO NOT
WORK IN ANY OTHER SECTION OF THE TEST.

Section 4

25 Questions • Time—30 Minutes

Directions: Solve the following problems using any available space on the page for scratchwork. On your answer sheet, fill in the choice that best corresponds to the correct answer.

Notes: The figures accompanying the problems are drawn as accurately as possible unless otherwise stated in specific problems. Again, unless otherwise stated, all figures lie in the same plane. All numbers used in these problems are real numbers. Calculators are permitted for this test.

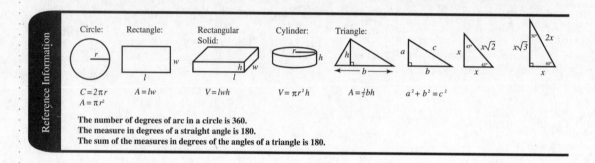

The number of degrees of arc in a circle is 360.
The measure in degrees of a straight angle is 180.
The sum of the measures in degrees of the angles of a triangle is 180.

Part 1: Quantitative Comparison Questions

Directions: For each of the following questions, two quantities are given—one in Column A, the other in Column B. Compare the two quantities and mark your answer sheet as follows:

(A) if the quantity in Column A is greater

(B) if the quantity in Column B is greater

(C) if the quantities are equal

(D) if the relationship cannot be determined from the information given

Notes:

(1) Information concerning one or both of the compared quantities will be centered above the two columns for some items.

(2) Symbols that appear in both columns represent the same thing in Column A as in Column B.

(3) Letters such as x, n, and k are symbols for real numbers.

Examples

	Column A	Column B

$$a > 0$$

$$x > 0$$

E1. $\boxed{a - x}$ $\boxed{a + x}$

E2. $\boxed{\begin{array}{c}\text{The average of}\\ \text{17, 19, 21, 23}\end{array}}$ $\boxed{\begin{array}{c}\text{The average of}\\ \text{16, 18, 20, 22}\end{array}}$

Answers

E1. Ⓐ ● Ⓒ Ⓓ   DO NOT MARK
                     CHOICE (E) FOR
                     THESE QUESTIONS.

E2. ● Ⓑ Ⓒ Ⓓ   THERE ARE ONLY
                       FOUR ANSWER
                     CHOICES.

practice test

	Column A	Column B		Column A	Column B

$r = -3$

1. $\boxed{r^3 + 5r^2 - 6r + 4}$ $\boxed{3r^2 - 7r - 8}$

$x \neq 0$

2. $\boxed{x}$ $\boxed{\dfrac{1}{x}}$

3. $\boxed{\text{The average of } a, b, \text{ and } c}$ $\boxed{b}$

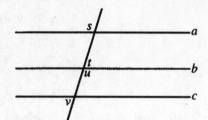

4. $\boxed{\angle ABC}$ $\boxed{\angle ACB}$

$a \parallel b \parallel c$
$\angle u > \angle v$

5. $\boxed{s}$ $\boxed{t}$

$R > r$

6. $\boxed{\begin{array}{c}\text{Circumference}\\\text{of circle}\\\text{with radius } r\end{array}}$ $\boxed{\begin{array}{c}\text{Area of}\\\text{circle with}\\\text{radius } R\end{array}}$

$s > t$

7. $\boxed{s^2}$ $\boxed{t^2}$

Questions 8–10 refer to the figure below.

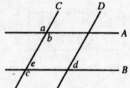

$C \parallel D$
$A \parallel B$
$a = 100°$

8. $\boxed{a + b}$ $\boxed{b + d}$

9. $\boxed{180}$ $\boxed{b + c}$

10. $\boxed{d}$ $\boxed{180 - a}$

$\left(\dfrac{1}{2}\right)x - \left(\dfrac{1}{2}\right)a = 4$

11. $\boxed{x}$ $\boxed{a}$

12. $\boxed{6\% \text{ of } 200}$ $\boxed{7\% \text{ of } 300}$

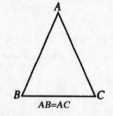

AB=AC

13. $\boxed{\angle A}$ $\boxed{\angle B}$

Column A	Column B

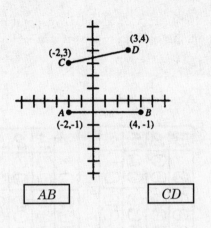

14. $\boxed{AB}$ $\boxed{CD}$

Column A	Column B

$$A * B = \frac{A}{4} + 2B$$

15. $\boxed{\left(\dfrac{1}{4}\right) * 2}$ $\boxed{5 * \left(\dfrac{1}{2}\right)}$

practice test

Part 2: Student-Produced Response Questions

Directions: Solve each of these problems. Write the answer in the corresponding grid on the answer sheet and fill in the ovals beneath each answer you write. Here are some examples.

Answer: $\frac{3}{4}$ (=.75; show answer either way)   Answer: 325

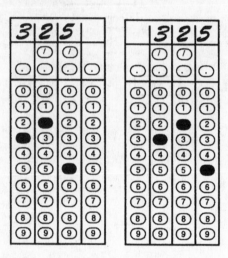

Note: A mixed number such as $3\frac{1}{2}$ must be gridded as 7/2 or as 3.5. If gridded as "3 1/2," it will be read as "thirty-one halves."

Note: Either position is correct.

16. What is the ratio of 6 minutes to 6 hours?

17. At Ungerville High School, the ratio of girls to boys is 2:1. If $\frac{3}{5}$ of the boys are on a team and the remaining 40 boys are not, how many girls are in the school?

18. Jerry grew 5 inches in 2003, and 2 inches more in 2004 before reaching his final height of 5 feet 10 inches. What percentage of his final height did his 2003–2004 growth represent?

19. Seth bought $4\frac{5}{6}$ pounds of peanuts. He gave $\frac{1}{4}$ of his purchase to his sister. How many pounds of peanuts did Seth keep for himself?

20. If $p = 2r = 3s = 4t$, then $\frac{pr}{st} =$

21. $\sqrt{7+9+7+9+7+9+7+9} =$

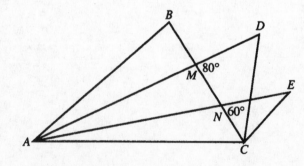

DA and EA trisect angle A.

22. In the figure above, if m$\angle DMC = 80°$ and m$\angle ENC = 60°$, then angle $A =$

(Do not grid the degree symbol.)

23.
$$\frac{\dfrac{7}{8}+\dfrac{7}{8}+\dfrac{7}{8}}{\dfrac{8}{7}+\dfrac{8}{7}+\dfrac{8}{7}}=$$

24. The average of 8 numbers is 6; the average of 6 other numbers is 8. What is the average of all 14 numbers?

25. If the ratio of 4a to 3b is 8 to 9, what is the ratio of 3a to 4b?

STOP

END OF SECTION 4. IF YOU HAVE ANY TIME LEFT, GO OVER YOUR WORK IN THIS SECTION ONLY. DO NOT WORK IN ANY OTHER SECTION OF THE TEST.

Section 5

12 Questions • Time—15 Minutes

> **Directions:** The two passages given below deal with a related topic. Following the passages are questions about the content of each passage or about the relationship between the two passages. Answer the questions based upon what is stated or implied in the passages and in any introductory material provided. Mark the letter of your choice on your answer sheet.

Questions 1–12 are based on the following passages.

In 1848, a Woman's Rights Convention was held at Seneca Falls, New York. Sponsored by Lucretia Mott, Martha Wright, Elizabeth Cady Stanton, and Mary Ann McClintock, the convention featured the creation of a "Declaration of Sentiments," a document based on America's Declaration of Independence, in which men's unfair dominion over women was described. Crusader for the rights of African Americans and women, Sojourner Truth was born a slave on a Dutch estate around 1797 and named Isabella. The first edition of her biography was written by Olive Gilbert, a white friend of hers, and published in 1850.

PASSAGE 1—Declaration of Sentiments

The history of mankind is a history of repeated injuries and usurpations on the part of man toward woman, having in direct object the establishment of an
(5) absolute tyranny over her. To prove this, let facts be submitted to a candid world.

He has never permitted her to exercise her inalienable right to the elective franchise.
(10) He has compelled her to submit to laws, in the formation of which she had no voice. He has withheld from her rights which are given to the most ignorant and degraded men—both natives and
(15) foreigners.

Having deprived her of this first right of a citizen, the elective franchise, thereby leaving her without representation in the halls of legislation, he has
(20) oppressed her on all sides.

He has made her, if married, in the eye of the law, civilly dead.

He has taken from her all right in property, even to the wages she earns.
(25) He has made her, morally, an irresponsible being, as she can commit many crimes with impunity, provided they be done in the presence of her husband. In the covenant of marriage, she is com-
(30) pelled to promise obedience to her husband, he becoming, to all intents and purposes, her master—the law giving him power to deprive her of her liberty, and to administer chastisement.
(35) He has so framed the laws of divorce, as to what shall be the proper causes, and in the case of separation, to whom the guardianship of the children shall be given, as to be wholly regardless
(40) of the happiness of women—the law, in all cases, going upon a false supposition of the supremacy of man, and giving all power into his hands.

After depriving her of all rights as
(45) a married woman, if single, and the owner of property, he has taxed her to support a government which recognizes her only when her property can be made profitable to it.
(50) He has endeavored, in every way that he could, to destroy her confidence in her own powers, to lessen her self-respect, and to make her willing to lead a dependent and abject life.

PASSAGE 2—Sojourner Truth

(55) After emancipation had been decreed by the State, some years before the time fixed for its consummation, Isabella's master told her if she would do well, and be faithful, he would give her "free pa-
(60) pers," one year before she was legally free by statute. In the year 1826, she had a badly diseased hand, which greatly diminished her usefulness; but on the arrival of July 4, 1827, the time specified
(65) for her receiving her "free papers," she claimed the fulfillment of her master's promise; but he refused granting it, on account (as he alleged) of the loss he had sustained by her hand. She plead that
(70) she had worked all the time, and done many things she was not wholly able to do, although she knew she had been less useful than formerly; but her master remained inflexible. Her very faithful-
(75) ness probably operated against her now, and he found it less easy than he thought to give up the profits of his faithful Bell, who had so long done him efficient service.
(80) But Isabella inwardly determined that she would remain quietly with him only until she had spun his wool—about one hundred pounds—and then she would leave him, taking the rest of the time to
(85) herself. "Ah!" she says, with emphasis that cannot be written, "the slaveholders are TERRIBLE for promising to give you this or that, or such and such a privilege, if you will do thus and so; and when the
(90) time of fulfillment comes, and one claims the promise, they, forsooth, recollect nothing of the kind; and you are, like as not, taunted with being a LIAR; or, at best, the slave is accused of not having per-
(95) formed *his* part or condition of the contract." "Oh!" said she, "I have felt as if I could not live through the *operation* sometimes. Just think of us! *so* eager for our pleasures, and just foolish enough to keep
(100) feeding and feeding ourselves up with the idea that we should get what had been thus fairly promised; and when we think it is almost in our hands, find ourselves flatly denied! Just think! how
(105) *could* we bear it?"

1. Both passages concern themselves with a kind of
   (A) tyranny.
   (B) liberation.
   (C) government.
   (D) security.
   (E) autonomy.

2. The word *injuries* in line 2 of the Declaration of Sentiments might be replaced with the word
   (A) bruises.
   (B) prejudice.
   (C) mistreatment.
   (D) wounds.
   (E) shocks.

3. The Declaration of Sentiments compares the status of women with those of "ignorant and degraded men" (lines 13–14) in order to
   (A) condemn people with weak bodies.
   (B) poke fun at a segment of the population.
   (C) argue that even undereducated men deserve a chance to express their opinions.
   (D) state that they are equals.
   (E) highlight the ludicrousness of women's position in society.

4. When the Declaration of Sentiments states in (line 22) that a married woman is "civilly dead," this probably means that
   (A) the law ignores married women.
   (B) married women must treat their husbands courteously.
   (C) women must give up their lives to their husbands.
   (D) a man may kill his wife with impunity.
   (E) married women must not show undue emotion.

5. The word *her* as used throughout the Declaration of Sentiments refers to
   (A) an emancipated woman.
   (B) a married woman.
   (C) any woman.
   (D) the author of the Declaration.
   (E) a woman who is old enough to vote.

6. According to the Declaration of Sentiments, women are only seen as useful to the government when they
   (A) promote discord.
   (B) can provide it with profit.
   (C) vote.
   (D) marry.
   (E) earn wages.

7. The word *sustained* (line 69), most nearly means
   (A) experienced.
   (B) maintained.
   (C) improved.
   (D) nourished.
   (E) made plentiful.

8. The narrative of Sojourner Truth implies that slaveholders' cruelty is based on
   (A) twisted emotions.
   (B) desire for profit.
   (C) fear of confrontation.
   (D) racism.
   (E) misunderstanding.

9. Truth's main objection to her slaveholder is to his
   (A) harassment.
   (B) brutality.
   (C) unfairness.
   (D) bigotry.
   (E) rudeness.

10. When Truth refers to "us" (line 98), she means
    (A) African Americans.
    (B) slaveholders.
    (C) women.
    (D) writers.
    (E) slaves.

11. The tone of both passages might be described as
    (A) resigned.
    (B) calculating.
    (C) fierce.
    (D) embittered.
    (E) hopeful.

12. Would you expect Sojourner Truth to approve of the Declaration of Sentiments?
    (A) No, because the Declaration clearly represents only white women.
    (B) No, because slavery and sexual oppression have little in common.
    (C) Yes, because she, too, is taxed to support a government that does not represent her.
    (D) Yes, because she, too, is willing to be dependent.
    (E) Yes, because she understands as well as anyone what it means to have no rights.

STOP

END OF SECTION 5. IF YOU HAVE ANY TIME LEFT, GO OVER YOUR WORK IN THIS SECTION ONLY. DO NOT WORK IN ANY OTHER SECTION OF THE TEST.

Section 6

10 Questions • Time—15 Minutes

Directions: Solve the following problems using any available space on the page for scratchwork. On your answer sheet fill in the choice that best corresponds to the correct answer.

Notes: The figures accompanying the problems are drawn as accurately as possible unless otherwise stated in specific problems. Again, unless otherwise stated, all figures lie in the same plane. All numbers used in these problems are real numbers. Calculators are permitted for this test.

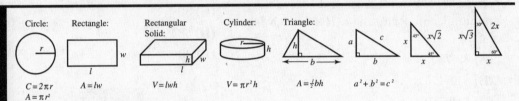

Circle: $C = 2\pi r$ $A = \pi r^2$

Rectangle: $A = lw$

Rectangular Solid: $V = lwh$

Cylinder: $V = \pi r^2 h$

Triangle: $A = \frac{1}{2}bh$ $a^2 + b^2 = c^2$

The number of degrees of arc in a circle is 360.
The measure in degrees of a straight angle is 180.
The sum of the measures in degrees of the angles of a triangle is 180.

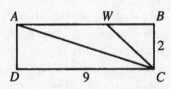

1. In the figure above, *BW* is one third the length of *AB*. What is the area of triangle *ACW*?

    (A) 4
    (B) 5
    (C) 6
    (D) 8
    (E) 9

2. Of the following, the one that is NOT equivalent to 376 is

    (A) $(3 \times 100) + (6 \times 10) + 16$
    (B) $(2 \times 100) + (17 \times 10) + 6$
    (C) $(3 \times 100) + (7 \times 10) + 6$
    (D) $(2 \times 100) + (16 \times 10) + 6$
    (E) $(2 \times 100) + (7 \times 10) + 106$

3. Emily can pack 6 cartons in *h* days. At this rate she can pack 3*h* cartons in how many days?

    (A) 18
    (B) $2h$
    (C) h^2
    (D) $\dfrac{h^2}{2}$
    (E) $2h^2$

4. What is the total length of fencing needed to enclose a rectangular area 46 feet by 34 feet (3 ft. = 1 yd.)?

(A) 26 yards 1 foot

(B) $26\frac{2}{3}$ yards

(C) 52 yards 2 feet

(D) $53\frac{1}{3}$ yards

(E) $37\frac{2}{3}$ yards

5. On an income of $15,000 a year, a clerk pays 15% in federal taxes and 10% of the remainder in state taxes. How much is left?

(A) $9,750

(B) $11,475

(C) $12,750

(D) $13,500

(E) $14,125

6. $(xa)^b =$

(A) $x \cdot a \cdot b$

(B) x^{a+b}

(C) x^{ab}

(D) $(ax)^b$

(E) b^{xa}

7. A is 300 miles from B. The path of all points equidistant from A and B can best be described as

(A) a line ∥ to AB and 150 miles north of AB.

(B) a transverse segment cutting through AB at a 45° angle.

(C) a circle with AB as its diameter.

(D) the perpendicular bisector of AB.

(E) the line AB.

8. If $y = x^2$, $z = x^3$, and $w = xy$, then $y^2 + z^2 + w^2 =$

(A) $x^4 + x^6 + x^{10}$

(B) $x^4 + 2x^5$

(C) $x^4 + 2x^6$

(D) $2x^9$

(E) $2x^{10}$

9. The number missing in the series 2, 6, 12, 20, ?, 42, 56, 72 is

(A) 24

(B) 30

(C) 36

(D) 38

(E) 40

10. The square and the equilateral triangle in the above drawing both have a side of 6. If the triangle is placed inside the square with one side of the triangle directly on one side of the square, what is the area of the shaded region?

(A) $36 - 18\sqrt{3}$

(B) $36 - 9\sqrt{3}$

(C) $36 - 6\sqrt{3}$

(D) $36 + 6\sqrt{3}$

(E) $36 + 9\sqrt{3}$

STOP

END OF SECTION 6. IF YOU HAVE ANY TIME LEFT, GO OVER YOUR WORK IN THIS SECTION ONLY. DO NOT WORK IN ANY OTHER SECTION OF THE TEST.

ANSWERS AND EXPLANATIONS
Section 1: Verbal

1.	B	8.	D	15.	C	22.	D	29.	D
2.	D	9.	B	16.	B	23.	A	30.	C
3.	E	10.	E	17.	A	24.	B	31.	D
4.	B	11.	D	18.	E	25.	A	32.	D
5.	A	12.	A	19.	B	26.	D	33.	B
6.	E	13.	C	20.	C	27.	E	34.	C
7.	E	14.	C	21.	C	28.	C	35.	D

Section 2: Math

1.	C	6.	E	11.	B	16.	E	21.	A
2.	C	7.	A	12.	C	17.	B	22.	A
3.	D	8.	A	13.	B	18.	C	23.	E
4.	C	9.	E	14.	E	19.	B	24.	A
5.	E	10.	A	15.	A	20.	C	25.	B

Section 3: Verbal

1.	B	8.	D	15.	A	22.	A	29.	A
2.	A	9.	C	16.	E	23.	B	30.	D
3.	D	10.	B	17.	B	24.	B	31.	E
4.	A	11.	C	18.	C	25.	B		
5.	C	12.	D	19.	A	26.	C		
6.	B	13.	A	20.	C	27.	E		
7.	A	14.	C	21.	E	28.	A		

Section 4: Math
Part 1

1.	C	4.	A	7.	D	10.	C	13.	D
2.	D	5.	A	8.	A	11.	A	14.	A
3.	D	6.	D	9.	B	12.	B	15.	A

Part 2

16.	$\frac{1}{60}$	18.	10	20.	6	22.	60	24.	$\frac{48}{7} = 6.86$
17.	200	19.	$\frac{29}{8} = 3.63$	21.	8	23.	.766	25.	$\frac{1}{2}$

Section 5: Verbal

1.	A	4.	A	7.	A	9.	C	11.	D
2.	C	5.	C	8.	B	10.	E	12.	E
3.	E	6.	B						

Section 6: Math

1.	C	3.	D	5.	B	7.	D	9.	B
2.	D	4.	D	6.	C	8.	C	10.	B

> **Note:** A [calculator icon] following a math answer explanation indicates that a calculator could be helpful in solving that particular problem.

Section 1

1. **The correct answer is (B).** The word *finally* suggests that the woman agreed to sell the farm only after being *importuned*, or repeatedly urged, to do so by her family.

2. **The correct answer is (D).** The ghost urges, or *exhorts*, Hamlet to take revenge.

3. **The correct answer is (E).** Concern for the children's safety would logically lead a father to *inculcate* (teach by constant repetition) in them a *wary* attitude toward strangers.

4. **The correct answer is (B).** With a life full of hardship and poverty, they are surely *inured* (accustomed) to discomfort.

5. **The correct answer is (A).** The author probably withdrew from the project because he was displeased with the novel's *adaptation*, or change, required to turn the novel into a television program.

6. **The correct answer is (E).** *Vacillation* means fluctuation of mind or changing from one purpose to another.

7. **The correct answer is (E).** A smile could be *devastating* or *bright*, but it could logically only *dazzle* all those who saw it.

8. **The correct answer is (D).** The word *although* indicates that the blanks will be filled by opposites as in choice (D): *penurious* (stingy) and *generous*.

9. **The correct answer is (B).** To disarm someone in a single motion requires sure and swift, or *deft*, action.

10. **The correct answer is (E).** The platypus, with its curious duckbill and habit of laying eggs, is a biological *anomaly* (abnormality).

11. **The correct answer is (D).** A *teacher* gives *instruction*, and a *guard* gives *protection*.

12. **The correct answer is (A).** An *usher* shows people to their seats in a theater, just as a *conductor* shows people to their seats on the *train*.

13. **The correct answer is (C).** A *rink* is a place to *skate*; a *bed* is a place to *repose*.

14. **The correct answer is (C).** A *sapling* is a young *tree*, and a *puppy* is a young *dog*.

15. **The correct answer is (C).** To *fret* is by definition not to *relax*, and to *fight* is necessarily not to *submit*.

16. **The correct answer is (B).** To *stutter* impedes *talking*; to *stumble* impedes *walking*.

17. **The correct answer is (A).** *Damage* is a much less intense degree of destruction than *demolish*. Similarly, *whimper* is much less intense than *wail*.

18. **The correct answer is (E).** A *hose* is used to conduct *water*, just as a *chimney* is used to conduct *smoke*.

19. **The correct answer is (B).** *Exercise* is a way to build *strength*. *Practice* is a way to build *skill*.

20. **The correct answer is (C).** A *sergeant* trains *soldiers* just as a *coach* trains *players*.

21. **The correct answer is (C).** *Volatile* means lacking in *stability*, just as *wanton* means lacking in *restraint*.

22. **The correct answer is (D).** A *scientist* works in a *laboratory*, and a *teacher* works in a *classroom*.

23. **The correct answer is (A).** To be *jocular* is to lack *solemnity*. To be *latent* is to lack *visibility*.

24. **The correct answer is (B).** The Power of Place is the main subject of the passage. Dolores Hayden, choice (D), is important only because she is the founder and spokesperson of this organization; while she would probably agree with choices (A) and (C), those answers are too broad.

25. **The correct answer is (A).** The juxtaposition in lines 1 and 2 of "outsider" and "Los Angeles" indicates that "civic" should be taken in its original sense of "having to do with the city." That the city's feelings might be "bruised" by a criticism suggests that these feelings consist of a loyalty to allegiance to one's home city.

26. **The correct answer is (D).** According to the author, the modernization of Los Angeles threatens to rob the city of its naturally diverse cultural history.

27. **The correct answer is (E).** See lines 6–11. Choices (A) and (B), while they may reflect Hayden's opinions, are not what she means while quoting Stein's statement.

28. **The correct answer is (C).** This answer summarizes Hayden's point in saying that 98 percent of landmarks memorialize Anglo Americans while less than half the population of Los Angeles is Anglo American (lines 26–31).

29. **The correct answer is (D).** Answer I is supported by the contrast between the "landholders, bankers, business leaders" of lines 34–35 and the workers described in the fifth paragraph. Answer II is supported in lines 41–44. Answer III is not supported in the passage; in fact, Hayden's respect for the economic contributions of working people is mentioned in lines 45–51.

30. **The correct answer is (C).** This is the point of the third paragraph, especially lines 47–51.

31. **The correct answer is (D).** See lines 58–65.

32. **The correct answer is (D).** The author describes the site as "ethnically evocative" (line 72) and identifies several different ethnic groups that worked there.

33. **The correct answer is (B).** This answer summarizes Hayden's views as they are expressed not only in lines 44–51 but throughout the passage. "Placemaking" is intended to make the site "more redolent of its past" (line 88), and the point of this redolence, as described by the first three paragraphs, is to give Los Angeles a better sense of place.

34. **The correct answer is (C).** The tree is a miracle only in contrast to its surroundings as described in lines 95–99.

35. **The correct answer is (D).** Chances are that a monument such as city hall garners significant attention from the mainstream community. After all, it is an official government landmark. The other listed attributes are more likely to get lost in the shuffle.

Section 2

1. **The correct answer is (C).** This is easily solved by plugging in the numbers:

$$(4-1) \times (5-2) \times (6-3)$$
$$= 3 \times 3 \times 3 = 27$$

2. **The correct answer is (C).** If $2n$ is an even number, $2n + 1$ is odd.

3. **The correct answer is (D).** Solving the equation for x gives x a value of $-\frac{1}{2}$, and $x^2 = \left(-\frac{1}{2}\right)^2 = \frac{1}{4}$.

4. **The correct answer is (C).** Setting up a ratio,

$$\frac{88 \text{ ft./sec.}}{60 \text{ mi./hr.}} = \frac{1100 \text{ ft./sec.}}{x \text{ mi./hr.}}$$
$$88x = (1100)(60)$$
$$x = 750 \text{ mi./hr.}$$

5. **The correct answer is (E).** Setting up a ratio,

$$\frac{\frac{1}{4} \text{ in.}}{12 \text{ in.}} = \frac{3\frac{3}{8} \text{ in.}}{x \text{ in.}}$$

$$\left(\frac{1}{4}\right)x = (12)\left(3\frac{3}{8}\right)$$

$$x = 162 \text{ in.} = 13\frac{1}{2} \text{ ft.}$$

6. **The correct answer is (E).** Let x be the second angle. The first angle is $3x$, and the third angle is $x + 20$. The angles of a triangle must equal 180°, so $3x + x + (x + 20) = 180$, $5x = 160$, and $x = 32$.

7. **The correct answer is (A).**

By substitution, $x + y^2 - \frac{1}{2}$ becomes

$$\frac{3}{2} + (2)^2 - \frac{1}{2} = \frac{3}{2} + 4 - \frac{1}{2} = \frac{3}{2} + \frac{8}{2} - \frac{1}{2} = \frac{10}{2} = 5.$$

8. **The correct answer is (A).** $14 + 17 = 31$ Therefore, there are 4 students who must be enrolled in all three courses. Note that $\frac{4}{27}$ is slightly larger than $\frac{4}{28}$. The answer must be slightly larger than $\frac{1}{7}$, which is $4\frac{2}{7}\%$.

9. **The correct answer is (E).** The volume of the container is the area of the circle at one end times the height. The area of the circle is $A = \pi 7^2 \approx 154$ sq. in. The volume is $154 \times 6 = 924$ cu. in. The capacity of the tank is 924 cu. in. ÷ 231 cu. in./ gal. = 4 gallons.

10. **The correct answer is (A).**

$$\frac{1}{x+y} = 6$$

$$\frac{1}{2+y} = 6$$

$$6(2+y) = 1$$

$$12 + 6y = 1$$

$$6y = -11$$

$$y = -\frac{11}{6}$$

11. **The correct answer is (B).** If there are 28.35 grams per ounce, then 28.35 grams per ounce ÷ 1,000 grams per kilogram = .02835 kilograms per ounce. Since there are 16 ounces to the pound, .02835 kilograms per ounce times 16 ounces per pound = 0.45 kilograms per pound.

12. **The correct answer is (C).** The square root of .16 is .4, so .16 is a perfect square. The square root of 16 is 4, so 16 is a perfect square. The square root of 1,600 is 40, so 1,600 is a perfect square. The square root of .0016 is .04, so .0016 is a perfect square. Only 1.6 is not a perfect square.

13. **The correct answer is (B).** Let's start by pointing out that we do not know the size of angles 1, 2, 3, or 4. We do know that the two lines are parallel and therefore 8 and 6 can be moved to their corresponding locations on the top line. Since all straight lines have 180 degrees, III and IV each equal 180 degrees.

14. **The correct answer is (E).** The maximum value is obtained by making x as large as possible and y as small as possible. Thus, we set up a fraction:

$$\frac{\frac{1}{2}}{\frac{3}{4}} = \frac{1}{2} \times \frac{4}{3} = \frac{4}{6} = \frac{2}{3}$$

15. **The correct answer is (A).** Start by finding the area of the largest circle. The radius of the largest circle is 9, so the area is 81π. The middle circle has a radius of 5, so the area is 25π. The smallest circle has a radius of 2, so the area is 4π. To find the shaded region, subtract the smaller circle from the middle and get 21π. The fraction is thus $\frac{21\pi}{81\pi}$, which can be simplified to $\frac{7}{27}$.

16. **The correct answer is (E).** The answer can quickly be obtained by using a numerical example. Let $n = 5$ and $d = 2$.

I. $\frac{2}{5}$

II. $\frac{3}{6}$

III. $\frac{1}{4}$

IV. $\frac{5}{2}$

V. $\frac{4}{1}$

$$\frac{1}{4} < \frac{2}{5} < \frac{3}{6} < \frac{5}{2} < 4$$

17. The correct answer is (B). Let the time the train is scheduled to arrive be t. At 40 mph the train arrives in $t + \frac{10}{60} = t + \frac{1}{6}$ hours. At 30 mph the train takes $t + \frac{16}{60} = t + \frac{4}{15}$ hours. The distance is the speed times the time.

$$40\left(t + \frac{1}{6}\right) = 30\left(t + \frac{4}{15}\right)$$
$$40t + \frac{40}{6} = 30t + 8$$
$$10t = 8 - \frac{40}{6}$$
$$10t = 1\frac{1}{3}\ hr = 80 \text{ min.}$$
$$t = 8 \text{ min.}$$

The distance between towns is:

$$d = \left(40 \text{ mph}\right)\left(\frac{8}{6} + \frac{10}{60}\right)\text{hr.}$$
$$= 40 \times \frac{18}{60}$$
$$= 12 \text{ miles}$$

18. The correct answer is (C). When you are given the diagonal of a square, you can find the length of the side by dividing the diagonal by 2 and multiplying by $\sqrt{2}$.

19. The correct answer is (B).

$m\angle TSP = 60°$

Since $mPSR = 90°$, $m\angle TSR = 90 - 60 = 30°$.

Since $TS = PS = SR$, $\angle RTS = -TRS$. Thus,

$$\angle TRS = \frac{1}{2}\left(180° - 30°\right) = \frac{1}{2}\left(150°\right) = 75°$$

20. The correct answer is (C).

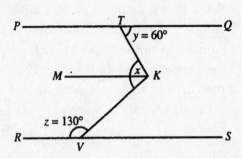

Through point K, draw KM parallel to PQ and RS. Then,

$m\angle x = m\angle MKV + m\angle MKT$

$m\angle MKV = m\angle KVS = 180 - 130 = 50°$

$m\angle MKT = m\angle QTK = 60°$

$m\angle x = 60° + 50° = 110°$

21. The correct answer is (A). Draw OP. Then, in right triangle OPS,

$$OP^2 = PS^2 + OS^2 = 6^2 + 8^2 = 10^2$$

$$OP = 10$$

Then, $m\,\overset{\frown}{QR} = \frac{1}{4} \bullet 2\pi r = \frac{1}{4} \bullet 2\pi \bullet 10 = 5\pi$.

22. The correct answer is (A).

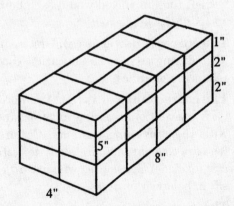

The 2-inch ice cube will fit only in the 8- by 4-inch by 4-inch part of the compartment. The upper inch cannot be used. Hence,

$$\frac{8 \times 4 \times 4}{2 \times 2 \times 2} = 16 \text{ cubes.}$$

23. The correct answer is (E). Since it takes Paul 2 hours to paint 1 fence, he paints $\frac{1}{2}$ of the fence in one hour. Fred paints $\frac{1}{3}$ of the fence per hour. Together their speed is $\frac{1}{2}+\frac{1}{3}=\frac{5}{6}$ fence/hr. The time to paint this fence working together is 1 fence $\div \frac{5}{6}$ fence/hr. = 1.2 hours.

24. The correct answer is (A). $\frac{3}{4}$ evaporates the second day; therefore, there is $\frac{1}{4}$ of the $\frac{2}{3}$ of liquid left after evaporation the first day. $\frac{1}{4}$ of $\frac{2}{3}=\frac{1}{6}$, so $\frac{1}{6}$ of the original contents remains after two days.

25. The correct answer is (B). The time it takes the driver to arrive at her destination is 60 miles $\div$ 40 miles per hour = $1\frac{1}{2}$ hours. The time it takes to return is 60 miles $\div$ 30 miles per hour = 2 hours, making the total time for this 120-mile trip $1\frac{1}{2}+2=3\frac{1}{2}$ hours. The average speed for the entire trip is 120 miles $\div 3\frac{1}{2}$ hours = $34\frac{2}{7}$ miles per hour.

Section 3

1. The correct answer is (B). Acting together, those involved would each be *responsible* for an *element*.

2. The correct answer is (A). Unwise *neglect* during someone's education could result in *ignorance*.

3. The correct answer is (D). A conformist is conventional, acting in accordance with the prevailing customs. Children who are conventional are likely to *ostracize* (exclude) classmates who are *different* in behavior or dress.

4. The correct answer is (A). The date chosen for a king's coronation would most likely be *propitious* (lucky).

5. The correct answer is (C). A poem dripping with venom is apt to be *redolent* with (suggestive of) scorn.

6. The correct answer is (B). If the rites were kept secret, the members never *divulged* (revealed) them. Furthermore, fraternity rites are very likely to be *esoteric* (known to only a select few).

7. The correct answer is (A). A composer who praised the work of a musician he detested would be considered *magnanimous* (extremely generous).

8. The correct answer is (D). *Goodwill* is a genuine asset, but it is necessarily *intangible* (incapable of being touched in the physical sense).

9. The correct answer is (C). Clearly, the law's actual result was different from its *ostensible* (apparent) purpose. By curtailing false advertising, it also tended to *circumscribe* (limit) free speech.

10. The correct answer is (B). An *awl* is used to *puncture*, and a *cleaver* is used to *cut*.

11. The correct answer is (C). A *jungle* is characteristically *lush*; a *desert* is characteristically *barren*.

12. The correct answer is (D). *Hands* may become *gnarled* (knotted and twisted) with age, just as *brows* may become *creased* (wrinkled or ridged) with age.

13. The correct answer is (A). A *planet* *rotates* on its axis just as a *top spins*.

14. The correct answer is (C). *Milk* that *spoils* loses its original freshness. *Wood* that *rots* deteriorates from its original condition.

15. The correct answer is (A). Something *munificent* is characterized by great *generosity*. Something *dolorous* is characterized by great *sorrow*.

16. The correct answer is (E). According to the first paragraph, the bear "changes its haunts with the seasons" in order to obtain "suitable food" and security.

17. The correct answer is (B). This is the only possible conclusion one can reach among those listed. Nothing indicates that Audubon hunts, choice (A), and he never denies that bears are dangerous, choice (D).

18. The correct answer is (C). Low, rich lands bordering a river are likely to be composed largely of river-deposited sediments.

19. The correct answer is (A). The bears scratch bark with their teeth and claws, but they do not eat it. Each of the other choices is specifically mentioned.

20. The correct answer is (C). Lines 82–83 puts forth Audubon's theory. Others, he says, believe in theories, choices (A), (B), and (E).

21. The correct answer is (E). Audubon draws back and addresses the reader directly in lines 44–46, remarking that "you well know" and "you also know" about bears' honey eating and ability to climb.

22. The correct answer is (A). The first comparison comes in lines 7–14 and the second comes at the end of the passage, in lines 79–90.

23. The correct answer is (B). Audubon makes much of the positive traits of the bear, focusing on its strength and pragmatism. He brushes over any indications that bears are fearsome, choice (A), or alarming, choice (D).

24. The correct answer is (B). A careful reading of paragraph 1 will tell you this. Although choices (B) and (C) are true in some cases, they have nothing to do with the opinion of the author.

25. The correct answer is (B). Whether or not you know this word in another context, you should be able to comprehend its meaning by reading the surrounding passage. The word is used to describe a plant with an extremely short life cycle.

26. The correct answer is (C). Not all herbaceous plants are annuals; line 38 refers to biennial herbaceous plants, and lines 49–65 cover herbaceous perennials. Thus, statement I is false. Only very short-lived annuals are called *ephemeral*. Thus, statement III is false. Since only II is correct, the answer is (C).

27. The correct answer is (E). The definition of *biennial* appears in paragraph 3.

28. The correct answer is (A). This is a key idea in the passage, most of which deals with the five characteristic life spans of plants and their respective differences and similarities.

29. The correct answer is (A). The paragraph deals mainly with suffrutescent shrubs, which fall somewhere between herbaceous perennials and true shrubs.

30. The correct answer is (D). According to lines 74–75, a woody perennial is a tree or shrub. Of the four choices given, only an oak fits this definition.

31. The correct answer is (E). Since it is the end of the eight-state life cycle, it should be easy to determine the meaning of *senescent*.

Section 4
Part 1

1. **The correct answer is (C).** Substituting $r = -3$ into Column A, $(-3)^3 + 5(-3)^2 - 6(-3) + 4 = -27 + 45 + 18 + 4 = 40$. Doing the same for Column B, $3(-3)^2 - 7(-3) - 8 = 27 + 21 - 8 = 40$. Therefore, Columns A and B are equal.

2. **The correct answer is (D).** If $x > 1$ or $-1 < x < 0$, then any number $x > \frac{1}{x}$. But if $x < -1$ or $0 < x < 1$, then any number $x < \frac{1}{x}$. Therefore, it is not possible to tell which column is larger.

3. **The correct answer is (D).** Without knowing the value of any of the variables, it is impossible to make a determination.

4. **The correct answer is (A).** The angles of triangle ABC are $2m + 3m + 90° = 180°$, $.5m = 90°$ and $m = 18°$. Angle ACB is $2m = 2 \times 18 = 36°$. Angle ABC is $3m = 3 \times 18 = 54°$. Thus, angle ABC is the larger angle.

5. **The correct answer is (A).** Since $a \parallel b \parallel c$ angle t = angle v, being opposite exterior angles. Therefore, since angle $u >$ angle v, angle $u >$ angle t. Also angle $s =$ angle u, since they are opposite exterior angles. Therefore, $u = s > t$. Column A is the larger.

6. **The correct answer is (D).** The circumference of a circle with radius r is $2\pi r$. The area of a circle with radius R is πR^2. If $R > r \geq \sqrt{2}$, then $\pi R^2 > 2\pi r$. But if $0 < r < R < \sqrt{2}$, then $2\pi r > \pi R^2$. Therefore, it is not possible to tell which column is larger.

7. **The correct answer is (D).** If $s > t > 0$, then $s^2 > t^2$. But if $0 > s > t$, then $s^2 < t^2$. It is not possible to tell which column is the larger.

8. **The correct answer is (A).** a and b are equal, so $a + b = 2a = 2(100°) = 200°$. b and d are supplementary angles, so $b + d = 180°$. Column A is larger than Column B.

9. **The correct answer is (B).** In Column B, $a = b = c$, so $b + c = 100° + 100° = 200°$, which is more than Column A's value of $180°$.

10. **The correct answer is (C).** Since a and d are supplementary angles, $d = 180° - a$.

11. **The correct answer is (A).** $\left(\frac{1}{2}\right)x - \left(\frac{1}{2}\right)a = 4$. Multiplying both sides of the equation by 2, $x - a = 8$, and $x = 8 + a$. Adding 8 to any real number will make it larger; therefore, x is the larger number.

12. **The correct answer is (B).** The values of Column A and Column B are 12 and 21, respectively. Therefore, Column B is the larger.

13. **The correct answer is (D).** Since $AB = AC$, $\triangle ABC$ is isosceles, and it can be assumed that $\angle B$ and $\angle C$ are equal. This information, though, does not provide any clues as to which is bigger, $\angle A$ or $\angle B$.

14. **The correct answer is (A).** It is obvious that the length of $\overline{AB}$ is 6. The length of CD is $\sqrt{[3-(-2)]^2 + (4-3)^2} = \sqrt{26}$, or approximately 5.10. Therefore, AB is longer.

15. **The correct answer is (A).** The value of Columns A and B are $4\frac{1}{16}$ and $2\frac{1}{4}$, respectively. Therefore, Column A is larger than Column B.

Part 2

16. $\dfrac{6 \text{ minutes}}{6 \text{ hours}} = \dfrac{6 \text{ minutes}}{6(60) \text{ minutes}} = \dfrac{1}{60}$

17.

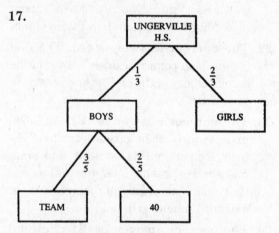

$\dfrac{2}{5}$ (Boys) $= 40$

$\therefore$ Boys $= 100$

There are twice as many girls as boys.

$\therefore$ girls $= 200$

18. First convert Jerry's final height to inches:

$5 \times 12 = 60 \quad 60 + 10 = 70$.

Jerry's 7-inch growth is 10% of 70 inches.

19. He kept $\frac{3}{4}$ of his peanuts.

$$\frac{3}{4}\left(4\frac{5}{6}\right)=\frac{3}{4}\left(\frac{29}{6}\right)=\frac{29}{8}=3\frac{5}{8}=3.625$$

Use 3.63.

20. $\dfrac{pr}{st}=\dfrac{p\left(\frac{p}{2}\right)}{\left(\frac{p}{3}\right)\left(\frac{p}{4}\right)}=\dfrac{\frac{p^2}{2}}{\frac{p^2}{12}}=\dfrac{p^2}{2}\cdot\dfrac{12}{p^2}=6$

21. $\sqrt{7+9+7+9+7+9+7+9}=$

$\sqrt{4(7+9)}=\sqrt{4(16)}=\sqrt{64}=8$

22 $x+y=60$ (Exterior angle = sum of the 2 remote interior angles.)

    $2x+y=80$ (Exterior angle = sum of the 2 remote interior angles.)

$$\begin{array}{r}2x+y=80\\-(x+y=60)\\\hline x=20\end{array}$$

$\therefore\angle A=3x=60$

23. $\dfrac{\frac{7}{8}+\frac{7}{8}+\frac{7}{8}}{\frac{8}{7}+\frac{8}{7}+\frac{8}{7}}=\dfrac{3\left(\frac{7}{8}\right)}{3\left(\frac{8}{7}\right)}=\dfrac{\frac{7}{8}}{\frac{8}{7}}$

$=\dfrac{7}{8}\cdot\dfrac{7}{8}=\dfrac{49}{64}=.766$

24. Average $=\dfrac{\text{Sum}}{\text{Number of items}}$

$\therefore$ Sum $=\big(\text{Avg.}\big)\big(\text{No. of items}\big)$

$48=\big(8\big)\big(6\big)$

$\dfrac{+\ 48}{96}=\big(6\big)\big(8\big)$

Average $=\dfrac{96}{14}=6\dfrac{6}{7}=\dfrac{48}{7}=6.86$

25. $\dfrac{4a}{3b}=\dfrac{8}{9}$

Multiply each side of the equation by $\frac{9}{16}$.

$$\dfrac{\overset{1}{\cancel{4}}a}{\underset{1}{\cancel{3}}b}\cdot\dfrac{\overset{3}{\cancel{9}}}{\underset{4}{\cancel{16}}}=\dfrac{\overset{1}{\cancel{8}}}{\underset{1}{\cancel{9}}}\cdot\dfrac{\overset{1}{\cancel{9}}}{\underset{2}{\cancel{16}}}$$

$\dfrac{3a}{4b}=\dfrac{1}{2}$

Section 5

1. **The correct answer is (A).** The Declaration speaks of the tyranny of men over women; Truth speaks of the tyranny of the slaveholder over his slaves.

2. **The correct answer is (C).** The word *injuries* signifies general mistreatment of women by men. The forms of mistreatment that are listed are primarily legal and social; "bruises," "prejudice," "wounds," and "shocks" are never mentioned.

3. **The correct answer is (E).** The Declaration does not equate the two, as is argued in choice (D). The comparison is made to argue that if undereducated foreigners have basic rights, so too should the average American woman.

4. **The correct answer is (A).** "In the eye of the law" is the clue here; a woman who marries is dead in the law's eyes, or ignored by the law.

5. **The correct answer is (C).** Look back at the first paragraph and you will see that the authors of the Declaration are referring to the tyranny of man over woman throughout history. *He* is all men; *her* refers to all women.

6. **The correct answer is (B).** The proof of this is in lines 46–49, wherein the woman is taxed to "support a government which recognizes her only when her property can be made profitable to it."

7. **The correct answer is (A).** In this context, *sustained* means *experienced*. The master experienced a loss in productivity because of the slave's diseased hand.

8. **The correct answer is (B).** This opinion is implied in lines 68–69 ("the loss he had sustained by her hand"); and 77–78 ("to give up the profits of his faithful Bell . . .").

9. **The correct answer is (C).** We see no signs of brutality (D), but Truth's owner is clearly pictured as unfair. He breaks his promises despite Isabella's faithfulness.

10. The correct answer is (E). Truth is referring to those who are eager for freedom but foolish enough to believe that they will get it—slaves, in other words.

11. The correct answer is (D). The passages as cited cannot be considered *resigned,* choice (A), or *hopeful,* choice (E). Each is essentially a catalog of sins by an aggrieved victim.

12. The correct answer is (E). In fact, Sojourner Truth went on to work hard for the rights of women. Even if you did not know that, however, you could predict her approval based on the fact that her description of slavery parallels so thoroughly the Declaration's description of sexual oppression.

Section 6

1. The correct answer is (C). Area $= \left(\frac{1}{2}\right)bh$. The base is AW, which is $\frac{2}{3}$ of AB, or $\frac{2}{3}(9) = 6$. The height is 2.

$$a = \frac{1}{2}(6)(2) = 6$$

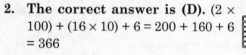

2. The correct answer is (D). $(2 \times 100) + (16 \times 10) + 6 = 200 + 160 + 6 = 366$

3. The correct answer is (D). This is a direct proportion.

$$\frac{\text{cartons}}{\text{days}} \Rightarrow \frac{6}{h} = \frac{3h}{x}$$
$$6x = 3h^2$$
$$x = \frac{h^2}{2}$$

4. The correct answer is (D). The perimeter of a 46' × 34' rectangle is 160 feet, which equals $53\frac{1}{3}$ yards.

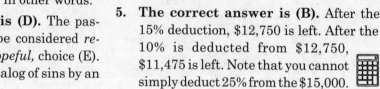

5. The correct answer is (B). After the 15% deduction, $12,750 is left. After the 10% is deducted from $12,750, $11,475 is left. Note that you cannot simply deduct 25% from the $15,000.

6. The correct answer is (C). By definition, $(x^a)^b$ is the same as $x^{a \cdot b}$.

7. The correct answer is (D). The path of all points equidistant from two points is the perpendicular bisector of the segment that connects the two points. Therefore, the line that is perpendicular to AB and intersects it at 150 miles from A is the perpendicular bisector of AB. (Remember, A and B are 300 miles apart.)

8. The correct answer is (C).

$$w = xy = x(x^2) = x^3$$

$$y^2 + z^2 + w^2 = (x^2)^2 + (x^3)^2 + (x^3)^2$$

$$= x^4 + x^6 + x^6 = x^4 + 2x^6$$

9. The correct answer is (B). The difference between the numbers increases by 2; therefore, $? - 20 = 10$, so $? = 30$.

10. The correct answer is (B). The area of the square is 36. Since the triangle is equilateral, we can use the 30-60-90 rule to solve. By dropping a perpendicular we find the altitude to be $3\sqrt{3}$. Then, the area of the triangle is $9\sqrt{3}$. Thus, the shaded area is $36 - 9\sqrt{3}$.

COMPUTING YOUR SCORES

Now that you've completed the fourth practice examination, it's time to check your progress. To get a sense of your scores on this exam, you need to compute individual verbal and mathematical raw scores. Once you have computed these, use the conversion scales in the section that follows to compute your SAT scaled scores (200–800). Keep in mind that these formulas have been simplified to give you a "quick and dirty" sense of where you are scoring, not a perfectly precise score.

To Compute Your Raw Scores

1 Enter the number of correct answers for each verbal and mathematical reasoning section into the boxes marked Number of Questions Correct.

2 Enter the number of incorrect answers (not blanks) for each verbal and mathematical reasoning section into the boxes marked Number of Questions Incorrect.

3 Total the number correct and number incorrect.

4 Follow this formula: Take the total correct and minus one quarter of the total incorrect. Round up in your favor to compute your raw score.

Verbal Section	Total Number of Questions	Number of Questions Correct	Number of Questions Incorrect
1	35		
3	31		
5	12		
Totals	78	Total Correct:	Total Incorrect:

Verbal Raw Score = Total Correct – ($\frac{1}{4}$× Total Incorrect) = _____

Math Section	Total Number of Questions	Number of Questions Correct	Number of Questions Incorrect
2	25		
4	25		
6	10		
Totals	60	Total Correct:	Total Incorrect:

Math Raw Score = Total Correct – ($\frac{1}{4}$× Total Incorrect) = _____

CONVERSION SCALES

VERBAL REASONING

Raw Score	Scaled Score	Raw Score	Scaled Score
75	800	35	520
70	800	30	480
65	760	25	440
60	710	20	410
55	670	15	370
50	620	10	340
45	590	5	290
40	550	0	230

MATHEMATICAL REASONING

Raw Score	Scaled Score	Raw Score	Scaled Score
60	800	25	510
55	760	20	480
50	690	15	440
45	650	10	410
40	610	5	340
35	580	0	200
30	550		

Although you now have some idea of what your scores would look like had they been scaled according to unofficial ETS standards, you will probably want to know how to interpret your raw scores in more familiar terms. If so, use the following Self-Evaluation Charts to see what your raw scores actually mean.

SELF–EVALUATION CHARTS

VERBAL REASONING: Raw Score		MATHEMATICAL REASONING: Raw Score	
Excellent	60–75	Excellent	50–60
Good	50–59	Good	40–49
Average	30–49	Average	20–39
Fair	20–29	Fair	10–19
Poor	0–19	Poor	0–9

PRACTICE TEST 5

Answer Sheet

If a section has fewer questions than answer ovals, leave the extra ovals blank.

SECTION 1

1 Ⓐ Ⓑ Ⓒ Ⓓ Ⓔ	11 Ⓐ Ⓑ Ⓒ Ⓓ Ⓔ	21 Ⓐ Ⓑ Ⓒ Ⓓ Ⓔ	31 Ⓐ Ⓑ Ⓒ Ⓓ Ⓔ
2 Ⓐ Ⓑ Ⓒ Ⓓ Ⓔ	12 Ⓐ Ⓑ Ⓒ Ⓓ Ⓔ	22 Ⓐ Ⓑ Ⓒ Ⓓ Ⓔ	32 Ⓐ Ⓑ Ⓒ Ⓓ Ⓔ
3 Ⓐ Ⓑ Ⓒ Ⓓ Ⓔ	13 Ⓐ Ⓑ Ⓒ Ⓓ Ⓔ	23 Ⓐ Ⓑ Ⓒ Ⓓ Ⓔ	33 Ⓐ Ⓑ Ⓒ Ⓓ Ⓔ
4 Ⓐ Ⓑ Ⓒ Ⓓ Ⓔ	14 Ⓐ Ⓑ Ⓒ Ⓓ Ⓔ	24 Ⓐ Ⓑ Ⓒ Ⓓ Ⓔ	34 Ⓐ Ⓑ Ⓒ Ⓓ Ⓔ
5 Ⓐ Ⓑ Ⓒ Ⓓ Ⓔ	15 Ⓐ Ⓑ Ⓒ Ⓓ Ⓔ	25 Ⓐ Ⓑ Ⓒ Ⓓ Ⓔ	35 Ⓐ Ⓑ Ⓒ Ⓓ Ⓔ
6 Ⓐ Ⓑ Ⓒ Ⓓ Ⓔ	16 Ⓐ Ⓑ Ⓒ Ⓓ Ⓔ	26 Ⓐ Ⓑ Ⓒ Ⓓ Ⓔ	36 Ⓐ Ⓑ Ⓒ Ⓓ Ⓔ
7 Ⓐ Ⓑ Ⓒ Ⓓ Ⓔ	17 Ⓐ Ⓑ Ⓒ Ⓓ Ⓔ	27 Ⓐ Ⓑ Ⓒ Ⓓ Ⓔ	37 Ⓐ Ⓑ Ⓒ Ⓓ Ⓔ
8 Ⓐ Ⓑ Ⓒ Ⓓ Ⓔ	18 Ⓐ Ⓑ Ⓒ Ⓓ Ⓔ	28 Ⓐ Ⓑ Ⓒ Ⓓ Ⓔ	38 Ⓐ Ⓑ Ⓒ Ⓓ Ⓔ
9 Ⓐ Ⓑ Ⓒ Ⓓ Ⓔ	19 Ⓐ Ⓑ Ⓒ Ⓓ Ⓔ	29 Ⓐ Ⓑ Ⓒ Ⓓ Ⓔ	39 Ⓐ Ⓑ Ⓒ Ⓓ Ⓔ
10 Ⓐ Ⓑ Ⓒ Ⓓ Ⓔ	20 Ⓐ Ⓑ Ⓒ Ⓓ Ⓔ	30 Ⓐ Ⓑ Ⓒ Ⓓ Ⓔ	40 Ⓐ Ⓑ Ⓒ Ⓓ Ⓔ

SECTION 2

1 Ⓐ Ⓑ Ⓒ Ⓓ Ⓔ	11 Ⓐ Ⓑ Ⓒ Ⓓ Ⓔ	21 Ⓐ Ⓑ Ⓒ Ⓓ Ⓔ	31 Ⓐ Ⓑ Ⓒ Ⓓ Ⓔ
2 Ⓐ Ⓑ Ⓒ Ⓓ Ⓔ	12 Ⓐ Ⓑ Ⓒ Ⓓ Ⓔ	22 Ⓐ Ⓑ Ⓒ Ⓓ Ⓔ	32 Ⓐ Ⓑ Ⓒ Ⓓ Ⓔ
3 Ⓐ Ⓑ Ⓒ Ⓓ Ⓔ	13 Ⓐ Ⓑ Ⓒ Ⓓ Ⓔ	23 Ⓐ Ⓑ Ⓒ Ⓓ Ⓔ	33 Ⓐ Ⓑ Ⓒ Ⓓ Ⓔ
4 Ⓐ Ⓑ Ⓒ Ⓓ Ⓔ	14 Ⓐ Ⓑ Ⓒ Ⓓ Ⓔ	24 Ⓐ Ⓑ Ⓒ Ⓓ Ⓔ	34 Ⓐ Ⓑ Ⓒ Ⓓ Ⓔ
5 Ⓐ Ⓑ Ⓒ Ⓓ Ⓔ	15 Ⓐ Ⓑ Ⓒ Ⓓ Ⓔ	25 Ⓐ Ⓑ Ⓒ Ⓓ Ⓔ	35 Ⓐ Ⓑ Ⓒ Ⓓ Ⓔ
6 Ⓐ Ⓑ Ⓒ Ⓓ Ⓔ	16 Ⓐ Ⓑ Ⓒ Ⓓ Ⓔ	26 Ⓐ Ⓑ Ⓒ Ⓓ Ⓔ	36 Ⓐ Ⓑ Ⓒ Ⓓ Ⓔ
7 Ⓐ Ⓑ Ⓒ Ⓓ Ⓔ	17 Ⓐ Ⓑ Ⓒ Ⓓ Ⓔ	27 Ⓐ Ⓑ Ⓒ Ⓓ Ⓔ	37 Ⓐ Ⓑ Ⓒ Ⓓ Ⓔ
8 Ⓐ Ⓑ Ⓒ Ⓓ Ⓔ	18 Ⓐ Ⓑ Ⓒ Ⓓ Ⓔ	28 Ⓐ Ⓑ Ⓒ Ⓓ Ⓔ	38 Ⓐ Ⓑ Ⓒ Ⓓ Ⓔ
9 Ⓐ Ⓑ Ⓒ Ⓓ Ⓔ	19 Ⓐ Ⓑ Ⓒ Ⓓ Ⓔ	29 Ⓐ Ⓑ Ⓒ Ⓓ Ⓔ	39 Ⓐ Ⓑ Ⓒ Ⓓ Ⓔ
10 Ⓐ Ⓑ Ⓒ Ⓓ Ⓔ	20 Ⓐ Ⓑ Ⓒ Ⓓ Ⓔ	30 Ⓐ Ⓑ Ⓒ Ⓓ Ⓔ	40 Ⓐ Ⓑ Ⓒ Ⓓ Ⓔ

SECTION 3

Answer spaces for Section 3 are on the back of this Answer Sheet.

SECTION 4

1 Ⓐ Ⓑ Ⓒ Ⓓ Ⓔ	11 Ⓐ Ⓑ Ⓒ Ⓓ Ⓔ	21 Ⓐ Ⓑ Ⓒ Ⓓ Ⓔ	31 Ⓐ Ⓑ Ⓒ Ⓓ Ⓔ
2 Ⓐ Ⓑ Ⓒ Ⓓ Ⓔ	12 Ⓐ Ⓑ Ⓒ Ⓓ Ⓔ	22 Ⓐ Ⓑ Ⓒ Ⓓ Ⓔ	32 Ⓐ Ⓑ Ⓒ Ⓓ Ⓔ
3 Ⓐ Ⓑ Ⓒ Ⓓ Ⓔ	13 Ⓐ Ⓑ Ⓒ Ⓓ Ⓔ	23 Ⓐ Ⓑ Ⓒ Ⓓ Ⓔ	33 Ⓐ Ⓑ Ⓒ Ⓓ Ⓔ
4 Ⓐ Ⓑ Ⓒ Ⓓ Ⓔ	14 Ⓐ Ⓑ Ⓒ Ⓓ Ⓔ	24 Ⓐ Ⓑ Ⓒ Ⓓ Ⓔ	34 Ⓐ Ⓑ Ⓒ Ⓓ Ⓔ
5 Ⓐ Ⓑ Ⓒ Ⓓ Ⓔ	15 Ⓐ Ⓑ Ⓒ Ⓓ Ⓔ	25 Ⓐ Ⓑ Ⓒ Ⓓ Ⓔ	35 Ⓐ Ⓑ Ⓒ Ⓓ Ⓔ
6 Ⓐ Ⓑ Ⓒ Ⓓ Ⓔ	16 Ⓐ Ⓑ Ⓒ Ⓓ Ⓔ	26 Ⓐ Ⓑ Ⓒ Ⓓ Ⓔ	36 Ⓐ Ⓑ Ⓒ Ⓓ Ⓔ
7 Ⓐ Ⓑ Ⓒ Ⓓ Ⓔ	17 Ⓐ Ⓑ Ⓒ Ⓓ Ⓔ	27 Ⓐ Ⓑ Ⓒ Ⓓ Ⓔ	37 Ⓐ Ⓑ Ⓒ Ⓓ Ⓔ
8 Ⓐ Ⓑ Ⓒ Ⓓ Ⓔ	18 Ⓐ Ⓑ Ⓒ Ⓓ Ⓔ	28 Ⓐ Ⓑ Ⓒ Ⓓ Ⓔ	38 Ⓐ Ⓑ Ⓒ Ⓓ Ⓔ
9 Ⓐ Ⓑ Ⓒ Ⓓ Ⓔ	19 Ⓐ Ⓑ Ⓒ Ⓓ Ⓔ	29 Ⓐ Ⓑ Ⓒ Ⓓ Ⓔ	39 Ⓐ Ⓑ Ⓒ Ⓓ Ⓔ
10 Ⓐ Ⓑ Ⓒ Ⓓ Ⓔ	20 Ⓐ Ⓑ Ⓒ Ⓓ Ⓔ	30 Ⓐ Ⓑ Ⓒ Ⓓ Ⓔ	40 Ⓐ Ⓑ Ⓒ Ⓓ Ⓔ

TEAR HERE

SECTION 5

1 (A)(B)(C)(D)(E)	6 (A)(B)(C)(D)(E)	11 (A)(B)(C)(D)(E)
2 (A)(B)(C)(D)(E)	7 (A)(B)(C)(D)(E)	12 (A)(B)(C)(D)(E)
3 (A)(B)(C)(D)(E)	8 (A)(B)(C)(D)(E)	13 (A)(B)(C)(D)(E)
4 (A)(B)(C)(D)(E)	9 (A)(B)(C)(D)(E)	14 (A)(B)(C)(D)(E)
5 (A)(B)(C)(D)(E)	10 (A)(B)(C)(D)(E)	15 (A)(B)(C)(D)(E)

SECTION 6

1 (A)(B)(C)(D)(E)	6 (A)(B)(C)(D)(E)	11 (A)(B)(C)(D)(E)
2 (A)(B)(C)(D)(E)	7 (A)(B)(C)(D)(E)	12 (A)(B)(C)(D)(E)
3 (A)(B)(C)(D)(E)	8 (A)(B)(C)(D)(E)	13 (A)(B)(C)(D)(E)
4 (A)(B)(C)(D)(E)	9 (A)(B)(C)(D)(E)	14 (A)(B)(C)(D)(E)
5 (A)(B)(C)(D)(E)	10 (A)(B)(C)(D)(E)	15 (A)(B)(C)(D)(E)

SECTION 3

1 (A)(B)(C)(D)(E)	6 (A)(B)(C)(D)(E)	11 (A)(B)(C)(D)(E)
2 (A)(B)(C)(D)(E)	7 (A)(B)(C)(D)(E)	12 (A)(B)(C)(D)(E)
3 (A)(B)(C)(D)(E)	8 (A)(B)(C)(D)(E)	13 (A)(B)(C)(D)(E)
4 (A)(B)(C)(D)(E)	9 (A)(B)(C)(D)(E)	14 (A)(B)(C)(D)(E)
5 (A)(B)(C)(D)(E)	10 (A)(B)(C)(D)(E)	15 (A)(B)(C)(D)(E)

Note: ONLY the answers entered on the grid are scored.

Handwritten answers at the top of the column are NOT scored.

TEAR HERE

16. 17. 18. 19. 20.

21. 22. 23. 24. 25.

PRACTICE TEST 5
Section 1

31 Questions • Time—30 Minutes

> **Directions:** Each of the following questions consists of an incomplete sentence followed by five words or pairs of words. Choose that word or pair of words that, when substituted for the blank space or spaces, best completes the meaning of the sentence and mark the letter of your choice on your answer sheet.

Example

> **Q** In view of the extenuating circumstances and the defendant's youth, the judge recommended ____.
>
> **(A)** conviction
>
> **(B)** a defense
>
> **(C)** a mistrial
>
> **(D)** leniency
>
> **(E)** life imprisonment
>
> **A** Ⓐ Ⓑ Ⓒ ● Ⓔ

1. ____ the activities of her employees, the director refused to ____ their methods.

   (A) Disarming..condone

   (B) Applauding..question

   (C) Repudiating..reward

   (D) Handling..oversee

   (E) Approving..arrogate

2. The ____ soldier ____ at the idea that he was to go to battle.

   (A) luckless..rejoiced

   (B) youthful..retired

   (C) unwilling..recoiled

   (D) frail..relapsed

   (E) vigorous..repined

3. The ____ treatment of the zoo animals resulted in community-wide ____.

   (A) curious..apathy

   (B) popular..neglect

   (C) critical..distention

   (D) adequate..revulsion

   (E) inhumane..criticism

4. Unlike gold, paper money has no ____ value; it is merely a representation of wealth.

   (A) financial

   (B) inveterate

   (C) economic

   (D) intrinsic

   (E) fiscal

5. His untimely death, at first thought to be due to a ____ fever, was later ____ to poison.

   (A) degenerative..relegated

   (B) debilitating..ascribed

   (C) raging..reduced

   (D) sanguine..abdicated

(E) pernicious..prescribed

6. To strengthen her client's case, the lawyer sought to put the ____ of the witness in doubt.

   (A) laxity

   (B) posterity

   (C) probity

   (D) onus

   (E) sensitivity

7. During the campaign, the politicians engaged in ____ debate, accusing each other of gross misdeeds.

   (A) capricious

   (B) acrimonious

   (C) altruistic

(D) facetious

(E) chimerical

8. His carelessness produced a(n) ____ report that left everyone ____.

   (A) intelligent..inept

   (B) ambiguous..confused

   (C) complete..mollified

   (D) acceptable..angry

   (E) insipid..inspired

9. Only a ____ person could be ____ to the suffering of the starving child.

   (A) churlish..receptive

   (B) dour..disposed

   (C) placid..detrimental

   (D) pious..uncivil

   (E) callous..oblivious

Directions: Each of the following questions consists of a capitalized pair of words followed by five pairs of words lettered (A) to (E). The capitalized words bear some meaningful relationship to each other. Choose the lettered pair of words whose relationship is most similar to that expressed by the capitalized pair and mark its letter on your answer sheet.

Example

Q DAY : SUN ::

   (A) sunlight : daylight

   (B) ray : sun

   (C) night : moon

   (D) heat : cold

   (E) moon : star

A Ⓐ Ⓑ ● Ⓓ Ⓔ

10. MICROSCOPE : INSTRUMENT ::

   (A) autobiography : novel

   (B) hammer : metal

   (C) necktie : accessory

   (D) oar : boat

   (E) telescope : stars

11. SKETCH : PAINTING ::

   (A) original : replica

   (B) camera : photo

   (C) scene : play

   (D) draft : thesis

   (E) illustration : cartoon

12. GATE : PLANE ::

   (A) latch : door

   (B) fence : yard

   (C) track : train

   (D) highway : car

   (E) driver : bus

practice test

13. SWEAR : OATH ::

   (A) laugh : smile

   (B) grab : boulder

   (C) sign : contract

   (D) neglect : demand

   (E) disregard : notice

14. SPELUNKER : CAVE ::

   (A) astronaut : space

   (B) teacher : student

   (C) miner : ore

   (D) pilot : airplane

   (E) bear : den

15. LAUGHTER : AMUSEMENT ::

   (A) vigor : optimism

   (B) squalor : filth

   (C) stealth : openness

   (D) pride : humility

   (E) pallor : illness

Directions: Each passage below is followed by a set of questions. Read each passage, then answer the accompanying questions, basing your answers on what is stated or implied in the passage and in any introductory material provided. Mark the letter of your choice on your answer sheet.

Questions 16–23 are based on the following passage.

The following speech has been adapted from A Citizen is Entitled to Vote *by Susan B. Anthony, a nineteenth-century campaigner for women's rights. At the time of the speech, women were not guaranteed the right to vote.*

Friends and fellow citizens:—I stand before you tonight under indictment for the alleged crime of having voted at the last presidential election, without hav-
(5) ing a lawful right to vote.

It shall be my work this evening to prove to you that in thus voting, I not only committed no crime, but instead, simply exercised my *citizen's rights*, guar-
(10) anteed to me and all United States citizens by the National Constitution, beyond the power of any State to deny.

The preamble of the Federal Constitution says: "We, the people of the
(15) United States, in order to form a more perfect union, establish justice, insure *domestic* tranquility, provide for the common defense, promote the general welfare, and secure the blessings of liberty
(20) to ourselves and our posterity, do ordain and establish this Constitution for the United States of America."

It was we, the people, not we, the white male citizens; but we, the whole
(25) people, who formed the Union. And we formed it, not to give the blessings of liberty, but to secure them; not to the half of ourselves and the half of our posterity but to the whole people—
(30) women as well as men. And it is a downright mockery to talk to women of their enjoyment of the blessings of liberty while they are denied the use of the only means of securing them provided by this
(35) democratic-republican government—the ballot.

For any State to make sex a qualification that must ever result in the disfranchisement of one entire half of
(40) the people is a violation of the supreme law of the land. By it the blessings of liberty are forever withheld from women and their female posterity. To them this government has no just powers derived
(45) from the consent of the governed. To

them this government is not a democracy. It is not a republic. It is a hateful oligarchy of sex. An oligarchy of learn-
(50) ing, where the educated govern the ignorant, might be endured; but this oligarchy of sex, which makes father, brothers, husband, sons, the oligarchs or rulers over the mother and sisters, the wife and daughters of every house-
(55) hold—which ordains all men sovereigns, all women subjects, carries dissension, discord and rebellion into every home of the nation.

Webster's Dictionary defines a citi-
(60) zen as a person in the United States, entitled to vote and hold office.

The only question left to be settled now is, Are women persons? And I hardly believe any of our opponents will have
(65) the hardihood to say they are not. Being persons, then, women are citizens; and no State has a right to make any law, or to enforce any old law, that shall abridge their privileges or immunities. Hence,
(70) every discrimination against women in the constitutions and laws of the several States is today null and void.

16. Anthony talks as if she were a

(A) defendant on trial.

(B) chairperson of a committee.

(C) legislator arguing for a new law.

(D) judge ruling at a trial.

(E) lawyer in court.

17. Anthony broadens her appeal to her audience by showing how her case could affect all

(A) existing laws.

(B) United States citizens.

(C) women.

(D) uneducated persons.

(E) children.

18. Anthony quotes the preamble to the Constitution in order to

(A) impress the audience with her intelligence.

(B) share common knowledge with her audience.

(C) point out which part of the preamble needs to be changed.

(D) add force to her argument.

(E) utilize a common legalistic trick.

19. According to this speech, one reason for forming the Union was to

(A) establish an aristocracy.

(B) limit the powers of the states.

(C) insure domestic harmony.

(D) draw up a Constitution.

(E) provide an international power.

20. Anthony argues that a government that denies women the right to vote is not a democracy because its powers do not come from

(A) the Constitution of the United States.

(B) the rights of the states.

(C) the consent of the governed.

(D) the vote of the majority.

(E) both houses of Congress.

21. According to this speech, an oligarchy of sex would cause

(A) women to rebel against the government.

(B) men to desert their families.

(C) poor women to lose hope.

(D) problems to develop in every home.

(E) the educated to rule the ignorant.

22. In this speech, a citizen is *defined* as a person who has the right to vote and also the right to

(A) change laws.

(B) acquire wealth.

(C) speak publicly.

(D) hold office.

(E) pay taxes.

23. Anthony argues that state laws that discriminate against women are

(A) being changed.

(B) null and void.

(C) helpful to the rich.

(D) supported only by men.

(E) supported by the Constitution.

Questions 24-31 are based on the following passage.

The Indianists were musicians who borrowed freely from Native American motifs, rhythms, and musical structures to create a style of music that was unique. The passage outlines a history of this movement.

In the late nineteenth and early twentieth centuries, Euro-American composers known as the "Indianist" school chose and adapted elements of Indian song for
(5) their own work. Certain elements of Indian song styles could easily be used by these American-born but typically European-trained composers; other elements were not assimilated so easily
(10) into musical structures built on harmony and into a musical aesthetic that preferred an open-throated singing style. For example, a choral setting of the "Navajo War Dance," composed by
(15) Arthur Farwell (1872–1952), does not give the illusion of being an actual Navajo song. But the elements of Navajo style that caught Farwell's attention are clear: the sparse sound (few harmonies),
(20) the typical Navajo melodic skips, the pulsing beat.

Farwell got his ideas about Indian music from visits to southwestern reservations and from studying transcrip-
(25) tions of melodies collected by Alice Fletcher, a noted scholar of Omaha ceremonial traditions. Other composers also borrowed material from Fletcher's collections. The opening motif and basic
(30) melodic outline for perhaps the most famous Indianist composition, Charles Wakefield Cadman's "From the Land of the Sky Blue Waters" (published in 1901), are fairly literal reproductions of
(35) an Omaha flute call and love song in Fletcher's collection. But, unlike Farwell, Cadman did not try to replicate Indian sounds. He embedded the tune in pure Euro-American harmonic structures and
(40) rhythms. What seems more "Indian" is the song's narrative, describing a fearless captive maid courted by a flute player.

It is the text that marks many
(45) Indianist compositions, but the words do not usually reflect direct tribal experience. The Indianists were Romantics who seized on universal themes of love, war and death cloaked in American In-
(50) dian dress. One could not know from these compositions that native peoples had an everyday world of work, education, childbearing, and food preparation. The images selected for Indianist
(55) compositions are just that: selections from a much broader array of experiences.

As the Indianist composers selected sounds from or notions about Native
(60) American music for their purposes, native groups chose and adapted items from Euro-American musical practice. For example, while many drum groups use a wooden drum covered with raw-
(65) hide, others choose a Western-style bass drum turned on its side; in its decoration and use, it becomes a Native American instrument. Similarly, many Canadian and Alaskan indigenous people have
(70) adopted the fiddle as a means of cultural self-expression. This adaptation reflects Euro-American influence, but native

traditions are also represented, for example, in the way songs are introduced, (75) typically identifying the occasion for the song's composition, and in accompanying activities, such as community feasts.

Perhaps the most far-reaching result of European contact is the develop- (80) ment of a pantribal style. The very concept of "American Indian" is probably a product of contact. Though there were tribal confederacies prior to contact with Europeans, there was no need for an identity (85) that spanned a continent to include tribal neighbors, rivals, and strangers—and no outside view to lump together people as diverse as the Kwakiutl, the Hopi, the Cuna, the Pawnee, and the Natchez. (90) However, "American Indian" and "Native American" are now recognized concepts both inside and outside the societies so identified. Though tribal affiliation is a primary source of identification for most (95) individuals, sometimes the category "American Indian" takes precedence.

One drum group that includes Arizona Pima and Kansas Potawatomi singers, for example, performs songs rep- (100) resentative of the Northern Plains rather than of the Southwest or Central Plains. Indeed, the wide-range Northern Plains-style song has come to represent "American Indian" music. Its characteristic (105) forms, sung with tense throat and pulsating voice, make it most different from Euro-American singing, and the most difficult aural pattern for a non-Indian to assimilate, let alone replicate. By dif- (110) ferentiating as much as possible from the dominant culture, by staking out that which is most markedly unique and displaying it to the outside world, native musical groups that perform in the (115) Northern Plains style confirm their cultural identity.

24. In using and adapting Native American music, the Indianist composers attempted to

(A) reflect the gamut of Native American experiences.

(B) popularize Native American music among Euro-Americans.

(C) reproduce faithfully the style and content of the music they were copying.

(D) address universal concerns using Native American motifs.

(E) indicate their appreciation of the musical form.

25. According to the passage, both Arthur Farwell and Charles Wakefield Cadman

(A) studied with Native American musicians.

(B) attempted to reproduce Native American harmonies and rhythms.

(C) used material from Alice Fletcher's collections.

(D) studied musical composition in Europe.

(E) adapted Native American melodies to European harmonies.

26. The word *marks* in line 44 most nearly means

(A) grades.

(B) distinguishes.

(C) notices.

(D) imprints.

(E) symbolizes.

27. The use of a Western-style drum by some Native American drum groups is an example of how some Native Americans have

    (A) put aside their own traditions in favor of Euro-American forms of cultural expression.

    (B) adopted some Euro-American material goods, but not other aspects of Euro-American culture.

    (C) borrowed aspects of European culture and adapted these aspects to their own use.

    (D) adapted to the scarcity of traditional instruments by using instruments that are more readily available.

    (E) indicated an inclination to embrace more and more Western forms.

28. The "development of a pantribal style" of music (lines 79–80) is an example of the way in which

    (A) cultural groups select and adapt aspects of each other's culture when two groups meet.

    (B) Native American groups formed tribal confederacies to resist the advance of the Europeans.

    (C) tribal identification transcends musical style.

    (D) members of the Pima and Potawatomi peoples have learned to work together.

    (E) a group's culture can be modified when the group meets another cultural group.

29. In saying that the "very concept of 'American Indian' is probably a product of contact" (lines 80–82), the author means that

    (A) Native Americans could begin to think of themselves as "American Indians" only after they learned to speak English.

    (B) a cross-cultural identity became necessary as Native American groups came into contact with each other.

    (C) Europeans were the first to see the various Native American peoples as one group.

    (D) Native Americans identify with their tribe and do not accept the Euro-American designation of "American Indian."

    (E) the American Indian did not exist prior to contact with Europeans.

30. The passage suggests that the Indianist composers would have had the most difficulty in using and adapting which of the following aspects of Native American music?

    (A) melodic lines

    (B) harmonic styles

    (C) vocal techniques

    (D) rhythmical patterns

    (E) all of the above

31. According to the passage, the Northern Plains-style music has come to stand for Native American music in general because

(A) the Northern Plains-style is so different from Euro-American musical styles that it sets the singers clearly apart as Native Americans.

(B) Europeans, when they first heard Northern Plains-style music, wrongly assumed that it was representative of all Native American music.

(C) Northern Plains-style music is more easily comprehended and enjoyed by Euro-Americans than most other styles of Native American music.

(D) Northern Plains tribes are predominant among Native American tribes today.

(E) Northern Plains music has been the most widely distributed music.

STOP

END OF SECTION 1. IF YOU HAVE ANY TIME LEFT, GO OVER YOUR WORK IN THIS SECTION ONLY. DO NOT WORK IN ANY OTHER SECTION OF THE TEST.

Section 2

25 Questions • Time—30 Minutes

Directions: Solve the following problems using any available space on the page for scratchwork. On your answer sheet fill in the choice that best corresponds to the correct answer.

Notes: The figures accompanying the problems are drawn as accurately as possible unless otherwise stated in specific problems. Again, unless otherwise stated, all figures lie in the same plane. All numbers used in these problems are real numbers. Calculators are permitted for this test.

Reference Information

Circle: Rectangle: Rectangular Solid: Cylinder: Triangle:

$C = 2\pi r$
$A = \pi r^2$ $A = lw$ $V = lwh$ $V = \pi r^2 h$ $A = \frac{1}{2}bh$ $a^2 + b^2 = c^2$

The number of degrees of arc in a circle is 360.
The measure in degrees of a straight angle is 180.
The sum of the measures in degrees of the angles of a triangle is 180.

1. If $3x + 2 > 2x + 7$, then x is

   (A) 5
   (B) < 5
   (C) > 5
   (D) < 1
   (E) < −1

2. If $x \neq \frac{2}{3}$, then $\dfrac{6x^2 - 13x + 6}{3x - 2} =$

   (A) $3x - 2$
   (B) $3x - 3$
   (C) $2x - 6$
   (D) $2x - 3$
   (E) $2x^2 + 3x - 3$

3.

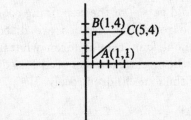

   What is the length of AC?
   (A) $2\frac{1}{2}$
   (B) 5
   (C) 7
   (D) 11
   (E) 25

4. If 3! means $3 \cdot 2 \cdot 1$ and 4! means $4 \cdot 3 \cdot 2 \cdot 1$, then what does $\frac{8!}{9!}$ equal?

(A) 9

(B) $\frac{8}{9}$

(C) $\frac{1}{9}$

(D) $\frac{1}{89}$

(E) 0

5. If a distance estimated at 150 feet is really 140 feet, the percent of error in this estimate is

(A) 10%

(B) $7\frac{1}{7}\%$

(C) $6\frac{2}{3}\%$

(D) 1%

(E) 0.71%

6. There are x cookies in a cookie jar. One child eats $\frac{1}{4}$ of all the cookies. A second child eats $\frac{1}{3}$ of the remaining cookies. If the remaining cookies are distributed among four other children, what fraction of the original number of cookies did each of the four children receive?

(A) $\frac{7}{12}$

(B) $\frac{1}{2}$

(C) $\frac{5}{12}$

(D) $\frac{1}{6}$

(E) $\frac{1}{8}$

7. $|2y - 4| = 6$, $y =$

(A) $-5, 1$

(B) -8

(C) $-4, 3$

(D) $5, -1$

(E) 0

8. Given the system of equations $3x + 2y = 4$ and $6x - 3y = 6$, what does y equal?

(A) 14

(B) $\frac{14}{6}$

(C) 2

(D) $\frac{11}{7}$

(E) $\frac{2}{7}$

9. If the radius of a circle is diminished by 20%, the area is diminished by

(A) 20%

(B) 36%

(C) 40%

(D) 64%

(E) 400%

10. If $x - y = 10$ and $x + y = 20$, then what is the value of $x^2 - y^2$

(A) 400

(B) 200

(C) 100

(D) 30

(E) It cannot be determined from the information given.

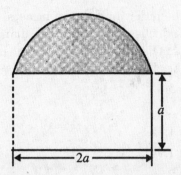

11. A semicircle surmounts a rectangle whose length is $2a$ and whose width is a, as shown in the above diagram. A formula for finding the area of the whole figure is

(A) $2a^2 + \dfrac{\pi a^2}{2}$

(B) $2\pi a^2$

(C) $3\pi a^2$

(D) $2a^2 + \pi a^2$

(E) $2a^2 + 2\pi a^2$

12. An airplane flies 550 yards in 3 seconds. What is the speed of the airplane, expressed in miles per hour? (5,280 ft. = 1 mi.)

(A) 1,125

(B) 375

(C) 300

(D) 125

(E) 90

13. Given that 1 meter = 3.28 ft., the distance run in a 100-meter race approximates most closely

(A) 100 yards.

(B) 90 yards.

(C) 105 yards.

(D) 110 yards.

(E) 103 yards.

14. Of the following sets of fractions, the set that is arranged in increasing order is

(A) $\dfrac{7}{12}, \dfrac{6}{11}, \dfrac{3}{5}, \dfrac{5}{8}$

(B) $\dfrac{6}{11}, \dfrac{7}{12}, \dfrac{5}{8}, \dfrac{3}{5}$

(C) $\dfrac{6}{11}, \dfrac{7}{12}, \dfrac{3}{5}, \dfrac{5}{8}$

(D) $\dfrac{3}{5}, \dfrac{5}{8}, \dfrac{6}{11}, \dfrac{7}{12}$

(E) $\dfrac{7}{12}, \dfrac{6}{11}, \dfrac{5}{8}, \dfrac{3}{5}$

15. If one pipe can fill a tank in $1\frac{1}{2}$ hours and another can fill the same tank in 45 minutes, then how many hours will it take the two pipes to fill the tank if they are working together?

(A) $\dfrac{1}{3}$

(B) $\dfrac{1}{2}$

(C) $\dfrac{5}{6}$

(D) 1

(E) $1\dfrac{1}{2}$

16. If the sum of the lengths of the edges of a cube is 48 inches, the volume of the cube in cubic inches is

(A) 64

(B) 96

(C) 149

(D) 512

(E) 1,728

17. If the length of each side of a square is $\frac{2x}{3}+1$, the perimeter of the square is

(A) $\frac{8x+4}{3}$

(B) $\frac{8x+12}{3}$

(C) $\frac{2x}{3}+4$

(D) $\frac{2x}{3}+16$

(E) $\frac{4x}{3}+2$

18. Equilateral triangle ABC has a perpendicular line drawn from point A to point D. If the triangle is "folded over" on the perpendicular line so that points B and C meet, the perimeter of the new triangle is approximately what percent of the perimeter of the triangle before the fold?

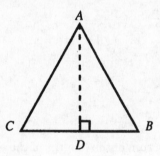

(A) 100%

(B) 78%

(C) 50%

(D) 32%

(E) It cannot be determined from the information given.

19. To find the radius of a circle whose circumference is 60 inches,

(A) multiply 60 by π.

(B) divide 60 by 2π.

(C) divide 30 by 2π.

(D) divide 60 by π and extract the square root of the result.

(E) multiply 60 by $\frac{\pi}{2}$.

20. If the outer diameter of a metal pipe is 2.84 inches and the inner diameter is 1.94 inches, the thickness of the metal in inches is

(A) .45

(B) .90

(C) 1.42

(D) 1.94

(E) 2.39

21.

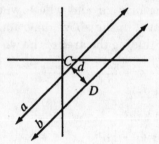

Line $a \parallel b$, while d is the distance between a and b at points C and D.

The length of segment d

(A) steadily increases as it is moved along lines a and b to the right.

(B) steadily decreases as it is moved toward the left.

(C) fluctuates in both directions.

(D) remains constant.

(E) is none of the above.

22. $(x + 9)(x + 2) =$

(A) $x^2 + 18$

(B) $11x$

(C) $x^2 + 11$

(D) $x^2 + 11x + 18$

(E) $9(x + 2) + 2(x + 9)$

23. The points $(3, 1)$ and $(5, y)$ are $\sqrt{13}$ units apart. What does y equal?

(A) -3

(B) 4

(C) $\sqrt{17}$

(D) 10

(E) 17

24. In a baseball game, a pitcher needs to throw nine strikes to complete an inning. If a pitcher is able to throw strikes on 85% of his pitches; how many pitches to the nearest whole number would it take for him to throw the necessary number of strikes for a nine-inning game?

(A) 95

(B) 97

(C) 103

(D) 105

(E) 111

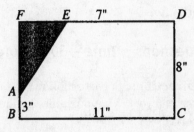

Note: Figure not drawn to scale.

25. Triangle *AFE* is cut from the rectangle as shown in the figure above. The area of the remaining polygon *ABCDE* in square inches is

(A) 29

(B) 68

(C) 78

(D) 88

(E) 98

STOP

END OF SECTION 2. IF YOU HAVE ANY TIME LEFT, GO OVER YOUR WORK IN THIS SECTION ONLY. DO NOT WORK IN ANY OTHER SECTION OF THE TEST.

Section 3

25 Questions • Time—30 Minutes

Directions: Solve the following problems using any available space on the page for scratchwork. On your answer sheet fill in the choice that best corresponds to the correct answer.

Notes: The figures accompanying the problems are drawn as accurately as possible unless otherwise stated in specific problems. Again, unless otherwise stated, all figures lie in the same plane. All numbers used in these problems are real numbers. Calculators are permitted for this test.

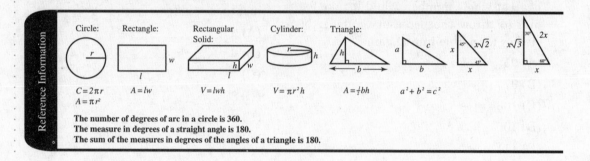

Circle: Rectangle: Rectangular Solid: Cylinder: Triangle:

$C = 2\pi r$
$A = \pi r^2$ $A = lw$ $V = lwh$ $V = \pi r^2 h$ $A = \tfrac{1}{2}bh$ $a^2 + b^2 = c^2$

The number of degrees of arc in a circle is 360.
The measure in degrees of a straight angle is 180.
The sum of the measures in degrees of the angles of a triangle is 180.

Reference Information

Part 1: Quantitative Comparison Questions

Directions: For each of the following questions, two quantities are given—one in Column A, and the other in Column B. Compare the two quantities and mark your answer sheet as follows:

(A) if the quantity in Column A is greater

(B) if the quantity in Column B is greater

(C) if the two quantities are equal

(D) if the relationship cannot be determined from the information given

Notes:

(1) Information concerning one or both of the compared quantities will be centered above the two columns for some items.

(2) Symbols that appear in both columns represent the same thing in Column A as in Column B.

(3) Letters such as x, n, and k are symbols for real numbers.

Examples

	Column A	Column B

$$a > 0$$

$$x > 0$$

E1. $\boxed{a - x}$ $\boxed{a + x}$

E2. $\boxed{\begin{array}{c}\text{The average of}\\ \text{17, 19, 21, 23}\end{array}}$ $\boxed{\begin{array}{c}\text{The average of}\\ \text{16, 18, 20, 22}\end{array}}$

Answers

E1.   Ⓐ ● Ⓒ Ⓓ   DO NOT MARK
CHOICE (E) FOR
THESE QUESTIONS.

E2.   ● Ⓑ Ⓒ Ⓓ   THERE ARE ONLY
FOUR ANSWER
CHOICES.

practice test

	Column A	Column B
		$s > t$
1.	$s - t$	$t - s$
2.	The cost of a complete stereo system that is discounted 30%	The cost of a pair of speakers that is discounted 30%

$p > 0$

$q < 0$

3.	$p + q$	$p - q$

Distance from A to B is 12 miles
Distance from A to C is 10 miles

4.	Distance from A to B	Distance from B to C

5.	The number that 63 is 7% of	7% of 63

$r = \dfrac{1}{2}$

6.	$2r^3 - 12r + 7$	$r^2 + 1$

$x \neq 0$

7.	$\dfrac{1}{x^2}$	x^2

$m^3 = 64$

$\sqrt{n} = 16$

8.	m	n

	Column A	Column B

$x = y = z$

9.	s	t
10.	Area of a rectangle with a length of 4 and a width of π	Area of a circle with radius 4

11.	Surface area of the cube	Cutting the cube in half to form 2 smaller boxes: the sum of the surface both the boxes

$r < 0 < s$

12.	r^5	s^4

$x^2 = 25$

$2y + 3 = 27$

13.	x	y

Column A	Column B		Column A	Column B

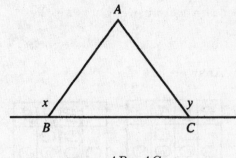

$$AB = AC$$

14. $\boxed{x}$ $\boxed{y}$

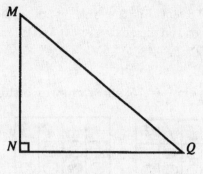

∠*MNQ* is a right angle

15. $\boxed{m\angle M + m\angle Q}$ $\boxed{45^\circ}$

Part 2: Student-Produced Response Questions

Directions: Solve each of these problems. Write the answer in the corresponding grid on the answer sheet and fill in the ovals beneath each answer you write. Here are some examples.

Answer: $\frac{3}{4}$ (=.75; show answer either way) **Answer:** 325

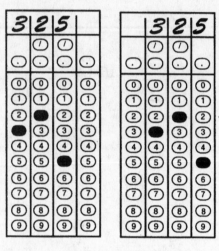

Note: A mixed number such as $3\frac{1}{2}$ must be gridded as 7/2 or as 3.5. If gridded as "3 1/2," it will be read as "thirty-one halves."

Note: Either position is correct.

16.

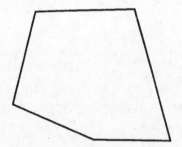

In the pentagon shown, what is the maximum number of different diagonals that can be drawn?

17. If $4x = 2(2 + x)$ and $6y = 3(2 + y)$, then $2x + 3y =$

18. Let the "JOSH" of a number be defined as three less than three times the number. What number is equal to its "JOSH"?

19. Machine A produces flue covers at a uniform rate of 2,000 per hour. Machine B produces flue covers at a uniform rate of 5,000 in $2\frac{1}{2}$ hours. After $7\frac{1}{4}$ hours, Machine A has produced how many more flue covers than Machine B?

20. .01 is the ratio of .1 to what number?

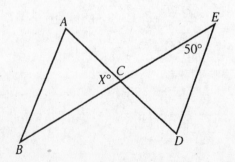

21. In the figure above, AB is parallel to ED and $AC = BC$. If angle E is 50°, then $x =$

22. At NJL High School, $\frac{1}{4}$ of the school's population are seniors, $\frac{1}{5}$ are juniors, and $\frac{1}{3}$ are sophomores. If there are 390 freshmen, what is the total school population?

23. From the town of Williston Park to Albertson there are 3 different roads. From the town of Albertson to Mineola there are 5 routes. How many different paths are there to go from Williston Park to Mineola through Albertson?

24. If 12 candies cost $1.70, how many of these candies can be bought for $10.20?

25. Two roads intersect at right angles. A pole is 30 meters from one road and 40 meters from the other road. How far (in meters) is the pole from the point where the roads intersect?

STOP

END OF SECTION 3. IF YOU HAVE ANY TIME LEFT, GO OVER YOUR WORK IN THIS SECTION ONLY. DO NOT WORK IN ANY OTHER SECTION OF THE TEST.

practice test

Section 4

35 Questions • Time—30 Minutes

Directions: Each of the following questions consists of an incomplete sentence followed by five words or pairs of words. Choose that word or pair of words that, when substituted for the blank space or spaces, best completes the meaning of the sentence and mark the letter of your choice on your answer sheet.

Example

Q In view of the extenuating circumstances and the defendant's youth, the judge recommended ____.

(A) conviction

(B) a defense

(C) a mistrial

(D) leniency

(E) life imprisonment

A (A) (B) (C) ● (E)

1. The society was not ____ and required much outside aid.

    (A) destitute

    (B) self-sufficient

    (C) democratic

    (D) impoverished

    (E) benevolent

2. The new regime immediately ____ laws implementing the promised reforms.

    (A) vouchsafed

    (B) ensconced

    (C) augmented

    (D) promulgated

    (E) parlayed

3. The machines were ____, and because of the below-zero temperature, it was feared they would ____.

    (A) frozen..dehydrate

    (B) brittle..shatter

    (C) frosty..slide

    (D) icy..capsize

    (E) shiny..expand

4. A long illness can ____ even the strongest constitution.

    (A) obviate

    (B) inculcate

    (C) bolster

    (D) enervate

    (E) disparage

5. With ____ attention to detail, the careful researcher churned out his reports.

    (A) prosaic

    (B) painless

    (C) meticulous

    (D) appealing

    (E) atypical

6. A shy look from the beautiful Laura ____ him, and soon they were married.

    (A) released

    (B) controlled

    (C) enchanted

    (D) ensconced

    (E) jilted

7. The city ____ to the advancing invaders without firing a single shot.
   (A) extolled
   (B) regressed
   (C) equivocated
   (D) dissembled
   (E) capitulated

8. When the two opposing sides failed to reach a ____, the long-anticipated strike became ____.
   (A) consensus..impossible
   (B) transition..general
   (C) compromise..inevitable
   (D) rationale..culpable
   (E) precedent..potential

9. Her new neighbor was ____ and charming, the ____ of the bumbling yokel she had expected.
   (A) urbane..antithesis
   (B) callow..exemplar
   (C) provincial..precursor
   (D) obtuse..tableau
   (E) petulant..delegate

10. If you find peeling potatoes to be ____, perhaps you'd prefer to scrub the floors?
    (A) felicitous
    (B) remunerative
    (C) onerous
    (D) vilifying
    (E) redundant

Directions: Each of the following questions consists of a capitalized pair of words followed by five pairs of words lettered (A) to (E). The capitalized words bear some meaningful relationship to each other. Choose the lettered pair of words whose relationship is most similar to that expressed by the capitalized pair and mark its letter on your answer sheet.

Example

 DAY : SUN ::
   (A) sunlight : daylight
   (B) ray : sun
   (C) night : moon
   (D) heat : cold
   (E) moon : star

11. OSCILLATE : PENDULUM ::
    (A) obligate : promise
    (B) float : fish
    (C) turn : car
    (D) spin : gyroscope
    (E) learn : student

12. PREMIERE : MOVIE ::
    (A) unveiling : statue
    (B) rookie : football
    (C) debutante : teenager
    (D) ruler : subject
    (E) celluloid : film

13. CARPENTER : AWL ::
    (A) artist : canvas
    (B) computer : disc
    (C) film : camera
    (D) gardener : hose
    (E) miner : pick

14. ROOF : PITCH ::
    (A) triangle : side
    (B) basement : cement
    (C) mountain : grade
    (D) tree : sap
    (E) ceiling : rafter

15. COG : WATCH ::

   (A) plant : biome
   (B) piston : engine
   (C) scale : fish
   (D) handle : pot
   (E) leash : dog

16. EQUESTRIAN : HORSE ::

   (A) veterinarian : hospital
   (B) taxi : cab
   (C) cyclist : bicycle
   (D) cow : farmer
   (E) camel : desert

17. RECLUSE : SOLITARY ::

   (A) socialite : gregarious
   (B) hermit : old
   (C) monk : lowly
   (D) soldier : political
   (E) hut : squalid

18. DIFFUSE : CONCENTRATION ::

   (A) spread : expansion
   (B) diffident : shyness
   (C) indelicate : coarseness
   (D) incongruous : harmony
   (E) anger : resentment

19. APPLE : FRUIT ::

   (A) dog : bone
   (B) tree : bush
   (C) sparrow : bird
   (D) robin : owl
   (E) elm : birch

20. TEN : DECADE ::

   (A) score : century
   (B) discount : percent
   (C) miles : odometer
   (D) era : eon
   (E) thousand : millennium

21. ZEALOT : FERVOR ::

   (A) charlatan : honesty
   (B) rogue : sobriety
   (C) fledgling : experience
   (D) dotard : youth
   (E) sage : wisdom

22. CURE : PHYSICIAN ::

   (A) prescribe : pharmacist
   (B) discuss : writer
   (C) entertain : comedian
   (D) train : athlete
   (E) trust : police officer

23. SYMPHONY : MOVEMENT ::

   (A) dollar : cent
   (B) strings : section
   (C) chorus : soloist
   (D) play : act
   (E) action : reason

Directions: The reading passage below is followed by a set of questions. Read the passage and answer the accompanying questions, basing your answers on what is stated or implied in the passage. Mark the letter of your choice on your answer sheet.

Questions 24–35 are based on the following passage.

Anton Chekhov is the Russian playwright responsible for some of our most enduring dramas—The Sea Gull, The Cherry Orchard, Uncle Vanya, and others. In this letter he writes to another important playwright, Maxim Gorky, about Gorky's latest work.

Moscow. Oct. 22, 1901
Five days have passed since I read your play (*The Petty Bourgeois*). I have not written to you till now because I could
(5) not get hold of the fourth act; I have kept waiting for it, and—I have still not got it. And so I have read only three acts, but that I think is enough to judge of the play. It is, as I expected, very good,
(10) written á la Gorky, original, very interesting; and, to begin by talking of the defects, I have noticed only one, a defect incorrigible as red hair in a red-haired man—the conservatism of the form. You
(15) make new and original people sing new songs to an accompaniment that looks second-hand; you have four acts, the characters deliver edifying discourses, there is a feeling of alarm before long
(20) speeches, and soon, and so on. But all that is not important, and it is all, so to speak, drowned in the good points of the play. Perchikhin—how living! His daughter is enchanting, Tatyana and
(25) Piotr also, and their mother is a splendid old woman. The central figure of the play, Nil, is vigorously drawn and extremely interesting! In fact, the play takes hold of one from the first act. Only,
(30) God preserve you from letting anyone act Perchikhin except Artyom, while Alekseyev-Stanislavsky must certainly play Nil. Those two figures will do just

what's needed; Piotr—Meierkhold. Only,
(35) Nil's part, a wonderful part, must be made two or three times as long. You ought to end the play with it, to make it the leading part. Only, do not contrast him with Piotr and Tatyana, let him be
(40) by himself and them by themselves, all wonderful, splendid people independent of one another. When Nil tries to seem superior to Piotr and Tatyana, and says of himself that he is a fine fellow—the
(45) element so characteristic of our decent working man, the element of modesty, is lost. He boasts, he argues, but you know one can see what kind of man he is without that. Let him be merry, let him
(50) play pranks through the whole four acts, let him eat a great deal after his work— and that will be enough for him to conquer the audience with. Piotr, I repeat, is good. Most likely you don't even sus-
(55) pect how good he is. Tatyana, too, is a finished figure, only,—(a) she ought really to be a schoolmistress, ought to be teaching children, ought to come home from school, ought to be taken up with
(60) her pupils and exercise-books, and—(b) it ought to be mentioned in the first or second act that she has attempted to poison herself; then, after that hint, the poisoning in the third act will not seem
(65) so startling and will be more in place. Teterev talks too much: such characters ought to be shown bit by bit among others, for in any case such people are everywhere merely incidental—both in
(70) life and on the stage. Make Elena dine with all the rest in the first act, let her sit and make jokes, or else there is very little of her, and she is not clear. . . .

24. By " á la Gorky" (line 10) Chekhov seems to mean
   (A) plagiarized from another playwright.
   (B) in the manner of Maxim's father.
   (C) quirky.
   (D) fascinating and creative.
   (E) full of defects.

25. The word *incorrigible* (line 13) means
   (A) offensive.
   (B) irreparable.
   (C) pessimistic.
   (D) alarming.
   (E) impossible.

26. When Chekhov compares the book to the red-haired man in lines 13–14, his comments are
   (A) inflammatory.
   (B) pessimistic.
   (C) harsh.
   (D) supportive.
   (E) condescending.

27. When Chekhov states that the "accompaniment looks second-hand" (lines 16–17), he means that
   (A) the music should be rewritten.
   (B) the minor characters are stereotypes.
   (C) the form of the play is old-fashioned.
   (D) very few new characters are introduced.
   (E) the set is shabby.

28. By "all that" in lines 20–21, Chekhov is referring to
   (A) the dramatic highlights of the play.
   (B) the superior development of the play's characters.
   (C) the work's traditional trappings.
   (D) the poor acting.
   (E) the bizarre elements of "The Petty Bourgeois."

29. When Chekhov refers to Perchikhin as "living" (line 23), he means that the character
   (A) dies later in the act.
   (B) seems authentic.
   (C) is incredibly active.
   (D) lives well.
   (E) seethes with rage.

30. From the passage you can infer that Nil is most likely a(n)
   (A) intellectual.
   (B) ordinary working man.
   (C) aristocrat.
   (D) murderer.
   (E) revolutionary.

31. Chekhov objects to Nil's lack of
   (A) willpower.
   (B) contrast.
   (C) superiority.
   (D) modesty.
   (E) energy.

32. Chekhov's advice about Elena (lines 70–73) is meant to
   (A) elucidate her character.
   (B) startle Gorky.
   (C) remove her from the first act.
   (D) contrast her behavior with that of Nil.
   (E) lengthen the play.

33. The word *incidental* (line 69) means
   (A) insignificant.
   (B) accidental.
   (C) coincidental.
   (D) essential.
   (E) characteristic.

34. Chekhov expresses definite opinions on each of these points EXCEPT

(A) who should play the part of Nil.

(B) whose part should be extended.

(C) what Tatyana should do for a living.

(D) how Teterev's part should be cut.

(E) how the third act should end.

35. Chekhov suggests change in all of the following characters EXCEPT

(A) Tatyana.

(B) Elena.

(C) Nil.

(D) Teterev.

(E) Piotr.

STOP

END OF SECTION 4. IF YOU HAVE ANY TIME LEFT, GO OVER YOUR WORK IN THIS SECTION ONLY. DO NOT WORK IN ANY OTHER SECTION OF THE TEST.

Section 5

12 Questions • Time—15 Minutes

> **Directions:** The two passages given below deal with related topics. Following the passages are questions about the content of each passage or about the relationship between the two passages. Answer the questions based upon what is stated or implied in the passages and in any introductory material provided. Mark the letter of your choice on your answer sheet.

Questions 1–12 are based on the following passages.

President Lincoln referred to Harriet Beecher Stowe as "the little woman who made the great war," largely because of the furor caused by the publication of her antislavery novel Uncle Tom's Cabin. *In Passage 1, Stowe reflects on the writing of that novel. In Passage 2, Frederick Douglass, a slave who fled to freedom, speaks of his fear on the eve of his second—and successful—attempt to escape to the North from slavery.*

PASSAGE 1—Harriet Beecher Stowe, from a letter to Mrs. Follen (1853)

I had two little curly-headed twin daughters to begin with, and my stock in this line was gradually increased, till I have been the mother of seven children, the
(5) most beautiful and the most loved of whom lies buried near my Cincinnati residence. It was at his dying bed and at his grave that I learned what a poor slave mother may feel when her child is
(10) torn away from her. In those depths of sorrow which seemed to me immeasurable, it was my only prayer to God that such anguish might not be suffered in vain. There were circumstances about
(15) his death of such peculiar bitterness, of what seemed almost cruel suffering, that I felt that I could never be consoled for it unless this crushing of my own heart might enable me to work out some great
(20) good to others. . . .

I allude to this here because I have often felt that much that is in that book ("Uncle Tom") had its root in the awful scenes and bitter sorrows of that sum-
(25) mer. It has left now, I trust, no trace on my mind except a deep compassion for the sorrowful, especially for mothers who are separated from their children. . . .

I am now writing a work which will
(30) contain, perhaps, an equal amount of matter with *Uncle Tom's Cabin*. It will contain all the facts and documents upon which that story was founded, and an immense body of facts, reports of trial,
(35) legal documents, and testimony of people now living South, which will more than confirm every statement in *Uncle Tom's Cabin*.

I must confess that till I began the
(40) examination of facts in order to write this book, much as I thought I knew before, I had not begun to measure the depth of the abyss. The law records of courts and judicial proceedings are so
(45) incredible as to fill me with amazement whenever I think of them. It seems to me that the book cannot but be felt, and, coming upon the sensibility awaked by the other, do something.
(50) I suffer exquisitely in writing these things. It may be truly said that I suffer with my heart's blood. Many times in writing *Uncle Tom's Cabin* I thought my heart would fail utterly, but I prayed
(55) earnestly that God would help me till I got through, and still I am pressed beyond measure and above strength. . . .

PASSAGE 2—Recollection of Frederick Douglass

... It is impossible for me to describe my feelings as the time of my contemplated
(60) start grew near. I had a number of warm-hearted friends in Baltimore,—friends that I loved almost as I did my life,—and the thought of being separated from them forever was painful beyond ex-
(65) pression. It is my opinion that thousands would escape from slavery, who now remain, but for the strong cords of affection that bind them to their friends. The thought of leaving my friends was
(70) decidedly the most painful thought with which I had to contend. The love of them was my tender point, and shook my decision more than all things else. Besides the pain of separation, the dread
(75) and apprehension of a failure exceeded what I had experienced at my first attempt. The appalling defeat I then sustained returned to torment me. I felt assured that, if I failed in this attempt,
(80) my case would be a hopeless one—it would seal my fate as a slave forever. I could not hope to get off with anything less than the severest punishment, and being placed beyond the means of es-
(85) cape. It required no very vivid imagination to depict the most frightful scenes through which I would have to pass, in case I failed. The wretchedness of slavery, and the blessedness of freedom,
(90) were perpetually before me. It was life and death with me. But I remained firm and according to my resolution, on the third day of September, 1838, I left my chains, and succeeded in reaching New
(95) York without the slightest interruption of any kind.

1. Harriet Beecher Stowe traces her compassion for slave mothers to her
   (A) writing of *Uncle Tom's Cabin.*
   (B) hatred of injustice.
   (C) meeting a young woman in Cincinnati.
   (D) reading of legal documents and testimony.
   (E) loss of her own son.

2. Stowe is writing a new book that will be
   (A) as long as *Uncle Tom's Cabin.*
   (B) fictional, like *Uncle Tom's Cabin.*
   (C) more successful than *Uncle Tom's Cabin.*
   (D) both A and B.
   (E) both B and C.

3. By "the depth of the abyss" (line 43), Stowe refers to
   (A) the endless array of documentation.
   (B) the cruelty of the judicial process.
   (C) the suffering of young mothers.
   (D) the horrors of slavery.
   (E) the immeasurable intensity of grief.

4. In line 50, the word *exquisitely* most nearly means
   (A) lavishly.
   (B) expensively.
   (C) enormously.
   (D) indefinitely.
   (E) superficially.

5. Stowe believes that her new book will
   (A) prompt readers to read her last book.
   (B) arouse empathy in readers.
   (C) cause readers intense suffering.
   (D) console readers of *Uncle Tom's Cabin.*
   (E) infuriate readers of *Uncle Tom's Cabin.*

6. Why does Stowe want to write a follow-up to *Uncle Tom's Cabin*?

   I. She believes that the book needs a sequel to complete the story.

   II. She feels the need to substantiate claims that she made in the original novel.

   III. She feels that a presentation of more facts will deepen the reader's understanding of the first book.

(A) I only

(B) II only

(C) I and II only

(D) III only

(E) II and III only

7. Stowe is obviously a writer who

(A) wrote with little effort.

(B) conducted little research for her writing.

(C) was deeply and emotionally involved in her work.

(D) did not understand the demands of writing.

(E) was not an enduring literary force.

8. The main idea of Passage 1 is that

(A) Stowe was in the right place at the right time.

(B) a successful writer is born, not made.

(C) Stowe was successful because she lived at a time when significant events were occurring in our nation.

(D) without Lincoln, Stowe would not have succeeded.

(E) a writer's life is a deeply felt one.

9. In Passage 2, Douglass acknowledges which of the following as a reason for many slaves not attempting to escape?

(A) fear

(B) ties to their friends

(C) lack of education

(D) lack of courage

(E) inability to make contact with people in the North

10. According to the passage, what, in particular, tormented Douglass as he waited to make his second attempt at escape?

(A) fear of reprisals

(B) memories of his failed first attempt to escape

(C) the wretchedness of slavery

(D) the blessedness of freedom

(E) pain of separation

11. Douglass was especially frightened at this attempt to escape because

(A) it was not as well-planned as his first attempt.

(B) his northern contact had not been established.

(C) he was going alone.

(D) failure would result in the severest punishment.

(E) he was leaving his friends.

12. From the picture of Douglass portrayed in Passage 2, which phrase below best describes him?

(A) fearful and indecisive

(B) bitter and angry

(C) friendless and alone

(D) confused and troubled

(E) brave and persistent

STOP

END OF SECTION 5. IF YOU HAVE ANY TIME LEFT, GO OVER YOUR WORK IN THIS SECTION ONLY. DO NOT WORK IN ANY OTHER SECTION OF THE TEST.

Section 6

10 Questions • Time—15 Minutes

Directions: Solve the following problems using any available space on the page for scratchwork. On your answer sheet fill in the choice that best corresponds to the correct answer.

Notes: The figures accompanying the problems are drawn as accurately as possible unless otherwise stated in specific problems. Again, unless otherwise stated, all figures lie in the same plane. All numbers used in these problems are real numbers. Calculators are permitted for this test.

Reference Information

Circle: $C = 2\pi r$ $A = \pi r^2$

Rectangle: $A = lw$

Rectangular Solid: $V = lwh$

Cylinder: $V = \pi r^2 h$

Triangle: $A = \frac{1}{2}bh$

$a^2 + b^2 = c^2$

The number of degrees of arc in a circle is 360.
The measure in degrees of a straight angle is 180.
The sum of the measures in degrees of the angles of a triangle is 180.

1. If a triangle of base 7 is equal in area to a circle of radius 7, what is the altitude of the triangle?

   (A) 8π

   (B) 10π

   (C) 12π

   (D) 14π

   (E) It cannot be determined from the information given.

2. If the following numbers are arranged in order from the smallest to the largest, what will be their correct order?

   I. $\frac{9}{13}$

   II. $\frac{13}{9}$

   III. 70%

   IV. $\frac{1}{.70}$

   (A) II, I, III, IV

   (B) III, II, I, IV

   (C) III, IV, I, II

   (D) II, IV, III, I

   (E) I, III, IV, II

3. The coordinates of the vertices of quadrilateral $PQRS$ are $P(0,0)$, $Q(9,0)$, $R(10,3)$, and $S(1,3)$, respectively. What is the area of $PQRS$?

   (A) $9\sqrt{10}$

   (B) $\frac{9}{2}\sqrt{10}$

   (C) $\frac{27}{2}$

   (D) 27

   (E) It cannot be determined from the information given.

4. If $8x + 4 = 64$, then $2x + 1 =$

   (A) 12

   (B) 13

   (C) 16

   (D) 24

   (E) 60

5. A circle whose radius is 7 has its center at the origin. Which of the following points are outside the circle?

   I. (4, 4)

   II. (5, 5)

   III. (4, 5)

   IV. (4, 6)

   (A) I and II only

   (B) II and III only

   (C) II, III, and IV only

   (D) II and IV only

   (E) III and IV only

6. What is the difference in area between a square with side = 9 and the surface area of a cube with edge = 3?

   (A) 516

   (B) 432

   (C) 72

   (D) 27

   (E) 18

7. A set of numbers is "quarked" if the sum of all the numbers in the set is evenly divisible by each of the numbers in the set. Which of the following sets is "quarked"?

   (A) (1, 3, 5, 7)

   (B) (4, 6, 8)

   (C) (6, 7, 8, 9)

   (D) (2, 4, 6)

   (E) (5, 10, 15, 20)

8. If $x \neq -2$, $\dfrac{3\left(x^2 - 4\right)}{x+2} =$

   (A) $3x^2 + 4$

   (B) $3x - 2$

   (C) $3x - 2$

   (D) $3x - 6$

   (E) $3x + 6$

9. An ice-cream truck runs down a certain street 4 times a week. This truck carries 5 different flavors of ice-cream bars, each of which comes in 2 different designs. Considering that the truck runs Monday through Thursday, and Monday was the first day of the month, by what day of the month could a person, buying one ice-cream bar each truck run, purchase all the different varieties of ice-cream bars?

   (A) 11th
   (B) 16th
   (C) 21st
   (D) 24th
   (E) 30th

10. If $N! = N(N-1)(N-2)\ldots[N-(N-1)]$, what does $\dfrac{N!}{(N-2)!}$ equal?

   (A) $N^2 - N$
   (B) $N^5 + N^3 - N^2 + \dfrac{N}{N^2}$
   (C) $N + 1$
   (D) 1
   (E) 6

STOP

END OF SECTION 6. IF YOU HAVE ANY TIME LEFT, GO OVER YOUR WORK IN THIS SECTION ONLY. DO NOT WORK IN ANY OTHER SECTION OF THE TEST.

ANSWERS AND EXPLANATIONS
Section 1: Verbal

1. B	8. B	14. A	20. C	26. B
2. C	9. E	15. E	21. D	27. C
3. E	10. C	16. A	22. D	28. E
4. D	11. D	17. B	23. B	29. C
5. B	12. C	18. D	24. D	30. C
6. C	13. C	19. C	25. C	31. A
7. B				

Section 2: Math

1. C	6. E	11. A	16. A	21. D
2. D	7. D	12. B	17. B	22. D
3. B	8. E	13. D	18. B	23. B
4. C	9. B	14. C	19. B	24. A
5. B	10. B	15. B	20. A	25. C

Section 3: Math
Part 1

1. A	4. D	7. D	10. B	13. B
2. D	5. A	8. B	11. B	14. C
3. B	6. C	9. C	12. B	15. A

Part 2

16. 5	18. $1.5 = \frac{3}{2}$	20. 10	22. 1800	24. 72
17. 10	19. 0	21. 80	23. 15	25. 50

Section 4: Verbal

1. B	8. C	15. B	22. C	29. B
2. D	9. A	16. C	23. D	30. B
3. B	10. C	17. A	24. D	31. D
4. D	11. D	18. D	25. B	32. A
5. C	12. A	19. C	26. D	33. A
6. C	13. E	20. E	27. C	34. E
7. E	14. C	21. E	28. C	35. E

Section 5: Verbal

1. E	4. C	7. C	9. B	11. D
2. A	5. B	8. E	10. B	12. E
3. D	6. E			

Section 6: Math

1. D	3. D	5. D	7. D	9. B
2. E	4. C	6. D	8. D	10. A

> **Note:** A ⌨ following a math answer explanation indicates that a calculator could be helpful in solving that particular problem.

Section 1

1. **The correct answer is (B).** If the director *applauds* her employees' activities, she is not likely to *question* their methods.

2. **The correct answer is (C).** An *unwilling* soldier would *recoil* at the idea of going to battle.

3. **The correct answer is (E).** The *inhumane* treatment of the zoo animals would result in *criticism*.

4. **The correct answer is (D).** Paper money is merely a representation of wealth; therefore, unlike gold, it has no *intrinsic* (inherent) value.

5. **The correct answer is (B).** The fever could be *degenerative, debilitating, raging,* or *pernicious.* However, only *ascribed* (attributed) makes sense in the second blank.

6. **The correct answer is (C).** If the lawyer can cast doubt on the *probity* (honesty or integrity) of the witness, she can probably strengthen her client's case.

7. **The correct answer is (B).** A debate in which candidates fling accusations at each other is likely to be *acrimonious* (harsh or bitter).

8. **The correct answer is (B).** Because they result from *carelessness*, both blanks should be filled by negative words. *Carelessness* is likely to produce an *ambiguous* (vague or unclear) report, which may leave everyone *confused.*

9. **The correct answer is (E).** Only a *callous* or insensitive person could be *oblivious* to, or unmindful of, the suffering of a starving child.

10. **The correct answer is (C).** A *microscope* is an *instrument,* and a *necktie* is an *accessory.*

11. **The correct answer is (D).** A *sketch* precedes a finished *painting* as a *draft* precedes a finished *thesis.*

12. **The correct answer is (C).** A *plane* arrives at and departs from an assigned *gate,* just as a *train* arrives at and departs from an assigned *track.*

13. **The correct answer is (C).** One *swears* an oath and signs a *contract.* Both actions show commitment.

14. **The correct answer is (A).** A *spelunker* is a person who explores a *cave.* An *astronaut* is one who explores *space.*

15. **The correct answer is (E).** *Laughter* is a sign of *amusement; pallor* is a sign of *illness.*

16. **The correct answer is (A).** The second sentence of the passage states: "I stand before you tonight under indictment for the alleged crime . . ." A defendant on trial would be under indictment for a supposed crime.

17. **The correct answer is (B).** The fourth paragraph discusses how ". . . not we, the white male citizens; but we, the whole people . . . formed the Union" to secure the blessings of liberty ". . . to the whole people—women as well as men."

18. **The correct answer is (D).** Quoting the preamble of the Constitution adds weight to her argument that all citizens, not merely white, male citizens, should have the right to vote.

19. The correct answer is (C). Lines 24–29 state: ". . . we, the whole people, who formed the Union . . . not to give the blessings of liberty, but to secure them . . . to the whole people . . . ."

20. The correct answer is (C). Lines 43–48 state: "To them this government has no just powers derived from the consent of the governed . . . . It is a hateful oligarchy of sex."

21. The correct answer is (D). Lines 55–57 describe an oligarchy of sex as a government where "all men [are] sovereigns [and] all women subjects, [inciting] dissension, discord and rebellion [in] every home . . . ."

22. The correct answer is (D). Lines 60–61 present the definition of a citizen ". . . as a person in the United States, entitled to vote and hold office."

23. The correct answer is (B). The last sentence of the passage states that ". . . every discrimination against women in the constitutions and laws of the several States is today null and void."

24. The correct answer is (D). As stated in lines 47–49, "The Indianists . . . seized on universal themes . . . cloaked in American Indian dress."

25. The correct answer is (C). Lines 24–26 say that Farwell used Fletcher's collections; lines 34–36 show that Cadman used melodies from the same collection.

26. The correct answer is (B). Substitution of each choice for the word *marks* in context shows that "It is the text that *distinguishes* many Indianist compositions."

27. The correct answer is (C). Lines 58–68 state the point of the examples in the fifth paragraph.

28. The correct answer is (E). The final paragraph contains the best explanation for this thesis. Choice (A), while it expresses the main idea of the passage as a whole, does not apply to the development of a pantribal style of music because in this case the Native Americans are not adapting a European cultural expression.

29. The correct answer is (C). Lines 82–86, directly following the quoted sentence, explain the author's meaning.

30. The correct answer is (C). Lines 5–6 say that "certain elements of Indian song styles" could not be easily assimilated into European "musical structures built on harmony and . . . a musical aesthetic that preferred an open-throated singing style." The fact that Farwell used a Navaho harmonic style in "Navajo War Dance" (line 14) eliminates choice (B) as the best choice, while the discussion of Europeans' difficulty with Northern Plains-style singing "with tense throat and pulsating voice" in the final paragraph confirms that vocal techniques are the most difficult aspect of Native American music for Euro-American composers to assimilate.

31. The correct answer is (A). See lines 103–109.

Section 2

1. The correct answer is (C).

$$3x + 2 > 2x + 7$$
$$x + 2 > 7$$
$$x > 5$$

2. The correct answer is (D). By long division:

$$\require{enclose}
\begin{array}{r}
2x-3 \\
3x-2 \enclose{longdiv}{6x^2-13x+6} \\
\underline{6x^2-4x} \\
-9x+6 \\
\underline{-9x+6} \\
0
\end{array}$$

3. **The correct answer is (B).** It can easily be seen that $AB = 3$ and $BC = 4$. By the Pythagorean theorem, $(3)^2 + (4)^2 = (AC)^2$ and $AC = 5$. Also, the distance formula can be used.

$$d = \sqrt{\left(x - x_1\right)^2 + \left(y - y_1\right)^2}$$
$$= \sqrt{\left(5 - 1\right)^2 + \left(4 - 1\right)^2}$$
$$= \sqrt{\left(4\right)^2 + \left(3\right)^2} = \sqrt{25} = 5$$

4. **The correct answer is (C).**

$$\frac{8!}{9!} = \frac{8 \times 7 \times 6 \times 5 \times 4 \times 3 \times 2 \times 1}{9 \times 8 \times 7 \times 6 \times 5 \times 4 \times 3 \times 2 \times 1}$$

Dividing out common factors in the numerator and denominator leaves $\frac{1}{9}$.

5. **The correct answer is (B).** There was an error of 150 ft. − 140 ft. = 10 ft. The percent of error is the error divided by the actual distance, 10 ft. ÷ 140 ft. = .0714 × 100% or about $7\frac{1}{7}\%$.

6. **The correct answer is (E).** The first child leaves $\frac{3}{4}$ of the cookies. The second child eats $\frac{1}{3}$ of $\frac{3}{4}$ and that leaves $\frac{1}{2}$. If the $\frac{1}{2}$ is divided among four children, then $\frac{1}{2}$ divided by 4 is $\frac{1}{8}$.

7. **The correct answer is (D).** $|2y - 4| = 6$ means that $2y - 4 = 6$ or $2y - 4 = -6$. Solving the first equation, $y = \frac{10}{2} = 5$, and solving the second equation gives y a value of −1. Therefore, y = both 5 and −1.

8. **The correct answer is (E).** To solve this system of equations for y, the first equation must be multiplied by 2.

$$3x + 2y = 4 \rightarrow 6x + 4y = 8$$

$$6x - 3y = 6 \rightarrow 6x - 3y = 6$$

Subtracting the two equations on the right gives $7y = 2$. Therefore, $y = \frac{2}{7}$.

9. **The correct answer is (B).** If the radius r of a circle is diminished by 20%, the new radius is $r - .20r$. The new area is $\pi(r - .20r)^2 = \pi(.64r^2)$. The new area is 64% of the old area. Thus, the area was diminished by 100% − 64% = 36%.

10. **The correct answer is (B).**

$$x^2 - y^2 = (x + y)(x - y) = 10 \times 20 = 200$$

11. **The correct answer is (A).** The area of the rectangle is $(2a) \times a = 2a^2$. The area of a semicircle is $\frac{1}{2}$ the area of a circle. The radius of the semicircle is $\frac{1}{2}(2a) = a$; therefore, the area is $\frac{\pi a^2}{2}$. Add the areas of the rectangle and semicircle to get the total area, $2a^2 + \frac{\pi a^2}{2}$.

12. **The correct answer is (B).** In one second the plane flies about 550 yds. ÷ 3 sec. = 183 yd./sec. There are 3,600 seconds in one hour, so the plane flies 183 yd./sec. × 3,600 sec./hr. = 658,800 yd./hr. There are 1,760 yards in one mile, so the plane flies 658,800 yd./hr. ÷ 1,760 yd./mi. ≈ 375 mi./hr.

13. **The correct answer is (D).** One meter equals approximately 1.10 yds. 100 meters is 100 m. × 1.10 yds. per m. = 110 yds.

14. **The correct answer is (C).** The least common denominator of all the fractions is 1,320. Reducing each fraction to have 1,320 as the denominator, we have

$$\frac{6}{11} = \frac{720}{1320}, \frac{7}{12} = \frac{770}{1320}, \frac{3}{5} = \frac{792}{1320},$$

and $\frac{5}{8} = \frac{825}{1320}$.

15. The correct answer is (B). The first pipe can fill the tank in $1\frac{1}{2}$ or $\frac{3}{2}$ hours, or it can do $\frac{2}{3}$ the work in 1 hour. The second pipe can fill the tank in 45 minutes or $\frac{3}{4}$ hour, doing $\frac{4}{3}$ of the job in 1 hour. Thus, together the two pipes can do $\frac{4}{3}+\frac{2}{3}=\frac{6}{3}$ of the job in 1 hour. Therefore, the pipes working together could fill the entire tank in $\frac{1}{2}$ hour.

16. The correct answer is (A). There are 12 edges on a cube, so each edge is 48 in. $\div$ 12 = 4 inches. The volume of the cube is $(s)^3 = (4 \text{ in.})^3 = 64$ cu. in.

17. The correct answer is (B). Since the perimeter of a square is four times the length of a side, it is

$$4\left(\frac{2x}{3}+1\right), \text{ or } \frac{8x+12}{3}.$$

18. The correct answer is (B). This is more easily solved by using real numbers. If we assign a value of 6 to AB, then we can figure out that the perpendicular AD is $3\sqrt{3}$. The old perimeter was 18 and the new perimeter is $6 + 3 + 3\sqrt{3}$, or about 14.1. The fraction $\frac{14}{18}$ can be simplified to $\frac{7}{9}$, which is about 78%.

19. The correct answer is (B). If the circumference is 60 inches, since $C = 2\pi r$, substitute $C = 60$; therefore, $r = \frac{60}{2\pi}$.

20. The correct answer is (A). The radii of the pipe are 1.42 in. and 0.97 in. The thickness is their difference, or .45 in.

21. The correct answer is (D). By definition, parallel lines are everywhere equidistant. Therefore, the length of segment d remains constant.

22. The correct answer is (D). By using the FOIL method,

$$(x + 9)(x + 2) = x^2 + 9x + 2x + 18$$

By combining like terms, this is simplified to:

$$x^2 + 11x + 18.$$

23. The correct answer is (B). If the points $(3, 1)$ and $(5, y)$ are $\sqrt{13}$ units apart, then by the distance formula,

$$\sqrt{13} = \sqrt{(5-3)^2 + (y-1)^2}.$$

Solving for y: $13 = (2)^2 + (y-1)^2$

$$9 = (y-1)^2$$
$$y = 4$$

24. The correct answer is (A). The total number of strikes that a pitcher must throw in a game is 9×9, or 81. Since only 85% of his pitches are strikes, he must throw 81/.85, or 95, pitches a game.

25. The correct answer is (C). The area of the rectangle is length $\times$ width = 11" $\times$ 8" = 88 sq. in. The area of the triangle is $\frac{1}{2}$ (base) $\times$ (height). Its base is 8" $-$ 3" = 5"; its height is 11" $-$ 7" = 4". The area of the triangle is $\frac{1}{2} \times 5" \times 4" = 10$ sq. in. The area of the polygon is 88 $-$ 10 = 78 sq. in.

Section 3

Part 1

1. The correct answer is (A). For any real numbers s and t, as long as $s > t$, the difference of the smaller from the larger, $s - t$, will always be greater than the larger from the smaller, $t - s$.

2. **The correct answer is (D).** There is no way to determine the cost of the total system or the speakers; therefore, there is no way to determine the discounted price.

3. **The correct answer is (B).** If $p > 0$ and $q < 0$, then $p - q$ is equivalent to $p + |q|$ and $p + q$ is equivalent to $p - |q|$. Since Column B is adding rather than subtracting, Column B is larger.

4. **The correct answer is (D).** Since we know nothing about the placement of A, B, and C, we cannot determine anything about their distances.

5. **The correct answer is (A).** The value of Column A is found by computing $\frac{63}{.07}$, which equals 900. The value of Column B is $(.07)(63) = 4.41$. Hence, Column A is larger.

6. **The correct answer is (C).** Substituting $\frac{1}{2}$ for r in Column A,
$$2r^3 - 12r + 7 = 2\left(\frac{1}{2}\right)^3 - 12\left(\frac{1}{2}\right) + 7 = 1\frac{1}{4}.$$
Doing the same in Column B,
$$r^2 + 1 = \left(\frac{1}{2}\right)^2 + 1 = 1\frac{1}{4}.$$
The columns are equal.

7. **The correct answer is (D).** We cannot judge which is the larger since if $-1 < x < 1$, $\frac{1}{x^2} > x^2$, but, if $x > 1$ or $x < -1$, $x^2 > \frac{1}{x^2}$.

8. **The correct answer is (B).** Solving the two equations: first, $m^3 = 64$, $m = \sqrt[3]{64} = 4$, and second, $\sqrt{n} = 16$, $n = (16)^2 = 256$. Therefore, $n > m$, making Column B greater than Column A.

9. **The correct answer is (C).** Since the measures of angles x, y, and z are equivalent, the triangle is an equilateral triangle with all sides equal. Therefore, $s = t$.

10. **The correct answer is (B).** In Column A, the area of the rectangle is $4 \times \pi = 4\pi$. In Column B, the area of the circle is $\pi(4)^2$

$= 16\pi$. Therefore, the area of the circle is larger, and Column B is the correct choice.

11. **The correct answer is (B).** The surface area of the whole cube is $6(3)^2 = 54$. The new boxes formed by cutting the cube in half have the same surface area as the cube as a whole, but have added surface area on each cube where the cut was made. This is an addition of $3^2 = 9$ for each cube, making the total surface area $54 + 9 + 9 = 72$. Column B is the larger.

12. **The correct answer is (B).** Since r is a negative number, r^5 will also be a negative number. s^4 is always positive and, consequently, larger than r^5.

13. **The correct answer is (B).**
If $x^2 = 25$, $x = \pm 5$.
If $2y + 3 = 27$, $2y = 24$, so $y = 12$.
y is larger whether x is $+5$ or -5.

14. **The correct answer is (C).** Triangle ABC is isosceles with sides AB and AC equal; therefore, angles ABC and ACB are equal. Angles x and y are supplementary angles of angles ABC and ACB, respectively, and thus must be equal to each other.

15. **The correct answer is (A).** The angles of all triangles add up to 180°. Angle $MNO = 90°$; therefore, the sum of angles M and Q must also equal 90°. Column A is larger than Column B.

Part 2

16. 5

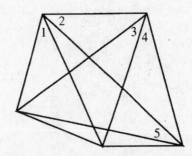

17. $4x = 2(2 + x)$ $\qquad$ $6y = 3(2 + y)$

$\quad 4x = 4 + 2x$ $\qquad$ $6y = 6 + 3y$

$\quad 2x = 4$ $\qquad\qquad$ $3y = 6$

$\quad 2x + 3y = 4 + 6 = 10$

18. "JOSH" $= 3n - 3$

$\qquad n = 3n - 3$

$\qquad -2n = -3$

$\qquad n = \dfrac{3}{2} = 1.5$

19. Machine A produces:

2,000 flue covers/hour.

Machine B produces:

$5,000/\dfrac{5}{2}$ hr. $= 5,000\left(\dfrac{2}{5}\right) = 2,000/$hr.

Since the rates are the same, they produce the same amount of flue covers during any period of time. So Machine A has produced 0 more than Machine B.

20. $.01 = \dfrac{.1}{x}$

$\dfrac{1}{100} = \dfrac{\frac{1}{10}}{x} = \dfrac{1}{10} \cdot \dfrac{1}{x} = \dfrac{1}{10x}$

$\dfrac{1}{100} = \dfrac{1}{10x}$

$10x = 100$

$x = 10$

21.

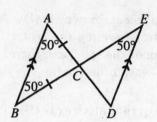

Since $ED \parallel AB$,

angle E = angle $B = 50°$.

(alternate interior angles)

Since $AC = BC$, angle A = angle $B = 50°$.

(In a triangle, opposite equal sides are equal angles.)

In $\triangle ABC$:

$\quad 50 + 50 + x = 180$

$\qquad\qquad\quad x = 80.$

22. Let p = the school's population.

$\dfrac{1}{4}p + \dfrac{1}{5}p + \dfrac{1}{3}p + 390 = p$

$\dfrac{15p + 12p + 20p}{60} + 390 = p$

$60\left(\dfrac{47p}{60} + 390 = p\right)$

$47p + 390(60) = 60p$

$13p = 390(60)$

$p = \dfrac{\overset{30}{\cancel{390}}(60)}{13} = 30(60) = 1800$

23.

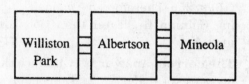

There are $3 \times 5 = 15$ different paths from Williston Park to Mineola through Albertson.

24. Establish a ratio of candies to cents.

Note: $1.70 = 170 cents and $10.20 = 1020 cents.

$$\frac{\text{candies}}{\text{cents}} : \frac{12}{170} = \frac{x}{1020}$$

$$170x = 12(1020)$$

$$x = 72$$

25.

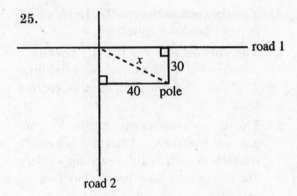

Using the Pythagorean theorem:

$$(30)^2 + (40)^2 = x^2$$

$$900 + 1,600 = x^2$$

$$2,500 = x^2$$

$$x = 50$$

Section 4

1. **The correct answer is (B).** The fact that the society required outside aid indicates that it could not totally support itself. In other words, it was not *self-sufficient*.

2. **The correct answer is (D).** Since the regime is new, the laws must be newly announced and put into effect, or *promulgated*.

3. **The correct answer is (B).** *Brittle* machines might *shatter*.

4. **The correct answer is (D).** When illness strikes, even a person with a strong constitution can be *enervated* (weakened and drained of energy).

5. **The correct answer is (C).** A careful researcher would be *meticulous*.

6. **The correct answer is (C).** A shy look might *enchant* someone into matrimony, but it would not *release, control, ensconce,* or *jilt* someone to that end.

7. **The correct answer is (E).** A city that has failed to fire a single shot against an invading army has clearly *capitulated* (surrendered).

8. **The correct answer is (C).** A *compromise* (agreement) between two opposing sides might avert a strike, but without one the strike becomes *inevitable* (unavoidable).

9. **The correct answer is (A).** A neighbor who is charming is also likely to be *urbane* (suave and sophisticated). Such a person would be the opposite, or *antithesis*, of a bumbling yokel.

10. **The correct answer is (C).** Peeling potatoes and scrubbing floors are both tasks that are *onerous* (burdensome and unpleasant).

11. **The correct answer is (D).** A *pendulum* is designed to *oscillate* and a *gyroscope* to *spin*.

12. **The correct answer is (A).** The first showing of a *movie* is its *premiere* and the first showing of a *statue* is its *unveiling*.

13. **The correct answer is (E).** An *awl* is a pointed tool used by a *carpenter* to make holes in wood. A *pick* is a pointed tool used by a *miner* to break up soil or rock.

14. **The correct answer is (C).** The degree of incline of a *roof* is its *pitch*. The degree of incline of a *mountain* is its *grade*.

15. **The correct answer is (B).** A *cog* is a moving part of a *watch* as a *piston* is a moving part of an *engine*.

16. **The correct answer is (C).** An *equestrian* rides a *horse*; a *cyclist* rides a *bicycle*.

17. **The correct answer is (A).** A *recluse* is *solitary*, preferring to be without company. A *socialite* is *gregarious*, or fond of company.

18. **The correct answer is (D).** *Diffuse* means lacking *concentration*. Similarly, *incongruous* means lacking *harmony*.

19. **The correct answer is (C).** An *apple* is a kind of *fruit* and a *sparrow* is a kind of *bird*.

20. **The correct answer is (E).** A *decade* is *ten* years just as a *millennium* is a *thousand* years.

21. **The correct answer is (E).** A *zealot* (ardent supporter of a cause) is characterized by *fervor* (passion) as a *sage* (wise man) is characterized by *wisdom*.

22. **The correct answer is (C).** A *physician* cures and a *comedian entertains*.

23. **The correct answer is (D).** Plays and symphonies are performed. A *movement* is a part of a *symphony*, and an *act* is part of a *play*.

24. **The correct answer is (D).** Chekhov is praising the play. He is presumably familiar with Gorky's style, and thus compares this play to previous plays with this compliment.

25. **The correct answer is (B).** Red hair on a red-haired man cannot be corrected; it is a natural "flaw." Chekhov means that the "defect" in the play is natural and cannot be repaired.

26. **The correct answer is (D).** Even though Chekhov is being critical in lines 11–15, he makes the point that the play's problems are unavoidable. As a result, his criticism is more supportive than it is negative.

27. **The correct answer is (C).** The play's only defect, according to Chekhov, is "the conservatism of the form" (lines 14–15), which undermines Gorky's new and original characters.

28. **The correct answer is (C).** Chekhov explains that "all that"—the play's unavoidable flaws—stem from the work's conservative structure, i.e., its traditional trappings.

29. **The correct answer is (B).** Chekhov seems concerned throughout with realism. This answer is the only one that makes sense in context.

30. **The correct answer is (B).** As stated in lines 44–46, Nil's modesty is "the element so characteristic of our decent working man."

31. **The correct answer is (D).** Lines 46–47 reveal Chekhov's concern.

32. **The correct answer is (A).** Chekhov is concerned that Elena "is not clear" (line 73); his suggestions attempt to correct that.

33. **The correct answer is (A).** "Both on life and on the stage," Chekhov considers characters such as Teterev unimportant. For this reason, he suggests that Teterev talk less.

34. **The correct answer is (E).** (A) is covered in lines 31–33, (B) in lines 34–36, (C) in lines 55–60, and (D) in lines 66–70. Chekhov has ideas about the ending of the play, which has four acts, but never discusses the ending of the third act.

35. **The correct answer is (E).** Chekhov comments that Piotr "is good. Most likely you don't even suspect how good he is." His only suggestion is that Piotr should be portrayed by the actor Meierkhold.

Section 5

1. **The correct answer is (E).** Stowe says as much in lines 7–10 and in paragraph 2.

2. **The correct answer is (A).** The book will "contain facts and documents" (line 32), so it will not be fictional (B). It will "contain, perhaps, an equal amount of matter" as the previous book (lines 30–31); in other words, it may be as long.

3. **The correct answer is (D).** Rereading this paragraph and the one before proves that Stowe is referring to the horrors of slavery, which she thought she knew, but now finds she "had not begun to measure."

4. **The correct answer is (C).** In this context, the word *exquisitely* means enormously, not its more conventional definitions—expensively, lavishly, or ostentatiously.

5. **The correct answer is (B).** "It seems to me that the book cannot but be felt . . . ." (lines 46–49). Stowe thinks that her readers will feel the pain she documents.

6. **The correct answer is (E).** Nowhere in the passage is it stated that Stowe feels that *Uncle Tom's Cabin* needs a sequel. But she does imply that a second book would support her original work (statement II) and that a presentation of more factual information will strengthen the reader's understanding.

7. **The correct answer is (C).** The passage vividly conveys the emotionalism with which Stowe approaches her writing.

8. **The correct answer is (E).** While there is some truth to (C), it is not implied in the passage. The entire passage concerns Stowe's deeply felt emotions concerning the evils of slavery.

9. **The correct answer is (B).** While all of the answers may have had something to do with slaves not escaping, only choice (B) is cited in the passage.

10. **The correct answer is (B).** The passage specifically states (lines 77–79) that Douglass's failed first attempt haunted him.

11. **The correct answer is (D).** Since this was his second attempt at escape, Douglass knew that he would be severely punished if he did not succeed.

12. **The correct answer is (E).** Although choice (D) has some appeal, it is obvious from the last sentence that "brave and persistent" is the best choice.

Section 6

1. **The correct answer is (D).** Since both areas are equal, $\frac{1}{2}bh = \pi r^2$. Thus, knowing the base of the triangle and radius of the circle, $\frac{1}{2}(7)h = \pi(7)^2$, so $h = 14\pi$.

2. **The correct answer is (E).** $70\% = \frac{70}{100}$ and $\frac{7}{10} \cdot \frac{1}{.70} = \frac{100}{70} = \frac{10}{7} \cdot \frac{13}{9}$ and $\frac{1}{.70}$ are the only fractions larger than 1. Comparing them by finding a common denominator of 63, $\frac{10}{7} = \frac{90}{63}, \frac{13}{9} = \frac{91}{63}$, we find $\frac{10}{7} < \frac{13}{9}$. Comparing $\frac{9}{13}$ and $\frac{7}{10}$, which are both less than 1, we find $\frac{9}{13} = \frac{90}{130}, \frac{7}{10} = \frac{91}{130}$, so $\frac{9}{13} < \frac{7}{10}$. Therefore, $\frac{9}{13} < 70\% < \frac{1}{.70} < \frac{13}{9}$.

3. **The correct answer is (D).** The quadrilateral *PQRS* is a parallelogram as shown:

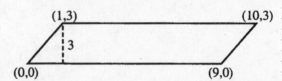

It has a height of 3 and a base of 9. The area is, like that of a rectangle, bh, or 27.

4. **The correct answer is (C).** One simple way to solve this problem is to divide each side of the given equation by 4.

$$\frac{8x+4}{4} = \frac{64}{4}$$
$$2x+1 = 16$$

5. **The correct answer is (D).** Since the center is at the origin, each coordinate point is the length of a leg of a triangle. The hypotenuse of each triangle is the radius of a new circle with its center at the origin. If the hypotenuse of the triangle is greater than 7, the points are outside the circle.

$(4,4)$: $= \sqrt{4^2 + 4^2} = 5.7$, so $(4,4)$ is inside the circle. $(5,5)$: $= \sqrt{5^2 + 5^2} = 7.07$, so $(5,5)$ is outside the circle. $(4,5)$: $= \sqrt{4^2 + 5^2} = 6.4$, so

(4,5) is inside the circle. (4,6): $= \sqrt{4^2 + 6^2} = 7.2$, so (4,6) is outside the circle.

6. **The correct answer is (D).** The area of a square with side = 9 is $9 \cdot 9 = 81$. The surface area of a cube with edge = 3 is $3 \cdot 3 \cdot 6 = 9 \cdot 6 = 54$. The difference, therefore, is $81 - 54 = 27$.

7. **The correct answer is (D).** $2 + 4 + 6 = 12$ and 12 is evenly divisible by all three.

8. **The correct answer is (D).**

$$\frac{3(x^2 - 4)}{(x+2)} = \frac{3(x+2)(x-2)}{(x+2)}$$
$$= 3(x-2)$$
$$= 3x - 6$$

9. **The correct answer is (B).** There are $5 \times 2 = 10$ different varieties of ice-cream bars on the truck. Since the truck only runs four times a week, it would take a person 2 weeks + 2 days to purchase all the different varieties of ice-cream bars. Therefore, the day would be the 16th of the month.

10. **The correct answer is (A).**

$$\frac{N!}{(N-2)} =$$

$$\frac{N(N-1)(N-2)(N-3)(N-4)...[N-(N-1)]}{(N-2)(N-3)(N-4)...[N-(N-1)]}$$

Dividing out common factors in the numerator and the denominator leaves only

$$\frac{N(N-1)}{1} = N(N-1) = N^2 - N$$

COMPUTING YOUR SCORES

You are now ready to check your progress by calculating your scores for the fifth practice examination. To begin, you need to compute individual verbal and mathematical raw scores. Once you have computed these, use the conversion scales in the section that follows to compute your SAT scaled scores (200-800). Keep in mind that these formulas have been simplified to give you a "quick and dirty" sense of where you are scoring, not a perfectly precise score.

To Compute Your Raw Scores

1 Enter the number of correct answers for each verbal and mathematical reasoning section into the boxes marked Number of Questions Correct.

2 Enter the number of incorrect answers (not blanks) for each verbal and mathematical reasoning section into the boxes marked Number of Questions Incorrect.

3 Total the number correct and number incorrect.

4 Follow this formula: Take the total correct and minus one quarter of the total incorrect. Round up in your favor to compute your raw score.

Verbal Section	Total Number of Questions	Number of Questions Correct	Number of Questions Incorrect
1	31		
4	35		
5	12		
Totals	**78**	**Total Correct:**	**Total Incorrect:**

Verbal Raw Score = Total Correct – ($\frac{1}{4}$ × Total Incorrect) = _____

Math Section	Total Number of Questions	Number of Questions Correct	Number of Questions Incorrect
2	25		
3	25		
6	10		
Totals	**60**	**Total Correct:**	**Total Incorrect:**

Math Raw Score = Total Correct – ($\frac{1}{4}$ × Total Incorrect) = _____

CONVERSION SCALES

VERBAL REASONING

Raw Score	Scaled Score	Raw Score	Scaled Score
75	800	35	520
70	800	30	480
65	760	25	440
60	710	20	410
55	670	15	370
50	620	10	340
45	590	5	290
40	550	0	230

MATHEMATICAL REASONING

Raw Score	Scaled Score	Raw Score	Scaled Score
60	800	25	510
55	760	20	480
50	690	15	440
45	650	10	410
40	610	5	340
35	580	0	200
30	550		

Although you now have some idea of what your scores would look like had they been scaled according to unofficial ETS standards, you will probably want to know how to interpret your raw scores in more familiar terms. If so, use the following Self-Evaluation Charts to see what your raw scores actually mean.

SELF–EVALUATION CHARTS

VERBAL REASONING: Raw Score		MATHEMATICAL REASONING: Raw Score	
Excellent	60–75	Excellent	50–60
Good	50–59	Good	40–49
Average	30–49	Average	20–39
Fair	20–29	Fair	10–19
Poor	0–19	Poor	0–9

PART VIII

THE PSAT/NMSQT

CHAPTER 17   Preparing for the PSAT/NMSQT

Preparing for the PSAT/NMSQT

OVERVIEW

- Find out how to register for the PSAT/NMSQT
- Learn why the student search survey is important
- Understand how the PSAT differs from the SAT
- Get to know the PSAT format
- Make sense of your PSAT scores
- Know how your selection index can qualify you for National Merit
- Take a PSAT Practice Test

The Preliminary SAT (PSAT) is a test that is designed to help students practice for the SAT. The exam is also called the National Merit Scholarship Qualifying Test (NMSQT) because students who do well on it are eligible for scholarships awarded by the National Merit Scholarship Corporation. The test is cosponsored by the College Board and the National Merit Scholarship Corporation. In this chapter, you will learn about the PSAT content and format, how this exam differs from the SAT, and what role the PSAT plays in your bid for National Merit scholarships. You will also learn how to make sure that you're registered for the PSAT, how to interpret your scores, and how to use your scores as a tool for SAT preparation.

HOW TO REGISTER FOR THE PSAT/NMSQT

The PSAT/NMSQT is offered on two days in October of every year (but only on one day at any single location). You'll probably take this test in October of your junior year in high school. It is usually given on a Tuesday or a Saturday, depending upon your school's testing policy. Some schools have students take the exam in tenth grade for extra practice. But only when you take the exam during your junior year do you become eligible to compete for National Merit scholarships.

Most high school guidance departments automatically register juniors to take the PSAT. This means no fees and no hassles. But to be safe and certain, check with your guidance counselor or contact:

PSAT/NMSQT
P.O. Box 6720
Princeton, NJ 08541-6720
www.collegeboard.com

ALERT!

At the end of your sophomore year, or immediately when you begin your junior year of high school, be sure to ask your guidance counselor or grade advisor when your school is offering the test. You should be registered automatically, but it's better not to assume anything.

WHY THE STUDENT SEARCH SURVEY IS IMPORTANT

The answer sheet for the PSAT/NMSQT includes a "student search" survey where you provide information about your possible college major and your career interests. This information is then sent to colleges and universities, which will contact you with admission information. When you receive your score report, it will include information about the courses and skills you need to follow the academic major you've chosen. The report also lists information about career opportunities for graduates.

Make sure that you also complete the Scholarship Programs sections, if you are interested in participating. One of the sections covers general eligibility, and two other sections ask about your qualifications to enter the National Achievement Scholarship Program for Outstanding Negro Students or the National Hispanic Scholar Recognition Program.

HOW THE PSAT DIFFERS FROM THE SAT

Some of you may have heard that the PSAT is easier than the SAT. Others may have heard the opposite. Neither assessment is accurate. The substance of the PSAT is virtually identical to that of the SAT—no easier, no harder. The PSAT has fewer sections than the SAT, but you'll find the same types of questions: analogies, critical reading, sentence completions, multiple-choice math, quantitative comparisons, and grid-ins. After you have taken the sample PSAT/NMSQT, evaluate which types of questions give you the most trouble. To review different areas, see earlier chapters of this book.

A big difference between the tests is that the PSAT has recently added a 30-minute section that tests writing skills. *This section is not on the SAT.* The writing section includes questions that ask you to identify errors in sentences, rephrase sentences to make the meaning clearer, and revise paragraphs to improve sentence structure and organization. If you are shooting for National Merit recognition, then improving your score on this section is important. And if you plan to take the SAT II Writing Test, then this score is an early indicator of how you would do. But if the SAT is your main concern, you shouldn't spend too much time worrying about your performance on this section.

Probably the biggest difference between the PSAT and SAT is that PSAT scores do not "count" in terms of your bid for college admission. Colleges do not use PSAT scores when they make admissions decisions. On the other hand, every SAT score you earn throughout high school shows up on your testing transcript, so your performance on every SAT you take is critical.

GET TO KNOW THE PSAT FORMAT

As we said earlier in this chapter, the PSAT has fewer sections than the SAT, but the PSAT questions are just like those on the SAT. As you'll note in the following table, the PSAT contains analogies, critical reading, sentence completions, multiple-choice math, quantitative comparisons, and student-produced responses. The writing skills section of the PSAT, however, may represent new territory for you—the SAT doesn't have such a section. But don't worry—you get a chance to preview this portion of the PSAT in the practice test in this book.

FORMAT OF A TYPICAL PSAT/NMSQT

Section	Number of Questions	Time Allowed
Section 1: Verbal	26	25 minutes
Sentence Completions	6	
Analogies	7	
Critical Reading	13	
Section 2: Mathematics	20	25 minutes
Multiple-Choice Math	20	
Section 3: Verbal	26	25 minutes
Analogies	6	
Sentence Completions	7	
Critical Reading	13	
Section 4: Mathematics	20	25 minutes
Quantitative Comparisons	12	
Student-Produced Responses	8	
Section 5: Writing Skills	39	30 minutes
Identifying Sentence Errors	19	
Improving Sentences	14	
Improving Paragraphs	6	

HOW TO INTERPRET AND USE YOUR PSAT SCORES

This is what you really want to know, isn't it? You'll have to wait about six weeks, but then your school will give you your score report and original test book. This will make it easy for you to review your results and identify your weaknesses.

Here's a breakdown of how the PSAT/NMSQT is scored:

Each correct answer	1 point
Each unanswered question	0 points
Each incorrect answer to a 4-choice multiple-choice question	minus $\frac{1}{3}$ point
Each incorrect answer to a 5-choice multiple-choice question	minus $\frac{1}{4}$ point
Each incorrect answer to a Student-Produced Response question	0 points

NOTE

If you're a home-schooled student, you should make arrangements to register for the PSAT/NMSQT well before the test dates in mid-October. The preceding June, contact the principal or a guidance counselor at a local public or private high school to arrange your test registration. Your scores will be sent directly to your home. When you take the test, you will fill out some basic information; be sure to enter your state's home school code in the "school code" section. The test supervisor will give you this code.

Your score report will include separate scores for verbal, math, and writing skills, each reported on a scale of 20 to 80. This scale corresponds perfectly to the SAT scoring scale of 200 to 800. So to translate a PSAT score into an SAT score, just add a "0" to the end of each math and verbal score. (Remember: The writing section is not on the actual SAT so such a translation is unnecessary.) For example, if Jane received a 49 on verbal, 56 on math, and 44 on writing, that would correspond to a 490 on the SAT verbal and 560 on the SAT math. To get a sense of what these individual scores mean, you will receive three separate percentiles for each of your three separate scores. These percentiles tell you how your scores compare with those of everyone else who took the test.

The report will also indicate your estimated verbal and math scores for the SAT I and your estimated score on the SAT II writing test. But if you prepare thoroughly before the SAT, you should be able to surpass ETS's predictions!

NOTE

Over 2 million students took the PSAT/NMSQT in 1998—44% of high school juniors and 22% of sophomores.

The score report gives you some valuable information that will help you prepare for the SAT. It tells you the correct answer for every question that you missed and it indicates the difficulty level of those questions. With this information, you can review the questions that you answered incorrectly (or didn't answer at all), and then use the skills and strategies you've learned in this book to find the best ways to overcome the problems that contributed to your mistakes. When you review your PSAT/NMSQT answers, ask yourself if incorrect answers or omissions were the result of time pressures. Maybe a few hard questions took up too much of your time, and as a result, you omitted some easy questions that could have added to your score. Maybe you could have eliminated some of the answer choices on a few of the hard questions that you passed over. Use this analysis of your PSAT performance to focus your SAT preparation, and you'll get the most from *both* test experiences.

HOW YOUR SELECTION INDEX CAN QUALIFY YOU FOR NATIONAL MERIT

If you score well on the PSAT and want to shoot for National Merit recognition, you should be more concerned with your "selection index" than with your three individual scores. Your selection index is the sum of your three separate scores. So if we revisit Jane's performance, her selection index would be 149 (49 + 56 + 44). The National Merit Scholarship Corporation (NMSC) takes this index and compares it with those of every other high school junior in her state. The NMSC identifies the highest selection indices and awards these students with some form of National Merit recognition. Unfortunately, many students are not usually alerted of their National Merit status until fall of senior year.

Becoming a Commended Scholar

If your selection index places you in roughly the top 5 percent in your state, you will receive a National Merit Letter of Commendation and become a "commended scholar." This is an impressive academic honor that you should indicate on your college applications. In 1997, a selection index of 199 was required to become a commended scholar in New York state. Keep in mind that these cutoffs vary from state to state and year to year, depending upon the strength of the competition. So if you earn a selection index of 199 on your PSAT, be proud, but don't celebrate prematurely.

Becoming a Semifinalist and Applying for Scholarships

If your selection index places you in roughly the top 1 percent in your state, you will become a National Merit Semifinalist, an even more impressive feat. If you become a semifinalist, you have to submit an application to the NMSC to qualify to become a finalist and receive scholarships. Ultimately, candidates are awarded scholarships by the NMSC, colleges, and universities based on scores, academic records, and other criteria.

TIP

If you haven't decided what you want to major in, just choose something general from the list. No one will hold you to this choice if you want to change your mind in a year.

SUMMARY

What You Need to Know about the PSAT/NMSQT

- The PSAT/NMSQT is designed to help students practice for the SAT. It's also used to determine the test-taker's eligibility for scholarships awarded by the National Merit Scholarship Corporation.

- The PSAT/NMSQT is offered on one of two days in October at individual sites across the nation. Most students take this test in their junior year of high school.

- Colleges don't use the results of this test to determine your eligibility for admission.

- The exam answer sheet contains a "student search" survey; the information you enter on this survey is sent to colleges and universities, which then can send appropriate course and majors information to you.

- The PSAT offers the same format and question types that you find on the SAT. The PSAT differs from the SAT in that it now contains a 30-minute writing skills section. Your results on this section can help you in your bid for National Merit recognition and it can help you prepare for the SAT II writing exam (if you're planning on taking that exam).

- Your PSAT scores are computed to form a selection index; your final selection index is compared to that of every other junior test-taker in the state to determine your eligibility for National Merit recognition.

PSAT/NMSQT PRACTICE TEST

Answer Sheet

Section 1—Verbal 25 minutes
1 Ⓐ Ⓑ Ⓒ Ⓓ Ⓔ
2 Ⓐ Ⓑ Ⓒ Ⓓ Ⓔ
3 Ⓐ Ⓑ Ⓒ Ⓓ Ⓔ
4 Ⓐ Ⓑ Ⓒ Ⓓ Ⓔ
5 Ⓐ Ⓑ Ⓒ Ⓓ Ⓔ
6 Ⓐ Ⓑ Ⓒ Ⓓ Ⓔ
7 Ⓐ Ⓑ Ⓒ Ⓓ Ⓔ
8 Ⓐ Ⓑ Ⓒ Ⓓ Ⓔ
9 Ⓐ Ⓑ Ⓒ Ⓓ Ⓔ
10 Ⓐ Ⓑ Ⓒ Ⓓ Ⓔ
11 Ⓐ Ⓑ Ⓒ Ⓓ Ⓔ
12 Ⓐ Ⓑ Ⓒ Ⓓ Ⓔ
13 Ⓐ Ⓑ Ⓒ Ⓓ Ⓔ
14 Ⓐ Ⓑ Ⓒ Ⓓ Ⓔ
15 Ⓐ Ⓑ Ⓒ Ⓓ Ⓔ
16 Ⓐ Ⓑ Ⓒ Ⓓ Ⓔ
17 Ⓐ Ⓑ Ⓒ Ⓓ Ⓔ
18 Ⓐ Ⓑ Ⓒ Ⓓ Ⓔ
19 Ⓐ Ⓑ Ⓒ Ⓓ Ⓔ
20 Ⓐ Ⓑ Ⓒ Ⓓ Ⓔ
21 Ⓐ Ⓑ Ⓒ Ⓓ Ⓔ
22 Ⓐ Ⓑ Ⓒ Ⓓ Ⓔ
23 Ⓐ Ⓑ Ⓒ Ⓓ Ⓔ
24 Ⓐ Ⓑ Ⓒ Ⓓ Ⓔ
25 Ⓐ Ⓑ Ⓒ Ⓓ Ⓔ
26 Ⓐ Ⓑ Ⓒ Ⓓ Ⓔ

Section 2—Math 25 minutes
1 Ⓐ Ⓑ Ⓒ Ⓓ Ⓔ
2 Ⓐ Ⓑ Ⓒ Ⓓ Ⓔ
3 Ⓐ Ⓑ Ⓒ Ⓓ Ⓔ
4 Ⓐ Ⓑ Ⓒ Ⓓ Ⓔ
5 Ⓐ Ⓑ Ⓒ Ⓓ Ⓔ
6 Ⓐ Ⓑ Ⓒ Ⓓ Ⓔ
7 Ⓐ Ⓑ Ⓒ Ⓓ Ⓔ
8 Ⓐ Ⓑ Ⓒ Ⓓ Ⓔ
9 Ⓐ Ⓑ Ⓒ Ⓓ Ⓔ
10 Ⓐ Ⓑ Ⓒ Ⓓ Ⓔ
11 Ⓐ Ⓑ Ⓒ Ⓓ Ⓔ
12 Ⓐ Ⓑ Ⓒ Ⓓ Ⓔ
13 Ⓐ Ⓑ Ⓒ Ⓓ Ⓔ
14 Ⓐ Ⓑ Ⓒ Ⓓ Ⓔ
15 Ⓐ Ⓑ Ⓒ Ⓓ Ⓔ
16 Ⓐ Ⓑ Ⓒ Ⓓ Ⓔ
17 Ⓐ Ⓑ Ⓒ Ⓓ Ⓔ
18 Ⓐ Ⓑ Ⓒ Ⓓ Ⓔ
19 Ⓐ Ⓑ Ⓒ Ⓓ Ⓔ
20 Ⓐ Ⓑ Ⓒ Ⓓ Ⓔ

Section 3—Verbal 25 minutes
27 Ⓐ Ⓑ Ⓒ Ⓓ Ⓔ
28 Ⓐ Ⓑ Ⓒ Ⓓ Ⓔ
29 Ⓐ Ⓑ Ⓒ Ⓓ Ⓔ
30 Ⓐ Ⓑ Ⓒ Ⓓ Ⓔ
31 Ⓐ Ⓑ Ⓒ Ⓓ Ⓔ
32 Ⓐ Ⓑ Ⓒ Ⓓ Ⓔ
33 Ⓐ Ⓑ Ⓒ Ⓓ Ⓔ
34 Ⓐ Ⓑ Ⓒ Ⓓ Ⓔ
35 Ⓐ Ⓑ Ⓒ Ⓓ Ⓔ
36 Ⓐ Ⓑ Ⓒ Ⓓ Ⓔ
37 Ⓐ Ⓑ Ⓒ Ⓓ Ⓔ
38 Ⓐ Ⓑ Ⓒ Ⓓ Ⓔ
39 Ⓐ Ⓑ Ⓒ Ⓓ Ⓔ
40 Ⓐ Ⓑ Ⓒ Ⓓ Ⓔ
41 Ⓐ Ⓑ Ⓒ Ⓓ Ⓔ
42 Ⓐ Ⓑ Ⓒ Ⓓ Ⓔ
43 Ⓐ Ⓑ Ⓒ Ⓓ Ⓔ
44 Ⓐ Ⓑ Ⓒ Ⓓ Ⓔ
45 Ⓐ Ⓑ Ⓒ Ⓓ Ⓔ
46 Ⓐ Ⓑ Ⓒ Ⓓ Ⓔ
47 Ⓐ Ⓑ Ⓒ Ⓓ Ⓔ
48 Ⓐ Ⓑ Ⓒ Ⓓ Ⓔ
49 Ⓐ Ⓑ Ⓒ Ⓓ Ⓔ
50 Ⓐ Ⓑ Ⓒ Ⓓ Ⓔ
51 Ⓐ Ⓑ Ⓒ Ⓓ Ⓔ
52 Ⓐ Ⓑ Ⓒ Ⓓ Ⓔ

Section 4—Math
25 minutes

21 Ⓐ Ⓑ Ⓒ Ⓓ Ⓔ
22 Ⓐ Ⓑ Ⓒ Ⓓ Ⓔ
23 Ⓐ Ⓑ Ⓒ Ⓓ Ⓔ
24 Ⓐ Ⓑ Ⓒ Ⓓ Ⓔ
25 Ⓐ Ⓑ Ⓒ Ⓓ Ⓔ
26 Ⓐ Ⓑ Ⓒ Ⓓ Ⓔ
27 Ⓐ Ⓑ Ⓒ Ⓓ Ⓔ
28 Ⓐ Ⓑ Ⓒ Ⓓ Ⓔ
29 Ⓐ Ⓑ Ⓒ Ⓓ Ⓔ
30 Ⓐ Ⓑ Ⓒ Ⓓ Ⓔ
31 Ⓐ Ⓑ Ⓒ Ⓓ Ⓔ
32 Ⓐ Ⓑ Ⓒ Ⓓ Ⓔ

Section 5—Writing Skills
30 minutes

1 Ⓐ Ⓑ Ⓒ Ⓓ Ⓔ   15 Ⓐ Ⓑ Ⓒ Ⓓ Ⓔ   29 Ⓐ Ⓑ Ⓒ Ⓓ Ⓔ
2 Ⓐ Ⓑ Ⓒ Ⓓ Ⓔ   16 Ⓐ Ⓑ Ⓒ Ⓓ Ⓔ   30 Ⓐ Ⓑ Ⓒ Ⓓ Ⓔ
3 Ⓐ Ⓑ Ⓒ Ⓓ Ⓔ   17 Ⓐ Ⓑ Ⓒ Ⓓ Ⓔ   31 Ⓐ Ⓑ Ⓒ Ⓓ Ⓔ
4 Ⓐ Ⓑ Ⓒ Ⓓ Ⓔ   18 Ⓐ Ⓑ Ⓒ Ⓓ Ⓔ   32 Ⓐ Ⓑ Ⓒ Ⓓ Ⓔ
5 Ⓐ Ⓑ Ⓒ Ⓓ Ⓔ   19 Ⓐ Ⓑ Ⓒ Ⓓ Ⓔ   33 Ⓐ Ⓑ Ⓒ Ⓓ Ⓔ
6 Ⓐ Ⓑ Ⓒ Ⓓ Ⓔ   20 Ⓐ Ⓑ Ⓒ Ⓓ Ⓔ   34 Ⓐ Ⓑ Ⓒ Ⓓ Ⓔ
7 Ⓐ Ⓑ Ⓒ Ⓓ Ⓔ   21 Ⓐ Ⓑ Ⓒ Ⓓ Ⓔ   35 Ⓐ Ⓑ Ⓒ Ⓓ Ⓔ
8 Ⓐ Ⓑ Ⓒ Ⓓ Ⓔ   22 Ⓐ Ⓑ Ⓒ Ⓓ Ⓔ   36 Ⓐ Ⓑ Ⓒ Ⓓ Ⓔ
9 Ⓐ Ⓑ Ⓒ Ⓓ Ⓔ   23 Ⓐ Ⓑ Ⓒ Ⓓ Ⓔ   37 Ⓐ Ⓑ Ⓒ Ⓓ Ⓔ
10 Ⓐ Ⓑ Ⓒ Ⓓ Ⓔ   24 Ⓐ Ⓑ Ⓒ Ⓓ Ⓔ   38 Ⓐ Ⓑ Ⓒ Ⓓ Ⓔ
11 Ⓐ Ⓑ Ⓒ Ⓓ Ⓔ   25 Ⓐ Ⓑ Ⓒ Ⓓ Ⓔ   39 Ⓐ Ⓑ Ⓒ Ⓓ Ⓔ
12 Ⓐ Ⓑ Ⓒ Ⓓ Ⓔ   26 Ⓐ Ⓑ Ⓒ Ⓓ Ⓔ
13 Ⓐ Ⓑ Ⓒ Ⓓ Ⓔ   27 Ⓐ Ⓑ Ⓒ Ⓓ Ⓔ
14 Ⓐ Ⓑ Ⓒ Ⓓ Ⓔ   28 Ⓐ Ⓑ Ⓒ Ⓓ Ⓔ

TEAR HERE

PSAT/NMSQT PRACTICE TEST

Section 1

26 Questions (1–26) • Time—25 Minutes

> **Directions:** Each of the following questions consists of an incomplete sentence followed by five words or pairs of words. Choose that word or pair of words that, when substituted for the blank space or spaces, best completes the meaning of the sentence and mark the letter of your choice on your answer sheet.

Example

Q In view of the extenuating circumstances and the defendant's youth, the judge recommended ____.
(A) conviction
(B) a defense
(C) a mistrial
(D) leniency
(E) life imprisonment

1. The speaker fascinated us with his knowledge, but his ____ toward the end onto other topics confused us.
(A) digression
(B) removal
(C) preoccupation
(D) tipoff
(E) apprehension

2. My accountant suggested that I should organize my ____ more carefully.
(A) regulations
(B) annals
(C) profits
(D) remainders
(E) receipts

3. He swept into the room like a ____, blowing papers and journals off the desk.
(A) tyrant
(B) zephyr
(C) cyclone
(D) viper
(E) satyr

4. If you make a ____ movement, you might ____ the bear.
(A) vast..disturb
(B) sudden..startle
(C) graceful..perturb
(D) slow..aggrieve
(E) rash..promote

5. Because the motorist had been unable to control his car, the police officer questioned his ____.
(A) sobriety
(B) fecundity
(C) passivity
(D) frailty
(E) virility

6. After the recital we all ____ to the salon for tea and cakes.
(A) retired
(B) restored
(C) retorted
(D) reviewed
(E) remanded

Directions: Each of the following questions consists of a capitalized pair of words followed by five pairs of words lettered (A) to (E). The capitalized words bear some meaningful relationship to each other. Choose the lettered pair of words whose relationship is most similar to that expressed by the capitalized pair and mark its letter on your answer sheet.

Example

Q DAY : SUN ::

(A) sunlight : daylight

(B) ray : sun

(C) night : moon

(D) heat : cold

(E) moon : star

  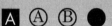

7. COLLAR : NECK ::

(A) hat : head

(B) mitten : hand

(C) lapel : jacket

(D) cuff : wrist

(E) sock : ankle

8. MASTER : CHESS ::

(A) prodigy : game

(B) genius : contest

(C) acme : skill

(D) slave : fashion

(E) virtuoso : music

9. SNOW : BLIZZARD ::

(A) rain : fog

(B) hail : tornado

(C) story : building

(D) English : French

(E) scale : music

10. SONG : LYRICIST ::

(A) tune : musician

(B) play : dramatist

(C) poet : author

(D) show : cast

(E) book : publisher

11. GEOMETRY : MATHEMATICS ::

(A) painting : calculation

(B) astronomy : accounting

(C) hygiene : health care

(D) art : arithmetic

(E) botany : science

12. DOLLAR : DIME ::

(A) decade : year

(B) century : time

(C) nickel : quarter

(D) metal : paper

(E) value : cost

13. GRAMMAR : LANGUAGE ::

(A) training : puppy

(B) hanger : clothing

(C) story : building

(D) English : French

(E) scale : music

Directions: Each reading passage below is followed by a set of questions. Read the passage and answer the accompanying questions, basing your answers on what is stated or implied in the passage. Mark the letter of your choice on your answer sheet.

Questions 14–26 are based on the following passages.

In 1891 in China, a collection of descriptive essays on other countries was compiled by a native of Kiangsu named Wang Hsi-ch'i. This excerpt is from an essay entitled "Europe to a Chinese Observer."

Europe's people are all tall and white. Only those who live in the northeast where it is very cold are short, and dwarfish. They have big noses and deep eyes.
(5) But their eyes are not of the same color, with brown, green, and black being most frequent. They have heavy beards that go up to their temples, or are wound around their jaws. Some of their beards
(10) are straight like those of the Chinese. Some are crooked and twisted like curly hairs. Some shave them all off. Some leave them all on. Some cut their beards but leave their mustaches. Some cut off
(15) their mustaches and leave their beards. They do what they wish. Whether old or young, all have beards. They let their hair grow to two or three inches. But if it gets longer they cut it. The women leave
(20) on all of their hair. The women dress their hair somewhat like Chinese women, but gather it together in a net. The color of their whiskers and hair is different. They have yellow, red, mottled,
(25) or black, all kinds. The men wear flat-topped, tubelike, narrow-brimmed hats of different heights ranging from four inches to over one foot. They are made of felt or silk. When they meet people, they
(30) lift their hats as a sign of respect. Their clothes are narrow and their sleeves are tight. The length only goes down to their bellies. Their trousers are bound tightly around their waists. But their outer
(35) garments are loose and long, and reach as far down as their knees. They wear collars in front and back. Their inner garments are of cotton, but their outer garments are of wool. They often wear
(40) boots which are made of leather.
Women's clothes are also tight and their sleeves stick to their bodies. They wear skirts which are long and brush the ground. This is how they generally
(45) dress. For their ceremonial hats, ceremonial clothes, their military helmets and garments, they have different practices.
For their eating and drinking utensils they use gold, silver, and ceramics.
(50) When they eat they use knife and fork, and they do not use chopsticks. They eat mainly bread. Potatoes are staple. They mostly roast or broil fowl and game.
(55) They usually season it with preserves or olive oil. They drink spirits and soda water, as well as coffee in which they mix sugar. Its fragrance enlivens teeth and jaws, and makes the spirit fresh and
(60) clear.

14. When Wang Hsi-ch'i says that European people's "eyes are not of the same color" (line 5), he means that

(A) they often have two eyes that do not match in color.

(B) their eyes are different from Chinese people's eyes.

(C) different Europeans have different-colored eyes.

(D) their eyes are a different color from their hair.

(E) northern Europeans have eyes that are a different color from those of southern Europeans.

15. The word *dress* (line 20) is used to mean

(A) clothe.

(B) attire.

(C) style.

(D) bandage.

(E) decorate.

16. How does paragraph 3 differ from paragraphs 1 and 2?

(A) It does not refer to personal appearance.

(B) It compares European ways to Chinese ways.

(C) It does not discuss European customs.

(D) Both A and B

(E) Both B and C

17. This passage was intended primarily as

(A) entertainment and amusement.

(B) digression and exchange.

(C) persuasion and argument.

(D) narration and diversion.

(E) description and instruction.

18. How does Wang Hsi-ch'i feel about European customs?

(A) They are not to be trusted.

(B) They are unusual but interesting.

(C) They are bizarre and hilarious.

(D) They are pathetic.

(E) They are preferable to Chinese customs.

Charles Darwin (1809–1882) was best known for his own observational studies, which led to his theory of natural selection, but he was quite capable of using other people's observations to support his theories, as shown in this excerpt from The Descent of Man.

Birds sometimes exhibit benevolent feelings; they will feed the deserted young ones even of distinct species, but this perhaps ought to be considered as a
(5) mistaken instinct. They will feed, as shown in an earlier part of this work, adult birds of their own species which have become blind. Mr. Buxton gives a curious account of a parrot which took
(10) care of a frost-bitten and crippled bird of a distinct species, cleansed her feathers and defended her from the attacks of the other parrots which roamed freely about his garden. It is a still more curious fact
(15) that these birds apparently evince some sympathy for the pleasures of their fellows. When a pair of cockatoos made a nest in an acacia tree "it was ridiculous to see the extravagant interest taken in
(20) the matter by the others of the same species." These parrots also evinced unbounded curiosity and clearly had "the idea of property and possession." They have good memories, for in the Zoologi-
(25) cal Gardens they have plainly recognized their former masters after an interval of some months.

Birds possess acute powers of observation. Every mated bird, of course,
(30) recognizes its fellow. Audubon states that a certain number of mating thrushes (*Mimus polyglottus*) remain all the year round in Louisiana, while others migrate to the Eastern States; these latter
(35) on their return are instantly recognized and always attacked by their southern brethren. Birds under confinement distinguish different persons, as is proved by the strong and permanent antipathy
(40) or affection which they show without any apparent cause toward certain individuals. I have heard of numerous instances with jays, partridges, canaries, and especially bullfinches. Mr. Hussey
(45) has described in how extraordinary a manner a tamed partridge recognized everybody; and its likes and dislikes were very strong. This bird seemed "fond of gay colors, and no new gown or cap
(50) could be put on without catching his attention." Mr. Hewitt has described the habits of some ducks (recently descended from wild birds) which at the approach of a strange dog or cat would rush head-
(55) long into the water and exhaust themselves in their attempts to escape; but

they knew Mr. Hewitt's own dogs and cats so well that they would lie down and bask in the sun close to them. They
(60) always moved away from a strange man, and so they would from the lady who attended them if she made any great change in her dress. Audubon relates that he reared and tamed a wild turkey
(65) which always ran away from any strange dog; this bird escaped into the woods, and some days afterward Audubon saw, as he thought, a wild turkey and made his dog chase it; but to his astonishment
(70) the bird did not run away, and the dog when he came up did not attack the bird, for they mutually recognized each other as old friends.

Mr. Jenner Weir is convinced that
(75) birds pay particular attention to the colors of other birds, sometimes out of jealousy and sometimes as a sign of kinship. Thus he turned a reed-bunting (*Emberiza schoeniculus*), which had ac-
(80) quired its black headdress, into his aviary, and the newcomer was not noticed by any bird except by a bullfinch, which is likewise black-headed. This bullfinch was a very quiet bird, and had never
(85) before quarreled with any of its comrades, including another reed-bunting, which had not as yet become black-headed; but the reed-bunting with a black head was so unmercifully treated
(90) that it had to be removed.

19. Why does Darwin cite Mr. Buxton?

(A) To support his theory about birds' powers of observation

(B) To support his statement about birds' benevolence

(C) To contrast with his own observations of birds

(D) Both A and B

(E) Both B and C

20. The word *distinct* (line 11) is used to mean

(A) special.

(B) apparent.

(C) intelligible.

(D) definite.

(E) different.

21. The word *antipathy* (line 39) means

(A) dislike.

(B) remedy.

(C) disappointment.

(D) amusement.

(E) argument.

22. Why does Darwin mention jays, partridges, canaries, and bullfinches?

(A) To explain why some birds cannot be trained

(B) To educate his reader on types of local birds

(C) To contrast with a later discussion of shore birds

(D) To support his discussion of birds' memories

(E) To show the variety of birds in England

23. The word *reared* (line 64) is used to mean

(A) backed.

(B) raised.

(C) leaped.

(D) ended.

(E) constructed.

24. What does Darwin mean by "a sign of kinship" (lines 77–78)?

(A) Mark of common parentage

(B) Premonition of future union

(C) Symbol of compatibility

(D) Evidence of family relationship

(E) Indication of mutual interest

25. A good title for paragraph 3 might be

(A) "Different-Colored Birds."

(B) "Bullfinches and Their Colors."

(C) "An Example of Color Recognition in Birds."

(D) "Captive Birds."

(E) "Birds in Peace and War."

26. The main purpose of this passage is to

(A) contrast birds with humans.

(B) compare three species of birds.

(C) review current studies of birds.

(D) compare wild birds to confined birds.

(E) discuss some traits of birds.

STOP

END OF SECTION 1. IF YOU HAVE ANY TIME LEFT, GO OVER YOUR WORK IN THIS SECTION ONLY. DO NOT WORK IN ANY OTHER SECTION OF THE TEST.

Section 2

20 Questions (1–20) • Time—25 Minutes

Directions: Solve the following problems using any available space on the page for scratchwork. On your answer sheet fill in the choice that best corresponds to the correct answer.

Notes: The figures accompanying the problems are drawn as accurately as possible, unless otherwise stated in specific problems. Again, unless otherwise stated, all figures lie in the same plane. All numbers used in these problems are real numbers. Calculators are permitted for this test.

Reference Information

Circle:
$C = 2\pi r$
$A = \pi r^2$

Rectangle:
$A = lw$

Rectangular Solid:
$V = lwh$

Cylinder:
$V = \pi r^2 h$

Triangle:
$A = \tfrac{1}{2}bh$

$a^2 + b^2 = c^2$

The number of degrees of arc in a circle is 360.
The measure in degrees of a straight angle is 180.
The sum of the measures in degrees of the angles of a triangle is 180.

1. $0.1 \times 0.01 \times 0.001 =$
   - **(A)** .01
   - **(B)** .03
   - **(C)** .003
   - **(D)** .0001
   - **(E)** .000001

2. The average height of the four-member gymnastics squad is 5 feet. Three of the girls are 4 feet 10 inches tall. How tall is the fourth member?
   - **(A)** 5 feet
   - **(B)** 5 feet 2 inches
   - **(C)** 5 feet 4 inches
   - **(D)** 5 feet 6 inches
   - **(E)** It cannot be determined from the information given.

3. $\frac{1}{5}$ times its reciprocal is
   - **(A)** $\dfrac{2}{5}$
   - **(B)** $\dfrac{1}{25}$
   - **(C)** 1
   - **(D)** 5
   - **(E)** 25

4. How many sixteenths are in $5\frac{1}{4}$?
   - **(A)** 17
   - **(B)** 20
   - **(C)** 80
   - **(D)** 81
   - **(E)** 84

5. Whenever a particular organism reproduces, it doubles in number each hour. If you start with one organism at 3:00, how many will you have by 6:00?

   (A) 4

   (B) 6

   (C) 8

   (D) 24

   (E) 120

6. If $x = \frac{1}{4}y$, what is the value of $\frac{x}{4}$?

   (A) 16

   (B) $\frac{y}{16}$

   (C) $\frac{y}{4}$

   (D) y

   (E) $4y$

7. If the sides of a square are tripled, what always happens to its perimeter?

   (A) It remains the same.

   (B) It is cubed.

   (C) It increases by 100%.

   (D) It is tripled.

   (E) It increases by 900%.

8. If $\triangle ABC$ is an isosceles triangle in the figure below, what is the value of z?

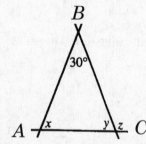

   (A) 60

   (B) 90

   (C) $2y$

   (D) 100

   (E) 105

9. Leo is 67. His son Robert is 29. In how many years will Robert be exactly half his father's age?

   (A) 2

   (B) 5

   (C) 7

   (D) 9

   (E) 12

10. When the numbers $\frac{1}{4}, \frac{3}{10}$, 0.23, and $\frac{4}{15}$ are arranged in ascending order of size, the result is

   (A) $0.23, \frac{3}{10}, \frac{1}{4}, \frac{4}{15}$

   (B) $\frac{1}{4}, 0.23, \frac{3}{10}, \frac{4}{15}$

   (C) $0.23, \frac{1}{4}, \frac{3}{10}, \frac{4}{15}$

   (D) $\frac{4}{15}, \frac{3}{10}, \frac{1}{4}, 0.23$

   (E) $0.23, \frac{1}{4}, \frac{4}{15}, \frac{3}{10}$

11. If $a + b = 12$ and $\frac{b}{a} = 3$, then

   (A) $a = 9$

   (B) $b = \frac{a}{3}$

   (C) $12 = 3b$

   (D) $b - a = 9$

   (E) $ab = 27$

12. The side of a square forms the radius of a circle with a circumference of 10. What is the perimeter of the square?

   (A) $\frac{5}{\pi}$

   (B) $\frac{10}{\pi}$

   (C) $\frac{20}{\pi}$

   (D) 4π

   (E) 100π

13. Station KBAZ is on the air 24 hours a day. Yesterday it sold ads and took in money at this rate: 20% from drive-time ads at $20/minute, 50% from daytime ads at $10/minute, and 30% from nighttime ads at $5/minute. If the station made $500 yesterday, how much air time was dedicated to ads?

(A) 30 minutes

(B) 1 hour

(C) 2 hours

(D) 3 hours

(E) 3 hours, 30 minutes

14. In the figure below, the area of the circle is equivalent to

(A) $\dfrac{AB}{\pi}$

(B) AB

(C) πAB

(D) $\pi\left(\dfrac{AC}{2}\right)^2$

(E) $\pi AC2$

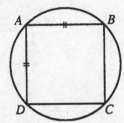

15. A motorist drives 90 miles at an average speed of 50 miles per hour and returns at an average speed of 60 miles per hour. Approximately what is her average speed in miles per hour for the entire trip?

(A) 53

(B) 54.5

(C) 56.5

(D) 58

(E) It cannot be determined from the information given.

16. If $17x - 32 = 308$, what is $\dfrac{x}{4}$?

(A) 5

(B) 10

(C) 20

(D) 50

(E) 85

17. In the square below, $\triangle UQR$ and $\triangle RST$ are equal in area. If $QR = 2$, what is the area of triangle RUT?

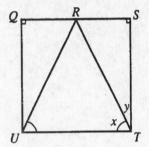

(A) 2

(B) 4

(C) 8

(D) 12

(E) 16

18. If the radius of a circle is increased by 10%, the area of the circle is increased by

(A) 10%

(B) 21%

(C) 100%

(D) 110%

(E) 121%

19. If 2* means 2×3 and 3* means 3×4, what does 7* + 8* mean?

(A) 56

(B) 128

(C) 392

(D) 448

(E) 4,032

20. If one faucet fills the sink in 3 minutes and the other fills it in 2 minutes, how long will it take both faucets to fill the sink if both are turned on together?

(A) .5 minute

(B) 1 minute

(C) 1.2 minutes

(D) 1.5 minutes

(E) 1.8 minutes

STOP

END OF SECTION 2. IF YOU HAVE ANY TIME LEFT, GO OVER YOUR WORK IN THIS SECTION ONLY. DO NOT WORK IN ANY OTHER SECTION OF THE TEST.

Section 3

26 Questions (27–52) • Time—25 Minutes

Directions: Each of the following questions consists of an incomplete sentence followed by five words or pairs of words. Choose that word or pair of words that, when substituted for the blank space or spaces, best completes the meaning of the sentence and mark the letter of your choice on your answer sheet.

Example

Q In view of the extenuating circumstances and the defendant's youth, the judge recommended ____.

(A) conviction

(B) a defense

(C) a mistrial

(D) leniency

(E) life imprisonment

A Ⓐ Ⓑ Ⓒ ● Ⓔ

27. He soon ____ that she was making fun of him; with that ____ came a feeling of intense shame.

(A) forgot..withdrawal

(B) apprised..wisdom

(C) realized..contentment

(D) recognized..awareness

(E) believed..contrivance

28. Her easy win in the cross-country ski race gained her much ____ from skiers in her northern community.

(A) condemnation

(B) consternation

(C) tribulation

(D) demarcation

(E) approbation

29. The house looked ____ situated on the crumbling cliff.

(A) prudently

(B) precariously

(C) predominantly

(D) vicariously

(E) aimlessly

30. Should we allow Paul to ____ his brother's time at the computer?

(A) usurp

(B) renege

(C) depict

(D) marshal

(E) entail

31. The treaty was ____ almost as soon as the signatures were ____.

(A) broken..revamped

(B) abrogated..affixed

(C) signed..appended

(D) funded..initialed

(E) prepared..fulfilled

32. The stark trees were ____ against the grey sky.

(A) silhouetted

(B) shackled

(C) established

(D) conflicted

(E) oscillated

33. It makes no difference what we ____; her opinion is ____.

   (A) understand..reflective

   (B) assert..unwavering

   (C) opine..shifting

   (D) modify..subversive

   (E) delineate..volatile

Directions: Each of the following questions consists of a capitalized pair of words followed by five pairs of words lettered (A) to (E). The capitalized words bear some meaningful relationship to each other. Choose the lettered pair of words whose relationship is most similar to that expressed by the capitalized pair and mark its letter on your answer sheet.

Example

Q DAY : SUN ::

   (A) sunlight : daylight

   (B) ray : sun

   (C) night : moon

   (D) heat : cold

   (E) moon : star

Ⓐ Ⓐ Ⓑ ● Ⓓ Ⓔ

34. WHEEL : WAGON ::

   (A) runner : sled

   (B) circle : square

   (C) fin : fish

   (D) engine : automobile

   (E) skate : blade

35. DEFEND : PROSECUTE ::

   (A) protect : serve

   (B) allay : berate

   (C) fortify : assail

   (D) liberate : free

   (E) deliberate : judge

36. SAPPHIRE : BLUE ::

   (A) ruby : red

   (B) tree : green

   (C) silver : tarnished

   (D) gem : polished

   (E) jewelry : ornate

37. CASTOFFS : CLOTHING ::

   (A) closet : coat

   (B) castaway : ship

   (C) rummage : sale

   (D) trash : garbage

   (E) scrap : metal

38. FOX : KIT ::

   (A) pup : seal

   (B) manx : cat

   (C) male : female

   (D) lion : cub

   (E) wolf : pack

39. SHARECROPPER : PLANTATION ::

   (A) renter : apartment

   (B) farmer : crop

   (C) worker : job

   (D) assembly line : factory

   (E) potato : root

Directions: The reading passage below is followed by a set of questions. Read the passage and answer the accompanying questions, basing your answers on what is stated or implied in the passage. Mark the letter of your choice on your answer sheet.

Questions 40-44 are based on the following passage.

Kate Chopin wrote a number of short stories about the Louisiana Creoles, but she is famous for her novel of a woman trapped in a stifling marriage. The Awakening is a strange, moody book, basing much of its appeal on a strong sense of character and setting. In this excerpt from the beginning of the novel, we meet the main characters.

Mr. Pontellier finally lit a cigar and began to smoke, letting the paper drag idly from his hand. He fixed his gaze upon a white sunshade that was ad-
(5) vancing at snail's pace from the beach. He could see it plainly between the gaunt trunks of the water-oaks and across the stretch of yellow camomile. The gulf looked far away, melting hazily into the
(10) blue of the horizon. The sunshade continued to approach slowly. Beneath its pink-lined shelter were his wife, Mrs. Pontellier, and young Robert Lebrun. When they reached the cottage, the two
(15) seated themselves with some appearance of fatigue upon the upper step of the porch, facing each other, each leaning against a supporting post.

"What folly! to bathe at such an
(20) hour in such heat!" exclaimed Mr. Pontellier. He himself had taken a plunge at daylight. That was why the morning seemed long to him.

"You are burnt beyond recognition,"
(25) he added, looking at his wife as one looks at a valuable piece of personal property which has suffered some damage. She held up her hands, strong, shapely hands, and surveyed them critically, drawing
(30) up her lawn sleeves above the wrists. Looking at them reminded her of her

rings, which she had given to her husband before leaving for the beach. She silently reached out to him, and he,
(35) understanding, took the rings from his vest pocket and dropped them into her open palm. She slipped them upon her fingers; then clasping her knees, she looked across at Robert and began to
(40) laugh. He sent back an answering smile.

"What is it?" asked Pontellier, looking lazily and amused from one to the other. It was some utter nonsense; some adventure out there in the water, and
(45) they both tried to relate it at once. It did not seem half so amusing when told. They realized this, and so did Mr. Pontellier. He yawned and stretched himself. Then he got up, saying he had
(50) half a mind to go over to Klein's hotel and play a game of billiards.

"Come go along, Lebrun," he proposed to Robert. But Robert admitted quite frankly that he preferred to stay
(55) where he was and talk to Mrs. Pontellier.

"Well, send him about his business when he bores you, Edna," instructed her husband as he prepared to leave.

"Here, take the umbrella," she ex-
(60) claimed, holding it out to him. He accepted the sunshade, and lifting it over his head descended the steps and walked away.

40. The word *folly* (line 19) is used to mean

(A) temerity.

(B) gaiety.

(C) clumsiness.

(D) tactlessness.

(E) foolishness.

41. The narrator refers to "a valuable piece of personal property" (line 26) to

(A) show how very much her husband values Mrs. Pontellier.

(B) imply that Mr. Pontellier considers his wife to be his possession.

(C) remind the reader of Mr. Pontellier's great wealth.

(D) show how much the author values Mrs. Pontellier.

(E) contrast Mrs. Pontellier with her beach property.

42. The incident with Mrs. Pontellier's rings symbolizes

(A) her bondage.

(B) her love for Lebrun.

(C) her traditional values.

(D) her desire to grow.

(E) her bravery.

43. The word *relate* (line 37) is used to mean

(A) unite.

(B) recount.

(C) integrate.

(D) involve.

(E) compare.

44. How does the narrator feel about Mr. Pontellier?

(A) He is mischievous.

(B) He is dull.

(C) He is rude.

(D) He is vain.

(E) He is fiendish.

Directions: The two passages given below deal with a related topic. Following the passages are questions about the content of each passage or about the relationship between the two passages. Answer the questions based upon what is stated or implied in the passages and in any introductory material provided. Mark the letter of your choice on your answer sheet.

Questions 45–52 are based on the following passages.

As many in pre-Revolutionary Virginia cried for conciliation with Britain, Patrick Henry advocated preparing for war in a speech to the delegates to the Continental Congress. A year later, a group of writers who signed themselves Hutchinson, Cooper, Cato, & c. submitted a stinging article to the Pennsylvania Evening Post.

PASSAGE 1—Patrick Henry to the Virginia Delegation, March 23, 1775

No man thinks more highly than I do of the patriotism, as well as abilities, of the very worthy gentlemen who have just addressed the House. But different

(5)   men often see the same subject in different lights; and, therefore, I hope it will not be thought disrespectful to those gentlemen, if, entertaining as I do opinions of a character very opposite to theirs,

(10) I shall speak forth my sentiments freely and without reserve. This is no time for ceremony. The question before the House is one of awful moment to this country. For my own part, I consider it

(15) as nothing less than a question of freedom or slavery. . . .

Mr. President, it is natural to man to indulge in the illusions of hope. We are apt to shut our eyes against a painful (20) truth, and listen to the song of that siren till she transforms us into beasts. Is this the part of wise men, engaged in a great and arduous struggle for liberty? Are we disposed to be of the number of those (25) who, having eyes, see not, and, having ears, hear not, the things which so nearly concern their temporal salvation? For my part, whatever anguish of spirit it may cost, I am willing to know the whole (30) truth; to know the worst, and to provide for it.

I have but one lamp by which my feet are guided, and that is the lamp of experience. I know of no way of judging (35) the future but by the past. And judging by the past, I wish to know what there has been in the conduct of the British ministry for the last ten years to justify those hopes with which gentlemen have (40) been pleased to solace themselves and the House.

PASSAGE 2—In the *Pennsylvania Evening Post*, June 1, 1776

Notwithstanding the savage treatment we have met with from the King of Britain, and the impossibility of the colonies (45) ever being happy under his government again, according to the usual operation of natural and moral causes, yet we still find some people wishing to be dependent once more upon the crown of Brit-(50) ain. I have too good an opinion of the human understanding, to suppose that there is a man in America who believes that we ever shall be happy again in our old connection with that crown. I, there-(55) fore, beg leave to oblige the advocates for dependence to speak for themselves in the following order:—

1. I shall lose my office. 2. I shall lose the honor of being related to men in (60) office. 3. I shall lose the rent of my houses for a year or two. 4. We shall have no more rum, sugar, tea nor coffee, in this country, except at a most exorbitant price. 5. We shall have no more gauze or (65) fine muslins imported among us. 6. The New England men will turn Goths and Vandals, and overrun all the Southern Colonies. N.B.—It is the fashion with the people who make this objection to (70) independence, to despise the courage and discipline of the New England troops, and to complain that they are unwilling to fight out of their own colonies. 7. The church will have no king for a head. 8. (75) The Presbyterians will have a share of power in this country. N.B.—These people have been remarked, ever since the commencement of our disputes with Great Britain, to prefer a Quaker or an (80) Episcopalian, to one of their own body, where he was equally hearty in the cause of liberty. 9. I shall lose my chance of a large tract of land in a new purchase. 10. I shall want the support of the first (85) officers of government, to protect me in my insolence, injustice, and villany. 11. The common people will have too much power in their hands. N.B.—The common people are composed of tradesmen (90) and farmers, and include nine-tenths of the people of America.

Finally.—Sooner than submit to the chance of these probable evils, we will have our towns burnt, our country (95) desolated, and our fathers, brothers, and children butchered by English, Scotch, and Irishmen. . . . And, after all, such of us as survive these calamities, will submit to such terms of slavery as King (100) George and his Parliament may impose upon us.

45. The phrase "awful moment" (line 13) is used by Henry to mean

(A) terrible time.

(B) unpleasant point.

(C) dreadful value.

(D) great importance.

(E) sudden amazement.

46. Why does Henry refer to the myth about the siren?

(A) To remind us that sweet sounds may lull us falsely

(B) To advise us to prepare for war as the Greeks once did

(C) To compare our democracy with that of the Greeks

(D) To persuade us to heed the song as it is sung

(E) To stress the need for alarm

47. The numbered list in Passage 2 contains

(A) articles of confederation.

(B) arguments in favor of independence from Britain.

(C) moral causes.

(D) the author's opinions about independence.

(E) supposed excuses for remaining dependent on Britain.

48. "Goths and Vandals" (line 66–67) are used as examples of

(A) haphazard events.

(B) tribal rites.

(C) games.

(D) barbaric peoples.

(E) famous cowards.

49. The word *want* (line 84) is used in Passage 2 to mean

(A) covet.

(B) need.

(C) lack.

(D) crave.

(E) prefer.

50. How does the author of Passage 2 feel about commoners?

(A) They must be tolerated.

(B) They have too much power.

(C) They are in the majority.

(D) Both A and B

(E) Both B and C

51. Passage 1 differs from Passage 2 in its

(A) politics.

(B) tone.

(C) attitude toward the British.

(D) both A and B

(E) both B and C

52. With which of the following would both authors agree?

(A) The question is one of freedom or slavery.

(B) Men indulge in illusions of hope.

(C) The British have done nothing to inspire hope.

(D) All of the above

(E) None of the above

STOP

END OF SECTION 3. IF YOU HAVE ANY TIME LEFT, GO OVER YOUR WORK IN THIS SECTION ONLY. DO NOT WORK IN ANY OTHER SECTION OF THE TEST.

Section 4

20 Questions (21–40) • Time—25 Minutes

Directions: Solve the following problems using any available space on the page for scratchwork. On your answer sheet fill in the choice that best corresponds to the correct answer.

Notes: The figures accompanying the problems are drawn as accurately as possible unless otherwise stated in specific problems. Again, unless otherwise stated, all figures lie in the same plane. All numbers used in these problems are real numbers. Calculators are permitted for this test.

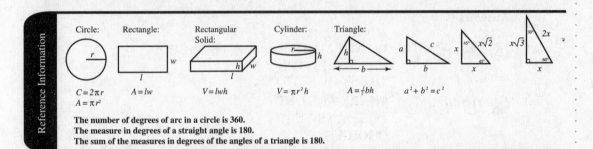

$C = 2\pi r$
$A = \pi r^2$
Circle:

Rectangle: $A = lw$

Rectangular Solid: $V = lwh$

Cylinder: $V = \pi r^2 h$

Triangle: $A = \frac{1}{2}bh$ $a^2 + b^2 = c^2$

The number of degrees of arc in a circle is 360.
The measure in degrees of a straight angle is 180.
The sum of the measures in degrees of the angles of a triangle is 180.

Part 1: Quantitative Comparison Questions

Directions: Questions 21–32 each consist of two quantities—one in Column A, the other in Column B. Compare the two quantities and mark your answer sheet as follows:

(A) if the quantity in Column A is greater

(B) if the quantity in Column B is greater

(C) if the quantities are equal

(D) if the relationship cannot be determined from the information given

Notes:

(1) Information concerning one or both of the compared quantities will be centered above the two columns for some items.

(2) Symbols that appear in both columns represent the same thing in Column A as in Column B.

(3) Letters such as x, n, and k are symbols for real numbers.

Examples

	Column A	Column B

$$a > 0$$

$$x > 0$$

E1. $\boxed{a - x}$ $\boxed{a + x}$

E2.   The average of 17, 19, 21, 23   The average of 16, 18, 20, 22

Answers

E1.   Ⓐ ● Ⓒ Ⓓ   DO NOT MARK CHOICE (E) FOR THESE QUESTIONS.

E2.   ● Ⓑ Ⓒ Ⓓ   THERE ARE ONLY FOUR ANSWER CHOICES.

	Column A	Column B		Column A	Column B
21.	Area of a circle with a radius of z	Area of a square with sides measuring z			

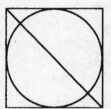

$$\frac{a}{2} = -b$$

	Column A	Column B		Column A	Column B
22.	ab	$\dfrac{a}{b}$	**28.**	The perimeter of the triangle	The circumference of the circle
23.	The number of odd numbers greater than 3 and less than or equal to 13	4	**29.**	5% of 7	7% of 5

a and b are positive integers

$$x^2 = 144$$
$$2y - 18 = 32$$

	Column A	Column B		Column A	Column B
24.	$2x$	y	**30.**	$(a + b) - a$	$(b + a) - b$
			31.	$(x + 2)(x - 2)$	$x^2 - 4$

$m < n$

	Column A	Column B		Column A	Column B
25.	$\dfrac{m}{n}$	$\dfrac{n}{m}$	**32.**	The average of the even numbers greater than 2 and less than 12	The average of the odd numbers greater than 3 and less than 13
26.	$\dfrac{1}{3}(c + d)$	$\dfrac{c}{3} + \dfrac{d}{3}$			

Two dice packed exactly into a box

	Column A	Column B
27.	The volume of the box	The volumes of the dice added together

practice test

Part 2: Student-Produced Response Questions

Directions: Solve each of these problems. Write the answer in the corresponding grid on the answer sheet and fill in the ovals beneath each answer you write. Here are some examples.

Answer: $\frac{3}{4}$ (=.75; show answer either way)   Answer: 325

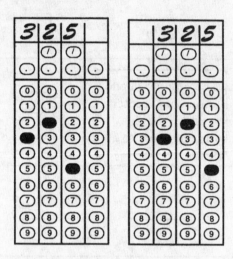

Note: A mixed number such as $3\frac{1}{2}$ must be gridded as 7/2 or as 3.5. If gridded as "3 1/2," it will be read as "thirty-one halves."

Note: Either position is correct.

33. If $4x - 9 = 27$, what is x^3?

34. One half of the contents of a container evaporates in one week, and three fourths of the remainder evaporates in the following week. At the end of two weeks, what fractional part of the original contents remains? Express your answer in simplest form.

35. The distance from the center of a circle to the midpoint of a chord is 3. If the length of the chord is 8, what is the length of the radius of the circle?

36. Three friends decide to split the cost of a pizza, with each chipping in $3.25. If two more friends join them, and each pays an equal share, how much less will each of the three friends have to pay?

37. Five members of the baseball team weigh 130, 115, 120, 140, and 145 pounds. If the average weight of the nine-person team is 130 pounds, what is the average weight in pounds of the remaining four players?

38. In the figure below, what is the measure in degrees of angle n?

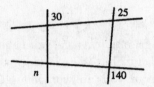

39. If $a + b = -4$ and $b^2 = 49$, what positive whole number can a be?

40. Danielle ate $\frac{1}{4}$ of a bag of popcorn and gave $\frac{1}{6}$ of the remainder to Phil. How much of the original container was left? Express your answer in simplest form.

STOP

END OF SECTION 4. IF YOU HAVE ANY TIME LEFT, GO OVER YOUR WORK IN THIS SECTION ONLY. DO NOT WORK IN ANY OTHER SECTION OF THE TEST.

practice test

Section 5

39 Questions (1–39) • Time—30 Minutes

Directions: The sentences below contain errors in grammar usage, word choice, and idiom. Parts of each sentence are underlined and lettered. Decide which underlined part contains the error and mark its letter on your answer sheet. If the sentence is correct as it stands, mark (E) on your answer sheet. No sentence contains more than one error.

1. <u>Not wanting</u> them to be <u>unnecessary</u>
        A   B
   <u>distressed</u>, I didn't tell them about our
        C
   <u>mishap</u> with the car. <u>No error</u>.
        D   E

2. By the time he <u>reached</u> the cabin, the
                          A
   <u>mercury</u> had dropped and his hands were
        B
   <u>nearly</u> <u>froze</u>. <u>No error</u>.
        C   D   E

3. We <u>ought to</u> <u>set</u> our prejudices aside and
            A   B
   <u>except</u> each other as <u>equals</u>. <u>No error</u>.
        C   D   E

4. Every <u>athlete</u> has <u>their</u> own <u>way</u> of
              A   B   C
   <u>preparing</u> for a game. <u>No error</u>.
        D   E

5. As a <u>documentary</u> photographer for the
              A
   Farm Security Administration during the
   <u>Depression</u>, Dorothea Lange <u>recorded</u> the
        B   C
   hardships and desperation of America's
   <u>dispossessed</u>. <u>No error</u>.
        D   E

6. The Piltdown man, one of the most extraordinary scientific <u>hoax</u> of all time,
                               A
   was <u>accepted</u> by <u>anthropologists</u> as
            B   C
   the "<u>missing link</u>" between man and
              D
   the apes. <u>No error</u>.
                  E

7. Lifeguards <u>have been known</u> to <u>effect</u>
                      A   B
   rescues <u>even</u> <u>during</u> tumultuous storms.
              C   D
   <u>No error</u>.
        E

8. The <u>mayor</u> <u>expressed</u> concern about the
            A   B
   large <u>amount</u> of people injured at street
              C
   <u>crossings</u>. <u>No error</u>.
        D   E

9. "<u>Leave</u> us <u>face</u> the fact that <u>we're</u> in
        A   B   C
   <u>trouble</u>!" he shouted. <u>No error</u>.
        D   E

10. Jones seems <u>slow</u> on the track, but you
    ⠀⠀⠀⠀⠀⠀A

    will find few boys <u>quicker</u> <u>than</u> <u>him</u> on the
    ⠀⠀⠀⠀⠀⠀⠀⠀⠀⠀⠀B⠀⠀⠀⠀C⠀⠀D

    basketball court. <u>No error</u>.
    ⠀⠀⠀⠀⠀⠀⠀⠀⠀⠀⠀⠀⠀⠀E

11. We had <u>swam</u> <u>across</u> the lake <u>before</u> the
    ⠀⠀⠀⠀⠀⠀A⠀⠀⠀⠀B⠀⠀⠀⠀⠀⠀⠀⠀⠀C

    sun <u>rose</u>. <u>No error</u>.
    ⠀⠀⠀⠀D⠀⠀⠀⠀E

12. The <u>loud noise</u> of the cars and trucks
    ⠀⠀⠀⠀⠀⠀A

    <u>annoys</u> those <u>who</u> live <u>near the road</u>.
    ⠀⠀B⠀⠀⠀⠀⠀⠀⠀C⠀⠀⠀⠀⠀⠀D

    <u>No error</u>.
    ⠀⠀⠀E

13. I know that you <u>will enjoy</u> <u>receiving</u>
    ⠀⠀⠀⠀⠀⠀⠀⠀⠀⠀⠀⠀A⠀⠀⠀⠀⠀⠀⠀B

    flowers that <u>smell</u> so <u>sweetly</u>. <u>No error</u>.
    ⠀⠀⠀⠀⠀⠀⠀⠀⠀C⠀⠀⠀⠀D⠀⠀⠀⠀⠀E

14. He is <u>at least</u> ten years <u>older</u> <u>then</u> <u>she</u> is.
    ⠀⠀⠀⠀⠀A⠀⠀⠀⠀⠀⠀⠀⠀⠀⠀B⠀⠀⠀C⠀⠀D

    <u>No error</u>.
    ⠀⠀⠀E

15. To go out <u>dancing</u>, to have a couple of
    ⠀⠀⠀⠀⠀⠀⠀A

    beers, and <u>staying</u> out late <u>is</u> <u>my idea</u> of
    ⠀⠀⠀⠀⠀⠀⠀⠀⠀B⠀⠀⠀⠀⠀⠀⠀⠀C⠀⠀⠀D

    relaxation. <u>No error</u>.
    ⠀⠀⠀⠀⠀⠀⠀⠀⠀⠀E

16. All of the children <u>have</u> grown
    ⠀⠀⠀⠀⠀⠀⠀⠀⠀⠀⠀⠀⠀A

    <u>considerable</u> since the last time <u>their</u> uncle
    ⠀⠀⠀B⠀⠀⠀⠀⠀⠀⠀⠀⠀⠀⠀⠀⠀⠀⠀⠀⠀⠀C

    <u>visited.</u> <u>No error</u>.
    ⠀⠀D⠀⠀⠀⠀E

17. What <u>does</u> <u>either</u> Rick or Alice <u>know</u> about
    ⠀⠀⠀⠀⠀A⠀⠀⠀B⠀⠀⠀⠀⠀⠀⠀⠀⠀⠀⠀C

    disease, hunger, or <u>being poor</u>? <u>No error</u>.
    ⠀⠀⠀⠀⠀⠀⠀⠀⠀⠀⠀⠀⠀⠀D⠀⠀⠀⠀⠀⠀E

18. A bad <u>conscious</u> made him give <u>himself</u>
    ⠀⠀⠀⠀⠀A⠀⠀⠀⠀⠀⠀⠀⠀⠀⠀⠀⠀⠀⠀B

    up, <u>though</u> no one had suspected him <u>of</u>
    ⠀⠀⠀⠀C⠀⠀⠀⠀⠀⠀⠀⠀⠀⠀⠀⠀⠀⠀⠀⠀D

    the crime. <u>No error</u>.
    ⠀⠀⠀⠀⠀⠀⠀⠀E

19. <u>In his effort</u> to reach a wise decision about
    ⠀⠀A

    these <u>truants</u>, the attendance officer
    ⠀⠀⠀⠀⠀B

    <u>conferred</u> many times with the dean and
    ⠀C

    <u>I</u>. <u>No error</u>.
    ⠀D⠀⠀⠀E

> **Directions:** The sentences below contain problems in grammar, sentence construction, word choice, and punctuation. Part or all of each sentence is underlined. Select the lettered answer that contains the best version of the underlined section. Answer (A) always repeats the original underlined section exactly. If the sentence is correct as it stands, select (A).

20. The hunter stalked the tiger slowly, cautiously, <u>and in a silent manner</u>.

   (A) and in a silent manner

   (B) and silently

   (C) and by acting silently

   (D) and also used silence

   (E) and in silence

21. The doctor believed that exercise and a hot bath were <u>equally as effective as, and less addictive than</u>, a sedative for relieving anxiety.

   (A) equally as effective as, and less addictive than

   (B) equally as affective as, and less addictive than

   (C) as effective as, and less addictive than

   (D) equally as effective, and less addictive than

   (E) equally as effective as, while being less addictive than

22. <u>When describing</u> the accident, a tone of self-justification creeps into his voice.

   (A) When describing

   (B) In describing

   (C) When there is a description of

   (D) When describing about

   (E) When he describes

23. <u>Expressing a radically different idea is Dorothy Sayers, who believes</u> that women all through history have been oppressed by men.

   (A) Expressing a radically different idea is Dorothy Sayers, who believes

   (B) Dorothy Sayers expresses a radically different idea—

   (C) Expressing a radically different idea is Dorothy Sayers, believing

   (D) Dorothy Sayers, expressing a radically different idea believes

   (E) Dorothy Sayers is expressing a radically different idea

24. How much <u>has fuel costs raised</u> during the past year?

   (A) has fuel costs raised

   (B) have fuel costs raised

   (C) has fuel costs risen

   (D) have fuel costs risen

   (E) has fuel costs rose

25. <u>Being that</u> it was raining, we decided to postpone the hike.

   (A) Being that

   (B) Being as how

   (C) In view of the fact that

   (D) Considering the fact that

   (E) Because

26. Many critics consider James Joyce's *Ulysses*, a novel once banned as obscene, to be the greatest novel of the twentieth century.

   (A) *Ulysses*, a novel once banned as obscene, to be

   (B) *Ulysses*, a novel once banned as obscene to be

   (C) *Ulysses*, which is a novel that was once banned as obscene, to be

   (D) *Ulysses*, a once banned as obscene novel, to be

   (E) *Ulysses*, a novel once banned as obscene, being

27. About three hundred people gathered, they were there protesting the construction of a nuclear power plant.

   (A) gathered, they were there protesting

   (B) gathered—they were there protesting

   (C) gathered, they were there protesting against

   (D) gathered to protest

   (E) gathered for the purpose of protesting

28. I think they, as a rule, are much more conniving than us.

   (A) as a rule, are much more conniving than us

   (B) as a rule are much more conniving than us

   (C) as a rule, are much more conniving than we

   (D) as a rule; are much more conniving than us

   (E) are, as a rule, much more conniving than us

29. The public health officer warned his audience about the danger of mixing alcohol and pills and driving after drinking also.

   (A) about the danger of mixing alcohol and pills and driving after drinking also

   (B) about the danger both of mixing alcohol and pills and of driving after drinking

   (C) about the dangerous nature of mixing alcohol and pills and driving after drinking also

   (D) about the danger of mixing alcohol and pills, and driving after drinking also

   (E) about the danger both of mixing alcohol and pills and driving after drinking

30. If you disobey traffic regulations, you will loose your driver's license.

   (A) you will loose your driver's license

   (B) you'll loose your driver's license

   (C) you will lose your driver's license

   (D) you will loose your drivers' license

   (E) your driver's license will be lost

31. "When my husband will come home, I'll tell him you called," the housewife sighed into the phone.

   (A) will come home,

   (B) will come home

   (C) will have come home

   (D) comes home,

   (E) has come home,

32. Robert did not want to set the table because <u>he did not know what time they were coming home</u>.

(A) he did not know what time they were coming home.

(B) he did not know what time they were coming home at.

(C) he did not know what time it would be when they came home.

(D) he did not know at what time they were coming home at.

(E) he did not know what the time was that they were coming home.

33. Neither Marty <u>or Christine knows</u> how to speak French.

(A) or Christine knows

(B) or Christine knew

(C) nor Christine knows

(D) nor Christine know

(E) or Christine know

Directions: Questions 34–39 are based on a passage that might be an early draft of a student's essay. Some sentences in this draft need to be revised or rewritten to make them both clear and correct. Read the passage carefully; then answer the questions that follow it. Some questions require decisions about diction, usage, tone, or sentence structure in particular sentences or parts of sentences. Other questions require decisions about organization, development, or appropriateness of language in the essay as a whole. For each question, choose the answer that makes the intended meaning clearer and more precise, and that follows the conventions of standard written English.

---

(1) When my family came to the United States to live, we spoke no English. (2) My parents luckily got a job and my sister and I were very young and we did what many other immigrant children did. (3) We learned English in public school and learned our native language and culture at home with our family. (4) It was not long before we all realized that success in the United States would depend on our ability to be fluent in English.

(5) Because of my own case I think that bilingual education is not as good as English in school, native language at home. (6) But I know of other people who found a bilingual education to be just what they needed, in fact it was essential to their progress since their English was so limited. (7) However, some people I knew did drop out of school later on. (8) Some of them had been labeled learning disabled. (9) It was really just a language problem. (10) And some of my friends' parents felt that their children's bilingual education was ineffective or harmful, while others felt it was very good for them.

(11) As a result, I cannot decide for certain whether English is being taught better to foreigners today than it was in the past. (12) But I think that I would like to see small groups of non-native speakers taught in English by caring, well-trained professionals. (13) Then I would like them to be moved into regular classrooms as soon as possible. (14) In that way, I think they would be best served by a school system that has not always done justice to their needs. (15) Perhaps that would be one way to solve the problem of how to help them to succeed in school and in their life in the United States.

34. Which of the following is the best way to revise sentence (2)?

(A) My parents luckily got a job. My sister and I were young. We did what many other immigrated children did.

(B) My parents luckily got a job and my sister and I were very young so we did what many other immigrants did.

(C) My parents got jobs, luckily; my very young sister and I did what many others did.

(D) Luckily, my parents got jobs. My sister and I, who were very young, did what many other immigrant children did.

(E) Luckily, my parents got jobs and my sister and I were very young. We did what many other immigrant children did.

35. Which of the following is the best way to revise sentence (5)?

(A) Because of my own experience, I think that a bilingual education is not so good as learning English in school and the family's native language at home.

(B) In my own case, bilingual education is not so good as English in school and native language at home.

(C) I think that because of my own experience, English in school, native language at home is better than bilingual education.

(D) As a result of my own case, I think that bilingual education is not as good as students who learn English in school and their native language at home.

(E) Because of my own case, I consider bilingual education less effective than learning English in school and their native language at home.

36. Which of the following is the best revision of the underlined portion of sentence (6) below?

But I know of other people who found a bilingual education to be just what they <u>needed, in fact it was essential</u> to their progress since their English was so limited.

(A) needed; in fact it being essential

(B) needed, being that it was essential

(C) needed; in fact it was essential

(D) needed; essential as it was in fact

(E) needed. In fact essential

37. Which of the following is the best way to combine sentences (8) and (9)?

(A) Although it was really just a language problem; some had been labeled learning disabled.

(B) Some of them were labeled learning disabled, it was really just a language problem.

(C) Some of them has been labeled learning disabled, even though what they really had was a language problem.

(D) Some of them were learning disabled with a language problem.

(E) Some of them had a language problem that made them learning disabled.

38. Which of the following is the best revision of sentence (10)?

(A) Some of my friends' parents felt that their children's bilingual education was ineffective or harmful, while others felt it was very good for them.

(B) Some felt that their child's bilingual education was ineffective or harmful, but other of my friends' parents felt it was very good for them.

(C) Though some of my friends' parents felt it was very good for them, some felt that bilingual education was ineffective or harmful.

(D) Although some of my friends' parents felt it was very good, some felt that their children's bilingual education was ineffective or harmful.

(E) Ineffective or harmful though it may have been to some, others of my friends' parents felt that their children's bilingual education has been very good.

39. Which of the following would be the best way to improve the last paragraph?

(A) Incorporate transitional words or phrases

(B) Eliminate the specious argument presented.

(C) Present a more personal point of view.

(D) Adopt a less sympathetic tone.

(E) Be more exact and concise in wording.

STOP

END OF SECTION 5. IF YOU HAVE ANY TIME LEFT, GO OVER YOUR WORK IN THIS SECTION ONLY. DO NOT WORK IN ANY OTHER SECTION OF THE TEST.

ANSWERS AND EXPLANATIONS

Section 1: Verbal

1.	A	7.	D	13.	E	19.	B	25.	C
2.	E	8.	E	14.	C	20.	E	26.	E
3.	C	9.	A	15.	C	21.	A		
4.	B	10.	B	16.	A	22.	D		
5.	A	11.	E	17.	E	23.	B		
6.	A	12.	A	18.	B	24.	D		

Section 2: Math
(Code: A = Arithmetic; AL = Algebra; G = Geometry; O = Other)

1.	E (A)	5.	C (A)	9.	D (AL)	13.	B (A)	17.	C (G)
2.	D (A)	6.	B (AL)	10.	E (AL)	14.	D (G)	18.	B (G)
3.	C (A)	7.	D (G)	11.	E (AL)	15.	B (A)	19.	B (O)
4.	E (A)	8.	E (G)	12.	C (G)	16.	A (AL)	20.	C (O)

Section 3: Verbal

27.	D	33.	B	39.	A	45.	D	51.	B
28.	E	34.	A	40.	E	46.	A	52.	D
29.	B	35.	C	41.	B	47.	E		
30.	A	36.	A	42.	A	48.	D		
31.	B	37.	E	43.	B	49.	C		
32.	A	38.	D	44.	B	50.	C		

Section 4: Math

Part 1

21.	A	25.	D
22.	B	26.	C
23.	A	27.	C
24.	B	28.	A

Part 2

29.	C	33.	729	37.	130
30.	D	34.	$\frac{1}{8}$	38.	45
31.	C	35.	5	39.	3
32.	B	36.	1.30	40.	$\frac{5}{8}$

Section 5: Writing Skills

1.	B	9.	A	17.	D	25.	E	33.	C
2.	D	10.	D	18.	A	26.	A	34.	D
3.	C	11.	A	19.	D	27.	D	35.	A
4.	B	12.	E	20.	B	28.	C	36.	C
5.	E	13.	D	21.	C	29.	B	37.	C
6.	A	14.	C	22.	E	30.	C	38.	D
7.	E	15.	B	23.	B	31.	D	39.	E
8.	C	16.	B	24.	D	32.	A		

Section 1

1. **The correct answer is (A).** The word *confused* is your clue. The speaker has made a *digression*, or departure from the topic.

2. **The correct answer is (E).** What might concern an accountant? *Profits* (C) are one possibility, but they could not be *organized*, as the sentence indicates. *Receipts*, on the other hand, might be.

3. **The correct answer is (C).** The words *swept* and *blowing* indicate a windlike movement. A *zephyr* (B) is a kind of wind, but it is very gentle. Only *cyclone*, of the choices given, names a big, blustery wind.

4. **The correct answer is (B).** Both words must fit the context here. In choice (A), only the second word fits; the first makes no sense. In choices (C) and (D), if the first is true, the second is not; and choice (E) makes no sense at all.

5. **The correct answer is (A).** A motorist who cannot control a car may be intoxicated; in other words, lacking in *sobriety*.

6. **The correct answer is (A).** *Retired* has many meanings, and the one that means "retreated" or "withdrew" is the one used here.

7. **The correct answer is (D).** A *collar* fastens around the *neck* just as a *cuff* fastens around a wrist.

8. **The correct answer is (E).** A very great chess player is a *master*, and a very great musician is a *virtuoso*.

9. **The correct answer is (A).** A *blizzard* is a storm characterized by heavy, blowing *snow*, and a *typhoon* is a storm characterized by strong *wind*.

10. **The correct answer is (B).** The writer of a *song* is called a *lyricist*, and the writer of a *play* is called a *dramatist*. A musician may write a tune choice (A), but the more accurate word is *composer*. In addition, both lyricists and dramatists deal in words.

11. **The correct answer is (E).** As *geometry* is a branch of *mathematics*, so *botany* is a branch of *science*.

12. **The correct answer is (A).** Think of relative values here. A *dollar* equals ten *dimes*, and a *decade* equals ten *years*.

13. **The correct answer is (E).** *Grammar* is the structure on which *language* is built. In a similar way, *scales* are used to structure *music*.

14. **The correct answer is (C).** Return to the cited line, and you will see that the only eyes referred to are those of the Europeans, which come in brown, green, and black.

15. **The correct answer is (C).** Any of these might be a synonym for *dress*, but only *style* fits the context of fixing hair.

16. **The correct answer is (A).** Paragraph 3 *does* compare European ways to Chinese ways and discuss European customs. However, it deals with eating habits rather than with personal appearance.

17. **The correct answer is (E).** Looking at the passage as a whole, you can see that it primarily describes the people and customs of Europe, all with an instructive tone.

18. **The correct answer is (B).** The author rarely inserts himself into the passage, and he certainly says nothing negative, as choices (A), (C), and (D) would suggest. Nor does he ever imply that European customs are better than Chinese customs. He focuses on the strangeness of what he observes, stressing what his reader might find most interesting.

19. **The correct answer is (B).** Mr. Buxton is cited in paragraph 1. His account of a parrot that took care of a crippled bird is clearly included to support the discussion of benevolent behavior in birds.

20. **The correct answer is (E).** *Distinct* has several meanings, but in this case, the bird is of a *different* species from the parrot.

21. **The correct answer is (A).** The birds show "antipathy or affection," two opposite reactions.

22. **The correct answer is (D).** The list of birds appears in paragraph 2 as supporting evidence for Darwin's discussion of birds' powers of observation and recall.

23. **The correct answer is (B).** Returning to the cited phrase, you will see that only *raised* fits the context.

24. **The correct answer is (D).** Test the choices in context, and you will find that, while (A) and (C) are close, (D) is the best choice.

25. **The correct answer is (C).** Choice (A) is too broad, and choice (B) is too narrow. Choices (D) and (E) are off the mark. Only choice (C) is an accurate summary of the author's intent.

26. **The correct answer is (E).** You might be fooled into choosing choice (C), but Darwin really only cites studies to support his own observations, and there is no indication whether they are "current studies," unscientific observations by friends, or writings from long ago. Only choice (E) is accurate.

Section 2

1. **The correct answer is (E).** You can solve simply by counting decimal places to the right of the decimal and recognizing that the answer will have six (1 + 2 + 3).

2. **The correct answer is (D).** Convert first to inches. The average height is 60 inches. Three girls are 58 inches tall. The fourth is x.

    $(58 + 58 + 58 + x) \div 4 = 60$

    $(174 + x) = 240$

    $x = 66$ inches, or 5 feet 6 inches

3. **The correct answer is (C).** *Any* number times its reciprocal is 1.

4. **The correct answer is (E).** Think:

    $$5\frac{1}{4} = \frac{x}{16}$$

    $$\frac{21}{4} = \frac{84}{16}$$

5. **The correct answer is (C).** This lends itself to a draw-a-picture strategy.

    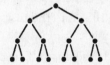

6. **The correct answer is (B).** You know that $x = \frac{y}{4}$. Therefore, stated in terms of y, $\frac{x}{4} = \frac{y}{4} \times 4$, or $\frac{y}{4} \times \frac{1}{4}$, or $\frac{y}{16}$.

7. **The correct answer is (D).** If you have any doubts, simply plug in a few numbers to test your ideas. If the side of a square = 2, the perimeter = 4×2, or 8. If the side is tripled to 6, the perimeter = 4×6, or 24. The perimeter is tripled.

8. **The correct answer is (E).** The sum of the angles of a triangle = 180°. Because $\triangle ABC$ is an isosceles triangle, $x = y$

    $$30. \pm x + y = 180..$$
    $$x + y = 150.$$
    $$2x = 150.$$
    $$x = 75...$$
    $$y = 75...$$

    AC is a straight line.

    The sum of the angles of a straight line = 180°.

    $$y + z = 180...$$
    $$75. \pm z = 180...$$
    $$z = 180. \div .75.$$
    $$z = 105...$$

9. **The correct answer is (D).** The easiest way to solve is to determine the age Leo was when Robert was born: $67 - 29 = 38$. Then you know that when Robert reaches age 38, he will be half his father's age. That will occur in x years, where $29 + x = 38$ years. In 9 years, Robert will be 38, and his father will be $67 + 9 = 76$ years old—twice Robert's age.

10. **The correct answer is (E).** You can rename all the numbers to fractions with the same denominator and compare them:

$$\frac{75}{300}, \frac{90}{300}, \frac{69}{300}, \frac{80}{300}$$

Alternatively, you can use a calculator to do the division and compare the numbers in decimal form.

11. **The correct answer is (E).** You know that $\frac{b}{a} = 3$, so you can refer to b as $3a$. Plugging that into the first number sentence, you get

$a + 3a = 12$, so $4a = 12$, so $a = 3$.

Since $b = 3a$, $b = 9$.

Therefore, $ab = 27$.

12. **The correct answer is (C).** First, draw the picture.

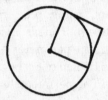

The reference information tells you that the circumference, 10, equals $2\pi r$.

Therefore, $\pi r = 5$.

Since $r = \frac{5}{\pi}$, the perimeter of the square = $4 \times \frac{5}{\pi}$, or $\frac{20}{\pi}$.

13. **The correct answer is (B).** The station got $500 in all. Of this, 20%, or $100, was from drive-time ads at $20/minute—5 minutes of ads. 50%, or $250, was from daytime ads at $10/minute—25 minutes of ads. Finally, 30%, or $150, was from nighttime ads at $5/minute—30 minutes of ads. Add the numbers of minutes:

$5 + 25 + 30 = 60$ minutes, or 1 hour.

14. **The correct answer is (D).** You should not need to do any calculating here. You know that the area of any circle is equal to πr^2. The radius of the circle pictured is equal to $\frac{AC}{2}$.

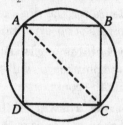

Therefore, the circle's area is $\pi \left(\frac{AC}{2}\right)^2$.

15. **The correct answer is (B).** On the first leg of the trip, the motorist drives 90 miles per hour.

$\text{Time} = \frac{\text{Distance}}{\text{Rate}}$

$\text{Time} = \frac{90}{50} = 1.8$

On the return trip, the motorist drives the 90 miles at 60 miles per hour.

$\text{Time} = \frac{\text{Distance}}{\text{Rate}}$

$\text{Time} = \frac{90}{60} = 1.5$

The total time for the trip is

$$\begin{array}{r} 1.5 \\ + \ 1.8 \\ \hline 3.3 \text{ hours.} \end{array}$$

$\text{Rate} = \frac{\text{Distance}}{\text{Time}}$

$\text{Rate} = \frac{180}{3.3} \approx 54.5$ miles per hour

16. **The correct answer is (A).** Solve for x:

$17x - 32 = 308$

$17x = 340$

$x = 20$

Knowing the value of x, you can see that $\frac{x}{4} = 5$.

17. The correct answer is (C). The area of any triangle is $\frac{1}{2}$ base × height. Since ΔUQR and ΔRST are equal in area and have equal heights, they must also have equal bases. In other words, $QR = RS$, and each equals 2. That means that $QS = 4$, so each side of the square = 4.

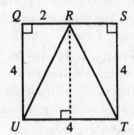

Now, to find the area of ΔRUT,

$$\frac{1}{2} UT \times ST = \frac{1}{2}(4 \times 4) = 8$$

18. The correct answer is (B). This is trickier than it looks. Express the increase in the radius as $r + .1r$. Then the area, which before was πr^2, now is $\pi (r + .1r)^2$, or $\pi (1.1r)^2$. $(1.1)^2 = 1.21$, so the new area is 21% greater than the old.

19. The correct answer is (B). The sign * appears to mean "multiply the number by the next greater whole number." Therefore, $7* = 7 \times 8$, and $8* = 8 \times 9$. Solving for $7* + 8*$, you add $56 + 72$ for a sum of 128.

20. The correct answer is (C). In one minute, the faucets working together will fill $\frac{1}{3} + \frac{1}{2}$ of the sink. In two minutes, they will fill $\frac{2}{3} + \frac{2}{2}$ overflowing the sink. Returning to the first set of numbers, you can see that the faucets will fill $\frac{2}{6} + \frac{3}{6}$, or $\frac{5}{6}$ of the sink in one minute. If $\frac{5}{6}x = 1$, then $x = \frac{6}{5}$, $1\frac{1}{5}$, or 1.2 minutes.

Section 3

27. The correct answer is (D). A parallelism is set up in this sentence; the second word will be an extension of the first. Once you recognize that, you will see that only choice (D) works.

28. The correct answer is (E). She would not be *condemned*, choice (A), or "criticized" for her win; nor would other skiers be *consternated*, choice (B), or "alarmed." *Tribulation*, choice (C), means "hardship," and *demarcation*, (D), means "limitation." Only *approbation*, meaning "congratulations" or "praise," has the proper meaning.

29. The correct answer is (B). If the house is on a crumbling cliff, it does not look *prudently* or "carefully" situated, choice (A). It looks *precariously* or "shakily" positioned.

30. The correct answer is (A). The words *allow* and *time* are your clues here. If Paul *usurped*, or "took over," his brother's computer time, that might be a questionable offense.

31. The correct answer is (B). Both words must fit in order for your choice to be correct. In choice (A), the first word fits, but signatures cannot be *revamped*. Choice (C) is absurd—the treaty would be signed at exactly the same time as the signatures were appended. Choice (D) makes no sense, because a treaty would not be *funded*, and choice (E) makes no sense, because signatures cannot be *fulfilled*. The answer is choice (B)—the treaty was *abrogated*, or "broken," almost as soon as the signatures were *affixed*, or "added."

32. The correct answer is (A). The sentence has to do with appearance. The trees were *silhouetted*—only their outlines were apparent.

33. The correct answer is (B). Try filling in the second word first. That means choices (B), (C), and (D) are possibilities. Now add the first word, and you will see that only choice (B) is logical.

34. The correct answer is (A). The *wheel* helps propel the *wagon* in the same way that the *runner* helps propel the *sled*. A fin might help propel a fish (C), but it works more like a rudder than like a wheel. An engine might help propel an automobile (D), but it does not do it in the same way that a wheel does.

35. The correct answer is (C). These words are used in their antithetical meanings. Of the answer choices, the only one that is a pair of opposites is choice (C), *fortify* and *assail*.

36. The correct answer is (A). A *sapphire* is a *blue* gem, and a *ruby* is a *red* gem. A tree may be green (B), but it is not a gem.

37. The correct answer is (E). We call discarded clothing "*castoffs*," and we call discarded metal "*scrap*."

38. The correct answer is (D). A *kit* is a baby *fox*, and a *cub* is a baby *lion*.

39. The correct answer is (A). A *sharecropper* has a relationship to a *plantation* much as a *renter* does to an *apartment*—neither has ownership; both lease the space.

40. The correct answer is (E). Mr. Pontellier regards much of his wife's actions as *folly*, by which he means "foolishness" rather than the more negative connotations.

41. The correct answer is (B). If you read the introduction, you know that this is the story of a woman "trapped in a stifling marriage." Even if you didn't know this, you could infer from Mr. Pontellier's amused and patronizing attitude toward his wife that choice (B) is the correct answer.

42. The correct answer is (A). Mrs. Pontellier has removed her rings, including, presumably, her wedding ring, and has left them in the care of her husband while she set off for a morning of freedom. The scene in question makes it seem as though Mrs. Pontellier is putting out her arms to be handcuffed once more.

43. The correct answer is (B). Of all of these synonyms, only *recount*, meaning "retell," has the meaning that fits the context.

44. The correct answer is (B). We see Mr. Pontellier moving ponderously about, mystified by the laughter of others, and confined to a routine. There is no support for any of the other choices, but the author plainly feels he is dull.

45. The correct answer is (D). This is *awful* as meaning "full of awe" and *moment* as the root of *momentous*. Henry means that this is a time of great importance.

46. The correct answer is (A). Rereading the entire sentence in which the reference is found will help you recognize that this myth is referred to as a parallel for those men who cling to false hope.

47. The correct answer is (E). If you understand the passage at all, you will see that the list is one of excuses those who advocate dependence use to explain why America should remain connected to Britain.

48. The correct answer is (D). The clues in the sentence are *men* and *overrun*. The author suggests that people fear that New Englanders will take over the South, much as the barbarian Goths and Vandals took over Europe long ago.

49. The correct answer is (C). One fear cited is that the independent Americans will *want*, or "lack," protection.

50. The correct answer is (C). This is delineated in one of the N.B. asides. The author does not believe (B); he believes that those in favor of dependence believe it.

51. The correct answer is (B). The passages share the same political bent and attitude toward the British, but whereas Passage 1 is heartfelt and solemn, Passage 2 is tongue-in-cheek and ironic.

52. **The correct answer is (D).** Both authors refer to slavery—in line 16 in Passage 1, and in line 86 in Passage 2. Both remark on the fact that some people have deluded themselves with vain hopes about the British, despite the fact that the British have done nothing to inspire such hope. Since choices (A), (B), and (C) are correct, the answer is (D).

Section 4

Part 1

21. **The correct answer is (A).** Draw a picture to help you solve this problem. Just looking at the picture will convince you that the area of the circle will be greater than that of the square.

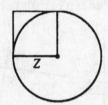

22. **The correct answer is (B).** Try plugging in some numbers. Suppose a is a positive number such as 4.

$$\frac{4}{2} = -(-2)$$

In that case, ab, $4(-2)$, equals -8.

$\frac{a}{b}$, $\frac{4}{-2}$, equals -2.

Now suppose a is a negative number such as -4.

$$\frac{-4}{2} = -2$$

In that case, ab, $-4(2)$, equals -8 again.

$\frac{a}{b}$, $\frac{-4}{2}$, equals -2.

23. **The correct answer is (A).** There are five odd numbers greater than 3 and less than or equal to 13: 5, 7, 9, 11, and 13.

24. **The correct answer is (B).** If $x^2 = 144$, $x = 12$, and $2x = 24$.

If $2y - 18 = 32$, $2y = 50$, and $y = 25$.

25. **The correct answer is (D).** There is not enough information to solve this. If m and n are positive whole numbers, then $\frac{n}{m}$ is greater, but if n is positive and m negative, then $\frac{m}{n}$ is greater.

26. **The correct answer is (C).** One glance should tell you that these numbers are equivalent, but if you wish, try some numbers in place of c and d. If $c = 1$ and $d = 2$, $\frac{1}{3}(c+d) = 1$

$\frac{c}{3} + \frac{d}{3} = \frac{1}{3} + \frac{2}{3} = 1$.

27. **The correct answer is (C).** You may wish to draw a picture to check this.

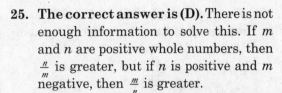

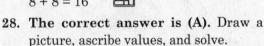

The volume of the large box =

$2 \times 4 \times 2 = 16$.

The volume of each of the dice =

$2 \times 2 \times 2 = 8$.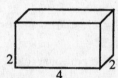

$8 + 8 = 16$

28. **The correct answer is (A).** Draw a picture, ascribe values, and solve.

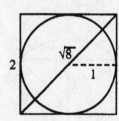

The perimeter of the triangle $= 2 + 2 + \sqrt{8}$.

The circumference of the circle $= 2\pi r$, and since $r = 1$, you can restate that as 2π.

$\pi \approx 3.14$, so $2\pi \approx 6.28$.

$\sqrt{8}$ lies between 2.8 and 2.9, so $2 + 2 + \sqrt{8} = 6.8$ or 6.9.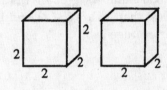

29. **The correct answer is (C).** If you do not recognize the equivalence immediately, use your calculator to solve.

5% of 7 = .35

7% of 5 = .35

30. **The correct answer is (D).** Unless you know which is greater, a or b, you cannot answer this question.

31. **The correct answer is (C).**

$(x + 2)(x - 2) = x^2 - 2x - 2x - 4$, or $x^2 - 4$.

32. **The correct answer is (B).** The even numbers greater than 2 and less than 12 are 4, 6, 8, and 10. Their average is 7. The odd numbers greater than 3 and less than 13 are 5, 7, 9, and 11. Their average is 8.

Part 2

33. **(729)**

$4x - 9 = 27$, so $4x = 36.9^3 = 729$

34. $\left(\frac{1}{8}\right)$ At the end of week 2, you have the following:

$$1 - \left[\frac{1}{2} + \left(\frac{1}{2} \times \frac{3}{4}\right)\right] =$$

$$1 - \left(\frac{4}{8} + \frac{3}{8}\right) = \frac{1}{8}$$

35. **(5)** If the chord is 8, half of it is 4, which sets you up with a nice 3-4-5 right triangle, as here:

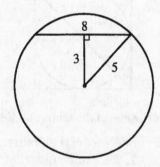

36. **(1.30)** The pizza costs $3 \times \$3.25$, or $\$9.75$. If that is now divided by 5, each person pays $\$9.75 \div 5$, or $\$1.95$. That is $\$1.30$ less for each of the original friends. (Although you will not record a dollar sign, do not forget the final 0.)

37. **(130)** This is less difficult than it may at first seem. Average the five players you know:

$(130 + 115 + 120 + 140 + 145) \div 5 = 130$.

In order to maintain the 130 average, the average weight of the remaining players must be 130 as well.

38. **(45)** You can solve this if you recall that the sum of the measures of the angles of a quadrilateral will equal 360. Redraw the picture, writing in all the measures you know or can calculate:

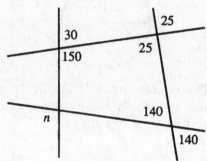

$360 - (150 + 25 + 140) = 45$.

39. **(3)** The key to this is the phrase "positive whole number." If a is positive, b must be negative, and the only negative number whose square is 49 is -7. If $a + (-7) = -4$, $a = 3$.

40. $\left(\frac{5}{8}\right)$ Express the consumed popcorn this way:

$$1 - \left[\frac{1}{4} + \left(\frac{3}{4} \times \frac{1}{6}\right)\right] =$$

$$1 - \left(\frac{1}{4} + \frac{3}{24}\right) =$$

$$1 - \left(\frac{2}{8} + \frac{1}{8}\right) = \frac{5}{8}$$

Section 5

1. **The correct answer is (B).** The adverbial form *unnecessarily* is required to modify an adjective, *distressed*.

2. **The correct answer is (D).** The past participle of *freeze* is *frozen*.

3. **The correct answer is (C).** The verb meaning "receive willingly" or "agree to" is *accept*, not *except*.

4. **The correct answer is (B).** The pronoun should be singular (either *his* or *his or her*) to agree with the singular subject.

5. **The correct answer is (E).** This sentence is correct.

6. **The correct answer is (A).** The plural of *hoax* is *hoaxes*.

7. **The correct answer is (E).** This sentence is correct.

8. **The correct answer is (C).** Use *number* for a quantity thought of as a collection of individual things or people.

9. **The correct answer is (A).** The use of *leave* to mean "allow" is nonstandard; use *let*.

10. **The correct answer is (D).** The complete comparison would be *quicker than he is*; the shortened form is *quicker than he*.

11. **The correct answer is (A).** The past participle of *swim* is *swum*.

12. **The correct answer is (E).** This sentence is correct.

13. **The correct answer is (D).** The verb *smell* takes a predicate adjective, *sweet*.

14. **The correct answer is (C).** The word used in comparisons is *than*.

15. **The correct answer is (B).** Parallel structure requires a third infinitive, *to stay*.

16. **The correct answer is (B).** The adverbial form *considerably* is required.

17. **The correct answer is (D).** Items in a series should be grammatically parallel. A third noun, *poverty*, is needed to balance the nouns *disease* and *hunger*.

18. **The correct answer is (A).** The word for a sense of right and wrong is *conscience*. *Conscious* is an adjective meaning "awake" or "aware."

19. **The correct answer is (D).** The object of a preposition (*with*) should be in the objective case (*me*).

20. **The correct answer is (B).** Items in a series should be parallel in form. In this case, a third adverb, *silently*, is required.

21. **The correct answer is (C).** The construction *or . . . as* expresses the notion of equality. The use of *equally* is therefore redundant.

22. **The correct answer is (E).** The original makes it seem as if the tone is describing the accident. The dangling phrase may be replaced by a dependent clause containing its own subject, *he*.

23. **The correct answer is (B).** The original sentence is awkward.

24. **The correct answer is (D).** The correct verb form is *have risen*, plural to agree with the plural subject *costs*. *Risen* is the past participle of the intransitive verb *to rise*.

25. **The correct answer is (E).** The use of *being that* to mean "because" or "since" is nonstandard.

26. **The correct answer is (A).** The sentence is correct.

27. **The correct answer is (D).** The original version is a run-on sentence.

28. **The correct answer is (C).** In a comparison introduced by *than* or *as*, use the case of the pronoun that you would use if you were completing the comparison. The complete version here would be *they are more conniving than we are conniving*, so the shortened form is *they are more conniving than we*.

29. **The correct answer is (B).** The awkwardness of the original sentence is removed by the construction *both of . . . and of . . .* used with parallel verbs.

30. **The correct answer is (C).** As a verb, *to loose* means "to set free."

31. **The correct answer is (D).** The present tense is used to express future time in subordinate clauses beginning with *if, when, after, before, until,* and *as soon as.*

32. **The correct answer is (A).** This sentence is correct.

33. **The correct answer is (C).** Use *neither* with *nor* and *either* with *or.*

34. **The correct answer is (D).** What is required is a grammatically sound and precisely worded revision. The adverb *luckily* is best placed at the beginning of the sentence. Choice (D) is best.

35. **The correct answer is (A).** The only choice that is not awkward, and does not misrepresent the material given, is choice (A).

36. **The correct answer is (C).** A comma cannot join two independent clauses as in sentence (6). Choice (C) corrects this error by replacing the comma with a semicolon. In choices (A) and (D), the words following the semicolon do not form an independent clause. The use of *being that* in choice (B) is incorrect. Choice (E) creates a fragment.

37. **The correct answer is (C).** The word *it* in sentence (9) has no clear reference. Choices (A) and (B) have the same problem. In addition, choice (A) has a fragment, and choice (B) has a comma splice error. Choices (D) and (E) change the intended meaning. Choice (C) correctly eliminates the vague *it* and makes it clear that these students had a language problem.

38. **The correct answer is (D).** Choices (A), (B), and (C) are poor since the antecedent of the pronoun *them* is not clear. Choice (E) is wrong since the sentence is awkwardly phrased. Choice (D) is best.

39. **The correct answer is (E).** The use of the pronouns *they* and *them* in sentences (13), (14), and (15) is not always clear. One is not certain to whom the pronoun refers. Often, a precise noun would be a better choice.

COMPUTING YOUR SCORES

To get a sense of how your performance on this diagnostic test would be scored on a "real" PSAT/ NMSQT, you first need to compute individual verbal, mathematical, and writing raw scores. Once you have computed these, use the conversion scales in the section that follows to compute your PSAT scaled scores (20–80). Keep in mind that these formulas have been simplified to give you a "quick and dirty" sense of where you are scoring, not a perfectly precise score.

To Compute Your Raw Scores

1. Enter the number of correct answers for each verbal and mathematical reasoning section into the boxes marked Number of Questions Correct.

2. Enter the number of incorrect answers (not blanks) for each verbal and mathematical reasoning section into the boxes marked Number of Questions Incorrect.

3. Total the number correct and number incorrect.

4. Follow this formula: Take the total correct and minus one quarter of the total incorrect. Round up in your favor to compute your raw score.

Verbal Section	Total Number of Questions	Number of Questions Correct	Number of Questions Incorrect
1	26		
3	26		
Totals	**52**	**Total Correct:**	**Total Incorrect:**

Verbal Raw Score = Total Correct – ($\frac{1}{4}$ × Total Incorrect) = _____

Math Section	Total Number of Questions	Number of Questions Correct	Number of Questions Incorrect
2	20		
4	20		
Totals	**40**	**Total Correct:**	**Total Incorrect:**

Math Raw Score = Total Correct – ($\frac{1}{4}$ × Total Incorrect) = _____

Writing Section	Total Number of Questions	Number of Questions Correct	Number of Questions Incorrect
5	39		
Totals	**40**	**Total Correct:**	**Total Incorrect:**

Writing Raw Score = Total Correct – ($\frac{1}{4}$ × Total Incorrect) = _____

To Compute Your Scaled PSAT Score

Add a "0" to the end of your mathematical and verbal scaled scores.

PINPOINTING RELATIVE STRENGTHS AND WEAKNESSES ON THE PSAT/NMSQT

Verbal Question Types

Sentence Completions

1. Count up the number of sentence completions you answered correctly (Section 1: 1–6 and Section 3: 27–33).

2. Write that number in the box marked Number of Questions Correct.

3. Divide that number by the Total Number of Questions and write down your percentage.

Analogies

1. Count up the number of analogies you answered correctly (Section 1: 7–13 and Section 3: 34–39).

2. Write that number in the box marked Number of Questions Correct.

3. Divide that number by the Total Number of Questions and write down your percentage.

Critical Reading

1. Go back through the test's passages and count up the number of questions that you answered correctly.

2. Write that number in the box marked Number of Questions Correct.

3. Divide that number by the Total Number of Questions and write down your percentage.

Type of Verbal Question	Number of Questions Correct	Total Number of Questions	Percent Correct (number correct/total)
Sentence Completions		13	
Analogies		13	
Critical Reading		26	

Compare these three percentages to assess your relative strengths and weaknesses within the subtopic areas of the PSAT verbal tests. If any individual percentage was considerably lower than others, you've found an area upon which you need to focus further study. To work on that area, read the appropriate strategy chapter in Part III and do the exercises.

If sentence completions and analogies gave you difficulty, you should work through Part V to upgrade your vocabulary. Learning vocabulary words is a critical step to improving on these sections of the PSAT.

Math Question Types

Multiple-Choice Math

1. Count up the number of multiple-choice questions you answered correctly (Section 2).
2. Write that number in the box marked Number of Questions Correct.
3. Divide that number by the Total Number of Questions and write down your percentage.

Quantitative Comparisons

1. Count up the number of quantitative comparisons you answered correctly (Section 4: 21–32).
2. Write that number in the box marked Number of Questions Correct.
3. Divide that number by the Total Number of Questions and write down your percentage.

Grid-Ins

1. Count up the number of grid-ins that you answered correctly (Section 4: 33–40).
2. Write that number in the box marked Number of Questions Correct.
3. Divide that number by the Total Number of Questions and write down your percentage in the shaded box.

Type of Verbal Question	Number of Questions Correct	Total Number of Questions	Percent Correct (number correct/total)
Multiple Choice		20	
Quantitative Comparison		12	
Grid-In		8	

Compare these three percentages to assess your relative strengths and weaknesses within the math subject areas of the PSAT. If any individual section produced a percentage that is considerably lower than others, that question type deserves more of your preparation study and attention. To work on PSAT math subject areas, read the appropriate strategy chapter in Part IV and do the exercises.

Math Subtopics

To get an even more in-depth look at your performance, look back at the answer key to the multiple-choice math questions (Section 2). You'll notice that each question has been subdivided into one of four categories—arithmetic, algebra, geometry, and other.

Arithmetic

1 Count up the number of arithmetic multiple-choice questions you answered correctly.

2 Write that number in the box marked Number of Questions Correct.

3 Divide that number by the Total Number of Questions and write down your percentage.

Algebra

1 Count up the number of algebra multiple-choice questions you answered correctly.

2 Write that number in the box marked Number of Questions Correct.

3 Divide that number by the Total Number of Questions and write down your percentage.

Geometry

1 Count up the number of geometry multiple-choice questions you answered correctly.

2 Write that number in the box marked Number of Questions Correct.

3 Divide that number by the Total Number of Questions and write down your percentage.

Type of Math Subtopic	Number of Questions Correct	Total Number of Questions	Percent Correct (number correct/total)
Arithmetic		8	
Algebra		4	
Geometry		6	

Compare these three percentages to assess your relative strengths and weaknesses by mathematical subcategory. If an individual percentage is considerably lower than others, you've found an SAT math subtopic in which you need to concentrate further study. Read the appropriate math chapter in Part 6 and do the exercises.

Writing Skills

Error Identifications

1 Count up the number of error identifications you answered correctly (Section 5: 1–19).

2 Write that number in the box marked Number of Questions Correct.

3 Divide that number by the Total Number of Questions and write down your percentage.

Improving Sentences

1 Count up the number of sentence corrections you answered correctly (Section 5: 20–33).

2 Write that number in the box marked Number of Questions Correct.

3 Divide that number by the Total Number of Questions and write down your percentage.

Improving Paragraphs

1 Count up the number of questions you answered correctly (Section 5: 34–39).

2 Write that number in the box marked Number of Questions Correct.

3 Divide that number by the Total Number of Questions and write down your percentage.

Type of Writing Question	Number of Questions Correct	Total Number of Questions	Percent Correct (number correct/total)
Error Identifications		19	
Improving Sentences		14	
Improving Paragraphs		6	

Compare these three percentages to assess your relative strengths and weaknesses. If any individual percentage was considerably lower than others, you need to concentrate further study in that area.

MEASURING YOUR PROGRESS

As you visit chapters and do exercises, don't forget to compare your performance on those exercises with the verbal and mathematical percentages you calculated here. Down the road, you can also measure your progress very easily by comparing how you did on this PSAT test with how you do on other practice SATs. Remember: The difficulty levels of the PSAT and SAT are comparable.

Take note of whether you had difficulty finishing any particular part of the test. It might be that you are spending too long on certain questions and not allotting enough time for others. This should improve as you work through the strategy sections of this book and increase your familiarity with the test and question format. If you are worried about spending too long on particular question types, see Chapter 16 for a discussion of timing drills.

VERBAL		MATH		WRITING	
Raw Score	SCORE	Raw Score	SCORE	Raw Score	SCORE
52	80	40	80	39	80
47	74	35	69	34	75
42	68	30	63	29	67
37	62	25	57	24	60
32	57	20	51	19	54
27	52	15	45	14	49
22	47	10	39	9	43
17	42	5	33	4	37
12	37	2	28	2	34
7	31	0	24	0	31
2	24	minus 1	22	minus 1	30
0	21	minus 2	20	minus 5	24
minus 1	20			minus 9	20

PART IX

THE SAT AND BEYOND

The New SAT and PSAT

You may have heard that the SAT is going to change. But when will it happen? How will it change? And most importantly, what does it all mean for you?

WHEN?

The test in question is the SAT I: Reasoning Test, commonly referred to as just the plain old SAT. The modified SAT will be introduced in March 2005. If you will be a high school senior graduating and looking to enter college in 2006, you will take the new exam. If you will be a high school senior graduating and looking to enter college before 2006, you will take the current version of the exam. The PSAT will be changing, too. The new PSAT will be introduced in October 2004.

WHAT?

The current SAT consists of two sections, Verbal and Math. Changes will be made to each of the existing sections, and a new Writing section will be created. Some of the changes relate to the actual content being tested, while others relate to the question types used to test it.

Verbal

The first change to the Verbal section is its name. On the new SAT, this section will be called Critical Reading. This change signals the recognition of the importance of reading as a part of high school curricula and as a skill vital to success in college. This focus will be carried through to the content of the section. The second change to the Verbal section is the elimination of the analogy questions. Analogies require students to detect the relationship between a pair of words in the question stem and then to select the pair of words in the answer choices that reflects the same relationship. This question type is being eliminated so that this section on the new exam will consist entirely of critical reading questions, which will test reading skills at the sentence, paragraph, and passage level. The third change to the Verbal section is the addition of paragraph-length critical reasoning questions, to supplement the existing question types of sentence completions and reading comprehension passages. The topics of the given texts will represent a wide range of subjects, including science, literature, humanities, and history.

appendix A

Math

The Math section of the SAT will also change. Algebra II material will be tested on the new exam in order to better align the SAT with the math curriculum being taught in high school classrooms. Since most high school students in general and the vast majority of college-bound high school students complete Algebra II, it makes sense for this content to be a part of the exam. It also makes sense since most four-year colleges require three years of high school math.

The second change to the Math section is the elimination of quantitative comparisons. This question type requires students to compare quantities in two columns and decide if one or the other is greater, if they are equal, or if it is impossible to determine based on the information given. The other two current math question types, 5-choice multiple-choice and student-produced responses, will remain on the exam.

Writing

Essay

The biggest change to the SAT will be the introduction of a new Writing section. This change is designed to provide an additional measure for college admissions purposes as well as to emphasize the importance of writing for success in school and professional life. The Writing section will consist of two parts: an essay and a multiple-choice section. Students will be given 25 minutes to respond to a prompt and construct a well-organized essay that effectively addresses the task. The essay question may require students to complete a statement, to react to a quote or excerpt, or to agree or disagree with a point of view. In any case, a good essay will support the chosen position with specific reasons and examples from literature, history, art, science, current affairs, or even a student's own experiences.

Essays will be scored based on the procedures for the current SAT II: Writing Test. Essays will be graded by two independent readers on a scale of 1–6, and their two scores will be combined to form an essay subscore that ranges from 2 to 12. Should the readers' scores vary by more than 2 points, a third reader will score the essay. The readers will be high school teachers and college professors who teach composition. They will score essays using a rubric that evaluates the compositions based upon how effectively the task in the question is addressed, how well the essay is organized, the use of appropriate examples, the facility of language, and the variety of sentence structure and vocabulary. To ensure that essays will be scored in a timely manner, they will be scanned and made available to readers on the Internet for grading purposes.

Multiple-Choice

The Writing section will also include multiple-choice grammar and usage questions. Some of these questions will call upon students to improve given sentences and paragraphs. Others will present students with sentences and require them to identify mistakes in diction, grammar, sentence construction, subject–verb agreement, proper word usage, and wordiness. Questions like this already appear on both the SAT II: Writing Test and the Writing Skills section of the PSAT.

The highest possible score on the new Writing section will be 800. Scores on the essay and multiple-choice section will be combined to produce a single score. A writing sub-score will also be assigned. The highest possible scores on the Critical Reading and Math sections will remain 800 each, making a perfect score on the new SAT 2400.

PSAT

The PSAT will be changing, too. In fact, the current PSAT already differs from the current SAT in that it includes a Writing Skills test of multiple-choice questions like those mentioned above. Like the new SAT, the new PSAT will omit Analogies and Quantitative Comparisons. However, the new PSAT will not require students to write an essay. It will also not include Algebra II content, since the PSAT will be taken by sophomores and juniors who may not yet have encountered this content. As mentioned earlier, the new PSAT will be introduced in October 2004.

CHANGES AT A GLANCE

Critical Reading	Current SAT I	New SAT I
Time	Two 30-minute sections	Two 25-minute sections
	One 15-minute section	One 20-minute section
	Total: 75 minutes	Total: 70 minutes
Content	Analogical reasoning	Critical reading
	Critical reading	Sentence-level reading
	Sentence-level reading	
Question Types	Analogies	Reading comprehension
	Reading comprehension	Sentence completions
	Sentence completions	Paragraph-length critical reading
Score	800	800

Math	Current SAT I	New SAT I
Time	Two 30-minute sections One 15-minute section Total: 75 minutes	Two 25-minute sections One 20-minute section Total: 70 minutes
Content	Algebra I Geometry Data analysis and statistics	Algebra I Algebra II Geometry Data analysis and statistics
Question Types	5-choice multiple-choice Quantitative comparisons Student-produced responses	5-choice multiple-choice Student-produced responses
Score	800	800

Writing	Current SAT I	New SAT I
Time	N/A	25-minute essay 25-minute multiple-choice section Total: 50 minutes
Content	N/A	Grammar, usage, word choice, and idiom writing
Question Types	N/A	Essay Multiple-choice section
Score	N/A	800; Essay subscore 2–12

Total	Current SAT I	New SAT I
Time	3 hours (including 30-minute experimental section)	3 hours 35 minutes (including 25-minute experimental section)
Score	1600	2400

WHY?

These changes to the SAT come on the heels of complaints by educators about the current exam. They assert that the SAT as it stands is not an accurate enough indicator of the content taught in high school classrooms. The test has also been accused of being too susceptible to tricks and coaching techniques and as being biased against less affluent students. The College Board has stated that it has three goals in revising the exam:

- To better align it with high school curricula and college requirements
- To provide college admissions officers with a measure of a student's writing skills
- To emphasize how crucial writing is to success in college and beyond

WHAT DOES IT MEAN FOR YOU?

How does all this affect you? If you are going to graduate from high school and enter college before 2006, you will not be affected by any of these changes. You will take the current exam. If, however, you are going to graduate from high school in 2006 or later, you will take the new exam. There are several ways in which your testing experience will be impacted. The coveted perfect SAT score will rise from 1600 to 2400. The new test will be more than half an hour longer than the current test. The additional personnel required to score the essays will result in a higher fee for the exam. Early estimates suggest that the test fee may increase by $10 or $12. And the changes to the content and format of the exam will obviously affect your preparation.

The College Board plans to release practice materials for the new exam well in advance of its introduction in 2005. Prior to this, current SAT II: Writing Test and PSAT Writing Section materials would be good prep for the proposed Writing Test. If you use current SAT I materials to prepare for the Math and Critical Reading sections, you will not need to focus on the analogy or quantitative comparison sections.

Choosing the Right College

WHICH COLLEGE IS RIGHT FOR YOU?

Choosing a college is a long and arduous process—but it can also be a lot of fun.

This will be one of the most important decisions you'll ever make. You're choosing where you're going to spend the next four (or more!) years of your life, where you're going to learn the skills you'll need for your adult life, and where you'll meet friends you will cherish for *all* of your life. You don't want to make the wrong choice, but you still have to make a choice—and probably sooner than you'd like!

So, how do you determine which is the right college for you?

First, make sure you choose the college that offers the best mix of academics, environment, and extracurricular activities for your particular needs and wants. Don't choose a school just on its academic merits; remember, you'll be spending the next four years of your life there, so you better make sure you enjoy the nonacademic life on campus, too!

You also have to take into account *where* the college is (how far away from your parents do you *really* want to be?) and *how much* it costs to attend. Your dream school might be too far away or simply cost too much to make it practical. (Although even if a college appears out of reach monetarily, you should always evaluate the potential for financial aid at that institution.)

If you have an idea of what career you wish to pursue after graduation, you should look for universities that are known for their excellence in the field that interests you. When comparing the merits of different schools, be sure to examine the caliber of the faculty, average class size in upper division courses, its academic reputation, and finally, the facilities. Visiting the prospective campus can be the most decisive factor in your choice of a school.

Even if a school meets *your* requirements, you might not meet *theirs*. You should examine the admissions requirements very carefully to determine which ones offer the most realistic opportunities for gaining admission. Consider things like the school's SAT and ACT standards and whether or not they require an interview. Don't waste your time, money, or hope applying to schools that you have little, if any, chance of getting into.

669

In a nutshell, then, here are some of the key points to consider when choosing a college:

- **Size.** Are you more comfortable at a college (1,000–2,500 population), a small university (2,500–6,000), or a big university (7,000 and up)? Colleges and small universities might offer a more comfortable environment with more extracurricular comradery, while big universities offer more extracurricular activities and more class and subject selection.

- **Location.** Do you prefer a school situated in a rural setting, a town, a small city, or a megalopolis? Does the location of the school in any way enhance the curriculum? How far away from home do you want to be—one hour, one gas tank, or one airplane ticket? How much will it cost you to travel home and how often will you be making the trip? What are the local transportation options? Can you park a car on campus or do you have to take the bus?

- **Curriculum.** Which is most important to you, a liberal arts, professional, or technical degree? What is the school known for? What are its academic strengths and weaknesses? Do they offer the courses and the degree track that you really want?

- **Faculty.** What percentage of the faculty has attained the terminal degree (doctorate, master's, etc.) in their field? Are professors available to meet with students outside of their classrooms? How many classes will actually be taught by a professor versus a teaching assistant? Is there an academic advising program? What about tutoring?

- **Job placement.** What percentage of students have job offers when they graduate? What percentage of alums continue on to graduate school? How strong is the alumni network?

- **Admissions requirements.** Are they academically rigorous? Too much so? Can you pass muster—or can too many others pass muster?

- **Costs and financial aid.** Can you afford this particular institution? What financial aid can you obtain to help you afford it? Are there any "hidden" costs of living on this campus?

- **Housing/food.** Are there different types of on-campus housing options? Do you have to live in a dorm? With how many roommates? What off-campus housing is available? What about fraternities and sororities? What are your dining options? Just how bad is the dorm food? Where is the closest pizza place and does it deliver?

- **Extracurricular activities.** What do you like to do outside of class? What sports activities are available for nonathletic majors? What about music, theater, and clubs? Where are the closest nightspots?

- **Social atmosphere/student body.** Is this a fun place to live? Too much fun? Is the school known as a "party" campus? Is it elitist or populist? Are the students there people you'd choose to hang out with, given the choice?

How do you find the answers to all these questions? There are numerous sources of information available to you, from official university brochures to comprehensive college selection Web sites. However, the best sources of information are often the college's students—and you can meet them either on campus or on line.

TIPS ON VISITING CAMPUSES

You should try to visit as many schools as possible before deciding where to apply. This is helpful in many ways, especially if you get accepted into more than one school and have to choose between them. A campus visit is even more important if you're applying under an early decision plan and must commit to that school if you're accepted. Remember, the school you choose is going to be your home for the next four to five years; make sure it's a place you really want to live.

Here are some things to look for when you visit a school:

- **Walk around.** By all means, check out the campus. Take in the sights. Does it seem cold and impersonal, or warm and friendly? Is this a campus you'll remember twenty years from now? Visit the student center, and find out what activities the college has to offer—free movies, games, lectures, etc. See whether or not the classrooms and lecture halls are relatively close together. Will you have to do a great deal of walking? What is the campus transportation like? How will you get to your favorite off-campus places for shopping, eating, and socializing?

- **Check out the weather.** Learn the weather patterns of the area. What are the winters like? How cold does it get—and how much snow will you have to hike through between classes? How much rain can you expect? When does it start warming up—and how hot does it get? What about the humidity? Make sure that, weather-wise, this can be a comfortable place for you to live.

- **Visit the dorms.** Take a look at everything—the bathrooms, bedrooms, lounges, you name it. Are the rooms big enough? Are they clean? Quiet enough for studying? If possible, stay the night and take a trip to the dining hall and try the food. Can you keep it down? If there is more than one dorm or dining area, then check out several, and determine your preferences.

- **Visit the classrooms.** Stop by the departments that you might be majoring in, and pick up their course lists. Take the time to ask questions of the people working in each department. Find out a little about the first-year professors you might have.

- **Talk to people!** Most importantly, stop and strike up conversations with some of the students. Ask them what they think about the school, their coursework, the social scene, the Greek system, the dorms, the dorm food, or anything else that you were wondering about. Find out from the students what are the best dorms, which places have the best pizza, where are the best parties, who are the best professors. Maybe you'll even make a few new friends and exchange phone numbers or e-mail addresses. Students are your best resource—use them!

TIP

Whenever possible, contact the college admission's office a week or two ahead of time to arrange some portions of your on-campus visit. Their assistance can help make your visit more productive. They'll send you a campus map, and they can help you set up meetings with faculty, give you directions to specific classrooms, or arrange for sleeping accommodations in a dorm.

When you do go, visit during the school year, not during spring, summer, or Christmas break. You should also try to avoid making visits during midterms and finals, or during the first few weeks of a new school year, before students are truly settled in. Also, it's probably better to visit during the week, if you can; a lot of students go home on weekends, and the atmosphere isn't quite the same.

HANGING OUT WITH OTHER STUDENTS ON LINE

If you can't hang out with college students in person, you can do so on line, in *Usenet newsgroups* and in *e-mail mailing lists*. Newsgroups and mailing lists are like topic-specific discussion groups where you post messages (called *articles*) and read articles posted by similarly interested users; they're a great way to interact with others electronically.

Usenet Newsgroups

Usenet newsgroups are the easiest discussion forums to find and to use. Since Usenet is part of the Internet, you need a computer and Internet access to visit them. You'll also need a *newsreader* software program. Two of the most popular newsreader programs are Microsoft Outlook Express (included free with both Windows 98 and Microsoft Internet Explorer) and Netscape Messenger (included free with the Netscape Communicator suite, which also includes the Netscape Navigator Web browser). If you access the Internet via America Online, just go to the keyword "newsgroups" to use AOL's built-in newsreader.

Newsgroups are arranged in hierarchies, so that all "alternative" newsgroups start with "alt.," and alternative newsgroups related to colleges start with "alt.college.", and on down the hierarchy. Here are some of the better newsgroups to peruse:

- alt.college
- alt.college.food
- alt.college.fraternities
- alt.college.greek.organizations
- alt.college.sororities
- alt.college.us
- alt.education.higher.stu-affairs
- alt.penpals.college
- alt.student.affairs.net
- soc.college
- soc.college.admissions
- soc.college.financial-aid

E-Mail Mailing Lists

You can also communicate with college students through e-mail mailing lists. Mailing lists are like newsgroups, except you do all your message posting and reading via normal e-mail, and the lists are typically moderated (resulting in less unwanted "noise" and spam).

You can find a master list of all available mailing lists at the Liszt Web site (http://www.liszt.com); also try **fresch,** the weekly newsletter of scholarship and financial aid information. Go to http://www.freschinfo.com for more information.

Check Out College and Student Web Pages

Almost every college has its own Web site. These sites often include a lot of good information about the school, the faculty, the classes, and the campus. In many cases you'll also be able to access individual student Web pages directly from the main college Web site.

To search for college Web sites, go to Yahoo! College Search, at http://education.yahoo.com/college/essentials. Enter the name of the college you're looking for and click the Search button. You can also search for schools by major, location, enrollment, and "wiredness" (level of PC use on campus).

In addition to the official college Web sites, it's also fun and informative to check out the Web pages created by students of a particular college. While you can access some student pages from some college Web sites, you can also find listings of student pages at the following independent sites:

- **Student.com** (http://www.student.com) lists more than 200,000 student Web pages.
- **Personal Pages Worldwide** (http://www.utexas.edu/world/personal/index.html) links to collections of personal pages at colleges and universities worldwide.
- **Student Homepages** (http://www.westegg.com/students/) lists student pages from more than three hundred different colleges.

TIP

Here's a quick way to find most schools' Web sites: In your browser, type *http://www.college.edu/,* where "college" is the college's name or initials. For example, type *http://www.duke.edu/* to connect to Duke University's Web site, or enter *http://www.ucla.edu/* to go to UCLA's home page.

COLLEGE SITES ON THE INTERNET

You'll also find dozens, if not hundreds, of sites on the Web devoted to helping you learn more about a college. Here's just a small list of the best and most popular of these college selection sites.

- **All about College** (http://www.allaboutcollege.com), compiling thousands of links to college and university Web sites around the world. Includes admissions office e-mail addresses for most schools.

- **Best College Picks** (http://www.bestcollegepicks.com), after completing a survey, Best College Picks will match you with colleges that fit your interests and future goals.

- **Campus Tours** (http://www.campustours.com), online virtual tours of thousands of college campuses, complete with interactive maps, college webcams, QuickTime VR tours, campus movies, and pictures. A great way to "tour" a school without actually being there!

- **College Bound.net** (http://www.cbnet.com), a resource that bills itself as "a student's interactive guide to college life," with sections on money, college profiles, sports, and food.

- **College E-Mail Addresses** (http://www.qucis.queensu.ca/FAQs/college-email/college.html), an extremely useful site that explains how to find e-mail addresses for undergraduate and graduate students, faculty, and staff at various colleges and universities.

- **Colleges.com** (http://www.colleges.com), a "virtual campus" that provides an online community for college students across the country. Sections include entertainment, academics, sports, music, books, games, research, and search engines.

- **Educational Resources Information Center** (http://www.eric.ed.gov), the site of the National Library of Education. Includes the ERIC database, the world's largest source of education information, with more than 950,000 abstracts of documents and journal articles. This site also lets you access a large inventory of brochures for parents.

- **Getting Ready for College Early** (http://www.ed.gov/pubs/GettingReadyCollegeEarly/), an online handbook for parents of students in the middle and junior high school years, from the U.S. government.

- **Mapping Your Future** (http://mapping-your-future.org), guides you on paying for school, selecting a school, and planning a career. Includes guided tours for middle and high school students, nontraditional students, and parents.

- **National Association for College Admission Counseling** (http://www.nacac.com), a site created by the education association of secondary school counselors, college and university admission officers, and other student counselors. This association sponsors the National College Fair program, and the site includes a comprehensive listing of college fairs.

- **Petersons.com** (http://www.petersons.com), online databases of academic programs, colleges and universities, and scholarship programs, as well as test-prep information and practice material.

- **Preparing Your Child for College** (http://www.ed.gov/pubs/Prepare), an online resource for parents, from the U.S. government.

- **The Student Survival Manual** (http://www.thesurvivalmanual.com), last but far from least, a wonderful little self-published resource guide for success in college. Includes Ten Tips for Survival in the Classroom, Ten Campus Organizations to Look Into, Ten Tips for Surviving the Registration Process, Ten Tips for Deciding On or Changing Your Major, Ten Ways to Improve Your Social Life, and numerous other lists of "Tens" to help you make your way through your first year at school.

As you can see, there are a lot of resources available for you to use on the Internet. It's best to take your time, settle back with a soft drink or glass of juice, and cruise through a number of these Web sites to see what they have to offer. At the end of your Web surfing, you'll be a lot more informed about where you want to go than you were when you first started out!

Applying to the College of Your Choice

WHEN TO APPLY

Once you've narrowed down your list of possible colleges to a handful of schools, it's time to start the application process.

All schools fall into one of three types of admission categories:

· **Selective admission,** with firm applications deadlines, which generally fall in January.

· **Rolling admission,** where there is no firm application deadline, and applicants are accepted (and rejected) until the freshman classes are full.

· **Open admission,** used by many two-year colleges, where there is no admission deadline and the schools accept anyone with a high school diploma until classes begin.

All that said, you should probably start preparing your applications in November and December, and submit all your applications no later than January. There is little benefit to submitting much earlier than that, but much downside if you submit later. When in doubt, contact the college of your choice to find out its recommended application date.

About the Early Action and Early Decision Options

Some colleges offer Early Action and Early Decision plans that enable you to apply early to your first-choice schools and receive early notification of your acceptance, or rejection, often as early as December. These plans have benefits for both you and the schools. Early applicants get the first chance at financial aid packages, fellowships, and student housing, and they can put the whole college application process behind them and enjoy the rest of their senior year. The colleges get to start constructing their freshman class profile—with a group of students who are really committed to attending *their* school. The plans have drawbacks, as well, so let's look at them in a bit more detail.

TIP

Many schools offer honors programs and honors scholarships. These programs and scholarships often have earlier application deadlines, sometimes as early as the fall.

Under most Early Action plans, you can apply to schools as early as November and receive notification of acceptance as early as January or February. Most Early Action plans require that you accept or reject admission by May 1. You can apply to a number of schools (if they offer this plan, that is) and compare the financial aid packages and offers before you accept. If you are relatively certain which schools you're really interested in attending, and if you fit the "profile" of their average applicant, Early Action gives you a chance to compete in a smaller applicant pool and let your first-choice schools know right up front that you're interested in them. If you need time to shop around, though, or if you need as much time as possible to boost your academic performance, Early Action may not be for you. Check each college's published guidelines for its Early Action plan before you commit to this route.

Early Decision plans offer many of the same benefits as Early Action, but they involve some restrictions, too. Under most Early Decision plans you can only have one Early Decision application underway at any one time. You can apply to other schools, but only under their regular admissions plan. And, most Early Decision plans require you to accept admission if they offer it and if it's accompanied by an adequate financial aid package. If you're accepted by your first-choice school, you have to withdraw all other outstanding applications. Obviously, this plan can prevent you from comparing financial aid offers from other schools. Because it may be a binding agreement, Early Decision is right for a more select group of students. It's well worth considering if

TIP

You really should visit your first-choice school before you opt for its Early Decision plan. If you commit to an Early Decision plan without first having visited the campus, you're committing yourself to a largely unknown academic destination. Take the time to look before you leap!

- You know with certainty your first-choice school, and you fit its applicant profile.
- You don't need time to boost your academic performance prior to applying.
- You don't need to negotiate the highest possible financial aid package.

And, as with Early Action plans, before you decide to participate in Early Decision, carefully read the college's published guidelines for the program.

HOW TO APPLY

When you're ready to apply, what is involved? While each school has its own specific admissions guidelines (and you should contact each school to get a copy of these), there are some general guidelines used by most major institutions. In fact, many colleges are now using something called the Common Application, an eight-page form created by the National Association of Secondary School Principals.

For any school using the Common Application, you only have to fill out one form, which can then go to multiple colleges. You can get copies of the Common Application from your high school guidance office; you'll have to get institution-specific application forms from the individual schools.

In addition, many schools now accept applications either via software or via online forms. (See the next section for more information on applying online.) If your school is one of those that let you apply online, take advantage of the opportunity—at the very least, it will save you a few stamps!

FILLING OUT THE APPLICATION

The Common Application and most private application forms include the following sections:

- **Personal data,** including information such as your name, address, possible areas of concentration, language spoken, and whether or not you'll be applying for financial aid.

- **Educational data,** such as the school you currently attend, your graduation date, the name of your high school counselor, etc.

- **Test information,** specifically your SAT or ACT scores.

- **Family,** information about your family—father's name, mother's name, where they went to school, their occupations, that sort of thing.

- **Academic honors,** where you should describe any scholastic distinctions or honors you have won (since the ninth grade).

- **Extracurricular, Personal, and Volunteer Activities,** where you get to impress the judges with all the things you do outside of school. This is more important than it might sound, most often the second item read by admission officers, who want to make sure you have a well-rounded background. Make sure you include sports, volunteer work (not paid work!), and other nonacademic activities—and list them in order of importance.

- **Work experience,** where you list all the jobs you've held during the past three years. Don't forget to fill in the section where you elaborate on the most important of these activities (work and other) and why they were important to you.

- **Personal statement,** otherwise known as "the essay." Some schools require this, many don't. For those that do, you're often asked to evaluate an important experience in your life; discuss a national, local, or personal issue; or describe how one person has influenced your life. Take your time with these, and make sure what you write has meaning, and is written well.

OTHER MATERIALS TO SUBMIT

In addition to the application form, you'll also need to submit some or all of the following, depending on school guidelines:

- **Recommendation letters** from one or more of your teachers (although some colleges have predefined forms they use instead of free-form letters).

- **Counselor form** (also known as the "school report"), often a separate form that must be completed by your school counselor.

- **SAT/ACT results**, which some colleges require to be submitted directly by your high school.

- **Major-specific requirements.** Some individual schools and majors have their own specific requirements. For example, most schools require music majors to arrange and pass an audition.
- **Application fee**

You should submit these materials directly to the admissions offices of the colleges you have selected—unless you're applying online.

COLLEGE ADMISSIONS TIME LINE

The following table provides you with a detailed time line to plan your college admissions activities.

COLLEGE ADMISSIONS TIME LINE

When	What to do

Junior Year of High School

When	What to do
September	Make sure that PSAT/NMSQT registration is handled by your guidance counselor staff (except in regions where the ACT is prevalent). Find out and save the date.
	Ask your guidance department about college fairs in your area and college admission-representative visits to the school. Attend fairs and sessions with reps at school.
	Familiarize yourself with guidance-office resources.
October	Make sure PSAT/NMSQT date is on your calendar. Read the student bulletin and try the practice questions.
	Schedule a day trip to visit nearby colleges. Don't worry if these are places where you won't apply; the goal is to explore different types of schools, so aim for variety. Discuss which characteristics are attractive and which aren't.
December	Questions about PSAT scores? Contact your guidance counselor. If necessary, discuss strategies for improving weak areas. Evaluate different SAT prep options, as needed.
	Take advantage of college students home for vacation. Ask them questions.
	Take an introductory look at financial aid forms, just to see what you'll need by this time next year.

When	What to do
January	Evaluate your academic progress so far. Are your grades up to par? Are course levels on target? Do your study habits need improvement?
	Begin thinking about worthwhile summer plans (job, study, camp, volunteer work, travel, etc.)
	Mark projected SAT I and II or ACT test dates on your calendar. Also mark registration deadlines.
February	Look ahead to SAT or ACT registration deadlines for the tests you plan to take. Are you about to miss one? Mark appropriate dates on your calendar. (A few juniors have reason to take the SAT I in March. If you will do so, heed the February registration deadline.)
	Buy a general guidebook to U.S. colleges and universities. Start checking out prospective schools via their Web sites.
March	Consider and plan spring-vacation college visits.
	Begin listing target colleges in a notebook or computer spreadsheet or database.
	Begin calling, writing, or e-mailing target colleges to request publications.
	Set aside an area for college propaganda. Invest in folders for materials from front-runner schools.
	Look ahead to SAT or ACT registration deadlines for the tests you plan to take. Are you about to miss one? Mark appropriate test and registration dates on your calendar.
	Make sure you discuss plans to take advanced placement exams with teachers and your guidance counselor as needed.
April	Look ahead to SAT or ACT registration deadlines for the tests you plan to take. Are you about to miss one? Mark appropriate test and registration dates on your calendar.
	Decide on senior-year classes. Include at least one math course or lab science, as well as the most challenging courses possible. Recognize that colleges weigh senior classes and grades as heavily as the junior record.
	Update your activities record.
May	Look ahead to SAT or ACT registration deadlines for the tests you plan to take. Are you about to miss one? Mark the appropriate test and registration dates on your calendar.
	Assess the need for and affordability of special services such as standardized test-prep courses, independent college counselors, and private group-tour programs.

When	What to do
May *(contd)*	Do you need to take the TOEFL (Test of English as a Foreign Language)? Select date and oversee registration.
June	Look ahead to SAT or ACT registration deadlines for the tests you plan to take. Are you about to miss one? Mark the appropriate test and registration dates on your calendar.
Summer	Make sure you have a job or constructive activities throughout most of the summer. Study, jobs, and volunteer work always rate high with admission officials. Consider and plan summer and fall college visits. Request publications from additional target colleges. Plan and execute supplemental submissions such as audition tapes and art slides/portfolio, if required and appropriate. Review and update target college list. Include pros and cons. Make tentative plans for fall visits. Begin to explore Early Action and Early Decision options at first-choice schools. Get the materials you need and read them carefully.

Senior Year of High School

When	What to do
September	Discuss plans and goals for the months ahead. Include pros and cons of target schools. Look ahead to SAT or ACT registration for the tests you plan to take. Are you about to miss one? Mark the appropriate test and registration dates on your calendar. Ask your guidance counselor about college fairs in your area and college admission representative visits to the school. Make certain that you attend fairs and sessions with reps at schools. Finalize fall college-visit plans. Include campus overnights, where possible. Request additional publications and applications from target colleges. If applicable, take appropriate Early Action and Early Decision application steps, as outlined in the published guidelines of your first-choice schools.
October	Look ahead to SAT or ACT registration for the tests you plan to take. Are you about to miss one? Mark the appropriate test and registration dates on your calendar.

When	What to do
	Draw up a master schedule of application and financial aid due dates, and then put them on your calendar.
	Begin considering essay topics and requesting teacher recommendations.
	Visit colleges. Include interviews on campus (or with local alumni representatives).
	Attend college fairs.
	For another look at college life, rent a movie like *Animal House* or *School Daze*.
	Again, review Early Decision and Early Action options and requirements, and take appropriate actions.
November	Look ahead to SAT or ACT registration for the tests you plan to take. Are you about to miss one? Mark the appropriate test and registration dates on your calendar.
	Reduce target college "long list" to a "short list," where applications will be made.
	Plan a Thanksgiving break that includes college visits (to almost-empty campuses).
	What is the status of your applications? Get someone to proofread your applications and essay(s).
December	Look ahead to SAT or ACT registration for the tests you plan to take. Are you about to miss one? Mark the appropriate test and registration dates on your calendar.
	Pick up financial aid material from guidance office and attend planning workshops, if available. Check out financial aid resources on the Internet.
	Make sure that teachers and guidance counselors are up-to-date with reference forms and that transcripts are being sent to all short-list colleges.
	Some Early Decision notifications may be sent this month—be on the lookout if you've applied under this plan.
January	Begin filling out financial aid forms. Finish and mail these forms as soon as possible and *never* late.
	Complete all applications, including those with later deadlines. Don't forget to photocopy everything and save in accordion files.
	If SATs are being taken this month, are "rush" scores required? Ask target colleges, if you're not certain.

When	What to do
February	Unless confirmations have been received, call colleges to check on completion of applications. Record the name of the person you spoke with. Track down missing records.
	If you've made Early Action applications, colleges should send notifications by the end of this month. Be on the lookout for yours, and follow up if necessary.
March	WAIT!
April	Keep in mind that "thin" letters aren't always rejections. Some schools send out enrollment forms later.
	Rejoice in acceptances; keep rejections in perspective.
	Plan "crunch-time" visits to campuses, as needed, to help prompt final decisions.
	Compare financial aid decisions, where applicable. Contact financial aid offices with questions.
	Make sure you return "wait-list" cards, as needed. Contact admission offices to check on wait-list status. Send updated records and other information, if available. Write an upbeat "Please take me, and this is why you should" letter.
	Make your final decision. Have your parents send the required deposit. Don't dawdle and miss the May 1 deadline or colleges can give away your place. Also notify those schools you won't be attending, especially if an aid offer was made.
May	Take AP exams, if appropriate.
	Stay abreast of housing choices, etc. When will forms be mailed? Should you be investigating living-situation options? When is a freshman orientation? (Some schools have spring and summer programs.) When is course registration?
June	Write a thank-you note to anyone who may have been especially helpful. Guidance counselors are often unsung heroes. Don't forget teachers who wrote recommendations, admissions counselors or secretaries, tour guides, or other students.
	Consider summer school if you want to accelerate or place out of requirements. ALWAYS check with colleges first to make sure credits will count. Get permission in writing when it's questionable.
	Make sure that a final high-school transcript is sent to the college you will attend. (Most schools should do this automatically.)

Finding Financial Aid

FIGURING OUT FINANCIAL AID

Once you know what different schools might cost, it's time to work out what you and your family can afford to pay. Then you'll know how much financial aid you can apply for. The principle behind financial aid is that students who can't afford the full cost of college should still have the opportunity to go.

WHAT YOU WILL PAY

Taking the difference between what the college costs (including room and board, books, and other supplies) and what you can afford to pay gives the amount of your need. This deceptively simple term, "need," doesn't necessarily mean what you think it ought to mean, or what you would like for it to mean. It's a specific, technical term for the amount you cannot pay on your own—the amount left after your Expected Family Contribution (EFC) is subtracted from your cost of education.

Your EFC is the total amount that you, as a family, are expected to contribute toward college costs. This number is determined by analyzing your overall financial circumstances and comparing them to the circumstances of other families. Family income is the major factor in determining your EFC, *not* the balances of your savings accounts or the worth of trust funds, your parents' home, and other assets.

Your EFC figure may vary from school to school, depending on which formula the college uses to determine financial need. Although your EFC may seem to be an unattainable amount, it can be financed if you carefully plot out a strategy that combines different economic sources, including loans, savings, a part-time job for the student, and current income.

WHAT'S COVERED BY FINANCIAL AID

Financial aid, which makes up the difference between the EFC and the cost of attending the school of your choice, comes in three basic flavors:

- **Grants and scholarships** don't need to be repaid or maintained by a job. Grants are usually based on need alone, while scholarships are given to students who have met some criteria, such as academic or athletic merit.

appendix D

- **Loans** are the most widely available source of financial aid. They must be repaid some day, but the interest rates for student loans are often lower than for commercial loans, and payments are deferred until after the student has completed college.

- **Work-study** lets students work 10 to 15 hours per week in order to gain the money to pay for school.

You and the financial aid officer at the college of your choice will negotiate a financial assistance package that will probably contain a combination of all three of these varieties of aid.

SOURCES OF FINANCIAL AID

Your aid will most likely come from a number of sources, from the most massive federal programs down to institutional funds unique to your school. Aid might come from the state, private foundations, the college, or even an employer. If the aid comes from a federal government program or a state agency, it is known as public aid; sources like employers, donors, and foundations are known as private aid.

Federal Aid

The federal government is by far the largest source of financial aid, providing nearly 70 percent of the aid that is awarded each year. In 2001–02, the federal government, through the Department of Education, made available more than $60 billion in student aid. So, it pays to know something about the major federal programs, since they will be your first source of aid.

Pell Grants

The Pell Grants program was once known as the Basic Educational Opportunity Grant program, and you might still see it referred to as such in older materials. Pell Grants are distributed based on family need and education costs at your school. The maximum grant available is currently $4,000 per year, but this figure changes from year to year depending on how Congress funds the program.

Eligibility for Pell Grants is determined by the standard Federal Methodology formula that was passed into law by Congress and is used to calculate your EFC. If that figure falls below a certain threshold, you'll be eligible for a Pell Grant. Once you've applied for aid, you'll receive a student aid report that gives your EFC number and tells you if you qualify. The amount of the grant you may receive is not standardized. Different schools, with their varying tuitions, disburse different amounts.

Federal Loan Programs

There are two main kinds of low-interest loans for students and parents: the Federal Direct Student Loans (Direct Loan) program and the Federal Family Education Loan (FFEL) program. Collectively, they're called Stafford Loans.

Direct Loans come directly from the federal government. Federal Family Education Loans involve private lenders like banks, credit unions, and savings and loans. Aside from that difference, the two loan programs are pretty much the same; which program you get your money from depends on which program your school participates in. The interest rate on these loans varies from year to year, but the maximum is 8.25 percent, and often the interest rate is lower while you're in school. You'll also have to pay a fee of up to 4 percent, deducted from each loan disbursement; this money goes to the federal government to help reduce the cost of the loans.

If financial need remains after subtracting your EFC, your Pell Grant eligibility, and aid from other sources, you can borrow a Stafford Loan to cover all or part of the remaining need. This is a subsidized loan; the government pays the interest while you're in school and for six months after you graduate.

Even if you have no remaining need, you can still borrow a Stafford Loan for your EFC or the annual Stafford Loan borrowing limit, whichever is less. (The borrowing limit ranges from $2,625 to $10,500 a year, depending on a number of factors, including your year in school and whether you're classified as an independent or dependent student.) However, this is an unsubsidized loan; you're responsible for paying all of the interest.

Parents who are applying for the financial aid go for what are called PLUS Loans. Like the Stafford Loans, PLUS Loans are available from both the Direct Loan and the FFEL program. The yearly borrowing limit on PLUS Loans is equal to the cost of attending the college *minus* any financial aid you get; so if it costs $6,000 per year to attend college and the student has received $4,000 in other financial aid, that student's parents can borrow up to $2,000. The interest rate varies from year to year, but the maximum is 9 percent.

Campus-Based Programs

"Campus-based" simply means that financial aid officers at each school administer the programs. Three of the federal programs are campus-based (not all schools participate in all three programs):

- **Federal Supplemental Educational Opportunity Grants (FSEOG):** These grants are awarded to undergraduates based on financial need—"exceptional financial need" is the way the government brochures put it. Pell Grant recipients with the lowest EFCs will be the first in line for one of these grants. Depending on your need, when you apply, and the funding level at your school, you may receive between $100 and $4,000 a year.

- **Federal Work-Study (FWS):** This is basically a part-time job. Most undergraduates are paid by the hour and often at minimum wage (graduate students may receive a salary). Jobs are awarded based on need, the size of FWS funds at your school, and the size of your aid package. The program encourages community service work and work related to your field of study, so it can also help you get your foot in the door by giving you work experience in your chosen field.

- **Federal Perkins Loans:** These are low-interest loans for students with "exceptional" financial need. They're also an exceptionally good deal at just 5 percent interest, and you don't have to start repaying until nine months after you graduate. Undergraduates can borrow $4,000 a year, up to a total of $20,000.

How much aid you receive from a campus-based program is based on your financial need, how much other aid you're receiving, and the availability of funds at your school. Unlike Pell Grants or Stafford Loans, the campus-based programs aren't entitlement programs. The government gives each school a set amount of cash; when it's gone, it is really gone—no more campus-based aid can be had until the next year's allotment comes through. Not every eligible student will receive aid from these programs. The schools set their own deadlines, so ask at your school's financial aid office and apply as early as possible to catch some of the money before it runs out.

Other Federal Aid

The Department of Education is not alone in providing financial aid; the federal government has several other ways of helping students get through school. Scholarships, loans, job training, and money to pay back existing loans are all available from a variety of federal programs, including the following:

- The branches of the armed forces maintain ROTC units on many campuses, which are a rich lode of scholarships geared toward helping minority students and boosting the number of students entering important-but-strained career fields, such as the health professions. For more information, call (800) USA-ROTC.

- The Department of Veterans Affairs (VA) offers aid for veterans, reservists, those who serve in the National Guard, and widows and orphans of veterans. For more information on these programs, call (800) 827-1000 and speak with a Veterans Benefits Counselor or visit www.va.gov.

- The Corporation for National and Community Service administers a program called AmeriCorps that enables students to pay for education in exchange for one year of public service. Visit www.americorps.com for more information.

- The U.S. Public Health Service provides a variety of loan, scholarship, and loan repayment programs to students studying to enter the health professions. Visit www.hhs.gov for more information.

- The Department of Labor administers the Workforce Investment Act, a tuition aid program for the economically disadvantaged and others facing employment barriers. For more information, visit www.doleta.gov.

State Aid

It's part of a continuing trend among the states to increase their support for higher education, and all fifty states offer grant aid. However, each state is different, and some states spend far more than others. Five states—California, Illinois, New Jersey, New York, and Pennsylvania—award about 60 percent of the national total, $1.5 billion altogether, in undergraduate need-based aid.

College Funds

This money includes everything from athletic to academic (or merit) scholarships, which don't take need into account; merit aid is used by colleges to attract the students that they want. Next to the federal government, colleges are the largest sources of aid.

The last few years have also been building years for college and university endowments, with hundreds of millions of dollars flowing into schools as diverse as Harvard University and the University of Washington. Some, but certainly not all, of this endowment money has gone into scholarship funds. Other college funds might find their way to students in the form of tuition discounts for prepayment, aid in receiving loans, and other innovative programs. Most schools also keep funds on hand for short-term emergency loans for students.

Employers

Many employers help put students through college through the burgeoning field of cooperative education, in which students alternate semesters of school with semesters of work. Not only does this provide professional skills and a leg up in the employment game, but it also puts money into the student's pocket. It is best developed at technical and engineering schools like Georgia Tech, which places hundreds of students into positions in a five-year degree program, but all kinds of institutions offer cooperative education programs—almost 1,000 schools boast such programs.

Private Scholarships

This is a relatively small part of the financial aid picture, and many carry daunting eligibility requirements—the old "red-haired, left-handed cricket player from Alaska" problem. There's a lot more money to be drawn from federal and state programs, but hundreds of millions of dollars are nonetheless available in private scholarships—not an amount to turn up your nose at. Just remember to go after the big money first and early, and then look around for whatever private scholarships you can pick up.

FINDING FINANCIAL AID ON LINE

The Internet contains a treasure trove of financial aid resources, including applications that you can file electronically, in-depth information about grants and loans, college connections, scholarship searches, and more.

Almost every financial aid agency that you'll deal with—from the Department of Education to your college's financial aid office—maintains a Web site that provides applications, deadline dates, the latest news, and more important information that you need to know. There are also numerous Web sites from "unofficial" third-party sources that can help you with researching financial aid; these sites often include insider advice, tips, and tricks that the official sources won't give you.

The Department of Education

A great place to start looking into the nuts and bolts of student financial aid is the source of so much of it—the federal government. The Department of Education maintains three separate Web sites that provide a great deal of reliable information:

- The **Office of Postsecondary Education** will tell you about the different kinds of federal aid and how to go about applying for that aid. You'll also find a free electronic version of the federal financial application that you can submit directly from the site. Go to: http://www.ed.gov/offices/OPE/Students/index.html.

- **Project EASI** (Easy Access for Students and Institutions) is a program aimed at streamlining the financial aid process. The Web site takes you step-by-step through the entire process and offers down-to-earth, straightforward advice. Go to: http://easi.ed.gov/.

- **Think College** is the college preparation information resource. This site provides information about recently enacted government programs that help pay for college, such as the higher education tax credits of the Taxpayer Relief Act. The site also offers good advice geared toward parents and high school students on how to prepare for paying for college. Go to: http://www.ed.gov/thinkcollege/.

State Programs

All fifty states offer innovative financial aid programs, such as prepaid tuition funds and college savings plans. And, of course, you can find up-to-date information about the majority of these programs on the Web.

For a comprehensive list of college savings programs by state, go to the listing at the College Savings Plans Network Web site (http://www.collegesavings.org/). In addition, you may find more information about such plans by contacting your state's financial aid office.

Other Lenders

The National Financial Services Network has published an online directory of lenders who provide education loans, organized by state. Searching the directory is probably the fastest way to locate a lender. Go to: http://www.nfsn.com/personal/index.htm.

College Web Sites

It's getting hard to find a college these days that doesn't have a home page on the Web to advertise itself to prospective students. Of course, surfing the Web sites of schools that you're interested in is a fun—and effective—way to narrow down your list. But many colleges' sites also have pointers to the information provided by the school's financial aid office. This online financial aid "office" can be an extremely valuable resource, giving you access to up-to-date application deadlines, required forms, available scholarships, and more for your school of choice. So, surf over to your new school and check out its Web site!

To get started, search for the Web sites of specific college aid offices at the FinAid site (http://www.finaid.org/).

Third-party Resources

There's a great deal of excellent unofficial information on the Web as well. The absolute best place to start is FinAid, produced by Mark Kantrowitz, author of several collegial financial aid books. The Web page is a gold mine. It includes access to scholarship and fellowship databases, information on grants and loans, an extensive bibliography, and links to school financial aid offices. Like all good Web pages, this one contains links to most of the other important sources of financial aid information contained on other computer systems. So we won't go into a long list of Web page addresses here, since one leads to the other. Go to: http://www.finaid.org/.

Another nice resource is Peterson's *Get a Jump! The Financial Aid Answer Book*, which gives parents and students advice and information on the ins and outs of the financial aid process.

A STEP-BY-STEP GUIDE TO APPLYING FOR FINANCIAL AID

While the financial aid application process may seem dauntingly complex, when you break it down into its separate steps, there's really not that much to it. Much of your time will be spent filling out the requisite financial aid forms and then waiting to see what you get.

Before You Apply: Assembling the Paperwork

Before you start accumulating forms and wearing down the point of your number-2 pencil, you should prepare for your applications by assembling the following records, necessary for many of the common aid forms:

- Earned income for the year
- Federal taxes paid for the year
- Untaxed income received (such as Social Security benefits)

One of the best sites for finding things online is yahoo.com, which organizes a gigantic directory of Web sites in outline form so that you can track down information by category. You can also search the entire Web for certain words or phrases by using such sites as Altavista.com, Excite.com, and Lycos.com.

- Money held in checking and savings accounts
- Value of any current investments
- Value of any business or farm owned by your family

For each item on this list, you'll need both the student's and the parents' records, unless you're an independent student—in which case you'll need these records for you and for your spouse.

Getting and Filling out Financial Aid Forms

The forms that you'll need to fill out in order to apply for financial aid vary from state to state and from institution to institution, depending on the "need analysis service" used by that state or institution. Your school will let you know which forms you must complete and will provide them to you. While not easy, none of these forms is impossible to fill out on your own.

The most common forms are the following:

- the U.S. Department of Education's Free Application for Federal Student Aid (FAFSA)

- the College Scholarship Service's (CSS) Financial Aid PROFILE (available in high school guidance counselor offices, college financial aid offices, and on line at http://www.collegboard.com/)

- the Pennsylvania Higher Education Assistance Agency's Application for Pennsylvania State Grant and Federal Student Aid (PHEAA)

- the Student Aid Application for California (SAAC)

- the Illinois State Scholarship Commission's Application for Federal and State Student Aid (AFSSA)

Your school's application instructions will give you the information you need about applying for other forms of aid—several states, for instance, require that you fill out still more forms to apply for their own aid programs. It's also a good idea for students applying for private or institutional funds to check with the schools they are interested in to see if additional forms are required or if other procedures must be followed. The school's own application and the state applications might have separate deadlines that you have to pay heed to.

Once you've applied, the processing agency will take between four and six weeks to turn your application around. You may be asked to confirm information or to correct the forms and then return them to be processed again. The reprocessing will add another two or three weeks to your wait.

Getting the FAFSA

There are a number of ways to apply for federal financial aid—but it all starts with the FAFSA. You have several options for getting a copy of the FAFSA and submitting it to a federal aid processing center:

- You can apply electronically through your school.
- You can apply electronically through the Department of Education's Web site: http://www.fafsa.ed.gov/
- You can use the FAFSA Express software; it runs on computers that use the Windows operating system and have a modem. Computers with the FAFSA Express program can be found at many high schools, public libraries, and Educational Opportunity Centers. Or you can order the software on diskette by calling (800) 801-0576, or download a copy yourself from the Department of Education's Web site.
- You can forego technology altogether and get the version of the form that comes on old-fashioned paper. Ask at your high school guidance office, college financial aid office, or write directly to:

Federal Student Aid Information Center
P.O. Box 84
Washington, DC 20044-0084
(800) 4-FEDAID

Filling out the FAFSA

Be as accurate and as neat as you can when completing the FAFSA. Use a pen with black ink or a number-2 pencil that can easily be read by a computer. Don't jot notes in the margin that may interfere with processing the form. And don't attach any explanatory documents like tax returns—they'll just wind up in the shredder.

Keeping Track of Paperwork: What to Do With the Student Aid Report

After processing your data, you'll begin to receive a lot of paper. Your application for federal aid through the FAFSA or the other forms will be used to generate a Student Aid Report (SAR), which arrives within four weeks after submitting the FAFSA. The SAR compares all your data and generates a Student Aid Index number (which lets you know whether you qualify for a Pell Grant) and an Estimated Family Contribution (EFC) number (which will be used to see whether you qualify for campus-based programs like FSEOG, Federal Work-Study, Federal Perkins Loans, and the Stafford Loan programs).

TIP

Some schools offer financial aid applications in electronic form, so you don't have to worry about your eraser rubbing through the paper. You can also submit forms faster electronically and have the computer check for errors before you submit the forms.

TIP

Always save a copy of your application and worksheets as a backup, whether filing electronically or submitting a paper form. The school may need to see these copies later, or you may need to refer to them if you find errors in your aid package.

If you qualify for a Pell Grant, your SAR will arrive in three parts:

- Part 1, the Information Summary, tells you how to check the SAR for errors.
- Part 2, the Information Review Form, is used to correct any errors in the SAR.
- Part 3, the Pell Grant Payment Document, is used by your school to decide how much money you will receive.

Immediately make copies of Part 1 and send one to the financial aid office of each school that you applied to. You'll submit all three parts of the SAR to the school that you ultimately decide to attend.

Didn't get the Pell Grant? Don't worry—very few applicants do. But now you have something very important—your EFC number. Send that information to your financial aid administrator, who will use it to figure out whether you qualify for other federal student aid.

Receiving Your Award Letter

Once the school has all the information it needs, it can put together an aid package that will probably include a combination of grants (precious few), loans (too many), and work-study employment. You're notified of what your aid package contains in an award letter. This document gives you an idea of your probable cost of attendance, how your need was determined, what your need turned out to be, and the composition of that aid package. If you're satisfied with the aid package, you sign the documents that come with the form and send them back to the school.

Even if you haven't decided which school to attend, you should move quickly to accept the aid package from each school that offers one. Accepting the aid package does not obligate you to attend the school, but it's the only way to keep your options open. Schools set response deadlines: If you don't respond to your aid letter within that time, you could miss out on the funds that have been offered to you. This isn't to say that you should keep a number of colleges on a string—choose your college as quickly as possible so that the schools you don't choose can distribute the money to other students.

But before you leap to accept that award letter, evaluate your offers with a cold eye. Don't be fooled by big numbers; pay special attention to how much of the offer is made up of grants and how much is made up of loans. Are all the costs of attending the school listed in the aid package, or will the costs of books, personal expenses, and travel add on to that amount? Which schools are tossing in special awards for academic or athletic merit? If scholarships are offered, are they renewable or are they one-shot wonders that will leave you high and dry next year? Break out your calculator and compare the loan interest rates offered by different institutions, and check out whether the payback requirements for those loans are especially onerous. And as for work-study offers, keep in mind the study load before you, and ask yourself whether you'll be able to juggle work and school right off the bat. And remember, financial aid offers may be negotiable.

Compare all of the offers that you receive, then contact the admissions office of any school with which you want to negotiate. Your offer may be nonnegotiable, but you won't know until you ask.

PUTTING IT ALL TOGETHER: THE FINANCIAL AID CALENDAR

The following table presents a calendar of important dates to remember when applying for college and for financial aid. Use this calendar as a checklist to ensure that you get everything done on time; to get the most aid, get applications in early.

CALENDAR OF IMPORTANT FINANCIAL AID DATES

When	What to Do
Junior Year of High School	
October	Take the PSAT/NMSQT.
Fall/Winter	Send for college brochures and financial aid information.
Spring	Begin campus tours; talk to financial aid advisers at colleges.
	Sign up for AP courses for senior year, if available.
Senior Year of High School	
September–December	Narrow down your college choices.
	Ask schools for admission applications and financial aid forms.
	Get a copy of the FAFSA.
	Send in applications for admission to college.
	Take the SAT or ACT.
January 1	Send in the FAFSA and other required financial aid applications.
February–March	Make sure that the colleges received your applications and that you've completed all the required financial aid applications for each college.
April 1	Most college acceptances and rejections have been sent out by now; send in your nonrefundable deposit to the college of your choice.
May	Take any AP tests.
	Follow up with housing, financial aid, and other college offices.
June 30	Your financial aid application must be received by the processing agency listed on the form.
	Your school's financial aid office must have received your application and student aid report.

NOTE

Remember that if you've applied under an Early Decision plan, your notification time—and subsequent obligations—differ. See "About the Early Action and Early Decision Options" in Appendix C for more details.

TIP

Remember that the money from campus-based programs, state programs, and the college's own awards are often given out much earlier than the June 30 deadline for filing your FAFSA. To have more of your need met, get your financial aid applications in as soon after January 1 as possible.

NOTES

NOTES

NOTES

NOTES

NOTES